The Playbill® Broadway Yearbook

Fourth Annual Edition
2007–2008

Robert Viagas
Editor

Amy Asch
Assistant Editor

Kesler Thibert
Art Director

Aubrey Reuben   Ben Strothmann
Photographers

David Gewirtzman
Production Coordinator

Kristen Luciani
Photo Coordinator

The Playbill Broadway Yearbook: Fourth Annual Edition, June 1, 2007–May 31, 2008
Robert Viagas, Editor

ISBN-978-1-55783-746-2
ISSN-1932-1945

Published by PLAYBILL® BOOKS
525 Seventh Avenue, Suite 1801
New York, NY 10018
Email: yearbook@playbill.com
Internet: www.playbill.com

Printed by WALSWORTH PUBLISHING COMPANY
Commercial Book Group
389 Piedmont Street
Waterbury, CT 06706

Exclusively distributed by APPLAUSE THEATRE & CINEMA BOOKS/Hal Leonard Corporation.

Applause Theatre & Cinema Books
19 West 21st Street, Suite 201
New York, NY 10010
Phone: (212) 575-9265
Fax: (212) 575-9270
info@applausepub.com
www.applausepub.com

Page 1 Photo Credits: Joan Marcus,
Paul Kolnik, Carol Rosegg, Manuel
Harlan and Michael Brosilow.

Special Thanks

Special thanks to Amy Asch, David Gewirtzman, Kristen Luciani, Kesler Thibert, Aubrey Reuben, Ben Strothmann, Pam Karr, Greg Kalafatas, Maria Somma, Natasha Williams, Jim Ayala, Matt Blank, Andrew Gans, Kenneth Jones, Ernio Hernandez, David Sutch, Jenny Shoemaker, Nathan Stufflebean, The Rodgers and Hammerstein Organization, Matt Shea, Jackie Green, Ed Lefferson, Jane Grey, Roy Harris, Brian Landrine, Bobby Maguire, Lori Steiger-Perry, and our interns Scott Hamilton and Craig Stekuer whose help made this year's edition possible.

We also thank the Fourth Edition *Yearbook* Correspondents who shared their stories with such wit and insight:

Heather Ayers, Dylan Baker, Nili Bassman, Jeremy Bobb, John Bolton, Carolee Carmello, Jill Cordle, Mara Davi, Diane Davis, Eisa Davis, James FitzSimmons (for the third time), Artie Gaffin, Jared Gertner, Gwen Gillian, Leslie Goddard, Mandy Gonzalez, Jamie Greathouse, Jane Grey, Kathryn Hahn, Jim Harker (for the second time), Roy Harris (for the second time), Nevin Hedley, Rodney Hicks, Curtis Holbrook, MaryAnn Hu, Eddie Korbich (for the third time), Leigh Ann Larkin, Jeanne Lehman, Michael Longoria, Patti LuPone, Paul McGill, Lindsay Mendez, Cass Morgan (for the third time), Orfeh, Kris Koop Ouellette (for the fourth time), Patrick Page, Mary Beth Peil, Tory Ross, Seth Rudetsky, Bethany Russell, Jimmi Simpson, Rick Steiger, Barclay Stiff (for the third time), Jason Viarengo (for the third time), Ron Vodicka, Max Von Essen, Hannah Waddingham, Ben Walker, Karen Walsh.

And we thank the folks on each show who shared their photographs and lent sparkle to the Scrapbook pages:

Matt Blank, Rex Bonomelli, Jay Brady, Theresa DiStasi, Sara Inbar, Sanford Kaplan, Scott Landis, Leigh Ann Larkin, Maryann Lopinto, Brittany Marcin, Michael Portantiere, Anita Shevett, Morgan Shevett, Steve Shevett, Jonny Rueda, Thomas Vrzala and Alissa Zulvergold.

Also the Broadway press agents who helped set up interviews and photo sessions: especially Chris Boneau, Adrian Bryan-Brown, John Barlow, Michael Hartman, Pete Sanders, Richard Kornberg, Jeffrey Richards, Marc Thibodeau, Philip Rinaldi, Gary Springer, Sam Rudy, Tony Origlio, Rick Miramontez, and their respective staffs.

Plus Joan Marcus, Paul Kolnik, Carol Rosegg, Bruce Glikas and all the fine photographers whose work appears on these pages.

And, most of all, thanks to the great show people of Broadway who got into the spirit of the *Yearbook* and took time out of their busy days to pose for our cameras. There's no people like them.

Preface to the Fourth Edition

The 2007-2008 Broadway season presented a classic feast-or-famine scenario. Despite a growing recession exacerbated by the costs of food and fuel, box offices were humming. Humming, that is, except for 19 days in November when all but a handful of shows were shut down by a strike of IATSE Local 1, the stagehands' union, protesting producers' unilateral changes in work rules. Sister unions honored their picket lines. The strike gouged a hole out of everyone's income (and the audience's fun) at the peak of the holiday rush. The strike and its after-effects cast a shadow over the entire season—which you'll see reflected in many of our *Yearbook* Correspondents' reports on the Scrapbook pages.

Broadway enjoyed a flood of new blood this season, with most of the big plays and musicals being written by Broadway first-timers, including playwright Tracy Letts, whose family drama *August: Osage County* won every playwriting award in sight, and Lin-Manuel Miranda, whose Latino neighborhood musical *In The Heights*, which he conceived in college, took four Tony Awards including Best Musical and Best Score.

While veteran writers like Mel Brooks (*Young Frankenstein*) and Alan Menken (*The Little Mermaid*) presented works that weren't embraced by most critics, two of the biggest hits of the season, revivals of *Gypsy* and *South Pacific*, proved that Broadway audiences still love the great classics. (It was, for some reason, the first time *South Pacific* had ever been revived on Broadway.) Both of those revivals showcased their large orchestras, running counter to the trend in recent years toward smaller ensembles and electronic music. *Gypsy*, which transferred from the "Encores!" Summer 2007 production, had its orchestra on stage; *South Pacific* deployed its musicians under the thrust stage at the Vivian Beaumont Theatre, but engineered the stage to roll back during the overture and entr'acte and let the classic score fill the air.

The Playbill Broadway Yearbook was also very lucky in its selection of Correspondents from each show. Just a few of the highlights:

Carolee Carmello tells of ghostly encounters backstage at *Mamma Mia!* at the Winter Garden. Seth Rudetsky recounts how the "horribly inappropriate" Broadway medley was assembled for *The Ritz*. Hannah Waddingham recounts her experience as a Brit on Broadway in *Monty Python's Spamalot*.

Eddie Korbich gives a seagull's-eye-view of life backstage at *The Little Mermaid*. Kris Koop Ouellette, who has chronicled backstage life at *Phantom of the Opera* in each of the three previous yearbooks, is back with stories of how the cast of the Andrew Lloyd Webber musical spent their 20th year on Broadway.

Gypsy Correspondent Leigh Ann Larkin was in the middle of compiling her report when star Patti LuPone asked to get involved. She jumped in as co-Correspondent with lively backstage observations from one of the grandest Broadway Dames of our era.

Those are just a few of the names of our five dozen correspondents recording for posterity the backstage lives of Broadway show peple.

Yearbook User's Manual

Which Shows Are Included? *The Playbill Broadway Yearbook 2007-2008* covers the Broadway season, which ran, as per tradition, from June 1, 2007 to May 31, 2008. Each of the seventy shows that played at a Broadway theatre under a Broadway contract during that time got a chapter in this edition. That includes new shows which opened during that time, like *In The Heights*; shows from the previous season that ran just a few performances into the new season, like *Journey's End*; older shows from seasons past that closed during this season, like *Beauty and the Beast*; and older shows from seasons past that ran throughout this season and continue into the future (and into the next *Yearbook*), like *The Phantom of the Opera*.

How Is It Decided Which Credits Page Will Be Featured? Each show's credits page (which PLAYBILL calls a "billboard page") changes over the year as cast members come and go. We use the opening-night billboard page for most new shows. For most shows that carry over from the previous season we use the billboard page from the first week in October. Occasionally, sometimes at the request of the producer, we use a billboard page from another part of the season, especially when a major new star joins the cast.

What Are "Alumni" and "Transfer Students"? Over the course of a season some actors leave a production; others take their place. To follow our "Yearbook" concept, the ones who left a show between the start of the season and the date of the billboard page are listed as "Alumni"; the ones who joined the cast are called "Transfer Students." If you see a photo appearing in both "Alumni" and "Transfer Students" sections, it's not a mistake; it just means that they went in and out of the show during the season and were not present on the billboard date.

What Is a "Correspondent" and How Is One Chosen? We ask each show to appoint a Correspondent to record anecdotes of backstage life at their production. Sometimes the show's press agent picks the Correspondent; sometimes the company manager, the stage manager or the producer does the choosing. Each show gets to decide for itself. They bring a richness of experience to the job and help tell the story of backstage life on Broadway from many different points of view.

Who Gets Their Picture in the *Yearbook*? Everyone who works on Broadway can get their picture in the *Yearbook*. That includes actors, producers, writers, designers, assistants, stagehands, ushers, box office personnel, stage doormen and anyone else employed at a Broadway show or a support organization. PLAYBILL maintains a database of headshots of all Broadway actors and most creators. We send our staff pho-tographers to all opening nights and all major Broadway-related events. We also schedule in-theatre photo shoots at every production. No one is required to appear in the *Yearbook*, but all are invited. A few shows declined to host a photo shoot this year or were unable to schedule one before our printing deadline. We hope they'll join us in 2009.

Welcome to Kristen Luciani

Here at *The Playbill Broadway Yearbook*, we welcomed an important new staff member. Kristen Luciani, who performed so superbly as our intern in spring 2007, joined the staff as Photo Coordinator. It has been her job to work with each show to schedule photos of all those groups of stagehands, ushers, musicians, doormen, not to mention corralling the good people who run the guilds, unions, trade groups, ancillary businesses, charities and service organizations we humorously call Faculty. These are very busy people and we thank them for taking a few minutes to gather for our cameras.

Kristen Luciani

During the course of the year, Luciani completed her Junior year at New York University where she majors in Theater at the associated Playwrights Horizons Studio and pursues a minor in Producing. Aside from her work at PLAYBILL, she's also the associate producing intern at The Public Theater, under Associate Producer Jenny Gersten. She said, "I hope to one day become a famous circus clown after escaping the clutches of *The Playbill Broadway Yearbook*...or if that doesn't work out, I suppose I'll pursue both acting and producing!"

The rest of the *Yearbook* editorial staff has a second job running PLAYBILL's newest venture, Playbill Radio, a web radio station (PlaybillRadio.com) that broadcasts show music around the clock, punctuated on weekdays by hourly news reports from our studios on 38th Street, just below Times Square, and enhanced throughout the week by interviews and special programming from backstage at the Broadway theatres. If you like the *Yearbook*, we hope you'll give PlaybillRadio.com a listen. Both of them come from the same place.

Robert Viagas
June 2008

TABLE OF CONTENTS

Timeline 2007-2008

Opening Nights, News Headlines and Other Significant Milestones of the Season

A busy season of new musicals and plays meant that Broadway continued to boom despite a strike and a looming recession.

Broadway 2007-2008 was also a season of construction around Times Square, with scaffolding not only surrounding Duffy Square where the new TKTS booth was being built, but on seemingly every side street where new office buildings and residential towers were rising. One of the towers belonged to the Square's namesake, *The New York Times*, which moved from West 43rd Street to Eighth Avenue and 41st.

Here are some of the season's biggest headlines on the Great White Way.

June 8, 2007—*The New York Times* is edited from its Times Square office for the last time. Plywood boxes go up around the Times' loading docks opposite Shubert Alley for the rest of the season as the interior of the building is dismantled.

June 10, 2007—The 2007 Tony Awards are held at Radio City Music Hall. *Spring Awakening* is named Best Musical, Tom Stoppard's *The Coast of Utopia* trilogy is named Best Play. *Company* and *Journey's End* are named Best Revivals.

June 19, 2007—The Tony Awards Administration Committee announces it will add two new competitive categories for future Tony Awards: Best Sound Design of a Play and Best Sound Design of a Musical. With the inclusion of these new categories, the Tony Awards now have a total of 27 competitive categories.

June 2007—Irving Berlin's daughters Mary Ellin Barrett, Linda Emmet and Elizabeth Peters, sell their portion of the Music Box Theatre to the Shubert Organization. The theatre has been owned half by the Shuberts and half by the Berlin estate for decades.

June 28, 2007—The first production of the season is a revival of John van Druten's 1940 comedy, *Old Acquaintance*, about two women whose longtime friendship is tested by conflicts over marriage, lifestyles, and how one of the women is raising her daughter.

July 2007—The Shubert Organization begins a renovation of the Longacre Theatre that takes it out of use for most of the rest of the season.

July 10, 2007—*Xanadu*, a new musical based on the cult-flop film about how the Greek muses help a young man fulfill his dream of running a roller disco, opens to surprisingly positive reviews. Credit goes to librettist Douglas Carter Beane, who has retrofitted the story and score with a tongue-in-cheek book. The show supplies backstage drama as leading man James Carpinello injures himself in an onstage roller-skating accident. Cheyenne Jackson goes on for him during the final previews and opening night as well.

July 20, 2007—Opening day for the film adaptation of the 2003 Tony Award-winning Best Musical *Hairspray*, starring John Travolta, Nikki Blonsky and Christopher Walken. It will go on to earn more than $200 million internationally.

July 29, 2007—*Beauty and the Beast*, Disney's inaugural producing venture on Broadway, closes after 5461 performances, a 13-year run. It is the sixth-longest running show in Broadway history.

August 19, 2007—The second musical of the season is a revival of perennial favorite *Grease*, whose leads were cast via a multi-week televi-

What are these folks doing out on 45th Street at curtain time? See November 10, 2007.

sion reality show, "You're the One That I Want," the previous winter and spring. The chosen couple, Max Crumm as Danny and Laura Osnes as Sandy, make their Broadway debuts with this production.

September 1, 2007—The official roll-out of PlaybillRadio.com, the 24/7 web radio station that plays showtunes, theatre news and Broadway interviews around the clock.

September 18, 2007—Tony-nominee *Legally Blonde* is filmed in its entirety, live, for broadcast on the MTV cable TV network.

September 24, 2007—Actors' Equity Association's Advisory Committee on Chorus Affairs names the ensemble of Broadway's *Legally Blonde* as winner of its new ACCA Award for Outstanding Broadway Chorus. It's being billed as the first industry award to honor "the distinctive talents and contributions made by the chorus."

October 2, 2007—Mayor Bloomberg proclaims the block of 47th Street between Eighth and Ninth Avenues "Forbidden Broadway" in honor of the 25th anniversary of Gerard

Alessandrini's parody revue of that title, which plays at the 47th St Theatre. Chita Rivera appears at a ceremony to hang the new street sign.

October 4, 2007—Playwright Theresa Rebeck makes her Broadway debut with *Mauritius*, a drama about two sisters who inherit an enormously valuable postage stamp, and the effect it has on their relationship and on the people around them.

October 10, 2007—The Theatre Development Fund announces that the stalled rebuilding of the TKTS discount ticket booth in Times Square is back on track for a spring 2008 reopening. Underway since May 1, 2006, the $14.5 million project ran into construction delays. TKTS has been operating out of temporary quarters in the ground floor of the Marriott Marquis Hotel on 46th Street. By the end of the season, however, the booth is still not ready.

October 11, 2007—The first revival of Terrence McNally's 1975 farce *The Ritz*, involving a man (Kevin Chamberlin) on the run from the mob, who hides out in a gay bath house. The production features Rosie Perez, Brooks Ashmanskas and Seth Rudetsky.

October 13, 2007—The premiere broadcast of *Legally Blonde: The Musical* on MTV.

October 18, 2007—David Grindley stages a rare revival of George Bernard Shaw's *Pygmalion* (the source material for *My Fair Lady*) starring Jefferson Mays as Henry Higgins and Claire Danes as Eliza Doolittle.

October 25, 2007—Chazz Palminteri fulfills his dream to open his one-man Off-Broadway show *A Bronx Tale*—which has already been adapted as a successful film—on Broadway. The acclaimed actor tells of his upbringing in the world of gangsters.

November 1, 2007—Kevin Kline plays Edmond Rostand's hypertrophic warrior-poet in a major revival of *Cyrano de Bergerac*, co-starring Jennifer Garner and Daniel Sunjata.

November 4, 2007—Tom Stoppard recalls the brief 1968 "Prague Spring" uprising of Czechoslovakians against the Soviet occupation of their country in the drama *Rock 'n' Roll*, starring Rufus Sewell, Sinéad Cusack and Brian Cox.

November 5, 2007—The Broadway audience is getting a little younger and more diversified, according to the annual demographics report from The League of American Theatres and Producers. The report, which surveyed audiences in the 2006-2007 season, found that the average age of the Broadway theatregoer was 41.2 years, the lowest in recent years, while those under 18 bought 1.42 million tickets, a 23 percent jump in that category in just one year. Also, the study found that 26 percent of theatregoers were non-Caucasians, half again as many as five years ago. The League also found that tourists—both domestic U.S. and interna-

Timeline 2007-2008

tional—bought 65 percent of the 12.3 million tickets sold for Broadway shows last season. Overall, foreign tourists comprised 16 percent of Broadway audiences, which is the highest in recent history.

November 8, 2007—Opening night for *Young Frankenstein*—officially *The New Mel Brooks Musical Young Frankenstein*, a musical stage adaptation of his cult film parody of old-time horror movies with a full score by Brooks. Roger Bart, Sutton Foster, Andrea Martin and Shuler Hensley star in the production, directed and choreographed by Susan Stroman. The show comes under strong criticism—including some by the first night critics—for setting aside some tickets at a top price of $450. Brooks and the producers say they're only trying to get back some of what scalpers charge for premium tickets.

Jujamcyn to allow *The Grinch* to resume, and it does, this same evening.

November 28, 2007—An overall contract agreement is reached late this evening, and the strike ends.

November 29, 2007—Nearly all Broadway shows resume performances tonight after settlement of the 19-day stagehands' strike, which is estimated to have cost the theatre industry and the New York economy nearly $40 million. Many shows that had been previewing at the time of the strike now scramble to schedule new opening dates over the next two weeks.

December 2007—Nina Lannan, new chair of the League of American Theatres and Producers, announces that the group is being rechristened simply The Broadway League.

December 2, 2007— Michael Cerveris, John Cullum, Martha Plimpton, Jonathan Cake and

playing cards in their midst on Christmas Eve might just be Satan.

December 9, 2007—David Ives adapts Mark Twain's long-lost comedy *Is He Dead?*, originally written in 1898, about an artist who pretends to be dead so he'll become famous. Michael Blakemore directs a cast that includes Norbert Leo Butz, Jenn Gambatese, Byron Jennings, Michael McGrath and John McMartin.

December 12, 2007—One of the last vestiges of bad old Times Square vanishes with the demolition of the Playpen Theatre on Eighth Avenue near 44th Street. It opened in 1916 as the Ideal Theatre, a cinema and vaudeville house, but spent its later years as a porn palace.

December 16, 2007— Raúl Esparza, Ian McShane, Eve Best, and Michael McKean star in a revival of Harold Pinter's *The Homecoming*, about an estranged brother's return to his menacing family.

December 17-18, 2007—Surviving members of the original cast of *West Side Story* reunite to mark the show's 50th anniversary at the annual "Gypsy of the Year" celebration. Among participants on the stage of the New Amsterdam Theatre are original Maria, Carol Lawrence, and original Anita, Chita Rivera.

December 21, 2007—Tim Burton's film of the Tony-winning 1979 Best Musical *Sweeney Todd: The Demon Barber of Fleet Street* opens, starring Johnny Depp and Helena Bonham Carter. The film will go to earn more than $150 million internationally.

December 31, 2007—Year-end accounting by the Broadway League shows that Broadway earned $938 million in calendar 2007 (a fiscal year with 53 weeks), up 3.5 percent over 2006. Only the losses incurred during the November strike prevented the total from topping $1 billion for the first time. Attendance rose to 12.29 million in 2007, about 2.7 percent more than in 2006. Average ticket price for 2007: $76.32.

January 10, 2008—A stage adaptation of the Disney animated film *The Little Mermaid* features the original movie score by Alan Menken and the late Howard Ashman, plus ten new songs by Menken and Glenn Slater. Francesca Zambello directs a cast led by Sierra Boggess as Ariel the mermaid, and Sherie Rene Scott as Ursula, the tentacled sea witch.

January 13, 2008—Tim Burton's *Sweeney Todd* movie wins the Golden Globe Award as Best Motion Picture—Musical or Comedy. Johnny Depp is named Best Actor in a Motion Picture—Musical or Comedy.

January 15, 2008—An unusual tongue-in-cheek stage adaptation of the Alfred Hitchcock film thriller *The 39 Steps* arrives on Broadway from London, with the story's dozens of characters performed, quick-change style, by an ensemble of four—and possibly five—actors.

January 17, 2008—In the midst of the presidential primary season, David Mamet opens

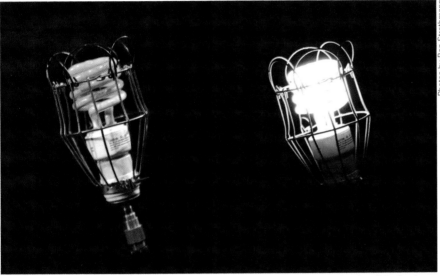

Broadway Goes Green: A CFL bulb replaces the traditional incandescent bulb in the ghostlight that burns all night at the Biltmore Theatre. See Spring 2008.

Photos by Ben Strothmann

November 9, 2007—Return engagement of the holiday show *Dr. Seuss' How the Grinch Stole Christmas!—The Musical*, starring Patrick Page as the Grinch.

November 10, 2007—Local 1 of IATSE, the stagehands' union, goes on strike, shutting down most Broadway shows.

November 16, 2007—CBS begins offering free WiFi access throughout Times Square.

November 18, 2007—After an extended negotiating session, talks between producers and stagehands break down and producers cancel performances over the Thanksgiving holiday weekend.

November 19, 2007—Local 1 agrees to allow *The Grinch* to reopen when the producers present evidence that their contract is separate from the one in dispute. In response, St. James theatre owners announce a lockout of *The Grinch*.

November 26, 2007—A judge orders

Phylicia Rashad star in William Shakespeare's rarely-produced romance *Cymbeline*, directed by Mark Lamos.

December 3, 2007— The head of the RCA corporation battles wits with a young prodigy for control of a new invention called television in Aaron Sorkin's fact-based drama, *The Farnsworth Invention*, starring Hank Azaria and Jimmi Simpson, and directed by Des McAnuff.

December 4, 2007—Transfer of Steppenwolf Theatre Company's run of Tracy Letts' drama *August: Osage County*, about what happens when a far-flung rural Oklahoma family gathers after the family patriarch goes missing. The show will go on to sweep all the Broadway Best Play awards of 2008.

December 6, 2007—The Royal National Theatre's production of Conor McPherson's Dublin-set play *The Seafarer* is about a group of men who discover that the mysterious stranger

his political comedy, *November*, about an entertainingly corrupt U.S. President (Nathan Lane), who tries to leverage a turkey-pardoning into a surprise second term.

January 18, 2008—"American Idol" runner-up Clay Aiken joins the cast of *Monty Python's Spamalot* as "bravely bold" Sir Robin.

January 24, 2008—S. Epatha Merkerson plays a woman trying to cope with loneliness, longing and an alcoholic husband (Kevin Anderson) in a revival of William Inge's 1950 drama *Come Back, Little Sheba*.

February 10, 2008—The original cast recording of *Spring Awakening* wins the Grammy Award as Best Musical Show Album.

February 20, 2008—The Tony Award-winning 2006 revival of *Company* is broadcast on PBS.

February 21, 2008—A hit London production of another Sondheim musical, *Sunday in the Park With George*, comes to Studio 54 with London leads Daniel Evans as George and Jenna Russell as Dot. Directed by Sam Buntrock, the production is notable for the use of animated drawings (designed by Timothy Bird) to illustrate the progress of the painting that forms the show's centerpiece.

February 25, 2008—A television adaptation of the Tony-winning revival of *A Raisin in the Sun*, starring Sean Combs, Phylicia Rashad and Audra McDonald, is broadcast on ABC after debuting at the Sundance Film Festival.

February 28, 2008—A young black Californian who feels trapped by his religious suburban upbringing goes on a coming-of-age odyssey to Bohemian Amsterdam and Berlin in *Passing Strange*, a musical narrated by the rock musician Stew, who co-composed the score with Heidi Rodewald.

March 6, 2008—Anika Noni Rose and James Earl Jones star as Maggie and Big Daddy in Debbie Allen's all-black revival of *Cat on a Hot Tin Roof*, also featuring Phylicia Rashad as Big Mama and Terrence Howard as Brick.

March 9, 2008—Transfer of the Off-Broadway musical *In The Heights*, about life among the Latino residents of Manhattan's Washington Heights neighborhood. Lin-Manuel Miranda co-wrote and stars in the show, along with Mandy Gonzalez, Karen Olivo and Priscilla Lopez.

Spring 2008—Skyrocketing energy costs and a desire to be eco-friendly prompt theatre managers to find ways to conserve. As a symbolic gesture, electricians replace standard incandescent bulbs with CFL bulbs in the ghostlights that burn all night on Broadway stages.

March 27, 2008—Patti LuPone brings her summer 2007 "Encores!" revival of the musical *Gypsy* to Broadway, co-starring Laura Benanti and Boyd Gaines. Librettist Arthur Laurents directs.

April 3, 2008—The first-ever Broadway revival of Rodgers and Hammerstein's *South Pacific* stars Kelli O'Hara and Brazilian opera

Where is this ticket buyer? See October 10, 2007.

singer Paulo Szot, directed by Bartlett Sher. Unbilled co-star is the 30-piece orchestra, one of the largest on Broadway.

April 3, 2008—After a months-long internet gag campaign to get their Off-Broadway musical to Broadway, life imitates art for the creators of *[title of show]*, who announce that real-life producers have indeed stepped up to move the show to Broadway in the coming summer.

April 7, 2008—*August: Osage County* wins the Pulitzer Prize for Drama, beginning its sweep of Best Play awards.

April 7, 2008—Also today, a proposal by Mayor Michael Bloomberg to charge drivers eight dollars to enter Manhattan below 60th Street—including the entire Times Square theatre district—fails to come to a vote in Albany, effectively killing the measure.

April 8, 2008—Shakespeare's bloody tragedy *Macbeth* returns to Broadway with Patrick Stewart in the title role of a murderous nobleman who ascends to the throne with the aid of his plotting wife, played by Kate Fleetwood. The stylish Chichester Festival Theatre production is directed by Rupert Goold.

April 15, 2008—Television star Mario Lopez makes his Broadway debut as Zach in the revival of *A Chorus Line* at the Schoenfeld Theatre.

April 17, 2008—Harvey Fierstein is librettist and co-star of *A Catered Affair*, a musical adaptation of the film of the same title, with music and lyrics by John Bucchino. Faith Prince, Tom Wopat, Leslie Kritzer and Matt Cavenaugh co-star in this show about a working class couple trying to stage a grand wedding for their only daughter. Directed by John Doyle.

April 24, 2008—*Hairspray* librettists Mark O'Donnell and Thomas Meehan fashion a musical from another John Waters film, *Cry-Baby*, set in the world of "Squares" and "Drapes" in 1950s Baltimore. Mark Brokaw directs a cast that includes James Snyder, Harriet Harris and Elizabeth Stanley, perform-

ing a score by Broadway newcomers Adam Schlesinger and David Javerbaum.

April 27, 2008—Morgan Freeman, Frances McDormand, Peter Gallagher and Chip Zien star in a revival of *The Country Girl*, Clifford Odets' backstage drama about an alcoholic actor trying to make a comeback. Directed by Mike Nichols.

April 30, 2008—Laurence Fishburne stars in the solo drama *Thurgood*, about the life of Civil Rights activist and Supreme Court Justice Thurgood Marshall.

May 1, 2008—Laura Linney and Ben Daniels star in a revival of *Les Liaisons Dangereuses*, Christopher Hampton's 1780s-set Parisian drama of sex and scheming among the aristocracy.

May 4, 2008—Broadway transfer of the hit London revival of *Boeing-Boeing*, Marc Camoletti's sex farce about a swinging bachelor and his three stewardess girlfriends. It stars Mark Rylance, Bradley Whitford, Christine Baranski and Gina Gershon, and is directed by Matthew Warchus.

May 6, 2008—*Glory Days*, coming-of-age pop musical, written by young newcomers Nick Blaemire (music and lyrics) and James Gardiner (book), transfers to Broadway from a hit run at Signature Theatre in Virginia. Its stay is brief, however: it closes after 17 previews and a single regular performance, the first Broadway show to do so since *The Oldest Living Confederate Widow Tells All* in 2003, and first Broadway musical to do so since a revival of *Take Me Along* in 1985. It earns the nickname "Glory Day."

May 7, 2008—Manhattan Theatre Club revives *Top Girls*, Caryl Churchill's play about the price a professional woman pays to rise to the top of the workplace ladder. Elizabeth Marvel, Martha Plimpton and Marisa Tomei star.

May 10, 2008—The creators and marketers of *Xanadu* create a viral Tony campaign centered on the adventures of a 10-year-old "mogul" named Cubby Bernstein, who schmoozes his way around Broadway trying to drum up votes for his show...which is subsequently shut out of the Tony Awards.

May 31, 2008—Broadway closes the books on the 2007-2008 season, with the boxoffice down slightly, owing partly to the fall stagehands' strike. Thirty-six new productions opened during the season, one more than the previous year. For this 52-week period ending May 25, 2008, paid attendance at Broadway shows was 12.27 million, down two tenths of a percent from last season, according to figures released by The Broadway League. Broadway shows grossed approximately $937.5 million, compared to the previous season's record of $938.5 million. League officials estimate that had the strike not occurred, all-time records for both box-office grosses and attendance would have been set with an estimated $975 million in grosses, still just short of the elusive billion-dollar season.

Head of the Class

Trends, Extraordinary Achievements and Peculiar Coincidences of the Season

Most Tony Awards to a Musical: *South Pacific* (7, a record for a revival).

Most Tony Awards to a Play *August: Osage County* (5).

Catchphrases and Memorable Quotes: "I'm running things now," *August: Osage County*. "She gave me her key," *Passing Strange*. "E-evil woman," *Xanadu*.

Self-Starters: Want to star in a Broadway show? Write one for yourself, like these people. Lin-Manuel Miranda in *In The Heights*, Stew and Heidi Rodewald in *Passing Strange*, Harvey Fierstein in *A Catered Affair*, Bob Martin in *Drowsy Chaperone*, Chazz Palmenteri in *A Bronx Tale*.

Women Drivers: Once the preserve of male directors, this Broadway season saw many of its biggest productions staged by women: Maria Aitken (*The 39 Steps*), Debbie Allen (*Cat on a Hot Tin Roof*), Annie Dorsen (*Passing Strange*), Kathleen Marshall (*Grease*), Anna D. Shapiro (*August: Osage County*), Susan Stroman (*Young Frankenstein*), Francesca Zambello (*The Little Mermaid*).

Awards They Should Give: #1 Best New Showtune. Our nominees: "Don't Ever Stop Saying I Love You" from *A Catered Affair*. "I Want the Good Times Back" from *The Little Mermaid*. "It Won't Be Long Now" from *In The Heights*. "Love Like That" from *Passing Strange*. "The Brain" from *Young Frankenstein*.

Non-Traditional Casting: The entire cast of *Cat on a Hot Tin Roof*; S. Epatha Merkerson in *Come Back, Little Sheba*; Morgan Freeman in *The Country Girl*; Audra McDonald in *110 in the Shade*, Phylicia Rashad in *Cymbeline*, Norm Lewis in *The Little Mermaid*; The black Seabees in *South Pacific*.

Class of the Head (Coiffure-Related Titles): *Hairspray, Legally Blonde, Grease*, the Central Park concert production of *Hair*.

Hey, We're Over Here! (Posters Showing the Back of People's Heads): *A Chorus Line, The Farnsworth Invention, Jersey Boys, The Little Mermaid, The Radio City Christmas Show*.

Omigod You Guys! Year II: Shows With Pre-Teen, Teenage or Barely Post-Teen Girls As Lead or Important Characters (Though Not Always Played By Teens): *August: Osage County, The Color Purple, Cry-Baby, Grease, Grey Gardens, Gypsy, Hairspray, Legally Blonde, Les Misérables, The Little Mermaid, Mary Poppins, Spelling Bee, Spring Awakening, Top Girls, Wicked*.

Awards They Should Give: #2 Best Special Effects. Our nominees: The animated drawings in *Sunday in the Park With George*. The transition from ocean surface to ocean floor (and back) in *The Little Mermaid*. The simple set pieces that turn into trains, swamps, hotels, and Scotland in *The 39 Steps*. The reanimation of the monster in *Young Frankenstein*.

Broadway's Longest Runs

By number of performances. Asterisk (*) indicates show still running as of May 31, 2008. Totals are for original runs except where otherwise noted.

* *The Phantom of the Opera* 8463
Cats 7485
Les Misérables 6680
A Chorus Line 6137
Oh! Calcutta! (Revival) 5959
Beauty and the Beast 5461
* *Rent* 5027
* *Chicago* (Revival) 4780
* *The Lion King* 4412
Miss Saigon 4097
42nd Street 3486
Grease 3388
Fiddler on the Roof 3242
Life With Father 3224
Tobacco Road 3182
Hello, Dolly! 2844
* *Mamma Mia!* 2748
My Fair Lady 2717
The Producers 2502
* *Hairspray* 2385

Suicide or Threatened Suicide: *August: Osage County, Country Girl, Jersey Boys, Les Misérables, Macbeth, Spring Awakening*.

Roller Skating: *Xanadu* and *The Little Mermaid*.

Pullet Surprise: There were six Pulitzer Prize winners running on Broadway this season. Since the founding of the Pulitzer Prize for Drama in 1917 only seven musicals have won the coveted honor: *Of Thee I Sing* (1931), **South Pacific** (1949), *Fiorello* (1960), *How to Succeed in Business Without Really Trying* (1962), **A Chorus Line** (1976), **Sunday in the Park With George** (1984) and *Rent* (1996). Of them, four were playing on Broadway in spring 2008 (the ones in boldface type). Two more Pulitzer-winning plays joined them: the revival of **Cat on a Hot Tin Roof** (1954) and the 2008 winner **August: Osage County**.

Step on It! Taxicab ownership presented moral dilemmas in two musicals this season. Taxi or wedding? (*A Catered Affair*). Taxi or college education? (*In The Heights*).

Awards They Should Give: #3 Hottest Couple. Paulo Szot and Kelli O'Hara in *South Pacific*, Sean Palmer and Sierra Boggess in *The Little Mermaid*, Terrence Howard and Anika Noni Rose in *Cat on a Hot Tin Roof*, Leslie Kritzer and Matt Cavenaugh in *A Catered Affair*, Max Crumm and Laura Osnes in *Grease*. Kerry Butler and Cheyenne Jackson in *Xanadu*.

Plots About Deals Gone Bad: *Boeing-Boeing, Chicago, Cymbeline, Cyrano de Bergerac, The Farnsworth Invention, Is He Dead?, The Little Mermaid, Macbeth, Mauritius, November, Old Acquaintance, The Seafarer, Top Girls*.

Getting Married Today (Shows with Weddings): *A Catered Affair, Avenue Q, The Color Purple, Company, Drowsy Chaperone, Grey Gardens, Legally Blonde, The Little Mermaid, Lovemusik, Mamma Mia!, The Pirate Queen, Tarzan, Young Frankenstein*.

Point/Counterpoint: "I'm as normal as blueberry pie."—*South Pacific*. "Goodbye to blueberry pie."—*Gypsy*.

Awards They Should Give: #4 Best New Rendition of an Old Song in a Revival or Jukebox Musical. Our nominees: Patti LuPone's "Everything's Coming Up Roses" in *Gypsy*. Mary Testa's and Jackie Hoffman's "Evil Woman" in *Xanadu*. Jenna Russell's and Daniel Evans' "Move On" in *Sunday in the Park With George*. Paulo Szot's "This Nearly Was Mine" in *South Pacific*. Kelli O'Hara's "A Wonderful Guy" in *South Pacific*. Seth Rudetsky's "Magic To Do" in *The Ritz*.

Shows With Jail Scenes: *Chicago, The Color Purple, Cry-Baby, Hairspray, Inherit the Wind, Legally Blonde, Les Misérables, The Pirate Queen*.

Fastest Quick-Changes: Twelve in 40 seconds: Arnie Burton and Cliff Saunders in *The 39 Steps*.

Coolest Program Credit: "Card Shark Consultant" (Laura Linney on *Les Liaisons Dangereuses*).

Awards They Should Give: #5 Best Show-stopping Moment. Retracting the stage to reveal the 30-piece orchestra in *South Pacific*. Patti LuPone's "Rose's Turn" in *Gypsy*. Colman Domingo's turn as a ranting German performance artist in *Passing Strange*.

Suppertime (Shows With Meal Scenes): *August: Osage County, A Catered Affair, Gypsy, Rent, Top Girls*.

Mount Rushmore (Eminences Grise Working on Broadway This Season): Stephen Sondheim, James Earl Jones, Phylicia Rashad, Morgan Freeman, John Waters, Arthur Laurents, Mel Brooks, Frank Langella, Christopher Plummer, Brian Dennehy, Hal Prince, Patrick Stewart, John Cullum, Tony Roberts, Vanessa Redgrave, Angela Lansbury, Marian Seldes, Mike Nichols and John Kander.

Working Hard: Boyd Gaines had major roles in three shows this season: *Journey's End, Pygmalion* and *Gypsy*.

Vanity Titles (Just in Case We Didn't Already Know): Actual official titles: *Dr. Seuss' How the Grinch Stole Christmas—The Musical!, Monty Python's Spamalot, The New Mel Brooks Musical Young Frankenstein, Rodgers and Hammerstein's South Pacific*.

Autographs

The Playbill Broadway Yearbook

2007 • 4 • 2008

shows

August: Osage County

First Preview: October 30, 2007. Opened: December 4, 2007.
Still running as of May 31, 2008.

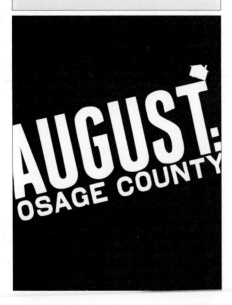

CAST

Beverly Weston	DENNIS LETTS
Violet Weston	DEANNA DUNAGAN
Barbara Fordham	AMY MORTON
Bill Fordham	JEFF PERRY
Jean Fordham	MADELEINE MARTIN
Ivy Weston	SALLY MURPHY
Karen Weston	MARIANN MAYBERRY
Mattie Fae Aiken	RONDI REED
Charlie Aiken	FRANCIS GUINAN
Little Charles	IAN BARFORD
Johnna Monevata	KIMBERLY GUERRERO
Steve Heidebrecht	BRIAN KERWIN
Sheriff Deon Gilbeau	TROY WEST

SETTING

A large country home outside Pawhuska, Oklahoma,
60 miles northwest of Tulsa, Oklahoma.

UNDERSTUDIES/STANDBYS

For Charles, Beverly: MUNSON HICKS
For Violet, Mattie Fae: SUSANNE MARLEY
For Steve, Bill, Sheriff Deon Gilbeau:
JAY PATTERSON
For Barbara, Karen, Ivy: DEE PELLETIER
For Jean: MOLLY RANSON
For Johnna: KRISTINA VALADA-VIARS
For Little Charles: TROY WEST

---

⑤ IMPERIAL THEATRE
249 West 45th Street
A Shubert Organization Theatre

Gerald Schoenfeld, *Chairman*   Philip J. Smith, *President*

Robert E. Wankel, *Executive Vice President*

Jeffrey Richards   Jean Doumanian   Steve Traxler   Jerry Frankel
Ostar Productions   Jennifer Manocherian   The Weinstein Company
Debra Black/Daryl Roth   Ronald & Marc Frankel/Barbara Freitag
Rick Steiner/Staton Bell Group

PRESENT

The Steppenwolf Theatre Company production of

BY

Tracy Letts

with

Ian Barford   Deanna Dunagan   Kimberly Guerrero   Francis Guinan
Brian Kerwin   Dennis Letts   Madeleine Martin   Mariann Mayberry   Amy Morton
Sally Murphy   Jeff Perry   Rondi Reed   Troy West

SCENIC DESIGN	COSTUME DESIGN	LIGHTING DESIGN	SOUND DESIGN
Todd Rosenthal	Ana Kuzmanic	Ann G. Wrightson	Richard Woodbury

ORIGINAL MUSIC	DRAMATURG	ORIGINAL CASTING
David Singer	Edward Sobel	Erica Daniels

NEW YORK CASTING	FIGHT CHOREOGRAPHER	DIALECT COACH
Stuart Howard, Amy Schecter & Paul Hardt	Chuck Coyl	Cecilie O'Reilly

PRODUCTION STAGE MANAGER	PRODUCTION SUPERVISOR	TECHNICAL SUPERVISOR
Deb Styer	Jane Grey	Theatersmith, Inc./Smitty

PRESS REPRESENTATIVE	MARKETING SERVICES	GENERAL MANAGEMENT
Jeffrey Richards Associates	TMG The Marketing Group	Richards/Climan, Inc.

DIRECTED BY

Anna D. Shapiro

"August: Osage County" was commissioned by Steppenwolf Theatre Company and the World Premiere was presented at
Steppenwolf Theatre Company, Chicago, IL. Martha Lavey, Artistic Director and David Hawkanson, Executive Director

The Producers wish to express their appreciation to the Theatre Development Fund for its support of this production.

 LIVE BROADWAY

12/4/07

Deanna Dunagan (standing)
with members of the
ensemble.

Photo by Michael Brosilow

August: Osage County

Ian Barford
Little Charles

Deanna Dunagan
Violet Weston

Kimberly Guerrero
Johnna Monevata

Francis Guinan
Charlie Aiken

Brian Kerwin
Steve Heidebrecht

Dennis Letts
Beverly Weston

Madeleine Martin
Jean Fordham

Mariann Mayberry
Karen Weston

Amy Morton
Barbara Fordham

Sally Murphy
Ivy Weston

Jeff Perry
Bill Fordham

Rondi Reed
Mattie Fae Aiken

Troy West
Sheriff Deon Gilbeau

Munson Hicks
u/s Charles, Beverly

Susanne Marley
u/s Violet, Mattie Fae

Jay Patterson
u/s Steve, Bill, Sheriff

Dee Pelletier
u/s Barbara, Karen, Ivy

Molly Ranson
u/s Jean

Kristina Valada-Viars
u/s Johnna

Tracy Letts
Playwright

Anna D. Shapiro
Director

Todd Rosenthal
Set Design

Ana Kuzmanic
Costume Design

Ann G. Wrightson
Lighting Design

Richard Woodbury
Sound Design

David Singer
Original Music

Chuck Coyl
Fight Choreographer

Christopher C. Smith,
Smitty/
Theatersmith, Inc.
Technical Supervisor

David R. Richards and Tamar Haimes,
Richards/Climan, Inc.
General Manager

Jeffrey Richards
Producer

Jean Doumanian
Producer

Steve Traxler
Producer

Jerry Frankel
Producer

Bill Haber,
Ostar Productions
Producer

August: Osage County

Jennifer Manocherian
Producer

Bob Weinstein, The Weinstein Company
Producer

Harvey Weinstein, The Weinstein Company
Producer

Debra Black
Producer

Daryl Roth
Producer

Barbara Freitag
Producer

Rick Steiner/ Staton Bell Group
Producer

Martha Lavey
Artistic Director, Steppenwolf Theatre Company

David Hawkanson,
Executive Director, Steppenwolf Theatre Company

Anne Berkowitz
Understudy for Jean

Michael McGuire
Beverly Weston

Aaron Serotsky
Understudy for Little Charles/Sheriff Dean Gilbeau

CREW
Front Row (L-R): Jay Satterwite, Neil Rosenberg, Joshua Rosenberg, Jane Grey, Deb Styer.

Back Row (L-R): Paul Dean, Jr., Valerie Spradling, Rob Bevenger, Walter Bullard, Cambra Overend, Mary Miller, David Marquez.

BOX OFFICE
(L-R): Catherine Harbula, Bill Carrick, John Zameryka.

FRONT OF HOUSE STAFF
Front Row (L-R): Victor Perez, Carmella Giacomin, Ed Phillips, Michael Knowles, Emanuel Billingslea, Frances Barbaretti, Martin Werner.

Back Row (L-R): James Young, Jerry Gallagher, Jeffrey Cobbs, Crystal Walker, Dennis Norwood.

DOORMAN
Kevin Kennedy

August: Osage County

STAFF FOR *AUGUST: OSAGE COUNTY*

GENERAL MANAGEMENT
RICHARDS/CLIMAN, INC.
David R. Richards   Tamar Haimes
Laura Janik Cronin

GENERAL PRESS REPRESENTATIVE
JEFFREY RICHARDS ASSOCIATES
IRENE GANDY
Judith Hansen   Noah Himmelstein   Elon Rutberg

ASSISTANT PRODUCERS
MARK BARBER   PATRICK DALY   BEN WEST

COMPANY MANAGER
MARY MILLER

MARKETING SERVICES
TMG – THE MARKETING GROUP
Tanya Grubich   Laura Matalon
Victoria Cairl   Jessica Morris

PRODUCTION STAGE MANAGER ....Deb Styer
PRODUCTION SUPERVISOR ....Jane Grey
TECHNICAL SUPERVISOR ....Christopher C. Smith
Assistant Director ....Henry Wishcamper
Assistant Set Designers ....Kevin Depinet,
    Matthew D. Jordan, Martin Andrew Orlowicz,
    Stephen T. Sorenson
Assistant Costume Designer ....Amelia Dombrowski
Assistant Lighting Designer(s) ....Kathleen Dobbins/
    Kristina Kloss
Assistant Sound Designer ....Joanna Lynne Staub
Assistant to Mr. Richards................Noah Himmelstein
Assistant to Ms. Doumanian ....Jon Weissberg
Assistant to Mr. Traxler ....Brandi Preston
General Management Associate ....Jeromy Smith
General Management Intern ....Kayla Shriner-Cahn
Production Assistant ....Catherine Mancuso
Production Carpenter ....Don Oberpriller
Production Electrician ....Neil McShane
Production Props ....Neil Rosenberg
Production Sound ....Valerie Spradling
Head Carpenter ....Walter Bullard
Head Electrician ....Paul Dean, Jr.
Head Props..............................Jay Satterwite

Wardrobe Supervisor ....Rob Bevenger
Dresser ....Kathy Guida
Dialect Coach ....Cecilie O'Reilly
Advertising ....SpotCo./
    Drew Hodges, Jim Edwards
    Lauren Hunter, Josh Fraenkel
Website Design/
    Internet Marketing ....Situation Marketing/
    Damian Bazadona, John Lanasa
Banking ....JP Morgan Chase Bank/
    Richard Callian, Margaret Wong
Accountants ....FK Partners/
    Robert Fried, Elliott Aronstam
Legal Counsel ....Lazarus & Harris, LLP/
    Scott R. Lazarus, Esq.,
    Robert C. Harris, Esq., Diane Viale
Insurance ....DeWitt Stern Group, Inc./Joe Bower
Payroll ....CSI/Lance Castellana
Group Sales ....Broadway Inbound, Inc.
Merchandising ....Desiree
Production Photographer ....Joan Marcus
Company Mascots ....Joker, Lottie, Mr. Moon,
    Skye and Buster

CREDITS
Scenery constructed by Hudson Scenic Studios. Lighting equipment by PRG Lighting. Sound equipment by Sound Associates. Additional props by The Spoon Group. Hair by Jennifer Sliter and Marcus Garcia/Robert G. Salon. Major League Baseball ®footage used with permission of Major League Baseball Properties, Inc. "Little Charles" music and lyrics by David Singer. "Sanford and Son Theme" words and music by Quincy Jones. Copyright ©1972 Hee Bee Dooinit Music (ASCAP). Worldwide rights for Hee Bee Dooinit Music administered by Cherry Lane Music Publishing Company, Inc. (ASCAP). "Lay Down Sally" (Eric Patrick Clapton, Marcy Levy and George E. Terry) ©(Renewed), Throat Music Ltd. (PRS) and Eric Patrick Clapton (PRS). All rights on behalf of Throat Music Ltd. and Eric Patrick Clapton administered by Warner-Tamerlane Publishing Corp. All rights on behalf of Throat Music Ltd. administered by WB Music Corp. All rights reserved. Used by permission. Permissions cleared by B/Z Rights & Permission, Inc.

August: Osage County

SCRAPBOOK

Correspondent: Jane Grey, Stage Manager

Opening Night Gifts: Getting back on the boards after the Local 1 strike.

Most Exciting Celebrity Visitor and What They Did/Said: Warren Beatty & Annette Bening and their kids came back and lauded us with compliments. Julia Roberts sent a case of Perrier-Jouët to the cast after seeing the show. Diane Keaton sent a gorgeous bouquet of flowers to the company.

Who Has Done the Most Shows in Their Career: Rondi Reed has performed more than 60 productions at Steppenwolf alone.

Special Backstage Rituals: The character of Little Charles gives the character of Ivy a little charm bracelet each night before the show to jump start their backstory.

Favorite Moment During Each Performance: Sharing the love and the chicken during the Dinner Scene.

Favorite In-Theatre Gathering Place: Chitra's Third Act Lounge a.k.a. the SM Office

Favorite Off-Site Hangout: Pigalle.

Favorite Snack Food: Chocolate.

Favorite Therapies: Purell, Emergen-C, Ricola.

Memorable Ad-Libs: Dennis Letts, in response to the question, "What pills does she take?" said "A couple of them start with A," instead of "Valium, vicodin. Darvon, Darvocet, Percodan, Percocet. Xanax for fun. Oxycontin in a pinch. Some Black Mollies once, just to make sure I was still paying attention. And of course Dilaudid. I shouldn't forget Dilaudid." (Not an A in the bunch!)

Amy Morton made the Freudian slip "Hatey Mom" instead of "Howdy Mom" to which Deanna Dunagan replied accordingly "What's hatey about it?"

Memorable Press Encounter: Every Press

**Dennis Letts
1934-2008**

Encounter with Irene Gandy (press rep) is memorable.

Fastest Costume Change: Ain't nothin' goes fast in Oklahoma.

Busiest Day at the Box Office: Day After Opening: $600,000.

Memorable Directorial Note: "Choose between Bits. Pick One."

Nickname: Madeleine Martin, our 15-year-old company member: "Mad Dog."

Sweethearts Within the Company: Actor Ian Barford and Director Anna D. Shapiro.

Embarrassing Moment: An actress who shall remain nameless passed wind onstage and the audience heard it.

Mascot: Broadway Buster.

Coolest Thing About Being in This Show: It's a big fat-titty hit and you get a free meal every night onstage.

Memorable Opening Night Letter: From Gary Sinise, a founding member of Steppenwolf:

In the 33 years of the theatre's history, this is a first. We have achieved many things as a company over the years. We have performed in NY and around the world. We have won Tony Awards for adaptation and for revival. Our actors have gone on to great success in many aspects of the performing arts.

But we have never opened a world premiere on Broadway of an original play generated by one of our ensemble members. Not only is it an original play, but it is going to clean up and our writer is going to be hailed as the next great American playwright.

In 1995 we initiated the New Plays Project under Anna's supervision.

Twelve years later, our goal of discovering a great new American voice at the level of a Mamet or a Shepard has been achieved. So many new writers have come from theatres like The Public, Manhattan Theatre Club and Playwrights Horizons.

Now, thanks to Tracy and the hard work of Martha, Anna, Ed and all who have participated in the New Plays Initiative, Steppenwolf stands on a new plateau. Tracy is that great new American voice and he is shouting from the rooftops.

Congratulations to everyone who has worked so hard for this moment. Enjoy every bit of it. I am very proud.

Best,

Gary

1. The cast gathers on stage.
2. Company mascot, Broadway Buster.
3. What's wrong with this picture? For a brief time in spring 2008, when *August: Osage County* was moving from the Imperial Theatre to the Music Box, the show's logo appeared on both theatres' marquees.

Avenue Q

First Preview: July 10, 2003. Opened: July 31, 2003.
Still running as of May 31, 2008.

PLAYBILL®

CAST

(in order of appearance)

Princeton, Rod .... HOWIE MICHAEL SMITH
Brian .... EVAN HARRINGTON
Kate Monster, Lucy & others .... MARY FABER
Nicky, Trekkie Monster,
   Bear & others .... DAVID BENOIT
Christmas Eve .... ANN SANDERS
Gary Coleman .... HANEEFAH WOOD
Mrs. T., Bear & others .... JENNIFER BARNHART
Ensemble .... JONATHAN
                       ROOT,
               MATT SCHREIBER

Place: an outer borough of New York City
Time: the present

UNDERSTUDIES

For Princeton/Rod, Brian, Nicky/Trekkie/Bear:
JONATHAN ROOT, MATT SCHREIBER
For Kate Monster/Lucy:
JENNIFER BARNHART, AYMEE GARCIA,
SHARON WHEATLEY
For Mrs. T./Bear:
CARMEN RUBY FLOYD, AYMEE GARCIA,
SALA IWAMATSU, SHARON WHEATLEY
For Christmas Eve:
AYMEE GARCIA, SALA IWAMATSU
For Gary Coleman:
CARMEN RUBY FLOYD

Continued on next page

---

⑥ GOLDEN THEATRE
A Shubert Organization Theatre
Gerald Schoenfeld, *Chairman*   **Philip J. Smith,** *President*

Robert E. Wankel, *Executive Vice President*

Kevin McCollum   Robyn Goodman   Jeffrey Seller
Vineyard Theatre   and   The New Group
present

Music and Lyrics by   Book by   Based on an Original Concept by
Robert Lopez and Jeff Marx   **Jeff Whitty**   **Robert Lopez and Jeff Marx**

with
**Jennifer Barnhart, David Benoit, Mary Faber, Evan Harrington,
Ann Sanders, Howie Michael Smith, Haneefah Wood**

Puppets Conceived and Designed by
Rick Lyon

Set Design	Costume Design	Lighting Design	Sound Design
Anna Louizos	**Mirena Rada**	**Howell Binkley**	**Acme Sound Partners**

Animation Design	Music Director and Incidental Music	Music Coordinator
Robert Lopez	**Gary Adler**	**Michael Keller**

General Manager	Technical Supervisor	Production Stage Manager
John Corker	**Brian Lynch**	**Robert Witherow**

Press Representative	Casting	Associate Producers
Sam Rudy Media Relations	**Cindy Tolan**	**Sonny Everett Walter Grossman Mort Swinsky**

Music Supervision, Arrangements
and Orchestrations by
Stephen Oremus

Choreographer
Ken Roberson

Directed by
Jason Moore

Avenue Q was supported by a residency and public staged reading at the
2002 O'Neill Music Theatre Conference of the Eugene O'Neill Theater Center, Waterford, CT

www.avenueq.com

10/1/07

(L-R): Kate Monster, Sarah Stiles, Princeton and Howie Michael Smith.

Photo by Carol Rosegg

Avenue Q

Cast Continued

SWINGS
CARMEN RUBY FLOYD, AYMEE GARCIA,
SALA IWAMATSU, SHARON WHEATLEY

DANCE CAPTAIN
AYMEE GARCIA

BAND
Keyboard/Conductor:
GARY ADLER
Keyboard/Associate Conductor:
MARK HARTMAN
Reeds:
PATIENCE HIGGINS
Drums:
MICHAEL CROITER
Bass:
MARYANN McSWEENEY
Guitars:
BRIAN KOONIN

Photo by Carol Rosegg

Howie Michael Smith (R)
with Rod.

Jennifer Barnhart
Mrs. T., Bear & Others

David Benoit
Nicky, Trekkie, Bear & Others

Mary Faber
Kate Monster, Lucy & Others

Evan Harrington
Brian

Ann Sanders
Christmas Eve

Howie Michael Smith
Princeton/Rod

Haneefah Wood
Gary Coleman

Carmen Ruby Floyd
u/s for Gary Coleman, Mrs. T., Bear

Aymee E. Garcia
u/s Mrs. T., Bear & Others; Kate, Lucy; Christmas Eve

Sala Iwamatsu
u/s Christmas Eve, Mrs. T., Bear & Others

Jonathan Root
Ensemble

Matt Schreiber
Ensemble

Sharon Wheatley
u/s Mrs. T., Bear & Others; Kate, Lucy

Robert Lopez and Jeff Marx
Music and Lyrics, Original Concept

Jeff Whitty
Book

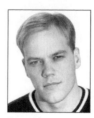

Jason Moore
Director

Ken Roberson
Choreographer

Stephen Oremus
Music Supervision/ Arrangements/ Orchestrations

Rick Lyon
Puppet Design

Avenue Q

Anna Louizos
Set Designer

Mirena Rada
Costume Design

Howell Binkley
Lighting Designer

Tom Clark, Mark Menard and Nevin Steinberg,
Acme Sound Partners
Sound Design

Gary Adler
*Musical Director/
Conductor/
Incidental Music*

Michael Keller
Music Coordinator

Brian Lynch/
Theatretech, Inc.
Technical Supervisor

John Corker
General Manager

Kevin McCollum
Producer

Robyn Goodman
Producer

Jeffrey Seller
Producer

Scott Elliott
Founding Artistic
Director,
The New Group
Producer

Sonny Everett
Associate Producer

Mort Swinsky
Associate Producer

Avenue Q
Alumni
2007-2008

Christian Anderson
*Nicky,
Trekkie Monster,
Bear & Others*

Minglie Chen
Christmas Eve

Hazel Anne
Raymundo
Swing

Jasmin Walker
*Understudy for Gary
Coleman*

Avenue Q
Transfer
Students
2007-2008

Christian Anderson
*Nicky,
Trekkie Monster,
Bear & Others*

Leo Daignault
Ensemble, Swing

Heather Hawkins
*Mrs. T., Bear &
Others*

Nicholas Kohn
Brian

Hazel Anne
Raymundo
Swing

Rashidra Scott
Gary Coleman

Sarah Stiles
*Kate Monster, Lucy
& Others*

Jasmin Walker
Swing

Avenue Q

Beauty and the Beast

First Preview: March 9, 1994. Opened: April 18, 1994.
Closed July 29, 2007 after 46 Previews and 5461 Performances.

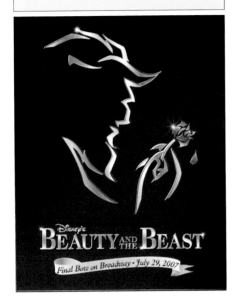

PLAYBILL

CAST

(in order of appearance)

Young Prince ....CONNOR GALLAGHER
Enchantress ....ELIZABETH POLITO
Beast ....STEVE BLANCHARD
Belle ....ANNELIESE VAN DER POL
Bookseller ....BILLY VITELLI
Lefou ....ALDRIN GONZALEZ
Gaston ....CHRIS HOCH
Three Silly Girls ....ALISA KLEIN,
TRACY RAE WILSON, TIA MARIE ZORNE
Maurice....................................JAMIE ROSS
Wolves ....ANA MARIA ANDRICAIN,
CHRISTOPHER DeANGELIS,
CONNOR GALLAGHER,
ELIZABETH POLITO
Cogsworth ....GLENN RAINEY
Lumiere ....DAVID deVRIES
Babette ....ANN MANDRELLA
Mrs. Potts ....JEANNE LEHMAN
Chip ....TREVOR BRAUN
(Wed. Eve., Thurs., Sat. Eve., Sun. Mat.)
MARLON SHERMAN
(Tues., Wed. Mat., Fri., Sat. Mat.)
Madame de la Grande Bouche ....MARY STOUT
Salt and Pepper .....CHRISTOPHER DeANGELIS,
GARRETT MILLER
Doormat ....CONNOR GALLAGHER
Cheesegrater ....ROD ROBERTS
Monsieur D'Arque ....BILLY VITELLI
Townspeople, Enchanted Objects ....
ANA MARIA ANDRICAIN,
CHRISTOPHER DeANGELIS,

Continued on next page

Continued on next page

⊰N⊱ LUNT–FONTANNE THEATRE
UNDER THE DIRECTION OF
JAMES M. NEDERLANDER AND JAMES L. NEDERLANDER

Disney Theatrical Productions
presents

STEVE BLANCHARD   ANNELIESE VAN DER POL
in

Disney's BEAUTY AND THE BEAST

Music by   *Lyrics by*   *Book by*
ALAN MENKEN   HOWARD ASHMAN & TIM RICE   LINDA WOOLVERTON

with

CHRIS HOCH   DAVID deVRIES   JEANNE LEHMAN
GLENN RAINEY   JAMIE ROSS

TREVOR BRAUN   ALDRIN GONZALEZ   ANN MANDRELLA
MARLON SHERMAN   MARY STOUT

ANA MARIA ANDRICAIN   CHRISTOPHER DeANGELIS   KEITH FORTNER   CONNOR GALLAGHER
ALISA KLEIN   DAVID E. LIDDELL   GARRETT MILLER   BILL NABEL   JAMES PATTERSON
ELIZABETH POLITO   ROD ROBERTS   DARIA LYNN SCATTON   JENNIFER SHRADER
DAVID SPANGENTHAL   GINA CARLETTE STATILE   ANN VAN CLEAVE   BILLY VITELLI
MARGUERITE WILLBANKS   TRACY RAE WILSON   TIA MARIE ZORNE

Scenic Design   *Costume Design*   *Lighting Design*
STANLEY A. MEYER   ANN HOULD-WARD   NATASHA KATZ

Sound Design   *Hair Design*   *Illusion Design*   *Prosthetics*
JONATHAN DEANS   DAVID H. LAWRENCE   JIM STEINMEYER   JOHN DODS
JOHN GAUGHAN

Associate Producer/Company Manager   *Production Supervisor*   *Production Stage Manager*
MARK ROZZANO   HARRIS PRODUCTION SERVICES   JOHN BRIGLEB

Casting   *Press Representative*
BINDER CASTING/MARK BRANDON   BONEAU/BRYAN-BROWN

Fight Direction   *Dance Arrangements*   *Music Coordinator*
RICK SORDELET   GLEN KELLY   JOHN MILLER

Musical Supervision   *Music Direction &*
& Vocal Arrangements   *Incidental Music Arrangements*
Orchestrations   DAVID FRIEDMAN   MICHAEL KOSARIN
DANNY TROOB

Choreography by
MATT WEST

Directed by
ROBERT JESS ROTH

Disney ON BROADWAY   © Disney

7/29/07

Anneliese van der Pol as Belle

Steve Blanchard as The Beast

11

Beauty and the Beast

MUSICAL NUMBERS

ACT ONE

Overture
Prologue
"Belle" ....Belle, Gaston, Lefou, Silly Girls, Townspeople
"No Matter What"* ....Maurice, Belle
"No Matter What"* (Reprise) ....Maurice
"Me"* ....Gaston, Belle
"Belle" (Reprise) ....Belle
"Home"* ....Belle
"Home"* (Reprise) ....Mrs. Potts
"Gaston" ....Lefou, Gaston, Silly Girls, Tavern Patrons
"Gaston" (Reprise) ....Gaston, Lefou
"How Long Must This Go On?"* ....Beast
"Be Our Guest" ....Lumiere, Mrs. Potts, Cogsworth, Madame de la Grande Bouche, Chip, Babette, Enchanted Objects
"If I Can't Love Her"* ....Beast

ACT TWO

Entr'acte/Wolf Chase
"Something There" ....Belle, Beast, Lumiere, Mrs. Potts, Cogsworth
"Human Again" ....Lumiere, Madame de la Grande Bouche, Cogsworth, Mrs. Potts, Babette, Chip, Enchanted Objects
"Maison des Lunes"* ....Gaston, Lefou, Monsieur D'Arque
"Beauty and the Beast" ....Mrs. Potts
"If I Can't Love Her"* (Reprise) ....Beast
"A Change In Me"* ....Belle
"The Mob Song" ....Gaston, Lefou, Monsieur D'Arque, Townspeople
"The Battle" ....The Company
"Transformation"* ....Beast, Belle
"Beauty and the Beast" (Reprise) ....The Company

*Music by Alan Menken and lyrics by Tim Rice.
All other lyrics by Howard Ashman and music by Alan Menken.

ORCHESTRA

Conductor : MICHAEL KOSARIN
Associate Conductor: KATHY SOMMER
Assistant Conductor: JOSEPH PASSARO
Assistant Conductor: AMY DURAN

Concertmaster:
SUZANNE ORNSTEIN
Violins:
LORRA ALDRIDGE, EVAN JOHNSON,
ROY LEWIS, KRISTINA MUSSER
Cellos:
CARYL PAISNER, JOSEPH KIMURA
Bass:
JEFFREY CARNEY
Flute:
KATHY FINK
Oboe:
VICKI BODNER
Clarinet/Flute:
KERIANN KATHRYN DiBARI

Flute/Clarinet:
TONY BRACKETT
Bassoon, Contrabassoon:
CHARLES McCRACKEN
Trumpets:
NEIL BALM, JAMES DE LA GARZA
French Horns:
JEFFREY LANG, ANTHONY CECERE,
ROBERT CARLISLE
Bass Trombone/Tuba:
PAUL FAULISE
Drums:
JOHN REDSECKER
Percussion:
JOSEPH PASSARO
Harp:
STACEY SHAMES
Keyboards:
KATHY SOMMER, MADELYN RUBINSTEIN

Music Coordinator: JOHN MILLER

Cast Continued

KEITH FORTNER, CONNOR GALLAGHER,
ALISA KLEIN, DAVID E. LIDDELL,
GARRETT MILLER, BILL NABEL,
JAMES PATTERSON, ELIZABETH POLITO,
ROD ROBERTS, DARIA LYNN SCATTON,
JENNIFER SHRADER,
DAVID SPANGENTHAL,
GINA CARLETTE STATILE,
ANN VAN CLEAVE, BILLY VITELLI,
MARGUERITE WILLBANKS,
TRACY RAE WILSON, TIA MARIE ZORNE

Voice of
Prologue Narrator: DAVID OGDEN STIERS

UNDERSTUDIES
Enchantress: DARIA LYNN SCATTON,
GINA CARLETTE STATILE
Young Prince: KEITH FORTNER,
DAVID E. LIDDELL
Beast: JAMES PATTERSON,
DAVID SPANGENTHAL
Belle: ANA MARIA ANDRICAIN,
JENNIFER SHRADER
Bookseller: KEITH FORTNER,
DAVID E. LIDDELL
Lefou: KEITH FORTNER,
CONNOR GALLAGHER
Gaston: JAMES PATTERSON,
DAVID SPANGENTHAL
Silly Girls: DARIA LYNN SCATTON,
GINA CARLETTE STATILE
Wolves: KEITH FORTNER,
DAVID E. LIDDELL,
DARIA LYNN SCATTON,
GINA CARLETTE STATILE
Maurice/Cogsworth: BILL NABEL,
BILLY VITELLI
Lumiere: CHRISTOPHER DeANGELIS,
BILL NABEL
Babette: ALISA KLEIN, TRACY RAE WILSON
Mrs. Potts/Madame de la Grande Bouche:
ANN VAN CLEAVE,
MARGUERITE WILLBANKS
Salt and Pepper/Doormat/Cheesegrater:
KEITH FORTNER, DAVID E. LIDDELL
Monsieur D'Arque: BILL NABEL,
DAVID SPANGENTHAL

SWINGS
KEITH FORTNER, DAVID E. LIDDELL,
DARIA LYNN SCATTON,
GINA CARLETTE STATILE

DANCE CAPTAIN
DARIA LYNN SCATTON

Beauty and the Beast

Steve Blanchard
Beast

Anneliese
van der Pol
Belle

Donny Osmond
Gaston (final performance)

David deVries
Lumiere

Jeanne Lehman
Mrs. Potts

Glenn Rainey
Cogsworth

Jamie Ross
Maurice

Trevor Braun
Chip at certain performances

Aldrin Gonzalez
Lefou

Ann Mandrella
Babette

Marlon Sherman
Chip at certain performances

Mary Stout
Madame de la Grande Bouche

Ana Maria Andricain
Ensemble

Christopher
DeAngelis
Ensemble/Salt

Keith Fortner
Ensemble/Swing

Connor Gallagher
Young Prince, Doormat, Ensemble

Alisa Klein
Ensemble/Silly Girl

David E. Liddell
Fight Captain/ Ensemble/Swing

Garrett Miller
Ensemble/Pepper

Bill Nabel
Ensemble

James Patterson
Ensemble

Elizabeth Polito
Enchantress/ Ensemble

Rod Roberts
Ensemble/ Cheesegrater

Daria Lynn Scatton
Ensemble/Swing/ Dance Captain

Jennifer Shrader
Ensemble

David Spangenthal
Ensemble

Gina Carlette Statile
Ensemble/Swing

Ann Van Cleave
Ensemble

Billy Vitelli
Ensemble/ Bookseller/ Monsieur D'Arque

Marguerite Willbanks
Ensemble

Tracy Rae Wilson
Ensemble/Silly Girl

Tia Marie Zorne
Ensemble/Silly Girl

Alan Menken
Composer

Howard Ashman
Lyricist

Tim Rice
Lyrics

Beauty and the Beast

Linda Woolverton
Book

Robert Jess Roth
Director

Matt West
Choreographer

Stanley A. Meyer
Scenic Designer

Ann Hould-Ward
Costume Designer

Natasha Katz
Lighting Design

Jonathan Deans
Sound Designer

David H. Lawrence
Hair Designer

Jim Steinmeyer
Illusions

John Dods
Prosthetics Designer

Binder Casting/
Mark Brandon
Casting

Rick Sordelet
Fight Director

John Miller
Music Coordinator

Danny Troob
Orchestrator

David Friedman
*Music Supervision/
Vocal Arrangements*

Michael Kosarin
*Music Direction/
Incidental Music
Arrangements*

Thomas Schumacher
*Disney Theatrical
Productions*

Tracy Generalovich
Ensemble/Silly Girl

Chris Hoch
Gaston

Stephanie Lynge
Ensemble

Jennifer Marcum
Ensemble/Silly Girl

Bret Shuford
Wolf

Beauty and the Beast

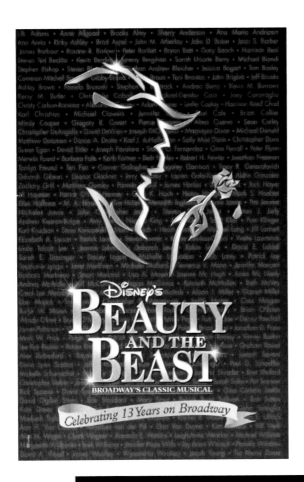

Disney's *Beauty and the Beast*
would like to thank the following for helping to keep the magic alive for 13 years on Broadway:

ALACER CORP	GREENBERG & HAMMER	NEW YORK SPACES/RIPLEY GRIER
ALCONE	HAIRESS	PENN & FLETCHER
AMERICAN PLUME & FANCY FEATHER	HAR-MAN BEADS	PERFORMING ARTS PHYSICAL THERAPY
AMY'S BREAD	HARRIS PRODUCTION SERVICES	PLAYBILL
ANDREW BENEPE	HELENA	PLUMA
ARNOLD LEVINE	HOCHIJOSE ORTEGA ASIATICO	PRG
B&J FABRICS	I. WEISS	RAY'S BEAUTY SUPPLY
BARBARA MATERA LTD	INTERNATIONAL COFFEE SYSTEMS	RICOLA
BLS LIMOUSINE SERVICE	IZQUIERDO STUDIO	ROSEBRAND
BOB KELLY WIG CREATIONS	JAUCHEM & MEEH	ROSEN & CHADWICK FABRICS
BRA-TENDERS	JC THEATRICALS	SCENIC TECHNOLOGIES
BULBTRONICS	JOHN DODS	SOUND ASSOCIATES
BURMAX COMPANY	JOHN JERARD STUDIO	STARLITE DELI
CAPEZIO	KIEHL'S	STEINLAUF & STOLLER
CARROLL MUSICAL INSTRUMENTS	LITTLE PIE COMPANY	STYLECREST FABRICS
COSTUME ARMOUR	LYNNE MACKEY	SUE HAMILTON
ELEGANT FABRICS	MANHATTAN MINI STORAGE	TO DEY
ENERGIZER	MANHATTAN WARDROBE SUPPLY	TOP HATS AMERICA
ERNEST WINZER THEATRICAL CLEANERS	MARIANNE CHALLIS	UNITED BEAUTY SUPPLY
GARDEN HARDWARE & SUPPLY	MB REGAN	UNITED CITY ICE CO
GENE MIGNOLA	MCKINNEY WELDING	VASILI SHOE REPAIR
GENIE INSTANT PRINTING CO	MICHAEL CURRY	WILTON ARMETALE
GOOD AND PLENTY	MP ASSOCIATES	WOODY SHELP
GRACE COSTUMES	NATIONAL FIBER TECHNOLOGIES	ZEE MEDICAL
	NEW DANCE GROUP STUDIO	

A Very Special Thanks To the Cast, Crew and Front of House Staff Who Are Members of the Following Theatrical Unions:

ACTORS' EQUITY ASSOCIATION	SOCIETY OF STAGE DIRECTORS AND CHOREOGRAPHERS (SSDC)
ASSOCIATION OF THEATRICAL PRESS AGENTS AND MANAGERS (ATPAM)	STAGEHANDS UNION LOCAL 1
ENGINEERS UNION LOCAL 30	TELEPHONE & MAIL ORDER CLERKS UNION LOCAL B-751
INTERNATIONAL ALLIANCE OF THEATRICAL STAGE EMPLOYEES (IATSE)	THEATRICAL WARDROBE UNION LOCAL 764
MAKE-UP ARTISTS & HAIRSTYLISTS UNION LOCAL 798	TREASURERS' & TICKET SELLERS' UNION LOCAL 751
MUSICIANS UNION LOCAL 802	UNITED SCENIC ARTISTS LOCAL 829
PORTERS' & CLEANERS' UNION LOCAL 32 BJ	USHERS & DOORMEN'S UNION LOCAL 306

On Wednesday, April 18th, Disney's *Beauty and the Beast* celebrated its 13th Anniversary with Broadway's biggest cast party! More than 125 past and present cast members gathered on stage at the Lunt-Fontanne Theatre to mark the occasion. These cast members represented the more than 250 actors who have starred in *Beauty and the Beast* on Broadway since the show's debut in 1994.

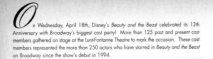

Photo by Lyn Hughes

In attendance were many notable past and present "Belles" including Deborah Gibson, Andrea McArdle and current "Belle" Anneliese van der Pol, star of Disney Channel's "That's So Raven," as well as many "Lumieres" from the last 13 years including Tony Award®-winning Gary Beach (original Lumiere), "All My Children" star Jacob Young and Disney Channel's "Johnny and the Sprites" star John Tartaglia. Many of the creative forces behind the show were also present to celebrate. Composer Alan Menken, director Robert Jess Roth, book writer Linda Woolverton, choreographer Matt West and scenic designer Stanley A. Meyer were among those who gathered together to "Be Our Guests" and to celebrate the success of Disney's inaugural Broadway production.

And there was quite a lot to celebrate! 'Beauty,' as it is affectionately called, is currently the 6th longest-running Broadway show of all time, logging in more performances than shows like *Miss Saigon*, *42nd Street*, *Fiddler on the Roof*, and *Hello, Dolly!*, among others. It holds records for the longest runs at both the Lunt-Fontanne Theatre and the Palace Theatre, its original Broadway home.

The highlight of the afternoon was an official proclamation from Mayor Bloomberg's office, naming April 18th, 2007, "*Beauty and the Beast* Day."

The magic behind Broadway's most enchanting musical.

BEAUTIFUL MILESTONES
On April 18, 1994, BEAUTY AND THE BEAST opened at the Palace Theatre.
On November 11, 1999, BEAUTY AND THE BEAST moved to the Lunt-Fontanne Theatre.
The show is the longest-running production at both the Palace Theatre and the Lunt-Fontanne Theatre.

On April 21, 2004, BEAUTY AND THE BEAST celebrated its 4,098th performance, passing "Miss Saigon" to become the 6th longest-running musical in Broadway history. It is the longest currently running American musical.

On July 29, 2007, BEAUTY AND THE BEAST plays its final performance on Broadway. The production will have played 46 previews and 5,464 regular performances.

WORLDWIDE SUCCESS
More than 26 million people have seen BEAUTY AND THE BEAST worldwide. The show has played in a total of 13 countries and 115 cities. The show has been translated into six languages including Chinese, Spanish, Japanese, German, Portuguese and Korean.

CELEBRITY CAST MEMBERS
More than 250 actors have performed on Broadway in BEAUTY AND THE BEAST. The show boasts a star-studded list of alumni performers including Toni Braxton (Belle), Ashley Brown (Belle), Tom Bosley (Maurice), Deborah Gibson (Belle), Andrea McArdle (Belle), Donny Osmond (Gaston), Christy Carlson Romano (Belle), Jamie-Lynn Sigler (Belle), John Tartaglia (Lumiere), Meshach Taylor (Lumiere), Anneliese van der Pol (Belle) and Jacob Young (Lumiere).

FUN FACTS
Over 120 wigs are worn on stage every night.
It took 20 pounds of human hair and over 400 man-hours to create the first Beast.
Belle's ball gown weighs over 40 pounds.
During "Be Our Guest," 36,000 top hats have been used.
Gaston has punched Lefou over 32,000 times.
The Beast has roared over 37,000 times.
There are enough lighting instruments on the set to light up a football stadium.
Over 1,500 beer mugs have been used in the "Gaston" number.
Maurice's invention has traveled over 375,000 feet.
More than 13,000 petals have fallen from the enchanted rose.

Beauty and the Beast

(L-R): Keith Cooper (Associate Company Manager), Tracey Malinowski (House Manager), Mark Rozzano (Associate Producer), Joe Olcese (Treasurer).

HOUSE PROPERTYMAN
Dennis Sabella

Photo by Sanford Kaplan

DRESSER
Michele Reisch

STAGE MANAGEMENT
(L-R): Michael Biondi, John Salvatore, Angela Piccinni and Elizabeth Larson.
Not Pictured: Margaret Howard, John Brigleb.

Photos by Ben Strothmann

Beauty and the Beast

FRONT OF HOUSE
Front Row (L-R):
Evelyn Fernandez (Ticket Taker), Lauren Banyai
(Usher), Angalic Cortes (Usher),
Barry Jenkins (Porter).

Second Row (L-R):
Carlo Mosarra (Usher), Hector Aguilar (Usher),
Paul Perez (Bag Checker),
Melody Rodriguez (Usher), Madeline Flores
(Directress), Joey Cintron (Usher).

Back Row (L-R):
Stephanie Martinez (Usher), Jessica Vargas
(Usher), Honey Owens (Directress),
Marlon Danton (Usher), Marisa Perez (Usher),
Mildred Villano (Usher),
Wil Pacheco (Usher), Roberto Calderon (Usher),
Jessica Gonzales and Susan Martin (Head Usher).

WARDROBE CREW
Front Row (L-R):
Michael Piatkowski, Teresia Larsen, Rose Keough,
Barbara Hladsky.

Back Row (L-R):
Eric Rudy (Assistant Wardrobe Supervisor),
Suzanne Sponsler, Joan Weiss, Claire Verlaet,
Billy Hipkins, Rita Santi and James Cavanaugh.

STAGE CREW
Front Row (L-R):
Jan Nebozenko (Sound),
Eddie McGarry (Spot Operator),
David Brickman (Spot Operator),
Eric Levy (Spot Operator).

Second Row (L-R):
Ned Hatton (Sound Effects Engineer),
George Dignam (Sound),
Gerald Schultz (Assistant Electrician/
Vari Lite Operator),
William C. Horton, Sr. (Assistant
Electrician/Special Effects Technician),
Peter Byrne (Head Electrician).

Back Row (L-R):
Mark Hallisey (Assistant Carpenter),
Mitch Christenson (Spot Operator),
Andrew D. Elman (Automation Carpenter),
Dana McDaniel (Automation Carpenter).

Beauty and the Beast

EVENING DOORMAN
Bob Garner

WIG CREW
Front Row (L-R): Amy Uhl, Elizabeth Mathews.
Second Row (L-R): Jennifer Mooney, Rene Kelly.
Back Row (L-R): Armando Licon, Mark Adam
Rampmeyer (Hair Supervisor).

BOX OFFICE
Joe Olcese (Treasurer) and Christine Desavino
(Box Office).

Photos by Ben Strothmann

STAFF FOR DISNEY'S *BEAUTY AND THE BEAST*

Company Manager ....MARK ROZZANO

Production Supervision ....Harris Production Services

General Press Representative ....Boneau/Bryan-Brown
Chris Boneau/Jim Byk/
Juliana Hannett

Production Stage Manager ....John Brigleb
Stage Manager ...............................M.A. Howard
Stage Manager ....John Salvatore
Stage Manager ....Elizabeth Larson
Dance Captain ....Daria Lynn Scatton
Fight Captain ....David E. Liddell

Puppet Design Consultant ....Michael Curry

Special Effects Consultant ....Jauchem & Meeh, NYC

Associate Production Supervisor ....Tom Bussey
Production Manager ....Elisa Cardone
Associate Scenic Designer ....Dennis W. Moyes
Principal Set Design Assistant ......Edmund A. LeFevre, Jr.
Set Design Assistants ....Stephen Carter,
Judy Gailen, Dana Kenn, Sarah Lambert
Associate Lighting Designers ....Gregory Cohen,
Dan Walker
Assistant Lighting Designers ....Rob Cangemi,
Maura Sheridan
Automated Lighting Programmers ....Aland Henderson,
Richard W. Knight
Associate Sound Designer ....John Petrafesa, Jr.
Original Pyrotechnic Designer ....Tylor Wymer

Automated Lighting Tracker ....John Viesta
Projection Effects ....Wendall K. Harrington
Associate Costume Designer ....Tracy Christensen
Assistants to Ms. Hould-Ward ....David C. Paulin,
Markas Henry, Mark Musters,
Fabio Toblini
Assistant to Mr. Lawrence ....Linda Rice
Synthesizer Programming .....Dan Tramon, Bruce Samuels

Production Carpenter ............................B.B. Baker
Production Flyman ....Peter H. Jackson III
Production Electrician ....Todd Davis
Production Property Master ....Joseph P. Harris, Jr.
Production Sound Engineer ....Scott Anderson
Production Wardrobe Supervisor ....Sue Hamilton
Production Hair Supervisor ....Wanda Gregory,
Mark Adam Rampmeyer
Production Prosthetics Supervisor ....Angela Johnson

Head Carpenter ................................B.B. Baker
Flyman ....Frank Frederico
Assistant Carpenter ....Mark Hallisey
Automation Carpenters ....Andrew D. Elman,
Hugh M. Hardyman
Head Electrician ....Peter Byrne
Assistant Electrician/Front Light ....Richard Sullivan
Assistant Electrician/
Special Effects Technician ....William C. Horton, Sr.
Assistant Electrician/Vari*Lite Operator .....Gerald Schultz
Head Sound Engineer ....Ned Hatton
Sound Effects Engineer ....George Dignam
Head Propertyman ....David L. Bornstein
Assistant Propertyman ....Joel DeRuyter
Wardrobe Supervisor ....Julie Ratcliffe
Assistant Wardrobe Supervisor ....Eric Rudy

Ms. van der Pol's Dresser ....Erin Byrne
Mr. Blanchard's Dresser ....Rita Santi
Wardrobe Crew ....James Cavanaugh, Joseph Davis,
Barbara Hladsky, Greg Holz,
Shannon Koger, Teresia Larsen,
Kimberly Mark, Michael Piatkowski,
Suzanne Sponsler, Claire Verlaet,
Joan Weiss
Makeup/Prosthetics Supervisor ....Eve Morrow
Hair Supervisor ....Mark Adam Rampmeyer
Assistant Hair Supervisor ....Paula Schaffer
Wig Crew ....Armando Licon, Elizabeth Mathews,
Jennifer Mooney, Amy Uhl

Additional Orchestrations ....Michael Starobin,
Ned Ginsberg
Music Preparation Supervisor ....Peter R. Miller,
Miller Music Service
Assistant to Mr. Menken ....Rick Kunis
Assistant to Mr. Rice ....Eileen Heinink
Assistant to John Miller ....Matthew P. Ettinger
Rehearsal Pianists ....Glen Kelly,
Madelyn Rubinstein, Amy Duran

Web Design Consultant ....Joshua Noah
Advertising ....Serino Coyne, Inc.
Press Associates ....Adrian Bryan-Brown,
Brandi Cornwell, Jackie Green,
Hector Hernandez, Allison Houseworth,
Jessica Johnson, Kevin Jones,
Aaron Meier, Christine Olver, Joe Perrotta,
Linnae Petruzzelli, Matt Polk, Matt Ross,
Heath Schwartz, Susanne Tighe

Casting Associates ....Jack Bowdan, C.S.A.;

Beauty and the Beast

Mark Brandon; Megan Larche;
Assistants: Allison Estrin, Nikole Vallins
Payroll Manager ....Cathy Guerra
Production Assistants ....Bari Kartowski,
Mika Hadani, Alison Miller
Production Photography ....Joan Marcus,
Marc Bryan-Brown
Production Travel ....Jill Citron
Children's Tutoring. ....On Location Education
Child Wrangler ....Alissa Zulvergold
Theatre Displays ....King Displays
Safety & Health Consultants ....CHSH, Inc.,
New York City
Originally Produced by
Robert W. McTyre ....Producer
Don Frantz ....Associate Producer

Based on the Disney Film Disney's
BEAUTY AND THE BEAST,
directed by Kirk Wise and Gary Trousedale.
Produced by Don Hahn.
Special thanks to all the artists and staff at
Walt Disney Feature Animation.
Tom Child, Initial Conceptual Development. Anthony
Stimac/Musical Theatre Works, Inc.

CREDITS

Scenic & Transformation Effect
Motion Control Featuring
Stage Command Systems™
by Scenic Technologies.
Scenic construction, sculpting and scenic painting by Scenic
Technologies. Additional scenery by Variety Scenic Studios;
Hudson Scenic Studios, Inc.; Draperies by Showbiz
Enterprises and I. Weiss & Sons, Inc. Lighting equipment
by Four Star Lighting. Automated lighting by Vari-Lite, Inc.
Pani Projection by Production Arts Lighting Inc. Sound
furnished by Sound Associates Inc. Custom built props by
Seitzer and Associates. Table cloths by Decor Couture
Designs. Window treatments, hand and table linens by
O'Neil. Costumes executed by Barbara Matera Ltd. Foliage
by Modern Artificial. Costumes executed by Grace
Costumes, Inc. Dyeing, screening and painting by Fabric
Effects Incorporated. Surface designs and costume crafts by
Martin Izquierdo Studios. Prosthetics by John Dods Studio.
Millinery by Douglas James, Arnold S. Levine, Janet Linville
and Woody Shelp. Footwear by Capezio and J.C. Theatrical.
Vacuform costume sculptor by Costume Armour, Inc. Wigs
created by Bob Kelly Wig Creations, Inc. Opticals by
Fabulous Fanny's Myoptics. Gloves by LaCrasia Glamour
Gloves. Beast muscle system by Andrew Benepe Studio.
Costume harness and supports by J. Gerard. Additional
supports by Danforth Orthopedic. Special Adhesives by
Adhesive Technologies, Inc. Illusions by John Gaughan and
Associates. Invention and Magic Mirror by Tom Talmon
Studio. Pyrotechnical special effects materials supplied by
MP Associates, Inc. Pyrotechnical Equipment supplied by
LunaTech. All sound recording by Sound Designers Studio,
New York City. Emer'gen-C super energy booster provided
by Alacer Corp. Throat lozenges supplied by Ricola, Inc.

Cover Art Design © Disney

BEAUTY AND THE BEAST
originally premiered at
Theatre Under The Stars
Houston, Texas
December 2, 1993

Inquiries regarding the licensing of stock and amateur
productions of *Beauty and the Beast* or Elton John and
Tim Rice's *Aida* should be directed to Music Theatre
International, 421 W. 54th St., New York, NY 10019. Tel:
212-541-4684; www.MTIshows.com

►N◄
NEDERLANDER

Chairman	**James M. Nederlander**
President	**James L. Nederlander**

Executive Vice President
Nick Scandalios

Vice President	Senior Vice President
Corporate Development	Labor Relations
Charlene S. Nederlander	**Herschel Waxman**

Vice President	Chief Financial Officer
Jim Boese	**Freida Sawyer Belviso**

STAFF FOR THE LUNT-FONTANNE

House Manager ....**Tracey Malinowski**
Treasurer ....Joe Olcese
Assistant Treasurer ....Gregg Collichio
House Carpenter ....Terry Taylor
House Electrician ....Dennis Boyle
House Propertyman ....Dennis Sabella
House Flyman ....Mike Walters
House Engineers .....Robert MacMahon, Joseph Riccio III

DISNEY THEATRICAL PRODUCTIONS

President ....Thomas Schumacher
SVP & General Manager ....Alan Levey
SVP, Managing Director & CFO ....David Schrader

Senior Vice President, Creative Affairs .....Michele Steckler
Senior Vice President, International ....Ron Kollen
Vice President, Operations ....Dana Amendola
Vice President, Labor Relations ....Allan Frost
Vice President, Domestic Touring ....Jack Eldon
Director, Domestic Touring ....Michael Buchanan
Vice President, Theatrical Licensing ....Steve Fickinger
Director, Casting &
    Development ....Jennifer Rudin Pearson
Director, Human Resources ....June Heindel
Manager, Labor Relations ....Stephanie Cheek
Manager, Human Resources ....Cynthia A. Young
Human Resources Representative ....Jewel Neal
Manager, Information Systems ....Scott Benedict
Senior Computer Support Analyst ....Kevin A. McGuire
IT/Business Analyst ....William Boudiette

Production

Executive Music Producer ....Chris Montan
Vice President, Physical Production ....John Tiggeloven
Senior Manager, Safety ....Canara Price
Manager, Physical Production ....Karl Chmielewski
Purchasing Manager ....Joseph Doughney
Staff Associate Designer ....Dennis W. Moyes

Dramaturg and Literary Manager ....Ken Cerniglia

Marketing

Vice President, Broadway ....Andrew Flatt
Vice President, International ....Fiona Thomas
Director, Broadway ....Kyle Young
Director, Education and Outreach ....Peter Avery
Senior Manager, Broadway ....Michele Groner
Website Manager ....Eric W. Kratzer
Online Marketing Manager ....Roseann Warren
Media Asset Manager ....Cara L. Moccia
Assistant Manager, Communications ....Dana Torres
Assistant Manager, Promotions ....Craig Buckley

Sales

Director, National Sales ....Bryan Dockett
Manager, Group Sales ....Jacob Lloyd Kimbro
Manager, Sales and Ticketing ....Nick Falzon
Assistant Manager, Group Sales ....Juil Kim

Business and Legal Affairs

Senior Vice President ....Jonathan Olson
Vice President ....Robbin Kelley
Executive Director ....Harry S. Gold
Senior Counsel ....Seth Stuhl
Paralegal/Contract Administration ....Colleen Lober

Finance

Director ....Joe McClafferty
Senior Manager, Finance ....Dana James
Manager, Finance ....Justin Gee
Manager, Finance ....John Fajardo
Production Accountants ....Joy Brown, Nick Judge,
Barbara Toben
Assistant Production Accountant ....Isander Rojas
Senior Financial Analyst ....Tatiana Bautista
Senior Analyst ....Liz Jurist

Controllership

Director, Accounting ....Leena Mathew
Senior Analysts ....Stephanie Badie, Mila Danilevich,
Adrineh Ghoukassian
Analysts ....Ken Herrell, Bilda Donado

Administrative Staff

Dusty Bennett, Amy Caldamone, Lauren Daghini, Jessica
Doina, Cristi Finn, Cristina Fornaris, Dayle Gruet, Lance
Gutterman, Gregory Hanoian, Jonathan Hanson, Jay
Hollenback, Connie Jasper, Tom Kingsley, Tivon Marcus,
Kerry McGrath, Lisa Mitchell, Ryan Pears, Roberta Risafi,
Kisha Santiago, David Scott, Andy Singh, Jason Zammit

BUENA VISTA THEATRICAL
MERCHANDISE, L.L.C.

Vice President ....Steven Downing
Operations Manager ....Shawn Baker
Merchandise Manager ....Neil Markman
Associate Buyer ....Violet Burlaza
Assistant Manager, Inventory ....Suzanne Jakel
Retail Supervisor ....Michael Giammatteo
On-Site Retail Manager ....Anjie Maraj
On-Site Assistant Retail Manager ....Jana Christiano

Disney Theatrical Productions • 1450 Broadway
New York, NY 10018
guestmail@disneytheatrical.com

Beauty and the Beast
SCRAPBOOK

Correspondent: Jeanne Lehman, "Mrs. Potts"

Closing Night: It was magical! It was enchanting! It was Disney at its best. July 29, 2007, was an emotional day, indeed, for the Broadway cast and crew of Disney's *Beauty and the Beast* when, after 13 years and 5,461 performances, the curtain came down for the last time and the enchantment ended at the Lunt-Fontanne Theatre.

The night ran the gamut of emotions from the excitement of an opening night to the tears and heartbreak of a door closing on the lives and hearts of all those behind the curtain as well as in front of it.

A closing night is always a magical, yet an intensely emotional night unto itself, but this one was even more so. There was an added excitement to it because the audience was filled with our theatre family, friends, fans, Disney

appearances and of forgiveness and hope. What a thrill to be a part of bringing those elements to life on stage. There was not a dry eye onstage or in the audience as we each felt the "tale as old as time" slip from our grasp, line by line, song by song.

There is nothing more exciting than hearing an overture begin. The music draws the audience and cast into the show and something inside us comes alive as we leave the cares of the world behind. A new energy emerges and we become part of an adventure. The energy on that last night was extraordinary and thrilling and tears welled up from the first downbeat.

Being in such a family-oriented production, it was delightful to hear the giggles and laughter and the excited responses from children in the audience. My heart would melt every time I would see a little girl dressed as Belle or see the

our dressing rooms and made plans for the future. Had the show closed suddenly, the loss would have been even more heart-wrenching. Still, it was difficult to see such a show come to an untimely close, one that was selling out and which continued, performance after performance, to touch the lives of so many people.

Beauty and the Beast was my favorite children's story when I was a child. It was through that Disney comic book that I learned the value of looking for truth beyond appearances. Then, much to my delight, in 1995-96, the story was brought to life for me when I was cast in the role of "Mrs. Potts" in the Los Angeles company of *Beauty and the Beast* with original cast members Susan Egan, Gary Beach, Burke Moses, and Tom Bosley. From then on, the child in me got to emerge and play with the adult. How often do we as adults get to say that? I loved being a Teapot! And, ten years later, I was overjoyed to become a part of the Broadway cast. The cast and crew became family…lives intertwined with support for each other through marriages, births, deaths, illnesses and other challenges. As is the case with long-running shows, many cast changes kept us on our toes, even up to closing night when Donny Osmond joined us to reprise his role as Gaston!

As each of us did that last night on Broadway, I treasured every little moment, from walking into my nearly empty dressing room to being one of the last to leave the festive closing night party at Cipriani. Cameras were at the ready to capture backstage memories; my hair dresser, Armando, put on my wig and "lid" for the last time; my hardworking dresser, Joan Weiss, cheerfully got me into my 30 lb. costume; cast members hugged in farewell before the show and embraced crew members who made the paths to and from stage safe and clear during every performance.

(L-R): Director Robert Jess Roth and librettist Linda Woolverton, Jeanne Lehman (Mrs. Potts), Aldrin Gonzalez (Lefou) and Ann Mandrella (Babette) at the final curtain call on closing night.

staff and the incredible creative team, which needed to take that last journey with us.

There is nothing so compelling, thought provoking and thrilling as live theatre in which the audience becomes part of the story being told, whether they respond through attentive silence, laughter or tears and, throughout our closing night, the atmosphere sizzled with electricity connecting the audience, performers and crew. The love and support that came full circle from the stage to audience and back to the stage again was overwhelming and the urgent need to deliver every heartfelt nuance, thought, and feeling of Linda Woolverton's wonderful story and Alan Menken, Howard Ashman and Tim Rice's incredible songs for one last time kept us going.

It was almost as if the audience had a power of its own, giving us the strength we needed to get through the difficult moments. We were all swept away into the world of Disney enchantment where, as children, we were once drawn into worlds of mystery, castles, menacing wolves, gargoyles and spells…and tales of human struggles for the healing powers of love and being loved in return, of learning to see beyond

wide-eyed faces of wonder and excitement on children and adults alike! Greeting fans at the stage door was an absolute pleasure, seeing and hearing about how the show inspired and delighted "children of all ages."

Men, dragged kicking and screaming to see a fairytale production, were often the first to express their surprise and joy at how much the show appealed to them. For many, children and adults alike, it was their first show and the memory would last a lifetime. It was especially fulfilling to see and hear the impact that live theatre had on hundreds of children…our future audiences.

Because theatre folk are a passionate lot, emotions are strong and loss is deeply felt. No matter how much notice is given to a cast, and we had several months' notice, the end seems abrupt, the "family" is dispersed, the music stops, the enchantment is broken. As with any loss, there is a need to mourn, to say goodbye to friends and colleagues and adjust to leaving a certain sense of security for the unknown. I think for most of us at the Lunt-Fontanne, that process of saying goodbye unfolded gradually during the final weeks as we slowly cleaned out

It was a terrific journey and it is with a grateful heart that I commend director Rob Jess Roth, choreographer Matt West, conductor Michael Kosarin, musical supervisor David Friedman and all the design team for bringing the animated version of *Beauty and the Beast* to life. It was an honor to share the final bow with them before the curtain fell.

Among the many farewell phone calls, cards and emails I received on closing night, one particular message stands out, summing up beautifully the sentiment felt by all of us. Helen Zelon wrote, "Sing out, Miss Jeanne, for the kids who are seeing the show tonight for the very first time and for those of us who know and love it and understand how much heart and passion you and the entire company have invested, day by day, show by show, eight times a week . . . heartbreak, triumph, all of it! Be strong, sing well and be very glad that you have had the chance to make a giant and enduring contribution to the lives of so many."

Indeed, that magical closing night and the spirit of Disney's *Beauty and the Beast,* which inspired and enchanted millions of people, will live "happily ever after" in our hearts.

Boeing-Boeing

First Preview: April 19, 2008. Opened: May 4, 2008.
Still running as of May 31, 2008.

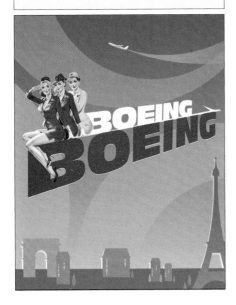

CAST
(in order of appearance)

Gloria	KATHRYN HAHN
Bernard	BRADLEY WHITFORD
Berthe	CHRISTINE BARANSKI
Robert	MARK RYLANCE
Gabriella	GINA GERSHON
Gretchen	MARY McCORMACK

SETTING

Bernard's apartment in Paris. One Saturday in April.
Early 1960s.

UNDERSTUDIES

For Bernard:
RAY VIRTA
For Berthe:
PIPPA PEARTHREE
For Gabriella, Gloria, Gretchen:
ROXANNA HOPE

CURTAIN-CALL CHOREOGRAPHY

KATHLEEN MARSHALL

Mark Rylance is appearing with the permission of
Actors' Equity Association.

⊕ LONGACRE THEATRE
220 West 48th Street
A Shubert Organization Theatre

Gerald Schoenfeld, *Chairman*   Philip J. Smith, *President*

Robert E. Wankel, *Executive Vice President*

SONIA FRIEDMAN PRODUCTIONS   BOB BOYETT   ACT PRODUCTIONS   MATTHEW BYAM SHAW   ROBERT G. BARTNER   THE WEINSTEIN COMPANY
SUSAN GALLIN/MARY LU ROFFE   BROADWAY ACROSS AMERICA   TULCHIN/JENKINS/DSM   THE ARACA GROUP

present

CHRISTINE BARANSKI   MARK RYLANCE   BRADLEY WHITFORD

in

BOEING BOEING

by
MARC CAMOLETTI

Translated by
BEVERLEY CROSS & FRANCIS EVANS

also starring
GINA GERSHON   KATHRYN HAHN   MARY McCORMACK

Scenic and Costume Design	Lighting Design	Original Music	Sound Design
ROB HOWELL	HUGH VANSTONE	CLAIRE VAN KAMPEN	SIMON BAKER
Stage Manager	U.S. Casting	Dialect Coach	Press Representative
WILLIAM JOSEPH BARNES	JIM CARNAHAN, C.S.A.	DEBORAH HECHT	BARLOW-HARTMAN

Sales and Marketing	Production Management	Associate Producer for RBT
ON THE RIALTO	AURORA PRODUCTIONS	TIM LEVY

UK General Management for SFP	General Management	Associate Producers
DIANE BENJAMIN	STUART THOMPSON PRODUCTIONS	JILL LENHART
MATTHEW GORDON		DOUGLAS G. SMITH

Directed by
MATTHEW WARCHUS

The Producers wish to express their appreciation to the Theatre Development Fund for its support of this production.

5/4/08

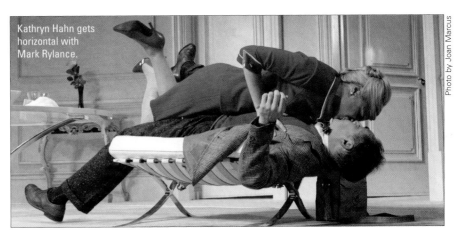

Kathryn Hahn gets horizontal with Mark Rylance.

Photo by Joan Marcus

Boeing-Boeing

Christine Baranski
Berthe

Mark Rylance
Robert

Bradley Whitford
Bernard

Gina Gershon
Gabriella

Kathryn Hahn
Gloria

Mary McCormack
Gretchen

Roxanna Hope
*Understudy for
Gabriella, Gloria,
Gretchen*

Pippa Pearthree
*Understudy for
Berthe*

Ray Virta
*Understudy for
Bernard*

Matthew Warchus
Director

Rob Howell
*Scenic and Costume
Design*

Hugh Vanstone
Lighting Design

Simon Baker
Sound Design

Jim Carnahan
Casting

Stuart Thompson
Productions
*General
Management*

Sonia Friedman
Productions
Producer

Bob Boyett
Producer

Bob Weinstein,
The Weinstein
Company
Producer

Harvey Weinstein,
The Weinstein
Company
Producer

DOORMAN
Enrico Bozzacco

FRONT OF HOUSE STAFF
Front Row (L-R): Bob Reilly, John Mallon,
Monica Caraballo, Janet Kay.

Middle Row (L-R): Jim McIntosh,
Dennis Norwood, Paula Raymond,
Joe Biamonte, Christina Gutierrez,
Kenny Weinstein.

Back Row (L-R): Denise Eckels,
Marla Karaliolios.

PROPS ASSISTANT
Alan C. Edwards

Photo by Ben Strothmann

Boeing-Boeing

Photo by Ben Strothmann

CREW
Front Row (L-R): Kim Prentice, Barry Doss, Billy Barnes, Elisa Acevedo, Robert Witherow, Ric Rogers.
Back Row (L-R): John Lofgren, Wilbur Graham, Wayne Smith.

STAFF FOR BOEING-BOEING

GENERAL MANAGEMENT
STUART THOMPSON PRODUCTIONS
Stuart Thompson   Caroline Prugh
James Triner   David Turner

COMPANY MANAGER
Cassidy J. Briggs

PRODUCTION MANAGEMENT
AURORA PRODUCTIONS INC.
Gene O'Donovan   W. Benjamin Heller II
Bethany Weinstein   Melissa Mazdra
John Horsman   Asia Evans

PRESS REPRESENTATIVE
BARLOW•HARTMAN
Michael Hartman   John Barlow
Dennis Crowley   Michelle Bergmann

Production Stage Manager ....William Joseph Barnes
Stage Manager ....Robert Witherow
Literal Translation by ....Chris Campbell
Associate Director ....Mark Schneider
Associate Scenic Designer ....Ted LeFevre
Associate Lighting Designer ....Anthony Pearson
Associate Sound Designer ....Christopher Cronin
Associate Costume Designer ....Brian Russman
Hair Design ....Larry Boyette
Makeup Design ....Erica Whelan
Assistant to Ms. Marshall ....Jennifer Savelli
Production Electrician ....Dan Coey
Production Sound Operator ....Wayne Smith
Production Properties ....Peter Sarafin
Production Properties Assistant ....Alan C. Edwards
Wardrobe Supervisor ....Kay Grunder
Dressers ....Barry Doss, Kimberly Prentice
Hair Supervisor ....Elisa Acevedo
Production Assistant ....Caroline Anderson
Casting Associate ....Kate Schwabe
UK Costume Supervisor ....Irene Bohan

General Management Assistants ....Megan Curren,
                    Aaron Thompson, Jacob Thompson
Banking ....City National Bank/
                                        Michele Gibbons
Payroll ....Castellana Services, Inc.
Accountant ....Fried & Kowgios CPA's LLP/
                                      Robert Fried, CPA
Controller ....J.S. Kubala
Insurance ....DeWitt Stern Group
Legal Counsel ....Lazarus & Harris/
            Scott Lazarus, Esq., Robert Harris, Esq.
Advertising ....SPOTCO/
                        Drew Hodges, Jim Edwards,
                        Jim Aquino, Kyle Hall
Sales and Marketing......................on the RIALTO/
                    Clint Bond Jr., Steven Rummer
Production Photographer ....Joan Marcus
Theatre Displays ....Going Signs

SONIA FRIEDMAN PRODUCTIONS
Producer ....Sonia Friedman
General Manager ....Diane Benjamin
Creative Producer ....Lisa Makin
Head of Production ....Pam Skinner
Associate Producer........................Matthew Gordon
Literary Associate ....Jack Bradley
CEO-NY ....David Lazar
Production Assistant ....Lucie Lovatt
Production Assistant ....Martin Ball
Production Assistant ....Jamie Hendry
Production Accountant ....Melissa Hay
SFP Board ....Helen Enright, Howard Panter,
                                        Rosemary Squire

For ACT PRODUCTIONS
Chairman ....Roger Wingate
Director of Production ....Nick Salmon
General Manager ....Nia Janis
Assistant Producer ....Imogen Kinchin

Makeup provided by
M•A•C Cosmetics

CREDITS
Scenery by Souvenir Scenic Studios Ltd. Lighting equipment from PRG Lighting. Sound equipment from Sound Associates. Costumes executed by Tricorne LLC. Millinery by Rodney Gordon Ltd. Custom footwear by Worldtone. Select vintage clothing by The Autumn Olive. Special thanks to Bra*Tenders for hosiery and undergarments.

Opening Night party courtesy of Nikki Midtown. Opening Night travel courtesy of EOS Airlines. Opening Night party services: Reed Hatkoff at Really Spectacular Events.

Boeing-Boeing

SCRAPBOOK

Correspondent: Kathryn Hahn, "Gloria"

Cherished Opening Night Memory: Being photographed on the toilet by Gina for my Broadway debut moment.

Opening Night Gifts: Our *Boeing-Boeing* flight bags.

Who Has Done the Most Shows in Their Career: Mark Rylance.

Favorite Moment During Each Performance: "The Beast" by Bradley.

Favorite In-Theatre Gathering Place: Stage Left quick-change room.

Favorite Off-Site Hangout: Hurley's, Food Emporium, Angus, Starbucks!!!

Favorite Snack Food: Christine's chocolate cookies.

Mascot: Gina

Favorite Therapies: Brad's blue exercise ball, Gina's dressing room pharmacy.

Most Memorable Ad-Lib: Gina: "Oh, look he's got a stiffy!"

Memorable Press Encounter: The stewardesses at a Brazilian meat restaurant with a *New York Times* reporter.

Fastest Costume Change: Gina and Mary into their stewardess outfits for the curtain call.

Heaviest/Hottest Costume: Mark's tweedy suit.

Who Wore the Least: Kathryn—in her flashing moment.

Catchphrases Only the Company Would Recognize: "The Beast." "Champions Adjust."

Company In-Jokes: The "What's under Kathryn's towel tonight?" guessing game.

1. Curtain call on opening night.
2. Kathryn Hahn at the opening night party at Nikki Beach.
3. Gina Gershon at the party.
4. Christine Baranski at Nikki Beach.
5. A group of former stewardesses attend the premiere at the Longacre Theatre.

A Bronx Tale

First Preview: October 4, 2007. Opened: October 25, 2007.
Closed February 24, 2008 after 18 Previews and 111 Performances.

Photo by Joan Marcus

Chazz Palminteri

WALTER KERR THEATRE

A JUJAMCYN THEATRE
ROCCO LANDESMAN
PRESIDENT

PAUL LIBIN
PRODUCING DIRECTOR

JACK VIERTEL
CREATIVE DIRECTOR

JORDAN ROTH
VICE PRESIDENT

GO PRODUCTIONS
JOHN GAUGHAN / TRENT OTHICK / MATT OTHICK
NEIGHBORHOOD FILMS
IN ASSOCIATION WITH
JUJAMCYN THEATERS
PRESENT

CHAZZ PALMINTERI

IN

a BRONX TALE

WRITTEN BY
CHAZZ PALMINTERI

Set Design
JAMES NOONE

Lighting Design
PAUL GALLO

Original Music and Sound Design
JOHN GROMADA

Production Stage Manager
JAMES HARKER

Wardrobe Provided by
ISAIA

Press Representative
BONEAU/BRYAN-BROWN

Promotions
HHC MARKETING

Production Management
AURORA PRODUCTIONS

General Management
STUART THOMPSON PRODUCTIONS / JAMES TRINER

Associate Producers
ROBERT H. MORETTI RICHARD CARRIGAN

Executive Producer
NICOLE KASTRINOS

DIRECTED BY
JERRY ZAKS

LIVE BROADWAY

The Producers wish to express their appreciation to the Theatre Development Fund for its support of this production.

10/25/07

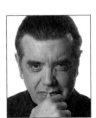

Chazz Palminteri
Playwright/ Performer

Jerry Zaks
Director

James Noone
Scenic Design

Paul Gallo
Lighting Design

A Bronx Tale

John Gromada
*Original Music and
Sound Design*

Stuart Thompson
Productions
*General
Management*

James Triner
General Manager

Rocco Landesman,
President,
Jujamcyn Theaters
Producer

FRONT OF HOUSE STAFF
Front Row (L-R): TJ D'Angelo, Jason Barker, Ralph Santos,
Juliette Cipriatti, Barbara Kagan.

Second Row (L-R): Brandon Houghton, Joy Sandell,
Adam Ferguson, Henry Linton

Back Row (L-R): Victoria Lauzun and Michelle Fleury.

Not Pictured: Susan Elrod.

STAGE DOORMAN
John Barker

Photos by Ben Strothmann

BOX OFFICE
Harry Jaffie and Gail Yerkovich.

CREW
Front Row (L-R): Lilliana Peeler, Vincent Valvo, Jr., Greg Peeler, George Fullum,
Cassidy Briggs, Jim Harker

Back Row (L-R): Jacqui Phillips, Thea Bradshaw Scott, Christel Murdock

A Bronx Tale
SCRAPBOOK

Correspondent: Jim Harker, Production Stage Manager.

Most Exciting Celebrity Visitors: Omar Minaya, Johnny Roast Beef.

Special Backstage Ritual: Six minutes with all the girls backstage right before he goes onstage.

Favorite In-Theatre Gathering Place: Wine in the wardrobe room after the Saturday evening show.

Favorite Off-Site Hangout: '089' on Arthur Avenue in the Bronx for pizza, between shows.

Favorite Snack Food: Susan's jar of chocolates.

Favorite Therapies: Green tea, or chicken soup from the Edison.

Catchphrase Only the Company Would Recognize: "Fat bastard."

Photos by Aubrey Reuben

1. (L-R): Chazz Palminteri and Robert De Niro at the opening night party at Bond 45.
2. Director Jerry Zaks on opening night.
3. Palminteri's well-wishers (L-R): Hollywood Roj, Vincent Pastore, Lennox Lewis and Stephen Baldwin at Bond 45.

STAFF FOR *A BRONX TALE*

GENERAL MANAGEMENT
STUART THOMPSON PRODUCTIONS
Stuart Thompson   Caroline Prugh   James Triner

COMPANY MANAGER
Cassidy J. Briggs

PRODUCTION MANAGEMENT
AURORA PRODUCTIONS INC.
Gene O'Donovan   W. Benjamin Heller II
Bethany Weinstein   Melissa Mazdra
John Horsman   Asia Evans

PRESS REPRESENTATIVE
BONEAU/BRYAN-BROWN
Adrian Bryan-Brown   Jackie Green   Matt Ross

Production Stage Manager . . . . .James Harker
Stage Manager . . . . .Thea Bradshaw Scott
Assistant Scenic Designer . . . . .Patrick Tennant
Assistant Lighting Designers . . . . .Michael Jones, Paul Hackenmueller
Assistant Sound Designers . . . . .Christopher Cronin, Sten Severson
Production Electrician . . . . .Dan Coey
Moving Light Programmer . . . . .David Arch
Production Sound .Greg Peeler

Wardrobe Supervisor . . . . .Christel Murdock
Makeup Artist . . . . .Jacqui Phillips
Production Assistant . . . . .Amanda Michaels
Assistant to Mr. Palminteri . . . . .Staci Gilchrist
Assistant to Mr. Zaks . . . . .Cat Parker
Assistant to Mr. Gallo . . . . .Travis Sawyer
General Management Assistants . . . . .Megan Curren, Aaron Thompson
Banking . . . . . . .JP Morgan Chase Bank/Margaret Wong
Payroll .Castellana Services, Inc.
Accountant . . . . .Fried & Kowgios CPA's LLP/ Robert Fried, CPA
Controller . . . . .Joe Kubala
Insurance . . . . .DeWitt Stern Group
Legal Counsel . . . . .Sendroff & Baruch, LLP/ Jason Baruch
Advertising . . . . .SPOTCO/ Drew Hodges, Jim Edwards, Lauren Hunter, Josh Fraenkel
Promotions . . . . .HHC Marketing/ Hugh Hysell, Michael Redman, Brandon Martin, Matt Sicoli, Jaime Roberts, Kayla Kuzbel, Candice Beckmann
Website Design and
Internet Marketing . . . . .Bay Bridge Productions/ Jean Strong, Laura Wagner
Production Photographer . . . . .Joan Marcus
Theatre Displays . . . . .King Displays, Inc.

Wardrobe . . . . .ISAIA/ Gianluca Isaia, Alban Lesne, Lauren Weiss
Special Thanks . . . . .Omar Aboudi

CREDITS
Scenery by Proof Productions, Inc. Lighting equipment from PRG Lighting. Sound equipment by Masque Sound.®

🎭 JUJAMCYN THEATERS

ROCCO LANDESMAN
President

PAUL LIBIN   **JACK VIERTEL**   **JORDAN ROTH**
Producing Director   Creative Director   Vice President

DANIEL ADAMIAN   **JENNIFER HERSHEY**
General Manager   Director of Operations

MEREDITH VILLATORE   **JERRY ZAKS**
Chief Financial Officer   Resident Director

STAFF FOR THE WALTER KERR THEATRE
Manager . . . . .Susan Elrod
Treasurer . . . . .Harry Jaffie
Carpenter . . . . .George A. Fullum
Propertyman . . . . .Timothy Bennet
Electrician . . . . .Vincent Valvo, Jr.
Engineer . . . . .Ralph Santos

A Catered Affair

First Preview: March 25, 2008. Opened: April 17, 2008.
Still running as of May 31, 2008.

PLAYBILL

CAST

(in order of appearance)

Winston	HARVEY FIERSTEIN
Pasha/Mrs. Halloran	LORI WILNER
Myra/Wedding Dress Saleswoman	KRISTINE ZBORNIK
Dolores/Caterer	HEATHER MAC RAE
Janey	LESLIE KRITZER
Ralph	MATT CAVENAUGH
Sam/Mr. Halloran	PHILIP HOFFMAN
Tom	TOM WOPAT
Aggie	FAITH PRINCE
Alice/Army Sergeant	KATIE KLAUS

UNDERSTUDIES

For Aggie:
JENNIFER ALLEN, LORI WILNER
For Tom:
PHILIP HOFFMAN, MARK ZIMMERMAN
For Winston, Sam/Mr. Halloran:
MARK ZIMMERMAN
For Janey:
KATIE KLAUS, BRITTA OLLMANN
For Ralph:
MATTHEW SCOTT
For Pasha/Mrs. Halloran, Myra/
Wedding Dress Saleswoman, Dolores/Caterer:
JENNIFER ALLEN
For Alice/Army Sergeant:
BRITTA OLLMANN

Continued on next page

○ WALTER KERR THEATRE

A JUJAMCYN THEATRE
ROCCO LANDESMAN
President

PAUL LIBIN	JACK VIERTEL	JORDAN ROTH
Producing Director	Creative Director	Vice President

Jujamcyn Theaters   Jordan Roth   Harvey Entertainment/Ron Fierstein   Richie Jackson   Daryl Roth
John O'Boyle/Ricky Stevens/Davis-Tolentino   Barbra Russell/Ron Sharpe   in association with   Frankel-Baruch-Viertel-Routh Group
Broadway Across America   True Love Productions   Rick Steiner/Mayerson-Bell-Staton-Osher Group   Jan Kallish

Present

Faith Prince   Tom Wopat
Harvey Fierstein

in

A Catered Affair

Book by
Harvey Fierstein

Music & Lyrics by
John Bucchino

Based on the Turner Entertainment motion picture distributed by Warner Brothers
and written by Gore Vidal, and the original teleplay by Paddy Chayefsky

Also Starring
Leslie Kritzer

Philip Hoffman   Katie Klaus   Heather Mac Rae   Lori Wilner   Kristine Zbornik
Jennifer Allen   Britta Ollmann   Matthew Scott   Mark Zimmerman

And
Matt Cavenaugh

Scenic Design by	Costume Design by	Lighting Design by	Sound Design by
David Gallo	Ann Hould-Ward	Brian MacDevitt	Dan Moses Schreier

Projection Design by	Hair Design by	Casting by	Associate Director
Zachary Borovay	David Lawrence	Telsey + Company	Adam John Hunter

Music Director & Arrangements	Orchestrations by	Music Coordinator	Associate Producers
Constantine Kitsopoulos	Jonathan Tunick	John Miller	Stacey Mindich Rhoda Mayerson

Press Representative	Marketing	Production Management	General Management
O&M Co.	Type A Marketing	Juniper Street Productions	Alan Wasser-Allan Williams

Directed by
John Doyle

WORLD PREMIERE AT THE OLD GLOBE THEATRE, San Diego, California
Louis G. Spisto, Executive Producer

4/17/08

(Clockwise from Bottom): Matt Cavenaugh,
Leslie Kritzer, Lori Wilner,
Harvey Fierstein, Philip Hoffman,
Tom Wopat and Faith Prince.

Photo by Jim Cox

A Catered Affair

MUSICAL NUMBERS

"Partners"	Tom and Sam, Ralph and Janey
"Ralph and Me"	Janey
"Married"	Aggie
"Women Chatter"	Myra, Pasha, Dolores
"No Fuss"	Aggie
"Your Children's Happiness"	Mr. and Mrs. Halloran
"Immediate Family"	Winston
"Our Only Daughter"	Aggie
"One White Dress"	Janey, Aggie
"Vision"	Aggie
"Don't Ever Stop Saying 'I Love You'"	Janey, Ralph
"I Stayed"	Tom
"Married" (Reprise)	Aggie
"Coney Island"	Winston
"Don't Ever Stop Saying 'I Love You'" (Reprise)	Ralph, Janey, Tom
"Coney Island" (Reprise)	Winston and Company

Cast Continued

SETTING

The Bronx, New York, the morning after Memorial Day and onward, 1953.

MUSICIANS

Conductor:
CONSTANTINE KITSOPOULOS

Associate Conductor/Piano:
ETHYL WILL

Concert Master:
DALE STUCKENBRUCK

Violin:
LIZ LIM-DUTTON

Viola:
KEN BURWARD-HOY

Cello:
SUSANNAH CHAPMAN

Bass:
JOHN ARBO

Woodwinds:
JIM ERCOLE, DON McGEEN

Trumpet/Flugel:
NEIL BALM

Percussion:
DEAN WITTEN

Music Coordinator:
JOHN MILLER

Music Copying:
KAYE-HOUSTON MUSIC/
ANNE KAYE, DOUG HOUSTON

Photo by Jim Cox

(L-R): Tom Wopat, Faith Prince and Harvey Fierstein.

Faith Prince
Aggie

Tom Wopat
Tom

Harvey Fierstein
Book Writer/Winston

Leslie Kritzer
Janey

Matt Cavenaugh
Ralph

Philip Hoffman
Mr. Halloran/Sam

Katie Klaus
Alice/Army Sergeant

Heather Mac Rae
Dolores/Caterer

Lori Wilner
Pasha/Mrs. Halloran

Kristine Zbornik
*Myra/
Dress Saleswoman*

Jennifer Allen
*u/s Aggie, Pasha/
Mrs. Halloran, Myra/
Wedding Dress
Saleswoman,
Dolores/Caterer*

Britta Ollmann
*u/s Janey, Alice/
Army Sergeant*

Matthew Scott
u/s Ralph

Mark Zimmerman
*u/s Tom, Winston,
Sam/Mr. Halloran*

A Catered Affair

John Bucchino
Music and Lyrics

John Doyle
Director

David Gallo
Scenic Design

Ann Hould-Ward
Costume Design

Brian MacDevitt
Lighting Design

Dan Moses Schreier
Sound Design

Jonathan Tunick
Orchestrations

Bernard Telsey,
Telsey + Company
Casting

Constantine
Kitsopoulos
*Music Director/
Arrangements*

John Miller
Music Coordinator

Guy Kwan, John Paull III, Hillary Blanken,
Kevin Broomell, Ana Rose Greene,
Juniper Street Productions
Production Manager

Angelina Avallone
Make-up Design

Louis G. Spisto,
Old Globe Theatre
Regional Production

Alan Wasser
Associates
*General
Management*

Rocco Landesman,
Jujamcyn Theaters
Producer

Jordan Roth
Producer

Daryl Roth
Producer

Rick Stevens
Producer

John O'Boyle
Producer

Richard Frankel,
Frankel-Baruch-
Viertel-Routh Group
Producer

Steven Baruch,
Frankel-Baruch-
Viertel-Routh Group
Producer

Tom Viertel,
Frankel-Baruch-
Viertel-Routh Group
Producer

Marc Routh,
Frankel-Baruch-
Viertel-Routh Group
Producer

Rick Steiner
Producer

Frederic H.
Mayerson,
Mayerson-Bell-
Staton-Osher Group
Producer

Marc Bell,
Mayerson-Bell-
Staton-Osher Group
Producer

Dan Staton,
Mayerson-Bell-
Staton-Osher Group
Producer

John and Bonnie
Osher,
Mayerson-Bell-
Staton-Osher Group
Producer

Rhoda Mayerson
Producer

Alan C. Edwards
Set Design Assistant

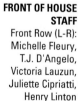

**FRONT OF HOUSE
STAFF**
Front Row (L-R):
Michelle Fleury,
T.J. D'Angelo,
Victoria Lauzun,
Juliette Cipriatti,
Henry Linton

Back Row (L-R):
Adam Ferguson,
Joy Sandell,
Brandon Houghton,
Tim Kodres

Photo by Claudia Lynch

A Catered Affair

Photo by Colleen Croft

ORCHESTRA
Front Row (L-R): Jonathan Tunick, Annie Kaye, Doug Houston, Liz Lim-Dutton, Don McGeen, Ethyl Will, Neil Balm

Back Row (L-R): John Miller, Constantine Kitsopoulos, Dean Witten, Susannah Chapman, Dale Stuckenbruck, Ken Burward-Hoy, John Arbo, Jim Ercole

Photo by Harvey Fierstein

STAGE MANAGEMENT
Claudia Lynch, Adam Hunter, Heather J. Weiss

Photo by Ben Strothmann

DOORMAN
John Barker

Photo by Ben Strothmann

BOX OFFICE
(L-R): Gail Yerkovich and Michael Loiacono

Photo by Ben Strothmann

PRODUCTION ASSISTANTS
(L-R): Heather Weiss (Assistant Stage Manager), Spencer Robinson (Production Assistant), Monica Cuoco (Production Assistant)

Photo by Harvey Fierstein

DOORMAN
Kevin Wallace

CREW
(From back left side): Chris Pantuso, Drayton Allison, Tim Bennet, Vincent Valvo, Jr., Danny Braddish, Eric "Speed" Smith, George Fullum, Lolly Totero, Stephanie Vetter, Jack Anderson, Keith Shaw, Penny Davis, Kevin O'Brien, Patrick Pummill.

Photo by Ben Strothmann

2007-2008 AWARD

DRAMA LEAGUE AWARD
Distinguished Production of Musical

A Catered Affair

GENERAL MANAGEMENT
ALAN WASSER ASSOCIATES
Alan Wasser   Allan Williams
Aaron Lustbader

COMPANY MANAGER
PENELOPE DAULTON

GENERAL PRESS REPRESENTATIVE
O&M Co.
Rick Miramontez
Jon Dimond   Molly Barnett   Jaron Caldwell

PRODUCTION STAGE MANAGER
ADAM JOHN HUNTER

CASTING
TELSEY + COMPANY
Bernie Telsey CSA, Will Cantler CSA, David Vaccari CSA,
Bethany Knox CSA, Craig Burns CSA,
Tiffany Little Canfield CSA, Rachel Hoffman CSA,
Carrie Rosson CSA, Justin Huff CSA, Joe Langworth,
Bess Fifer CSA, Patrick Goodwin

TECHNICAL SUPERVISION
JUNIPER STREET PRODUCTIONS
Hillary Blanken   Kevin Broomell
Guy Kwan   Ana Rose Greene

Associate General Manager ....Aaron Lustbader
Assistant General Manager ....Jake Hirzel
Stage Manager ....Claudia Lynch
Assistant Stage Manager ....Heather Weiss
Assistant Company Manager ....Ashley Berman
Associate Scenic Designer ....Josh Zangen
Associate Costume Designer ....Sidney Shannon
Associate Lighting Designer..............Jennifer Schriever
Assistant Lighting Designer ....Peter Hoerburger
Associate Sound Designer ....David Bullard
Associate Projection Designer ....Austin Switser
Assistant Hair Designer ....Jeannette Harrington
Automated Lighting Programmer ....Timothy F. Rogers
MAKE-UP DESIGN ....ANGELINA AVALLONE
DIALECT & VOCAL COACH ....DEBORAH HECHT
Production Carpenter ....Tony Menditto
Head Carpenter ....Jack Anderson
Automation Carpenter ....Geoff Vaughn
Flyman ....Dan Braddish
Production Electrician ....Michael S. LoBue
Head Electrician ....Drayton Allison
Production Sound Engineer ....Patrick Pummill
Assistant Sound Engineer ....Stephanie Vetter
Production Properties Supervisor ....Chris Pantuso
Assistant Properties Supervisor ....Eric Smith
Properties Assistant ....Manfred Bockwoldt
Wardrobe Supervisor ....Penny Davis
Dressers ....Kevin O'Brien, Keith Shaw, Lolly Totero
Hair Supervisor ....David H. Lawrence
Music Coordinator ....John Miller
Assistant to John Miller ....Melissa Heller
Music Preparation ....Kaye-Houston Music, Inc.
Music Transcription ....Mario Vaz De Mello
Advertising ....Serino Coyne, Inc./
Nancy Coyne, Sandy Block, Greg Corradetti,
Marci Kaufman, Danielle Boyle

Marketing ....Type A Marketing/
Anne Rippey, Nick Pramik,
Janette Roush, Maryana Geller
Illustration ....Charles Pyle
Theatre Displays ....King Displays
Interactive Agency ....Situation Marketing/
Damian Bazadona, Ryan Klink,
Kristen Butler
Legal Counsel ....Loeb & Loeb, LLP/
Seth Gelblum
Franklin, Weinrib, Rudell & Vasallo/
Elliot Brown
Accounting ....Rosenberg, Neuwirth & Kuchner/
Chris Cacace, Pat Pedersen
Assistant to Mr. Roth ....Ed Lefferson
Assistant to Ms. Roth ....Greg Raby
Assistant to Mr. Frankel ....Heidi Libby
Assistant to Mr. Baruch ....Sonja Soper
Assistant to Mr. Viertel ....Tania Senewiratne
Assistant to Mr. Routh ....Katie Adams
Assistant to Mr. Steiner ....Kathy Wall

General Management Associates ....Jim Brandeberry,
Connie Chong, Lane Marsh,
Thom Mitchell, Mark Shacket
General Management Office ....Christopher Betz,
Patty Montesi, Jennifer Mudge,
Dawn Kusinski
Press Associates ....Richard Hillman, Yufen Kung,
Philip Carrubba
Press Interns ....Elizabeth Wagner, Paul Iacono
Production Photographer ....Jim Cox
Production Assistants ....Monica Cuoco,
Spencer Robinson
Technical Production Assistants ....Elise Hanley,
Ally Paull
Additional Projection Artwork ....Brian Drucker
Insurance ....Ventura Insurance Brokerage/
Janice Brown
Banking ....Commerce Bank/
Barbara von Borstel
Payroll ....Castellana Services, Inc.
Merchandising ....Max Merchandising/
Randi Grossman
Opening Night Coordination ....The Lawrence Company/
Michael Lawrence
Group Sales ....Group Sales Box Office
BestOfBroadway.com
212-398-8383/800-223-7565
Rehearsal Studio ....New 42nd Street Studios

CREDITS AND ACKNOWLEDGEMENTS
Scenery and scenic effects built, painted and electrified by
PRG Scenic Technologies, New Windsor, NY, and the Old
Globe Theatre, San Diego, CA. Show control and scenic
motion control featuring Stage Command Systems® by
PRG Scenic Technologies, New Windsor, NY. Softgoods
built by I. Weiss and Sons, Inc., Long Island City, NY.
Lighting equipment provided by PRG Lighting, North
Bergen, NJ. Sound equipment provided by PRG Audio, Mt.
Vernon, NY. Video equipment provided by PRG Video, Mt.
Vernon, NY. Furniture and props executed by the Spoon
Group, Rahway, NJ, and the Old Globe Theatre, San Diego,
CA. Hauling by Clark Transfer, Inc. Men's wear by Scafati
Inc. Women's wear by John Kristiansen and the Old Globe
costume shop. Ms. Prince's clothes by Tricorne. Millinery by
Lynne Mackey. Shoes by TO Dey. Undergarments by

Bra*Tenders. Wigs by Bob Kelly Wig Creations.

SPECIAL THANKS
Kleinfeld Bridal, St. John Knits, Brooks Brothers, Cupcake
Café, Delta Airlines, Flatotel, Tavern on the Green,
IBA Limo

Makeup provided by M•A•C Cosmetics.

www.ACateredAffairOnBroadway.com

WORLD PREMIERE AT
THE OLD GLOBE THEATRE
San Diego, California
Louis G. Spisto, Executive Producer

The Old Globe Theatre Staff
Executive Producer ....Louis G. Spisto
Co-Artistic Director ....Jerry Patch
Co-Artistic Director ....Darko Tresnjak
General Manager ....Michael G. Murphy
Director of Production ....Robert Drake
Director of Marketing
and Communications ....Dave Henson
Director of Development ....Todd Schultz
Director of Finance ....Mark Somers
Technical Director ....Benjamin Thoron
Costume Director ....Stacy Sutton
Properties Director ....Neil Holmes
Lighting Director ....Chris Rynne
Sound Director ....Paul Peterson
Stage Manager ....Tracy Skoczelas

JUJAMCYN THEATERS

ROCCO LANDESMAN
President

| **PAUL LIBIN** | **JACK VIERTEL** | **JORDAN ROTH** |
| Producing Director | Creative Director | Vice President |

| **DANIEL ADAMIAN** | **JENNIFER HERSHEY** |
| General Manager | Director of Operations |

| **MEREDITH VILLATORE** | **JERRY ZAKS** |
| Chief Financial Officer | Resident Director |

STAFF FOR THE WALTER KERR THEATRE
Manager ....Susan Elrod
Treasurer ....Harry Jaffie
Carpenter ....George E. Fullum
Propertyman ....Timothy Bennet
Electrician ....Vincent Valvo, Jr.
Engineer ....Vladimir Belenky

A Catered Affair
SCRAPBOOK

1. Leslie Kritzer sings "Don't Ever Stop Saying I Love You" (with composer John Bucchino at the piano) at Kleinfeld Bridal press event.
2. Tom Wopat arrives in a taxi as publicity on opening night.
3. (L-R): Principals Matt Cavenaugh, Leslie Kritzer, Harvey Fierstein, Faith Prince and Tom Wopat at Kleinfeld's.
4. (L-R): Correspondent Lori Wilner with fellow cast members Kristine Zbornik and Heather MacRae at Kleinfeld's.
5. (L-R): Director John Doyle, librettist Harvey Fierstein and songwriter John Bucchino at the press event.

Correspondent: Lori Wilner, "Pasha/Mrs. Halloran."

Opening Night Gifts: Lots of taxis and wedding stuff. Tiffany taxi key chains, yellow taxi banks, cookies in the shape of elaborate wedding cakes, books on wedding etiquette.

Most Exciting Celebrity Visitor and What They Said: Debbie Reynolds (who was in the original movie) came to see the show and said, "This is a much better show than that ever was a movie!"

Who Has Done the Most Shows in Their Career: Probably Harvey, at around 70.

Special Backstage Rituals: We have two weekly rituals, which are a lot of fun. The first is Dollar Friday, which is simply a pool. Everyone who wants to play puts a dollar with their initials in the hat, and one is drawn. The winner takes the whole pot. And then we have "Saturday night on Broadway." I think Harvey Fierstein may have started it, because he did it in *Fiddler*, which is the first show I did with him. Harvey (or another actor in the show) writes a rhyming verse which reflects the events of the

week as it pertains to the show and he or she reads it over the loudspeaker right before the places call. The last line of the verse is always "It's Saturday night on Broadway, y'all!" Sometimes they're very funny, and they always add a little dose of gratitude, knowing that we are lucky to be working, and are part of a wonderful community.

Favorite Moment During Each Performance (On Stage or Off): Just my personal fave: at the curtain call, Harvey comes running out to take his bow. When he turns around to join the "line" of other actors, he mouths the words, "My mother," as if to explain to the rest of us why people are clapping so fervently.

Favorite In-Theatre Gathering Place: Definitely Harvey's dressing room. It's big and comfy, beautifully decorated, and he always has some fun thing playing on his iPod or computer, and there are usually snacks. A no-brainer!

Memorable Press Encounter: Tom Wopat did a series of photographs outside the theater on opening night. He was in costume, driving a

vintage checker cab up and down the block!

Fastest Costume Change: Leslie Kritzer changes from a period wedding gown with a train and a full veil to a dress in about twenty seconds. There are three people surrounding her to make it happen.

Busiest Day at the Box Office: Probably the day that the twelve Drama Desk nominations were announced.

Who Wore the Least: Leslie Kritzer and Matt Cavenaugh are nude at the top of the show, and proceed to get dressed under and over the covers in the opening number.

Catchphrases Only the Company Would Recognize: "In the box." John Doyle, our director, was constantly streamlining the production, so whatever wasn't absolutely necessary got cut. But at the beginning of rehearsal, he had a physical BOX where some of the props ended up if they were deemed non-essential. We were always wondering what was going to end up "in the box."

Memorable Directorial Note: "Sing worse. Your character doesn't sing that well."

Cat on a Hot Tin Roof

First Preview: February 12, 2008. Opened: March 6, 2008.
Still playing as of May 31, 2008.

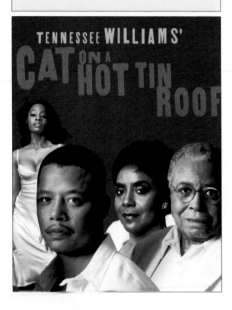

PLAYBILL

CAST

(in order of appearance)

Maggie ....ANIKA NONI ROSE
Brick ....TERRENCE HOWARD
Reverend Tooker ....LOU MYERS
Doctor Baugh ....COUNT STOVALL
Mae ....LISA ARRINDELL ANDERSON
Sonny ....SKYE JASMINE ALLEN-MCBEAN
Big Mama ....PHYLICIA RASHAD
Gooper ....GIANCARLO ESPOSITO
Sookey ....MARJA HARMON
Dixie..............................HEAVEN HOWARD
Trixie ....MARISSA CHISOLM
Lacey ....CLARK JACKSON
Big Daddy ....JAMES EARL JONES
Household Staff ....BETHANY BUTLER,
ROBERT CHRISTOPHER RILEY

TIME AND PLACE

An evening gathering at the Pollitt family estate in
Mississippi.

Saxophone Player:
GERALD HAYES

Continued on next page

Continued on next page

⊛BROADHURST THEATRE
235 West 44th Street
A Shubert Organization Theatre

Gerald Schoenfeld, *Chairman*   Philip J. Smith, *President*

Robert E. Wankel, *Executive Vice President*

FRONT ROW PRODUCTIONS and STEPHEN C. BYRD
With ALIA M. JONES
in Association with
CLARENCE J. CHANDRAN, NORM NIXON, MICHAEL FUCHS, ANTHONY LACAVERA,
EDWARD J. JONES, SHEANNA PANG, JOVAN VITAGLIANO, and AL WILSON

TERRENCE HOWARD
PHYLICIA RASHAD
ANIKA NONI ROSE
and
JAMES EARL JONES
in

TENNESSEE WILLIAMS'

CAT ON A HOT TIN ROOF

with
LISA ARRINDELL ANDERSON
LOU MYERS   COUNT STOVALL
and
GIANCARLO ESPOSITO

BETHANY BUTLER   MARISSA CHISOLM   LYNDA GRAVÁTT   MARJA HARMON   HEAVEN HOWARD
CLARK JACKSON   SKYE JASMINE-ALLEN MCBEAN   ROBERT CHRISTOPHER RILEY

Set Design	Costume Design	Lighting Design
RAY KLAUSEN	JANE GREENWOOD	WILLIAM H. GRANT III
Sound Design	Hair Design	Casting
JOHN H. SHIVERS	CHARLES G. LAPOINTE	PETER WISE & ASSOCIATES
Production Supervisor	Production Stage Manager	General Management
THEATRESMITH, INC.	GWENDOLYN M. GILLIAM	NLA/DEVIN KEUDELL
Press Agent	Original Music	Group Sales/Marketing
SPRINGER ASSOCIATES PR	ANDREW "TEX" ALLEN	MARCIA PENDELTON/WTGP

Associate Producers
BEATRICE L. RANGEL and TERRIE WILLIAMS

Directed by
DEBBIE ALLEN

3/6/08

Anika Noni Rose and
Terrence Howard.

Photo by Joan Marcus

Cat on a Hot Tin Roof

Cast Continued

UNDERSTUDIES

Understudy for Big Daddy:
COUNT STOVALL
Understudy for Brick, Rev. Tooker and Lacey:
ROBERT CHRISTOPHER RILEY
Understudy for Maggie and Mae:
MARJA HARMON
Understudy for Maggie and Mae:
BETHANY BUTLER
Understudy for Gooper, Dr. Baugh and Rev. Tooker:
CLARK JACKSON
Understudy for Big Mama:
LYNDA GRAVÁTT

2007-2008 AWARDS

DRAMA DESK AWARD
Special Award
(James Earl Jones)

OUTER CRITICS CIRCLE AWARD
Outstanding Featured Actor in a Play
(James Earl Jones)

Phylicia Rashad and
James Earl Jones.

Photo by Joan Marcus

Terrence Howard
Brick

James Earl Jones
Big Daddy

Phylicia Rashad
Big Mama

Anika Noni Rose
Maggie

Giancarlo Esposito
Gooper

**Lisa Arrindell
Anderson**
Mae

Lou Myers
Reverend Tooker

Count Stovall
Doctor Baugh

Lynda Gravátt
u/s Big Mama

Marja Harmon
Sookey

Clark Jackson
Lacey

Heaven Howard
Dixie

Marissa Chisolm
Trixie

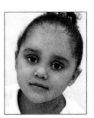

**Skye Jasmine
Allen-McBean**
Sonny

**Robert Christopher
Riley**
Household Staff

Bethany Butler
Household Staff

Tennessee Williams
Playwright

Debbie Allen
Director

Ray Klausen
Scenic Designer

Jane Greenwood
Costume Designer

Cat on a Hot Tin Roof

John H. Shivers
Sound Designer

Christopher C. Smith
Smitty/
Theatersmith, Inc.
*Production
Supervisor*

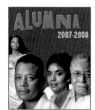

Jane White
*Understudy for Big
Mama*

Alessandra Chisolm
Dixie

Boris Kodjoe
Brick

FRONT OF HOUSE STAFF
Front Row (L-R): Selina Nelson, Hugh Lynch, Jose Morales.

Middle Row (L-R): Paul Rodriguez, Henry Bethea, Karen Diaz, La'Shone Cleveland.

Back Row (L-R): Julie Lugo, Jennifer Vega, Alfredo Rosario.

BOX OFFICE
(L-R): Cliff Cobb, Noreen Morgan, Al Crivelli.

CREW
Front Row (L-R): Gwendolyn M. Gilliam, Brian McGarty, Donna Holland, Michele Rutter, Charles Underhill, Ronnie Vitelli.

Back Row (L-R): Jake Hall, Peter Donovan, Charlie DeVerna, Phil Lojo, Kathy Guida, Tiffany N. Robinson, Elizabeth Talmadge.

Photos by Ben Strothmann

Cat on a Hot Tin Roof

SECURITY
(L-R): Aiden Redmond and Paul Johnson.

STAGE DOORMAN
Richard Jacob

Photos by Ben Strothmann

STAFF FOR *CAT ON A HOT TIN ROOF*

GENERAL MANAGER
NINA LANNAN ASSOCIATES

GENERAL MANAGER
Devin Keudell

COMPANY MANAGER
Paul Morer

GENERAL PRESS REPRESENTATIVE
SPRINGER ASSOCIATES PR
Gary Springer
Joe Trentacosta   Shane Marshall Brown
D'Arcy Drollinger   Jennifer Blum   Ethnee Lea

CASTING
PETER WISE CASTING & ASSOCIATES

Production Supervisor	Chris "Smitty" Smith
Production Stage Manager	Gwendolyn M. Gilliam
Stage Manager	Charles Underhill
Assistant to Director	Eartha Robinson
Associate Scenic Designer	Randall Parsons
Associate Costume Designer	MaryAnn D. Smith
Assistant to Costume Designer	Christina Bullard
Associate Lighting Designer	Temishia Johnson
Associate Sound Designer	David Patridge
Dramaturg	Shauneille Perry
Dialect Coach	Barbara Montgomery
Production Carpenter	Gerry Griffin
Production Electrician	Jimmy Fedigan
Head Electrician	Peter Donovan
Production Sound	Phil Lojo, Paul Delcioppo
Production Sound Mixer	David Patridge
Production Properties	Emiliano Pares,
	Laura McGarty, Ronnie Vitelli
Production Wardrobe Supervisor	Kathy Guida
Dressers	Stephanie Fox, Kristin Gardner,
	Donna Holland
Hair and Makeup Supervisor	Michele Rutter
Production Assistants	Tiffany N. Robinson,
	Zarinah Washington
Assistant to Mr. Howard	Kevin "Webb" Wigfall
Security/Transportation	Lucariello Inc./Mikey Garner
Assistant to Mr. Jones	Coddy Graham
Assistant to Ms. Rashad	Kim Tinsley
Advertising	SpotCo/Drew Hodges,
	Jim Edwards, Lauren Hunter,
	Josh Fraenkel
Marketing	Walk Tall Girl Productions/
	Marcia Pendleton
Production Photographer	Joan Marcus
Staff Photographer	Jeffry Fasano
Publicity Interns	Alexandra Leff, Kendall Henle,
	Joanna DiMattia
Web Design	ArtMeetsCommerce/
	Jim Glaub, Laurie Conner
Accounting	Rosenberg, Neuwirth and Kuchner/
	Chris Cacace, In Woo
Legal Counsel	Donald Farber, Jacob,
	Medinger and Finnegan, LLP
General Management Associates	Carol M. Oune
Insurance	DeWitt Stern Group, Inc./
	Yasmine Ramos
Banking	City National Bank
Payroll	Castellana Services, Inc.
Merchandising	Max Merchandising
Travel Agent	Tzell Travel/Andi Henig
Children's Tutoring	On-Location Education/
	Karin Farrell
Children's Teachers	Alana Serignese, Abby Dyer
Children's Wrangler	Elizabeth Daniels

Travel courtesy of the official airline of
Cat on a Hot Tin Roof
Continental Airlines
Felicia Daniels

CREDITS AND ACKNOWLEDGMENTS

Scenery constructed and painted by Hudson Scenic Studio, Inc. Lighting and sound equipment from PRG. Prop construction by the Spoon Group. Costumes by Eric Winterling, Inc.; Saint Laurie Merchant Tailors. Custom robes and pajamas by Auto Distinctive Shirtmakers. Hair services courtesy of Jason Wilkerson Salon. Housing by AKA, Korman Properties, Sharon Telesca and Eddie Gomez. Rehearsed at the New 42nd Street Studios.

SPECIAL THANKS
Sandra Sheppard
Terrie Williams, Cherine Anderson, Stephen Johnson, Flo Anthony, Nicole Kid, Kevin Bradley, Gerry Byrne, Felicia Taylor, David Friedman, John Travaligni, Ellen Krass, Trevor Brooks, Sylvia Rhone, Victoria Frederick, Marilyn and William Underdue, Pat Bransford, Brenda Braxton and Anthony Van Pattan of B. Braxton, Ricola natural herb cough drops courtesy of Ricola USA, Echo Spring, Heaven Hill Distilleries, Kecia Babb-Jordan/Amtrak, Matt Pyra/Verizon Wireless, Phillip Harvey

THE SHUBERT ORGANIZATION, INC.
Board of Directors

Gerald Schoenfeld Chairman	**Philip J. Smith** President
Wyche Fowler, Jr.	**John W. Kluge**
Lee J. Seidler	**Michael I. Sovern**
Stuart Subotnick	

Robert E. Wankel
Executive Vice President

Peter Entin Vice President – Theatre Operations	**Elliot Greene** Vice President – Finance
David Andrews Vice President – Shubert Ticketing Services	**John Darby** Vice President – Facilities

D.S. Moynihan
Vice President – Creative Projects

House Manager .... Hugh Barnett

Cat on a Hot Tin Roof
SCRAPBOOK

Photos by Aubrey Reuben

1. First day of rehearsal (L-R): Giancarlo Esposito, Lisa Arrindell Anderson, Phylicia Rashad, James Earl Jones, Terrence Howard, Anika Noni Rose, Lou Myers and Count Stovall.
2. Terrence Howard at the opening night party at Strata.915.
3. Phylicia Rashad, Debbie Allen and James Earl Jones take a curtain call at the Broadhurst Theatre on opening night.
4. Lisa Arrindell Anderson at the cast party.
5. Marissa Chisolm on opening night.

Correspondent: Gwen Gilliam, Stage Manager

Opening Night Gifts: Debbie gave a 3D picture of Times Square Broadway, which included the *Cat on a Hot Tin Roof* marquee. Received "Kat on a Hot Tin Roof" KitKat candy bars.

Most Exciting Celebrity Visitors: Aretha Franklin, Diana Ross, Hank Aaron.

Who Has Done the Most Shows in Their Career: James Earl Jones

Special Backstage Rituals: Anika meditates. Everybody eating.

Favorite Moments During Each Performance: The fight scene. Kids doing "Skinnamarink." James makes his entrance and the audience goes wild.

Favorite In-Theatre Gathering Places: Basement greenroom area/kids' lounge. Sitting at TV in front of Donna's picture wall.

Favorite Off-Site Hangouts: Sardi's, Angus, B. Smith's.

Favorite Snack Food: Lay's lightly salted potato chips, chocolate candy, green sour apple ribbons.

Mascot: Stage door teddy bear.

Favorite Therapy: Ricola.

Memorable Ad-Libs: The cast when Dr. Baugh (Count) didn't make his Act III entrance. Too much cigar smoke when someone pooted onstage.

Record Number of Cell Phone Rings During a Performance: Four in a row including a Beyonce ring tone.

Memorable Press Encounters: "CBS Sunday Morning" feature on James Earl Jones. "Today Show" hosts saying that we were robbed on Tony announcement day.

Memorable Stage Door Fan Encounter: Fans that wait an hour until Phylicia comes out.

Latest Audience Arrival: Half an hour before end of show.

Fastest Costume Change: Anika onstage getting out of her clothes.

Busiest Day at the Box Office: Every day.

Who Wore the Least: A tie between Anika and the Bricks (Terrence, Boris and Rob).

Catchphrases Only the Company Would Recognize: "It's time for 'Jeopardy'." "Get Fat Sunday, Get Fat Tuesday."

Memorable Directorial Note: When asked by a cast member if she could talk to director privately, she responded: "What? Just say it. Do I need to read somebody?!"

Company Legends: James Earl Jones and Phylicia Rashad.

Understudy Anecdote: Every u/s got to go on.

Nicknames: Slim pickin's. George Jefferson.

Ghostly Encounters Backstage: Anika has stuff that keeps disappearing and reappearing.

Coolest Thing About Being in This Show: The audience that it is attracting.

Also: Phylicia hosted the entire cast and crew to dinner at La Masseria after a Sunday show.

Chicago

First Preview: October 23, 1996. Opened: November 14, 1996.
Still running as of May 31, 2008.

THE CAST

(in order of appearance)

Velma Kelly ....BRENDA BRAXTON
Roxie Hart ....MICHELLE DeJEAN
Fred Casely ....GREGORY BUTLER
Sergeant Fogarty ....ADAM ZOTOVICH
Amos Hart ....ROB BARTLETT
Liz.....................MICHELLE M. ROBINSON
Annie ....SOLANGE SANDY
June ....DONNA MARIE ASBURY
Hunyak ....EMILY FLETCHER
Mona ....MELISSA RAE MAHON
Matron "Mama" Morton ....ADRIANE LENOX
Billy Flynn ....GEORGE HAMILTON
Mary Sunshine ....R. LOWE
Go-To-Hell Kitty ....MICHELLE POTTERF
Harry ....SHAWN EMAMJOMEH
Doctor ....BERNARD DOTSON
Aaron ....ERIC JORDAN YOUNG
The Judge ....BERNARD DOTSON
Bailiff ....DENNY PASCHALL
Martin Harrison ....MICHAEL CUSUMANO
Court Clerk ....DENNY PASCHALL
The Jury....................SHAWN EMAMJOMEH

THE SCENE:

Chicago, Illinois. The late 1920s.

Continued on next page

A Shubert Organization Theatre

Gerald Schoenfeld, *Chairman*   Philip J. Smith, *President*

Robert E. Wankel, *Executive Vice President*

Barry & Fran Weissler
in association with
Kardana/Hart Sharp Entertainment
present

**Michelle DeJean   Brenda Braxton
Rob Bartlett**
and
George Hamilton

in

CHICAGO

Lyrics by   Music By   Book by
Fred Ebb   John Kander   Fred Ebb & Bob Fosse

Original Production Directed and Choreographed by **Bob Fosse**

Based on the play by Maurine Dallas Watkins

with

Adriane Lenox   R. Lowe

and

**Donna Marie Asbury   Gregory Butler   Michael Cusumano
Bernard Dotson   Shawn Emamjomeh   Emily Fletcher   Gabriela Garcia
David Kent   J. Loeffelholz   Melissa Rae Mahon   Sharon Moore
Denny Paschall   Michelle Potterf   Michelle M. Robinson   Solange Sandy
Brian Spitulnik   Eric Jordan Young   Adam Zotovich**

Supervising Music Director   Music Director
Rob Fisher   **Leslie Stifelman**

Scenic Design   Costume Design   Lighting Design
John Lee Beatty **William Ivey Long** **Ken Billington**

Sound Design   Orchestrations   Dance Music Arrangements
Scott Lehrer   **Ralph Burns**   **Peter Howard**

Script Adaptation   Musical Coordinator   Hair Design
David Thompson   **Seymour Red Press**   **David Brian Brown**

Casting   Original Casting
Duncan Stewart   **Jay Binder**

Technical Supervisor   Dance Supervisor   Production Stage Manager
Arthur Siccardi   **Gary Chryst**   **David Hyslop**

Associate Producer   Presented in association with
Alecia Parker   **Live Nation**

General Manager   Press Representative
B.J. Holt   **Jeremy Shaffer
The Publicity Office**

Based on the presentation by City Center's Encores!℠

Choreography by
Ann Reinking
in the style of Bob Fosse

Directed by
Walter Bobbie

Cast Recording on RCA Victor

10/1/07

Brenda Braxton (center)
as Velma Kelly.

Photo by Paul Kolnik

Chicago

MUSICAL NUMBERS

ACT I

ALL THAT JAZZ	Velma and Company
FUNNY HONEY	Roxie
CELL BLOCK TANGO	Velma and the Girls
WHEN YOU'RE GOOD TO MAMA	Matron
TAP DANCE	Roxie, Amos and Boys
ALL I CARE ABOUT	Billy and Girls
A LITTLE BIT OF GOOD	Mary Sunshine
WE BOTH REACHED FOR THE GUN	Billy, Roxie, Mary Sunshine and Company
ROXIE	Roxie and Boys
I CAN'T DO IT ALONE	Velma
MY OWN BEST FRIEND	Roxie and Velma

ACT II

ENTR'ACTE	The Band
I KNOW A GIRL	Velma
ME AND MY BABY	Roxie and Boys
MISTER CELLOPHANE	Amos
WHEN VELMA TAKES THE STAND	Velma and Boys
RAZZLE DAZZLE	Billy and Company
CLASS	Velma and Matron
NOWADAYS	Roxie and Velma
HOT HONEY RAG	Roxie and Velma
FINALE	Company

ORCHESTRA

Orchestra Conducted by
LESLIE STIFELMAN
Associate Conductor:
SCOTT CADY
Woodwinds:
SEYMOUR RED PRESS, JACK STUCKEY,
RICHARD CENTALONZA
Trumpets:
JOHN FROSK, DARRYL SHAW
Trombones:
DAVE BARGERON, BRUCE BONVISSUTO
Piano
SCOTT CADY
Piano & Accordion:
JOHN JOHNSON
Banjo:
JAY BERLINER
Bass & Tuba:
RONALD RAFFIO
Violin:
MARSHALL COID
Drums & Percussion:
RONALD ZITO

Bianca Marroquin as Roxie Hart.

Photo by Len Prince

Cast Continued

UNDERSTUDIES

For Roxie Hart:
MELISSA RAE MAHON, MICHELLE POTTERF
For Velma Kelly:
DONNA MARIE ASBURY,
MELISSA RAE MAHON, SOLANGE SANDY
For Billy Flynn:
BERNARD DOTSON, ERIC JORDAN YOUNG
For Amos Hart:
ERIC JORDAN YOUNG, ADAM ZOTOVICH
For Matron "Mama" Morton:
DONNA MARIE ASBURY,
MICHELLE M. ROBINSON
For Mary Sunshine:
J. LOEFFELHOLZ
For Fred Casely/"Me and My Baby":
DAVID KENT, DENNY PASCHALL,
BRIAN SPITULNIK

For all other roles:
GABRIELA GARCIA, DAVID KENT,
SHARON MOORE, BRIAN SPITULNIK

Dance Captains:
GREGORY BUTLER, BERNARD DOTSON,
GABRIELA GARCIA

"Tap Dance" specialty performed by
BERNARD DOTSON, DENNY PASCHALL,
ERIC JORDAN YOUNG

"Me and My Baby" specialty performed by
MICHAEL CUSUMANO,
ERIC JORDAN YOUNG

"Nowadays" whistle performed by
ERIC JORDAN YOUNG

Original Choreography for "Hot Honey Rag" by
BOB FOSSE

Chicago

Michelle DeJean
Roxie Hart

Brenda Braxton
Velma Kelly

George Hamilton
Billy Flynn

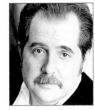
Rob Bartlett
Amos Hart

Adriane Lenox
*Matron "Mama"
Morton*

R. Lowe
Mary Sunshine

Donna Marie Asbury
June

Gregory Butler
*Fred Casely/
Dance Captain*

Michael Cusumano
Martin Harrison

Bernard Dotson
*Doctor/The Judge/
Dance Captain*

Shawn Emamjomeh
Harry/The Jury

Emily Fletcher
Hunyak

Gabriela Garcia
*Swing/
Dance Captain*

David Kent
Swing

J. Loeffelholz
*Standby
Mary Sunshine*

Melissa Rae Mahon
Mona

Sharon Moore
Swing

Denny Paschall
Bailiff/Court Clerk

Michelle Potterf
Go-To-Hell Kitty

Michelle M.
Robinson
Liz

Solange Sandy
Annie

Brian Spitulnik
Swing

Eric Jordan Young
Aaron

Adam Zotovich
Sergeant Fogarty

John Kander & Fred Ebb
Music; Book/Lyrics

Bob Fosse
Book

Walter Bobbie
Director

Ann Reinking
Choreographer

John Lee Beatty
Set Design

William Ivey Long
Costume Designer

Ken Billington
Lighting Designer

Rob Fisher
*Supervising Music
Director*

Peter Howard
*Dance Music
Arranger*

Seymour Red Press
Music Coordinator

Chicago

David Brian Brown
Wig/Hair Design

Arthur Siccardi,
Theatrical Services,
Inc.
Technical Supervisor

Barry and Fran Weissler
Producers

Morton Swinsky/
Kardana Productions
Producer

ALUMNI
2007-2008

Julio Agustin
Sergeant Fogarty

Eddie Bennett
*Bailiff, Court Clerk,
Harry, Tap Dance
Specialty, & The
Jury*

Raymond Bokhour
Amos Hart

Kate Dunn
June

Harry Hamlin
Billy Flynn

Robyn Hurder
Mona

Joey Lawrence
Billy Flynn

Dan LoBuono
*Fred Casely,
Sergeant Fogarty*

Bianca Marroquin
Roxie Hart

Angel Reda
Mona

Josh Rhodes
*Doctor, Tap Dance
Specialty, The Judge*

Lisa Rinna
Roxie Hart

Roz Ryan
*Matron "Mama"
Morton*

D. Sabella-Mills
Mary Sunshine

Tracy Shayne
Roxie Hart

Mark Anthony Taylor
*Understudy for
Amos Hart,
Fred Casely,
Me and My Baby*

Jennifer West
Swing

Tom Wopat
Billy Flynn

TRANSFER
STUDENTS
2007-2008

Nili Bassman
Hunyak

Raymond Bokhour
Amos Hart

Nicole Bridgewater
Annie, Liz

Maxwell Caulfield
Billy Flynn

Kelly Crandall
Annie

Dylis Croman
Annie

Kate Dunn
Annie

Nancy Lemenager
Velma Kelly

Kecia Lewis-Evans
*Matron "Mama"
Morton*

Dan LoBuono
*Bailiff, Court Clerk,
Tap Dance Specialty*

Chicago

Terra C. MacLeod
Velma Kelly

Bianca Marroquin
Roxie Hart

Jeff McCarthy
Billy Flynn

Brian McKnight
Billy Flynn

D. Micciche
Mary Sunshine

Jill Nicklaus
Hunyak

Ron Orbach
Amos Hart

Vincent Pastore
Amos Hart

Roz Ryan
Matron "Mama" Morton

John Schneider
Billy Flynn

Aida Turturro
Matron "Mama" Morton

(L-R): Scott Cady (Piano) and Leslie Stifelman (Conductor).

STAGE MANAGEMENT
(L-R): Terry Witter (Stage Manager), David Hyslop (Production Stage Manager), Mindy Farbrother (Stage Manager).

ORCHESTRA
Front Row (L-R): Marshall Coid, David Grego.

Middle Row (L-R): Shawn Edmonds, Ken Hitchcock, Jeff Schiller, Dave Bargeron, Leslie Stifelman, John Johnson, Jay Berliner, Dan Gross.

Back Row (L-R): Bruce Bonvissuto, Rick Centalonza.

FRONT OF HOUSE STAFF
Front Row (L-R): Tyrone Hendrix (Ticket Taker), Leeann Kelley (Dewynters Staff), Rachel Zeolla (Dewynters Staff), Tasha Allen (Usher), Dorothea Bentley (Head Usher), Mary Simcoe (Usher), Carole Hollenbeck (Usher), Carol Bokun (Directress).

Middle Row (L-R): Jack Donaghy (Usher), Rita Sussman (Sound Associates Rep.), Timothy Newsome (Usher), Danielle Banyai (Usher), Marilyn Wasbotten (Usher), Lottie Dennis (Usher), Beatrice Carney (Usher), Jessica Porcelli (Theatre Refreshment Staff).

Back Row (L-R): Matt Kuehl (Dewynters Manager), Bobbi Parker (Usher), Christopher Holmes (Theatre Refreshment Staff).

Chicago

BOX OFFICE
(L-R): James Gatens (Treasurer), William Roeder (Assistant Treasurer), James Lyons (Assistant Treasurer).

HAIR AND WARDROBE
(L-R): Kevin Woodworth (Wardrobe Supervisor), Jo-Ann Bethell (Dresser), Justen Brosnan (Hair Supervisor), Paula Davis (Dresser).

Photos by Ben Strothmann

CREW
Front Row (L-R): Jenny Montgomery (Props), John Montgomery (Production Sound), Eileen MacDonald (Deck Sound), Jim Werner (Front Light).

Back Row (L-R): Luciana Fusco (Head Electrician), Joe Mooneyham (Production Carpenter), Bob Hale (Front Light), Billy Rowland (House Electrician).

STAFF FOR *CHICAGO*

GENERAL MANAGEMENT
B.J. Holt, General Manager
Nina Skriloff, International Manager

PRESS REPRESENTATIVE
THE PUBLICITY OFFICE
Jeremy Shaffer   Marc Thibodeau
Michael Borowski   Matt Fasano

Production Stage Manager	**David Hyslop**
Company Manager	**Jean Haring**
Stage Managers	Terrence J. Witter, Mindy Farbrother
Associate General Manager	Hilary Hamilton
General Management Associate	Stephen Spadaro
Assistant Director	Jonathan Bernstein
Associate Lighting Designer	John McKernon
Assistant Choreographer	Debra McWaters
Dance Captains	Gregory Butler, Bernard Dotson, Gabriela Garcia
Assistant Set Designers	Eric Renschler, Shelley Barclay
Wardrobe Supervisor	Kevin Woodworth
Costume Assistant	Donald Sanders
Personal Asst. to Mr. Billington	Jon Kusner
Assistant to Mr. Lehrer	Thom Mohrman
Production Carpenter	Joseph Mooneyham
Production Electrician	James Fedigan
Head Electrician	Luciana Fusco
Front Lite Operator	Michael Guggino
Production Sound Engineer	John Montgomery
Hair Supervisor	Justen Brosnan
Production Propman	John Cagney
Dressers	Jo-Ann Bethell, Kathy Dacey, Paula Davis, Ronald Tagert, Eric Concklin
Banking	Chase Manhattan, Stephanie Dalton

Music Prep	Chelsea Music Services, Inc. Donald Oliver & Evan Morris
Payroll	Castellana Services, Inc.
Accountants	Rosenberg, Newirth & Kuchner Mark D'Ambrosi, Marina Flom
Insurance	Industrial Risk Specialists
Counsel	Seth Gelblum/Loeb & Loeb
Art Design	Spot Design
Advertising	SpotCo: Drew Hodges, Jim Edwards, Sara Fitzpatrick, Tom McCann, Steve Sosnowski
Education	Students Live/Amy Weinstein www.studentslive.net
Merchandising	Dewynters Advertising Inc.
Displays	King Display

NATIONAL ARTISTS MANAGEMENT CO.

Vice President of Marketing	Bob Bucci
Director of Business Affairs	Daniel M. Posener
Dramaturg/Creative Consultant	Jack DePalma
Chief Financial Officer	Bob Williams
Accounting	Marian Albarracin
Assistant to Mrs. Weissler	Brett England
Assistant to the Weisslers	Suzanne Evans
Assistant to Ms. Parker	Emily Dimond
Director of Marketing	Ken Sperr
Receptionist	Michelle Coleman

SPECIAL THANKS
Additional legal services provided by Jay Goldberg, Esq. and Michael Berger, Esq. Emer'gen-C super energy booster provided by Alacer Corp. Dry cleaning by Ernest Winzer Cleaners. Hosiery and undergarments provided by Bra*Tenders. Tuxedos by Brioni. Additional photography by Bruce Glikas.

CREDITS
Lighting equipment by PRG Lighting. Scenery built and painted by Hudson Scenic Studios. Specialty Rigging by United Staging & Rigging. Sound equipment by PRG Audio. Shoulder holster courtesy of DeSantis Holster and Leather Goods Co. Period cameras and flash units by George Fenmore, Inc. Colibri lighters used. Bible courtesy of Chiarelli's Religious Goods, Inc. Black pencils by Dixon-Ticonderoga. Gavel courtesy of The Gavel Co. Zippo lighters used. Garcia y Vega cigars used. Hosiery by Donna Karan. Shoes by T.O. Dey. Orthopaedic Consultant, David S. Weiss, M.D.

 THE SHUBERT ORGANIZATION, INC.
Board of Directors

Gerald Schoenfeld	**Philip J. Smith**
Chairman	President
Wyche Fowler, Jr.	**John W. Kluge**
Lee J. Seidler	**Michael I. Sovern**

Stuart Subotnick

Robert E. Wankel
Executive Vice President

Peter Entin	**Elliot Greene**
Vice President – Theatre Operations	Vice President – Finance
David Andrews	**John Darby**
Vice President – Shubert Ticketing Services	Vice President – Facilities

D.S. Moynihan
Vice President – Creative Projects

House Manager	Patricia Berry

Chicago
SCRAPBOOK

Correspondent: Eric Jordan Young, "Aaron"

Most Exciting Celebrity Visitor: Dame Shirley Bassey.

Actors Who Perform the Most Roles in This Show: It would definitely have to be our swings—David Kent, Brian Spitulnik, Gabriela Garcia, Sharon Moore.

Special Backstage Ritual: Running downstairs to the basement at intermission in hopes that there is cake to celebrate a birthday or a departing cast member. Sugar rush!!!!!

Favorite In-Theatre Gathering Places: The staircase on stage level, the basement in the costume shop and/or Brenda's dressing room (Velma).

Favorite Off-Site Hangout: Natsumi.

Favorite Snack Foods: Nerds, Gummi Bears, and any chocolate in the silver tin down in the basement.

Favorite Therapy: Packets of Emergen-C.

Record Number of Cell Phone Rings, Cell Phone Photos or Texting Incidents During a Performance: Honestly, too many to count.

Memorable Press Encounter: The company introduced a star from Japan stepping into the role of Velma in an all-Japanese production. The company welcomed her, and the new production set to open in Japan, on the Broadway stage following the show one evening. Unfortunately, many of us don't speak Japanese so we had no idea what she was saying to our audience.

Latest Audience Arrival: During "Me And My Baby" in Act II.

Fastest Costume Change: Costume change? Ha!

Busiest Day at the Box Office: In November, the day after the stagehands strike ended, when all of the seats in the house were 26 bucks.

Who Wore the Heaviest/Hottest Costume: Amos.

Who Wore the Least: Melissa Rae Mahon.

Catchphrases Only the Company Would Recognize: "Joooossssssssssshhhhhhhhhh!"

Sweethearts Within the Company: It's *Chicago*!! Everyone is a "sweetheart."

Memorable Directorial Note: To be "happy and excited" for Roxie's baby announcement.

Tales From The Put-In: *Chicago* doesn't have many put-ins but when we do they are always full out. Hee-hee.

Understudy Anecdote: I bit my tongue while singing "Cellophane" one night. I think it was... "If someone in a movie show yelled fire blah blah lah lah lah you'd notice him. OUCH!"

Nicknames: Otis Spunkmeyer, Old Buzzard, Cpt. Butler.

Embarrassing Moments: We had a Cartwheel Sunday once where everyone in the company took their bow by doing a cartwheel. One of our beautiful ladies had a ponytail that fell off during her cartwheel and it stayed center stage until someone else picked it up. Hilarious!

Coolest Thing About Being in This Show: No one ever tires of it. It really is the greatest show ever. Long live *Chicago*!

1. George Hamilton and ladies of the ensemble perform "All I Care About Is Love" on the rooftop of ABC Studios in Times Square for "Good Morning America."
2. (L-R): Darlene Love of *Hairspray* and Adriane Lenox of *Chicago* at the 2007 "Broadway on Broadway" event in Times Square.
3. Michelle DeJean (on lap) and Brian McKnight (seated) in rehearsal at MTC Studios.
4. To celebrate cast member Lisa Rinna's birthday, the entire company wore giant plastic wax lips and sang "Happy Birthday" to her at intermission.

A Chorus Line

First Preview: September 18, 2006. Opened: October 5, 2006.
Still running as of May 31, 2008.

PLAYBILL

A CHORUS LINE

CAST
(in alphabetical order)

Larry ....NICK ADAMS
Tricia ....MICHELLE ARAVENA
Roy ....DAVID BAUM
Zach ....MICHAEL BERRESSE
Tom ....MIKE CANNON
Butch.................E. CLAYTON CORNELIOUS
Diana ....NATALIE CORTEZ
Cassie ....CHARLOTTE d'AMBOISE
Val ....JESSICA LEE GOLDYN
Sheila ....DEIDRE GOODWIN
Greg ....MICHAEL GRUBER
Lois ....NADINE ISENEGGER
Paul ....BRYAN KNOWLTON
Richie...............................JAMES T. LANE
Maggie ....MELISSA LONE
Connie ....J. ELAINE MARCOS
Mark ....PAUL McGILL
Judy ....HEATHER PARCELLS
Bebe ....KRYSTA RODRIGUEZ
Don ....JASON PATRICK SANDS
Mike ....JEFFREY SCHECTER
Vicki ....KIM SHRIVER
Bobby ....WILL TAYLOR
Kristine ....KATHERINE TOKARZ
Frank ....GRANT TURNER
Al ....KEVIN WORLEY

The role of CASSIE will be played by
Nadine Isenegger on Thursdays
and Jessica Lea Patty on Sundays.

Continued on next page

⊗ **GERALD SCHOENFELD THEATRE**
236 West 45th Street
A Shubert Organization Theatre
Gerald Schoenfeld, *Chairman*   Philip J. Smith, *President*
Robert E. Wankel, *Executive Vice President*

Vienna Waits Productions

presents

A CHORUS LINE

Conceived and Originally Choreographed and Directed by
Michael Bennett

Book by   Music by   Lyrics by
James Kirkwood &   Marvin Hamlisch   Edward Kleban
Nicholas Dante

Originally Co-Choreographed by
Bob Avian

with

Nick Adams   Michelle Aravena   David Baum   Michael Berresse   Mike Cannon
E. Clayton Cornelious   Natalie Cortez   Charlotte d'Amboise   Dena DiGiacinto
Joey Dudding   Lyndy Franklin   Jessica Lee Goldyn   Deidre Goodwin   Michael Gruber
Nadine Isenegger   Bryan Knowlton   James T. Lane   Melissa Lone
J. Elaine Marcos   Paul McGill   Heather Parcells   Jessica Lea Patty
Krysta Rodriguez   Jason Patrick Sands   Jeffrey Schecter   Kim Shriver
Will Taylor   Katherine Tokarz   Grant Turner   Kevin Worley   Deone Zanotto

Scenic Design by   Costume Design by   Lighting Design by   Sound Design by
Robin Wagner   Theoni V. Aldredge   Tharon Musser   Acme Sound
                                                   Adapted by   **Partners**
                                                Natasha Katz

Music Direction & Supervision by   Orchestrations by   Vocal Arrangements by
Patrick Vaccariello   **Jonathan Tunick**   **Don Pippin**
                               Bill Byers & Hershy Kay

Choreography Re-Staged by
Baayork Lee

Directed by
Bob Avian

The original production of A CHORUS LINE was produced by The Public Theater, in association with Plum Productions.

10/1/07

Mario Lopez (center) as Zach.

Photo by Paul Kolnik

A Chorus Line

MUSICAL NUMBERS

I Hope I Get It	Company
I Can Do That	Mike
And	Bobby, Richie, Val, Judy
At the Ballet	Sheila, Bebe, Maggie
Sing!	Kristine, Al
Hello Twelve, Hello Thirteen, Hello Love	Company
Nothing	Diana
Dance: Ten; Looks: Three	Val
The Music and the Mirror	Cassie
One	Company
The Tap Combination	Company
What I Did for Love	Diana, Company
One: Reprise	Company

Cast Continued

SWINGS
DENA DiGIACINTO, JOEY DUDDING, LYNDY FRANKLIN, JESSICA LEA PATTY, DEONE ZANOTTO

Dance Captain: LYNDY FRANKLIN

UNDERSTUDIES
For Al, Mike:
DAVID BAUM, MIKE CANNON
For Bebe:
MICHELLE ARAVENA, DENA DiGIACINTO, LYNDY FRANKLIN
For Bobby:
DAVID BAUM, JOEY DUDDING
For Cassie:
NADINE ISENEGGER, JESSICA LEA PATTY
For Connie:
MICHELLE ARAVENA, DENA DiGIACINTO
For Diana:
MICHELLE ARAVENA, DENA DiGIACINTO, JESSICA LEA PATTY
For Don, Larry:
E. CLAYTON CORNELIOUS, GRANT TURNER
For Greg:
DAVID BAUM, GRANT TURNER
For Judy:
LYNDY FRANKLIN, KIM SHRIVER, DEONE ZANOTTO
For Kristine:
DENA DiGIACINTO, LYNDY FRANKLIN
For Maggie:
MICHELLE ARAVENA, LYNDY FRANKLIN, JESSICA LEA PATTY
For Mark:
JOEY DUDDING, MIKE CANNON
For Paul:
JOEY DUDDING, E. CLAYTON CORNELIOUS
For Richie:
MIKE CANNON, E. CLAYTON CORNELIOUS
For Sheila:
JESSICA LEA PATTY, KIM SHRIVER
For Val:
NADINE ISENEGGER, KIM SHRIVER
For Zach:
MICHAEL GRUBER, GRANT TURNER

AN AUDITION
TIME: 1975
PLACE: A Broadway Theatre

"This show is dedicated to anyone who has ever danced in a chorus or marched in step...anywhere."
—Michael Bennett

BOX OFFICE
(L-R): Gary Powers, Vigi Cadunz and Manny Rivera.

Photos by Ben Strothmann

DOORMAN
Lype O'Dell

ORCHESTRA
Conductor:
PATRICK VACCARIELLO
Associate Conductor/Keyboard 2:
JIM LAEV
Assistant Conductor/Keyboard 3:
MAGGIE TORRE
Woodwind 1:
TED NASH
Woodwind 2:
LINO GOMEZ
Woodwind 3:
DAVID YOUNG
Woodwind 4:
JACQUELINE HENDERSON
Trumpet 1:
JOHN CHUDOBA
Trumpet 2:
TREVOR NEUMANN
Trumpet 3:
SCOTT WENDHOLT
Trombone 1:
MICHAEL SELTZER

Trombone 2:
BEN HERRINGTON
Bass Trombone:
JACK SCHATZ
Bass:
BILL SLOAT
Keyboard 1:
ANN GERSCHEFSKI
Percussion:
DAN McMILLAN
Drums:
BRIAN BRAKE

Music Coordinator:
MICHAEL KELLER
Synthesizer Programmer:
BRUCE SAMUELS
Rehearsal Pianist:
JOHN O'NEILL

Music Copying:
EMILY GRISHMAN MUSIC PREPARATION/
KATHARINE EDMONDS, EMILY GRISHMAN

A Chorus Line

Nick Adams
Larry

Michael Berresse
Zach

Natalie Cortez
Diana

Charlotte d'Amboise
Cassie

Jessica Lee Goldyn
Val

Deidre Goodwin
Sheila

Michael Gruber
Greg

Bryan Knowlton
Paul

James T. Lane
Richie

Melissa Lone
Maggie

J. Elaine Marcos
Connie

Paul McGill
Mark

Heather Parcells
Judy

Krysta Rodriguez
Bebe

Jason Patrick Sands
Don

Jeffrey Schecter
Mike

Will Taylor
Bobby

Katherine Tokarz
Kristine

Kevin Worley
Al

Michelle Aravena
Tricia/Ensemble

David Baum
Roy/Ensemble

Mike Cannon
Tom/Ensemble

E. Clayton Cornelious
Butch/Ensemble

Dena DiGiacinto
Swing

Joey Dudding
Swing

Lyndy Franklin
Swing

Nadine Isenegger
Lois/Ensemble

Jessica Lea Patty
Swing

Kim Shriver
Vicki/Ensemble

Grant Turner
Frank/Ensemble

Deone Zanotto
Swing

Michael Bennett
*Conception,
Original Director/
Choreographer*

Marvin Hamlisch
Music

Baayork Lee
*Choreography
Re-Staging*

Robin Wagner
Scenic Design

A Chorus Line

Natasha Katz
Lighting Design

Tom Clark, Mark Menard and Nevin Steinberg,
Acme Sound Partners
Sound Design

Patrick Vaccariello
Music Direction and Supervision

Michael Keller
Music Coordinator

Jonathan Tunick
Orchestrator

Jay Binder C.S.A.
Casting

Alan Wasser
Associates
General Manager

Arthur Siccardi
Production Manager

John Breglio,
Vienna Waits
Productions
Producer

Ken Alan
Bobby

Brad Anderson
Don

Dylis Croman
*Understudy for
Cassie, Sheila*

Mara Davi
Maggie

Tyler Hanes
Larry

Pamela Jordan
Vicki

Denis Lambert
Swing

Courtney Laine
Mazza
Swing

Michael Paternostro
Greg

Alisan Porter
Bebe

Eric Sciotto
Swing

Yuka Takara
Connie

Josh Walden
Swing

Chryssie Whitehead
Kristine

Tony Yazbeck
Al

Deanna Aguinaga
Swing

Todd Anderson
Roy, Swing

Tommy Berklund
Greg

Kurt Domoney
Swing

Eric Dysart
Swing

Emily Fletcher
Vicki

Jenifer Foote
Vicki

Denis Lambert
Roy, Swing

A Chorus Line

Mario Lopez
Zach

Courtney Laine
Mazza
Swing

Kimberly Dawn
Neumann
*Understudy for
Cassie, Sheila*

Eric Sciotto
Swing

COMPANY MANAGEMENT
(L-R): Michael Altbaum, Adam Miller

FRONT OF HOUSE STAFF
Front Row (L-R): Annie Bree,
Kathleen Spock, Yvet Valdoquiin,
Nancy Barnicle, David M. Conte.

Middle Row (L-R): Roz Nyman,
Jason Bratton, Sarah Ricker,
Anthony Martinez.

Back Row (L-R): Bonny Hughes,
Michelle Moyna, Emily Christensen,
Geraldine White, Matt Blank.

ORCHESTRA
Sitting: Adam Kolker

Front Row (L-R): Scott Wendholt,
John "Sunshine" Chudoba, Rick Shapiro,
Mike Seltzer.

Middle Row (L-R): Rick Heckman,
Ann Gerschefski, Tony Facanga, Maggie
Torre, Jackie Henderson, Frank Lindquist,
Alan Ferber, Jason Aspinwall.

Back Row (L-R): Brian Brake,
Dan McMillan, Patrick Vaccariello.

CREW
Kevin Kenneally, Tim McWilliams, Brian Hutchinson, Tim Semon, Laurie Goldfeder, Billy Barnes, Peter Guernsey, Brian Cook, Leslie Kilian, Beth Berkeley,
Caitley Symons, Fritz Frizsell, Heidi Brown, Rory Powers, Scott Sanders, Eric Norris, Stephen Long, Libby Villanova, Hector Lugo, Shana Albery, Sarah Hench.

A Chorus Line
SCRAPBOOK

STAFF FOR *A CHORUS LINE*

GENERAL MANAGEMENT
ALAN WASSER ASSOCIATES
Alan Wasser   Allan Williams   Aaron Lustbader

GENERAL PRESS REPRESENTATIVE
BARLOW•HARTMAN
John Barlow   Michael Hartman
Wayne Wolfe

CASTING
JAY BINDER CASTING
Jay Binder, C.S.A.
Jack Bowdan, C.S.A.   Mark Brandon   Sara Schatz

PRODUCTION MANAGER
Arthur Siccardi

PRODUCTION STAGE MANAGER
William Joseph Barnes

COMPANY MANAGER
Susan Bell

Associate Company Manager .... Adam J. Miller
Stage Manager .... Laurie Goldfeder
Assistant Stage Manager .... Timothy R. Semon
Resident Choreographer .... Michael Gorman
Assistant Director .... Peter Pileski
Assistant Scenic Designer .... David Peterson
Associate Costume Designer .... Suzy Benzinger
Assistant Costume Designer .... Patrick Wiley
Wardrobe Consultant .... Alyce Gilbert
Associate Lighting Designer .... Yael Lubetzky
Assistant Lighting Designer .... Aaron Spivey
Assistant Sound Designer .... Michael Creason
Automated Lighting Programmer .... Matthew Hudson
Music Coordinator .... Michael Keller
Synthesizer Programmer .... Bruce Samuels
Production Carpenter .... Curtis Cowley
Head Carpenter .... Breffny Flynn
Production Electrician .... Jimmy Fedigan
Head Electrician .... Eric Norris
Assistant Electrician .... Stephen R. Long
Production Sound Engineer .... Scott Sanders
Advance Sound .... John Dory
Wardrobe Supervisor .... Rory Powers
Prop Coordinator .... Heidi Brown
Dressers .... Shana Albery, Sarah Hench,
Hector Lugo, Leo Namba,
Catherine Symons, Elizabeth Villanova
House Electrician .... Leslie Ann Kilian
Follow Spot Operators .... Peter W. Guernsey,
Fritz Frizsell
Deck Sound .... Brian "Cookie" Cook, Beth Berkeley

House Props .... Heidi L. Brown
House Carpenter .... Tim McWilliams
House Flyman .... Glenn Ingram

Advertising .... Serino Coyne/
Greg Corradetti,
Andrea Prince, Ryan Greer

Website Design &
Online Marketing
Strategy .... Situation Marketing LLC/
Damian Bazadona, Joey Oliva, Chris Powers

Marketing/Sponsorship
Services .... Apel, Inc./
David Sass, Harry Spero,
Matthew Farkash, Jessica Stock
Legal Counsel .... Paul Weiss Rifkind Wharton
& Garrison, LLP/Deborah Hartnett
Accounting .... Rosenberg, Neuwirth & Kuchner/
Chris Cacace,
Mark D'Ambrosi
Production Associate .... Deborah Hartnett
Administrative Assistant to
Mr. Breglio .... Helene Gaulrapp
Associate General Manager .... Aaron Lustbader
General Management Associates .... Jake Hirzel,
Thom Mitchell, Connie Yung
General Management Office .... Christopher Betz,
Christopher D'Angelo,
Jason Hewitt, Jennifer Mudge
Press Office Manager .... Bethany Larsen
Press Associates .... Leslie Baden, Michelle Bergmann,
Dennis Crowley, Tom D'Ambrosio,
Ryan Ratelle, Kevin Robak
Casting Assistants .... Nikole Vallins,
Allison Estrin
Production Assistant .... Annette Verga-Lagier
Production Photographer .... Paul Kolnik
Insurance .... Ventura Insurance Brokerage/
Janice Brown
Banking .... Commerce Bank/
Barbara von Borstel,
Ashley Elezi
Payroll .... Castellana Services, Inc.
Merchandising .... Max Merchandising/
Randi Grossman
Study Guide .... Peter Royston
Travel Services .... Road Rebel
Entertainment Touring
Assistants to Ms. Lee .... Steven Eng,
Cassey Kivnick
Opening Night
Coordination .... Tobak Lawrence Co./
Suzanne Tobak, Michael P. Lawrence
Physical Therapist .... Performing Arts Physical Therapy

Orthopedic Consultant .... Philip Bauman M.D.
Group Sales .... Theatre Direct International/
Broadway.com/
1-800-BROADWAY

www.achorusline.com

CREDITS AND ACKNOWLEDGEMENTS
Scenery built and electrified by Hudson Scenic Studio Inc. Automation equipment provided by Hudson Scenic Studio, Inc. Electric truss built by Scenic Technologies. Lighting equipment provided by PRG Lighting. Sound equipment provided by PRG Audio. Finale costumes by Barbara Matera, Ltd. Costumes by Lynne Baccus; Euro Co Costumes, Inc.; Rick Kelly; D. Barak; Catherine Stribling. Leotards by Bal Togs Industries. Custom shirts by Cego Custom Shirts. Custom knitwear by C.C. Wei. Fabric dyeing and painting by the Craft Show. Footwear by T.O. Dey, J.C. Theatricals. Rehearsal hats by Arnold S. Levine, Inc. Ms. d'Amboise's hair by Paul Labrecque. Mike Costa's shirts provided by Lacoste. Men's socks provided by Gold Toe Brands, Inc. Finale top hats by Rodney Gordon, Inc. Finale shoes by Capezio. Ricola natural herb cough drops courtesy of Ricola USA, Inc. Emergen-C super energy booster provided by Alacer Corp. Cover photography by Walter Iooss. Rehearsed at 890 Broadway.

A Chorus Line
SCRAPBOOK

Correspondent: Paul McGill, "Mark"

Memorable Note, Fax or Fan Letter: All the fan mail is great. I don't know if it has to do with the show or not, but I've gotten three letters from priests.

Anniversary Parties and Gifts: Christmas Party/One-Year Anniversary Party combined. I got a winter scarf embroidered "*A Chorus Line.*"

Most Exciting Celebrity Visitor: Daniel Radcliffe. We talked for about a half hour about the show, live theater versus film, and life. Cool guy!

"Gypsy of the Year" Sketch: It was a mini-musical called "*A Picket Line*" narrating the story of the 2007 IATSE/Local 1 strike. Shecky did most of the prep work, but all participants put their two cents in. It was Jeffrey Schecter, Melissa Lone, Krysta Rodriguez, Deidre Goodwin, Kat Tokarz, Bryan Knowlton, Nick Adams, (IATSE Member) Fritz Frizsell, Stage Managers Billy Barnes and Tim Semon, and me.

Actor Who Performed the Most Roles in This Show: Tie: Lyndy Franklin and Jessica Patty: eight roles each. HARD workers.

Special Backstage Rituals: Warming up... ALWAYS. "Purelling" has become a good luck charm...haha.

Favorite Moments During Each Performance: My personal favorite is in the "One" sequence when Zack says "Is this REALLY what you want to do?" Also: Heather's variety show during the "Ba-Da's." Standing upstage right with all the people who are not in "Mother." The "nervous breakdown" in the Montage or any spot to improv because it's so rare with the circumstance of the show. Our only times offstage, which are nice, are during "Nothing," the Cassie Dance, and the Paul Monologue...hahaha.

Favorite In-Theatre Gathering Places: Before the show...on- and backstage warming up, or in the Balcony getting Physical Therapy.

Since there's no greenroom: the stage management office or in our own dressing rooms.

Favorite Off-Site Hangouts: Performing Arts Physical Therapy. The OCCASIONAL Angus, Kodama, Irish Rogue, Delta Grill, or Chelsea Grill

Favorite Snack Foods: "The Fat Girl Drawer": Vienna Fingers, Oreos, and M&M's. James T. Lane has a piece of fruit every day during the Cassie Dance. Most birthdays are celebrated with Amy's Bread. The Candy Lady.

Mascot: It's still Latice...why? I have no idea.

Favorite Therapies: Ricola, Ben Gay, Throat-Coat Tea, Massage, Pilates, all of the above. We also have Physical Therapy five days a week as well as acupuncture every Monday and Massage every Thursday through the company.

Memorable Line Screwed-Up: "I used to run down the sidewalk...on my knees...at 5."

Memorable Press Encounters: The "Broadway's Back" photo shoot in Times Square. The "Broadway's Back" Concert was like Broadway threw up on the Marquis stage.

1. A backstage cake and champagne party marks the 500th performance, January 4, 2008.
2. At the "Broadway's Back" Concert (L-R): Patrick Page of *Dr. Seuss' How the Grinch Stole Christmas!* clowns with correspondent Paul McGill.

It was unbelievable for the participants as well as the audience. Shecky did "I Can Do That" at "Broadway on Broadway." 2007 NYC AIDS Walk "What I Did For Love."

Memorable Stage Door Fan Encounters: Tom always gives us gifts. George is so sweet at the stage door too.

Latest Audience Arrival: February 1 performance: A middle aged couple got into their orchestra center seats after "Dance:10 Looks: 3." I know this only because it happened the night I was filling out this survey.

Fastest Costume Change: Will Taylor (Bobby) on the "Finale" quick-change.

Busiest Day at the Box Office: Christmas. Isn't that standard?

Who Wore the Heaviest/Hottest Costume: The "Finale" costumes for the guys are VERY heavy, hot, and tight...but for the rest of the show, I think it's tie between the Greg costume and the Connie costume.

Who Wore the Least: Deidre Goodwin (Sheila), Heather Parcells (Judy), Emily Fletcher (Vicki), and Katherine Tokarz (Kristine) ... those are all leotards.

Catchphrases Only the Company Would Recognize: "4-4-4-8." "Standing by-y-y." "Appreciation Day! 1234...5678." "Just so you

A Chorus Line
Scrapbook

Photos courtesy Paul McGill

1. (L-R): McGill, Mara Davi, Heather Parcells, and James T. Lane outside of the Schoenfeld Theater.
2. McGill and Jonathan Groff of *Spring Awakening* at the "Broadway's Back" Concert.
3. Performing for the "Broadway's Back" photo shoot in Times Square
4. (L-R): Ali Porter, Chryssie Whitehead, E. Clayton Cornelious, Yuka Takara, Tony Yazbeck and James T. Lane backstage at the Schoenfeld
5. McGill and Krysta Rodriguez hanging out before the show.

know...." "A FIVE ... A SIX ... A FIVESIX SEVENEIGHT!"

Best In-House Parody Lyrics: "Oh scratch yourself...she can't get enough" —Grant Turner. "Sometimes I dance because I want to. Sometimes I dance because I have to."

Memorable Directorial Notes: "NUTS TO BUTTS!" –Baayork Lee. "Best show yet...Just say everything louder" –Bob Avian. "Let's do it once more so that you know that I know that you know." –Michael Gorman

Company In-Jokes: Jessica Goldyn and I joke around a LOT to each other. Here are a few: "CEASSY...Ya gunna come in hea in ya little red leataad and skoit thinkin ya sum koinda eacta...well guess what...YA CEANT EACT!" "The Bus...Jersey Transit." "HOT DOG JUICE!"

Company Legends: La Contessa.

Tales from the Put-in: We had an '80s-themed clean-up rehearsal!

Nicknames: Most everyone has a nickname.
Shecky—Jeffrey Schecter
Jalane—J. Elaine Marcos
Grubes—Michael Gruber
Kat—Katherine Tokarz
Granty—Grant Turner
Bereessie you so greasy—Michael Berresse
Lone Star—Melissa Lone
Wilma—Will Taylor
Dee—Deidre Goodwin
Nat—Natalie Cortez
Jess—Jessica Lee Goldyn
"RIGUEZ!"—Krysta Rodriguez
"GILL!"—Paul McGill
Nicki—Nick Adams
Cannon—Mike Cannon
Fletcha—Emily Fletcher
Betch—Bryan Knowlton
Cookie—Brian Cook (one of our sound guys)
Ro Po—Rory Powers (our wardrobe supervisor)
Sarah Friend—Sarah Hench (one of our dressers)
Lyndy Loo Hoo—Lyndy Franklin
Bauman—David Baum
Boo—E. Clayton Cornelious

Embarrassing Moment: Personally, for me, it's "I told the priest about the book's diagnosis for milky discharge and...he said...that...it... WASN'T milky discharge.... ANYWAY!..." Connie steps out, looks at me, looks at Zach, and sings, "Four foot ten...."

Superstitions That Turned Out To Be True: I cursed Michael Bennett for such a hard show during warmup, and that night after the show I broke my foot on the way down the stairs. Also, I said "Nadine, you're lucky you're not doing Cassie tonight." That night, Charlotte's back froze and Nadine finished the show.

Coolest Thing About Being in This Show: This show is so legendary. Being a part of Broadway History is the coolest thing, I think. When little boys and girls sing to your album in their rooms...you know you've made it. Haha!

Fan Club/Website: I run the Facebook group "A Chorus Line on Broadway." If you're not a member, JOIN!

The Color Purple

First Preview: November 1, 2005. Opened: December 1, 2005.
Closed February 24, 2008 after 30 Previews and 910 Performances.

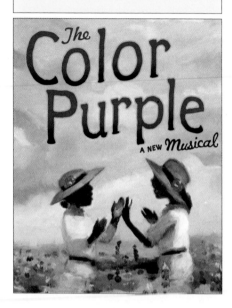

CAST

(in order of appearance)

Young Nettie,
   Mister's Daughter ....RUBY E. CRAWFORD
Young Celie, Mister's Daughter,
   Young Olivia, Henrietta ....JENNY MOLLET
Church Soloist ....KITRA WILLIAMS
Church Lady (Doris) ....YOLANDA WYNS
Church Lady (Darlene) ....TERESA STANLEY
Church Lady (Jarene),
   Daisy ....LEILANI N. BRYANT
Preacher, Prison Guard ....DOUG ESKEW
Pa ....JC MONTGOMERY
Nettie ....DARLESIA CEARCY
Celie ....FANTASIA
Mister ....ALTON FITZGERALD WHITE
Young Harpo, Young Adam ....RICKY SMITH
Harpo ....CHAZ LAMAR SHEPHERD
Sofia ....NaTASHA YVETTE WILLIAMS
Squeak ....KRISHA MARCANO
Shug Avery .....ELISABETH WITHERS-MENDES
Ol' Mister.......................LARRY MARSHALL
Buster, Chief....................GAVIN GREGORY
Grady...........................JC MONTGOMERY
Bobby...........................TODRICK D. HALL
Older Olivia................MARLA McREYNOLDS
Older Adam ....LEVENSKY SMITH

Continued on next page

⑤ BROADWAY THEATRE

1681 Broadway
A Shubert Organization Theatre

Gerald Schoenfeld, *Chairman*   Philip J. Smith, *President*

Robert E. Wankel, *Executive Vice President*

OPRAH WINFREY
SCOTT SANDERS   ROY FURMAN   QUINCY JONES
CREATIVE BATTERY   ANNA FANTACI & CHERYL LACHOWICZ   INDEPENDENT PRESENTERS NETWORK
DAVID LOWY   STEPHANIE P. McCLELLAND   GARY WINNICK   JAN KALLISH
NEDERLANDER PRESENTATIONS, INC.   BOB & HARVEY WEINSTEIN
ANDREW ASNES & ADAM ZOTOVICH   TODD JOHNSON

Present

The Color Purple

BASED UPON THE NOVEL WRITTEN BY ALICE WALKER
AND THE WARNER BROS./AMBLIN ENTERTAINMENT MOTION PICTURE

Book by   Music and Lyrics by

MARSHA NORMAN   **BRENDA**   **ALLEE**   **STEPHEN**
                              RUSSELL   **WILLIS**   **BRAY**

Starring
FANTASIA
ELISABETH WITHERS-MENDES   **NaTASHA YVETTE WILLIAMS**
CHAZ LAMAR SHEPHERD   **DARLESIA CEARCY**   **KRISHA MARCANO**
and **ALTON FITZGERALD WHITE**

with LEILANI N. BRYANT   TERESA STANLEY   YOLANDA WYNS
LARRY MARSHALL   KITRA WILLIAMS
DEIDRA H. BROOKS   LaTRISA A. COLEMAN   RUBY E. CRAWFORD   BOBBY DAYE   DOUG ESKEW
LaVON FISHER-WILSON   GUY FORTT   MONTEGO GLOVER   CHARLES GRAY   GAVIN GREGORY
STEPHANIE GUILAND-BROWN   TODRICK D. HALL   JAMES HARKNESS   FRANCESCA HARPER   CHAUNCEY JENKINS
ASHLEY RENEÉ JORDAN   KENYA UNIQUE MASSEY   MARLA McREYNOLDS   JENNY MOLLET   JC MONTGOMERY
ANGELA ROBINSON   KEMBA SHANNON   LEVENSKY SMITH   RICKY SMITH   JAMAL STORY

Scenic Design	Costume Design	Lighting Design	Sound Design
JOHN LEE BEATTY	PAUL TAZEWELL	BRIAN MacDEVITT	JON WESTON

Casting	Hair Design	Production Managers	Production Stage Manager
TELSEY + COMPANY	CHARLES G. LaPOINTE	ARTHUR SICCARDI PATRICK SULLIVAN	KRISTEN HARRIS

Press Representative	Marketing	General Management
BARLOW•HARTMAN	APEL, INC.	NLA/AMY JACOBS

Music Director	Dance Music Arrangements	Additional Arrangements	Music Coordinator
LINDA TWINE	DARYL WATERS	JOSEPH JOUBERT	SEYMOUR RED PRESS

Orchestrations	Music Supervisor & Incidental Music Arrangements
JONATHAN TUNICK	KEVIN STITES

Choreographed by
DONALD BYRD

Directed by
GARY GRIFFIN

World Premiere Produced by Alliance Theatre, Atlanta, GA
Susan V. Booth, Artistic Director   Thomas Pechar, Managing Director

10/1/07

The Company

Photo by Paul Kolnik

The Color Purple

MUSICAL NUMBERS

ACT ONE

Overture	Orchestra
Huckleberry Pie	Young Celie and Nettie
Mysterious Ways	Church Soloist, Church Ladies and Company
Somebody Gonna Love You	Celie
Our Prayer	Nettie, Celie, Mister
Big Dog	Mister and Field Hands
Hell No!	Sofia and Sisters
Brown Betty	Harpo and Men, Squeak
Shug Avery Comin' to Town	Mister, Celie and Company
Too Beautiful for Words	Shug Avery
Push Da Button	Shug Avery and Company
Uh Oh!	Church Ladies, Sofia, Squeak
What About Love?	Celie and Shug Avery

ACT TWO

African Homeland	Nettie, Celie, Olivia and Adam, Villagers
The Color Purple	Shug Avery
Celie's Curse	Mister
Miss Celie's Pants	Celie, Shug Avery, Sofia and Women
Any Little Thing	Harpo and Sofia
I'm Here	Celie
The Color Purple (Reprise)	Celie, Nettie and Company

(L-R): Fantasia and NaTasha Yvette Williams

Photo by Paul Kolnik

ORCHESTRA

Conductor:
LINDA TWINE
Associate Conductor:
JOSEPH JOUBERT

Trumpets:
BARRY DANIELIAN, STU SATALOF,
KAMAU ADILIFU
Trombones:
LARRY FARRELL, JASON JACKSON
Woodwinds:
LES SCOTT, LAWRENCE FELDMAN,
JAY BRANDFORD
Keyboards:
JOSEPH JOUBERT, SHELTON BECTON
Drums/Percussion:
BUDDY WILLIAMS, SHANE SHANAHAN

Guitars/Harmonica:
STEVE BARGONETTI
Bass:
BENJAMIN FRANKLIN BROWN
Violins:
PAUL WOODIEL, MINEKO YAJIMA
Viola:
DAVID CRESWELL
Cello:
CLAY RUEDE

Music Coordinator:
SEYMOUR RED PRESS
Copyists:
EMILY GRISHMAN MUSIC PREPARATION
KATHARINE EDMONDS/EMILY GRISHMAN
Synthesizer Programmer:
BRUCE SAMUELS

The Playbill Broadway Yearbook 2007-2008

ENSEMBLE

LEILANI N. BRYANT, LaTRISA A. COLEMAN,
RUBY E. CRAWFORD, DOUG ESKEW,
CHARLES GRAY, GAVIN GREGORY,
TODRICK D. HALL, JAMES HARKNESS,
FRANCESCA HARPER,
KENYA UNIQUE MASSEY,
MARLA McREYNOLDS, JENNY MOLLET,
JC MONTGOMERY, ANGELA ROBINSON,
LEVENSKY SMITH, RICKY SMITH,
TERESA STANLEY, JAMAL STORY,
KITRA WILLIAMS, YOLANDA WYNS

SWINGS

DEIDRA H. BROOKS, BOBBY DAYE,
LaVON FISHER-WILSON, GUY FORTT,
STEPHANIE GUILAND-BROWN,
CHAUNCEY JENKINS,
ASHLEY RENEÉ JORDAN,
KEMBA SHANNON

UNDERSTUDIES

For Celie:
DARLESIA CEARCY, MONTEGO GLOVER
For Shug Avery:
DEIDRA H. BROOKS, FRANCESCA HARPER,
ANGELA ROBINSON
For Sofia:
LaVON FISHER-WILSON, YOLANDA WYNS
For Nettie:
LaTRISA A. COLEMAN, MONTEGO GLOVER
For Mister:
CHARLES GRAY, JAMES HARKNESS,
JC MONTGOMERY
For Harpo:
GAVIN GREGORY, TODRICK D. HALL
For Squeak:
LaTRISA A. COLEMAN, FRANCESCA HARPER
For Ol' Mister:
DOUG ESKEW, CHARLES GRAY
For Young Harpo/Young Adam:
ASHLEY RENEÉ JORDAN, JENNY MOLLET

Dance Captain:
STEPHANIE GUILAND-BROWN
Assistant Dance Captain:
JAMAL STORY

SETTING

The story takes place in Georgia between 1909 and 1949.

The Color Purple

Fantasia
Celie

Elisabeth
Withers-Mendes
Shug Avery

Alton Fitzgerald
White
Mister

NaTasha Yvette
Williams
Sofia

Chaz Lamar
Shepherd
Harpo

Darlesia Cearcy
Nettie

Krisha Marcano
Squeak

Leilani N. Bryant
*Church Lady
[Jarene]/Daisy/
Ensemble*

Teresa Stanley
*Church Lady
[Darlene]/Ensemble*

Yolanda Wyns
*Church Lady [Doris]/
Ensemble*

Larry Marshall
Ol' Mister

Kitra Williams
*Church Soloist/
Ensemble*

Deidra H. Brooks
Swing

LaTrisa A. Coleman
*Ensemble/
Fight Captain*

Ruby E. Crawford
*Young Nettie/
Mister's Daughter*

Bobby Daye
Swing

Doug Eskew
*Preacher/
Prison Guard/
Ensemble*

LaVon Fisher-Wilson
Swing

Guy Fortt
Swing

Montego Glover
u/s Celie, Nettie

Charles Gray
Ensemble

Gavin Gregory
*Buster/Chief/
Ensemble*

Stephanie
Guiland-Brown
*Swing/
Dance Captain*

Todrick D. Hall
Bobby/Ensemble

James Harkness
Ensemble

Francesca Harper
Ensemble

Chauncey Jenkins
Swing

Ashley Reneé Jordan
Swing

Kenya Unique
Massey
Ensemble

Marla McReynolds
*Older Olivia/
Ensemble*

Jenny Mollet
*Mister's Daughter/
Young Olivia/
Henrietta/Ensemble*

JC Montgomery
Pa/Grady/Ensemble

Angela Robinson
Ensemble

Kemba Shannon
Swing

Levensky Smith
*Older Adam/
Ensemble*

The Color Purple

Ricky Smith
Young Harpo/
Young Adam

Jamal Story
Ensemble/
Assistant Dance
Captain

Alice Walker
Original Author

Marsha Norman
Bookwriter

Brenda Russell, Stephen Bray, Allee Willis
Composer/Lyricist

Gary Griffin
Director

Donald Byrd
Choreographer

John Lee Beatty
Set Design

Paul Tazewell
Costume Design

Brian MacDevitt
Lighting Design

Bernard Telsey,
Telsey + Company
Casting

Jonathan Tunick
Orchestrations

Linda Twine
Music Director

Angelina Avallone
Make-up Design

Joseph Joubert
Additional
Arrangements

Seymour Red Press
Music Coordinator

Arthur Siccardi
Production
Management

Oprah Winfrey
Producer

Scott Sanders
Lead Producer

Roy Furman
Producer

Quincy Jones
Producer

Stephanie P.
McClelland
Producer

James L.
Nederlander,
Nederlander
Presentations, Inc.
Producer

Bob Weinstein
Producer

Harvey Weinstein
Producer

Andrew Asnes
Producer

Adam Zotovich
Producer

Todd Johnson
Producer

Susan V. Booth,
Alliance Theatre
Original Production

Timothy George
Anderson
Swing

Jordan D. Bratton
Young Harpo,
Young Adam,
Ensemble

Shelby
Braxton-Brooks
Ensemble

Eric L. Christian
Swing

The Color Purple

Carol Dennis
*Church Soloist,
Ensemble*

Rosena M. Hill
*Church Lady
(Darlene), Ensemble*

Saycon Sengbloh
*Understudy for
Celie and Nettie*

Daniel J. Watts
Bobby

Marion Willis III
Ensemble

Shelby
Braxton-Brooks
Swing

Eric L. Christian
Swing

Darius Crenshaw
Swing

LaKisha Jones
*Sofia (matinée
performances)
Church Soloist,
Ensemble*

Chaka Khan
*Sofia (evening
performances)*

Zonya Love
Celie

BeBe Winans
Harpo

USHERS AND FRONT OF HOUSE
Front Row (L-R): Michael S.R. Harris, Lori Bokun.

Second Row (L-R): Mattie Robinson, May Park, Alfredo Rosario, Freddy Matos, John Hall, Nathaniel Wright, Santiago Ulises, Selina Nelson.

Third Row (L-R): William Phelan, Jorge Colon, Linda Engh.

Back Row (L-R): Tony Massey, Amy Wolk and Ji Ming.

BOX OFFICE
(L-R): Bob Belkin, Debbie Giarratano

DOORMAN
Fernando Sepulveda

COMPANY MANAGEMENT
(L-R): Tony Magner, Doug Gaeta

The Color Purple

ORCHESTRA
Front Row (L-R, kneeling): Mineko Yajima, Steve Bargonetti, Ben Brown.

Second Row (L-R): Buddy Williams, Jon Berger, Stu Satalof, Linda Twine (conductor), Shelton Becton.

Back Row (L-R): Clay Ruede, Scott Shachter, Kenny Rampton, Larry Farrell and Jason Webb.

STAGE MANAGEMENT
(L-R): Neveen Mahmoud, Kristen Harris, Lisa Dawn Cave, Kelly Stillwell.

STAGE CREW
Front Row (L-R): Neveen Mahmoud, Lisa Dawn Cave, Kenneth McAliece, Sonya Suzuki.

Second Row (L-R): Sabrena Armstrong, Shazia Saleem, Maureen George, Dora Bonilla, Dora Suarez, Betty Gillispie, Jay Woods, Kelly Stillwell, Thea Yatras.

Back Row (L-R): Kristen Harris, Timothy Harvey, Mia Neal, Peter Becker, Bob Beimers, David Grevengoed, Carin Ford, Valerie Frith, Charles Rasmussen, Renee Brunson, Declan McNeil and Richard DalCortivo.

Photos by David Gewirtzman

The Color Purple

STAFF FOR *THE COLOR PURPLE*

GENERAL MANAGER
NINA LANNAN ASSOCIATES
Amy Jacobs

COMPANY MANAGER
J. ANTHONY MAGNER
Associate Company Manager ....Doug Gaeta

GENERAL PRESS REPRESENTATIVE
BARLOW•HARTMAN

Michael Hartman	John Barlow
Wayne Wolfe	Kevin Robak

CASTING
Telsey + Company, C.S.A.:
Bernie Telsey, Will Cantler, David Vaccari,
Bethany Knox, Craig Burns,
Tiffany Little Canfield, Stephanie Yankwitt,
Carrie Rosson, Justin Huff, Joe Langworth

Associate Director ....Nona Lloyd
Assistant to the Choreographer ....Ruthlyn Salomons

PRODUCTION
    STAGE MANAGER ....KRISTEN HARRIS
Stage Manager ....Lisa Dawn Cave
Assistant Stage Manager ....Neveen Mahmoud
Assistant Stage Manager ....Kelly Stillwell
Associate Scenic Designer ....Eric L. Renschler
Assistant Scenic Designer ....Yoshi Tanokura
Associate Costume Designer ....Michael F. McAleer
Assistant Costume Designers...........Dennis E. Ballard,
                                Christine Field
Assistant to the Costume Designer ....Jacob A. Climer
Associate Lighting Designers ....Mark T. Simpson,
                            Jennifer M. Schriever
Assistant Lighting Designer................Benjamin Travis
Associate Sound Designer ....Jason Strangfeld
Automated Lighting Programmer ....David Arch
Fight Director ....J. Steven White
Fight Captain ....LaTrisa A. Coleman
Dialect Coach ....Deborah Hecht

Make-up Design ....Angelina Avallone

Production Carpenter ....Patrick Sullivan
Head Carpenter/Automation ....Charles A. Heulitt III
Assistant Carpenter/Flyman ....McBrien Dunbar
Assistant Carpenter ....Ryan Ensser
Production Electrician ....James J. Fedigan
Head Electrician ....Michael E. Cornell
Assistant Electrician ....Gary Marlin
Production Sound ....Carin Ford
Production Properties ....Michael Pilipski
Head Properties ....Rob Presley
Wardrobe Supervisor ....Deborah A. Cheretun
Assistant Wardrobe Supervisor ....James Hall
Star Dresser ....Betty A. Gillispie
Dressers ....Dora Bonilla, Renee Brunson,
        Suzanne Delahunt, Tara Delahunt,
        Tracey Diebold, Valerie Frith,
        Maureen George, David Grevengoed,
        Lizz Hirons, Holly Nissen, Franc Weinperl
Hair Supervisor ....Mia Neal
Assistant Hair Supervisor ....Timothy Harvey

Hairstylists ....Sabrena Armstrong, Joshua First,
                          Shazia Saleem
Rehearsal Musicians ....Damien A. Bassman,
        Shelton Becton, Joseph Joubert,
        Daryl Waters, Buddy Williams
Additional Music Copyists ....Singing Potato/Eidco
Production Assistants ....Kelly Stillwell,
                       Angelique Villegas
Child Wrangler ....Bridget Walders
Children's Tutoring ....On Location Education
Teachers ....Abigail Dyer, Maryanne Keller
Advertising ....Spotco/Drew Hodges, Jim Edwards,
        Tom Greenwald, Tom McCann,
        Stephen Sosnowski
Marketing, Sponsorship & Outreach ....Apel, Inc./
        David Sass, Harry Spero,
        Cherine Anderson, Mathew Farkash,
        Jessica Stock
Website Design & Online
    Marketing Strategy ....Situation Marketing LLC/
        Damian Bazadona, Ian Bennett,
        Lisa Cecchini, Lisa Donnelly
Legal Counsel ....M. Graham Coleman, Esq. and
        Robert J. Driscoll, Esq./
        Davis Wright Tremaine LLP
Comptroller ....Sarah Galbraith
Accounting...................Fried & Kowgios CPA's LLP/
        Robert Fried, CPA
General Management Associate ....Katherine McNamee
Press Associates ....Leslie Baden, Michelle Bergmann,
        Dennis Crowley, Tom D'Ambrosio,
        Ryan Ratelle, Kevin Robak
Press Office Manager ....Bethany Larsen
Production Photographers ....Joan Marcus, Paul Kolnik
Insurance ....Albert G. Ruben Company Inc./
        Claudia Kauffman
Banking ....City National Bank/Gregg Santos
Payroll ....Castellana Services, Inc.
Study Guide ....Camp Broadway
Merchandising...................Dewynters/James Decker
Travel Agent ....Tzell Travel/
        The "A" Team, Andi Henig
Assistant to Ms. Norman ....Brian Tucker
Assistant to Mr. Bray,
    Ms. Russell & Ms. Willis ....Richard Todd Loyd
Assistant to Mr. Sanders ....Adam Wachter
Assistant to Mr. Furman ....Eileen Williams
Assistant to Mr. MacDevitt ....Jessica Burgess
Music Dept. Assistant ....Nathan Kelly
SSDC Directing Intern ....Malinda Allen
Opening Night
    Coordination ....Tobak Lawrence Company/
        Michael P Lawrence

ALLIANCE THEATRE STAFF

Artistic Director .... Susan V. Booth
Managing Director ....Thomas Pechar
Associate Artistic Director ....Kent Gash
General Manager ....Max Leventhal
Director of Marketing ....Virginia Vann
Director of Finance ....Sallie Lawrence
Director of Development ....Andrea Dillenburg
Production Manager ....Rixon Hammond

www.colorpurple.com

CREDITS AND ACKNOWLEDGEMENTS

Scenery construction and automation equipment provided by Hudson Scenic Studio Inc. Costumes executed by Tricorne, Inc.; Barbara Matera Ltd.; Donna Langman Costumes; John Kristiansen New York. Custom millinery by Lynne Mackey Studio. African headdresses by Arnold S. Levine and Marie Schneggenburger. Custom shirts by the Shirt Store and DL Cerney. Custom eyewear by J. Kirby Harris. Custom Knitting by C.C. Wei. Custom shoes by T.O. Dey; JC Theatrical; Capezio. Fabric painting and distressing by Hochi Asiatico. Lighting equipment by PRG Lighting. Musical instruments provided by Yamaha Drums, Zildjian Cymbals Company, Aquarian Company. Sound equipment by PRG Audio. Marty at Latin Percussion. Props provided by Spoon Group; Cigar Box Studios Inc.; Paragon; Centerline Studios; Ellen Pilipski; The Alliance Theatre. Rehearsed at the New 42nd Street Studios and 37 Arts. Natural herb cough drops supplied by Ricola USA Inc. Makeup provided by M*A*C Cosmetics. Hair products provided by Motions Salon Products. Key art illustration by Peter Sylvada. Emergen-C super energy booster provided by Alacer Corp.

 THE SHUBERT ORGANIZATION, INC.
Board of Directors

Gerald Schoenfeld	**Philip J. Smith**
Chairman	President
Wyche Fowler, Jr.	**John W. Kluge**
Lee J. Seidler	**Michael I. Sovern**

Stuart Subotnick

Robert E. Wankel
Executive Vice President

Peter Entin	**Elliot Greene**
Vice President –	Vice President –
Theatre Operations	Finance
David Andrews	**John Darby**
Vice President –	Vice President –
Shubert Ticketing Services	Facilities

D.S. Moynihan
Vice President – Creative Projects

Theatre Manager ....Michael S.R. Harris

Come Back, Little Sheba

First Preview: January 3, 2008. Opened: January 24, 2008.
Closed March 16, 2008 after 27 Previews and 58 Performances.

PLAYBILL

come back, little sheba

CAST

(in order of appearance)

Doc	KEVIN ANDERSON
Marie	ZOE KAZAN
Lola	S. EPATHA MERKERSON
Turk	BRIAN J. SMITH
Postman	LYLE KANOUSE
Mrs. Coffman	BRENDA WEHLE
Milkman	MATTHEW J. WILLIAMSON
Messenger	DANIEL DAMON JOYCE
Bruce	CHAD HOEPPNER
Ed	KEITH RANDOLPH SMITH
Elmo	JOSEPH ADAMS

SETTING

A Midwestern city in the spring of 1950

Stage Manager ....BRYCE McDONALD

UNDERSTUDIES

For Doc:
JOSEPH ADAMS
For Elmo, Ed, Postman:
PHILLIP CLARK
For Lola:
CAROLINE STEFANIE CLAY
For Messenger:
CHAD HOEPPNER
For Turk, Milkman, Bruce:
DANIEL DAMON JOYCE
For Mrs. Coffman:
DARRIE LAWRENCE

BILTMORE THEATRE

manhattan theatre club

artistic director
lynne meadow

executive producer
barry grove

acting artistic director 2007-08 season
daniel sullivan

presents

come back, little sheba

by
william inge

with

joseph adams   kevin anderson   chad hoeppner
daniel damon joyce   lyle kanouse   zoe kazan
s. epatha merkerson   brian j. smith   keith randolph smith
brenda wehle   matthew j. williamson

scenic design
james noone

costume design
jennifer von mayrhauser

lighting design
jane cox

sound design
obadiah eaves

original music
peter golub

fight director
j. david brimmer

production stage manager
james fitzsimmons

casting
david caparelliotis

directed by
michael pressman

general manager
florie seery

associate artistic
director/production
mandy greenfield

director of marketing
debra a. waxman

press representatives
boneau/bryan-brown

production manager
kurt gardner

director of casting
nancy piccione

director of development
jill turner lloyd

This new perspective on COME BACK, LITTLE SHEBA is supported by American Express.

Manhattan Theatre Club wishes to express its appreciation to the Theatre Development Fund for its support of this production.

COME BACK, LITTLE SHEBA was produced by the Center Theatre Group at the Kirk Douglas Theatre from June 17 through July 15, 2007.

1/24/08

(L-R): Kevin Anderson and S. Epatha Merkerson.

Photo by Joan Marcus

Come Back, Little Sheba

Joseph Adams
Elmo

Kevin Anderson
Doc

Chad Hoeppner
Bruce

Daniel Damon Joyce
Messenger

Lyle Kanouse
Postman

Zoe Kazan
Marie

S. Epatha Merkerson
Lola

Brian J. Smith
Turk

Keith Randolph Smith
Ed

Brenda Wehle
Mrs. Coffman

Matthew J. Williamson
Milkman

Phillip Clark
u/s Elmo, Ed, Postman

Caroline Stefanie Clay
u/s Lola

Darrie Lawrence
u/s Mrs. Coffman

William Inge
Playwright

Michael Pressman
Director

James Noone
Scenic Design

Jennifer von Mayrhauser
Costume Design

Obadiah Eaves
Sound Design

2007-2008 AWARD

CLARENCE DERWENT AWARD
Most Promising Female Performer
(Zoe Kazan)

J. David Brimmer
Fight Director

Lynne Meadow
Artistic Director, Manhattan Theatre Club, Inc.

Barry Grove
Executive Producer, Manhattan Theatre Club, Inc.

Daniel Sullivan
Acting Artistic Director 2007-08 Season, Manhattan Theatre Club, Inc.

S. Epatha Merkerson calls for help.

Photo by Joan Marcus

Come Back, Little Sheba

MEMBERS OF THE CAST AND CREW
(L-R): Keith Sherman, Vaughn, Jeff Dodson, Tim Walsh, Lou Shapiro, Andrew Sliwinski, Marc Grimshaw, Jenn McNeil, Angie Simpson, S. Epatha Merkerson, Bryce McDonald, Jon Jordan, James Fitzsimmons

ALLIED BARTON FIRE SAFETY DIRECTOR
Danaci Santiago

FRONT OF HOUSE STAFF
Front Row (L-R): Russ Ramsey (Theatre Manager), Eric Dreier (Usher), Miranda Scopel (Asst. House Manager), Wendy Wright (Head Usher), Christine Ehren (Usher), Dinah Glorioso (Usher)

Back Row (L-R): Jackson Ero (Usher), Bru Dye (Usher), Ed Brashear (Ticket Taker), Thomas Jarus (Usher), Jorge Sarante (MTC Intern)

Come Back, Little Sheba

MANHATTAN THEATRE CLUB STAFF

Artistic Director	**Lynne Meadow**
Executive Producer	**Barry Grove**
Acting Artistic Director	
2007-08 Season	Daniel Sullivan
General Manager	**Florie Seery**
Associate Artistic Director/	
Production	**Mandy Greenfield**
Director of Artistic Administration/	
Assistant to the Artistic Director	Amy Gilkes Loe
Associate Director of Artistic Operations	Lisa McNulty
Artistic Assistant	Kevin Emrick
Administrative Assistant	Rebecca Stang
Director of Casting	**Nancy Piccione**
Casting Associate	Kelly Gillespie
Casting Assistant	Kristin Svenningsen
Literary Manager	**Raphael Martin**
Play Development Associate/	
Sloan Project Manager	Annie MacRae
Director of Musical	
Development	**Clifford Lee Johnson III**
Director of Development	**Jill Turner Lloyd**
Director, Institutional Giving	Josh Jacobson
Director, Individual Giving	Jon Haddorff
Manager, Individual Giving	Antonello Di Benedetto
Manager, Institutional Giving	Andrea Gorzell
Manager, Institutional Giving	Jessica Sadowski Comas
Development Associate/Special Events	Darra Messing
Development Associate/Institutional Giving	Laurel Bear
Development Associate/Individual Giving	Sage Young
Development Database Coordinator	Ann Mundorff
Patrons' Liaison	Samantha Mascali
Director of Marketing	**Debra A. Waxman**
Marketing Manager	Tom O'Connor
Marketing Associate	Andrea D. Paul
Director of Finance	**Jeffrey Bledsoe**
Business Manager	Holly Kinney
Human Resources Manager	Darren Robertson
Business & HR Associate	Adam Cook
Business Assistant	Charles Graytok
Receptionist/Studio Coordinator	Christina Prints
Manager of Systems Operations	Avishai Cohen
Systems Administrator	Mendy Sudranski
Associate General Manager	**Lindsey Brooks Sag**
Company Manager/NY City Center	Erin Moeller
General Management Assistant	Laura Roumanos
Assistant to the Executive Producer	Ashley Dunn
Director of Subscriber Services	**Robert Allenberg**
Associate Subscriber Services Manager	Andrew Taylor
Subscriber Services	
Representatives	Mark Bowers, Rebekah Dewald, Eric Gerdts, Matthew Praet, Rosanna Consalva Sarto
Director of Telesales and Telefunding	**George Tetlow**
Assistant Manager	Terrence Burnett
Director of Education	**David Shookhoff**
Asst. Director of Education/	
Coordinator, Paul A. Kaplan Theatre	
Management Program	Amy Harris
Education Assistants	Sarah Ryndak, Kelli Bragdon
MTC Teaching Artists	David Auburn, Michael Bernard, Carl Capotorto, Chris Ceraso, Charlotte Colavin, Dominic Colon, Gilbert Girion, Andy Goldberg, Elise Hernandez, Jeffrey Joseph, Julie Leedes, Kate Long, Louis D. Moreno, Andres Munar, Melissa Murray, Angela Pietropinto, Alexa Polmer, Alfonso Ramirez, Carmen Rivera, Judy Tate, Candido Tirado, Joe White
Theatre Management Interns	Caitlin Baird, Alex Barron, Julia Davis, Stephen Ferrell, Emily Gasser, Ryan Hudec, Caryn Morrow, Erin Ozer, Flora Pei, Jorge Sarante, Miranda Shutte, Rachel Slaven
Randy Carrig Casting Intern	Emily Hammond

Production Manager	**Kurt Gardner**
Associate Production Manager	Philip Naudé
Assistant Production Manager	Kelsey Martinez
Lighting and Sound Supervisor	**Matthew T. Gross**
Properties Supervisor	**Scott Laule**
Assistant Properties Supervisor	Julia Sandy
Props Carpenter	Peter Grimes
Costume Supervisor	**Erin Hennessy Dean**

GENERAL PRESS REPRESENTATION
BONEAU/BRYAN-BROWN

Chris Boneau	Aaron Meier
Heath Schwartz	Christine Olver

Script Readers .... Barbara Bleier, Erin Detrick, Liz Jones, Aaron Leichter, Sarah Schacter, Kathryn Walat, Ethan Youngerman

SERVICES

Accountants	ERE, LLP
Advertising	SpotCo/Drew Hodges, Jim Edwards, Dale Edwards, Laura Price
Web Design	Pilla Marketing Communications
Legal Counsel	John Breglio, Deborah Hartnett/ Paul, Weiss, Rifkind, Wharton and Garrison LLP
Real Estate Counsel	Marcus Attorneys
Labor Counsel	Harry H. Weintraub/ Glick and Weintraub, P.C.
Immigration Counsel	Theodore Ruthizer/ Kramer, Levin, Naftalis & Frankel, LLP
Sponsorship Consultant	Above the Title Entertainment/ Jed Bernstein
Technical Supervisor	
Consultant	Aurora Productions, Inc./ Gene O'Donovan
Special Projects	Elaine H. Hirsch
Insurance	Dewitt Stern Group, Inc./ Anthony Pittari
Maintenance	Reliable Cleaning
Production Photographer	Joan Marcus
Event Photography	Bruce Glikas
Cover Photo	Henry Leutwyler
Cover Design	SpotCo
Theatre Displays	King Display

PRODUCTION STAFF FOR
COME BACK, LITTLE SHEBA

Company Manager	**Seth Shepsle**
Production Stage Manager	**James Fitzsimmons**
Stage Manager	Bryce McDonald
Assistant Director	Jose Zayas
Assistant Scenic Designer	Patrick Tennant
Assistant Costume Designer	Suzanne Chesney
Associate Lighting Designer	Joshua Epstein
Associate Sound Designer	Ashley Hanson
Wig for Ms. Merkerson	Anita Crawford
Hair/Make-Up Supervisor	Jon Jordan
Lighting Programmer	Marc Polimeni
Dresser	Tracey Boone
Production Assistant	Jennifer McNeil
Magic Consultant	Eli Bosnick

CREDITS

Scenery by Showman Fabricators. Lighting equipment provided by PRG Lighting. Sound equipment provided by Masque Sound. Additional costumes provided by Helen Uffner Vintage Clothing and Center Theatre Group. Natural herbal cough drops courtesy of Ricola USA.

For more information visit
www.ManhattanTheatreClub.org

MANHATTAN THEATRE CLUB
BILTMORE THEATRE STAFF

Theatre Manager	**Russ Ramsey**
Assistant House Manager	Miranda Scopel
Box Office Treasurer	**David Dillon**
Assistant Box Office	
Treasurers	Tevy Bradley, Jeffrey Davis
Head Carpenter	Chris Wiggins
Head Propertyman	Timothy Walters
Sound Engineer	Louis Shapiro
Master Electrician	Jeff Dodson
Wardrobe Supervisor	Angela Simpson
Apprentices	Marc Grimshaw, Andrew Sliwinski
Chief Engineer	Deosarran
Maintenance Engineers	Robert Allen, Ricky Deosarran, Maximo Perez
Security	Initial Security
Lobby Refreshments	Sweet Concessions

Brian J. Smith and Zoe Kazan.

Photo by Joan Marcus

Come Back, Little Sheba
SCRAPBOOK

Correspondent: James FitzSimmons, Production Stage Manager

Opening Night Gifts: Epatha sewed the cast valuable bags (as seen on her appearance on Martha Stewart). She has been doing this for about 20 years now. She also gave the entire company bathrobes. (As Lola wears a ratty bathrobe for a good portion of the play.)

Most Exciting Celebrity Visitor and What They Did: So many–the entire history of "Law & Order" has passed through backstage. But the most impressive was Julie Harris meeting each company member—but her sobbing in Epatha's arms was incredible.

Who Has Done the Most Shows in Their Career: Well considering how many years she has been on "Law & Order"—Epatha. But Brenda Wehle and Lyle Kanouse have been around a bit!

Special Backstage Rituals: There are several: Kevin always takes a shower before the show. The daily viewing of "Law & Order" in the Stage Manager's office.

Favorite Moment During Each Performance (On Stage or Off): The escorting of the cast to their places onstage for each act. It's a bit of bonding time with cast and crew.

Favorite In-Theatre Gathering Place: The stage management office—it has cable and the computer. And occasionally the men's dressing room—when it wasn't too stinky!

Favorite Off-Site Hangout: Wherever there is alcohol. Rosie O'Grady's, Bar Centrale and especially Epatha's apartment. She has thrown several impromptu parties for the company and we all hang out, drink and play Wii.

Favorite Snack Food: Baked goods by Fitz and Jon Jordan and…the ever-present jar of chocolate.

Mascot: Sheba and Darby – Two stuffed dogs and our PA Jenn!

Favorite Therapy: Yoga for several company members. Ricola by the pound!

Most Memorable Ad-Lib: Kevin Anderson as the alcoholic Doc, as he is being carried off to the hospital—when he thought he was out of earshot—but not quite: "That's the last time I'll let you guys use the hot tub."

Record Number of Cell Phone Rings: Not a lot of rings but one cell phone perfectly timed to Epatha's finishing dialing the onstage phone. It caught her by surprise and the audience laughed.

Memorable Press Encounter: My appearance on Martha Stewart with Epatha.

Latest Audience Arrival: Midway through Act II and they decided to stay.

Busiest Day at the Box Office: The day after our *New York Times* review…sad but true.

Catchphrases Only the Company Would Recognize: "Muthaf..ker."

Company In-Jokes: The letters from "Eugene" and "Uncle Bill" (in reference to Inge).

Understudy Anecdote: On our first work-through of Act I, when we rang the doorbell, the actress covering Lola ran to the onstage

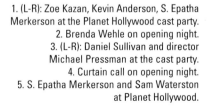

1. (L-R): Zoe Kazan, Kevin Anderson, S. Epatha Merkerson at the Planet Hollywood cast party.
2. Brenda Wehle on opening night.
3. (L-R): Daniel Sullivan and director Michael Pressman at the cast party.
4. Curtain call on opening night.
5. S. Epatha Merkerson and Sam Waterston at Planet Hollywood.

phone and started a whole other scene. The rehearsal basically stopped as everyone was rolling with laughter.

Nicknames: Bryce McDonald our ASM was nicknamed COOPAH by Epatha and Jenn was then nicknamed MINI-COOPAH. The rest can't be said in public.

Who Wore the Heaviest/Hottest Costume: Not heavy—but the most painful—Epatha's girdle.

Who Wore the Least: Brian J. Smith as Turk in his tightey whities.

Coolest Thing About Being in This Show: S. Epatha Merkerson!

Company

First Preview: October 30, 2006. Opened: November 29, 2006.
Closed July 1, 2007 after 34 Previews and 246 Performances.

PLAYBILL

⑧ ETHEL BARRYMORE THEATRE

243 West 47th Street
A Shubert Organization Theatre

Gerald Schoenfeld, *Chairman*   **Philip J. Smith,** *President*

Robert E. Wankel, *Executive Vice President*

Marc Routh   Richard Frankel   Tom Viertel   Steven Baruch
Ambassador Theatre Group   Tulchin/Bartner Productions
Darren Bagert and Cincinnati Playhouse in the Park

present

Raúl Esparza
in

COMPANY
A MUSICAL COMEDY

Music and Lyrics by

Stephen Sondheim

Book by

George Furth

with

Keith Buterbaugh   Matt Castle   Robert Cunningham   Angel Desai
Kelly Jeanne Grant   Kristin Huffman   Amy Justman   Heather Laws
Leenya Rideout   Fred Rose   Bruce Sabath   Elizabeth Stanley
Renée Bang Allen   Bradley Dean   Brandon Ellis   David Garry   Jason Ostrowski   Jane Pfitsch   Katrina Yaukey

and

Barbara Walsh

Set Design	Costume Design	Lighting Design	Sound Design
David Gallo	Ann Hould-Ward	Thomas C. Hase	Andrew Keister
Hair & Wig Design	Make-Up Design		Casting
David Lawrence	Angelina Avallone		Telsey + Company
Associate Director	Production Stage Manager		Resident Music Supervisor
Adam John Hunter	Gary Mickelson		Lynne Shankel
General Manager		Press Representative	Production Management
Richard Frankel Productions, Inc.		Barlow·Hartman	Juniper Street Productions, Inc.
Sammy Ledbetter			

Music Supervision & Orchestrations by

Mary-Mitchell Campbell

Direction and Musical Staging by

John Doyle

Proudly Sponsored by Fidelity Investments
The Producers wish to express their appreciation to the Theatre Development Fund for its support of this production.
This production of Company was originally produced by Cincinnati Playhouse in the Park
Edward Stern, Producing Artistic Director   Buzz Ward, Executive Director

LIVE BROADWAY

7/1/07

CAST

Robert	RAÚL ESPARZA
	Percussion
Joanne	BARBARA WALSH
	Orchestra Bells, Percussion
Harry	KEITH BUTERBAUGH
	Trumpet, Trombone
Peter	MATT CASTLE
	Piano/Keyboards, Double Bass
Paul	ROBERT CUNNINGHAM
	Trumpet, Drums
Marta	ANGEL DESAI
	Keyboard, Violin, Alto Sax
Kathy	KELLY JEANNE GRANT
	Flute, Alto Sax
Sarah	KRISTIN HUFFMAN
	Flute, Alto Sax, Piccolo
Susan	AMY JUSTMAN
	Piano/Keyboards, Orchestra Bells
Amy	HEATHER LAWS
	French Horn, Trumpet, Flute
Jenny	LEENYA RIDEOUT
	Violin, Guitar, Double Bass
David	FRED ROSE
	Cello, Alto Sax, Tenor Sax
Larry	BRUCE SABATH
	Clarinet, Drums
April	ELIZABETH STANLEY
	Oboe, Tuba, Alto Sax

Continued on next page

(L-R): Matt Castle, Bruce Sabath, Raúl Esparza, Keith Buterbaugh, Robert Cunningham and Fred Rose.

Photo by Paul Kolnik

Company

MUSICAL NUMBERS

ACT ONE

"Company" ....Robert and Company
"The Little Things You Do Together" ....Joanne and Company
"Sorry-Grateful" ....Harry, David, Larry
"You Could Drive a Person Crazy" ....April, Kathy, Marta
"Have I Got a Girl for You" ....Larry, Peter, Paul, David, Harry
"Someone Is Waiting" ....Robert
"Another Hundred People" ....Marta
"Getting Married Today" ....Amy, Paul, Susan and Company
"Marry Me a Little" ....Robert

ACT TWO

"Side by Side by Side" ....Robert and Company
"What Would We Do Without You?" ....Robert and Company
"Poor Baby" ....Sarah, Jenny, Susan, Amy, Joanne
"Barcelona" ....Robert, April
"The Ladies Who Lunch" ....Joanne
"Being Alive" ....Robert

Cast Continued

STANDBYS

For Robert:
BRADLEY DEAN; FRED ROSE

For Sarah, Joanne:
RENÉE BANG ALLEN
Flute, Alto Sax, Tenor Sax, Orchestra Bells, Percussion

For David, Paul:
BRANDON ELLIS
Cello, Drums, Double Bass, Guitar

For Harry, Larry, Paul:
DAVID GARRY
Trumpet, Trombone, Clarinet, Drums, Alto Sax, Tenor Sax

For Peter:
JASON OSTROWSKI
Piano/Keyboards, Double Bass

For Amy, Jenny, Susan:
JANE PFITSCH
French Horn, Trumpet, Flute, Violin, Piano/Keyboards, Orchestra Bells, Double Bass, Guitar

For Marta, Kathy, April:
KATRINA YAUKEY
Alto Sax, Flute, Oboe, Tuba, Trumpet, Keyboards

Dance Captain:
NEWTON COLE

(L-R): Elizabeth Stanley, Kelly Jeanne Grant and Angel Desai.

Photo by Paul Kolnik

Raúl Esparza
Robert

Barbara Walsh
Joanne

Keith Buterbaugh
Harry

Matt Castle
Peter

Robert Cunningham
Paul

Angel Desai
Marta

Kelly Jeanne Grant
Kathy

Kristin Huffman
Sarah

Amy Justman
Susan

Heather Laws
Amy

Company

Leenya Rideout
Jenny

Fred Rose
David

Bruce Sabath
Larry

Elizabeth Stanley
April

Renée Bang Allen
u/s Joanne, Sarah

Brandon J. Ellis
u/s Paul, David

David Garry
u/s Larry, Harry, Paul

Jason Ostrowski
u/s Peter

Jane Pfitsch
*u/s Amy, Jenny,
Susan*

Katrina Yaukey
*u/s April, Kathy,
Marta*

Stephen Sondheim
Music & Lyrics

George Furth
Book

John Doyle
Director

Mary-Mitchell
Campbell
*Music Supervision
and Orchestration*

David Gallo
Scenic Design

Ann Hould-Ward
Costume Design

Angelina Avallone
Makeup Design

Bernard Telsey,
Telsey + Company
Casting

Guy Kwan, John Paull, Hillary Blanken,
Kevin Broomell, Ana Rose Greene,
Juniper Street Productions
Production Manager

Marc Routh
Producer

Richard Frankel
*General
Management
and Producer*

Tom Viertel
Producer

Steven Baruch
Producer

Darren Bagert
Producer

Company

STAGE CREW
(L-R): Al C. Galvez (Carpenter), Philip W. Feller (House Prop Head), Dawn Makay (Head Properties Master), Jim Bay (Sound), Penny Davis (Wardrobe Supervisor), Chip White (Mr. Esparza's Dresser), Lolly Totero (Wardrobe), Tom Lawrey (Electrician), Vanessa Anderson (Hair Supervisor), Mike Wojchik (Sound), Jason Blair (Wardrobe) and Dan Landon (House Manager).

Photos by Robert Viagas

FRONT OF HOUSE STAFF
(L-R): Doris Buber (Head Usher), Cindy Acevedo (Usher), Angeline Montauban (Usher), Monica Orellana (Porter), A. John Dancy (Usher), Fran Barbareth, John Barbaretti (Ticket Taker), Aileen Kilburn (Usher), Michael Reilly (Usher), Dan Landon (Theatre Manager) and Peter Cooke (Concessions).

DOORMAN
Peter Condos

STAGE MANAGEMENT
(L-R): Newton Cole (Assistant Stage Manager), Gary Mickelson (Production Stage Manager) and Claudia Lynch (Assistant Stage Manager).

Company

STAFF FOR *COMPANY*

GENERAL MANAGEMENT
RICHARD FRANKEL PRODUCTIONS
Richard Frankel   Marc Routh   Laura Green
Sammy Ledbetter   Rod Kaats   Joe Watson

COMPANY MANAGEMENT
Company Manager ....Jason Pelusio
Assistant Company Manager ....Tanase Popa

GENERAL PRESS REPRESENTATIVE
BARLOW•HARTMAN
John Barlow   Michael Hartman
Leslie Baden

CASTING
TELSEY + COMPANY, CSA
Bernie Telsey   Will Cantler   David Vaccari
Bethany Knox   Craig Burns
Tiffany Little Canfield   Rachel Hoffman
Stephanie Yankwitt   Carrie Rosson
Justin Huff   Joe Langworth   Bess Fifer

Production Stage Manager ....**Gary Mickelson**
Stage Manager ....Newton Cole
Assistant Stage Manager ....Claudia Lynch
Production Manager ....Hillary Blanken
Production Management
Associates ....Guy Kwan, Kevin Broomell,
Ana Rose Greene, Elena Soderblom
Action Arrangement ....Drew Fracher
Associate Scenic Designer ....Mary Hamrick
Assistant Scenic Designer ....Josh Zangen
Scenic Model Builder ....Frank McCullough
Associate Costume Designer ....Sidney Shannon
Associate Lighting Designer ....Paul Miller
Assistant Lighting Designer ....Bradley Clements
Assistant Sound Designer ....Michael Bogden
Production Carpenter ....Fred Gallo
Advance Carpenter ....Jack Anderson
Production Electrician ....Jonathan Lawson
Lighting Board Operator ....Tom Lawrey
Sound Engineer ....Michael Wojchik
Production Property Master ....Joseph P. Harris, Jr.
Head Property Master ....Dawn Makay
Wardrobe Supervisor ....Penny Davis
Mr. Esparza's Dresser ....Chip White
Dressers ....Kevin O'Brien, Laura Totero
Hair & Wig Supervisor ....Vanessa Anderson
Assistant to Mr. Sondheim ....Steven Clar
Asst. to Mr. Baruch ....Sonja Soper
Asst. to Mr. Viertel ....Tania Senewiratne
Creative Director for Mr. Bagert ....Russell Owen
Operations Manager for Mr. Bagert ....Rob Fortier
Production Assistants ....Lauren Roth, Heather Weiss,
Rachel Sterner
Advertising ....Serino Coyne, Inc./
Sandy Block, Greg Corradetti,
Craig Sabbatino, Karen Girty
Press Associates ....Dennis Crowley, Carol Fineman,
Ryan Ratelle, Kevin Robak, Wayne Wolfe
Press Office Manager ....Bethany Larsen
Production Photography ....Paul Kolnik
Advertisement Photography ....|........Chris Callis
Cincinnati Photography ....Sandy Underwood
Web Design ....Bay Bridge Productions

Theatre Displays ....King Displays
Music Copying ....Kaye-Houston Music/
Anne Kaye, Doug Houston
Synthesizer Programming ....Randy Cohen
Insurance ....DeWitt Stern Group, Inc./
Peter Shoemaker, Mary E. De Spirt
Legal Counsel ....Patricia Crown, Esq./
Coblence & Associates
Banking ....Chase Manhattan Bank/Michele Gibbons
Payroll Service ....Castellana Services, Inc.
Accounting ....Fried & Kowgios Partners, CPAs, LLP
Exclusive Tour Direction ......On the Road/Simma Levine
New York Rehearsals ....New 42nd Street Studios
Opening Night Coordinator ....Jill Van Denburg

Group Sales ....Show Tix (212) 302-7000

RICHARD FRANKEL PRODUCTIONS STAFF
Finance Director ....**Michael Naumann**
Assistant to Mr. Frankel ....Jeff Romley
Assistant to Mr. Routh ....Rachel Kiwi
Assistant to Ms. Green ....Joshua A. Saletnik
Associate Finance Director ....John DiMeglio
Information Technology Manager ....Roddy Pimentel
Management Assistant ....Heidi Schading
Accounting Assistant ....Heather Le Blanc
Accounting Assistant ....Nicole O'Bleanis
National Sales and Marketing Director ..**Ronni Mandell**
Marketing Manager ....Melissa Marano
Marketing Coordinator ....Ashley Pitman
Sponsorship Manager ....Karen Sonet-Rosenthal
Director of Business Affairs ....**Michael Sinder**
Office Manager ....**Lori Steiger-Perry**
Assistant Office Manager ....Stephanie Adamczyk
Receptionists ....Risa Binder, Matt Maline
Interns ....Gabe Beck, Marco Biggio,
Jarrod Carland, Jennifer Cohen,
Annie Grappone, Margie Kment,
Jason Lane, Kristina Olson,
Kendra Swee, Philip Wilson

AMBASSADOR THEATRE GROUP LTD.
Chairman.......................Sir Eddie Kulukundis, OBE
Deputy Chairman ....Peter Beckwith
Managing Director ....Howard Panter
Executive Director ....Rosemary Squire
For *Company* New York:
Associate Producer ....Angela Edwards

CINCINNATI PLAYHOUSE IN THE PARK
Producing Artistic Director ....Edward Stern
Executive Director ....Buzz Ward
Production Manager ....Phil Rundle
Stage Manager..............................Suann Pollock
Technical Director ....Stirling Scot Shelton
Costume Shop Manager ....Gordon DeVinney

Piano by Steinway & Sons

CREDITS AND ACKNOWLEDGEMENTS
Scenery constructed by Showman Fabricators, Inc., Long Island City, NY. Lighting equipment from PRG Lighting, Inc. Sound equipment from Sound Associates. Costumes by Tricorne; Scafati, Inc.; Jennifer Love. Custom knitwear by Adele Recklies. Wigs by Bob Kelly Wig Creations. Hosiery and undergarments by Bra*Tenders. Natural herbal cough drops courtesy of Ricola USA, Inc. Thanks to Duke at Sam Ash, Don Robinson, Suann Pollock. Special thanks to Jo Porter.

Staff for The Ethel Barrymore
House Manager ....Dan Landon

(L-R): Raúl Esparza, Heather Laws, Angel Desai and Barbara Walsh.

Photo by Paul Kolnik

The Country Girl

First Preview: April 3, 2008. Opened: April 27, 2008.
Still running as of May 31, 2008.

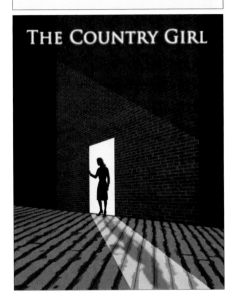

PLAYBILL

THE COUNTRY GIRL

CAST

(in order of speaking)

Bernie Dodd	PETER GALLAGHER
Larry	LUCAS CALEB ROONEY
Phil Cook	CHIP ZIEN
Nancy Stoddard	ANNA CAMP
Paul Unger	REMY AUBERJONOIS
Frank Elgin	MORGAN FREEMAN
Georgie Elgin	FRANCES McDORMAND
Ralph	JOE ROLAND

The year is 1950.

ACT I

Scene 1: The stage of a New York theatre
Scene 2: Frank's apartment, later the same day
Scene 3: The stage, ten days later
Scene 4: Frank's apartment, a week later
Scene 5: A dressing room in a Boston theatre,
after midnight, a week later

ACT II

Scene 1: The Boston dressing room,
a few nights later
Scene 2: The same, the next day
Scene 3: A dressing room in a New York theatre,
evening, some weeks later

UNDERSTUDIES

For Bernie, Larry: JOE ROLAND
For Nancy: AMANDA LEIGH COBB
For Frank: PETER RATRAY
For Georgie: ANGELA REED

 BERNARD B. JACOBS THEATRE

242 West 45th Street
A Shubert Organization Theatre

Gerald Schoenfeld, *Chairman*   Philip J. Smith, *President*

Robert E. Wankel, *Executive Vice President*

Ostar Productions   Bob Boyett   The Shubert Organization   Eric Falkenstein   Roy Furman   Lawrence Horowitz
Jam Theatricals   Stephanie P. McClelland   Bill Rollnick/Nancy Ellison Rollnick   Daryl Roth/Debra Black

In Association with

Jon Avnet/Ralph Guild   Michael Coppel   Jamie deRoy/Michael Filerman
Philip Geier/Donald Keough   Max OnStage   Mary Lu Roffe

Present

Morgan Freeman   Frances McDormand   Peter Gallagher

in

THE COUNTRY GIRL

By

Clifford Odets

Also Starring
**Remy Auberjonois   Anna Camp
Joe Roland   Lucas Caleb Rooney**
and **Chip Zien**

Scenic Design by **Tim Hatley**	Costume Design by **Albert Wolsky**	Lighting Design by **Natasha Katz**
Sound Design by **Acme Sound Partners**	Hair Design by **David Brian Brown**	Material Revisions by **Jon Robin Baitz**
Casting **Tara Rubin Casting**	Production Manager **Aurora Productions**	Production Stage Manager **Barclay Stiff**
Press Representative **Boneau/Bryan-Brown**	General Management **101 Productions Ltd.**	Associate Director **BT McNicholl**

Directed by

Mike Nichols

4/27/08

(L-R): Joe Roland,
Morgan Freeman,
Peter Gallagher and
Frances McDormand.

Photo by Brigitte Lacombe

The Country Girl

Morgan Freeman
Frank Elgin

Frances McDormand
Georgie Elgin

Peter Gallagher
Bernie Dodd

Remy Auberjonois
Paul Unger

Anna Camp
Nancy Stoddard

Joe Roland
Ralph

Lucas Caleb Rooney
Larry

Chip Zien
Phil Cook

Amanda Leigh Cobb
u/s Nancy

Peter Ratray
u/s Frank

Angela Reed
u/s Georgie

Clifford Odets
Playwright

Mike Nichols
Director

Tim Hatley
Scenic Design

Natasha Katz
Lighting Design

Tom Clark, Mark Menard and Nevin Steinberg,
Acme Sound Partners
Sound Designer

David Brian Brown
Wig/Hair Design

BT McNicholl
Associate Director

Tara Rubin,
Tara Rubin Casting
Casting

Bill Haber,
Ostar Productions
Producer

Bob Boyett
Producer

Gerald Schoenfeld,
Chairman,
The Shubert
Organization
Producer

Eric Falkenstein
Producer

Roy Furman
Producer

Lawrence C.
Horowitz, M.D.
Producer

Arny Granat,
Jam Theatricals
Producer

Steve Traxler,
Jam Theatricals
Producer

Stephanie P.
McClelland
Producer

Daryl Roth
Producer

Debra Black
Producer

Jon Avnet
Producer

Ralph Guild
Producer

Jamie deRoy
Producer

Michael Filerman
Producer

The Country Girl

CREW
Front Row (Sitting, L-R): Mike Van Praagh, Fred Ricci, Danny Carpio, Andy Meeker.

Back Row (Standing, L-R): Eddie Ruggiero, James Sturek, Herb Messing, Tyler Ricci, David Cohen and Mike Pitzer.

PROPS ASSISTANT
Alan C. Edwards

BOX OFFICE
Karen Coscia

CREW AND STAGE DOORMAN
(L-R): Eddie Ruggiero (Crew), Jerry Klein (Doorman)

Photos by Ben Strothmann

MERCHANDISE
Suzie Hepker

WARDROBE
Front Row (Sitting, L-R): Franc Weinperl, Kelly Saxon.

Back Row (Standing, L-R): Sandy Binion and Michael Abbate.

FRONT OF HOUSE STAFF
(Clockwise, from Top): William Mitchell (Manager), Kathleen Wehmeyer, Gary Cabana, Joyce Lumpkin, Patanne McEvoy, Al Nazario and John Minore.

The Country Girl

MANAGEMENT AND PRESS
(L-R): Alexis Shorter (Stage Manager), Jackie Green (Press Agent),
Barclay Stiff (Production Stage Manager), Steve Lukens (Company Manager).

BAR STAFF
(L-R): Richard Romero, Jerry Gallagher and Germaine Anthony.

Photos by Ben Strothmann

STAFF FOR *THE COUNTRY GIRL*

GENERAL MANAGEMENT
101 PRODUCTIONS, LTD.
Wendy Orshan   Jeffrey M. Wilson
David Auster

COMPANY MANAGEMENT
Barbara Crompton
Steven Lukens

GENERAL PRESS REPRESENTATIVE
BONEAU/BRYAN-BROWN
Adrian Bryan-Brown   Jackie Green
Matt Ross

PRODUCTION MANAGEMENT
AURORA PRODUCTIONS
Gene O'Donovan
W. Benjamin Heller II   Bethany Weinstein
John Horsman   Melissa Mazdra   Asia Evans

CASTING
TARA RUBIN CASTING
Tara Rubin, CSA, Eric Woodall, CSA
Laura Schutzel, CSA, Merri Sugarman, CSA
Rebecca Carfagna, Paige Blansfield, Dale Brown

Production Stage Manager	Barclay Stiff
Stage Manager	Alexis Shorter
Associate Director	BT McNicholl
Assistants to Mr. Nichols	Colleen O'Donnell, Daniel Murray
Makeup Design	**Angelina Avallone**
Associate Set Designer	Ted LeFevre
Associate Costume Designer	MaryAnn D. Smith
Associate Lighting Designer	Yael Lubetzky
Associate Sound Designer	Jeffrey Yoshi Lee
Assistant to the Costume Designer	Susan Kowarsh Hall
Costume Assistant	Marnie Russell

Production Carpenter	David M. Cohen
Assistant Carpenter	James Sturek
Production Electrician	Michael Pitzer
Production Sound	Daryl Kral
Production Props	Peter Sarafin
Production Prop Assistant	Alan Edwards
Head Props	Andrew Meeker
Wardrobe Supervisor	Kelly A. Saxon
Dressers	Mickey Abbate, Sandy Binion, Franc Weinperl

Hair Supervisor	Richard Orton
Production Assistants	Kyle Gates, Libby Unsworth

Associate Producer for Ostar Enterprises	Rachel Neuburger
Executive Assistant to Mr. Haber	Theresa Pisanelli
Assistant to Mr. Haber	Kristen Jackson

Producer, Boyett Theatricals	Tim Levy
Office Manager and Executive Asst., Boyett Theatricals	Diane Murphy
Staff, Boyett Theatricals	Michael Mandell, Keifer Mansfield, Evan Storey

Legal Counsel	Lazarus & Harris LLP/ Scott R. Lazarus, Esq., Robert C. Harris, Esq., Andrew Farber, Esq.
Accountant	Rosenberg, Neuwirth & Kushner, CPA's/ Chris Cacace, Kirill Baytalskiy
Music Consultant	Suzana Perić
Advertising	Serino Coyne, Inc./ Nancy Coyne, Angelo Desimini, Cara Christman, Tom Callahan, Sunil Ayyagari
Website Design	Situation Marketing/ Damian Bazadona, John Lanasa
Payroll Services	Castellana Services, Inc.
Production Photographer	Brigitte Lacombe
Director Finance/ Marketing for 101 Productions, Ltd.	Elie Landau
101 Productions, Ltd. Staff	Denys Baker, Mark Barna, Beth Blitzer, Danielle Fazio, Heidi Neven, Julie Anne Nolan, Robert Parkison, Mary Six Rupert, Samara Ungar, Hannah Wachtel
Press Representative Staff	Chris Boneau, Jim Byk, Joe Perrotta, Matt Polk, Susanne Tighe, Adriana Douzos, Jessica Johnson, Juliana Hannett, Aaron Meier, Heath Schwartz, Amy Kass, Christine Olver, Kelly Guiod, Ian Bjorklund, Brandi Cornwell, Kevin Jones, Linnae Petruzzelli
Press Interns	Ashley Pines, Marissa Schwartz
Opening Night Coordination	TLC/Michael Lawrence
Banking	City National Bank/Anne McSweeney
Insurance	Dewitt Stern, Inc./Jennifer Brown
Theatre Displays	King Displays, Inc.

CREDITS
Scenery by Hudson Scenic. Lighting equipment from Production Resource Group. Sound equipment from Sound Associates. Costumes by Western Costume Company, Eric Winterling Inc., Paul Chang Custom Tailor, Palace Costume Company, Anto Distinctive Shirtmakers and Izquierdo Studio. Special thanks to Eddie Marks. Prop dressing by Craig Grigg. Prop furniture by Monkey Business Props. Steamer trunks provided by TreasuredChests.com. Natural herb cough drops courtesy of Ricola USA, Inc. Emergen-C super energy booster provided by Alacer Corp. Coffee makers generously provided by Keurig.

SPECIAL THANKS
Peter Lawrence, Rachel Wolff, Bones Malone
and Sten Severson.

The Country Girl rehearsed at
New 42nd Street Studios.

To learn more about the production, please visit
TheCountryGirlonBroadway.com

THE SHUBERT ORGANIZATION, INC.
Board of Directors

Gerald Schoenfeld Chairman	**Philip J. Smith** President
Wyche Fowler, Jr.	**John W. Kluge**
Lee J. Seidler	**Michael I. Sovern**

Stuart Subotnick

Robert E. Wankel
Executive Vice President

Peter Entin Vice President – Theatre Operations	**Elliot Greene** Vice President – Finance
David Andrews Vice President – Shubert Ticketing Services	**John Darby** Vice President – Facilities

D.S. Moynihan
Vice President – Creative Projects

House Manager	William Mitchell

Cry-Baby

First Preview: March 15, 2008. Opened: April 24, 2008.
Still running as of May 31, 2008.

PLAYBILL

CAST

(in order of appearance)

Mrs. Vernon-Williams	HARRIET HARRIS
Baldwin	CHRISTOPHER J. HANKE
Allison	ELIZABETH STANLEY
Skippy Wagstaff	RYAN SILVERMAN
Pepper	CARLY JIBSON
Wanda	LACEY KOHL
Mona	TORY ROSS
Dupree	CHESTER GREGORY II
Cry-Baby	JAMES SNYDER
Lenora	ALLI MAUZEY
The Whiffles	NICK BLAEMIRE, COLIN CUNLIFFE, PETER MATTHEW SMITH
Bailiff	MARTY LAWSON
Judge Stone	RICHARD POE
Father Officer O'Brien	STACEY TODD HOLT
Radio DJ	MICHAEL BUCHANAN

Ensemble ....CAMERON ADAMS,
ASHLEY AMBER, NICK BLAEMIRE,
MICHAEL BUCHANAN, ERIC L. CHRISTIAN,
COLIN CUNLIFFE, STACEY TODD HOLT,
LAURA JORDAN, MARTY LAWSON,
SPENCER LIFF, MAYUMI MIGUEL,
ERIC SCIOTTO, RYAN SILVERMAN,
PETER MATTHEW SMITH,
ALLISON SPRATT, CHARLIE SUTTON

SWINGS

LISA GAJDA, MICHAEL D. JABLONSKI,
BRENDAN KING, COURTNEY LAINE MAZZA

Continued on next page

The Playbill Broadway Yearbook 2007-2008

 **MARQUIS THEATRE**
UNDER THE DIRECTION OF JAMES M. NEDERLANDER AND JAMES L. NEDERLANDER

Adam Epstein   Allan S. Gordon   Élan V. McAllister
and Brian Grazer
James P. MacGilvray   Universal Pictures Stage Productions
Anne Caruso   Adam S. Gordon   Latitude Link   The Pelican Group
in association with Philip Morgaman   Andrew Farber/Richard Mishaan

Present

CRY-BABY
The MUSICAL

Book by
**Mark O'Donnell &
Thomas Meehan**

Songs by
**David Javerbaum &
Adam Schlesinger**

Based on the Universal Pictures film written and directed by John Waters

James Snyder   Elizabeth Stanley
Chester Gregory II   Christopher J. Hanke   Alli Mauzey
Carly Jibson   Lacey Kohl   Richard Poe   Tory Ross
Cameron Adams   Ashley Amber   Nick Blaemire   Michael Buchanan   Eric L. Christian
Colin Cunliffe   Lisa Gajda   Stacey Todd Holt   Michael D. Jablonski   Laura Jordan   Brendan King
Marty Lawson   Spencer Liff   Courtney Laine Mazza   Mayumi Miguel   Eric Sciotto
Ryan Silverman   Peter Matthew Smith   Allison Spratt   Charlie Sutton
and
Harriet Harris

Scenic Design by	*Costume Design by*	*Lighting Design by*	*Sound Design by*
Scott Pask	**Catherine Zuber**	**Howell Binkley**	**Peter Hylenski**

Hair Design by	*Make-Up Design by*	*Fight Direction by*
Tom Watson	**Randy Houston Mercer**	**Rick Sordelet**

Orchestrator	*Dance Music Arranger*	*Music Producer*	*Music Coordinator*
Christopher Jahnke	**David Chase**	**Steven M. Gold**	**John Miller**

Production Manager	*Production Stage Manager*	*Associate Choreographer*	*Marketing*
Juniper Street Productions	**Rolt Smith**	**Joey Pizzi**	**HHC Marketing**

Press Representatives	*Casting by*	*General Management*
Richard Kornberg **Don Summa**	**Telsey + Company**	**Alan Wasser** **Allan Williams**

Creative Consultant
John Waters

Incidental Music, Arrangements and Music Direction by
Lynne Shankel

Choreographed by
Rob Ashford

Directed by
Mark Brokaw

World Premiere of Cry-Baby Produced by La Jolla Playhouse
Christopher Ashley, Artistic Director & Steven Libman, Managing Director

4/24/08

The Ensemble performs "The Anti-Polio Picnic."

Photo by Joan Marcus

Cry-Baby

MUSICAL NUMBERS

ACT ONE

"The Anti-Polio Picnic"	Mrs. Vernon-Williams, Allison, Baldwin and Ensemble
"Watch Your Ass"	Pepper, Wanda, Mona, Dupree, Cry-Baby and Ensemble
"I'm Infected"	Allison, Cry-Baby and Ensemble
"Squeaky Clean"	Baldwin and the Whiffles
"Nobody Gets Me"	Cry-Baby, Pepper, Wanda, Mona and Ensemble
"Nobody Gets Me" (Reprise)	Allison
"Jukebox Jamboree"	Dupree
"A Whole Lot Worse"	Pepper, Wanda and Mona
"Screw Loose"	Lenora
"Baby Baby Baby Baby Baby (Baby Baby)"	Cry-Baby, Allison and Ensemble
"Girl, Can I Kiss You…?"	Cry-Baby, Allison and Ensemble
"I'm Infected" (Reprise)	Allison and Cry-Baby
"You Can't Beat the System"	Full Company

ACT TWO

"Misery, Agony, Helplessness, Hopelessness, Heartache and Woe"	Allison, Cry-Baby, Dupree, Pepper, Wanda, Mona, Mrs. Vernon-Williams and Ensemble
"All in My Head"	Baldwin, Lenora and Ensemble
"Jailyard Jubilee"	Dupree and Ensemble
"A Little Upset"	Cry-Baby, Dupree, Allison and Ensemble
"I Did Something Wrong…Once"	Mrs. Vernon-Williams
"Thanks for the Nifty Country!"	Baldwin and the Whiffles
"This Amazing Offer"	Baldwin and the Whiffles
"Do That Again"	Cry-Baby and Allison
"Nothing Bad's Ever Gonna Happen Again"	Full Company

UNDERSTUDIES

For Cry-Baby:
RYAN SILVERMAN, ERIC SCIOTTO
For Allison:
ALLISON SPRATT, CAMERON ADAMS
For Mrs. Vernon-Williams:
LAURA JORDAN, TORY ROSS
For Judge Stone:
STACEY TODD HOLT,
PETER MATTHEW SMITH
For Baldwin:
COLIN CUNLIFFE,
PETER MATTHEW SMITH
For Pepper:
TORY ROSS, LISA GAJDA
For Mona:
LISA GAJDA
For Wanda:
ASHLEY AMBER, COURTNEY LAINE MAZZA
For Dupree:
ERIC L. CHRISTIAN, MICHAEL BUCHANAN
For Lenora:
ALLISON SPRATT,
COURTNEY LAINE MAZZA

Dance Captain ....SPENCER LIFF

MUSICIANS

Conductor:
LYNNE SHANKEL
Associate Conductor:
HENRY ARONSON
Keyboard 1:
LYNNE SHANKEL
Keyboard 2/Accordion:
HENRY ARONSON
Guitars:
JOHN BENTHAL, CHRIS BIESTERFELDT
Violin/Mandolin:
CENOVIA CUMMINS, MAXIM MOSTON
Violin/Viola:
ORLANDO WELLS
Cello:
SARAH SEIVER
Bass:
STEVE COUNT
Drums:
FRANK PAGANO
Reeds:
SCOTT KREITZER, CLIFF LYONS,
ROGER ROSENBERG
Trumpet:
BRIAN O'FLAHERTY

Trombone:
DAN LEVINE
Percussion:
JOE MOWATT

Music Coordinator:
JOHN MILLER
Music Copying:
KAYE-HOUSTON MUSIC/
ANNE KAYE, DOUG HOUSTON

Synthesizer Programmer:
RANDY COHEN

(L-R): James Snyder and Elizabeth Stanley.

Harriet Harris with members of the Ensemble.

Photos by Joan Marcus

Cry-Baby

James Snyder
Cry-Baby

Elizabeth Stanley
Allison

Harriet Harris
Mrs. Vernon-Williams

Christopher J. Hanke
Baldwin

Alli Mauzey
Lenora

Chester Gregory II
Dupree

Carly Jibson
Pepper

Lacey Kohl
Wanda

Richard Poe
Judge Stone

Tory Ross
Mona

Cameron Adams
Ensemble

Ashley Amber
Ensemble

Nick Blaemire
Ensemble

Michael Buchanan
Ensemble

Eric L. Christian
Ensemble

Colin Cunliffe
Ensemble

Lisa Gajda
Swing

Stacey Todd Holt
Ensemble

Michael D. Jablonski
Swing

Laura Jordan
Ensemble

Brendan King
Swing/Fight Captain

Marty Lawson
Ensemble

Spencer Liff
Ensemble/Assistant Choreographer/Dance Captain

Courtney Laine Mazza
Swing

Mayumi Miguel
Ensemble

Eric Sciotto
Ensemble

Ryan Silverman
Ensemble

Peter Matthew Smith
Ensemble

Allison Spratt
Ensemble

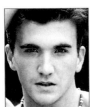
Charlie Sutton
Ensemble

Mark O'Donnell
Book

Thomas Meehan
Book

John Waters
Creative Consultant

Mark Brokaw
Director

Rob Ashford
Choreographer

Cry-Baby

Scott Pask
Scenic Designer

Howell Binkley
Lighting Designer

Catherine Zuber
Costume Designer

Peter Hylenski
Sound Designer

Tom Watson
Hair and Wig Design

Rick Sordelet
Fight Director

Christopher Jahnke
Orchestrations

John Miller
Music Coordinator

Guy Kwan, John Paull III, Hillary Blanken, Kevin Broomell, Ana Rose Greene, Juniper Street Productions
Production Manager

Richard Kornberg & Associates
Press Representative

Bernard Telsey, Telsey + Company
Casting

Alan Wasser
General Manager

Adam Epstein
Producer

Allan S. Gordon
Producer

Élan V. McAllister
Producer

Christopher Ashley
Artistic Director, La Jolla Playhouse

Ivor Royston, The Pelican Group
Producer

Courtney Balan
Mona

Andrew C. Call
Ensemble

BOX OFFICE (L-R): Richard Thigpen and Larry Waxman.

Photo by Ben Strothmann

Courtney Balan
Mona

2007-2008 AWARDS

DRAMA DESK AWARD
Outstanding Choreography
(Rob Ashford)

OUTER CRITICS CIRCLE AWARD
Outstanding Choreography
(Rob Ashford)

THEATRE WORLD AWARD
First Major New York Stage Appearance
(Alli Mauzey)

FRED & ADELE ASTAIRE AWARDS
Best Choreography on Broadway
(Rob Ashford)
Best Male Dancer on Broadway
(Spencer Liff)

Cry-Baby

WARDROBE
Sitting (L-R): Philip Heckman, Tom Bertsch, Andrea Gonzalez.

Standing (L-R): Pamela Pierzina, Charlie Catanese, Del Miskie, Julie Hilimire, Christina Ainge, Michael Berglund, Kimberly Mark, John Webber.

HAIR
(L-R): Katie Beatty, Carla Muniz, Barry Lee Moe, Mitch Ely.

STAGE MANAGEMENT
(L-R): Jenny Slattery (Assistant Stage Manager), Rolt Smith (Production Stage Manager), Andrea O. Saraffian (Stage Manager).

STAGE CREW
Front Row (L-R): David Bornstein (Head Props), Hugh Hardyman (Carpenter), Jesse Stevens (Sound), David Dignazio (Head Sound).

Back Row (L-R): Pat Amari (Props), Matty Lynch (Head Carpenter), Scott Mecionis (Props), Dave Fulton (Carpenter), Rick Poulin (Electrician).

Cry-Baby

FRONT OF HOUSE STAFF
Front Row (L-R): Rosaire Lulu Caso (Chief Usher), Austin Nathaniel (Associate Manager).

Second Row: Michael Newsome, Daisy Irizarry, Karen Garcia-Ortiz, Peter Shayne.

Back Row: Phyllis Weinsaft, Hugh Dill, Mildred Dinato, Donna Flaherty, Nancy Diaz, Stanley Seidman.

ORCHESTRA
Front Row (L-R): Henry Aronson, Chris Biesterfeldt, Lynne Shankel, John Benthal.

Middle Row (L-R): Kenny Rampton, Frank Pagano, Roger Rosenberg, Dan Levine, Orlando Wells, Robert Moose.

Back Row (L-R): Justin Smith, Steve Count, Cliff Lyons, Joe Mowatt, Scott Kreitzer.

Not Pictured: Cenovia Cummins, Barry Danielian Max Moston, Sarah Seiver.

Photos by Ben Strothmann

ASSOCIATE COMPANY MANAGER
Christopher D'Angelo

DOORMAN
Rey Concepcion

THEATRE MANAGER
David Calhoun

Cry-Baby

SCRAPBOOK

Correspondent: Tory Ross, "Hatchet-Face"
Opening Night Gifts: The best gift (and there were some good ones!) was a 40-page glossy, color, gold-foil stamped yearbook chronicling the characters, clubs and activities of "Waters High: 1953-1954." It had a limited printing of 65 copies.
Who Got the Gypsy Robe and What Did They Put on It: Lisa Gajda, one of our swings, received the Gypsy Robe. *Cry-Baby* is her 10th Broadway show. She actually took the responsibility very seriously. After running around the circle three times and posing for photographs, she went to every dressing room and huffily announced it "BLESSED." Apparently this isn't her first time around the Broadway block.
Actor Who Performed the Most Roles in This Show: I have actually played the most roles in *Cry-Baby* to date! After Carly got side-lined by the "Turkey Two" drop during the gypsy run, I played Pepper for the first 21 previews. Then I went back into my cigarette box for eight shows during which Courtney Balan hurt her knee. I subsequently took over the role of Hatchet-Face. Lisa Gajda, our Gypsy Robe recipient, had been on for the cheerleader portion of my track
Continued on next page

STAFF FOR *CRY-BABY*

GENERAL MANAGEMENT
ALAN WASSER ASSOCIATES
Alan Wasser   Allan Williams
Connie Chong

COMPANY MANAGER
Laura Kirspel

GENERAL PRESS REPRESENTATIVE
RICHARD KORNBERG & ASSOCIATES
Richard Kornberg   Don Summa
Alyssa Hart   Billy Zavelson

CASTING
TELSEY + COMPANY
Bernie Telsey CSA, Will Cantler CSA, David Vaccari CSA,
Bethany Knox CSA, Craig Burns CSA,
Tiffany Little Canfield CSA, Rachel Hoffman CSA,
Carrie Rosson CSA, Justin Huff CSA, Joe Langworth,
Bess Fifer CSA, Patrick Goodwin

PRODUCTION MANAGER
JUNIPER STREET PRODUCTIONS
Hillary Blanken   Guy Kwan
Kevin Broomell   Ana Rose Greene

Associate Company Manager	Christopher D'Angelo
Production Stage Manager	Rolt Smith
Stage Manager	Andrea O. Saraffian
Assistant Stage Manager	Jenny Slattery
Associate Director	Moritz von Stuelpnagel
Associate Choreographer	Joey Pizzi
Assistant Choreographer/Dance Captain	Spencer Liff
Assistant Choreographer	Christopher Bailey
Assistant Dance Captain	Courtney Laine Mazza
Fight Captain	Brendan King
Baton Sequences	Pamela Remler

Associate Scenic Designer	Orit Jacoby Carroll
Assistant Scenic Designer	Jeffrey A Hinchee
Associate Costume Designer	Holly Cain
Assistant Costume Designers	Lynn Bowling, Court Watson
Associate Lighting Designer	Ryan O'Gara
Assistant Lighting Designer	Carrie J. Wood
Associate Sound Designer	Keith Caggiano

Production Carpenter	Fred Gallo
Head Carpenter	Matthew Lynch
Flyman	Andrew D. Elman
Automation Carpenter	Hugh Hardyman
Assistant Carpenter	David Fulton
Production Electrician	Randall Zaibek
Head Electrician	Michael Cornell

Automated Lights Programmer	Eric Norris
Production Properties Supervisor	Joseph Harris, Jr.
Head Props	David Bornstein
Production Sound Engineer	David Dignazio
Assistant Sound	Jesse Stevens
Production Wardrobe Supervisor	Patrick Bevilacqua
Assistant Wardrobe Supervisor	Tom Bertsch
Dressers	Christina Ainge, Philip Heckman, John Webber, Michael Berglund, Charlie Catanese, Melissa Crawford, Julie Hilimire, Kimberly Mark, Del Miskie, Andrea Gonzalez, Pamela Kurz, Kimberly Prentice, Sarah Schaub, Chip White
Hair Supervisor	Katie Beatty
Hairdressers	Timothy Harvey, Barry Lee Moe, Carla L. Muniz
Associate Conductor/Rehearsal Pianist	Henry Aronson
Music Preparation	Kaye-Houston Music Inc.
Synthesizer Programmer	Randy Cohen
Assistant Synth Programmer	Jim Mironchik
Assistant to John Miller	Charles Butler

Photo Illustration	Richie Fahey
Advertising	Serino Coyne Inc./ Nancy Coyne, Angelo Desimini, Sandy Block, Miriam Naggar
Marketing	HHC Marketing/ Hugh Hysell, Michael Redman
Website Design and Internet Marketing	Bay Bridge Productions/ Jean Strong, Laura Wagner
National Marketing/Sponsorship	Charlie Katz
Merchandising	Broadway NY Marketing Group LLC
Legal Counsel	Franklin, Weinrib, Rudell & Vassallo
Comptroller	Sarah Galbraith/ Sarah Galbraith Company
Accountants	Robert Fried CPA/ Fried & Kowgios CPAs LLP

General Management Office	Christopher Betz, Jake Hirzel, Dawn Kusinski, Patty Montesi, Jennifer Mudge
General Management Associates	Jim Brandeberry, Aaron Lustbader, Lane Marsh, Mark Shacket
Production Assistants	Ruth Zang, Colleen Danaher, Ginene Licata, Elise Hanley
Assistant to Mr. Epstein	Cameron Leel
Production Photographer	Joan Marcus
Insurance	DeWitt Stern Group/ Peter Shoemaker
Banking	Commerce Bank/ Barbara von Borstel, Olivia Cassin
Payroll	Castellana Services, Inc.
Travel Services	Tzell Travel Group/Andi Henig
Massage Therapy	Russell Beasley, LMT

Opening Night Coordination	Classic Entertainment Group
Rehearsal Studio	New 42nd Street Studios

www.crybabyonbroadway.com

myspace.com/crybabyonbroadway

CREDITS AND ACKNOWLEDGEMENTS
Scenery and scenic effects built and electrified by PRG Scenic Technologies, New Windsor, NY. Scenery painted by Scenic Arts Studios, Cornwall, NY. Show control and scenic motion control featuring Stage Command Systems by PRG Scenic Technologies. Additional scenery and props by La Jolla Playhouse. Softgoods built by I. Weiss and Sons, Inc., Long Island City, NY. Lighting equipment provided by PRG Lighting, North Bergen, NJ. Sound equipment provided by PRG Audio, Mt. Vernon, NY. Props built by Cigarbox Studios, Newburgh, NY; The Spoon Group, Rahway, NJ; and Portafiori Flowers, New York, NY. Costumes by Euro Co. Costumes; Jennifer Love Costumes; Carelli Costumes, Inc.; Timberlake Studios, Inc.; Claudia Diaz; Ed Dawson; Brian Hemesath; John Cowles; Arnold S. Levine, Inc.; Angels, the Costumiers; Worldtone Dance; and Hiatt Dance Boots. Natural herb cough drops courtesy of Ricola USA, Inc. Makeup provided by M•A•C. *Cry-Baby* exclusively uses Gibson & Epiphone guitars and Slingerland drums. Special thanks to Bra*Tenders for undergarments and hosiery.

⟩N⟨
NEDERLANDER

Chairman	**James M. Nederlander**
President	**James L. Nederlander**

Executive Vice President
Nick Scandalios

Vice President Corporate Development **Charlene S. Nederlander**	Senior Vice President Labor Relations **Herschel Waxman**
Vice President **Jim Boese**	Chief Financial Officer **Freida Sawyer Belviso**

STAFF FOR THE MARQUIS THEATRE

Manager	David Calhoun
Associate Manager	Austin Nathaniel
Treasurer	Rick Waxman
Assistant Treasurer	John Rooney
Carpenter	Joseph P. Valentino
Electrician	James Mayo
Property Man	Scott Mecionis

Cry-Baby

SCRAPBOOK

Curtain call on opening night.

as I injured my hamstring during the first week of rehearsals, and took over my full track when I was Pepper, then went on for Pepper (after I had become Hatchet-Face) when Carly caught the "*Cry-Baby* Crud" that we keep giving to each other because we have a song in which we all make out with one another. As of print time, we're still giving it to each other.

Special Backstage Rituals: There are many! Every night at half-hour, the Whiffles meet in Christopher's (Baldwin's) dressing room and run-through "Squeaky Clean" a capella. The Drapes all have a super-secret handshake that they do before entering from SR for "Watch Your Ass." Elizabeth Stanley (Allison) always practices her baton moves in the second wing of SR before the overture starts.

Favorite Moment During Each Performance: Many Scrapes (which is a Drape born into a Square's body) would admit that a highlight of the show is singing the button of the song "Girl, Can I Kiss You With Tongue." We've been crouched behind that glade so long that after we pop up and have to belt out that ridiculously long note, we almost pass out. Every time!

Favorite In-Theatre Gathering Place: During previews, we would have the SNOB party in the boys' dressing room. Saturday Night on Broadway...starring tequila, vodka and anything we could get our hands on.

Favorite Off-Site Hangout: In San Diego: Baja Betty's. In NYC: Arriba, Arriba. We have a thing for margaritas.

Favorite Snack Food: Red Vines for Chester Gregory (Dupree), lollipops for Alli Mauzey (Lenora) and any other sort of candy or chocolate for the rest of us, which is conveniently located on stage left and in the secret hidden box in the wardrobe room. God love the crew

for continuing to feed our sugar addictions. We also love a good ol' fashioned pizza party.

Mascot: The Squirlkin. "Don't they find a lot of dead bodies out there?" "That part of the woods is just filthy!" These are just a few of the myths surrounding the home of the elusive Squirlkin. Squirlkin corpses can be found all over the Glades at Turkey Point. For those of you who don't know, a Squirlkin is a rare crossbreed of a squirrel and a chicken. It is unclear who the 'mad scientist' behind this creation was. Nonetheless, their existence provides entertainment and joy to the community. Baltimoreans enjoy dressing up in Squirlkin regalia. It is difficult to find a live one. However, on February 19th, 1954, Baltimore resident Igneous Stone snapped the rare photo of a baby Squirlkin (Swing Brendan King's brand-new baby Avery who was born during rehearsals). Patent pending, Gill and Pendelton plan to make a popular television program including the lovable crimefighter, Jessyka Squirlkin. She solves mysteries sporting skinny jeans and a sensible ballet flat.

Favorite Therapies: The delightfully supple massage hands of Russell Beasley. And Altoids.

Most Memorable Ad-Lib: The most jaw-dropping ad-lib actually came during our rehearsal process. During the courtroom scene, Hatchet-Face's mom, Gertie (Laura Jordan) would make an appearance to tell the judge the following:

GERTIE: Throw the book at her! I read your diary, you banana-humping piece of trash.

MONA: I was experimenting!

GERTIE: Then pick a good clean American fruit.

It was genius. And it got cut (followed by tears of sorrow).

Best Cut Lyrics: Cry-Baby used to sing a song in the opening scene called "One Tear." It has

subsequently been replaced by the song "Nobody Gets Me" in the country club. However, in "One Tear," he sang the lyrics:

You don't know from broken hearted
So don't get me started.
If happiness was brains, I'd be borderline
retarded.

Also genius. Also cut.

Memorable Directorial Note: Mark enjoyed the phrase: "pass the baton."

Fastest Costume Change/Who Wore the Least: The fastest costume change is actually the three cheerleader girls dropping all their clothing to run across the stage naked, covered in nothing but a pom-pom. Nudity provided by: Ashley Amber, Mayumi Miguel and Cameron Adams.

Who Wore the Heaviest/Hottest Costume: It's a tie between the Apple Pie (Laura Jordan) and the Cigarette Box (Lisa Gajda/Tory Ross). However, I feel it only fair to mention all of the "Stars of Funland" at this juncture, which includes Uncle Sam (Michael Buchanan on stilts) and Stacey Todd Holt as the loveable 16th US President, Abraham Lincoln. "Stars of Funland" THEY ARE!

Catchphrases Only the Company Would Recognize: Ska ska. And scene five ("whuuuu-uuuuuuut??").

Nicknames: Every character in this show has a name. We played out of town and previewed for a LOOOONG time. Here are some of the best: Heath Huxtable (Eric Christian's Square), Beverly "Buttons" Lemonade (Laura Jordan's Square), Guilderoy de Lillias White (Michael Buchanan's Square), Indian Civil Kim (Andrew C. Call's Drape), Yinzer "Kobes" Kobalowski (Marty Lawson's Drape), and Pirate Sandy (Allison Spratt's Drape).

Sweethearts Within the Company: Ashley & Spencer, Mayumi & Charlie, and Peter & Nick (they're "straighting.")

Embarrassing Moments: Too many and too embarrassing to name.

Superstitions That Turned Out To Be True: Don't EVER smudge a theatre. If you do, it will invite injury, sickness and evil blogging onto your show.

Coolest Things About Being in This Show: Free tattoos, scars and Chapstick! No seriously, the coolest thing about being part of *Cry-Baby*, is the incredible group of people they managed to get into one room. Not only is everyone a quadruple threat: singer, dancer, actor and funny, everyone is also really nice and fun and a treat to spend three months in San Diego making absolutely no money with. We had amazing bonfires on the beach and that atmosphere followed us all the way back to the Marquis Theatre. Everyone in that building is a delight, from the crew, to the house staff, to our company and stage management. Working with these people has been a pleasure and a gift.

Fan Club Info: Check out our website: www.crybabyonbroadway.com and also our blog on MySpace!

Curtains

First Preview: February 27, 2007. Opened: March 22, 2007.
Still running as of May 31, 2008.

PLAYBILL

CAST

(in order of appearance)

Jessica Cranshaw	PATTY GOBLE
Randy Dexter	JIM NEWMAN
Niki Harris	JILL PAICE
Bambi Bernét	MEGAN SIKORA
Bobby Pepper	NOAH RACEY
Johnny Harmon	MICHAEL X. MARTIN
Georgia Hendricks	KAREN ZIEMBA
Aaron Fox	JASON DANIELEY
Carmen Bernstein	DEBRA MONK
Oscar Shapiro	MICHAEL McCORMICK
Christopher Belling	EDWARD HIBBERT
Lieutenant Frank Cioffi	DAVID HYDE PIERCE
Mona Page	MARY ANN LAMB
Harv Fremont	MATT FARNSWORTH
Roberta Wooster	DARCIE ROBERTS
Sidney Bernstein	ERNIE SABELLA
Detective O'Farrell	KEVIN BERNARD
Daryl Grady	JOHN BOLTON
Sasha Iljinsky	DAVID LOUD
Marjorie Cook	PAULA LEGGETT CHASE
Arlene Barruca	NILI BASSMAN
Roy Stetson	KEVIN BERNARD
Brick Hawvermale	WARD BILLEISEN
Jan Setler	SHANNON LEWIS
Connie Subbotin	PATTY GOBLE
Peg Prentice	BRITTANY MARCIN
Ronnie Driscoll	SEAN SAMUELS
Russ Cochran	CHRISTOPHER SPAULDING

Continued on next page

AL HIRSCHFELD THEATRE

A JUJAMCYN THEATRE

ROCCO LANDESMAN
PRESIDENT

PAUL LIBIN
PRODUCING DIRECTOR

JACK VIERTEL
CREATIVE DIRECTOR

JORDAN ROTH
VICE PRESIDENT

ROGER BERLIND   ROGER HORCHOW   DARYL ROTH
JANE BERGÈRE   TED HARTLEY   CENTER THEATRE GROUP

present

DAVID HYDE PIERCE *and* DEBRA MONK

in

CURTAINS

Book by
RUPERT HOLMES

Music by
JOHN KANDER

Lyrics by
FRED EBB

Original Book and Concept by
PETER STONE

Additional Lyrics by
JOHN KANDER *and* RUPERT HOLMES

Starring

KAREN ZIEMBA

JASON DANIELEY   JILL PAICE

and

EDWARD HIBBERT

Also Starring

JOHN BOLTON   MICHAEL X. MARTIN   MICHAEL McCORMICK
NOAH RACEY   ERNIE SABELLA   MEGAN SIKORA

with

NILI BASSMAN   KEVIN BERNARD   WARD BILLEISEN   PAULA LEGGETT CHASE   DAVID EGGERS   J. AUSTIN EYER
MATT FARNSWORTH   PATTY GOBLE   MARY ANN LAMB   LORIN LATARRO   SHANNON LEWIS   BRITTANY MARCIN
JIM NEWMAN   DARCIE ROBERTS   SEAN SAMUELS   CHRISTOPHER SPAULDING   JEROME VIVONA   STEPHANIE YOUELL

Set Design
ANNA LOUIZOS

Costume Design
WILLIAM IVEY LONG

Lighting Design
PETER KACZOROWSKI

Sound Design
BRIAN RONAN

Hair and Wig Design
PAUL HUNTLEY

Dance Arrangements
DAVID CHASE

Fight Direction
RICK SORDELET

Aerial Effects Design
PAUL RUBIN

Make-Up Design
ANGELINA AVALLONE

Associate Choreographer
JOANN M. HUNTER

Casting
JIM CARNAHAN, CSA

Production Supervisor
BEVERLEY RANDOLPH

Technical Supervisor
PETER FULBRIGHT

Music Coordinator
JOHN MONACO

General Management
101 PRODUCTIONS, LTD.

Marketing Services
TMG-
THE MARKETING GROUP

Press Representative
BONEAU/BRYAN-BROWN

Associate Producers
BARBARA AND PETER FODOR

Orchestrations
WILLIAM DAVID BROHN

Music Director/Vocal Arrangements
DAVID LOUD

Choreography by
ROB ASHFORD

Directed by
SCOTT ELLIS

LIVE BROADWAY

AMERICAN PREMIERE PRODUCED AT THE AHMANSON THEATRE BY CENTER THEATRE GROUP, LA'S THEATRE COMPANY

10/1/07

Jill Paice, David Hyde Pierce and Company perform "A Tough Act to Follow."

Photo by Joan Marcus

Curtains

MUSICAL NUMBERS

ACT I

"Wide Open Spaces"	Randy, Niki, Jessica, Bobby, Ensemble
"What Kind of Man?"	Carmen, Oscar, Aaron, Georgia
"Thinking of Him"	Georgia, Aaron, Bobby
"The Woman's Dead"	Entire Company
"Show People"	Carmen, Cioffi, Entire Company
"Coffee Shop Nights"	Cioffi
"In the Same Boat 1"	Georgia, Niki, Bambi
"I Miss the Music"	Aaron
"Thataway!"	Georgia, Bobby, Ensemble

ACT II

"He Did It"	Entire Company
"In the Same Boat 2"	Bobby, Randy, Harv
"It's a Business"	Carmen, Stagehands
"Kansasland"	Randy, Niki, Harv, Bobby, Bambi, Ensemble
"Thinking of Him"/"I Miss the Music" (Reprise)	Aaron, Georgia
"A Tough Act to Follow"	Cioffi, Niki, Ensemble
"In the Same Boat 3"	Entire Company
"A Tough Act to Follow" (Reprise)	Entire Company

(L-R): Noah Racey and Karen Ziemba perform "Thataway!"

Photo by Joan Marcus

ORCHESTRA

Conductor: DAVID LOUD
Flute, Piccolo Clarinet, Alto Sax: STEVE KENYON
Oboe, English Horn, Clarinet,
    Tenor Sax: AL HUNT
Clarinet, Alto Sax, Soprano Sax: OWEN KOTLER
Bassoon, Bass Clarinet, Baritone Sax, Flute, Clarinet:
    MARK THRASHER
French Horn 1: R.J. KELLEY
French Horn 2: ANGELA CORDELL
Trumpet 1: DON DOWNS
Trumpet 2: MATT PETERSON
Trombone 1, House Contractor:
    CHARLES GORDON
Bass Trombone, Tuba: JENNIFER WHARTON
Percussion: GREG LANDES
Drums: BRUCE DOCTOR
Acoustic Guitar, Electric Guitar, Banjo,
    Classical Guitar: GREG UTZIG
Acoustic Bass: ROBERT RENINO
Associate Music Director/Piano and Synthesizer:
    SAM DAVIS

Musical Coordinator: JOHN MONACO
Music Copying Services: LARRY H. ABEL,
    MUSIC PREPARATION INTERNATIONAL

Cast Continued

SWINGS
DAVID EGGERS, J. AUSTIN EYER,
LORIN LATARRO, JEROME VIVONA,
STEPHANIE YOUELL

UNDERSTUDIES
For Lieutenant Frank Cioffi & Christopher Belling:
KEVIN BERNARD
For Niki Harris:
NILI BASSMAN, STEPHANIE YOUELL
For Bambi Bernét:
LORIN LATARRO, SHANNON LEWIS
For Aaron Fox
KEVIN BERNARD, MATT FARNSWORTH
For Daryl Grady
MATT FARNSWORTH, MICHAEL X. MARTIN
For Carmen Bernstein
PAULA LEGGETT CHASE, PATTY GOBLE
For Oscar Shapiro & Sidney Bernstein
MICHAEL X. MARTIN, JEROME VIVONA
~~For Johnny Harmon~~
JIM NEWMAN, JEROME VIVONA
For Bobby Pepper
WARD BILLEISEN, DAVID EGGERS,
JIM NEWMAN
For Georgia Hendricks & Jessica Cranshaw
PAULA LEGGETT CHASE, DARCIE ROBERTS

Dance Captain:
DAVID EGGERS

SETTING
Act One
The Colonial Theatre in Boston, 1959, during the
out-of-town tryout of the new musical, *Robbin'
Hood!*

Act Two
The same, much later that night

Curtains

David Hyde Pierce
*Lieutenant
Frank Cioffi*

Debra Monk
Carmen Bernstein

Karen Ziemba
Georgia Hendricks

Jason Danieley
Aaron Fox

Jill Paice
Niki Harris

Edward Hibbert
Christopher Belling

John Bolton
Daryl Grady

Michael X. Martin
Johnny Harmon

Michael McCormick
Oscar Shapiro

Noah Racey
Bobby Pepper

Ernie Sabella
Sidney Bernstein

Megan Sikora
Bambi Bernét

Nili Bassman
Arlene Barruca

Kevin Bernard
*Roy Stetson,
Detective O'Farrell*

Ward Billeisen
Brick Hawvermale

Paula Leggett Chase
Marjorie Cook

David Eggers
*Swing,
Dance Captain*

J. Austin Eyer
Swing

Matt Farnsworth
Harv Fremont

Patty Goble
*Jessica Cranshaw,
Connie Subbotin*

Mary Ann Lamb
Mona Page

Lorin Latarro
*Swing,
Asst. Dance Captain*

Shannon Lewis
Jan Setler

Brittany Marcin
Peg Prentice

Jim Newman
Randy Dexter

Darcie Roberts
Roberta Wooster

Sean Samuels
Ronnie Driscoll

Christopher
Spaulding
Russ Cochran

Jerome Vivona
*Swing, 2nd Ass't.
Stage Manager*

Stephanie Youell
Swing

Beverley Randolph
*Production
Supervisor*

John Kander and Fred Ebb
Music, Additional Lyrics; Lyrics

Rupert Holmes
*Book,
Additional Lyrics*

Peter Stone
*Original Book &
Concept*

Curtains

Scott Ellis
Director

Rob Ashford
Choreographer

Anna Louizos
Set Design

William Ivey Long
Costume Design

Peter Kaczorowski
Lighting Design

Brian Ronan
Sound Design

William David Brohn
Orchestrations

Paul Huntley
Hair and Wig Design

Rick Sordelet
Fight Director

Paul Rubin
Aerial Effects Design

Angelina Avallone
Make-up Design

JoAnn M. Hunter
*Associate
Choreographer*

Dave Solomon
Assistant Director

Teressa Esposito
*Creative Associate
to Mr. Holmes*

Jim Carnahan, CSA
Casting

Roger Berlind
Producer

Roger Horchow
Producer

Daryl Roth
Producer

Jane Bergère
Producer

Ted Hartley
Producer

Michael Ritchie
*Artistic Director,
Center Theatre Group*

Charles Dillingham
*Managing Director,
Center Theatre Group*

Gordon Davidson,
*Founding Artistic
Director,
Center Theatre Group*

Ashley Amber
Swing

Jennifer Dunne
Jan Setler

Sean McKnight
Brick Hawvermale

Joe Aaron Reid
Ronnie Driscoll

Darcie Roberts
Roberta Wooster

Allison Spratt
Swing

Bridget Berger
Roberta Wooster

Callie Carter
Arlene Barruca

Erin Davie
Niki Harris

Jennifer Dunne
Jan Setler

Curtains

David Elder
Randy Dexter

Jennifer Frankel
Marjorie Cook

John MacInnis
Randy Dexter

Aaron Ramey
Harv Fremont

Joe Aaron Reid
Ronnie Driscoll

Julie Tolivar
Roberta Wooster

Gerry Vichi
Sidney Bernstein

Matt Wall
Randy Dexter

ORCHESTRA
Front Row (L-R): Dave Roth, Owen Kotler

Back Row (L-R): Julie Ferrara, Greg Utzig, Jeremy Miloszewicz, Jennifer Wharton, Mark Thrasher, Charles Gordon, Bruce Doctor, Bill Ellison, Ken Hitchcock

Photos by Ben Strothmann

WARDROBE
Front Row (L-R): Frank Scaccia, Valerie Frith, Margo Lawless

Back Row (L-R): Jason Blair, Theresa diStasi, Misty Fernandez, David Mitchell, Alice Bee, Lisa Preston, Kay Gowenlock

FRONT OF HOUSE STAFF
Front Row (L-R): Mary Marzan (Usher), Janice Rodriguez (Chief Usher), Jennifer DiDonato (Usher), Lorraine Feeks (Ticket Taker), Kerri Gillen (Usher), Julie Burnham (Director), Marisol Diaz (Usher), William Burke (Usher)

Second Row (L-R): Nicole Grillos (Usher), Henry Menendez (Usher), Tristan Blacer (Ticket Yaker), Alex Gutierrez (Usher), Maura Leahy (Max Merchandising), Louis Mazza (Engineer)

Back Row (L-R): Jose Nunez (Porter), Albert Kim (Theatre Manager), Michael Yeshion (Bartender), Donald Royal (Usher), Roberto Ellington (Porter), Hollis Miller (Usher), Ron Marto (Security Guard), Bart Ryan (Usher)

Curtains

HAIR
(L-R): Gay Boseker, Natasha Steinhagen, Larry Boyette, Brendan O'Neal.

DOORMAN
Neil Perez

PROPS
(L-R): Gene Manford, Sal Sclafani, Andy Trotto, Bob Adams.

COMPANY AND STAGE MANAGEMENT
(L-R): Kevin Bertolacci (Assistant Stage Manager), Scott Rollison (Stage Manager), Beverley Randolph (Production Supervisor/Production Stage Manager), Jerome Vivona (Assistant Stage Manager/Fight Captain), Beverly Edwards (Company Manager).

CARPENTERS
Front Row (L-R): Erik Hansen, Joe Maher, Angelo Grasso, Paul Wimmer.

On Staircase (L-R): Richie Fullum, Morgan Shevett, Gabe Harris, Angelo Torre, Kevin Maher, Tom Lowery.

ELECTRICS AND SOUND
(L-R): Richard Mortell, Danny Ansbro, Cletus Karamon, Rob Dagna, Bonnie Runk, John Blixt, Dennis Short, Chris Sloan, Michele Gutierrez.

Curtains

The Playbill Broadway Yearbook 2007-2008

STAFF FOR *CURTAINS*

GENERAL MANAGEMENT
101 PRODUCTIONS, LTD.
Wendy Orshan   Jeffrey M. Wilson
David Auster

COMPANY MANAGER
Bruce Klinger

GENERAL PRESS REPRESENTATIVE
BONEAU/BRYAN-BROWN
Chris Boneau   Jim Byk
Juliana Hannett   Matt Ross

CASTING
JIM CARNAHAN, CSA
Carrie Gardner, Stephen Kopel, Kate Schwabe

TECHNICAL SUPERVISOR
TECH PRODUCTION SERVICES, INC.
Peter Fulbright   Mary Duffe
Colleen Houlehen   Jackie Prats

Production Stage Manager ....Beverley Randolph
Stage Manager ....Scott Taylor Rollison
Assistant Stage Manager ....Kevin Bertolacci
Asst. Stage Manager/Fight Capt. ....Jerome Vivona
Associate Company Manager ....Beverly Edwards
Dance Captain ....David Eggers
Assistant Dance Captain ....Lorin Latarro
Creative Associate to Mr. Holmes ....Teressa Esposito
Assistant Director ....Dave Solomon
Assistant to Mr. Ellis ....Kathleen Bond
Associate Scenic Designer ....Michael Carnahan
Assistant Scenic Designer ....Zhanna Gurvich
Assistant to Ms. Louizos ....Gaetane Bertol
Associate Costume Designer ....Tom Beall
Assistant Costume Designer ....Rachel Attridge
Assistants to Mr. Long ....Cathy Parrott,
                                      Brenda Abbandandalo
Associate Lighting Designer ....Hilary Manners
Assistant Lighting Designer ....Joel E. Silver
Assistant to Mr. Kaczorowski ....Lisa Katz
Moving Light Programmer ....Josh Weitzman
Assistant Sound Designer ....Mike Farfalla
Keyboard Programmer ....Stuart Andrews
Production Carpenter ....Paul Wimmer
Fly Automation ....Erik Hansen
Deck Automation ....Rick Styles
Production Electrician ....Richard Mortell
Head Electrician ....Cletus Karamon
Assistant Electrician ....Sandy Paradise
Production Props Supervisor ....George Wagner
Head Props ....Robert Adams
Production Sound Supervisor ....Christopher Sloan
Wardrobe Supervisor ....Michael Growler
Assistant Wardrobe Supervisor ....Derek Moreno
Dressers ....Alice Bee, Kenneth Brown,
                         Theresa DiStasi, Misty Fernandez,
                               Katherine Gowenlock,
                          Jennifer Griggs-Cennamo,
                          Joseph Hickey, Margaret Horkey,
                          Pamela Kurz, David Mitchell,
                          Jeannie Naughton, Frank Scaccia,
                                           Chip White
Hair Supervisor ....Larry Boyette

Assistant Hair Supervisor ....Natasha Steinhagen
Hair Dressers ....Brendan O'Neal, Elizabeth Mathews
Rehearsal Pianists ....Paul Ford, Sue Anschutz
Rehearsal Drummer ....Bruce Doctor
Music Department Intern ....Aaron Fischer
Production Assistants ....Lauren Korba, Timothy Eaker,
                                          Helen Coney
SSDC Observer ....Andrew Parkhurst
Dialect Coach ....Kate Mare
Assistant to Mr. Berlind ....Jeffrey Hillock
Assistant to Mr. Horchow ....Donna Harper
Assistant to Ms. Roth ....Greg Raby
Assistant to Ms. Bergère ....Amanda Woods
Assistant to Mr. Hartley ....Doris Schwartz
Legal Counsel ....Loeb & Loeb/Seth Gelblum, Esq.
Accountant ....Fried and Kowgios Partners, LLP
Comptroller ....Sarah Galbraith
Advertising ....Serino Coyne/
                          Scott Johnson, Sandy Block,
                                          Jean Leonard
Marketing ....The Marketing Group/
                          Victoria Cairl, Liz Miller,
                          Sara Rosenzweig, Anne Rippey
Marketing ....Leanne Schanzer Promotions, Inc.
Assistant to the General Managers ....John Vennema
101 Productions
   Director of Finance/Marketing ....Elie Landau
101 Productions, Ltd. Staff ....Denys Baker,
                          Ashley Berman, Katharine Croke,
                          Sherra Johnston, Emily Lawson,
                          Heidi Neven, Kyle Pickles,
                                      Mary Six Rupert
Banking ....City National Bank/Anne McSweeney
Insurance ....DeWitt Stern, Inc./ Jennifer Brown
Risk Managers ....Stockbridge Risk Management/
                                          Neil Goldstein
Opening Night Coordinator ....Tobak-Lawrence/
                          Suzanne Tobak, Michael Lawrence
Physical Therapy ....PhysioArts/Jennifer Green
Orthopedist ....Phillip Bauman, M.D.
Theatre Displays ....King Displays, Inc.
Merchandising ....Max Merchandising, LLC
Website Design ....Situation Marketing, LLC/
                          Damian Bazadona, Lisa Cecchini
Production Photography ....Joan Marcus
Payroll Services ....Castellana Services, Inc.

CREDITS
Scenery and scenic effects by Showmotion, Inc, Norwalk,
CT, using the AC2 computerized motion control system.
Lighting equipment from PRG Lighting. Sound equipment
from PRG Audio. Costumes executed by Barbara Matera
Ltd., Carelli Costumes, Euro Co Costumes, JC Theatrical &
Custom Footwear, Jennifer Love, Luigi's Quality Tailoring,
Scafati, Schneeman Studios, Tricorne Inc., Timberlake
Studio, American Plume and Fancy Feather Co., Lynne
Baccus, Cego Shirts, Mrinalini Inc., Rodney Gordon,
Tohma, Vogue Too. Shoes by T.O. Dey, J.C. Theatrical &
Custom Footwear Inc., LaDuca Shoes, Pluma Handmade
Dance Footwear. Props by The Spoon Group LLC, John
Creech Design and Production. Natural herb cough drops
courtesy of Ricola USA, Inc. Special thanks to Bra*Tenders
for hosiery and undergarments. Makeup provided by
M•A•C Cosmetics. Shoulder holsters provided by
Kirkpatrick Leather, Laredo, Texas.

Group Sales:
Scott Mallalieu/Stephanie Lee (800) 223-7565

CURTAINS rehearsed at New 42nd Street Studios

SPECIAL THANKS
The director would like to thank Adam Brazier, Aldrin
Gonzalez, Alyson Turner, Ann Arvia, Anne L. Nathan,
Bernard Dotson, Betsy Wolfe, Boyd Gaines, Burke Moses,
Casey Nicholaw, Chip Zien, Dana Lynn Mauro, Daniel
Sherman, Danny Burstein, David Andrew McDonald,
Deborah Rush, Deven May, Elizabeth Mills, Erin Dilly,
Gavin Creel, Gerry Vichi, Gina Lamparella, Gregg
Edelman, Hunter Foster, James Clow, James Naughton,
Jennifer Laura Thompson, Jessica Lea Patty, Jessica Stone,
John Dossett, Kerry O'Malley, Kevin Ligon, Kristine
Nielson, Laura Benanti, Lawrence Clayton, Lee Wilkof,
Mary Catherine Garrison, Megan Hilty, Mel Johnson Jr.,
Melina Kanakaredes, Meredith Patterson, Michael
Cumpsty, Michael Mendel, Michele Pawk, Paul Michael
Valley, Peter Benson, Rachel Coloff, Randy Graff, Ric
Stoneback, Robert Walden, Rosena Hill, Ruthie Henshall,
Sally Wilfert, Sean Martin Hingston, Stephen Buntrock,
Stephen DeRosa, Stephen Lee Anderson, Todd Haimes and
the Roundabout Theatre Company, without whom
tonight's performance of *Curtains* would not have been
possible.

JUJAMCYN THEATERS

ROCCO LANDESMAN
President

PAUL LIBIN   **JACK VIERTEL**   **JORDAN ROTH**
Producing Director   Creative Director   Vice President
DANIEL ADAMIAN   **JENNIFER HERSHEY**
General Manager   Director of Operations
MEREDITH VILLATORE   **JERRY ZAKS**
Chief Financial Officer   Resident Director

Staff for the Al Hirschfeld Theatre
Manager ....Albert T. Kim
Treasurer ....Carmine La Mendola
Carpenter ....Joseph J. Maher, Jr.
Propertyman ....Sal Sclafani
Electrician ....Dermot J. Lynch
Engineer ....Henry Haywood

The Company

Photo by Joan Marcus

Curtains

SCRAPBOOK

Correspondents: John Bolton, "Daryl Grady"; and Nili Bassman, "Arlene Barruca."

Exciting Celebrity Visitors: Marge Champion, Joe Torre, Liza, Robert DeNiro.

Broadway Cares Events: We recorded "The Monotone Angel" and "Deck the Halls" for "Carols For a Cure," performed "Family Feud (Producers vs Stagehands)" at "Gypsy of the Year," had a rockin' table at the Flea Market and raised a buttload of money from audience appeals. Coolest BC/EFA moment—the guy who donated $12,500 for a backstage tour.

Actor Who Performed the Most Roles in the Show: Jerome Vivona.

Role Played by the Most Different Actors: Randy (7).

Who Has Done the Most Performances of *Curtains*: Off stage: House Carpenter Joe Maher. On stage: Michael McCormick

Special Backstage Rituals: Cinnamon roll, Megan's pre-show Krazy Dance, Impromptu Strips, Cletus's candy bowl, after-show toasts on the fourth floor, Dollar Friday, Banana Saturday, Jason's Sunday chocolate pail, nightly horoscopes with Fern Turtletaub, men's quick change quote wall, treehouse initiations.

Favorite Moment During Each Performance: Hanging out together behind the curtain during the overture.

Favorite In-Theatre Gathering Place: The stairwell.

Favorite Off-Site Hangout: PhysioArts.

Favorite Snack Food: Advil.

Mascot: Niles, the dummy that drops from the flies during the bows.

Fastest Costume Change: David Hyde Pierce.

Who Wore the Heaviest Costume: Women's Ensemble, Matt Farnsworth/Aaron Ramey.

Who Wore the Least: Megan Sikora, Jen Dunne.

Catchphrases Only the Company Would Recognize: "Man on a Horse," "Boston Beans," "May the Fourth Be With You," "Popcorns," "J'accuse!" and "Sorry, pure reflux."

Which Orchestra Member Played the Most Consecutive Performances: Bruce Doctor (drums).

Best In-House Parody Lyrics: Too many—and most are too filthy to print. The hard part was not singing those alternate lyrics in performance by mistake!

Best Comedy Routine: Stage combat class with Michael X and Jason's Joke of the Day.

Memorable Directorial Note: "Ba ba ba ba ba."

Company Legend: Mary Ann Lamb.

Put-In Ritual: Pizza.

Nicknames: "Hurtains."

Backstage Fun: Hirschfeld High with everyone's high school senior photos in the stairwell, Holiday Door Decorating Contest, Secret Santa, birthday cakes by Austin Eyer and Carmine LaMendola, alley cookout, Sunday waffles.

After-Hours Fun: DHP treating the company to Chita Rivera's show at The Carlyle and hanging with her afterward. John Kander's

1. Celebrating the anniversary on stage at the Hirschfeld Theatre.
2. Rooftop beefcake (L-R): Ward Billeisen, Kevin Bernard, Christopher Spaulding, Joe Aaron Reid.
3. (L-R): Backstage tribute to the show's late lyricist and librettist.

surprise 80th Birthday party at Rain which was a Who's Who of American Theatre, party in the Hamptons, Deb's birthday at Angus, DHP's birthday at 44, East Village bash at Chris's, Darcie singing at Sardi's, Jason at The Metropolitan Room, Noah's Town Hall concert starring half the cast.

Most Embarrassing Moment: Deb Monk wearing her red slippers on stage by mistake.

Extracurricular Activities: John Kander tribute at The Westport Playhouse, gala honoring Roger Berlind at The Rainbow Room, the Alzheimer's Association's Memory Walk in Riverside Park, Broadway On Broadway, Broadway in Bryant Park.

Memorable Story #1: The entire company watching DHP win his Tony. Screams, projectile tears, grabbing whoever was standing closest and jumping up and down and feeling like we all won.

Memorable story #2: Doing Act II unplugged old-style when the sound went out. Magical.

Coolest Things About Being in This Show: Literally: Standing on the air conditioning vent on stage. Figuratively: Laughing every single day at work.

ALMA MATER

O Hirschfeld, hail we sing to thee
O'er the Great White Way
Your hallowed halls will welcome all
Be they hetero or gay.

'Neath neon Al and sky blue sign
Thine edifice gives rise
On Forty-Five we work and thrive
'Tween Charley O's and Private Eyes.

And when we all shall leave thy walls
Our tears away we'll mop
True we'll stay and hope and pray
Your shows will never flop.

Curtains
SCRAPBOOK

1. In costume at "places" just before the show begins.

2. Debra Monk (6th from left) and the group taking part in the "Broadway on Broadway" event.

3. View down the passageway to the green room.

4. (L-R): Brittany Marcin, Lorin Latarro and Stephanie Youell in their dressing room.

5. A visit from Broadway legend Chita Rivera (center).

6. The show's Local 1 members (and family) walk the picket line.

7. A picnic buffet in the alley next to the theatre.

Photo by Brittany Marcin

Photo by Morgan Shevett

Photo by Theresa DiStasi

Photo by Brittany Marcin

Photo by Theresa DiStasi

Photo by Morgan Shevett

Photo by Theresa DiStasi

Cymbeline

First Preview: November 1, 2007. Opened: December 2, 2007.
Closed January 6, 2008 after 24 Previews and 40 Performances.

PLAYBILL

Shakespeare's
Cymbeline

CAST

IN BRITAIN, in the time of the Roman Empire

Cymbeline, King of Britain ....JOHN CULLUM
Princess Imogen (later in disguise as the boy Fidele),
   secretly married
   to Posthumus ....MARTHA PLIMPTON
Helen, a lady
   attending Imogen ...GORDANA RASHOVICH
Queen, second wife of Cymbeline, and
   step-mother of Imogen ....PHYLICIA RASHAD
Lord Cloten, her son ......ADAM DANNHEISSER
Posthumus Leonatus, a poor gentleman raised
   at court, secretly married
   to Imogen ....MICHAEL CERVERIS
Pisanio, his servant ....JOHN PANKOW
Cornelius, a doctor ....HERB FOSTER
Two Gentlemen ....RICHARD TOPOL,
                      DANIEL BREAKER

IN ITALY

Philario, Posthumus' host ....DANIEL ORESKES
Iachimo, an Italian ....JONATHAN CAKE
A Frenchman ....ANTHONY COCHRANE
A Dutchman ....JEFF WOODMAN
A Spaniard...........................NOSHIR DALAL

ROMANS IN BRITAIN

Caius Lucius, Roman Ambassador,
   later General of the invading
   Roman Army ....EZRA KNIGHT
A Roman Captain ......ANTHONY COCHRANE
Philarmonus,
   a Soothsayer ....MICHAEL W. HOWELL

Continued on next page

LINCOLN CENTER THEATER AT THE VIVIAN BEAUMONT

under the direction of
André Bishop and Bernard Gersten
presents

Cymbeline

BY
William Shakespeare

WITH (IN ALPHABETICAL ORDER)

Jeffrey M. Bender   Daniel Breaker   Jonathan Cake   Michael Cerveris
Anthony Cochrane   John Cullum   Noshir Dalal   Adam Dannheisser
Jordan Dean   Herb Foster   David Furr   Adam Greer
Michael W. Howell   Ezra Knight   LeRoy McClain   Paul O'Brien
Daniel Oreskes   John Pankow   Martha Plimpton   Phylicia Rashad
Gordana Rashovich   Nancy Rodriguez   Michael Rossmy
Richard Topol   Gregory Wooddell   Jeff Woodman

SETS	COSTUMES	LIGHTING
Michael Yeargan	Jess Goldstein	Brian MacDevitt

ORIGINAL MUSIC   SOUND
Mel Marvin   Tony Smolenski IV and Walter Trarbach

MOVEMENT CONSULTANT	FIGHT DIRECTOR	STAGE MANAGER
Seán Curran	Rick Sordelet	Michael McGoff

CASTING	DRAMATURG	GENERAL PRESS AGENT
Daniel Swee	Anne Cattaneo	Philip Rinaldi

DIRECTOR OF DEVELOPMENT	DIRECTOR OF MARKETING
Hattie K. Jutagir	Linda Mason Ross

GENERAL MANAGER	PRODUCTION MANAGER
Adam Siegel	Jeff Hamlin

DIRECTED BY
Mark Lamos

CYMBELINE is supported by the Doris Duke Charitable Foundation Endowment Fund at LCT.

This production is also supported, in part, by public funds from the New York City Department of Cultural Affairs and the New York State Council on the Arts.

American Airlines is the official airline of Lincoln Center Theater.

Merrill Lynch is a 2007 season sponsor of Lincoln Center Theater.

LCT wishes to express its appreciation to Theatre Development Fund for its support of this production.

12/2/07

Martha Plimpton and Michael Cerveris as Imogen and Posthumus.

Photo by Paul Kolnik

Cymbeline

A NOTE ON THE PLAY

Cymbeline is one of Shakespeare's late plays, a "romance" that was perhaps created to utilize the technology of an indoor space, the Blackfriars, though we know it also played at the Globe. In these last four plays (*Pericles, The Winter's Tale* and *The Tempest* are the others) the playwright seems to be interested in resurrection, reunion and grace. Families are reunited; magical visions appear and disappear; those who were thought dead are found to be alive or are miraculously brought to life. Coincidences here are celebrated as a part of a great natural design. Myth, fairy tale and history are combined to create a landscape capable of encompassing both magic and meaning.

The continual experimenter and shape-shifter, Shakespeare here seems to be drawing together many of the themes and character types he created and reconstituted throughout his career. At the center is Imogen, his most mature female heroine. Briefly, the story begins as Imogen is imprisoned in her father's court by her wicked stepmother. Her husband Posthumus is banished, and she is "tested" by the wicked Iachimo at the behest of her husband, who is sure of her honesty. Iachimo leads Posthumus to believe that his wife has betrayed him, and events spiral out of control. As the story progresses, threads of the characters' pasts are woven into their present travails, and a clash of armies leads to visions and revelations at the play's end.

The story is set during the reign of an actual ancient Briton ruler, Kymbeline, a man of peace whose reign coincided with the birth of Christ. Its major events take place in Wales at Milford Haven, a hallowed place in British history — where the line of Tudor kings began and where the Roman settlement of the island was perhaps also born. The union of Rome and Britain is one of the outcomes of the design of *Cymbeline*.

Shakespeare uses these myths and histories, familiar to Jacobean audiences, to develop a work of synthesis, psychic shock, light humor, pageantry and renewal. His design is masterful, lock-tight, revelatory. We sense a grand design at work — and the writer places us in the position of gods: we know more than the characters do, and therefore we are asked to grant them grace, forgiveness, understanding.

Anne Cattaneo
Dramaturg, Lincoln Center Theater

UNDERSTUDIES

For Lord Cloten:
JEFFREY M. BENDER
For Caius Lucius, Jupiter and Philario:
ANTHONY COCHRANE
For Ghost of Posthumus' brother:
NOSHIR DALAL
For Guiderius:
JORDAN DEAN
For Cymbeline:
HERB FOSTER
For Posthumus Leonatus:
DAVID FURR
For Arviragus, Gentleman and
Ghost of Posthumus' brother:
ADAM GREER
For Pisanio:
EZRA KNIGHT

For Frenchman and Roman Captain:
LeROY McCLAIN
For Belarius:
DANIEL ORESKES
For Queen:
GORDANA RASHOVICH
For Helen, Ghost of Posthumus' mother and
Princess Imogen:
NANCY RODRIGUEZ
For Dutchman and Spaniard:
MICHAEL ROSSMY
For Iachimo:
GREGORY WOODDELL
For Cornelius, Gentleman,
Ghost of Posthumus' father and Philarmonus:
JEFF WOODMAN

Cast Continued

IN WALES, Living as Outcasts

Belarius, once known as Morgan, a Lord banished
  from Cymbeline's Court,
  who thereupon stole
  Cymbeline's two infant sons .....PAUL O'BRIEN
Guiderius, now called Polydore,
  lost son of Cymbeline ....DAVID FURR
Arviragus, now called Cadwal,
  his brother ....GREGORY WOODDELL

APPARITIONS

The Ghost of Posthumus' father,
  Sicilius Leonatus ....HERB FOSTER
The Ghost of his
  mother ....GORDANA RASHOVICH
The Ghosts of his two
  brothers .....NOSHIR DALAL, ADAM GREER
Jupiter ....DANIEL ORESKES

Officers, Captains, Soldiers, Lords, Ladies,
  Messengers, Attendants ...JEFFREY M. BENDER,
    JORDAN DEAN, LeROY McCLAIN,
    NANCY RODRIGUEZ, MICHAEL ROSSMY

Assistant Stage Manager ......ELIZABETH MILLER

Adam Dannheisser and Phylicia Rashad as Lord Cloten and the Queen.

Photo by Paul Kolnik

Cymbeline

Jeffrey M. Bender
Ensemble

Daniel Breaker
Gentleman

Jonathan Cake
Iachimo

Michael Cerveris
Posthumus

Anthony Cochrane
*Frenchman,
Roman Captain*

John Cullum
Cymbeline

Noshir Dalal
Ensemble

Adam Dannheisser
Cloten

Jordan Dean
Ensemble

Herb Foster
*Cornelius, Ghost of
Posthumus' father*

David Furr
Guiderius

Adam Greer
Ensemble

Michael W. Howell
Philarmonus

Ezra Knight
Caius Lucius

LeRoy McClain
Ensemble

Paul O'Brien
Belarius

Daniel Oreskes
Philario, Jupiter

John Pankow
Pisanio

Martha Plimpton
Princess Imogen

Phylicia Rashad
Queen

Gordana Rashovich
*Helen, Ghost of
Posthumus' mother*

Nancy Rodriguez
Ensemble

Michael Rossmy
Ensemble

Richard Topol
Gentleman

Gregory Wooddell
Arviragus

Jeff Woodman
Ensemble

Mark Lamos
Director

Michael Yeargan
Sets

Jess Goldstein
Costumes

Brian MacDevitt
Lighting

Mel Marvin
Original Music

Seán Curran
*Movement
Consultant*

Rick Sordelet
Fight Director

Elizabeth Smith
Vocal Consultant

André Bishop and
Bernard Gersten,
Lincoln Center
Theatre

Cymbeline

COSTUMES
Front Row (L-R):
Douglas Couture (Dresser), Patti Luther (Dresser), Kathy Karadza (Dresser), Leo Namba (Dresser), David Caudle (Dresser)

Back Row (arm on rack):
Lynn Bowling (Wardrobe Supervisor).

HAIR
(L-R):
Carrie Rohm (Hair Assistant),
Raul Hernandez (Hair Assistant),
Cindy Demand (Hair Supervisor).

FRONT OF HOUSE STAFF
Front Row (L-R):
Mim Pollock (Chief Usher), Jodi Gigliobianco (Usher), Susan Lehman (Usher).

Middle Row (L-R): Eleanor Rooks (Usher), Jeff Goldstein (Usher), Matt Barnaba (Usher).

Back Row (L-R): Nick Andois (Usher), Christine Owen (Usher), Beatrice Gilliard (Usher), Judith Fanelli (Usher), Douglas Charles (Security), Emmanuel Billingslea (Usher) and Robert De Barros (Usher).

Photos by Ben Strothmann

RUNNING CREW
Front Row (L-R):
Karl Rausenberger (Production Propman), Gary Simon (Sound Deck), Matt Altman (Followspot), Andrew Belits (Carpenter), Ray Skillin (Deck Carpenter), Bill Burke (Deck Electrician), Juan Bustamante (Deck Automation), Joe Pizzuto (Followspot), Mark Dignam (Props), John Ross (Props), Rudy Wood (Props).

Back Row (L-R):
Marc Salzberg (Production Soundman), John Weingart (Production Flyman), Bruce Rubin (Electrician/ Board Operator), Paul Gruen (Carpenter), Bill Nagle (Production Carpenter), Pat Merryman (Production Electrician), Nick Irons (Followspot), Jeff Ward (Follow Spot Operator), Scott Jackson (Props), Charlie Rausenberger (Props), Frank Linn (Electrician/Automation Tech).

Cymbeline

STAGE MANAGEMENT

(L-R): Elizabeth Miller (Assistant Stage Manager), Rachel Zack (Production Assistant), Monica A. Cuoco (Production Assistant) with Clyde the rat, Michael McGoff (Stage Manager) with Yips the dog

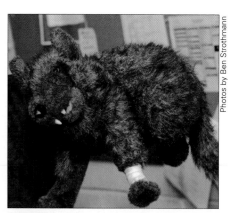

Photos by Ben Strothmann

MASCOT
Yips the dog

LINCOLN CENTER THEATER
ANDRÉ BISHOP   **BERNARD GERSTEN**
ARTISTIC DIRECTOR   **EXECUTIVE PRODUCER**

ADMINISTRATIVE STAFF
GENERAL MANAGER ....ADAM SIEGEL
Associate General
    Manager ....Jessica Niebanck
General Management
    Assistant ....Meghan Lantzy
Facilities Manager ....Alex Mustelier
Assistant Facilities
    Manager ....Michael Assalone
GENERAL PRESS AGENT ....PHILIP RINALDI
Press Associate ....Barbara Carroll
PRODUCTION MANAGER ....JEFF HAMLIN
Associate Production
    Manager ....Paul Smithyman
DIRECTOR OF
    DEVELOPMENT ....HATTIE K. JUTAGIR
Associate Director
    of Development ....Rachel Norton
Manager of Special Events and
    Young Patron Program ....Karin Schall
Grants Writer ....Neal Brilliant
Manager, Patron Program ....Sheilaja Rao
Assistant to the
    Director of Development ....Marsha Martinez
Development Assistant/
    Special Events ....Nicole Lindenbaum
Development Associate ....Raelyn Richards
DIRECTOR OF FINANCE..........DAVID S. BROWN
Controller ....Susan Knox
Systems Manager ....Stacy Valentine
Finance Assistant ....Megan Wildebour
DIRECTOR OF
    MARKETING ....LINDA MASON ROSS
Marketing Associate ....David Hatkoff
Marketing Assistant ....Kristin Miller
DIRECTOR OF EDUCATION ....KATI KOERNER
Associate Director of
    Education ....Dionne O'Dell
Assistant to the
    Executive Producer ....Barbara Hourigan
Office Assistant ....Kenneth Collins
Messenger ....Esau Burgess
Reception ....Terra Gillespie, Michelle Hamill

ARTISTIC STAFF
ASSOCIATE DIRECTORS ......GRACIELA DANIELE,
                              NICHOLAS HYTNER,
                              JACK O'BRIEN,
                              SUSAN STROMAN,
                              DANIEL SULLIVAN
DRAMATURG and DIRECTOR,
    LCT DIRECTORS LAB ....ANNE CATTANEO
CASTING DIRECTOR   DANIEL SWEE, CSA
MUSICAL THEATER
    ASSOCIATE PRODUCER...........IRA WEITZMAN
Artistic Administrator ....Julia Judge
Casting Associate ....Camille Hickman
Education/Lab Assistant ....Jill MacLean

HOUSE STAFF
HOUSE MANAGER ....RHEBA FLEGELMAN
Production Carpenter ....William Nagle
Production Electrician ....Patrick Merryman
Production Propertyman ....Karl Rausenberger
Production Flyman ....John Weingart
House Technician ....Linda Heard
Chief Usher ...............................M.L. Pollock
Box Office Treasurer ....Fred Bonis
Assistant Treasurer ....Robert A. Belkin

SPECIAL SERVICES
Advertising ....Serino-Coyne/Jim Russek
                            Roger Micone, Jill Jefferson
Principal Poster Artist ....James McMullan
Poster Art for Cymbeline ....James McMullan
Counsel ....Charles H. Googe, Esq.;
                            and Carol Kaplan, Esq. of
            Paul, Weiss, Rifkind, Wharton & Garrison
Immigration Counsel ....Theodore Ruthizer, Esq.;
                            Mark D. Koestler, Esq.
            of Kramer, Levin, Naftalis & Frankel LLP
Auditor ....Douglas Burack, CPA
                            Lutz & Carr, LLP
Insurance ....Jennifer Brown of
                            DeWitt Stern Group
Photographer ....Paul Kolnik
Travel ....Tygon Tours
Consulting Architect..........................Hugh Hardy,
            H3 Hardy Collaboration Architecture
Construction Manager ....Yorke Construction
Payroll Service ....Castellana Services, Inc.

STAFF FOR *Cymbeline*
COMPANY MANAGER........MATTHEW MARKOFF
Assistant Company Manager ...Jessica Perlmeter Cochrane
Assistant Director ....Jennifer Vellenga
Assistant to the Director ....Jeff Miller
Assistant Set Designers ....Timothy R. Mackabee,
                            Mikiko Suzuki
Associate Costume Designer ....China Lee
Assistant Costume Designer ....Matthew Hemesath
Associate Lighting Designer ....Michael O'Connor
Assistant Lighting Designer ....Jennifer Schriever
Associate Sound Design ....Drew Levy
Associate Composer ....Curtis Moore
Wig and Hair Design ....Charles LaPointe
Make-Up Designer ....Angelina Avallone
Props ....Scott Laule
Fight Captains ....Jeff Bender, Michael Rossmy
Wardrobe Supervisor ....Lynn Bowling
Dressers ....David Caudle, Douglas Couture,
            Kathy Karadza, Patti Luther, Leo Namba
Hair Supervisor ....Cindy Demand
Hair Assistants ....Carrie Rohm, Raul Hernandez
Production Assistants ....Rachel Zack,
                            Monica A. Cuoco

Vocal Consultant ....Elizabeth Smith

CREDITS
Scenery fabrication by PRG-Scenic Technologies, a division of Production Resource Group, LLC, New Windsor, NY. Show control and scenic motion control featuring Stage Command Systems® by PRG-Scenic Technologies, a division of Production Resource Group, LLC, New Windsor, NY. Costumes by Carelli Costumes and Brian Hemesath. Millinery by Carelli Costumes and Elizabeth Flauto. Boots by Fred Longtin Handmade Shoes. Sound equipment by Masque Sound. Lighting equipment from PRG Lighting. Puppets constructed by Jerard Studios, Inc. Head and body casting by Den Design. Natural herb cough drops courtesy of Ricola USA, Inc.

Visit www.lct.org

For groups of 20 or more:
Caryl Goldsmith Group Sales
(212) 889-4300

Lobby refreshments by Sweet Concessions.

Cyrano de Bergerac

First Preview: October 12, 2007. Opened: November 1, 2007.
Closed: January 6, 2008 after 21 Previews and 56 Performances.

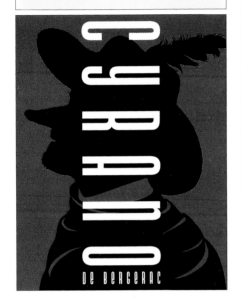

CAST

Cyrano de Bergerac .... KEVIN KLINE
Roxane .... JENNIFER GARNER
Christian de Neuvillette .... DANIEL SUNJATA
Comte de Guiche .... CHRIS SARANDON
Ragueneau .... MAX BAKER
Le Bret .... JOHN DOUGLAS THOMPSON
Roxane's Duenna/
   Sister Marthe .... CONCETTA TOMEI
Ligniere/
   Theophraste Renaudot .... EUAN MORTON
Carbon de
   Castel-Jaloux .... PETER JAY FERNANDEZ
Jodelet/A Capuchin/
   Gascony Cadet .... MACINTYRE DIXON
Vicomte de Valvert/
   Gascony Cadet .... CARMAN LACIVITA
Montfleury/Porter/Gascony Cadet .. TOM BLOOM
Marquis de Cuigy/
   Gascony Cadet .... BAYLEN THOMAS
Marquis de Brissaille/
   Gascony Cadet .... PITER MAREK
Musketeer/Gascony
   Cadet .... DANIEL STEWART SHERMAN
Lise/
   Mother Marguerite .... NANCE WILLIAMSON
Cellist/Poet/Gascony Cadet .... FRED ROSE
Theatregoer/Poet/
   Gascony Cadet .... THOMAS SCHALL
Page/Cook/Cadet/
   Guitar Player, Drums .... LUCAS PAPAELIAS

Continued on next page

RICHARD RODGERS THEATRE
UNDER THE DIRECTION OF JAMES M. NEDERLANDER AND JAMES L. NEDERLANDER

susan bristow llc   James L. Nederlander
Terry Allen Kramer   Stewart F. Lane/Bonnie Comley   Barbara Manocherian
Stephanie P. McClelland   Jon B. Platt

PRESENT

KEVIN   JENNIFER   DANIEL
KLINE   GARNER   SUNJATA

IN

CYRANO de BERGERAC

BY

EDMOND ROSTAND

TRANSLATED AND ADAPTED BY

ANTHONY BURGESS

ALSO STARRING

MAX BAKER EUAN MORTON CHRIS SARANDON JOHN DOUGLAS THOMPSON CONCETTA TOMEI

STEPHEN BALANTZIAN TOM BLOOM KEITH ERIC CHAPPELLE MacINTYRE DIXON

DAVIS DUFFIELD AMEFIKA EL-AMIN PETER JAY FERNANDEZ KATE GUYTON GINIFER KING

CARMAN LACIVITA PITER MAREK LUCAS PAPAELIAS FRED ROSE LEENYA RIDEOUT THOMAS SCHALL

DANIEL STEWART SHERMAN ALEXANDER SOVRONSKY BAYLEN THOMAS NANCE WILLIAMSON

SET DESIGN BY	COSTUME DESIGN BY	LIGHTING DESIGN BY
TOM PYE	**GREGORY GALE**	**DON HOLDER**

SOUND DESIGN BY	HAIR & WIG DESIGN BY	CASTING BY	PRESS REPRESENTATIVE
DAVID VAN TIEGHEM	**TOM WATSON**	**JV MERCANTI**	**BARLOW·HARTMAN**

TECHNICAL SUPERVISION	PRODUCTION STAGE MANAGER	GENERAL MANAGEMENT
HUDSON THEATRICAL ASSOCIATES	**MARYBETH ABEL**	**THE CHARLOTTE WILCOX COMPANY**

DIRECTED BY

DAVID LEVEAUX

11/1/07

Kevin Kline with
the Ensemble

Photo by Carol Rosegg

Cyrano de Bergerac

Cast Continued

Page/Cook/Cadet/Violin, Mandolin,
    Tin Whistle, Fife Player,
    Drums .... ALEXANDER SOVRONSKY
Foodseller/Nun .... KATE GUYTON
Actress/Sister Claire .... GINIFER KING
Theatregoer's Son/
    Gascony Cadet .... DAVIS DUFFIELD
Guard/Poet/
    Gascony Cadet ..... KEITH ERIC CHAPPELLE
A Lady/Singer/Nun .... LEENYA RIDEOUT
Gascony Cadet .... STEPHEN BALANTZIAN
Gascony Cadet .... AMEFIKA EL-AMIN

UNDERSTUDIES

For Cyrano de Bergerac:
THOMAS SCHALL
For Roxane:
GINIFER KING
For Christian de Neuvillette:
BAYLEN THOMAS
For Comte de Guiche:
STEPHEN BALANTZIAN
For Ragueneau:
DANIEL SHERMAN
For Le Bret:
STEPHEN BALANTZIAN
For Roxane's Duenna/Sister Marthe:
KATE GUYTON
For Carbon de Castel-Jaloux:
KEITH ERIC CHAPPELLE
For Capuchin/Jodelet:
THOMAS SCHALL
For Vicomte de Valvert:
KEITH ERIC CHAPPELLE
For Montfleury:
DANIEL SHERMAN
For Lise/Mother Marguerite:
KATE GUYTON

Musical arrangements and incidental music by
Lucas Papaelias and Alexander Sovronsky.
Additional musical arrangements by Fred Rose.
Vocal arrangements by Leenya Rideout.

(L-R): Jennifer Garner and Daniel Sunjata

Kevin Kline
Cyrano

Jennifer Garner
Roxane

Daniel Sunjata
Christian de Neuvillette

Max Baker
Ragueneau

Euan Morton
Ligniere/ Theophraste Renaudot

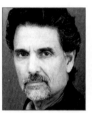

Chris Sarandon
Comte de Guiche

John Douglas Thompson
Le Bret

Concetta Tomei
Roxane's Duenna/ Sister Marthe

Stephen Balantzian
Cadet

Tom Bloom
Montfleury/Porter/ Cadet

Keith Eric Chappelle
Guard/Poet/Cadet

MacIntyre Dixon
Jodelet/Capuchin/ Cadet

Davis Duffield
Son/Cadet

Amefika El-Amin
Cadet

Peter Jay Fernandez
Carbon de Castel-Jaloux

Kate Guyton
Foodseller/Nun

Ginifer King
Actress/Sister Claire

Carman Lacivita
Vicomte de Valvert/ Cadet/Fight Captain

Piter Marek
Marquis de Brissaille/Cadet

Lucas Papaelias
Page/Cook/Cadet/ Musician

Photo by Carol Rosegg

Cyrano de Bergerac

Leenya Rideout
A Lady/Singer/Nun

Fred Rose
Cellist/Poet/Cadet

Thomas Schall
Theatregoer/Poet/Cadet

Daniel Stewart Sherman
Musketeer/Cadet

Alexander Sovronsky
Page/Cook/Cadet/Musician

Baylen Thomas
Marquis de Cuigy/Cadet

Nance Williamson
Lise/Mother Marguerite

David Leveaux
Director

Tom Pye
Scenic Design

Gregory Gale
Costume Design

Donald Holder
Lighting Design

Tom Watson
Hair and Wig Design

The Charlotte Wilcox Company
General Manager

James L. Nederlander
Producer

Stephanie P. McClelland
Producer

Terry Allen Kramer
Producer

Stewart F. Lane
Producer

Bonnie Comley
Producer

Jon B. Platt
Producer

Barbara Manocherian
Producer

STAGE MANAGEMENT AND PRODUCTION ASSISTANTS
(L-R): J. Jason Daunter (Production Assistant), Marybeth Abel (Production Stage Manager), Andrew Neal (Stage Manager), Jami Talbott (Production Assistant)

FRONT OF HOUSE STAFF
Front Row (L-R): Julian Ciego (Porter), Fran Eppy (Usher), Maureen Dabreo (Usher), Carmen Frank (Usher), Adam Souza (Merchandise)

Second Row (L-R): Kevin Corrigan (Usher), Dorothy Darby (Head Usher), Richard Dahlia (Ticket Taker), Joe Melchiorre (Usher), Beverly Thornton (Usher), Giovanny Lopez (Usher)

Third Row (L-R): Timothy Pettolina (House Manager), Dianne Hosang (Usher), Florence Coulter (Directress), Jennie Encarnacion (Usher), Jackie Corrigan (Usher)

Back Row (L-R): Fred Santore, Jr (Treasurer), Katherine Maldonado (Usher), Nadia Earle (Usher)

Photos by Ben Strothmann

Cyrano de Bergerac

CREW
Front Row (L-R): Danny Mura, Robert Guy, Steve Carver, Brian Aman, Eric Nahaczewski, Dana Gracey, Andy Bentz, Alice Ramos

Second Row (L-R): Vincent Schicchi, Kimberly Baird, Michael Louis, Mike Smanko, Arlene Watson, Robin Cook, Dan Terril

Back Row (L-R): Ronnie, Elisa Acevedo, Susan J. Wright , Tim Miller, Bill Ruger, Kevin Camus, Carlos Martinez, Jason Wilkosz, Kevin Crawford

DOORMAN
Jimmy Russell

STAFF FOR *CYRANO DE BERGERAC*

GENERAL MANAGEMENT
THE CHARLOTTE WILCOX COMPANY
Charlotte W. Wilcox
Matthew W. Krawiec   Dina Steinberg
David Roth   Steve Supeck   Margaret Wilcox

GENERAL PRESS REPRESENTATIVE
BARLOW•HARTMAN
John Barlow   Michael Hartman
Leslie Baden   Kevin Robak

COMPANY MANAGER
Alexandra Gushin

FIGHT DIRECTOR
Mark Deklin

MAKE UP & PROSTHETICS DESIGNER
Todd Kleitsch

PRODUCTION STAGE MANAGER .....Marybeth Abel
Stage Manager ....Andrew Neal
Associate Director ....Eli Gonda
Fight Captain ....Carman Lacivita
Management Associate ....Abigail Rose Solomon
Associate Scenic Designer ....Frank McCullough
Assistant Scenic Designers ....Lauren Alvarez,
Robert Braun, Christine Peters
Assistant Costume Designers ....Colleen Kesterson,
Sky Switser, Abby Taylor Redmond
Costume Intern ....Julia Broer
Associate Lighting Designers ....Hilary Manners,
Michael P. Jones
Associate Lighting Designer/
Moving Lights ....Warren Flynn
Sound System Design .........................T.J. McEvoy
Assistant Sound Designer ....David Stollings
Production Properties Coordinator ....Kathy Fabian
Associate Properties Coordinators ....Rose Howard,
Elisa Kuhar
Technical Supervisor ....Neil A. Mazzella
Associate Technical Supervisor ....Irene Wang

Production Electrician ....Brian Aman
Automation Carpenter ....Joseph Gracey
Head Electrician ....Jason Wilkosz
Head Properties ....Mike Smanko
Sound Engineer ....William Ruger
Wardrobe Supervisor ....Robert Guy
Mr. Kline's Dresser ....Susan Wright
Ms. Garner's Dresser ....Kimberly Baird
Mr. Sunjata's Dresser ....Michael Louis
Dressers ....Robin Cook, Danny Mura, Arlene Watson
Swing Dresser ....Kyle O'Connor
Laundry ....Renee Borys
Hair Supervisor ....Elisa Acevedo
Assistant Hair Supervisor ....Alice Ramos
Hairdresser ....Tim Miller
Make Up Supervisor ....Vincent Schicchi
Dialect and Voice Coach ....Deborah Hecht
Production Assistants ....J. Jason Daunter, Jami Talbott
Legal Counsel ....Levine, Plotkin & Menin LLP/
Loren Plotkin, Susan Mindell
Accountants ......Rosenberg, Neuwirth & Kuchner, CPAs/
Mark A. D'Ambrosi, Patricia Pederson
Advertising...SpotCo/
Drew Hodges, Jim Edwards,
Lauren Hunter, Josh Fraenkel
Website Design ....David Risley
Press Office Associates ....Michelle Bergmann,
Melissa Bixler, Dennis Crowley,
Tom D'Ambrosio, Bethany Larsen,
Ryan Ratelle, Wayne Wolfe
Production Photography ....Carol Rosegg
Theater Displays ....King Displays, Inc.
Banking ....JP Morgan Chase/Richard Callian
Payroll Service ....Castellana Services, Inc.
Merchandise ....Quasi World Merchandise
Insurance Consultant ....AON/Albert G. Ruben Co./
Claudia Kaufman
Computer Consultant ....Marion Finkler Taylor
Travel Services ....Andi Henig

CREDITS
Scenery and automation by Hudson Scenic Studio, Inc. Specialty furniture fabrication by Cigar Box Studios; Plumb Square. Properties by Propstar. Costumes constructed by EuroCo Costumes, Inc.; Eric Winterling, Inc.; Jennifer Love Costumes. Hosiery and undergarments by Bra*Tenders. Millinery constructed by Lynne Mackey Studio. Shoes constructed by Frederick Longtin. Custom gloves constructed by Pamela Woods. Costume painting by Hochi Asiatico Studio. Costume distressing and ageing by Jeff Fender. Custom quilting by Hall-Craft Associates. Lighting equipment supplied by PRG Lighting. Sound equipment by Masque Sound. Flame proofing by Turning Star.

Makeup provided by Make Up For Ever and Alcone Company.

SPECIAL THANKS
Special thanks to Jill B.C. Du Boff, Robin Engelman and Denys Baker.

NEDERLANDER

Chairman ....**James M. Nederlander**
President ....**James L. Nederlander**

Executive Vice President
Nick Scandalios

Vice President	Senior Vice President
Corporate Development	Labor Relations
Charlene S. Nederlander	**Herschel Waxman**

Vice President	Chief Financial Officer
Jim Boese	**Freida Sawyer Belviso**

HOUSE STAFF FOR
THE RICHARD RODGERS THEATRE
House Manager ....Timothy Pettolina
Box Office Treasurer ....Fred Santore Jr.
Assistant Treasurer ....Daniel Nitopi
Electrician ....Steve Carver
Carpenter ....Kevin Camus
Propertymaster ....Stephen F. DeVerna
Engineer ....Sean Quinn

Deuce

First Preview: April 11, 2007. Opened: May 6, 2007.
Closed August 19, 2007 after 27 Previews and 121 Performances.

CAST

(in order of appearance)

An Admirer ....MICHAEL MULHEREN
Midge Barker ....MARIAN SELDES
Leona Mullen ....ANGELA LANSBURY
Ryan Becker ....BRIAN HALEY
Kelly Short ....JOANNA P. ADLER

STANDBYS

For Midge:
JENNIFER HARMON
For Leona:
DIANE KAGAN
For Kelly:
LINDA MARIE LARSON
For Ryan/An Admirer:
ROBERT EMMET LUNNEY

THE MUSIC BOX
THE ESTATE OF IRVING BERLIN AND THE SHUBERT ORGANIZATION, OWNERS
239 W. 45th STREET

SCOTT RUDIN   STUART THOMPSON   MABERRY THEATRICALS
THE SHUBERT ORGANIZATION   ROGER BERLIND   DEBRA BLACK
BOB BOYETT   SUSAN DIETZ   DARYL ROTH

present

ANGELA LANSBURY   MARIAN SELDES

in

by

TERRENCE McNALLY

with

JOANNA P. ADLER   BRIAN HALEY   MICHAEL MULHEREN

Set Design	Costume Design	Lighting Design
PETER J. DAVISON	ANN ROTH	MARK HENDERSON
Video & Projection Design	Sound Design	Casting
SVEN ORTEL	PAUL CHARLIER	TELSEY + COMPANY
Production Stage Manager	Production Management	Company Manager
STEVEN BECKLER	AURORA PRODUCTIONS	BRIG BERNEY

Press Representative	General Management
BONEAU/BRYAN-BROWN	STP/JAMES TRINER

Directed by

MICHAEL BLAKEMORE

LIVE BROADWAY

The producers wish to express their appreciation to
Theatre Development Fund for its support of this production.

8/19/07

(L-R): Marian Seldes
and Angela Lansbury

Photo by Joan Marcus

Deuce

Angela Lansbury
Leona

Marian Seldes
Midge

Joanna P. Adler
Kelly

Brian Haley
Ryan

Michael Mulheren
An Admirer

Jennifer Harmon
Standby for Midge

Diane Kagan
Standby for Leona

Linda Marie Larson
Standby for Kelly

Robert Emmet Lunney
*Standby for Ryan/
An Admirer*

Terrence McNally
Playwright

Michael Blakemore
Director

Peter J. Davison
Set Designer

Ann Roth
Costume Design

Mark Henderson
Lighting Designer

Sven Ortel
*Video & Projection
Designer*

Paul Charlier
Sound Designer

Bernard Telsey,
Telsey + Company
Casting

Paul Huntley
Wig Designer

James Triner
General Manager

Scott Rudin
Producer

Stuart Thompson
Producer

Gerald Schoenfeld,
Chairman,
The Shubert
Organization
Producer

Roger Berlind
Producer

Debra Black
Producer

Bob Boyett
Producer

Susan Dietz
Producer

Daryl Roth
Producer

BOX OFFICE STAFF
Mike Taustine, Bob Kelly

FRONT OF HOUSE STAFF
(L-R): Joseph Lopez, Kenneth Kelly, Nic Stavola, Tom Cassano, Joe Amato, Michael Composto, Laura Scanlon, Dennis Scanlon, Jenna Scanlon, Matthew Wickert

Photos by Ben Strothmann

Deuce

STAGE AND COMPANY MANAGEMENT
(L-R): Mary MacLeod, Steve Beckler, Brig Berney.

STAGE CREW
(L-R): Dennis Maher, David Cohen, Brian McGarity, Lee Iwanski, Maeve Fiona Butler, Paul Delcioppo, Kristin Gardner.

STAFF FOR *DEUCE*

GENERAL MANAGEMENT
STUART THOMPSON PRODUCTIONS
Stuart Thompson Caroline Prugh James Triner

COMPANY MANAGER
Brig Berney

PRODUCTION MANAGEMENT
AURORA PRODUCTIONS INC.
Gene O'Donovan W. Benjamin Heller II
Bethany Weinstein Melissa Mazdra
Meghan VonVett

PRESS REPRESENTATIVE
BONEAU/BRYAN-BROWN
Chris Boneau Jim Byk Danielle Crinnion

CASTING
TELSEY + COMPANY, C.S.A.
Bernie Telsey, Will Cantler, David Vaccari,
Bethany Knox, Craig Burns,
Tiffany Little Canfield, Rachel Hoffman,
Stephanie Yankwitt, Carrie Rosson,
Justin Huff, Joe Langworth, Bess Fifer

Production Stage Manager	Steven Beckler
Stage Manager	Mary MacLeod
Sub Stage Manager	Caroline Andersen
Associate Costume Designer	Michelle Matland
Associate Lighting Designer	Daniel Walker
Associate Sound Designers	Walter Trarbach,
	Tony Smolenski IV
Makeup Consultant	Angelina Avallone
Production Electrician	Brian GF McGarity
Head Electrician	Peter Donovan
Production Sound Operator	Paul Delcioppo
Production Carpenter/	
Projections Operator	David Cohen
Wardrobe Supervisor	Kristin Gardner
Miss Lansbury's Dresser	Maeve Fiona Butler
Hair Supervisor	Anna Hoffman
Wardrobe Daywork	Kathy Guida

Production Assistant	John Bantay
Assistant to Mr. Rudin	Nathan Kelly
Assistant to Messrs. Kirdahy & Elliott	Diana Short
Assistant to Mr. Berlind	Jeffrey Hillock
Assistant to Ms. Black	Ana Pilar Camacho
Assistant to Ms. Roth	Greg Raby
Assistant to Mr. Boyett	Diane Murphy
Assistant to Ms. Dietz	Angela Sidlow
Assistant to Mr. McNally/Dramaturg	Tessa LaNeve
Assistant Director	Kim Weild
Tennis Consultant	Tom Santopietro
General Management Assistants	Megan Curren,
	Aaron Thompson
Banking	JP Morgan Chase/
	Michele Gibbons
Payroll	Castellana Services, Inc.
Accountant	Fried & Kowgios CPA's LLP/
	Robert Fried, CPA
Controller	Joseph Kubala
Insurance	DeWitt Stern Group
Legal Counsel	Loeb & Loeb Inc./
	Seth Gelblum, Esq.
Advertising	SPOTCO/
	Drew Hodges, Jim Edwards,
	Tom Greenwald, Jim Aquino, Y. Darius Suyama
Marketing	Leanne Schanzer Promotions, Inc.
Press Associates	Adrian Bryan-Brown,
	Jackie Green, Steven Padla,
	Joe Perrotta, Matt Polk, Susanne Tighe
Production Photographer	Michal Daniels
Immigration	Traffic Control Group, Inc./
	David King
Theatre Displays	King Displays, Inc.
Merchandise	Marquee Merchandise/Matt Murphy

Angela Lansbury's appearance by arrangement with
Corymore Entertainment, Inc.

Ms. Seldes' wig by Paul Huntley.

CREDITS
Scenery from Hudson Scenic Studio, Inc. Lighting equipment supplied by GSD Production Services, Inc., West Hempstead, NY. Sound equipment from Masque Sound.

Costumes constructed by Studio Rouge. Video projection system provided by Scharff Weisberg, Inc. *Deuce* rehearsed at the New 42nd Street Studios. Tennis umpire voiced by Rich Kaufman. Make-up provided by M•A•C Cosmetics.

STAFF FOR THE MUSIC BOX THEATRE
HOUSE MANAGER	Jonathan Shulman
Box Office Treasurer	Robert D. Kelly
Assistant Treasurers	Michael Taustine,
	Brendan Berberich, Victoria Radolinski
House Carpenter	Dennis Maher
House Electrician	F. Lee Iwanski
House Propertyman	Kim Garnett
Chief of Staff	Dennis Scanlon
Accountant	William C. Grother

THE SHUBERT ORGANIZATION, INC.
Board of Directors

Gerald Schoenfeld	**Philip J. Smith**
Chairman	President
Wyche Fowler, Jr.	**John W. Kluge**
Lee J. Seidler	**Michael I. Sovern**
Stuart Subotnick	

Robert E. Wankel
Executive Vice President

Peter Entin	**Elliot Greene**
Vice President –	Vice President –
Theatre Operations	Finance
David Andrews	**John Darby**
Vice President –	Vice President –
Shubert Ticketing Services	Facilities

D.S. Moynihan
Vice President – Creative Projects

Dr. Seuss' How the Grinch Stole Christmas!

First Preview: November 1, 2007. Opened: November 9, 2007.
Closed January 6, 2008 after 13 Previews and 96 Performances.

PLAYBILL

Dr. Seuss'
How The GRINCH STOLE CHRISTMAS!
THE MUSICAL

TM & ©1957, 2007 Dr. Seuss Enterprises, L.P.

CAST

(in order of appearance)

Old Max	ED DIXON
Cindy-Lou Who	
– Red Cast	CAROLINE LONDON
– White Cast	ATHENA RIPKA
Papa Who	AARON GALLIGAN-STIERLE
Mama Who	TARI KELLY
Grandpa Who	DARIN DE PAUL
Grandma Who	JAN NEUBERGER
Boo Who	
– Red Cast	JORDAN SAMUELS
– White Cast	JOHNNY SCHAFFER
Annie Who	
– Red Cast	KATIE MICHA
– White Cast	SAMI GAYLE
Danny Who	
– Red Cast	SKY FLAHERTY
– White Cast	ANDY RICHARDSON
Betty-Lou Who	
– Red Cast	JANELLE VISCOMI
– White Cast	JAHAAN AMIN

Citizens of Whoville .... HUNTER BELL,
JANET DICKINSON, CARLY HUGHES,
JOSEPHINE ROSE ROBERTS,
WILLIAM RYALL, JEFF SKOWRON

Little Whos
- Red Cast .... BRIANNA GENTILELLA,
MICHAEL HOEY, MARINA MICALIZZI,
SIMON PINCUS, TIANNA JANE STEVENS

Continued on next page

♩ **ST. JAMES THEATRE**
A JUJAMCYN THEATRE
ROCCO LANDESMAN
PRESIDENT

PAUL LIBIN	JACK VIERTEL	JORDAN ROTH
PRODUCING DIRECTOR	CREATIVE DIRECTOR	VICE PRESIDENT

RUNNING SUBWAY
EMI Music Publishing, Michael Speyer,
Allen Spivak, Janet Pailet
Amy Jen Sharyn, Maximum Entertainment
Present

Dr. Seuss'
How The GRINCH STOLE CHRISTMAS!
THE MUSICAL
Presented by Citi

Based on the book *How the Grinch Stole Christmas* by Dr. Seuss

Book & Lyrics by	Music by
Timothy Mason	**Mel Marvin**

Additional music and lyrics by Albert Hague and Dr. Seuss

Starring
Patrick Page

with
Ed Dixon   Rusty Ross

Darin De Paul, Aaron Galligan-Stierle, Tari Kelly, Caroline London, Jan Neuberger, Athena Ripka

Jahaan Amin, Juliette Allen Angelo, Hunter Bell, Caitlin Belcik, Janet Dickinson, Sky Flaherty, Eamon Foley, Sami Gayle,
Brianna Gentilella, Amy Griffin, Joseph Harrington, Michael Hoey, Carly Hughes, Liesl Jaye, Kurt Kelly, Jess LeProtto,
Marina Micalizzi, Katie Micha, Jillian Mueller, Jacob Pincus, Simon Pincus, Andy Richardson, Josephine Rose Roberts,
William Ryall, Jordan Samuels, Johnny Schaffer, Jeff Skowron, Tianna Jane Stevens, Heather Tepe, Janelle Viscomi

Set Designer	Lighting Designer	Costume Designer	Sound Designer
John Lee Beatty	Pat Collins	Robert Morgan	Acme Sound Partners
Puppet Designer	Wig/Hair Designer	Make-up Designer	Special Effects Designer
Michael Curry	Thomas Augustine	Angelina Avallone	Gregory Meeh
Musical Direction, Incidental Music and Vocal Arrangements	Orchestrator	Dance Music Arranger	Music Coordinator
Joshua Rosenblum	Michael Starobin	David Krane	Seymour Red Press
Technical Supervisor	Production Stage Manager	Casting by	Press Representative
Don S. Gilmore	Daniel S. Rosokoff	Telsey + Co.	Alison Brod Public Relations
Associate Producer	Producer	VP Marketing	General Manager
Audrey Geisel	Joshua Rosenblum	Tomm Miller	David Waggett

Co-Choreographer	Executive Producer
Bob Richard	James Sanna

Original Choreography by	Directed by
John DeLuca	Matt August

Original Production Conceived and Directed by
Jack O'Brien

Based on the production produced at The Old Globe, San Diego, California.
Jack O'Brien, Artistic Director   Louis G. Spisto, Executive Director
Originally commissioned by and produced at The Children's Theatre Company, Minneapolis, Minnesota.

Produced by permission of Dr.Seuss Enterprises. L.P.

11/9/07

The cast reprises "Who Likes Christmas?" at the finale.

Photo by Paul Kolnik

Dr. Seuss' How the Grinch Stole Christmas!

MUSICAL NUMBERS

"Who Likes Christmas?" ....Citizens of Whoville

"This Time of Year" ....Old Max and Young Max

"I Hate Christmas Eve" ....The Grinch, Young Max, Papa Who, Mama Who,
Grandma Who, Grandpa Who, Cindy-Lou Who,
Betty-Lou Who, Danny Who, Annie Who and Boo Who

"Whatchama Who" ....The Grinch, Little Whos

"Welcome, Christmas"* ....Citizens of Whoville

"I Hate Christmas Eve (Reprise)" ....The Grinch

"It's the Thought That Counts" ....Mama Who, Papa Who, Grandma Who, Grandpa Who,
Citizens of Whoville and Little Whos

"One of a Kind" ....The Grinch

"Now's the Time" ....Papa Who, Mama Who, Grandma Who, Grandpa Who

"You're a Mean One, Mr. Grinch"* ....Old Max, Young Max, The Grinch

"Santa for a Day" ....Cindy-Lou Who, The Grinch

"You're a Mean One, Mr. Grinch* (Reprise)" ....Old Max

"Who Likes Christmas? (Reprise)" ....Citizens of Whoville

"One of a Kind (Reprise)" ....Young Max, The Grinch, Cindy-Lou Who

"This Time of Year (Reprise)" ....Old Max

"Welcome, Christmas* (Reprise)" ....Citizens of Whoville

"Santa for a Day (Reprise)" ....The Grinch, Cindy-Lou Who and Citizens of Whoville

"Who Likes Christmas? (Reprise)" ....The Grinch, Young Max, Old Max and Whos Everywhere

*Music by Albert Hague and lyrics by Dr. Seuss. Published by EMI Robbins Catalog Inc.

Cast Continued

Little Whos
- White Cast .....JULIETTE ALLEN ANGELO,
CAITLIN BELCIK, JOSEPH HARRINGTON,
JILLIAN MUELLER, JACOB PINCUS
Young Max ....RUSTY ROSS
The Grinch ....PATRICK PAGE

SWINGS
KURT KELLY, EAMON FOLEY (Red Cast),
AMY GRIFFIN, LIESL JAYE (Red Cast),
JESS LePROTTO (White Cast),
HEATHER TEPE (White Cast)

UNDERSTUDIES
For Grinch:
WILLIAM RYALL, JEFF SKOWRON
For Old Max:
DARIN DE PAUL, WILLIAM RYALL
For Young Max:
HUNTER BELL, KURT KELLY
For Papa Who:
HUNTER BELL
For Grandpa Who:
JEFF SKOWRON
For Mama Who:
CARLY HUGHES
For Grandma Who:
JANET DICKINSON
For Cindy-Lou Who:
JULIETTE ALLEN ANGELO (White Cast),
TIANNA JANE STEVENS (Red Cast)

The cast sings "Santa for a Day."

ORCHESTRA

Conductor:
JOSHUA ROSENBLUM
Associate Conductor:
SUE ANSCHUTZ
Assistant Conductor:
MARK C. MITCHELL

Woodwinds:
STEVEN KENYON, ROBERT DeBELLIS,
TERRENCE COOK, JOHN WINDER
Trumpets:
CHRISTIAN JAUDES, PHILIP GRANGER,
WAYNE Du MAINE
Trombones:
WAYNE GOODMAN, ROBERT FOURNIER
Keyboards:
MARK C. MITCHELL, SUE ANSCHUTZ

Bass:
LOUIS BRUNO
Drums:
GREGORY LANDES
Percussion:
DAVE ROTH

Music Coordinator:
SEYMOUR RED PRESS
Music Copying:
EMILY GRISHMAN MUSIC
PREPARATION/EMILY GRISHMAN,
KATHARINE EDMONDS
Synthesizers Programmed by:
BRUCE SAMUELS

Photos by Paul Kolnik

Patrick Page as The Grinch.

Dr. Seuss' How the Grinch Stole Christmas!

Patrick Page
The Grinch

Ed Dixon
Old Max

Rusty Ross
Young Max

Darin De Paul
Grandpa Who

Aaron
Galligan-Stierle
Papa Who

Tari Kelly
Mama Who

Caroline London
Cindy-Lou Who - Red Cast

Jan Neuberger
Grandma Who

Athena Ripka
Cindy-Lou Who - White Cast

Juliette Allen Angelo
Ensemble

Jahaan Amin
Betty-Lou Who - White Cast

Caitlin Belcik
Ensemble - White Cast

Hunter Bell
Ensemble

Janet Dickinson
Ensemble

Sky Flaherty
Danny Who - Red Cast

Eamon Foley
Swing - Red Cast

Sami Gayle
Annie Who - White Cast

Brianna Gentilella
Ensemble - Red Cast

Amy Griffin
Swing

Joseph Harrington
Ensemble - White Cast

Michael Hoey
Ensemble - Red Cast

Carly Hughes
Ensemble

Liesl Jaye
Swing - Red Cast

Kurt Kelly
Swing

Jess LeProtto
Swing - White Cast

Marina Micalizzi
Ensemble - Red Cast

Katie Micha
Annie Who - Red Cast

Jillian Mueller
Ensemble - White Cast

Jacob Pincus
Ensemble - White Cast

Simon Pincus
Ensemble - Red Cast

Andy Richardson
Danny Who - White Cast

Josephine Rose Roberts
Ensemble

William Ryall
Ensemble

Jordan Samuels
Boo Hoo - Red Cast

Johnny Schaffer
Boo Who - White Cast

Dr. Seuss' How the Grinch Stole Christmas!

Jeff Skowron
Ensemble

Tianna Jane Stevens
*Ensemble -
Red Cast*

Heather Tepe
*Swing -
White Cast*

Janelle Viscomi
*Betty-Lou Who -
Red Cast*

Dr. Seuss
Writer

Jack O'Brien
*Original Conceiver/
Director*

Mel Marvin
Composer

Matt August
Director

John Lee Beatty
Scenic Designer

Pat Collins
Lighting Designer

Tom Clark, Mark Menard and Nevin Steinberg,
Acme Sound Partners
Sound Designer

Michael Curry
Puppet Designer

Angelina Avallone
Makeup Designer

Joshua Rosenblum
*Musical Direction,
Incidental Music
and Vocal
Arrangements/
Producer*

Michael Starobin
Orchestrator

Seymour Red Press
Music Coordinator

Bernard Telsey,
Telsey + Company
Casting

Allen Spivak
Producer

Eric Falkenstein,
Spark Productions
Producer

Louis G. Spisto
*Executive Director,
The Old Globe*

Jerry Patch
*Resident Artistic
Director,
The Old Globe*

Patrick Page (R) waits for the Whos to discover he has stolen their Christmas things in a scene from the 2006 Broadway visit of the show.

Photo by Paul Kolnik

Dr. Seuss' How the Grinch Stole Christmas!

PRODUCTION STAFF

GENERAL MANAGEMENT
RUNNING SUBWAY
David Waggett   Kathryn Schwarz

COMPANY MANAGER
Heidi Neven

GENERAL PRESS REPRESENTATIVE
Alison Brod Public Relations
Alison Brod, Jodi Hassan, Jen Roche,
Annabelle Abouab

CASTING
Telsey + Company, C.S.A.
Bernie Telsey, Will Cantler, David Vaccari,
Bethany Knox, Craig Burns,
Tiffany Little Canfield, Rachel Hoffman,
Carrie Rosson, Justin Huff, Joe Langworth,
Bess Fifer, Patrick Goodwin

MARKETING & ADVERTISING
RUNNING SUBWAY
Tomm Miller, Abby Endres,
Megan Skord, Natalie Gilhome
WE ARE GIGANTIC,
TAG WORLDWIDE,
GARDNER COMMUNICATIONS

DR. SEUSS ENTERPRISES, L.P.
Legal Representation ....Karl ZoBell, Esq./DLA Piper
Agency Representation ....Herb Cheyette/
International Creative Management, Inc.

Production Stage Manager ....Daniel S. Rosokoff
1st Assistant Stage Manager ....James D. Latus
2nd Assistant Stage Manager ....Pamela Edington
2nd Assistant Stage Manager ....Nancy Elizabeth Vest
Assistant Company Manager ....Erica Ezold
Assistant Company Manager ....Bruce Perry
Assistant Director ....Caitlin Moon
Associate Choreographer to Mr. Richard ....Shane Rhoades
Dance Captain ....Kurt Kelly
Assistant Scenic Designer ....Yoshinori Tanokura
Associate Lighting Designer ...................D.M. Wood
1st Assistant Lighting Designer ....Benjamin Travis
2nd Assistant Lighting Designer ....Lauren Phillips
Projection Consultant......................Mark Mongold
Associate Projection Consultant ....Michael Zaleski
Associate Costume Designer ....Nancy Palmatier
Assistant Costume Designer ....Sarah Smith
Assistant Sound Designer ....Jeffrey Yoshi Lee
Assistant Special Effects Designer ....Jeremy Chernick
Production Carpenter ....James Kane

Production Electrician ....Michael S. LoBue
Production Sound ....Daniel Robillard
Production Props Supervisor ....Michael Pilipski
Production Wardrobe/
    Hair Supervisor ....Thomas Augustine
Head Carpenter ....Timothy McDonough
House Fly Men ....Timothy McDonough Jr.,
                                        Ryan McDonough
Head Electrician ....Albert Sayers
Moving Light Programmer ....David Arch
Head Follow Spot Operator ....Michele Gutierrez
Head Props ....Barnett Epstein
Props ....Thomas Thomson, Richard Anderson,
                                        Robert Colgan
Deck Automation ....David Brown
Carpenters ....Tom Fitzsimons, Glen Ingram,
                                        James Devins
Follow Spot ....Robert Miller, Susan Pelkofer
Deck Electrician/Moving Light Tec ....Emile LaFargue
Deck Electrician ....Thomas Maloney
Sound Console Operator ....Paul Verity
RF Sound Tech/Back Up Mixer ....Mike Wojchik
RF Sound Tech ....Joseph Lenihan
Wardrobe Supervisor ....Robbie Amodeo
Assistant Wardrobe Supervisor ....Dawn Reynolds
Dressers ....Danny Paul, Olivia Booth,
                        Lillian Colon, Chad Jason, Tim Hanlon,
                        Jennifer Barnes, Stephanie Rudnick
Laundress ....Alexa Burt
Associate Wig Designer/Supervisor ....Carmel Vargyas
Assistant Hair Supervisor ....Brannon Gray
Wig Stylist ....Jeff Silverman, Tommy Matos
Make-up Supervisor ....Angelina Avallone
Assistant Make-up Artists ....Rex Tucker Moss,
                        Barry Berger, Craig Lindberg,
                                        Darci Snyder
Head Child Wrangler ....DeeAnne Dimmick
Child Wranglers ....Kenny Noth, Jennifer Noth
Children's Tutoring ....On Location Education
Tutors ....Beverly Brennan, Janna Kahr,
                        Jacquie Saul, Rachel Truman
Legal Counsel ....Frankfurt Kurnit Klein and Selz/
                                        Mark Merriman
Accountant ....Schall and Ashenfarb/Ira Schall
Banking ....JP Morgan Chase/
                        Brenda Steinacher, Margaret Wong
Insurance ....AON/Albert G. Ruben Company/
                                        Claudia Kauffman
Physical Therapy ....Performing Arts Physical Therapy
Theatre Displays ....King Displays, Inc.
Concession Manager ....Thia Calloway
Payroll Services ....Axium International/Ginger Hege
Sponsorship ....Revolution Marketing/Andrew Klein
Promotional Merchandising ....Max Merchandising/
                        Randi Grossman, Meridith Maskara

CREDITS
Scenery by Hudson Scenic Studio. Scenery built and painted by F&D Scene Changes LTD. Lighting equipment and special lighting effects by PRG Lighting. Sound equipment from Sound Associates. Props by Spoon Group. Projection equipment from Scharff-Weisberg. Special effects equipment from Jauchem & Meeh, Inc. Costumes executed by Tricorne. Shoes by Capezio, Capri of California, Spears Specialty Clown Shoes, Foot-So-Port. Costume painting by Hochi Asiatico. Fabric dying by Gene Mignola. Grinch finger extensions by Zoe Morsette. Grinch heart by Craig Griggs. Millinery by Rodney Gordon. Knitting by Karen Eifert. Special projects by Material Girl/Arnold Levine. Wigs made by Bob Kelly Wig Creations and Augustine Studios. Emergen-C health and energy drink mix supplied by Alacer Corp. Natural herb cough drops courtesy of Ricola USA, Inc. Hosiery and undergarments supplied by Bra*Tenders.

FOR RUNNING SUBWAY
Executive Producer ....James Sanna
Producer ....Joshua Rosenblum
Producer ....Stacey Lender
General Manager ....David Waggett
Vice President Marketing ....Tomm Miller
Director of Marketing ....Abby Endres
Assistant General Manager ....Kathryn Schwarz
Marketing Coordinator ....Megan Skord
Assistant Producer ....Natalie Gilhome

SPECIAL THANKS
James Claffey Jr., Tom Walsh, Frank Gallagher, Naomi Major, Louise Foisy, Martin Schulman, Mary Landolfi, Harvey Mars, Disney Theatrical Productions

JUJAMCYN THEATERS
ROCCO LANDESMAN
President

PAUL LIBIN   **JACK VIERTEL**   **JORDAN ROTH**
Producing Director   Creative Director   Vice President

DANIEL ADAMIAN   **JENNIFER HERSHEY**
General Manager   Director of Operations

MEREDITH VILLATORE   **JERRY ZAKS**
Chief Financial Officer   Resident Director

STAFF FOR THE ST. JAMES THEATRE
Manager ....Daniel Adamian
Treasurer ....Vincent Sclafani
Carpenter ....Timothy McDonough
Propertyman ....Barnett Epstein
Electrician ....Albert Sayers

Dr. Seuss' How the Grinch Stole Christmas!
SCRAPBOOK

Photos by Aubrey Reuben

1. (L-R): Patrick Page takes his curtain call on opening night with Rusty Ross.
2. Director Jack O'Brien enjoys a Grinch-colored libation at the opening night party at the Hawaiian Tropic Zone.

Correspondent: Patrick Page, "The Grinch."

Opening Night Messages and Gifts: Opening night was so exciting, but we'd been hearing all these rumors of a strike. We didn't even know if our curtain would go up. So there was an increased excitement and tension when the curtain finally did go up. Faxes came in from all the other shows, which can be so exciting when it's your first Broadway show and you look for people's signatures who you recognize. The kids in our show all got together and they bought great red fleece robes with *How the Grinch Stole Christmas!* emblems on them with each person's name on it.

Memorable Celebrity Visitor: The first night visitor was Teri Hatcher and her daughter and that was a blast. She came to the dressing room and we took a lot of pictures.

Favorite In-Theatre Gathering Place: "There's no green room here at the St. James Theatre, so the hangout for our kids is on the stairs. When I'm coming down the stairs to go to my entrance, they're all sitting all along the stairs talking to each other. All of the kids and a lot of the adults have taken up knitting to raise money for charity, so everybody you pass has a ball of yarn and needles."

Favorite Off-Site Hangout: Sometimes we'll go to Angus McIndoe because it's right next door and they put in a children's menu just for us. I think it's chicken fingers and spaghetti and stuff like that. Sardi's did the same thing—very smart to do for these kids. But to tell you the truth, there isn't a lot of hanging out because we're on a special contract that lets us do fifteen shows a week. So when you finish an evening show and you know you have to be back in the morning in time for an 11 AM matinee, it's pretty much go home and go to bed. The kids are also in tutoring this whole time.

Who Got the Gypsy Robe: Bill Ryall.

Favorite Snack Food: We have catering between shows from Starlight Deli and Tony's.

Favorite Therapy: We have a physical therapist, Sean, who comes every Saturday. And there's always the Ricolas backstage.

Mascot: My dog Sophie. She's a white Maltese.

Memorable Ad-Libs: There are a lot of ad-libs in our show because the audience is full of kids. Example: At the end when I'm struggling to get out the words "Merry Christmas" for the first time the kids will yell out "Christmas! Christmas!" So I tell them, "Don't rush me!"

Cell Phone Issues: We've got a great announcement at the beginning of the show. Bill Ryall says, "Turn the phones off, way off, you betcha! Turn the phones off or the Grinch just might getcha!" That scares 'em because I do go out in the audience several times, and I think they think I really will come and take the phones. I haven't yet—but I would. I absolutely would.

Memorable Press Encounter: We had "The CBS Early Show" and it was completely freezing outside and the wind was blowing like crazy. We had rehearsed a combination of "Santa for a Day" and "You're a Mean One, Mr. Grinch" but when we got there they said they wanted us to do four numbers. So that was certainly memorable.

Memorable Stage Door Fan Encounters: On the first day of the strike we had all those kids who were crying in front of the theatre. I'd go up to them and say, "I'm Patrick, I play the Grinch, and I just want to tell you I'm sorry there isn't a show." I'd sing a little song and sometimes give them a hug. And sometimes they did smile. That was memorable.

Heaviest/Hottest Costume: Mine! My amazing dresser, Danny Paul, has a bunch of ice packs, and a handheld fan. When I come off, he puts the fan on me and takes these big ice packs and stuffs them in my costume. So I've got ice in my back and ice on my head. He puts them in the hat and leaves them in the freezer all night, so when I put the hat on, it's actually frozen. It goes around my head and cools my head.

Who Wears the Least: For some reason, one night when Carly went on as Mama Who, her dress didn't have sleeves, which I thought was very weird for the middle of December.

Catchphrases Only the Company Would Recognize: "One take" and "Captain Kurt."

Story Everyone Tells: The strike, of course. And you know half our cast went to the courthouse to hear the decision come down to reopen the show. That's the most memorable thing.

Nicknames: Kurt Kelly the dance captain is "Captain Kurt." The costume designer named each of the Whos for the costume renderings so, for example, one Who who wears a watch became "Timey Who."

Backstage Sweethearts: I think some of the kids have gotten kind of sweet on each other.

Ghostly Encounters: None yet, but I'm in Ethel Merman's dressing room so I'm waiting to see the ghost of Merman.

Superstitions That Turned Out To Be True: The "Scottish Play" one is true. Rusty, who plays young Max, said the name of the play, so I made him go out in the freezing cold, turn around three times, spit and come back in. But even then I pulled something in my leg that night.

Coolest Thing About Being in This Show: Having our show reopened by a court order. I mean, that happens only once in your life.

Special Memory: When we sang "Who Likes Christmas?" and "Welcome, Christmas" outside the stage door on the first day of the strike. There was a picket line there and the whole audience, and, you know, there were a lot of tears in people's eyes.

The Drowsy Chaperone

First Preview: April 3, 2006. Opened: May 1, 2006.
Closed: December 30, 2007 after 32 Previews and 674 Performances.

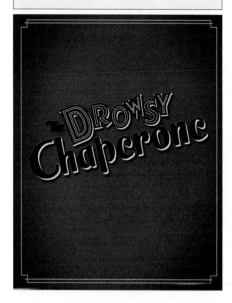

CAST
(in order of appearance)

Man in Chair	BOB SAGET
Mrs. Tottendale	JO ANNE WORLEY
Underling	PETER BARTLETT
Robert Martin	TROY BRITTON JOHNSON
George	PATRICK WETZEL
Feldzieg	GERRY VICHI
Kitty	JENNIFER SMITH
Gangster #1	JASON KRAVITS
Gangster #2	GARTH KRAVITS
Aldolpho	DANNY BURSTEIN
Janet Van De Graaff	MARA DAVI
The Drowsy Chaperone	BETH LEAVEL
Trix	KECIA LEWIS-EVANS
Super	MATT WALL
Ensemble	LINDA GABLER, DALE HENSLEY, MATT WALL, JOANNA YOUNG

SWINGS

JAY DOUGLAS, STACIA FERNANDEZ,
LINDA GRIFFIN,
MAMIE PARRIS, KILTY REIDY

Dance Captain:
LINDA GABLER
Assistant Dance Captain:
JAY DOUGLAS

Continued on next page

Continued on next page

MARQUIS THEATRE

UNDER THE DIRECTION OF JAMES M. NEDERLANDER AND JAMES L. NEDERLANDER

Kevin McCollum   Roy Miller   Boyett Ostar Productions
Stephanie McClelland   Barbara Freitag   Jill Furman

present

The DROWSY Chaperone

Music and Lyrics by
Lisa Lambert and Greg Morrison

Book by
Bob Martin and Don McKellar

by Special Arrangement with **Paul Mack**

Starring

Peter Bartlett   Danny Burstein   Mara Davi   Troy Britton Johnson
Garth Kravits   Jason Kravits   Beth Leavel   Kecia Lewis-Evans
Bob Saget   Jennifer Smith   Gerry Vichi   Patrick Wetzel   JoAnne Worley

and

Jay Douglas   Stacia Fernandez   Linda Gabler   Linda Griffin
Dale Hensley   Mamie Parris   Kilty Reidy   Matt Wall   Joanna Young

Scenic Design	Costume Design	Lighting Design	Sound Design
David Gallo	Gregg Barnes	Ken Billington Brian Monahan	Acme Sound Partners

Casting	Hair Design	Makeup Design
Telsey + Company	Josh Marquette	Justen M. Brosnan

Orchestrations by	Dance and Incidental Music Arrangements by	Music Direction and Vocal Arrangements by
Larry Blank	Glen Kelly	Phil Reno

Music Coordinator	Production Supervisors	Production Stage Manager
John Miller	Brian Lynch Chris Kluth	Karen Moore

Associate Producers	Press Representative	Marketing	General Management
Sonny Everett Mariano Tolentino, Jr.	Boneau/Bryan-Brown	TMG - The Marketing Group	The Charlotte Wilcox Company

Directed and Choreographed by
Casey Nicholaw

American Premiere produced at the Ahmanson Theatre by Center Theatre Group, LA's Theatre Company

The producers wish to express their appreciation to Theatre Development Fund for its support of this production.

LIVE BROADWAY

10/19/07

(L-R): Bob Saget and Mara Davi.

Photo by Joan Marcus

The Drowsy Chaperone

MUSICAL NUMBERS

Overture .... Orchestra
"Fancy Dress" .... Company
"Cold Feets" .... Robert, George
"Show Off" .... Janet, Company
"As We Stumble Along" .... Drowsy Chaperone
"I Am Aldolpho" .... Aldolpho, Drowsy Chaperone
"Accident Waiting to Happen" .... Robert, Janet
"Toledo Surprise" .... Gangsters, Feldzieg, Kitty, Aldolpho,
George, Janet, Robert, Underling,
Mrs. Tottendale, Drowsy Chaperone and Company
"Message From a Nightingale" .... Kitty, Gangsters, Aldolpho, Drowsy Chaperone
"Bride's Lament" .... Janet, Company
"Love Is Always Lovely in the End" .... Mrs. Tottendale, Underling
"I Do, I Do in the Sky" .... Trix and Company
"As We Stumble Along" (Reprise) .... Company

(L-R): JoAnne Worley and Peter Bartlett.

Photo by Joan Marcus

The Playbill Broadway Yearbook 2007-2008

UNDERSTUDIES

For Man in Chair:
JAY DOUGLAS, PATRICK WETZEL
For Janet:
MAMIE PARRIS, JOANNA YOUNG
For Robert:
JAY DOUGLAS, MATT WALL
For The Drowsy Chaperone:
STACIA FERNANDEZ, MAMIE PARRIS
For Mrs. Tottendale:
STACIA FERNANDEZ, LINDA GABLER,
LINDA GRIFFIN
For Aldolpho:
JAY DOUGLAS, DALE HENSLEY
For Underling:
DALE HENSLEY, KILTY REIDY
For Feldzieg:
JAY DOUGLAS, DALE HENSLEY
For Kitty:
MAMIE PARRIS, JOANNA YOUNG
For George:
KILTY REIDY, MATT WALL
For Gangsters #1 and #2:
DALE HENSLEY, KILTY REIDY, MATT WALL
For Trix:
STACIA FERNANDEZ, LINDA GABLER,
LINDA GRIFFIN

ORCHESTRA

Conductor:
PHIL RENO
Associate Conductor:
LAWRENCE GOLDBERG

Reeds:
EDWARD JOFFE, TOM MURRAY,
TOM CHRISTENSEN, RON JANNELLI
Trumpets:
DAVE STAHL, BRIAN O'FLAHERTY,
JEREMY MILOSZEWICZ
Trombones:
STEVE ARMOUR, JEFF NELSON
Guitar:
ED HAMILTON
Bass:
MICHAEL KUENNEN
Drums:
BILLY MILLER
Percussion:
BILL HAYES
Keyboards:
MATT PERRI, LAWRENCE GOLDBERG

Music Coordinator:
JOHN MILLER

The Drowsy Chaperone

Peter Bartlett
Underling

Danny Burstein
Aldolpho

Mara Davi
Janet Van De Graaff

Troy Britton Johnson
Robert Martin

Garth Kravits
Gangster #2

Jason Kravits
Gangster #1

Beth Leavel
The Drowsy Chaperone

Kecia Lewis-Evans
Trix

Bob Saget
Man in Chair

Jennifer Smith
Kitty

Gerry Vichi
Feldzieg

Patrick Wetzel
George

JoAnne Worley
Mrs. Tottendale

Jay Douglas
Swing

Stacia Fernandez
Swing

Linda Gabler
Ensemble

Linda Griffin
Swing

Dale Hensley
Ensemble

Mamie Parris
Swing

Kilty Reidy
Swing

Matt Wall
Ensemble, Super

Joanna Young
Ensemble

Lisa Lambert
Music & Lyrics

Greg Morrison
Music & Lyrics

Bob Martin
Book

Don McKellar
Book

Casey Nicholaw
Director & Choreographer

David Gallo
Scenic Design

Gregg Barnes
Costume Design

Ken Billington
Co-Lighting Design

Brian Monahan
Co-Lighting Design

Tom Clark, Mark Menard and Nevin Steinberg,
Acme Sound Partners
Sound Design

Bernard Telsey,
Telsey + Company
Casting

Josh Marquette
Hair Design

The Drowsy Chaperone

Justen M. Brosnan
Makeup Design

Larry Blank
Orchestrations

Phil Reno
*Music Direction &
Vocal Arrangements*

John Miller
Music Coordinator

Brian Lynch
*Production
Supervisor*

Casey Hushion
Assistant Director

Josh Rhodes
*Assistant
Choreographer*

Kevin McCollum
Producer

Roy Miller
Producer

Bob Boyett
Producer

Bill Haber,
OSTAR Enterprises
Producer

Stephanie P.
McClelland
Producer

Barbara Heller
Freitag
Producer

Jill Furman
Producer

Sonny Everett
Associate Producer

Mariano Tolentino, Jr.
Associate Producer

Charlotte Wilcox,
The Charlotte Wilcox
Company
General Manager

Andrea Chamberlain
Swing

Jonathan Crombie
Man in Chair

John Glover
Man in Chair

Tripp Hanson
Swing

Stacey Todd Holt
Swing

Janine LaManna
Janet Van De Graaff

Kate Loprest
Swing

Brian Marcum
Swing

Joey Sorge
Super, Ensemble

Lenny Wolpe
Feldzieg

Tripp Hanson
Swing

Joey Sorge
Super, Ensemble

Cindy Williams
Mrs. Tottendale

The Drowsy Chaperone

BOX OFFICE STAFF
(L-R): Larry Waxman, John Giebler, Richie Thigpen and John Rooney.

Photos by Ben Strothmann

WARDROBE DEPARTMENT
Top Row (L-R): Barry Hoff, Joby Horrigan (Assistant Wardrobe Supervisor), Charlie Catanese, Mel Hansen, Julien Havard.

Bottom Row (L-R): Pat Sullivan, John Glover (actor), Lyssa Everett, Margiann Flanagan, Philip R. Rolfe and Terri Purcell (Wardrobe Supervisor).

FRONT OF HOUSE STAFF
Top Row (L-R): (Ushers) Phyllis Weinsaft, Odalis Concepcion, Charlie Spencer, Stanley Seidman, Barbara Corey.

Middle Row (L-R): Lea Lefler, Lulu Caso, David Calhoun (House Manager), Ava Probst (Associate House Manager), Huey Dill.

Bottom Row (L-R): Carol Reilly, John Clark, and Nancy Diaz.

The Drowsy Chaperone

Photos by Ben Strothmann

STAGE CREW
Front Row (L-R): John Fullum, Chris Weigel, Augie Mericola, Kenny Sheehan.

Middle Row (L-R): Joe Sardo, Tim Donovan, Tim Shea, Joe Ippolito, Cheyenne Benson, Duke Wilson, Roland Weigel.

Back Row (L-R): Rick Poulin, Brady Jarvis and Keith Buchanan.

HAIR DEPARTMENT
(L-R): Sandy Schlender, Paul Zaya and Carla Muniz.

STAGE AND COMPANY MANAGEMENT
(L-R): Jeffrey Rodriguez (Production Assistant), Karen Moore (Production Stage Manager), Rachel McCutchen (Assistant Stage Manager) and Robert Jones (Assistant Company Manager).

ORCHESTRA
Front Row (L-R): Dave Stahl, Tom Murray.

Middle Row (L-R): Bill Hayes, Lawrence Goldberg (Associate Conductor), Matt Perri, Jeff Nelson.

Back Row (L-R): Steve Armour, Perry Cavari, Jeremy Miloszewicz, Ray Kilday, Ed Joffe, Ron Jannelli, Ed Hamilton, Glenn Drewes, Phil Reno (Music Director and Conductor) and Julie Ferrara.

The Drowsy Chaperone

STAFF FOR *THE DROWSY CHAPERONE*

GENERAL MANAGEMENT
THE CHARLOTTE WILCOX COMPANY
Charlotte W. Wilcox

Matthew W. Krawiec	Dina Steinberg
Steve Supeck	Margaret Wilcox
Beth Cochran	David Michael Roth

GENERAL PRESS REPRESENTATION
BONEAU/BRYAN-BROWN

Chris Boneau	Joe Perrotta
Heath Schwartz	Danielle Crinnion

COMPANY MANAGER
Seth Marquette

ASSISTANT COMPANY MANAGER
Robert E. Jones

CASTING
Telsey + Company, C.S.A.
Bernie Telsey, Will Cantler, David Vaccari,
Bethany Knox, Craig Burns,
Tiffany Little Canfield, Rachel Hoffman,
Stephanie Yankwitt, Carrie Rosson,
Justin Huff, Joe Langworth, Bess Fifer

PRODUCTION
STAGE MANAGER ....KAREN MOORE
Stage Manager ....Joshua Halperin
Assistant Stage Manager ....Rachel S. McCutchen
Assistant Director ....Casey Hushion
Assistant Choreographer ....Josh Rhodes
Asst. to Mr. McCollum ....Caitlyn Thomson
Assts. to Mr. Boyett ....Diane Murphy,
Michael Mandell
Assts. to Mr. Haber ....Theresa Pisanelli,
Kristen Jackson
Boyett-Ostar Development
and Strategic Planning .... Jan Gura
Associate Scenic Designer ....Charlie Smith
Assistant Scenic Designers ....Zhanna Gurvich,
Dustin O'Neill, Gaetane Bertol,
Bill Beilke, Mary Hamrick
Associate Costume Designer ....Sky Switser
Assistants to Costume Designers ....Cathy Parrot,
Sarah Sophia Turner
Costume Intern ....Katharine Sullivan
Associate Lighting Designer ....Stephen N. Boulmetis
Assistant Lighting Designer ....Anthony Pearson
Assistant Sound Designer ....Nick Borisjuk
Production Carpenter ....Chris Kluth
Production Properties ....George Wagner
Moving Lights Programmer ....Hillary Knox
Automation Flyman ....Cheyenne Benson
Production Electrician ....Keith Buchanan
Assistant Electrician ....Brady Jarvis
Production Sound...............................Daryl Kral
Head Properties ....Augie Mericola
Wardrobe Supervisor ....Terri Purcell
Assistant Wardrobe Supervisor ....Joby Horrigan
Dressers ....Michael Berglund, Charles Catanese,
Lyssa Everett, Margiann Flanagan,
Mel Hansen, Julien Havard,
Barry Hoff, Philip R. Rolfe,
Pat Sullivan

Hair Supervisor ....Richard Orton
Hairdressers ....Carla Muniz, Sandy Schlender,
Paul Zaya
Assistant to John Miller ....Kelly M. Rach
Synthesizer Programmer ....Jim Abbott
Music Preparation Service ....Hotstave, Ltd.
Music Copyists ....Anixter Rice Music Services
Rehearsal Pianists ....Lawrence Goldberg,
Glen Kelly, Matt Perri
Rehearsal Drummer ....Perry Cavari
Production Assistants ....Jeffrey Rodriguez,
Rachel Zack
Music Production Assistant ....Colleen Darnell
LA Casting ....Amy Lieberman, C.S.A.
NAMT Presentation Casting ....Cindi Rush Casting
Legal Counsel ....Levine, Plotkin & Menin LLP/
Loren Plotkin, Susan Mindell
Accountants ....Fried & Kowgios LLP/
Robert Fried
Advertising ....SpotCo/
Drew Hodges, Jim Edwards,
Pete Milano, Pete Duffy
Marketing ....TMG – The Marketing Group/
Tanya Grubich, Laura Matalon,
Meghan Zaneski
Press Representative Staff ....Adrian Bryan-Brown,
Jim Byk, Ian Bjorklund,
Brandi Cornwell, Adriana Douzos,
Jackie Green, Juliana Hannett,
Hector Hernandez, Jessica Johnson,
Kevin Jones, Amy Kass, Aaron Meier,
Christine Olver, Steven Padla,
Linnae Petruzzelli, Matt Polk,
Matt Ross, Susanne Tighe
Website Design ....Situation Marketing/
Damian Bazadona, Roger Ziegler,
Joey Oliva
Banking .............................J.P. Morgan Chase/
Stephanie Dalton
Payroll ....Castellana Services Inc./
Lance Castellana, Norman Seawell,
James Castellana
Group Sales ....Group Sales Box Office
Merchandising ....Max Merchandising LLC
Travel Arrangements ....Tzell Travel
Insurance Broker ....................D.R. Reiff Associates/
Dennis R. Reiff, Sonny Everett
Computer Consultant ....Marion Taylor
Opening Night Coordinator ....Tobak Lawrence Co./
Joanna B. Koondel, Suzanne Tobak
Production Photographer ....Joan Marcus
Gable and Stein Historian ....David Goldsmith
Theatre Displays ....King Displays

CREDITS
Scenery by Hudson Scenic Studio, Inc. Automation by Hudson Scenic Studio, Inc. Costume construction by Barbara Matera Limited, Carelli Costumes and Rodney Gordon. Custom made shoes built by Capri Shoes, J.C. Theatrical and T.O. Dey. Special thanks to Bra*Tenders for hosiery and undergarments. Chinese fan and feathers provided by American Plume and Fancy Feathers, New York, NY. Lights by Production Resource Group. Sound equipment by Sound Associates. Wigs by Ray Marston Wig Studios and Anne Devon Chambless. Natural herb cough drops courtesy of Ricola USA, Inc. Emergen-C super energy booster provided by Alacer Corp. Crash cymbals

courtesy of PAISTE America, Brea, CA. Rehearsed at the New 42nd Street Studios.

SPECIAL THANKS
Best Man Productions
Matt Watts
Frederick P. Bimbler, Esq.
Mirvish Productions
Michael Jenkins

Makeup provided by
M•A•C Cosmetics

www.DrowsyChaperone.com

THE DROWSY CHAPERONE was presented

n|a|m|t NATIONAL ALLIANCE *for* MUSICAL THEATRE

at the 2004 Festival of New Musicals
Kathy Evans, Executive Director   www.namt.org

NEDERLANDER

Chairman	**James M. Nederlander**
President	**James L. Nederlander**

Executive Vice President
Nick Scandalios

Vice President Corporate Development	Senior Vice President Labor Relations
Charlene S. Nederlander	**Herschel Waxman**

Vice President	Chief Financial Officer
Jim Boese	**Freida Sawyer Belviso**

STAFF FOR THE MARQUIS THEATRE
Manager ....David Calhoun
Associate Manager ....Ava Probst
Treasurer ....Rick Waxman
Assistant Treasurer ....John Rooney
Carpenter ....Joseph P. Valentino
Electrician...................................James Mayo
Property Man ....Roland Weigel

(L-R): Bob Saget and Beth Leavel.

Photo by Joan Marcus

The Drowsy Chaperone
SCRAPBOOK

Correspondent: Mara Davi: "Janet Van De Graaff"

Memorable Opening Night Fax: Mara received a fax from everyone over at *A Chorus Line*. That stayed on her wall for the rest of the run.

Opening Night Gifts: When Mara opened in the show, Beth Leavel gave her an angel which she kept at the theatre to watch over her, and Linda Gabler gave her a beautiful jewelry box (something Janet Van De Graaff definitely would have had).

Most Exciting Celebrity Visitor and What They Did/Said: Bob Saget came backstage after the show, shook everyone's hand enthusiastically and said "I have a lot of work to do." That was our first hint that he might be coming into the show. Elaine Stritch came backstage after the show. Sutton Foster was still there at this point. Sutton had on a bandana to cover up her wig cap. They were introduced and Ms. Stritch said "Oh, I thought you were the maid."

Who Wrote the Easter Bonnet Sketch: Stacia Fernandez.

"Carols for a Cure" Carol: "Drowsy on Christmas Day" by Garth Kravits and Lisa Lambert.

Which Actor Performed the Most Roles in This Show: The Swings of course. They covered everyone! And this was mainly a principal show. Only four fantastic ensemble members.

Who Has Done the Most Shows in Their Career: Jennifer Smith.

Special Backstage Rituals: We had a prayer circle before every show backstage left. It was a great way to get grounded and come together before the show. At the end of "Show Off" when everyone was frozen looking down into the hole in the stage, Stage Management would hold up a word scramble or a YouTube video for people to enjoy in the freeze. Also, every day there was a tableau during "Toledo Surprise" staged by our wardrobe supervisor Terri Purcell and her sidekicks. There were theme weeks. Broadway shows, Broadway flops, TV from the 60's, Grammy Award-winning songs, Oscar-winning movies...YOU NAME IT. It was very elaborate, with props and costumes.

Favorite Moment During Each Performance: When the Man in Chair starts singing "Stumble Along" and we all noticed him and stood looking at each other. It united us as a company. Watching Beth Leavel sing "Stumble" from the wings. When Danny Burstein would purrrr.

Favorite In-Theatre Gathering Place: Wherever there was food and a crowd. Our "Arabian Room" greenroom, especially on Bagel Saturday (a Sutton Foster tradition). Our wardrobe room—everyone adored the wardrobe department, headed by Terri Purcell and Joby Horrigan. It was extra crowded during Sunday Brunch. Also, stage management was a gathering place. Our lobby for Friday night themed parties. And the offstage monitor. We would take a rainbow of dry erase markers and

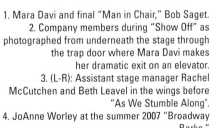

1. Mara Davi and final "Man in Chair," Bob Saget.
2. Company members during "Show Off" as photographed from underneath the stage through the trap door where Mara Davi makes her dramatic exit on an elevator.
3. (L-R): Assistant stage manager Rachel McCutchen and Beth Leavel in the wings before "As We Stumble Along".
4. JoAnne Worley at the summer 2007 "Broadway Barks."

circle the BLING in the audience on the monitor, or put elaborate drawings of costumes on our conductors!

Favorite Off-Site Hangout: Bar Centrale and Julien's house...it's always fun at LOVE Julien.

Favorite Snack Food: Pink Cake from Amy's Bread, and anything Gerry Vichi brought in. Almost every performance he would provide food for the company in the greenroom. It was always different: popcorn, chocolate, cake, cookies, cheese and meat, etc.

Mascot: Charlie Kravits

Favorite Therapy: Emergen-C. Our fantastic physical therapy provided by PhysioArts. Also, a group of us loved going to Reforming NY Pilates.

Catchphrases Only the Company Would Recognize: "Why ya' gotta put the line?" "Kick ball Lean." "Nicholaw, Nicholaw." "Salt and Pepper."

Most Memorable Ad-Lib: One night, Jay Douglas was playing Man in Chair. His microphone was not working right from the start. After the lights came up he continued the monologue but a stage manager was just off stage telling him to exit to get his mic fixed, so

The Drowsy Chaperone
SCRAPBOOK

Photos courtesy Mara Davi

1. The entire company poses in front of the Marquis Theatre.
2. (L-R): Mara Davi and television icon Cindy Williams as "Mrs. Tottendale."
3. (L-R): Joey Sorge, Mara Davi and Garth Kravits in costume for Mara's Olympic production number "Show Off."

he said "I always pee before I play my records" and left. When he came back on, his mic was working and he sat down with much relief and said "Ah, that's better." The audience cheered for two reasons!

Fastest Costume Changes: "Show Off." All of "Show Off."

Heaviest Costume: Janet's red "Show Off" opera coat, the elaborate headpieces in "Nightingale."

Hottest Costume: Aldolpho's Chinese robe in "Nightingale."

Who Wore the Least: The pastry chefs' bathing suits in "Show Off."

Which Orchestra Member Played the Most Instruments and What Were They: Ed Joffe (6 instruments): Piccolo, flute, Bb clarinet, Eb clarinet, soprano sax, alto sax.

Which Orchestra Member Played the Most Consecutive Performances Without a Sub: Dave Stahl (trumpet) - 54 performances.

Memorable Directorial Note: Keep it breezy.

Company In-Joke: Applegate (someone eating Eddie's apple).

Company Legends: Also Applegate. Who ate Eddie's apple? The world may never know…

Sweethearts Within the Company: Lyssa Everett and Jess Ferrara.

Coolest Things About Being in This Show: IT was a family to EVERYONE. And that family kept growing. During the run two weddings were planned, five babies were born, and three more are on the way!

Stacia Fernandez says: "Working with such a group of pros. The average age of this company in the beginning was 42!! That's experience. And also? Working with friends. And watching my pals Beth Leavel and Casey Nicholaw rise to this amazing place."

The Farnsworth Invention

First Preview: October 15, 2007. Opened: December 3, 2007.
Closed March 2, 2008 after 34 Previews and 104 Performances.

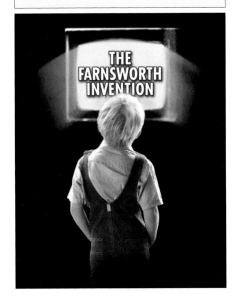

CAST
(in alphabetical order)

David Sarnoff .... HANK AZARIA
Lizette Sarnoff, Mary Pickford
   and others .... NADIA BOWERS
Pem's Father, Cliff Gardner
   and others .... KYLE FABEL
Atkins, Walter Gifford, Douglas Fairbanks
   and others .... MAURICE GODIN
Young Philo T. Farnsworth
   and others .... CHRISTIAN M. JOHANSEN
Wilkins, Analyst and others ...... AARON KROHN
George Everson, Vladimir Zworykin
   and others .... BRUCE McKENZIE
Young David Sarnoff
   and others .... MALCOLM MORANO
Stan Willis and others .... SPENCER MOSES
Leslie Gorrell
   and others .... MICHAEL MULHEREN
Justin Tolman, Jim Harbord, Doctor
   and others .... JIM ORTLIEB
Sarnoff's Father, Simms, Lippincott,
   Houston Control
   and others .... MICHAEL PEMBERTON
Betty and others .... KATHARINE POWELL
Harlan Honn, Radio Announcer, Lennox
   and others .... STEVE ROSEN
Philo T. Farnsworth .... JIMMI SIMPSON
Russian Officer, William Crocker
   and others .... JAMES SUTORIUS
Sarnoff's Mother, Pem's Mother, Agnes Farnsworth,
   Mina Edison and others .... MARGOT WHITE

Continued on next page

☆ THE MUSIC BOX
239 W. 45th Street
A Shubert Organization Theatre

Gerald Schoenfeld, *Chairman*　　Philip J. Smith, *President*

Robert E. Wankel, *Executive Vice President*

Dodger Properties and Steven Spielberg for Rabbit Ears, LLC
in association with Fred Zollo and Jeffrey Sine, Dancap Productions, Latitude Link/Pelican Group
present

Hank Azaria　　Jimmi Simpson

in

THE FARNSWORTH INVENTION

a new play by

Aaron Sorkin

with

Nadia Bowers　Kyle Fabel　Maurice Godin　Christian M. Johansen
Aaron Krohn　Bruce McKenzie　Malcolm Morano　Spencer Moses
Michael Mulheren　Jim Ortlieb　Michael Pemberton　Katharine Powell
Steve Rosen　James Sutorius　Margot White　Alexandra Wilson　William Youmans

Scenic Design	Costume Design	Lighting Design	Sound Design
Klara Zieglerova	David C. Woolard	Howell Binkley	Walter Trarbach

Hair and Wig Design	Movement	Fight Direction	Production Stage Manager
Mark Adam Rampmeyer	Lisa Shriver	Steve Rankin	Frank Hartenstein

East Coast Casting	West Coast Casting	Technical Supervisor	Company Manager
Tara Rubin Casting	Sharon Bialy C.S.A. Sherry Thomas C.S.A.	Peter Fulbright	Jennifer Hindman Kemp

Associate Producer	Executive Producer	Promotions	Press Representative
Lauren Mitchell	Sally Campbell Morse	HHC Marketing	Boneau/Bryan-Brown

Original Music by
Andrew Lippa

Directed by
Des McAnuff

Originally presented in the "Page To Stage" Program by La Jolla Playhouse, La Jolla, CA
Christopher Ashley, Artistic Director & Steven Libman, Managing Director

The producers wish to thank Theatre Development Fund for its support of this production.

12/3/07

Hank Azaria (far left), Jimmi Simpson (far right) and the rest of the cast await the first television image ever broadcast.

Photo by Joan Marcus

The Farnsworth Invention

Cast Continued

Pem Farnsworth
  and others .... ALEXANDRA WILSON
Wachtel and others .... WILLIAM YOUMANS

UNDERSTUDIES

For David Sarnoff:
STEVE ROSEN

For Philo T. Farnsworth:
SPENCER MOSES

For the roles played by Aaron Krohn,
Michael Mulheren, Jim Ortlieb, Michael Pemberton
and James Sutorius:
BRIAN RUSSELL

For the roles played by Maurice Godin,
Bruce McKenzie and Steve Rosen:
AARON KROHN

For the roles played by Kyle Fabel and
William Youmans:
SPENCER MOSES

For the roles played by Christian M. Johansen,
Malcolm Morano and Spencer Moses:
JAVIER PICAYO

For the roles played by Nadia Bowers, Katharine
Powell, Margot White and Alexandra Wilson:
KATE MacCLUGGAGE

Jimmi Simpson, as Philo T. Farnsworth, holds the first workable cathode ray tube.

Photo by Joan Marcus

Hank Azaria
David Sarnoff

Jimmi Simpson
Philo T. Farnsworth

Nadia Bowers
*Lizette Sarnoff,
Mary Pickford and
others*

Kyle Fabel
*Pem's Father,
Cliff Gardner and
others*

Maurice Godin
*Russian Officer,
Atkins,
Walter Gifford,
Douglas Fairbanks
and others*

Christian M.
Johansen
*Young Philo T.
Farnsworth and
others*

Aaron Krohn
*Wilkins, Analyst and
others*

Kate MacCluggage
Understudy

Bruce McKenzie
*George Everson,
Vladimir Zworykin
and others*

Malcolm Morano
*Young David Sarnoff
and others*

Spencer Moses
*Stan Willis and
others*

Michael Mulheren
*Leslie Gorrell and
others*

Jim Ortlieb
*Justin Tolman,
Harbord, Doctor and
others*

Michael Pemberton
*Sarnoff's Father,
Simms, Schenck,
Lippincott, Houston
Control and others*

Javier Picayo
Understudy

Katharine Powell
Betty and others

Steve Rosen
*Harlan Honn,
Radio Announcer,
Lennox and others*

Brian Russell
Understudy

James Sutorius
*Russian Officer,
William Crocker and
others*

Margot White
*Sarnoff's Mother,
Pem's Mother,
Agnes Farnsworth,
Mina Edison and
others*

The Farnsworth Invention

Alexandra Wilson
Pem Farnsworth and others

William Youmans
Wachtel and others

Aaron Sorkin
Playwright

Des McAnuff
Director

Andrew Lippa
Original Music

Klara Zieglerova
Scenic Design

David C. Woolard
Costume Design

Howell Binkley
Lighting Design

Lisa Shriver
Movement

Steve Rankin
Fight Direction

Tara Rubin Casting
East Coast Casting

Sharon Bialy and Sherry Thomas
West Coast Casting

Stephen Gabis
Dialect Coach

Michael David,
Dodger Properties
Producer

Edward Strong,
Dodger Properties
Producer

Rocco Landesman,
Dodger Properties
Producer

Steven Spielberg,
Rabbit Ears, LLC
Producer

Ivor Royston,
The Pelican Group
Producer

Lauren Mitchell
Associate Producer

Christopher Ashley,
Artistic Director,
La Jolla Playhouse
*Page to Stage
Producer*

Hank Azaria as David Sarnoff.

Photo by Joan Marcus

The Farnsworth Invention

CREW
Front Row (L-R): Kelly Martindale (Stage Manager), Bobby Minor (Propman), Michael Taylor (Production Head Electrician), Adam Biscow (Production Property Man)

Middle Row (L-R): Kim Garnett (House Head Propman), Stephanie Atlan (Stage Manager), Ray Harold (Production Head Carpenter), Jerry Pavon (Spot Operator)

Back Row (L-R): Michael Guggio (Spot Operator), F. Lee Iwanski (House Head Electrician), Dennis Maher (House Head Carpenter)

BOX OFFICE STAFF
(L-R): Robert D. Kelly (Treasurer), Vicki Radolinski

HAIR & WARDROBE
Front Row (L-R): Jackeva Hill (Dresser), Tony Hoffman (Dresser), Gay Boseker (Hair Assist Supervisor)

Back Row (L-R): Jane Rottenbach (Dresser), Teresia Larsen (Dresser), Pat Marcus (Hairdresser), Scott Westervelt (Wardrobe Supervisor), Renee Kelly (Hair Supervisor), Lyle Jones (Dresser)

The Farnsworth Invention

The Farnsworth Invention
SCRAPBOOK

1. Hank Azaria on opening night.
2. Curtain call at the Music Box on opening night.
3. (L-R): Andrew Lippa (music), Aaron Sorkin (playwright), Hank Azaria, Jimmi Simpson, Des McAnuff (director), Lisa Shriver (movement) at rehearsal at New 42nd St. Studios.
4. Coproducer Steven Spielberg at the debut.

Correspondent: Jimmi Simpson, "Philo T. Farnsworth."

Opening Night Gifts: An actual, vintage advertisement for the Farnsworth Television Company from our brilliant choreographer Lisa Shriver.

Most Exciting Celebrity Visitor: Warren Beatty! I was too mesmerized to really pay attention to what he was saying. I think it was something about some song being about him.

Actor Who Performed the Most Roles in This Show: Maurice Godin.

Who Has Done the Most Shows in Their Career: Either Michael Mulheren or Malcolm Morano. They're both legends.

Favorite Moment During Each Performance: Any of the several moments where Hank Azaria is telling me off and getting "all up in my business."

Special Backstage Rituals: Choking back the tears of self-doubt.

Favorite In-Theatre Gathering Place: Steve Rosen's dressing room... but you have to make a reservation.

Favorite Off-Site Hangout: Film Center Cafe for drinks. Hank's place for poker.

Favorite Snack Food: Sour Patch Kids.

Mascot: Javier Picayo.

Favorite Therapy: Sleep.

Most Memorable Ad-Lib: "Peenie."

Record Number of Cell Phone Rings, Cell Phone Photos or Texting Incidents During a Performance: Impossible to count. I guess the Music Box gets really great reception.

Catchphrases Only the Company Would Recognize: "What can I do with you?"

Memorable Directorial Note: "That choice should be taken out into the alley and shot."

Company In-Jokes: Christian Johansen's obsession with country music.

Company Legends: James Sutorius.

Nicknames: Bruce McKenzie ("Contrary Bruce"), Hank Azaria ("Joeboy").

Sweethearts Within the Company: Ummm....

Embarrassing Moments: Standing in a spotlight on center stage, realizing my fly was down and then making the inane decision to go ahead and zip it up in front of 1,000 people. I sold the hell out of it, though.

Ghostly Encounters Backstage: I bumped into Zero Mostel the other night. He tried to make out with me. I let him.

Coolest Thing About Being in This Show: The people. From the writer to the crew, from the stage door to the cast...the coolest group of people I've ever worked with.

Frost/Nixon

First Preview: March 31, 2007. Opened: April 22, 2007.
Closed August 19, 2007 after 23 Previews and 137 Performances.

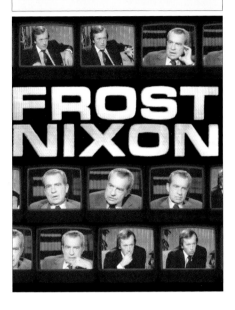

CAST
(in order of speaking)

Richard Nixon	FRANK LANGELLA
Jim Reston	STEPHEN KUNKEN
David Frost	MICHAEL SHEEN
Jack Brennan	COREY JOHNSON
Evonne Goolagong	SHIRA GREGORY
John Birt	REMY AUBERJONOIS
Manolo Sanchez	TRINEY SANDOVAL
Swifty Lazar/Mike Wallace	STEPHEN ROWE
Caroline Cushing	ROXANNA HOPE
Bob Zelnick	ARMAND SCHULTZ
Ensemble	MEGHAN ANDREWS, DENNIS COCKRUM, ANTONY HAGOPIAN

All other parts played by members of the company.

UNDERSTUDIES

For Richard Nixon: BOB ARI
For David Frost: REMY AUBERJONOIS
For Swifty Lazar, Bob Zelnick, Manolo Sanchez:
DENNIS COCKRUM
For John Birt, Jack Brennan, Manolo Sanchez:
ANTONY HAGOPIAN
For Evonne Goolagong, Caroline Cushing:
MEGHAN ANDREWS
For Jim Reston: TRINEY SANDOVAL

Michael Sheen is appearing with the permission of Actors' Equity Association pursuant to an exchange program between American Equity and UK Equity.

The Playbill Broadway Yearbook 2007-2008

---

⑧ BERNARD B. JACOBS THEATRE
242 West 45th Street
A Shubert Organization Theatre
Gerald Schoenfeld, *Chairman*   Philip J. Smith, *President*

Robert E. Wankel, *Executive Vice President*

ARIELLE TEPPER MADOVER   MATTHEW BYAM SHAW   ROBERT FOX   ACT PRODUCTIONS
DAVID BINDER   DEBRA BLACK   ANNETTE NIEMTZOW/HARLENE FREEZER   THE WEINSTEIN COMPANY

Present

THE DONMAR WAREHOUSE PRODUCTION

FRANK LANGELLA   MICHAEL SHEEN

A New Play By
PETER MORGAN

With

REMY AUBERJONOIS	SHIRA GREGORY	ROXANNA HOPE	COREY JOHNSON
STEPHEN KUNKEN	STEPHEN ROWE	TRINEY SANDOVAL	ARMAND SCHULTZ
MEGHAN ANDREWS	BOB ARI	DENNIS COCKRUM	ANTONY HAGOPIAN

Set and Costume Designer
CHRISTOPHER ORAM

Lighting Designer
NEIL AUSTIN

Composer and Sound Designer
ADAM CORK

Video Designer
JON DRISCOLL

Hair and Wig Designer
RICHARD MAWBEY

Casting
DANIEL SWEE

UK Casting
ANNE McNULTY

Press Representative
BONEAU/BRYAN-BROWN

Marketing
ERIC SCHNALL

General Management
101 PRODUCTIONS, LTD.

Production Stage Manager
RICK STEIGER

US Technical Supervisor
AURORA PRODUCTIONS

UK Technical Supervisor
PATRICK MOLONY

Directed by
MICHAEL GRANDAGE

LIVE BROADWAY

Frost/Nixon originally opened at The Donmar Warehouse on August 15, 2006.
Matthew Byam Shaw, Arielle Tepper Madover, Robert Fox, Act Productions transferred
The Donmar Warehouse Production to the Gielgud Theatre, Opening Night November 16, 2006.

The producers wish to express their appreciation to Theatre Development Fund for its support of this production.

Original Production Sponsor
BARCLAYS CAPITAL

8/19/07

(L-R): Michael Sheen and Frank Langella

Photo by Joan Marcus

Frost/Nixon

Frank Langella
Richard Nixon

Michael Sheen
David Frost

Remy Auberjonois
John Birt

Shira Gregory
Evonne Goolagong

Roxanna Hope
Caroline Cushing

Corey Johnson
Jack Brennan

Stephen Kunken
Jim Reston

Stephen Rowe
*Swifty Lazar/
Mike Wallace*

Triney Sandoval
Manolo Sanchez

Armand Schultz
Bob Zelnick

Meghan Andrews
Ensemble

Bob Ari
*Understudy for
Richard Nixon*

Dennis Cockrum
Ensemble

Antony Hagopian
Ensemble

Peter Morgan
Playwright

Michael Grandage
Director

Jon Driscoll
Video Designer

**Arielle Tepper
Madover**
Producer

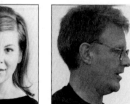
Robert Fox
Producer

Debra Black
Co-Producer

Harlene Freezer
Co-Producer

**Bob Weinstein,
The Weinstein
Company**
Co-Producer

**Harvey Weinstein,
The Weinstein
Company**
Co-Producer

Seth Sklar-Heyn
*Assistant to the
Director*

Sonya Walger
Caroline Cushing

STAGE MANAGEMENT
(L-R): Rick Steiger (Production Stage Manager), Lisa Buxbaum (Stage Manager) and Timothy Eaker (Production Assistant).

BOX OFFICE
Jose Hernandez and Karen Coscia.

Photos by Ben Strothmann

Frost/Nixon

STAGE CREW

Front Row (L-R): Joel Mendenhall (Hair Supervisor), Dave Fulton (Production Props), Alfred Ricci (House Props), Michael Van Praagh (House Carpenter), Edward Ruggiero (Flyman).

Back Row (L-R): Daniel Carpio (Props), John Alban (Props), Lyle Jones (Dresser), Kelly Saxon (Wardrobe Supervisor), Christopher Kurtz (Production Video), Philip Heckman (Dresser), Wayne Smith (Production Sound) and Herbert Messing (House Electrician).

DOORMAN
Jerry Klein

FRONT OF HOUSE STAFF
Seated (L-R): Rosa Pesante, Sean Cutler, Eva Laskow, Kathleen Wehmeyer.

Standing (L-R): Al Luongo, Billy Mitchell, Patanne McEvoy, John Minore, Al Nazario and Roxanne Gayol.

Frost/Nixon

Scrapbook

Correspondent: Rick Steiger, PSM
Opening Night Gifts: A special comic book created by Stephen Kunken. Beer glasses created by the wardrobe team. A fabulous martini set from our producers.
Most Roles in This Show: Shira Gregory
Most Shows in Career: Frank Langella
Special Backstage Rituals: Pre-show moving light dance with Reston (a.k.a. Stephen Kunken). Stopping at the mirror outside Frank Langella's dressing room.
Favorite In-Theatre Gathering Place: Outside Kunken's dressing room. The green room for Sunday brunch.

Favorite Moment During Each Performance: Drinking lemonade while onstage. "Crack investigators" disco move. That moment before the final Nixon closeup when you can hear a pin drop.
Favorite Off-Site Hangout: Vinyl Diner between shows. Angus after the show.
Favorite Snack Food: Chocolate and coffee.
Favorite Therapy: Starbucks.
Most Memorable Ad-Lib: After taking a pause for technical difficulties mid phone call, Michael Sheen returned to the stage, phone in hand, saying "I'm sorry we were cut off."
Nicknames: "Ma-Sheen." "Gong."

Memorable Stage Door Fan Encounter: (While leaving the stage door shared with *Avenue Q*:) "Which puppet were you?"
Heaviest/Hottest Costumes: Corey Johnson's military suit, which he was stuck in for the entire performance. Stephen Rowe's hairpiece.
Who Wore the Least: Michael Sheen, bathrobe and boxers.
Catchphrase Only the Company Would Recognize: "The way we did it in London."
Memorable Directorial Notes: "You won't ever hear us say 'The way we did it in London.'" "Don't declare your independence from the production."

STAFF FOR *FROST/NIXON*

GENERAL MANAGEMENT
101 PRODUCTIONS, LTD.
Wendy Orshan   Jeffrey M. Wilson
David Auster

COMPANY MANAGER
Alexandra Gushin

GENERAL PRESS REPRESENTATIVE
BONEAU/BRYAN-BROWN
Adrian Bryan-Brown   Steven Padla
Heath Schwartz

U.S TECHNICAL SUPERVISOR
AURORA PRODUCTIONS
Gene O'Donovan   W. Benjamin Heller II
Bethany Weinstein   Meghan Von Vett
Melissa Mazdra

Production Stage Manager	Rick Steiger
Stage Manager	Lisa Buxbaum
UK Technical Supervisor	Patrick Molony
Assistant Director	Seth Sklar-Heyn
Associate Costume Designer	Scott Traugott
Assistant Costume Designer	Brian Russman
Costume Design Assistants	Cory Ching, Robert Martin
Associate Lighting Designer	Daniel Walker
Associate Lighting Designer/ Moving Lights Programmer	Victoria Smerdon
Associate Sound Designer	Chris Cronin
Screen Technician	Colin Barnes
Casting Associate	Camille Hickman

Production Carpenter	Michael Van Praagh
Production Flyman	Edward Ruggiero
Production Electrician	Jon Lawson
House Electrician	Herbert Messing
Assistant Electrician (Video)	Christopher Kurtz
Production Props Supervisor	Dave Fulton
House Properties	Alfred Ricci
Prop Crew	John Alban, Daniel Carpio
Wardrobe Supervisor	Kelly A. Saxon
Mr. Langella's Dresser	Patrick Bevilacqua
Mr. Sheen's Dresser	Lyle Jones
Dresser	Philip Heckman
Hair Supervisor	Joel Mendenhall
Make-Up Designer	Angelina Avallone
Production Assistants	Timothy Eaker, Brian Maschka
Assistant to Ms. Tepper Madover	Holly Ferguson

Legal Counsel	Lazarus & Harris, LLP/ Scott R. Lazarus, Esq., Robert C. Harris, Esq.
Accountant	Fried & Kowgios
Controller	Galbraith & Co Inc./ Sarah Galbraith, Tabitha Falcone
Advertising	SPOTCO/ Drew Hodges, Jim Edwards, Tom McCann, Stephen Sosnowski
Assistant to the General Managers	John Vennema
101 Productions, Ltd. Staff	Denys Baker, Ashley Berman, Katharine Croke, Barbara Crompton, Laura Dickinson, Sherra Johnston, Emily Lawson, Heidi Neven, Kyle Pickles, Mary Six Rupert, Evan Storey
101 Productions, Ltd. Intern	Stewart Miller
Press Representative Staff	Chris Boneau, Brandi Cornwell, Linnae Petruzzelli, Jim Byk, Adriana Douzos, Jackie Green, Joe Perrotta, Matt Polk, Susanne Tighe, Juliana Hannett, Jessica Johnson, Aaron Meier, Hector Hernandez, Allison Houseworth, Kevin Jones, Ian Bjorklund, Danielle Crinnion, Amy Kass, Christine Olver, Matt Ross
Banking	City National Bank/Anne McSweeney
Insurance	Tanenbaum Harber Insurance Group/ Carol Bressi
Immigration	Traffic Control Group, Inc./ David King
Theatre Displays	King Displays, Inc.
Payroll Services	Castellana Services, Inc.
Production Photographers	Joan Marcus, Johan Persson (UK)
Website Design	Situation Marketing
Opening Night Coordinator	Tobak Lawrence Company/ Suzanne Tobak, Michael P. Lawrence

DONMAR WAREHOUSE

Artistic Director	Michael Grandage
Executive Producer	Lucy Davies
General Manager	James Bierman
Creative & Casting Associate	Anne McNulty
Marketing Manager	Ruth Waters
Literary Manager & Production Administrator	Sarah Nicholson
Executive Coordinator	Simon Woolley
General Assistant	Eleanor Lang
Development Director	Kate Mitchell
Development Manager	Tania Hutt
Development Officer	Aimée Barnett
Development Administrator	Nicola Stockley
Resident Assistant Director	Alex Sims

Deputy Production Manager	Lucy McEwan
Deputy Production Manager (Maternity Cover)	Lorna Cobbold
Press Representative	Kate Morley for Blueprint PR

CREDITS

London scenery by Rocket Scenery. Lighting by PRG. Sound equipment from Sound Associates. Video equipment by XL Video. Costumes executed by Leonard Logsdail Custom Tailor, Arel Studio, David Quinn, Allmeier Custom Shirts, Carlo Manzi, Keith Watson and Angels. Wigs made by Wig Specialities Ltd. Ricola products used. Video footage licensed by Huntley Film Archives. "Frost Over Australia" footage courtesy of Seven Network. Photo of Santa Pacifica courtesy of Getty Images. Special thanks to Bra-Tenders for hosiery and undergarments.

FROST/NIXON rehearsed at New 42nd Street Studios.

SPECIAL THANKS
Sarah Waling

www.frostnixononbroadway.com

THE SHUBERT ORGANIZATION, INC.
Board of Directors

Gerald Schoenfeld Chairman	**Philip J. Smith** President
Wyche Fowler, Jr.	**John W. Kluge**
Lee J. Seidler	**Michael I. Sovern**

Stuart Subotnick

Robert E. Wankel
Executive Vice President

Peter Entin Vice President – Theatre Operations	**Elliot Greene** Vice President – Finance
David Andrews Vice President – Shubert Ticketing Services	**John Darby** Vice President – Facilities

D.S. Moynihan
Vice President – Creative Projects

House Manager	William Mitchell

Glory Days

First Preview: April 22, 2008. Opened: May 6, 2008.
Closed May 6, 2008 after 17 Previews and 1 Performance.

PLAYBILL

glory days

CAST
(in order of appearance)

Will	STEVEN BOOTH
Andy	ANDREW C. CALL
Skip	ADAM HALPIN
Jack	JESSE JP JOHNSON

UNDERSTUDIES

For Will and Jack:
ALEX BRIGHTMAN

For Andy and Skip:
JEREMY WOODARD

ORCHESTRA

Conductor:
ETHAN POPP
Associate Conductor:
ALEC BERLIN
Electric Guitar:
ALEC BERLIN
Keyboards:
ETHAN POPP
Drums:
DAMIEN BASSMAN
Bass:
GARY BRISTOL
Music Coordinator:
MIKE KELLER
Music Copyist:
KAYE-HOUSTON MUSIC

CIRCLE IN THE SQUARE

UNDER THE DIRECTION OF
THEODORE MANN and PAUL LIBIN

JOHN O'BOYLE, RICKY STEVENS, RICHARD E. LEOPOLD,
LIZZIE LEOPOLD, THE MAX PRODUCTIONS, ALAN MINGO, JR.
and BROADWAY ACROSS AMERICA
in association with the SIGNATURE THEATRE

Present

Music & Lyrics by
NICK BLAEMIRE

Book by
JAMES GARDINER

STEVEN BOOTH	ANDREW C. CALL	ADAM HALPIN	JESSE JP JOHNSON

Scenic Design by	Costume Design by	Lighting Design by	Sound Design by
JAMES KRONZER	SASHA LUDWIG-SIEGEL	MARK LANKS	PETER HYLENSKI

Music Director	Vocal Arrangements by	Music Contractor
ETHAN POPP	NICK BLAEMIRE & JESSE VARGAS	MICHAEL KELLER

Casting by	Press Representative	Production Stage Manager
TARA RUBIN CASTING	BONEAU/ BRYAN-BROWN	GREGG KIRSOPP

Production Management by	General Management	Company Manager
JUNIPER STREET PRODUCTIONS, INC.	CARL D. WHITE RICKY STEVENS	LAUREN P. YATES

Music Supervision, Arrangements & Orchestrations by
JESSE VARGAS

Directed by
ERIC SCHAEFFER

Originally Produced January 2008 at Signature Theatre Arlington, Virginia Eric Schaeffer, Artistic Director

5/6/08

(L-R): Jesse JP Johnson, Steven Booth, Andrew C. Call and Adam Halpin

Photo by Scott Suchman

Glory Days

MUSICAL NUMBERS

"My Three Best Friends"	Will
"Are You Ready for Tonight?"	Will, Andy, Skip, Jack
"We've Got Girls"	Will and Andy
"Right Here"	Will, Andy, Skip, Jack
"Open Road"	Jack
"Things Are Different"	Will and Andy
"Generation Apathy"	Skip
"After All"	Will
"The Good Old Glory Type Days"	Will, Andy, Skip, Jack
"The Thing About Andy"	Will and Jack
"Forget About It"	Will, Andy, Skip, Jack
"Other Human Beings"	Jack and Andy
"My Turn"	Andy
"Boys"	Will and Skip
"My Next Story"	Will

Music & Lyrics by Nick Blaemire
Vocal Arrangements by Nick Blaemire and Jesse Vargas
Music Supervision, Arrangements and Orchestrations by Jesse Vargas

(L-R): Adam Halpin and Steven Booth

Steven Booth
Will

Andrew C. Call
Andy

Adam Halpin
Skip

Jesse JP Johnson
Jack

Alex Brightman
Understudy

Jeremy Woodard
Understudy

Nick Blaemire
*Music and Lyrics,
Vocal Arrangements*

James Gardiner
Book

Eric Schaeffer
Director

Peter Hylenski
Sound Design

Tara Rubin Casting
Casting

Guy Kwan, John Paull III, Hillary Blanken,
Kevin Broomell, Ana Rose Greene,
Juniper Street Productions
Production Manager

John O'Boyle
Producer

Ricky Stevens
Producer

Glory Days

Scrapbook

Photos by Aubrey Reuben

Photo by Kevin Hucke

1. (L-R): Librettist James Gardiner, Andrew C. Call, Jesse J.P. Johnson, Steven Booth, Adam Halpin and songwriter Nick Blaemire at rehearsals.
2. (L-R): Blaemire and Gardiner at the opening night party at Moda.
3. Curtain call on opening night.
4. Wardrobe Supervisor Ryan Rossetto mourns after the reviews came out.

STAFF FOR *GLORY DAYS*

GENERAL MANAGEMENT
Carl D. White
Ricky Stevens

GENERAL PRESS REPRESENTATIVE
BONEAU/BRYAN-BROWN
Adrian Bryan-Brown   Jim Byk
Adriana Douzos   Matt Ross

PRODUCTION MANAGEMENT
JUNIPER STREET PRODUCTIONS
Hillary Blanken   Guy Kwan
Kevin Broomell   Ana Rose Greene

Company Manager ....Lauren P. Yates
Production Stage Manager ....Gregg Kirsopp
Stage Manager ....Jess W. Speaker III
Assistant Director ....Matt Gardiner
Assistant Set Designer ....Larry Brown
Assistant to the Set Designer ....Jeremy Foil
Assistant Lighting Designer ....Nicholas Houfek
Associate Sound Designer ....Keith Caggiano
Wardrobe Supervisor ....Ryan Rossetto
Head Carpenter ....Robert Gordon
Head Electrician ....Stewart Wagner
Head Props..................................Owen Parmele
Music Department Coordinator ....Michael Keller
Production Assistant ....J. Jason Daunter
Legal Counsel .....Beigelman, Feldman & Associates, P.C./
Mark L. Beigelman,
T. Michael Wickersham
Controller ....Galbraith & Co Inc/Sarah Galbraith

Accountant ....Fried & Kowgios CPAs/Robert Fried
Advertising ....Serino Coyne Inc./
Greg Corradetti, Natalie Serota,
Danielle Boyle, Sandy Block,
Ryan Cunningham
Logo Art ....Design Army
Website Design ....Bay Bridge Productions
Production Photography ....Scott Suchman
Portrait Photography ....Carmelita Watkinson
General Management Associates ....Scott DelaCruz,
Steven DeLuca, Lauren P. Yates
Assistants to General Managers ....Natasha Burgos,
Emily Pye
Marketing Associates ....Mydra Kelly, Jessica Castro
Banking............................JP Morgan Chase Bank/
Margaret L. Wong, Richard Callian,
Salvatore Romano
Insurance ....C&S Int'l Insurance Brokers, Inc.
Risk Managers ....Debra Kozee
Theatre Displays................................King Display
Merchandising ....Max Merchandising/
Randi Grossman
Payroll Services.....................Castellana Services, Inc.
Group Sales ....Telecharge Group Sales
Rehearsal Studios ....Nola Studios

CREDITS
Scenery built by Showman Fabricators, Inc. Lighting equipment provided by PRG Lighting. Sound equipment provided by Masque Sound. Keyboards provided by Randy Cohen. Natural herb cough drops courtesy of Ricola USA, Inc.

To learn more about the production, please visit
GloryDaysBroadway.com

SPECIAL THANKS
David Sharrocks, Ryan Watkinson, Brian Spitulnik, Benj Pasek, Brian Mazzaferri, Jason Michael Snow, Danny Binstock, Justin Keyes, Ato Blankson-Wood, Jordan Price, Mark Bush, Josh Rouah, Jamie Cooper, Joel Bauer, Ryan Nealy, Charlie Brady, Jamie McGonnigal, Mark Christine, Eli Zoller, Jamie Burke, Theo Klose, Jason Miesner

CIRCLE IN THE SQUARE THEATRE
Thespian Theatre, Inc.
Under the direction of
Theodore Mann and Paul Libin
Vice President of Finance ....Susan Frankel
House Manager ....Shawn M. Fertitta
Head Carpenter ....Robert Gordon
Head Electrician ....Stewart Wagner
Prop Master ....Owen E. Parmele
FOH Sound Engineer ....Robert S. Lindsay
Box Office Treasurer ....Michael G. McCarthy
Administrative Assistant ....Abigail Saviteer
Assistant to Paul Libin ....Clark Mims Tedesco
Assistant to Theodore Mann ....Eric Vitale

CIRCLE IN THE SQUARE THEATRE SCHOOL
Staff
President ....Paul Libin
Artistic Director ....Theodore Mann
Theatre School Director ....E. Colin O'Leary
Administrative Assistant ....Jonathan Kronenberger
Administrative Assistant ....Virginia Tuller
Arts Education/Development ....Jonathan Mann

Grease

First Preview: July 24, 2007. Opened: August 19, 2007.
Still running as of May 31, 2008.

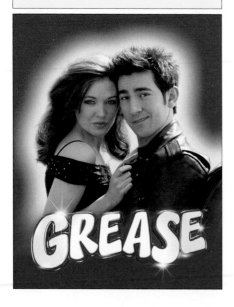

CAST

Danny Zuko	MAX CRUMM
Sandy Dumbrowski	LAURA OSNES
Kenickie	MATTHEW SALDÍVAR
Sonny LaTierri	JOSÉ RESTREPO
Roger	DANIEL EVERIDGE
Doody	RYAN PATRICK BINDER
Betty Rizzo	JENNY POWERS
Marty	ROBYN HURDER
Jan	LINDSAY MENDEZ
Frenchy	KIRSTEN WYATT
Patty Simcox	ALLISON FISCHER
Eugene Florczyk	JAMISON SCOTT
Miss Lynch	SUSAN BLOMMAERT
Vince Fontaine	JEB BROWN
Cha-Cha DiGregorio	NATALIE HILL
Teen Angel	STEPHEN R. BUNTROCK

Ensemble .... JOSH FRANKLIN,
CODY GREEN,
NATALIE HILL,
EMILY PADGETT,
KEVEN QUILLON,
BRIAN SEARS,
CHRISTINA SIVRICH,
ANNA AIMEE WHITE

Continued on next page

-N- BROOKS ATKINSON THEATRE
UNDER THE DIRECTION OF JAMES M. NEDERLANDER AND JAMES L. NEDERLANDER

Paul Nicholas and David Ian   Nederlander Presentations Inc.

Terry Allen Kramer

by arrangement with Robert Stigwood

present

GREASE

Book, Music and Lyrics by

Jim Jacobs and Warren Casey

Additional Songs by

Barry Gibb   John Farrar   Louis St. Louis   Scott Simon

Starring

Max Crumm   Laura Osnes

With

Ryan Patrick Binder   Susan Blommaert   Jeb Brown
Stephen R. Buntrock   Daniel Everidge   Allison Fischer
Robyn Hurder   Lindsay Mendez   Jenny Powers
José Restrepo   Matthew Saldívar   Jamison Scott   Kirsten Wyatt

and

Josh Franklin   Cody Green   Natalie Hill
Matthew Hydzik   Emily Padgett   Keven Quillon   Brian Sears
Christina Sivrich   Amber Stone   Anna Aimee White

Scenic Design	Costume Design	Lighting Design	Sound Design
Derek McLane	Martin Pakledinaz	Kenneth Posner	Brian Ronan

Wig & Hair Designer	Casting	Associate Director	Associate Choreographer
Paul Huntley	Jay Binder	Marc Bruni	Joyce Chittick
	Jack Bowdan/Megan Larche		

Orchestrations	Music Coordinator
Christopher Jahnke	Howard Joines

Production Supervisors	Production Stage Manager
Arthur Siccardi & Patrick Sullivan	David John O'Brien

Executive Producer	Press Representative	General Management
Max Finbow	Barlow • Hartman	Charlotte Wilcox Company

Director-Choreographer

Kathleen Marshall

8/19/07

Laura Osnes and Max Crumm (center) sing "Summer Nights" with the Company.

Grease

SCENES AND MUSICAL NUMBERS

ACT I

Prologue
Scene 1: Rydell High, 1959
"Grease" .... Company
Scene 2: Cafeteria/School Steps
"Summer Nights" .... Danny, Sandy and Company
Scene 3: Locker Room
"Those Magic Changes" .... Doody and Company
Scene 4: Marty's Bedroom
"Freddy, My Love" .... Marty and Pink Ladies
Scene 5: Street Corner
"Greased Lightnin'" .... Kenickie and Guys
Scene 6: Rydell High
"Rydell Fight Song" .... Sandy and Patty
Scene 7: Bleachers
"Mooning" .... Roger and Jan
"Look at Me, I'm Sandra Dee" .... Rizzo
"We Go Together" .... T-Birds and Pink Ladies

ACT II

Scene 1: School Gym/Sandy's Room
"Shakin' at the High School Hop" .... Company
"It's Raining on Prom Night" .... Jan and Sandy
"Born to Hand-Jive" .... Vince and Company
Scene 2: School Steps
"Hopelessly Devoted to You" .... Sandy
Scene 3: Outside Burger Palace
"Beauty School Dropout" .... Teen Angel and Girls
Scene 4: Drive-In Movie
"Sandy" .... Danny
Scene 5: Jan's Rec Room
"Rock 'n' Roll Party Queen" .... Doody and Roger
"There Are Worse Things I Could Do" .... Rizzo
"Look at Me, I'm Sandra Dee" (Reprise) .... Sandy
Scene 6: Inside Burger Palace
"You're the One That I Want" .... Danny, Sandy and Company
"We Go Together" (Reprise) .... Company

"Grease" (Barry Gibb); ©1978 Crompton Songs (BMI). All rights reserved. Used by permission.
"Hopelessly Devoted to You" (John Farrar); ©1978 Unichappell-Stigwood Music (BMI), John Farrar Music (BMI) and Ensign Music Corporation (BMI). All rights on behalf of John Farrar Music (BMI) and Ensign Music Corporation (BMI). Administered by Unichappell-Stigwood Music Inc. (BMI). All rights reserved. Used by permission.
"Sandy" (Scott Simon, Louis St. Louis); ©1978 Ensign Music Corporation (BMI). All rights administered by Unichappell Music Inc. (BMI). All rights reserved. Used by permission.
"You're the One That I Want" (John Farrar); ©1978 Unichappell-Stigwood Music (BMI), John Farrar Music (BMI) and Ensign Music Corporation (BMI). All rights on behalf of John Farrar Music (BMI) and Ensign Music Corporation (BMI). Administered by Unichappell-Stigwood Music Inc. (BMI). All rights reserved. Used by permission.

Cast Continued

UNDERSTUDIES

For Danny, Teen Angel:
JOSH FRANKLIN, MATTHEW HYDZIK
For Sandy, Patty Simcox:
EMILY PADGETT, ANNA AIMEE WHITE
For Kenickie:
CODY GREEN
For Sonny LaTierri:
CODY GREEN, KEVEN QUILLON
For Roger:
KEVEN QUILLON
For Doody, Eugene Florczyk:
BRIAN SEARS
For Betty Rizzo:
NATALIE HILL
For Marty:
NATALIE HILL, ANNA AIMEE WHITE
For Jan, Frenchy:
CHRISTINA SIVRICH, AMBER STONE
For Miss Lynch:
CHRISTINA SIVRICH
For Vince Fontaine:
JOSH FRANKLIN
For Cha-Cha DiGregorio:
AMBER STONE

SWINGS

MATTHEW HYDZIK, AMBER STONE

DANCE CAPTAIN

AMBER STONE

THE BAND

Conductor/Synthesizer:
KIMBERLY GRIGSBY
Associate Conductor/Piano/Synthesizer:
CHRIS FENWICK
Drums:
JOHN CLANCY
Bass:
MICHAEL BLANCO
Guitars:
MICHAEL AARONS, JIM HERSHMAN
Tenor Sax/Woodwinds:
JOHN SCARPULLA
Woodwinds:
JACK BASHKOW
Music Coordinator:
HOWARD JOINES

Grease

Max Crumm
Danny

Laura Osnes
Sandy

Ryan Patrick Binder
Doody

Susan Blommaert
Miss Lynch

Jeb Brown
Vince

Stephen R. Buntrock
Teen Angel

Daniel Everidge
Roger

Allison Fischer
Patty Simcox

Robyn Hurder
Marty

Lindsay Mendez
Jan

Jenny Powers
Rizzo

José Restrepo
Sonny

Matthew Saldívar
Kenickie

Jamison Scott
Eugene

Kirsten Wyatt
Frenchy

Josh Franklin
Ensemble

Cody Green
Ensemble

Natalie Hill
Cha-Cha, Ensemble

Matthew Hydzik
Swing

Emily Padgett
Ensemble

Keven Quillon
Ensemble

Brian Sears
Ensemble

Christina Sivrich
Ensemble

Amber Stone
*Swing,
Dance Captain*

Anna Aimee White
Ensemble

Kathleen Marshall
*Director and
Choreographer*

Derek McLane
Scenic Design

Martin Pakledinaz
Costume Design

Kenneth Posner
Lighting Designer

Brian Ronan
Sound Design

Paul Huntley
*Wig and Hair
Designer*

Joseph Dulude II
Make-Up Design

**Megan Larche,
Jay Binder C.S.A.**
Casting

Kimberly Grigsby
Music Director

Christopher Jahnke
Orchestrator

Grease

Howard Joines
Music Coordinator

Arthur Siccardi
Production Management

Marc Bruni
Associate Director

Joyce Chittick
Associate Choreographer

The Charlotte Wilcox Company
General Manager

James L. Nederlander, Nederlander Presentations Inc.
Producer

Terry Allen Kramer
Producer

Will Blum
Roger

Joe Komara
"Born to Hand Jive" Dance Specialty, Ensemble, Swing

Lauralyn McClelland
Swing

BOX OFFICE
(L-R):
Robert Wilamowski,
William O'Brien,
Peter Attanasio.

Photos by Ben Strothmann

PROPS
Front Row (Sitting, L-R): Billy Seelig, Steve DeVerna, Chuck Daique, Jim Kane.

Back Row (Standing, L-R): Joseph DePaulo, Chris Pantuso.

FRONT OF HOUSE STAFF
Front Row (L-R): Joan Heller, Marie Gonzalez, Kimberlee Imperato.

Second Row (L-R): Kaitlin Dato, Jamie Zurich, Ilona Figueroa, Brenden Imperato, Brenda Schwarz.

Back Row (L-R): Susan Martin, Stephen Flaherty, Sam Figert, Robert Banyai.

SOUND AND ELECTRICS
Front Row (L-R): Steve Clem, Manny Becker, Susanne Williams, Michael "Jersey" Van Nest.
Back Row (L-R): Jeff Koger, Christopher Robinson, Mike Farfalla.

Not Pictured: Brian GF McGarity

STAGE MANAGEMENT
(L-R): David John O'Brien,
Colleen Danaher,
Stephen R. Gruse.

CARPENTERS
(L-R): Tommy Lavaia, Mike Attianese, Ben Horrigan, Gerry Griffin, Jerry Urcivoli, Jason Erny, Joe McCormick, Richie Fideli.

Grease

Photo by Ben Strothmann

WARDROBE AND HAIR

Front Row (Sitting, L-R): Jack Curtin, Lisa Tucci.

Second Row (L-R): Dana Calahan, Jorie Malan, Cheryl Widner, Theresa DiStasi, Geoffrey Polischuk, Karen L. Eifert, Armando Licon, Hilda Garcia-Suli.

Back Row (Standing, L-R): Rosemary Keough, Wendall Goings.

STAFF FOR *GREASE*

GENERAL MANAGEMENT
THE CHARLOTTE WILCOX COMPANY
Charlotte W. Wilcox
Matthew W. Krawiec   Dina Steinberg
Steve Supeck   David Roth
Margaret Wilcox

GENERAL PRESS REPRESENTATIVE
BARLOW•HARTMAN
John Barlow   Michael Hartman
Ryan Ratelle

COMPANY MANAGER
James Lawson

ASSISTANT COMPANY MANAGER
Megan Trice

CASTING
JAY BINDER CASTING
Jay Binder CSA
Jack Bowdan CSA, Mark Brandon, Sara Schatz
Assistants: Nikole Vallins, Allison Estrin

PRODUCTION STAGE
   MANAGER ....DAVID JOHN O'BRIEN
Stage Manager ....Beverly Jenkins
Assistant Stage Manager ....Stephen R. Gruse
Dance Captain ....Amber Stone
Assistant to the Director ....Jenny Hogan
Associate Scenic Designer ....Ted LeFevre
Assistant Scenic Designers ....Anne Allen Goelz, Shoko Kambara
Assistants to the Scenic Designer ....Erica Hemminger, Court Watson
Associate Costume Designer ....Matthew Pachtman
Assistant Costume Designer ....Sarah Sophia Turner
Assistant to the Costume Designer ....Tescia Seufferlein
Associate Lighting Designer ....Aaron Spivey
Assistant Lighting Designer ....Kathleen Dobbins
Moving Light Programmer ....David Arch
Assistant Sound Designer ....Michael Creason
Production Electricians .....James Fedigan, Randall Zaibek
Production Carpenter ....Gerard Griffin
Production Flyman ....Brian Hutchinson
Automation Carpenter ....Benjamin Horrigan
Head Electrician ....Brian GF McGarity
Production Sound Engineer ....Michael Farfalla

Deck Sound ....TJ McEvoy
Production Properties ....Christopher Pantuso
Wardrobe Supervisor ....Lisa Tucci
Assistant Wardrobe Supervisor ....Karen L. Eifert
Dressers ....Elizabeth Cline, Hilda Garcia-Suli, Wendall Goings, Rosemary Keough, Geoffrey Polischuk, Cheryl Widner
Stitcher ....Dana Calahan
Associate Wig and Hair Designer .....Giovanna Calabretta
Hair Supervisor ....John "Jack" Curtin
Hair Dresser ....Armando Licon
Makeup Designer ....Joe Dulude II
Associate Conductor ....Chris Fenwick
Synthesizer Programmer ....Randy Cohen
Music Preparation Service ....Mark Cumberland
Rehearsal Pianist ....John Samorian
Rehearsal Drummers ....John Clancy, Joe Nero
Production Assistants ....Sally Sibson, Jami Talbott
Music Department Intern ....Eric Walton
Properties Intern ....Christopher Digsby
Sound Intern ....Kimberly Donowski
SDCF Observer ....Jacob Toth
Legal Counsel ....Franklin, Weinrib, Rudell & Vassallo, P.C.
Elliot H. Brown, Esq., Daniel Wasser, Esq.
Accountants ....Fried & Kowgios LLP
Robert Fried
Controller ....Sarah Galbraith, Galbraith & Co Inc.
Advertising ....Serino-Coyne
Angelo Desimini, Tom Callahan, Cara Christman, Matt Upshaw
Website Design ....David Risley/Pygmalion Designs
Press Office Manager ....Bethany Larson
Press Office Associates ....Leslie Baden, Michelle Bergman, Dennis Crowley, Tom D'Ambrosio, Justin Magri, Kevin Robak, Wayne Wolfe
Production Photography ....Joan Marcus
Theatre Displays ....King Displays, Inc.
Banking ....JPMorgan Chase
Stephanie Dalton
Payroll Service ....Castellana Services, Inc.
Opening Night Party Coordinator ...Christopher Raphael, Cristina Baldacci/ The Really Spectacular Company, Inc.
Physical Therapy ....PhysioArts
Massage Therapist ....Russell Beasley, LMT
Company Orthopedist ....David S. Weiss, MD
Merchandise ....Rick Steiner and MCM Limelight
Insurance Consultant ....Stockbridge Risk Management

Information Management Services ..Marion Finkler Taylor
Travel Services ....Andi Henig

CREDITS
Scenery by Hudson Scenic Studio, Inc. Automation by Hudson Scenic Studio, Inc. Costume construction by BaraCath Costumes; Barbara Matera Limited; Carelli Costumes, Inc.; Donna Langman Costumes; Eric Winterling, Inc.; Luigi's New York; Mardana; Maria Ficalora Knitwear, Ltd.; Paul Chang Custom Tailor; Seams Unlimited, Ltd.; Studio Rouge; and Tricorne, Inc. Custom fabric dyeing and printing by Gene Mignola, Inc., Jeff Fender. Millinery by Costume Armour, Lynne Mackey Studio, Arnold Levine, Marian "Killer" Hose and Leslie Norgate. Special thanks to Bra*Tenders for hosiery and undergarments. Custom footwear by LaDuca Shoes and Worldtone Dance. Lights by Hudson Sound & Light, LLC. Sound equipment by Production Resource Group. Drums provided by Yamaha. Rehearsal piano provided by Baldwin. Guitars provided by Gibson. Guitar strings provided by D'Addario. Drop painted by Ryan Kravitz. Rehearsed at the New 42nd Street Studios.

Makeup provided by M•A•C

STAFF FOR THE BROOKS ATKINSON THEATRE
House Manager ....Barbara Carrellas
Treasurer ....Keshave Sattaur
Assistant Treasurers ....William Dorso, William O'Brien
House Carpenter ....Thomas A. Lavaia
House Flyman ....Joseph J. Maher
House Electrician ....Manuel Becker
House Properties ....Joseph P. DePaulo
Engineer ....Kevin MacKay

N
NEDERLANDER
Chairman ....**James M. Nederlander**
President ....**James L. Nederlander**

Executive Vice President
Nick Scandalios

Vice President   Senior Vice President
Corporate Development   Labor Relations
Charlene S. Nederlander   **Herschel Waxman**

Vice President   Chief Financial Officer
Jim Boese   **Freida Sawyer Belviso**

Grease
SCRAPBOOK

Correspondent: Lindsay Mendez "Jan"

Most Exciting Celebrity Visitor: Definitely Richie Sambora. He was so excited to be there and had such wonderful things to say about the show. Meeting him and his family was definitely a treat for us, and for our band!

Actor Who Has Done the Most Shows in Their Career: The person who has done the most Broadway shows would have to be our beloved "Teen Angel" Stephen Buntrock. I believe *Grease* is his eighth!

Special Backstage Rituals: Every night as the house announcement starts, the T-Birds, Pink Ladies, "Danny" and "Sandy" gather backstage and put all of our hands in and cheer something different. Sometimes, it's as simple as "One down, one to go!" I think my favorite cheer we ever did was during the stomach flu season, when we looked around and chanted, "WOW...we're ALL here!"

Favorite Off-Site Hangout: On about any two-show day, you are bound to find some of our cast or crew dining at Tratoria Tre-Colori, which is this amazing Italian restaurant that opened up right around the time our show did. It happens to be RIGHT next door to us. We love the staff there and have enjoyed many celebrations there, including birthday and Christmas parties.

Mascot: That would have to be our own "Patty Simcox," Allison Fischer. She is the youngest member of our cast and embodies the *Grease* spirit on and off stage.

Favorite Therapy: I'd have to say our cast's favorite therapy is a result of our favorite therapist, Mr. Russ Beasley. EVERY show should have him working with them. He is with us every week, making sure we can perform to the best of our abilities! He has worked many wonders on our aches and pains!

Memorable Press Encounter: For me, it would have to be when the Pink Ladies sang the National Anthem at Madison Square Garden for a New York Rangers Game. We had the best time. It was SO amazing to feel the rush of that huge crowd! That is something I know the girls and I will not soon forget!

Memorable Stage Door Encounter: The very first preview night, when we finished the show and went to leave the theater, we couldn't! The stage door was SO bombarded with audience members that there was no way to get out. I think that was when we all kind of realized what we had gotten ourselves into! It was so crazy to see all of these people who just love the show.

Catchphrase Only the Company Would Recognize: That's simple: "It was a Maxident!"

Company Legends: "The Buntrocky Award" has been created for any person who royally messes up on stage. This award has been given to only three people thus far, and it includes a trophy and a serenade by our own Stephen Buntrock, Jeb Brown, and Matthew Saldívar.

Embarrassing Moment: At the end of the show, during "We Go Together," Max and Laura dance this incredibly fast duet, when Laura finally gets to cut loose and show off her

1. (L-R): Producer David Ian, director Kathleen Marshall and co-author Jim Jacobs on opening night.
2. Max Crumm and Laura Osnes attend the cast party at Roseland.
3. (L-R): Kirsten Wyatt, Lindsay Mendez, Robyn Hurder at the party.
4. Allison Fischer at Roseland.
5. (L-R): Laura Osnes with original Broadway "Sandy" Carole Demas.
6. More *Grease* alumni (L-R): Didi Conn ("Frenchy" in the film), Barry Pearl ("Doody" in the film). Marilu Henner (original Broadway production), Kenneth Waissman (original producer), Annette Cardona ("Cha Cha" in the film).

dancing skills! One night, as she kicked her leg to do a lay out, her wig completely fell off her head! Max picked it up, and turned his back to the audience while bopping his butt to cover her, while she tried to slip it back on. Meanwhile, all of the cast, and the audience, were DYING! It was hysterical, and the crowd ate it up!

Coolest Thing About Being in This Show: For me, it is definitely the company. We have such a great time together, onstage and off. How many people get to play around and re-live their high school antics every night? It is such a ball!

Photos by Aubrey Reuben

Grey Gardens

First Preview: October 3, 2006. Opened: November 2, 2006.
Closed July 29, 2007 after 33 Previews and 308 Performances.

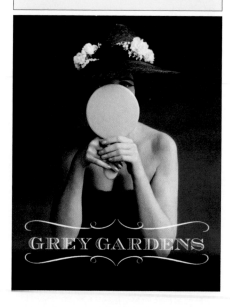

CAST
(in order of appearance)

PROLOGUE (1973)

Edith Bouvier Beale ......MARY LOUISE WILSON
"Little" Edie Beale ....CHRISTINE EBERSOLE

ACT ONE (1941)

Edith Bouvier Beale ....CHRISTINE EBERSOLE
Young "Little" Edie Beale ....ERIN DAVIE
George Gould Strong ....BOB STILLMAN
Brooks, Sr. ....MICHAEL POTTS
Jacqueline "Jackie" Bouvier ....SARAH HYLAND
Lee Bouvier ....KELSEY FOWLER
Joseph Patrick Kennedy, Jr. ...MATT CAVENAUGH
J.V. "Major" Bouvier ....JOHN McMARTIN

ACT TWO (1973)

Edith Bouvier Beale ......MARY LOUISE WILSON
"Little" Edie Beale ....CHRISTINE EBERSOLE
Brooks, Jr. ....MICHAEL POTTS
Jerry ....MATT CAVENAUGH
Norman Vincent Peale ....JOHN McMARTIN

Continued on next page

WALTER KERR THEATRE

A JUJAMCYN THEATRE
ROCCO LANDESMAN
PRESIDENT

PAUL LIBIN
PRODUCING DIRECTOR

JACK VIERTEL
CREATIVE DIRECTOR

JORDAN ROTH
VICE PRESIDENT

EAST OF DOHENY
STAUNCH ENTERTAINMENT   RANDALL L. WREGHITT / MORT SWINSKY
MICHAEL ALDEN   EDWIN W. SCHLOSS

in association with
PLAYWRIGHTS HORIZONS

present

CHRISTINE EBERSOLE

in

GREY GARDENS

Book by
DOUG WRIGHT

Music by
SCOTT FRANKEL

Lyrics by
MICHAEL KORIE

Based on the film "Grey Gardens" by David Maysles, Albert Maysles, Ellen Hovde, Muffie Meyer & Susan Froemke

Starring
MARY LOUISE WILSON

Featuring
MATT CAVENAUGH   ERIN DAVIE   KELSEY FOWLER
SARAH HYLAND   MICHAEL POTTS   BOB STILLMAN

and
JOHN McMARTIN

Scenic Design
ALLEN MOYER

Costume Design
WILLIAM IVEY LONG

Lighting Design
PETER KACZOROWSKI

Sound Design
BRIAN RONAN

Projection Design
WENDALL K. HARRINGTON

Hair and Wig Design
PAUL HUNTLEY

Orchestrations
BRUCE COUGHLIN

Music Director
LAWRENCE YURMAN

Music Coordinator
JOHN MILLER

General Management
ALAN WASSER -
ALLAN WILLIAMS

Production Stage Manager
JUDITH SCHOENFELD

Production Management
JUNIPER STREET
PRODUCTIONS

Press Representative
THE PUBLICITY OFFICE

Marketing
TMG -
THE MARKETING GROUP

Musical Staging by
JEFF CALHOUN

Directed by
MICHAEL GREIF

Grey Gardens was developed with the assistance of the Sundance Institute.

7/29/07

(L-R): Mary Louise Wilson as Edith Bouvier Beale and Christine Ebersole as "Little" Edie Beale

Photo by Joan Marcus

Grey Gardens

SONGS

PROLOGUE (1973)
"The Girl Who Has Everything"..Edith

ACT ONE (1941)
"The Girl Who Has Everything"..Edith
"The Five-Fifteen"...Edith, Gould, Jackie, Lee, Brooks
"Mother, Darling"..Edie, Edith, Gould
"Goin' Places"...Joe & Edie
"Marry Well"...............................Major Bouvier, Brooks, Jackie, Lee, Edie
"Hominy Grits"..Edith, Gould, Jackie, Lee
"Peas in a Pod"..Edie & Edith
"Drift Away"..Gould & Edith
"The Five-Fifteen" (Reprise)..Edith
"Daddy's Girl"...Edie
"The Telegram"...Edie
"Will You?"...Edith

ACT TWO (1973)
"The Revolutionary Costume for Today"..Edie
"The Cake I Had"..Edith
"Entering Grey Gardens"..Company
"The House We Live In"...Edie & Company
"Jerry Likes My Corn"..Edith & Edie
"Around the World"...Edie
"Will You?" (Reprise)..Edith & Edie
"Choose to Be Happy"...................Norman Vincent Peale & Company
"Around the World" (Reprise)..Edie
"Another Winter in a Summer Town"...............................Edie & Edith
"The Girl Who Has Everything" (Reprise)................................Edith & Edie

THE STORY OF THE EDIES

As a young society debutante in the early 1940s, "Little" Edie Bouvier Beale (1917-2002) was one of the brightest names in the social register. Known as "Body Beautiful Beale," she was the "It Girl" of her generation, even eclipsing her young cousin, Jacqueline Bouvier. In the years following World War II, however, life at Grey Gardens, their 28-room mansion, took an unexpected turn. While Jackie and her sister Lee Radziwill played out their lives on the world stage, Edie and her mother, Edith Bouvier Beale (1896-1977), became East Hampton's most notorious recluses. Filled with stray cats and in disrepair, the house was condemned by the Suffolk County Board of Health in 1972. Their squalid living conditions were plastered across the tabloids, and a public scandal erupted, forcing their famous relatives to step in and assist with the clean-up. In the end, the Edies proved to be indomitable, and their fierce individualism and nonconformist spirit has made them enduring icons.

In 1974, filmmakers Albert and David Maysles chronicled six weeks in the lives of the Beales at the Grey Gardens estate. The brothers would ultimately revolutionize documentary filmmaking with their series of landmark films, and *Grey Gardens* would become one of the most controversial examples of the emerging nonfiction style known as "cinema verite." The film is in the International Documentary Association's "Top Ten of All Time" list.

The musical *Grey Gardens*, which premiered Off-Broadway at Playwrights Horizons in March 2006, helped usher in a new resurgence in the *Grey Gardens* phenomenon. It was followed by the Maysles Brothers' own companion movie, *The Beales of Grey Gardens*, featuring previously unseen outtakes from the original documentary which is now available on DVD. The musical and the new film will be followed by several upcoming books on the Beales (including a collection of Edie's own poetry), and a documentary about the making of the musical.

STANDBYS
Standby for Christine Ebersole:
MAUREEN MOORE
For Mary Louise Wilson:
DALE SOULES
For Jacqueline Bouvier and Lee Bouvier:
ABIGAIL FERENCZY
For J.V. "Major" Bouvier/Norman Vincent Peale:
DONALD GRODY
For Brooks, Sr./Brooks, Jr.:
MICHAEL W. HOWELL
For Young "Little" Edie Beale:
MEGAN LEWIS
For Joseph Patrick Kennedy, Jr./Jerry and Gould:
ASA SOMERS

Dance Captain:
MEGAN LEWIS

SETTING
Act One takes place in July, 1941, Grey Gardens, East Hampton, Long Island, NY

Act Two takes place in 1973, Grey Gardens, East Hampton, Long Island, NY

The events of the play are based on both fact and fiction.

MUSICIANS
Conductor:
LAWRENCE YURMAN
Associate Conductor/Keyboards:
PAUL STAROBA

Violin:
ERIC DeGIOIA
Cello:
ANIK OULIANINE
Reeds:
KEN HITCHCOCK, TODD GROVES
Trumpet/Flugelhorn:
DANIEL URNESS
French Horn:
PATRICK PRIDEMORE
Acoustic Bass:
BRIAN CASSIER
Percussion/Drums:
TIM McLAFFERTY

Music Copying:
EMILY GRISHMAN MUSIC PREPARATION/
EMILY GRISHMAN, KATHARINE EDMONDS

Grey Gardens

Christine Ebersole
"Little" Edie Beale/
Edith Bouvier Beale

Mary Louise Wilson
Edith Bouvier Beale

John McMartin
J.V. "Major" Bouvier/
Norman Vincent
Peale

Matt Cavenaugh
Joseph Patrick
Kennedy, Jr./Jerry

Erin Davie
Young "Little"
Edie Beale

Kelsey Fowler
Lee Bouvier

Sarah Hyland
Jacqueline Bouvier

Michael Potts
Brooks, Sr./
Brooks, Jr.

Bob Stillman
George Gould Strong

Maureen Moore
Standby for Christine
Ebserole

Dale Soules
Standby for
Mary Louise Wilson

Donald Grody
Standby for
J.V. "Major" Bouvier/
Norman Vincent
Peale

Abigail Ferenczy
Standby for
Jacqueline Bouvier
& Lee Bouvier

Michael W. Howell
Standby for
Brooks, Sr./
Brooks, Jr.

Megan Lewis
Standby for Young
"Little" Edie Beale/
Dance Captain

Asa Somers
Standby for Joseph
Patrick Kennedy, Jr./
Jerry & Gould

Doug Wright
Book

Scott Frankel
Music

Michael Korie
Lyrics

Michael Greif
Director

Jeff Calhoun
Musical Staging

Allen Moyer
Scenic Designer

William Ivey Long
Costume Designer

Peter Kaczorowski
Lighting Designer

Brian Ronan
Sound Designer

Wendall K.
Harrington
Projections

Paul Huntley
Hair and Wig Design

Bruce Coughlin
Orchestrations

John Miller
Music Coordinator

Alan Wasser
Associates
General Manager

Guy Kwan, John Paull, Hillary Blanken,
Kevin Broomell, Ana Rose Greene,
Juniper Street Productions
Production Manager

Bernard Telsey,
Telsey + Company
Casting

Randall L. Wreghitt
Producer

Mort Swinsky
Producer

Grey Gardens

Michael Alden
Producer

Edwin W. Schloss
Producer

STAGE CREW
(L-R): P.J. Stasuk (Head Sound Engineer), Patrick McCormack (Stagehand), Jack Cennamo (Carpenter), Drayton Allison (Electrician), Angelo Torre (Production Props), Tim Bennet (Propman), George Fullum (Carpenter), Amber Adams (Assistant Sound Engineer), Lonny MacDougall (Electrician) and Matt Lynch (Automation).

STAGE MANAGERS
(L-R): Judith Schoenfeld, Vanessa Brown, Bryan Landrine and Colleen Danaher.

DOORMAN
John Raymond Barker

ORCHESTRA
Front Row Sitting (L-R): Anik Oulianine (Cello), Patrick Pridemore (Horn).

Back Row Standing (L-R): John Meyers (Percussion sub), Todd Groves (Reed 1), Lawrence Yurman (Conductor), Paul Staroba (Keyboard), Michael Blanco (Bass sub), Eric DeGioia (Violin) and Dan Urness (Trumpet).

Not Pictured: Brian Cassier (Bass), Tim McLafferty (Percussion), Ken Hitchcock (Reed 2).

Grey Gardens

HAIR
(L-R): Jodi Jackson (Hair Swing) and Erin Kennedy Lunsford (Hair Supervisor).

Photos by Ben Strothmann

WARDROBE
(L-R): Lisa Tucci (Wardrobe Supervisor), Vangeli Kaseluris (Dresser), Jill Frese (Dresser), Jane Rottenbach (Dresser) and Hilda Garcia-Suli (Dresser).

USHERS
(L-R): Michelle Fleury, TJ D'Angelo, Kelvin Loh, Victoria Lauzun, Alison Traynor and Henry Leo Linton.

USHER
Aaron Kendall

BOX OFFICE
(L-R): Stan Shaffer (Treasurer) and Gail Yerkovich (Ticket Seller).

MERCHANDISING
(L-R): Rodrigo Bolanos, Greg Watson, Molly Lehmann and Tammy Fowler.

Grey Gardens

(L-R): Erin Davie as young "Little" Edie Beale and John McMartin as Major Bouvier.

Photo by Joan Marcus

Gypsy

First Preview: March 3, 2008. Opened: March 27, 2008.
Still running as of May 31, 2008.

CAST

(in order of appearance)

Uncle Jocko	JIM BRACCHITTA
Georgie	BILL BATEMAN
Vladimir	KYRIAN FRIEDENBERG
Balloon Girl	KATIE MICHA
Baby June	SAMI GAYLE
Baby Louise	EMMA ROWLEY
Charlie	MATTHEW LOBENHOFER
Hopalong	RIDER QUENTIN STANTON
Rose	PATTI LuPONE
Pop	BILL RAYMOND
Driver	PEARCE WEGENER
Rich Boy	KYRIAN FRIEDENBERG
Tap Dancer	MATTHEW LOBENHOFER
Boy Scout	ANDY RICHARDSON
Weber	BRIAN REDDY
Herbie	BOYD GAINES
Dainty June	LEIGH ANN LARKIN
Louise	LAURA BENANTI
Yonkers	PEARCE WEGENER
L.A.	STEVE KONOPELSKI
Tulsa	TONY YAZBECK
Kansas	JOHN SCACCHETTI
Little Rock	GEO SEERY
East St. Louis	MATTY PRICE
Mr. Goldstone	BILL BATEMAN
Waitress	JESSICA RUSH
Miss Cratchitt	LENORA NEMETZ
Agnes	NICOLE MANGI
Marjorie May	ALICIA SABLE
Geraldine	MINDY DOUGHERTY

Continued on next page

🕁 ST. JAMES THEATRE

A JUJAMCYN THEATRE

ROCCO LANDESMAN
President

PAUL LIBIN	JACK VIERTEL	JORDAN ROTH
Producing Director	Creative Director	Vice President

Roger Berlind • The Routh • Frankel • Baruch • Viertel Group
Roy Furman Debra Black Ted Hartley Roger Horchow David Ian
Scott Rudin Jack Viertel

present

PATTI LuPONE
in

GYPSY

Book by	Music by	Lyrics by
Arthur Laurents	Jule Styne	Stephen Sondheim

Suggested by the memoirs of Gypsy Rose Lee

Starring

Boyd Gaines   Laura Benanti

Also Starring

Leigh Ann Larkin   Tony Yazbeck
Marilyn Caskey   Alison Fraser   Lenora Nemetz

With

Bill Bateman   Jim Bracchitta   Sami Gayle
Bill Raymond   Brian Reddy   Emma Rowley

Andrew Boyer Dorothy Stanley Beckley Andrews Nancy Renée Braun Mindy Dougherty Kyrian Friedenberg Matt Gibson
Sarah Marie Hicks Steve Konopelski Matthew Lobenhofer Nicole Mangi Katie Micha Matty Price Andy Richardson
Lisa Rohinsky Jessica Rush Alicia Sable John Scacchetti Geo Seery Rider Quentin Stanton Pearce Wegener

Scenery Designed by	Costumes Designed by	Lighting Designed by	Sound Designed by
James Youmans	Martin Pakledinaz	Howell Binkley	Dan Moses Schreier

Casting by	Wigs & Hair Designed by	Make Up Designed by	Production Stage Manager
Jay Binder	Paul Huntley	Angelina Avallone	Craig Jacobs

Orchestrations by	Dance Arrangements by		Music Coordination by
Sid Ramin and Robert Ginzler	John Kander		Seymour Red Press

General Management	Technical Supervision by	Press Representative	Based on the Presentation by
Richard Frankel Productions	Juniper Street	Barlow • Hartman	New York City Center
Laura Green	Productions, Inc.		*Encores!®* Summer Stars

Music Director and Arranger
Patrick Vaccariello

Choreography by

Jerome Robbins

Mr. Robbins's Choreography Reproduced by
Bonnie Walker

Direction by

Arthur Laurents

The Producers wish to express their appreciation to the Theatre Development Fund for its support of this production.

3/27/08

(L-R): Laura Benanti, Patti LuPone and Boyd Gaines.

Photo by Paul Kolnik

Gypsy

SCENES AND MUSICAL NUMBERS

ACT ONE

Overture ....The Orchestra
Scene 1: Vaudeville theatre stage. Seattle.
    "May We Entertain You" ....Baby June and Baby Louise
Scene 2: Kitchen. Seattle.
    "Some People" ....Rose
Scene 3: Road between Seattle and Los Angeles.
    Reprise: "Some People" ....Rose
Scene 4: Backstage of vaudeville theatre. Los Angeles.
    "Small World" ....Rose and Herbie
Scene 5: Stage of vaudeville theatre. Los Angeles.
    "Baby June and Her Newsboys" ....Baby June, Baby Louise and Newsboys
Scene 6: Hotel room. Akron.
    "Have an Eggroll, Mr. Goldstone" ....Rose, Herbie, June, Mr. Goldstone and Boys
    "Little Lamb" ....Louise
Scene 7: Chinese restaurant. New York.
    "You'll Never Get Away From Me" ....Rose and Herbie
Scene 8: Stage of Grantziger's Palace Theatre. New York.
    "Dainty June and Her Farmboys" ....Dainty June and Farmboys
Scene 9: Mr. Grantziger's Office.
    "If Momma Was Married" ....Louise and June
Scene 10: Theatre alley. Buffalo.
    "All I Need Is the Girl" ....Tulsa and Louise
Scene 11: Railway station. Omaha.
    "Everything's Coming Up Roses" ....Rose

ACT TWO

Entr'acte ....The Orchestra
Scene 1: Desert. Texas.
    "Madame Rose's Toreadorables" ....Louise and the Hollywood Blondes
    "Together Wherever We Go" ....Rose, Herbie and Louise
Scene 2: Backstage of a burlesque house. Wichita.
    "You Gotta Get a Gimmick" ....Mazeppa, Electra and Tessie Tura
Scene 3: Backstage corridor. Wichita.
Scene 4: Backstage and onstage: Wichita, Detroit, Philadelphia and Minsky's Burlesque.
    "The Strip" ....Louise
Scene 5: Louise's dressing room, Minsky's Burlesque.
Scene 6: Stage.
    "Rose's Turn" ....Rose

ORCHESTRA

Conductor: PATRICK VACCARIELLO
Violins: MARILYN REYNOLDS,
FRITZ KRAKOWSKI, ERIC DEGIOIA,
DANA IANCULOVICI
Violas: CRYSTAL GARNER, SALLY SHUMWAY
Cello: PETER PROSSER, VIVIAN ISRAEL
Bass: BRIAN CASSIER
Woodwinds: EDWARD SALKIN,
ADAM KOLKER, DENNIS ANDERSON,
RALPH OLSEN, JOHN WINDER

Trumpets: TONY KADLECK,
JAMES DELAGARZA, KAMAU ADILIFU
Trombones: BRUCE EIDEM,
WAYNE GOODMAN, ROBERT FOURNIER
French Horn: NANCY BILLMAN
Harp: SUSAN JOLLES
Keyboards: JEFFREY HARRIS
Drums: PAUL PIZZUTI
Percussion: THAD WHEELER
Music Coordinator: SEYMOUR RED PRESS

Cast Continued

Edna Mae ....NANCY RENÉE BRAUN
Carol Ann ....SARAH MARIE HICKS
Betsy Ann ....BECKLEY ANDREWS
Cigar ....BILL RAYMOND
Pastey ....JIM BRACCHITTA
Tessie Tura ....ALISON FRASER
Mazeppa ....LENORA NEMETZ
Electra ....MARILYN CASKEY
Renée ....JESSICA RUSH
Phil ....BRIAN REDDY
Bougeron-Cochon ....BILL BATEMAN

STANDBYS

Rose:
LENORA NEMETZ
Herbie:
JIM BRACCHITTA
Louise:
JESSICA RUSH
Dainty June:
MINDY DOUGHERTY
Tulsa:
PEARCE WEGENER
Tessie Tura, Mazeppa, Electra:
DOROTHY STANLEY
Miss Cratchitt:
JESSICA RUSH, DOROTHY STANLEY
Georgie:
MATT GIBSON
Bougeron-Cochon:
JOHN SCACCHETTI
Uncle Jocko:
ANDREW BOYER
Pastey:
PEARCE WEGENER, MATT GIBSON
Baby Louise, Baby June:
KATIE MICHA
Cigar:
BILL BATEMAN, ANDREW BOYER
Pop, Weber, Phil:
ANDREW BOYER
Balloon Girl, Agnes:
ALICIA SABLE
Military Boys:
KYRIAN FRIEDENBERG
Newsboys:
RIDER QUENTIN STANTON
Yonkers, L. A., Kansas:
MATTY PRICE, MATT GIBSON
Renée, Waitress:
LISA ROHINSKY

Swings:
MATT GIBSON, LISA ROHINSKY

Gypsy

Patti LuPone
Rose

Boyd Gaines
Herbie

Laura Benanti
Louise

Leigh Ann Larkin
Dainty June

Tony Yazbeck
Tulsa

Marilyn Caskey
Electra

Alison Fraser
Tessie Tura

Lenora Nemetz
*Mazeppa,
Miss Cratchitt,
Standby Rose*

Bill Bateman
*Georgie,
Mr. Goldstone,
Bougeron-Cochon,
Dance Captain*

Jim Bracchitta
Uncle Jocko, Pastey

Sami Gayle
Baby June

Bill Raymond
Pop, Cigar

Brian Reddy
Weber, Phil

Emma Rowley
Baby Louise

Andrew Boyer
*Standby
Uncle Jocko/Pop/
Cigar/Weber/Phil*

Dorothy Stanley
*Standby Electra/
Mazeppa/
Tessie Tura/
Miss Cratchitt*

Beckley Andrews
Betsy Ann, Ensemble

Nancy Renée Braun
Edna Mae, Ensemble

Mindy Dougherty
Geraldine

Kyrian Friedenberg
*Vladimir, Rich Boy,
Ensemble*

Sarah Marie Hicks
Carol Ann, Ensemble

Steve Konopelski
L.A., Ensemble

Matthew Lobenhofer
*Tap Dancer, Julius,
Ensemble*

Nicole Mangi
Agnes, Ensemble

Katie Micha
*Balloon Girl,
Ensemble*

Matty Price
East St. Louis

Andy Richardson
*Boy Scout, Charlie,
Ensemble*

Jessica Rush
Renée

Alicia Sable
*Marjorie May,
Ensemble*

John Scacchetti
Kansas, Ensemble

Geo Seery
Little Rock

Rider Quentin
Stanton
*Hopalong,
Military Boy,
Ensemble*

Pearce Wegener
*Driver, Yonkers,
Ensemble*

Matt Gibson
Swing

Lisa Rohinsky
Swing

Gypsy

Arthur Laurents
Book/Director

Stephen Sondheim
Lyrics

Jerome Robbins
*Original Direction/
Choreography*

Patrick Vaccariello
Music Director

Martin Pakledinaz
Costume Design

Howell Binkley
Lighting Design

Dan Moses Schreier
Sound Design

Jay Binder C.S.A.
Casting

Paul Huntley
Wig & Hair Design

Angelina Avallone
Make-up Design

John Kander
*Original Dance
Arrangements*

Seymour Red Press
Music Coordinator

**Laura Green,
Richard Frankel
Productions**
*General
Management*

**Roger Berlind,
Berlind Productions**
Producer

**Guy Kwan, John Paull III, Hillary Blanken,
Kevin Broomell, Ana Rose Greene,
Juniper Street Productions**
Production Manager

**Marc Routh,
The R/F/B/V Group**
Producer

**Richard Frankel,
The R/F/B/V Group**
Producer

**Steven Baruch,
The R/F/B/V Group**
Producer

**Tom Viertel,
The R/F/B/V Group**
Producer

Roy Furman
Producer

Debra Black
Producer

Ted Hartley
Producer

**Roger Horchow
Productions**
Producer

Jack Viertel
Producer

Boyd Gaines
and Laura
Benanti watch
as Patti LuPone
delivers
"Everything's
Coming Up
Roses."

Photo by Paul Kolnik

Gypsy

BOX OFFICE
(L-R): Vincent Sclafani, Vincent Siniscalchi, Michael Milione.

Photos by Ben Strothmann

HAIR DEPARTMENT
(L-R):Jeff Silverman, Danny Koye, Mia Neal, Carmel Vargyas (in photo),
Nathaniel Hathaway, Vanessa Anderson.

PROPS DEPARTMENT
(L-R): Rich Anderson, Tom Thompson, "Chowsie."

STAGE MANAGEMENT
Front Row (L-R): Liza Vest, Christine Rudakewycz
(Child Wrangler).

Back Row (L-R): Gary Mickelson, Craig Jacobs,
Tom Capps

DOORMAN
James Cline

Gypsy

Photos by Ben Strothmann

WARDROBE CREW
Front Row (L-R): Kimberly Baird, Marisa Lerette, Renee Borys.

Middle Row (L-R): Tree Sarvay, Lyle Jones, Michael Louis.

Back Row (L-R): Danny Mura, Robert Guy, Kurt Kielmann.

LIGHTING AND SOUND DEPARTMENT
Front Row (L-R): Al Sayers, Sue Pelkofer, Sandy Paradise.

Middle Row (L-R): Bob Miller, David Gotwald, Joe Lenihan.

Back Row (L-R): Scott Silvian, Ron Martin.

CARPENTERS
Front Row (L-R): John Paull, Mark Hallisey.

Middle Row (L-R): Dave Brown, Tim McDonough, Jr., Ryan McDonough.

Back Row (L-R): Tom Fitzsimons, Tim McDonough.

FRONT OF HOUSE STAFF
Front Row (L-R): Margaret McElroy, Catherine Junior, Cynthia Lopiano, Barbara Carrol, Harry Joshi.

Second Row (L-R): Julia Furay, Leonard Bernfeld Baron, Jim Barry.

Third Row (L-R): Chadwick Vogel, Sherry Przybyszewski, Kaiser Akram, Russ Buenteo, Amanda Rose.

Back Row (L-R): Jacobo Medrano, Francisco Medina, Antoin Ramirez, Beau Bisson, Juan Luis Acevedo, Justin Karr.

Gypsy

STAFF FOR *GYPSY*

GENERAL MANAGEMENT
RICHARD FRANKEL PRODUCTIONS
Richard Frankel   Marc Routh   Laura Green
Rod Kaats   Joe Watson

COMPANY MANAGER
Sammy Ledbetter
Associate Company Manager ....Townsend Teague

GENERAL PRESS REPRESENTATIVE
BARLOW•HARTMAN
John Barlow   Michael Hartman
Ryan Ratelle   Melissa Bixler

CASTING
JAY BINDER CASTING
Jay Binder CSA   Jack Bowdan CSA
Mark Brandon   Sara Schatz
Nicole Vallins   Allison Estrin

TECHNICAL SUPERVISION
JUNIPER STREET PRODUCTIONS
Hillary Blanken   Kevin Broomell
Guy Kwan   Ana Rose Greene

Production Stage Manager	**Craig Jacobs**
Stage Manager	Gary Mickelson
First Assistant Stage Manager	Tom Capps
Assistant Stage Manager	Nancy Elizabeth Vest
Assistant Director	Isaac Klein
Assistant Choreographer	Roger Preston Smith
Dance Captain	Bill Bateman
Associate Scenic Designer	Jerome Martin
Assistant Scenic Designer	Adrienne Kapalko
Associate Costume Designer	Martha Bromelmeier
Assistants to Martin Pakledinaz	Sarah Cubbage,
	Tescia Seufferlein
Associate Lighting Designer	Ryan O'Gara
Assistant Lighting Designer	Amanda Zieve
Associate Sound Designer	David Bullard
Assistant Sound Designer	David Stollings
Associate Wig Designer	Giovanna Calabretta
Company Management Intern	Emily Wright

Production Carpenter	Jack Anderson
Head Carpenter	John Paull
Assistant Carpenter	Mark Hallisey
Production Electrician	Dan Coey
Head Electrician	Ron Martin
Assistant Electrician	Sandy Paradise
Moving Light Programmer	Timothy F. Rogers
Head Sound Engineer	David Gotwald
Assistant Sound Engineer	Scott Silvian
Production Property Master	Tim Abel
Head Property Master	J. Marvin Crosland
Assistant Property Master	Thomas Thomson
Wardrobe Supervisor	Robert Guy
Assistant Wardrobe Supervisor	Kimberly Baird
Miss LuPone's Dresser	Pat White
Dressers	Renee Borys, Kurt Kielman,
	Michael Louis, Danny Mura,
	Tree Sarvay, Estella Marie Simmons,
	Arlene Watson, Lyle Jones
Hair & Wig Supervisor	Nathaniel A. Hathaway
Assistant Hair & Wig Supervisor	Carmel Vargyas

Hairdressers	Vanessa Anderson, Danny Koye,
	Jeff Silverman
Production Assistants	Emma Atherton, Elise Hanley,
	Laura Kimsey, Megan Loughran,
	Laura Skolnik, Alissa Zulvergold
Children's Tutoring	On Location Education, Alan Simon
Children's Guardian	Christine Rudakewycz

Music Director/Conductor	Patrick Vaccariello
Music Coordinator	Seymour Red Press
Associate Music Director/Conductor	Jeffrey Harris
Special Keyboard Arrangements	Danny Troob,
	Nathan Kelly
Synthesizer Programmer	Randy Cohen
Music Preparation	Anixter Rice Music Services
Rehearsal Pianist	Jim Laev
Dummer	Paul Pizzuti

Assistant to Stephen Sondheim	Steven Clar
Assistant to Roger Berlind	Jeffrey Hillock
Assistant to Steve Baruch	Sonja Soper
Assistant to Tom Viertel	Tania Senewiratne
Assistant to Roy Furman	Eileen Williams
Assistant to Debra Black	Rosemary Kenny
Assistant to Ted Hartley	David Woodard
Assistant to Roger Horchow	Donna Harper
Assistant to David Ian	Alison Kelly
Assistant to Scott Rudin	Adam Klaff
Assistant to Jack Viertel	Joanna Gang

Advertising	Serino Coyne, Inc./
	Sandy Block, Scott Johnson, Robert Jones
Press Associates	Leslie Baden, Michelle Bergmann,
	Dennis Crowley, Tom D'Ambrosio, Bethany Larsen,
	Richard Pineau, Kevin Robak, Wayne Wolfe
Promotions/Marketing	Broadway Print & Mail
Production Photography	Paul Kolnik
Web Design	Simma Park
Theatre Displays	King Displays
Music Copying	Anixter Rice Music Services
Insurance	DeWitt Stern Group, Inc./
	Peter Shoemaker, Mary DeSpirt
Legal Counsel	Patricia Crown, Esq.,
	Coblence & Associates
Banking	Chase Manhattan Bank/Michele Gibbons
Payroll Service	Castellana Services, Inc.
Accounting	Fried & Kowgios Partners, CPAs, LLP
New York Rehearsals	New 42nd Street Studios
Group Sales	Show Tix (212) 302-7000

RICHARD FRANKEL PRODUCTIONS STAFF

Finance Director	**Michael Naumann**
Assistant to Richard Frankel	Heidi Libby
Assistant to Marc Routh	Katie Adams
Assistant to Laura Green	Joshua A. Saletnik
Assistant Finance Director	Susan Bartelt
Information Technology Manager	Roddy Pimentel
Accounting Assistant	Heather Allen
National Sales and Marketing Director	**Ronni Mandell**
Director of Business Affairs	**Michael Sinder**
Marketing Manager	Melissa Marano
Promotions Manager	Alana Karpoff
Marketing Coordinator	Christina Papagjika
Office Manager	**Lori Steiger-Perry**
Office Management Assistant	Taryn Cagnina
Receptionists	Aubrey Ball, Christina Cataldo
Interns	Amanda Axelrod, Dario Dalla Lasta,

Dana Enis, Randi Fields, Andrew Gottlieb,
Leeann Kelley, Rebecca O'Connell, Corey Phillips,
Allison Raines, Samantha Saltzman,
Jessica Spota, Shannon Tooley, Irina Zheleznyak

Special thanks to Erik Preminger

The producers would like to acknowledge and thank the parents of each of the juvenile actors in *Gypsy*: Denise DeBella and Mike Stanton; Larissa & Douglas Friedenberg; Denise and Steve Johnson; Robin & Larry Klitzman; Angie & Lee Lobenhofer; Rita & Mike Richardson; Kathie & James Rowley.

Makeup provided by M•A•C Cosmetics

CREDITS AND ACKNOWLEDGEMENTS
Scenery and scenic effects built and electrified by PRG Scenic Technologies, New Windsor, NY and Black Walnut, Valley Cottage, NY. Scenery painted by Black Walnut, Valley Cottage, NY, and Scenic Art Studios, Cornwall, NY. Show control and scenic motion control featuring Stage Command Systems® by PRG Scenic Technologies, New Windsor, NY. Softgoods built by I. Weiss and Sons, Inc., Long Island City, NY. Lighting equipment provided by PRG Lighting, North Bergen, NJ. Sound equipment provided by PRG Audio, Mt. Vernon, NY. Furniture and props executed by The Spoon Group, Rahway, NJ, and Joe Props, Kane, PA. Hauling by Clark Transfer, Inc. Ms. LuPone's costumes by Barbara Matera, Ltd. & Eric Winterling, Inc. Ms. Benanti's costumes by Eric Winterling, Inc. Costumes by Tricorne Inc., Paul Chang Custom Tailors, Izquierdo Studio, Krostyne Studio, Seams Unlimited. Millinery by Lynne Mackey Studio, Arnold S. Levine Inc., Rodney Gordon Inc., Carelli Costumes, Ellen Christine. Shoes by Worldtone Dance, Capezio Dance, LaDuca Shoes, JC Theatrical, Freeds, Celebrity Shoes. Fabric dyeing and printing by Gene Mignola Inc., Ellen Steingraeber & Izquierdo Studios. "Electra"-fication by Chic Silber. Special thanks to Vintage Clothing Early Halloween New York City, Odds Costumes Rental, New York Vintage, Right to the Moon Alice, Odds and Adds. Lozenges provided by Ricola. Limousine services provided by Nice Guys Limousine, Inc. Special thanks to Barbara Crompton, Staci Levine, Tanase Popa, Michael Zande. Natural herb cough drops courtesy of Ricola USA, Inc. Special thanks to Bra*Tenders for undergarments and hosiery.

"Happy Birthday to You" (Mildred J. Hill, Patty Smith Hill); ©1935 (Renewed) Summy-Birchard Company (ASCAP). All rights reserved. Used by permission.

JUJAMCYN THEATERS

ROCCO LANDESMAN
President

PAUL LIBIN	**JACK VIERTEL**	**JORDAN ROTH**
Producing Director	Creative Director	Vice President
DANIEL ADAMIAN		**JENNIFER HERSHEY**
General Manager		Director of Operations
MEREDITH VILLATORE		**JERRY ZAKS**
Chief Financial Officer		Resident Director

STAFF FOR THE ST. JAMES THEATRE

Manager	Daniel Adamian
Treasurer	Vincent Sclafani
Carpenter	Timothy McDonough
Propertyman	Barnett Epstein
Electrician	Albert Sayers

Gypsy
SCRAPBOOK

Correspondents: Leigh Ann Larkin, "Dainty June"; and, her answers in red, Patti LuPone, "Rose."

Memorable Opening Night Letter, Fax or Note: Everyone in the cast wrote the most lovely notes. Also, I got notes and flowers from my friends. I was really touched.

Opening Night Gifts: Cancelled stock certificate from the Orpheum Circuit given to me by Patti LuPone. My parents being here to share the whole night with me!

Most Exciting Celebrity Visitor and What They Said: Angela Lansbury, who said she had just made up with Arthur [Laurents] on the stairs.

Erik Preminger, Gypsy Rose Lee's son, came to see the show with his wife. He told me how much his mother would have loved our show and told me how truthful I was being to his Aunt June. It was the highest compliment I could have ever been paid.

Actor Who Performed the Most Roles in This Show: Bill Bateman.

Actors Who Have Done the Most Shows in Their Career: Either me or Boyd. Is that showing our age?

Special Backstage Rituals: Show up and get ready!

Favorite Moment During Each Performance (On Stage or Off): Anything with Boyd, Laura and Leigh Ann. Singing "If Momma Was Married" with Laura and watching Patti from the wings performing "Rose's Turn."

Favorite In-Theatre Gathering Places: My dressing room. The "Dave Brown Lounge" and the stage manager's office.

Favorite Off-Site Hangout: Truthfully, I almost never go out, but I did go to Angus once and I had a blast!

Favorite Snack Food: Nuts, chocolates, alcohol—kidding! Starbucks and Swedish Fish.

Mascots: Adam Hunter, a PSM on another show. The lamb puppet and the cow.

Favorite Therapies: Massage, wash-outs, sleep. My personal vaporizer.

Record Number of Cell Phone Rings During a Performance: Very few, bless the Lord! None! Our announcement tells the audience to check to make sure their phones are off before both acts and so far, it's worked.

Memorable Press Encounter: Walking the red carpet and going through the press line on opening night! It was the best and most exciting night of my whole life!

Memorable Stage Door Fan Encounter: The first time I walked out the stage door after a performance. I was completely overwhelmed.

Latest Audience Arrival: Honestly, I don't ever look out into the audience because I have to focus on what's happening onstage.

Busiest Days at the Box Office: I would guess the weekend after we opened.

Memorable Directorial Note: "Have fun." Arthur once climbed up five flights of stairs to my dressing room at intermission to tell me how happy he was with my performance. It

1. Curtain call on opening night (L-R): Stephen Sondheim, Boyd Gaines, Patti LuPone, Laura Benanti, Marilyn Caskey, Alison Fraser, Lenora Nemetz, and Arthur Laurents.
2. (L-R): Laura Benanti and Yearbook Correspondent Leigh Ann Larkin backstage.
3. Two Junes (L-R): Sami Gayle and Leigh Ann Larkin.
4. Boyd Gaines and Leigh Ann Larkin backstage.

made my life!

Company Legends: Arthur Laurents! He's a pretty big legend to me!

Understudy Anecdote: Sami Gayle hurt herself, so her understudy Katie went on for opening night.

Sweethearts Within the Company and Crew: Joe and Carmel.

Embarrassing Moments: I won't say! Nothing too embarrassing yet, but once I punched a hole through the train and that didn't feel so great!

Ghostly Encounters Backstage: Not yet, but waiting.

Superstitions That Turned Out To Be True: The Scottish play. Arthur said "the title of the show that shall not be named" and one thing after another started happening. An air-conditioner grate fell on an audience member, light bulbs fell from a set piece on stage and a few other things happened as well. Patti had him lift the curse and things have been great!

Coolest Thing About Being in This Show: The sublime company of players, backstage crew, wardrobe, et al. I feel like I am a part of history and it's my Broadway debut! What could be cooler than that?

Fan Info: Send anything to the St. James Theatre—we love getting mail!

Hairspray

First Preview: July 18, 2002. Opened: August 15, 2002.
Still running as of May 31, 2008.

PLAYBILL

hairspray

CAST

(in order of appearance)

Tracy Turnblad	SHANNON DURIG
Corny Collins	LANCE BASS
Amber Von Tussle	ASHLEY SPENCER
Brad	KASEY MARINO
Tammy	HAYLEY PODSCHUN
Fender	DANIEL ROBINSON
Brenda	LESLIE GODDARD
Sketch	VAN HUGHES
Shelley	LORI EVE MARINACCI
IQ	TODD MICHEL SMITH
Lou Ann	LESLIE McDONEL
Link Larkin	ASHLEY PARKER ANGEL
Prudy Pingleton	SUSAN MOSHER
Edna Turnblad	PAUL C. VOGT
Penny Pingleton	NIKI SCALERA
Velma Von Tussle	MICHELE PAWK
Harriman F. Spritzer	KEVIN MEANEY
Wilbur Turnblad	JIM J. BULLOCK
Principal	KEVIN MEANEY
Seaweed J. Stubbs	TEVIN CAMPBELL
Duane	TRAVIS ROBERTSON
Gilbert	STEVEN CUTTS
Lorraine	TERITA R. REDD
Thad	DWAYNE COOPER
The Dynamites	IRIS BURRUSS, CARLA J. HARGROVE, JUDINE SOMERVILLE
Mr. Pinky	KEVIN MEANEY
Gym Teacher	SUSAN MOSHER
Inez	NATURI NAUGHTON

Continued on next page

NEIL SIMON THEATRE

UNDER THE DIRECTION OF JAMES M. NEDERLANDER AND JAMES L. NEDERLANDER

Margo Lion   Adam Epstein   The Baruch · Viertel · Routh · Frankel Group
James D. Stern/Douglas L. Meyer   Rick Steiner/Frederic H. Mayerson
SEL & GFO   New Line Cinema
In Association With
Live Nation   A. Gordon/E. McAllister
D. Harris/M. Swinsky   J. & B. Osher
Present

HAIRSPRAY

Book By	Music By	Lyrics By
Mark O'Donnell	Marc Shaiman	Scott Wittman
Thomas Meehan		Marc Shaiman

Based upon the New Line Cinema film written and directed by John Waters

Starring

Shannon Durig   **Paul C. Vogt**

With

Ashley Parker Angel   **Lance Bass**

Also Starring

Jim J. Bullock   Tevin Campbell   Scott Davidson   Kevin Meaney   Susan Mosher
Naturi Naughton   Niki Scalera   Ashley Spencer
with **Michele Pawk** and **Darlene Love**

With

Joe Abraham   Tracee Beazer   Gretchen Bieber   Iris Burruss   Dwayne Cooper   Steven Cutts   Michelle Dowdy
Brooke Leigh Engen   Leslie Goddard   Carla J. Hargrove   Van Hughes   Lori Eve Marinacci   Kasey Marino   Leslie McDonel
CJay Hardy Philip   Hayley Podschun   Terita R. Redd   Travis Robertson   Daniel Robinson   Robbie Roby
Todd Michel Smith   Judine Somerville   Tommar Wilson

Scenery Designed by	Costumes Designed by	Lighting Designed by
David Rockwell	William Ivey Long	Kenneth Posner

Sound Designed by	Casting by	Wigs & Hair Designed by
Steve C. Kennedy	Telsey + Company	Paul Huntley

Production Stage Manager	Associate Director	Associate Choreographer
Lois L. Griffing	Matt Lenz	Michele Lynch

Orchestrations by	Music Direction by	Arrangements by	Music Coordinator
Harold Wheeler	Lon Hoyt	Marc Shaiman	John Miller

General Management	Technical Supervisor	Press Representative	Associate Producers
Richard Frankel Productions	Tech Production	Richard Kornberg	Rhoda Mayerson
Laura Green	Services, Inc.	Don Summa	The Aspen Group
			Daniel C. Staton

Choreography by
Jerry Mitchell

Direction by
Jack O'Brien

The world premiere of "HAIRSPRAY" was produced with the 5th Avenue Theatre in Seattle, Washington David Armstrong, Producing Artistic Director; Marilynn Sheldon, Managing Director
The producers wish to express their appreciation to Theatre Development Fund for its support of this production.

ORIGINAL BROADWAY CAST RECORDING ON SONY CLASSICAL

LIVE BROADWAY

10/1/07

Ashley Parker Angel (center) with members of the Ensemble.

Darlene Love (center) with members of the Ensemble.

Photos by Paul Kolnik

Hairspray

SCENES & MUSICAL NUMBERS

Baltimore, 1962

ACT ONE

Prologue: "Good Morning Baltimore" ....Tracy & Company
Scene 1: TV Station WZZT & Turnblad Home
"The Nicest Kids in Town" ....Corny Collins & Council Members
Scene 2: At the Vanities
"Mama, I'm a Big Girl Now" ....Edna & Tracy, Velma & Amber, Penny & Prudy
Scene 3: TV Station WZZT
"I Can Hear the Bells" ....Tracy
"(The Legend of) Miss Baltimore Crabs" ....Velma & Council Members
Scene 4: Detention
Scene 5: Patterson Park High School Gymnasium
"The Madison" ....Corny & Company
Scene 6: WZZT & Turnblad Home
"The Nicest Kids in Town" (Reprise) ....Corny & Council Members
"It Takes Two" ....Link & Tracy
Scene 7: Turnblad Home and Streets of Baltimore
"Welcome to the '60s" ....Tracy, Edna, The Dynamites & Company
Scene 8: Patterson Park Playground
"Run and Tell That" ....Seaweed
Scene 9: Motormouth Maybelle's Record Shop
"Run and Tell That" ....Seaweed, Little Inez & Company
"Big, Blonde & Beautiful" ....Motormouth, Little Inez, Tracy, Edna, Wilbur

ACT TWO

Scene 1: Baltimore Women's House of Detention
"The Big Dollhouse" ....Women
"Good Morning Baltimore" (Reprise) ....Tracy
Scene 2: The Har-De-Har Hut
"Timeless to Me" ....Wilbur & Edna
Scene 3: Tracy's Jail Cell & Penny's Bedroom
"Without Love" ....Link, Tracy, Seaweed, Penny
Scene 4: Motormouth Maybelle's Record Shop
"I Know Where I've Been" ....Motormouth & Company
Scene 5: The Baltimore Eventorium
"Hairspray" ....Corny & Council Members
"Cooties" ....Amber & Council Members
"You Can't Stop the Beat" ....Tracy, Link, Penny, Seaweed,
Edna, Wilbur, Motormouth & Company

Cast Continued

Motormouth Maybelle ....DARLENE LOVE
Matron ....SUSAN MOSHER
Guard ....KEVIN MEANEY
Denizens of Baltimore ....IRIS BURRUSS,
DWAYNE COOPER, STEVEN CUTTS,
LESLIE GODDARD, CARLA J. HARGROVE,
VAN HUGHES, LORI EVE MARINACCI,
KASEY MARINO, LESLIE McDONEL,
KEVIN MEANEY, SUSAN MOSHER,
HAYLEY PODSCHUN, TERITA R. REDD,
TRAVIS ROBERTSON, DANIEL ROBINSON,
TODD MICHEL SMITH,
JUDINE SOMERVILLE

Dance Captains ....BROOKE LEIGH ENGEN,
ROBBIE ROBY

SWINGS

JOE ABRAHAM, TRACEE BEAZER,
GRETCHEN BIEBER,
BROOKE LEIGH ENGEN,
CJAY HARDY PHILIP, ROBBIE ROBY,
TOMMAR WILSON

UNDERSTUDIES

For Tracy Turnblad: MICHELLE DOWDY,
LORI EVE MARINACCI
For Edna Turnblad and Wilbur Turnblad:
SCOTT DAVIDSON, KEVIN MEANEY
For Velma Von Tussle: GRETCHEN BIEBER,
LESLIE McDONEL, SUSAN MOSHER
For Amber Von Tussle: GRETCHEN BIEBER,
LESLIE McDONEL, HAYLEY PODSCHUN
For Motormouth Maybelle:
CARLA J. HARGROVE, TERITA R. REDD
For Seaweed:
STEVEN CUTTS, TOMMAR WILSON
For Link Larkin:
VAN HUGHES, DANIEL ROBINSON
For Corny Collins: VAN HUGHES,
KASEY MARINO, DANIEL ROBINSON,
ROBBIE ROBY
For Penny Pingleton: LESLIE GODDARD,
HAYLEY PODSCHUN
For Inez: IRIS BURRUSS, CARLA J. HARGROVE
For Spritzer/Principal/Mr. Pinky/Guard:
ROBBIE ROBY, SCOTT DAVIDSON
For Prudy, Gym Teacher, Matron:
GRETCHEN BIEBER,
BROOKE LEIGH ENGEN,
LESLIE McDONEL
For Dynamites: NICOLE POWELL,
TERITA R. REDD, TOMMAR WILSON

ORCHESTRA

Conductor: LON HOYT
Associate Conductor: KEITH COTTON
Assistant Conductor: SETH FARBER
Guitars: DAVID SPINOZZA, PETER CALO
Keyboards: LON HOYT, KEITH COTTON,
SETH FARBER
Electric Bass: FRANCISCO CENTENO
Drums: CLINT DE GANON
Percussion: WALTER "WALLY" USIATYNSKI
Reeds: DAVID MANN, DAVE RIEKENBERG
Trumpet: BOB MILLIKEN
Trombone: BIRCH JOHNSON

Violins: ROB SHAW, CAROL POOL
Cello: SARAH HEWITT ROTH
Music Coordinator: JOHN MILLER

ONSTAGE MUSICIANS

Guitar: ASHLEY PARKER ANGEL
Keyboards: MICHELE PAWK
Glockenspiel: KEVIN MEANEY
Harmonica: NIKI SCALERA

Music Copying:
EMILY GRISHMAN MUSIC PREPARATION/
EMILY GRISHMAN, KATHARINE EDMONDS

Hairspray

Shannon Durig
Tracy Turnblad

Paul C. Vogt
Edna Turnblad

Ashley Parker Angel
Link Larkin

Lance Bass
Corny Collins

Michele Pawk
Velma Von Tussle

Darlene Love
Motormouth Maybelle

Jim J. Bullock
Wilbur Turnblad

Tevin Campbell
Seaweed J. Stubbs

Scott Davidson
u/s Edna Turnblad, Wilbur Turnblad, Harriman F. Spritzer, Principal, Mr. Pinky, Guard

Kevin Meaney
Harriman F. Spritzer, Principal, Mr. Pinky, Guard

Susan Mosher
Prudy Pingleton, Gym Teacher, Matron

Naturi Naughton
Inez

Niki Scalera
Penny Pingleton

Ashley Spencer
Amber Von Tussle

Joe Abraham
Swing

Tracee Beazer
Swing

Gretchen Bieber
Swing

Iris Burruss
Dynamite

Dwayne Cooper
Thad

Steven Cutts
Gilbert

Michelle Dowdy
u/s Tracy Turnblad

Brooke Leigh Engen
Dance Captain, Swing

Leslie Goddard
Brenda

Carla J. Hargrove
Dynamite

Van Hughes
Sketch

Lori Eve Marinacci
Shelley

Kasey Marino
Brad

Leslie McDonel
Lou Ann

CJay Hardy Philip
Swing

Hayley Podschun
Tammy

Terita R. Redd
Lorraine

Travis Robertson
Duane

Daniel Robinson
Fender

Robbie Roby
Dance Captain, Swing

Todd Michel Smith
IQ

Hairspray

Judine Somerville
Dynamite

Tommar Wilson
Swing

Mark O'Donnell
Book

Thomas Meehan
Book

Marc Shaiman
Music & Lyrics

Scott Wittman
Lyrics

Jack O'Brien
Director

Jerry Mitchell
Choreographer

David Rockwell
Scenic Designer

William Ivey Long
Costume Designer

Kenneth Posner
Lighting Designer

Steve Canyon
Kennedy
Sound Designer

Paul Huntley
Wig & Hair Design

John Waters
Consultant

Bernard Telsey,
Telsey + Company
Casting

Richard Kornberg &
Associates
Press Representative

Harold Wheeler
Orchestrations

Lon Hoyt
Music Director

John Miller
Music Coordinator

Laura Green,
Richard Frankel
Productions
*General
Management*

Matt Lenz
Associate Director

Michele Lynch
*Associate
Choreographer*

Margo Lion
Producer

Adam Epstein
Producer

Steven Baruch,
The Baruch•Viertel•
Routh•Frankel Group
Producer

Thomas Viertel,
The Baruch•Viertel•
Routh•Frankel Group
Producer

Marc Routh,
The Baruch•Viertel•
Routh•Frankel Group
Producer

Richard Frankel,
The Baruch•Viertel•
Routh•Frankel Group
Producer

Douglas L. Meyer
Producer

Rick Steiner
Producer

Frederic H.
Mayerson
Producer

Allan S. Gordon
Producer

Elan V. McAllister
Producer

Dede Harris
Producer

Morton Swinsky,
Kardana Swinsky
Productions
Producer

Hairspray

John and Bonnie
Osher
Producer

Daniel C. Staton
Associate Producer

Rhoda Mayerson
Associate Producer

David Armstrong
*Producing Artistic
Director,
5th Avenue Theatre*

Marilynn Sheldon
*Managing Director,
5th Avenue Theatre*

alumni
2007-2008

Cameron Adams
Swing

Jere Burns
Wilbur Turnblad

Ryan Christopher
Chotto
Swing

Michael Cunio
*Brad, Corny Collins,
Denizen of Baltimore*

Jonathan Dokuchitz
Corny Collins

Tyrick Wiltez Jones
*Duane,
Denizen of Baltimore*

Isabel Keating
Velma Von Tussle

Abdul Latif
Swing

Jerry Mathers
Wilbur Turnblad

Brynn O'Malley
Amber Von Tussle

Nicole Powell
Swing

Arbender J.
Robinson
*Gilbert,
Denizen of Baltimore*

Peter Mattew Smith
Swing

Alexa Vega
Penny Pingleton

Bryan West
*Sketch,
Denizen of Baltimore*

Willis White
Swing

Candice Marie
Woods
*Dynamite,
Denizen of Baltimore*

transfer
students
2007-2008

Cameron Adams
Swing

Mary Birdsong
Velma Von Tussle

Kirsten Bracken
*Lou Ann,
Denizen of Baltimore*

Ryan Christopher
Chotto
Swing

Carla Duren
Inez

Annie Funke
*Understudy for
Tracy Turnblad*

Curt Hansen
*Sketch,
Denizen of Baltimore*

Lauren Kling
Swing

Jenifer Lewis
*Motormouth
Maybelle*

Hairspray

Ken Marks
Wilbur Turnblad

Karen Mason
Velma Von Tussle

Matthew S. Morgan
Swing

Marissa Perry
Tracy Turnblad

Jacqui Polk
Swing

Nicole Powell
Swing

Ed Romanoff
*Understudy for
Edna Turnblad,
Spritzer/Principal/
Mr. Pinky/Guard,
Wilbur Turnblad*

Tom Rooney
Wilbur Turnblad

Clarke Thorell
Corny Collins

Aaron Tveit
Link Larkin

George Wendt
Edna Turnblad

STAGE MANAGEMENT
(L-R): Thom Gates (Asst. Stage Manager), Lois Griffing (Production Stage Manager).

ELEVATOR & PHONE
(L-R): Janine Peterson (Elevator Operator), Dawn Edmonds (Elevator Operator), Deborah Peterson (Phone Room).

WARDROBE
Sitting (L-R): Alesandro Ferdico, Kate McAleer, Liz Goodrum, Hiro Hosomizu.

Standing (L-R): Tanya Blue, Mindy Eng, Megan Bowers, Laura Horner, James Cavanaugh, David Ruble.

CARPENTRY, ELECTRIC, SOUND AND PROPS
Front Row (L-R): Paul Trapani, Jessica Morton, Steve Vessa, Bryan Davis, Art Lutz, John J. Kelly, Danny Viscardo, Sean Farrugia.

Back Row (L-R): Joel DeRuyter, Mike Bennet, Lorena Sullivan, Greg Reif, Ish, Joe Masucci, Tommy Green.

Photos by Ben Strothmann

Hairspray

BOX OFFICE
(L-R): Marc Needleman, William Dorso, Ed Waxman.

STAGE DOOR
(L-R): James Mosaphir, Roxanne Mosaphir.

ORCHESTRA
Sitting (L-R): Francisco Centeno, Lon Hoyt, Mike Davis, Seth Farber, Bob Milliken, Sarah Carter.

Standing (L-R): David Matos, Larry Saltzman, Dave Riekenberg, Mike Miggliore.

HAIR ROOM
Sitting: Alex "Parker" Bartlett.

Standing (L-R): Isabelle "Parker" Decauwert, Rich "Parker" Fabris, Mark "Parker" Manalansen, Johnny "Parker" Roberson.

FRONT OF HOUSE STAFF
Front Row (L-R): Maria Collado, Maureen Santos (Ticket Taker), Sharon Hauser, Michelle Vargas (Ticket Taker), Evelyn Olivero.

Second Row (L-R): Frances Banyai, Tara Delasnueces, Mary Ellen Palermo, Jose Lopez (Porter), Grace Darbasie, Jane Publik.

Third Row (L-R): Michelle Smith, Nadian Park, Dolores Banyai, Christine Bentley, Mickey Schechter, Dana Diaz, Adrienne Watson.

Back Row (L-R): Linwood Allen (Sound Associate), Shannon Marsh, Steve Ouellette (House Manager), Angel Diaz (Head Usher), Gene Ruda, Chris Langdon, Marisol Olavarrio.

Hairspray

Hairspray
SCRAPBOOK

Correspondent: Leslie Goddard, "Brenda."

Anniversary Party/Gift: We celebrated five years on Broadway with a huge party at Spotlight Live!!

Most Exciting Celebrity Visitor: JLo. She was sooo pregnant she had to come backstage a couple times during the show to use our bathrooms!! She delivered within a month of attending *Hairspray!*

Actor Who Has Done the Most Performances: Shannon Durig gave her 1000th performance as Tracy Turnblad on March 13, 2008. A party followed that performance...again at Spotlight Live! I don't know if she's done the most shows of anyone in the cast but 1000 performances as Tracy is pretty remarkable!

Tales from the Put-In: We started having themed put-ins thanks to our super-motivated dance captains, Robbie Roby and Brooke Leigh Engen. Check out the pictures from our Beach Party Put-In and our Awesome 80's Put-In!

1. Guest star Jerry Mathers (left) and the cast celebrate the show's 2000th performance backstage at the Neil Simon Theatre on June 5, 2007.

2. Awesome '80s Put-In: Dwayne Cooper, Leslie McDonel, Steven Cutts, Van Hughes, Lori Eve Marinacci, Suzy Mosher, Daniel Robinson, Todd Michel Smith, Michael Cunio, Joe Abraham, Alexa Vega, Tyrick Jones, Nicole Powell, Naturi Naughton, Candice Marie Woods, Michelle Dowdy, Leslie Goddard, Hayley Podschun, Judine Somerville, Carla Hargrove and Brooke Leigh Engen.

3. Beach Party Put-In: Tevin Campbell, Judine Somerville, Jonathan Dokuchitz, Robbie Roby, Isabel Keating, Daniel Robinson, Hayley Podschun, Steven Cutts, Michael Cunio, Dwayne Cooper, Brynn O'Malley, Lori Eve Marinacci, Leslie Goddard, Tommar Wilson, Shannon Durig, Keith Cotton, Carla J. Hargrove, Susan Mosher, Brooke Leigh Engen, Leslie McDonel, Candice Marie Woods, Gretchen Bieber, Joe Abraham, Todd Michel Smith, Terita R. Redd and Naturi Naughton.

The Homecoming

First Preview: December 4, 2007. Opened: December 16, 2007.
Closed April 13, 2008 after 15 Previews and 137 Performances.

PLAYBILL

CAST
(in order of speaking)

Max	IAN McSHANE
Lenny	RAÚL ESPARZA
Sam	MICHAEL McKEAN
Joey	GARETH SAXE
Teddy	JAMES FRAIN
Ruth	EVE BEST

SETTING

Summer
An old house in North London

UNDERSTUDIES/STANDBYS

For Max, Sam:
JARLATH CONROY
For Ruth:
FRANCESCA FARIDANY
For Lenny, Teddy, Joey:
CREIGHTON JAMES

Eve Best is appearing with the permission
of Actors' Equity Association.

⊛ CORT THEATRE
138 West 48th Street
A Shubert Organization Theatre

Gerald Schoenfeld, *Chairman*   Philip J. Smith, *President*

Robert E. Wankel, *Executive Vice President*

JEFFREY RICHARDS   JERRY FRANKEL   JAM THEATRICALS
ERGO ENTERTAINMENT   BARBARA & BUDDY FREITAG   MICHAEL GARDNER
HERBERT GOLDSMITH PRODUCTIONS   TERRY E. SCHNUCK   HAROLD THAU
MICHAEL FILERMAN/LYNNE PEYSER   RONALD FRANKEL/DAVID JAROSLAWICZ
in association with JOSEPH PIACENTILE

present

IAN McSHANE   RAÚL ESPARZA   EVE BEST
MICHAEL McKEAN   JAMES FRAIN   GARETH SAXE

in

THE HOMECOMING

by
HAROLD PINTER

Set Design by	Costume Design by	Lighting Design by
EUGENE LEE	JESS GOLDSTEIN	KENNETH POSNER

Sound Design by	Casting by	Production Stage Manager	Fight Director
JOHN GROMADA	TELSEY + COMPANY	ROY HARRIS	RICK SORDELET

Press Representatives	Marketing	Special Promotions
JEFFREY RICHARDS ASSOC.	HHC MARKETING	TMG
IRENE GANDY		THE MARKETING GROUP

General Management	Technical Supervision
ALBERT POLAND	HUDSON THEATRICAL ASSOCIATES

Directed by
DANIEL SULLIVAN

The producers wish to express their appreciation to Theatre Development Fund for its support of this production.

LIVE BROADWAY

12/16/07

(L-R): Gareth Saxe, Raúl Esparza and James Frain plot their next moves in Harold Pinter's drama.

Photo by Scott Landis

The Homecoming

Ian McShane
Max

Raúl Esparza
Lenny

Eve Best
Ruth

Michael McKean
Sam

James Frain
Teddy

Gareth Saxe
Joey

Jarlath Conroy
u/s Max, Sam

Francesca Faridany
u/s Ruth

Creighton James
u/s Lenny, Teddy, Joey

Harold Pinter
Playwright

Daniel Sullivan
Director

Eugene Lee
Set Design

Jess Goldstein
Costume Design

Kenneth Posner
Lighting Design

John Gromada
Sound Design

Rick Sordelet
Fight Director

Neil A. Mazzella,
Hudson Theatrical
Associates
Technical Supervisor

Bernard Telsey,
Telsey + Company
Casting

Albert Poland
General Manager

Jeffrey Richards
Producer

Jerry Frankel
Producer

Steve Traxler,
Jam Theatricals
Producer

Donny Epstein,
Ergo Entertainment
Producer

Yeeshai Gross,
Ergo Entertainment
Producer

Elie Landau,
Ergo Entertainment
Producer

Barbara Freitag
Producer

Michael Gardner
Producer

Harold Thau
Producer

Michael Filerman
Producer

2007-2008 AWARDS

OUTER CRITICS CIRCLE AWARD
Outstanding Revival of a Play

DRAMA DESK AWARD
Outstanding Ensemble Performance

The Homecoming

Photos by Ben Strothmann

STAGE CREW

Seated (L-R): Scott DeVerna (House Electrician), Patricia Peek (Hairdresser), Penny Davis (Wardrobe Supervisor), Kimberly Butler (Dresser)

Standing (L-R): Ed Diaz (House Carpenter), Jens McVoy (Sound Technician), Lonnie Gaddy (House Props), Kevin O'Brien (Dresser), Yvonne Jensen (Dresser), Denise Yaney (Stage Manager), Lolly Totero (Dresser)

FRONT OF HOUSE STAFF

Front Row (L-R): Dexter Luke (Chief), Robert DeJesus (Ticket Taker), Jessica Hidalgo (Usher), Lea Lefler (Usher), Danielle Smith (Director), Juan Luis Acevedo (Infrared Rep)

Back Row (L-R): Marilyn Molina (Porter), Christopher Santiago (Usher), Robert Evans (Usher)

The Homecoming

BOX OFFICE STAFF
(L-R): Diane Heatherington, Chuck Loesche,
Joshua Skidmore

DOORMAN
Mike Sawyer

STAFF FOR *THE HOMECOMING*

GENERAL MANAGEMENT
ALBERT POLAND

COMPANY MANAGER
DANIEL KUNEY

GENERAL PRESS REPRESENTATIVE
JEFFREY RICHARDS ASSOCIATES
IRENE GANDY

Judith Hansen	Noah Himmelstein
Rachel Murch	Elon Rutberg

CASTING
TELSEY + COMPANY, C.S.A.
Bernie Telsey, Will Cantler, David Vaccari,
Bethany Knox, Craig Burns,
Tiffany Little Canfield, Rachel Hoffman,
Carrie Rosson, Justin Huff, Joe Langworth,
Bess Fifer, Patrick Goodwin

ASSISTANT PRODUCER
MARK BARBER
PRODUCTION STAGE MANAGER .....ROY HARRIS
TECHNICAL SUPERVISOR ......NEIL A. MAZZELLA
Stage Manager ....Denise Yaney
Assistant Director ....Joshua Brody
Associate Set Designer ....Nick Francone
Assistant Set Designer ....Tristan Jeffers
Associate Costume Designer ....Anne Kenney
Associate Lighting Designer ....Aaron Spivey
Associate Sound Designer ....Chris Cronin
Assistant Sound Designer ....Bridget O'Connor
Props Coordinator ....Kathy Fabian
Associate Props Coordinator ....Carrie Hash
Assistant to Mr. Richards ....Noah Himmelstein
Assistant to Mr. Traxler......................Brandi Preston
Assistant to Mr. Poland ....Michael Altbaum
Associate Technical Supervisor ....Sam Ellis
Production Assistant ....Sean M. Thorne
Costume Intern ....Jessica Reiner
Production Carpenter ....Ed Diaz
Production Electrician ....Scott DeVerna
Production Props ....Lonnie Gaddy
Production Sound ....Jens McVoy
Wardrobe Supervisor ....Penny Davis
Mr. McShane's Dresser ....Kevin O'Brien
Mr. Esparza's Dresser ....Kimberly Butler
Ms. Best's Dresser ....Yvonne Jensen
Dresser ....Laura Totero
Fight Choreographer ....Rick Sordelet
Dialect Coach ....Liz Smith
Advertising ....Serino Coyne, Inc./
Greg Corradetti, Tom Callahan,
Andrea Prince
Marketing ....HHC Marketing/
Hugh Hysell, Michael Redman,
Matt Sicoli, Jaime Roberts,
Kayla Kuzbel, Candice Beckmann,
James Hewson, Brandon Martin,
Nicole Pando
Special Promotions.........TMG – The Marketing Group/
Tanya Grubich, Laura Matalon,
Victoria Cairl, Meghan Zaneski

Website Design ....Situation Marketing, LLC/
Damian Bazadona, Lisa Donnelly,
Jacqueline Bodley, Alex Bershaw
Banking ....Chase/Richard Callian
Insurance ....DeWitt Stern Group/Peter Shoemaker
Accountants .Rosenberg Neuwirth & Kuchner CPAs/Mark
A. D'Ambrosi,
Jana M. Jevnikar
Legal Counsel ....Nan Bases, Esq.
Immigration Attorney ....Lawrence S. Yudess, Esq.
Payroll ....CSI/Lance Castellana
Production Photographer ....Scott Landis
Company Mascots ....Lottie, Skye and Archie

CREDITS
Scenery by Hudson Scenic Studio, Inc. Lighting equipment
from PRG Lighting. Costumes executed by Studio Rouge
and Saint Laurie Merchant Tailors, New York City. Sound
equipment by Sound Associates. Props provided by
Propstar. Flame proofing by Turning Star. Rehearsed at
Roundabout Theatre Company rehearsal studios. Natural
herb cough drops courtesy of Ricola USA, Inc.

www.TheHomecomingOnBroadway.com

 THE SHUBERT ORGANIZATION, INC.
Board of Directors

Gerald Schoenfeld	**Philip J. Smith**
Chairman	President
Wyche Fowler, Jr.	**John W. Kluge**
Lee J. Seidler	**Michael I. Sovern**

Stuart Subotnick

Robert E. Wankel
Executive Vice President

Peter Entin	**Elliot Greene**
Vice President –	Vice President –
Theatre Operations	Finance
David Andrews	**John Darby**
Vice President –	Vice President –
Shubert Ticketing Services	Facilities

D.S. Moynihan
Vice President – Creative Projects

CORT THEATRE
House Manager ....Joseph Traina

The Homecoming
SCRAPBOOK

Correspondent: Roy Harris, Production Stage Manager.

Rehearsals for *The Homecoming* were delightful. Here are two of our favorite rehearsal quotes. During a notes session, in response to something Dan Sullivan, our director, said to him, an actor responded, "I believe there's a pause there." "Right now," Dan replied, "there's silence and curtain." A few days later, someone else said to Dan, "I'm confused by this blocking." "That's because I'm on strike today," Dan responded. (Yes, we rehearsed through the entire strike.) Also, during rehearsal, the company began work on a musical version of *The Homecoming*, tentatively called *Spanish Jacky!* Here are some lyrics (courtesy of Michael McKean) from a song entitled "Joey's Lament": "She's a tease. She's a tease./ I can't get her to open her knees."

Eve Best gave all five of her fellow actors individually monogrammed thongs for opening night. For several weeks in the run, we had "thong night," and the person who guessed how many actors were wearing their thongs was the winner. After several weeks, Sunday became "thong day," and only one of our actors wears his thong. Which actor? We'll never tell.

Our most memorable opening night letter was from Mr. Pinter himself. He sent a note which read "The best of all the best to you all"—MacGregor, Jesse, Pinter. MacGregor and Jesse are two characters not in the play but who figure prominently in all the background and history of five of the six characters.

Creighton James understudied Raúl Esparza, James Frain, and Gareth Saxe. So technically he played the most roles. However, in understudy rehearsals, assistant stage manager Denise Yaney had to play all five male roles. She never got to play Ruth.

Every night before they make their morning entrance in pajamas and nightgown near the end of the first act, James Frain and Eve Best as Teddy and Ruth would do a little Egyptian line dance on their way up the escape stairs to get into place.

During intermission you could often hear interesting, and sometimes confused, conversation about this very puzzling play. Our favorite overheard quote: "She: Who wrote this play? He: I think it was the Marquis de Sade."

Because the dressing rooms are not exactly palatial in these old Broadway theaters, the favorite gathering place of the company was the greenroom in the basement, which wardrobe supervisor Penny Davis set up next to her office. She always kept the "refreshment table" stocked with M&Ms, pretzels, goldfish, and other similarly "healthy" type snacks.

On Sundays before the matinee, we hosted our brunches there. Everyone who worked at the Cort took part: actors, dressers, stage managers, ushers, ticket takers, house manager, box office staff. And by the third or fourth Sunday, one of our producers Joe Piacentile of Love Bunny Entertainment, began sending various Italian pasta dishes, sometimes handcrafted by his wife Marci. These brunches were organized

1. (L-R): Michael McKean, Raúl Esparza, Ian McShane, James Frain and Gareth Saxe in rehearsal.
2. Eve Best, Raúl Esparza and Gareth Saxe rehearsing.
3. Director Daniel Sullivan at the opening night party at Bond 45.
4. Curtain call on opening night.
5. Eve Best at the cast party.

by our stage managers, Roy Harris and Denise Yaney, who've been working together off and on for ten years. At any one of these culinary events, you might find the following: Blueberry bread from Roy's kitchen, deviled eggs from Ms. Yaney, roasted new potatoes from dresser Lolly Totero, Dairy Maid eggs from Penny, homemade fried chicken from usher Robert Evans, New Year's Day egg casserole from Gareth Saxe, various delicious cookies and brownies from

Michael McKean, compliments of the baking skills of his wife, the actress Annette O'Toole; fruit and cheese from Ed Diaz, bagels and cream cheese from Scott DeVerna; and many other tasty treats. Brunch was a very popular event every Sunday.

Working on *The Homecoming* was an exciting and delightful experience for everyone involved. No one wanted our limited engagement to end—or the free food.

Inherit the Wind

First Preview: March 19, 2007. Opened: April 12, 2007.
Closed July 8, 2007 after 27 Previews and 100 Performances.

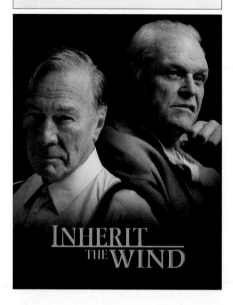

CAST

(in order of appearance)

Howard	CONOR DONOVAN
Melinda	AMANDA SPRECHER
Rachel	MAGGIE LACEY
Mr. Meeker	SCOTT SOWERS
Bert Cates	BENJAMIN WALKER
Mr. Goodfellow	HENRY STRAM
Mrs. Krebs	CHARLOTTE MAIER
Reverend Jeremiah Brown	BYRON JENNINGS
Sillers	ANDREW WEEMS
Dunlap	JAY PATTERSON
Bannister	BILL BUELL
Mrs. Loomis	ANNE BOWLES
Mrs. Blair	PIPPA PEARTHREE
Vendor	BILL CHRIST
Elijah	RAYNOR SCHEINE
Timmy	MATTHEW NARDOZZI
E.K. Hornbeck	DENIS O'HARE
Monkey Man	KEVIN C. LOOMIS
Matthew Harrison Brady	BRIAN DENNEHY
Mrs. Brady	BETH FOWLER
Mayor	JEFF STEITZER
Judge	TERRY BEAVER
Tom Davenport	JORDAN LAGE
Photographer	RANDALL NEWSOME
Henry Drummond	CHRISTOPHER PLUMMER
Reuters Reporter	ERIK STEELE
Esterbrook	ERIK STEELE
Gospel Quartet	CARSON CHURCH, KATIE KLAUS, MARY KATE LAW, DAVID M. LUTKEN

Continued on next page

Continued on next page

ⓈLYCEUM THEATRE

149 West 45th Street
A Shubert Organization Theatre

Gerald Schoenfeld, *Chairman*   **Philip J. Smith,** *President*

Robert E. Wankel, *Executive Vice President*

Boyett Ostar Productions   The Shubert Organization   Lawrence Horowitz
Jon Avnet/Ralph Guild   Roy Furman   Debra Black/Daryl Roth
Bill Rollnick/Nancy Ellison Rollnick   Stephanie McClelland

present

Christopher Plummer   Brian Dennehy

in

INHERIT THE WIND

By

Jerome Lawrence and Robert E. Lee

Also Starring
Byron Jennings

Terry Beaver   Anne Bowles   Steve Brady   Bill Buell   Bill Christ   Carson Church
Conor Donovan   Kit Flanagan   Beth Fowler   Sherman Howard   Katie Klaus
Maggie Lacey   Jordan Lage   Mary Kate Law   Philip LeStrange   Kevin C. Loomis
David M. Lutken   Charlotte Maier   Matthew Nardozzi   Randall Newsome
Jay Patterson   Pippa Pearthree   Raynor Scheine   Scott Sowers   Amanda Sprecher
Erik Steele   Jeff Steitzer   Henry Stram   Benjamin Walker   Andrew Weems

and

Denis O'Hare

Set & Costume Design	*Lighting Design*	*Original Music and Sound Design*
Santo Loquasto	**Brian MacDevitt**	**David Van Tieghem**

Hair & Wig Design	*Casting*
Paul Huntley	**Jay Binder/Jack Bowdan**

Production Stage Manager	*Technical Supervisor*	*Press Representative*
Michael Brunner	**Peter Fulbright**	**Boneau/Bryan Brown**

Marketing	*General Management*	*Associate Producer*
HHC Marketing	**101 Productions, Ltd.**	**Judith Resnick**

Directed by
Doug Hughes

7/8/07

(L-R): Christopher Plummer as Henry Drummond and Brian Dennehy as Matthew Harrison Brady.

Photo by Joan Marcus

Inherit the Wind

Cast Continued

Townspeople ... ANNE BOWLES, STEVE BRADY,
BILL CHRIST, KIT FLANAGAN,
SHERMAN HOWARD, PHILIP LeSTRANGE,
KEVIN C. LOOMIS, CHARLOTTE MAIER,
MATTHEW NARDOZZI,
RANDALL NEWSOME,
JAY PATTERSON, PIPPA PEARTHREE,
ERIK STEELE, ANDREW WEEMS

PLACE:
A small town.

TIME:
Summer. Not too long ago.

UNDERSTUDIES

Henry Drummond: SHERMAN HOWARD
Matthew Harrison Brady: JEFF STEITZER
E.K. Hornbeck: JORDAN LAGE
Rachel Brown: ANNE BOWLES
Mr. Meeker: KEVIN C. LOOMIS
Bert Cates: ERIK STEELE
Mr. Goodfellow: BILL CHRIST
Mrs. Krebs: KIT FLANAGAN
Reverend Jeremiah Brown: BILL CHRIST
Sillers: STEVE BRADY
Dunlap: STEVE BRADY
Bannister: PHILIP LeSTRANGE
Mrs. Blair: KIT FLANAGAN
Elijah: STEVE BRADY
Monkey Man: SHERMAN HOWARD
Mrs. Brady: KIT FLANAGAN
Mayor: PHILIP LeSTRANGE
Photographer: ERIK STEELE
Judge: PHILIP LeSTRANGE
Howard, Melinda: MATTHEW NARDOZZI
Reuters Reporter: KEVIN C. LOOMIS

Christopher Plummer
as Henry Drummond.

Christopher Plummer
Henry Drummond

Brian Dennehy
Matthew Harrison Brady

Denis O'Hare
E.K. Hornbeck

Byron Jennings
Reverend Jeremiah Brown

Terry Beaver
Judge

Beth Fowler
Mrs. Brady

Anne Bowles
Mrs. Loomis/ Townsperson

Steve Brady
Townsperson

Bill Buell
Bannister

Bill Christ
Vendor/Townsperson

Carson Church
Gospel Quartet

Conor Donovan
Howard

Kit Flanagan
Townsperson

Sherman Howard
Townsperson

Katie Klaus
Gospel Quartet

Maggie Lacey
Rachel Brown

Jordan Lage
Tom Davenport

Mary Kate Law
Gospel Quartet

Philip LeStrange
Townsperson

Kevin C. Loomis
Monkey Man/ Townsperson

Inherit the Wind

David M. Lutken
*Music Supervisor/
Gospel Quartet*

Charlotte Maier
*Mrs. Krebs/
Townsperson*

Matthew Nardozzi
Timmy

Randall Newsome
*Photographer/
Townsperson*

Jay Patterson
Dunlap/Townsperson

Pippa Pearthree
*Mrs. Blair/
Townsperson*

Raynor Scheine
Elijah

Scott Sowers
Mr. Meeker

Amanda Sprecher
Melinda

Erik Steele
*Esterbrook/
Reuters Reporter/
Townsperson*

Jeff Steitzer
Mayor

Henry Stram
Mr. Goodfellow

Benjamin Walker
Bert Cates

Andrew Weems
Sillers/Townsperson

Doug Hughes
Director

Santo Loquasto
*Set & Costume
Design*

Brian MacDevitt
Lighting Design

Paul Huntley
*Hair and Wig
Designer*

Jay Binder C.S.A.
Casting

Jack Bowdan C.S.A.
Casting

Bill Haber,
OSTAR Enterprises
Producer

Bob Boyett
Producer

Gerald Schoenfeld,
Chairman,
The Shubert
Organization
Producer

Lawrence Horowitz,
M.D.
Producer

Jon Avnet
Producer

Roy Furman
Producer

Debra Black
Producer

Daryl Roth
Producer

Stephanie P.
McClelland
Producer

Inherit the Wind

STAGE CREW
Front Row (L-R): Charley P. Mann (Production Carpenter), Talia Krispel (Child Wrangler), Kimberly Prentice (Dresser), Jennifer Barnes (Dresser), Jennifer Molloy (Dresser), Andrea Gonzalez (Dresser).

Back Row (L-R): Robin Day (Hair Supervisor), John Paull III (Head Props), William Rowland II (Head Electrician), Corina Frerotte (Spot Operator), Paul Riner (Dresser), Dave Rogers (Wardrobe Supervisor), Brien Brannigan (Production Sound Supervisor).

CAST
Front Row (L-R): Christopher Plummer, Brian Dennehy.

Second Row (L-R): Michael Brunner (Production Stage Manager), Benjamin Walker, Jordan Lage, Kevin C. Loomis, Jeff Steitzer, Byron Jennings, Philip LeStrange.

Third Row (L-R): Matthew Nardozzi, Carson Church, Raynor Scheine, Conor Donovan, Mary Kate Law, Denis O'Hare, Charlotte Maier, Terry Beaver.

Fourth Row (L-R): Beth Fowler, Jay Patterson, Maggie Lacey, Erik Steele, Kit Flanagan, Amanda Sprecher, Barclay Stiff (Stage Manager).

Fifth Row (L-R): Henry Stram, Randall Newsome, Andrew Weems, Steve Brady, Pippa Pearthree, Bill Buell, David Lutken, Bill Christ.

Back Row (L-R): Anne Bowles, Katie Klaus, Scott Sowers, Sherman Howard.

Photos by Ben Strothmann

BOX OFFICE
Tara Giebler and Mike Cadunz.

THEATRE STAFF
Front Row (L-R): Joann Swanson (House Manager), Susan Houghton (Ticket Taker), Carmen Sanchez (Assistant Porter).

Middle Row (L-R): Lorriane Aponte (Usher), Miriam Rincon (Cleaner), Laura Garanda (Cleaner).

Back Row: Neville Hinds (Doorman).

Inherit the Wind

STAFF FOR *INHERIT THE WIND*

GENERAL MANAGEMENT
101 PRODUCTIONS, LTD.
Wendy Orshan   Jeffrey M. Wilson
David Auster

COMPANY MANAGER
Gregg Arst

GENERAL PRESS REPRESENTATIVE
BONEAU/BRYAN-BROWN
Adrian Bryan-Brown   Jackie Green
Danielle Crinnion

PRODUCTION MANAGEMENT
TECH PRODUCTION SERVICES, INC.
Peter Fulbright, Mary Duffe,
Colleen Houlehen, Jackie Prats

CASTING
BINDER CASTING
Jay Binder, CSA
Jack Bowdan, CSA, Mark Brandon, Megan Larche
Assistants: Nikole Vallins, Allison Estrin

Production Stage Manager	Michael Brunner
Stage Manager	Barclay Stiff
Associate Director	Mark Schneider
Music Supervisor	David M. Lutken
Associate Scenic Designer	Jenny B. Sawyers
Scenic Assistants	Tobin Ost, Kanae Heike
Associate Costume Designer	Matthew Pachtman
Costume Assistant	Sarah Sophia Turner
Associate Lighting Designer	Michael O'Connor
Associate Sound Designer	Jill BC DuBoff

Production Carpenter	Charley P. Mann
Production Props Supervisor	Abraham Morrison
Production Electrician	Brian GF McGarity
Production Sound Supervisor	Brien Brannigan
Head Properties	John Paull III
Head Electrician	William Rowland II
Lighting Programmer	Marc Polimeni
Wardrobe Supervisor	Dave Olin Rogers
Mr. Plummer's Dresser	Andrea Gonzalez
Mr. Dennehy's Dresser	Kimberly Prentice
Dressers	Jennifer Barnes, Jennifer Molloy, Paul Riner
Hair Supervisor	Robin Maginsky Day
Production Assistant	Chris Munnell

Associate Producer for Ostar Enterprises	Rachel Neuburger
Executive Assistant to Mr. Haber	Theresa Pisanelli
Assistant to Mr. Haber	Andrew Cleghorn
Assistants to Mr. Boyett	Diane Murphy, Alex Libby, Michael Mandell
SVP, Strategic Partnerships & Developments	Jan Gura
Legal Counsel	Lazarus & Harris, LLP/ Scott Lazarus, Esq., Robert C. Harris, Esq.
Accountant	Rosenberg, Neuwirth, & Kushner, CPAs/ Chris Cacace, Patricia Pedersen, Alla Loyfman
Advertising	Serino Coyne, Inc./ Greg Corradetti, Tom Callahan, Steve Knight, Natalie Serota
Marketing	HHC Marketing/ Hugh Hysell, Amanda Pekoe, Kerry Minchinton

Children's Tutoring	On Location Education/ Alan Simon, Jodi Green, Anna Smith, Abigail Dyer, Irene Karasik
Child Guardian	Talia Krispel
Assistant to the General Managers	John Vennema
101 Productions, Ltd. Staff	Denys Baker, Ashley Berman, Katharine Croke, Barbara Crompton, Laura Dickinson, Sherra Johnston, Emily Lawson, Heidi Neven, Kyle Pickles, Mary Six Rupert, Evan Storey
101 Productions, Ltd. Intern	Stewart Miller
Press Associates	Chris Boneau, Ian Bjorklund, Jim Byk, Brandi Cornwell, Juliana Hannett, Allison Houseworth, Hector Hernandez, Jessica Johnson, Kevin Jones, Amy Kass, Aaron Meier, Christine Olver, Steven Padla, Joe Perrotta, Linnae Petruzzelli, Matt Polk, Matt Ross, Heath Schwartz, Suzanne Tighe
Banking	City National Bank/Anne McSweeney
Insurance	DeWitt Stern, Inc./Peter Shoemaker
Risk Managers	Stockbridge Risk Management, Inc./ Neil Goldstein
Theatre Displays	King Displays, Inc.
Merchandising	Max Merchandising, LLC/ Randi Grossman
Payroll Services	Castellana Services, Inc.
Website Design	Situation Marketing/ Damian Bazadona, Lisa Cecchini, Lisa Donnelly
Opening Night Coordination	Tobak Lawrence Company/ Suzanne Tobak, Michael P. Lawrence
Artwork Photography	Timothy White
SSDC Observer	Kel Haney

CREDITS

Scenery by Showmotion, Inc. Scenery automation and show control by Showmotion, Inc., Norwalk, CT, using the AC2 computerized motion control system. Lighting equipment from PRG Lighting. Sound equipment from Masque Sound. Costume construction by Euro Co Costumes, Werner Russold, Seamless Costumes, Felsen, Luigi Custom Tailors, Lynne Baccus and Arel Studios. Millinery by Leslie Norgate. Custom dyeing by Dye-Namix, Inc. Properties provided by Bergen Office Furniture, Waves Radio, Spoon Group Production. Tables by Golden Oldies Furniture. Audience chairs by Demolition Depot. Sconces by City Knickerbocker. Prop construction by Craig Grigg. Paper props by Pete Sarafin. Natural herb cough drops courtesy of Ricola USA, Inc. Emergen-C super energy booster provided by Alacer Corp. Special thanks to Bra*Tenders for hosiery and undergarments.

MUSIC CREDITS

"I Shall Not Be Moved," words by John Benson, Jr., music by Mrs. James A. Pate; "When the Roll Is Called Up Yonder" by James M. Black; "Faith of Our Fathers" by H.F. Hemy and J.G. Walton; "Not Made With Hands" by Ulysses Phillips; "Do Lord," arrangement Lewis G. Scharpf, Jr. © 1999, used by permission; "Dwelling in Beulah Land" by C. Austin Miles; "Shall We Gather at the River?" by Robert Lowry; "The Old Rugged Cross" by George Bennard; "This World Is Not My Home" by Albert E. Brumley; "You Can't Make a Monkey of Me" by Billy Rose; "Gospel Ship" by A.P. Carter; "Down by the Riverside";

"Farther Along" by J.R. Baxter and W.B. Stevens; "The Unclouded Day" by J.K. Alwood; "Love Lifted Me" by Howard E. Smith; "There's a Great Day Coming" by W.L. Thompson.

To learn more about the production, please visit
InheritTheWindOnBroadway.com

Inherit the Wind rehearsed at New 42nd Street Studios.

SPECIAL THANKS
The producers wish to thank
Eddie Marks and Western Costumes.

ACKNOWLEDGEMENTS
Online study guide provided courtesy of Novelguide.com. The producers also wish to thank Alan Dershowitz, the American Civil Liberties Union (ACLU), Kevin Anderson, AntiEssays.com, Berea College, Bryan College, Matthew Chapman, Scott Fowler, Edward Larson, Jennifer Leeson (Commemorative Collection Curator), Merriam-Webster Online Dictionary, Doug Sharp, Doug Stone, Robert Schneider, The Baltimore Sun, Jeffrey P. Moran, Peter Gordin, Max Gordin.

House Manager ....Joann Swanson

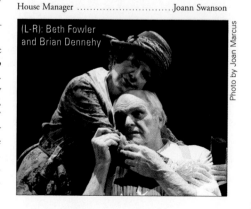

(L-R): Beth Fowler and Brian Dennehy

Photo by Joan Marcus

In The Heights

First Preview: February 14, 2008. Opened: March 9, 2008.
Still running as of May 31, 2008.

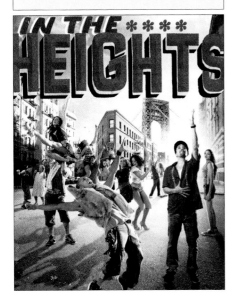

PLAYBILL

CAST
(in order of appearance)

Graffiti Pete	SETH STEWART
Usnavi	LIN-MANUEL MIRANDA
Piragua Guy	ELISEO ROMÁN
Abuela Claudia	OLGA MEREDIZ
Carla	JANET DACAL
Daniela	ANDRÉA BURNS
Kevin	CARLOS GOMEZ
Camila	PRISCILLA LOPEZ
Sonny	ROBIN DE JESÚS
Benny	CHRISTOPHER JACKSON
Vanessa	KAREN OLIVO
Nina	MANDY GONZALEZ
Ensemble	TONY CHIROLDES, ROSIE LANI FIEDELMAN, JOSHUA HENRY, AFRA HINES, NINA LAFARGA, DOREEN MONTALVO, JAVIER MUÑOZ, KRYSTA RODRIGUEZ, ELISEO ROMÁN, LUIS SALGADO, SHAUN TAYLOR-CORBETT, RICKEY TRIPP

SWINGS
MICHAEL BALDERRAMA,
BLANCA CAMACHO,
ROGELIO DOUGLAS JR.,
STEPHANIE KLEMONS

Continued on next page

RICHARD RODGERS THEATRE
UNDER THE DIRECTION OF JAMES M. NEDERLANDER AND JAMES L. NEDERLANDER

KEVIN McCOLLUM   JEFFREY SELLER   JILL FURMAN
SANDER JACOBS   GOODMAN/GROSSMAN   PETER FINE   EVERETT/SKIPPER

PRESENT

IN THE HEIGHTS

MUSIC AND LYRICS BY
LIN-MANUEL MIRANDA

BOOK BY
QUIARA ALEGRÍA HUDES

CONCEIVED BY
LIN-MANUEL MIRANDA

WITH

ANDRÉA BURNS   JANET DACAL   ROBIN DE JESÚS   CARLOS GOMEZ
MANDY GONZALEZ   CHRISTOPHER JACKSON   PRISCILLA LOPEZ   OLGA MEREDIZ
LIN-MANUEL MIRANDA   KAREN OLIVO   SETH STEWART

AND

TONY CHIROLDES   ROSIE LANI FIEDELMAN   JOSHUA HENRY   AFRA HINES
NINA LAFARGA   DOREEN MONTALVO   JAVIER MUÑOZ   KRYSTA RODRIGUEZ
ELISEO ROMÁN   LUIS SALGADO   SHAUN TAYLOR-CORBETT   RICKEY TRIPP
MICHAEL BALDERRAMA   BLANCA CAMACHO   ROGELIO DOUGLAS JR.   STEPHANIE KLEMONS

SET DESIGN	COSTUME DESIGN	LIGHTING DESIGN	SOUND DESIGN
ANNA LOUIZOS	PAUL TAZEWELL	HOWELL BINKLEY	ACME SOUND PARTNERS

ARRANGEMENTS & ORCHESTRATIONS
ALEX LACAMOIRE & BILL SHERMAN

MUSIC COORDINATOR
MICHAEL KELLER

CASTING	PRESS REPRESENTATIVE	MARKETING	COMPANY MANAGER
TELSEY + COMPANY	BARLOW·HARTMAN	SCOTT A. MOORE	BRIG BERNEY

GENERAL MANAGEMENT	TECHNICAL SUPERVISOR	PRODUCTION STAGE MANAGER	ASSOCIATE PRODUCERS
JOHN S. CORKER LIZBETH CONE	BRIAN LYNCH	J. PHILIP BASSETT	RUTH HENDEL HAROLD NEWMAN

MUSIC DIRECTION BY
ALEX LACAMOIRE

CHOREOGRAPHED BY
ANDY BLANKENBUEHLER

DIRECTED BY
THOMAS KAIL

DEVELOPMENT OF *IN THE HEIGHTS* WAS SUPPORTED BY THE EUGENE O'NEILL THEATER CENTER
DURING A RESIDENCY AT THE MUSIC THEATER CONFERENCE OF 2005.

INITIALLY DEVELOPED BY BACK HOUSE PRODUCTIONS.

INTHEHEIGHTSTHEMUSICAL.COM

LIVE BROADWAY

3/9/08

Lin-Manuel Miranda
(center) with members
of the ensemble.

Photo by Joan Marcus

In The Heights

MUSICAL NUMBERS

<table>
<tr><td colspan="2" align="center">ACT I</td></tr>
<tr><td>"In the Heights"</td><td>Usnavi, Company</td></tr>
<tr><td>"Breathe"</td><td>Nina, Company</td></tr>
<tr><td>"Benny's Dispatch"</td><td>Benny, Nina</td></tr>
<tr><td>"It Won't Be Long Now"</td><td>Vanessa, Usnavi, Sonny</td></tr>
<tr><td>"Inutil"</td><td>Kevin</td></tr>
<tr><td>"No Me Diga"</td><td>Daniela, Carla, Vanessa, Nina</td></tr>
<tr><td>"96,000"</td><td>Usnavi, Benny, Sonny, Vanessa, Daniela, Carla, Company</td></tr>
<tr><td>"Paciencia y Fe" ("Patience and Faith")</td><td>Abuela Claudia, Company</td></tr>
<tr><td>"When You're Home"</td><td>Nina, Benny, Company</td></tr>
<tr><td>"Piragua"</td><td>Piragua Guy</td></tr>
<tr><td>"Siempre" ("Always")</td><td>Camila</td></tr>
<tr><td>"The Club/Fireworks"</td><td>Company</td></tr>
</table>

<table>
<tr><td colspan="2" align="center">ACT II</td></tr>
<tr><td>"Sunrise"</td><td>Nina, Benny, Company</td></tr>
<tr><td>"Hundreds of Stories"</td><td>Abuela Claudia, Usnavi</td></tr>
<tr><td>"Enough"</td><td>Camila</td></tr>
<tr><td>"Carnaval del Barrio"</td><td>Daniela, Company</td></tr>
<tr><td>"Atencion"</td><td>Kevin</td></tr>
<tr><td>"Alabanza"</td><td>Usnavi, Nina, Company</td></tr>
<tr><td>"Everything I Know"</td><td>Nina</td></tr>
<tr><td>"No Me Diga (Reprise)"</td><td>Daniela, Carla, Vanessa</td></tr>
<tr><td>"Champagne"</td><td>Vanessa, Usnavi</td></tr>
<tr><td>"When the Sun Goes Down"</td><td>Nina, Benny</td></tr>
<tr><td>"Finale"</td><td>Usnavi, Company</td></tr>
</table>

(L-R): Carlos Gomez and Priscilla Lopez.

Photo by Joan Marcus

Cast Continued

UNDERSTUDIES

For Usnavi:
MICHAEL BALDERRAMA, JAVIER MUÑOZ, SHAUN TAYLOR-CORBETT
For Abuela Claudia:
BLANCA CAMACHO, DOREEN MONTALVO
For Nina:
JANET DACAL, NINA LAFARGA, KRYSTA RODRIGUEZ
For Benny:
ROGELIO DOUGLAS JR., JOSHUA HENRY
For Camila:
BLANCA CAMACHO, DOREEN MONTALVO
For Kevin:
TONY CHIROLDES, ELISEO ROMÁN
For Vanessa:
JANET DACAL, KRYSTA RODRIGUEZ
For Daniela:
BLANCA CAMACHO, DOREEN MONTALVO
For Carla:
STEPHANIE KLEMONS, KRYSTA RODRIGUEZ
For Sonny:
JAVIER MUÑOZ, SHAUN TAYLOR-CORBETT
For Graffiti Pete:
MICHAEL BALDERRAMA, RICKEY TRIPP

Dance Captain:
MICHAEL BALDERRAMA

BAND

Conductor:
ALEX LACAMOIRE
Associate Conductor:
ZACHARY DIETZ
Lead Trumpet:
RAUL AGRAZ
Trumpet:
TREVOR NEUMANN
Trombones:
JOE FIEDLER, RYAN KEBERLE
Reeds:
DAVE RICHARDS, KRISTY NORTER
Drums:
ANDRES FORERO
Percussion:
DOUG HINRICHS, WILSON TORRES
Bass:
IRIO O'FARRILL
Guitar:
MANNY MOREIRA
Keyboard 1:
ALEX LACAMOIRE
Keyboard 2:
ZACHARY DIETZ

In The Heights

Andréa Burns
Daniela

Janet Dacal
Carla

Robin De Jesús
Sonny

Carlos Gomez
Kevin

Mandy Gonzalez
Nina

Christopher Jackson
Benny

Priscilla Lopez
Camila

Olga Merediz
Abuela Claudia

Karen Olivo
Vanessa

Seth Stewart
Graffiti Pete

Tony Chiroldes
Ensemble

Rosie Lani Fiedelman
Ensemble

Joshua Henry
Ensemble

Afra Hines
Ensemble

Nina Lafarga
Ensemble

Doreen Montalvo
Ensemble

Javier Muñoz
Ensemble

Krysta Rodriguez
Ensemble

Eliseo Román
*Piragua Guy/
Ensemble*

Luis Salgado
*Ensemble;
Latin Assistant
Choreographer*

Shaun Taylor-Corbett
Ensemble

Rickey Tripp
Ensemble

Michael Balderrama
*Swing;
Dance Captain/
Fight Captain*

Blanca Camacho
Swing

Rogelio Douglas Jr.
Swing

Stephanie Klemons
Swing

Lin-Manuel Miranda
*Usnavi;
Music and Lyrics;
Original Concept*

Quiara Alegría Hudes
Book

Thomas Kail
Director

Andy Blankenbuehler
Choreographer

Alex Lacamoire
*Music Director,
Arranger,
Orchestrator*

Anna Louizos
Set Designer

Paul Tazewell
Costume Designer

Howell Binkley
Lighting Designer

Bill Sherman
*Arranger/
Orchestrator*

In The Heights

Tom Clark, Mark Menard and Nevin Steinberg,
Acme Sound Partners
Sound Designer

Michael Keller
Music Coordinator

Bernard Telsey,
Telsey + Company
Casting

John S. Corker
General Manager

Brian Lynch/
Theatretech, Inc.
Technical Supervisor

Casey Hushion
Assistant Director

Kevin McCollum
Producer

Jeffrey Seller
Producer

Jill Furman
Producer

Robyn Goodman,
Goodman/Grossman
Producer

Sonny Everett,
Everett/Skipper
Producer

Ruth Hendel
Associate Producer

DOORMEN
Top: James Russell.
Bottom: Angelo Gonzalez.

STAGE MANAGERS AND COMPANY MANAGER
Front Row (L-R): Heather Hogan (Stage Manager),
Amber Wedin (Stage Manager).

Back Row (L-R): J. Philip Bassett (Stage
Manager), Brig Berney (Company Manager).

BOX OFFICE
Saheed Baksh and Daniel Nitopi.

Photos by Ben Strothmann

In The Heights

CREW
Front Row (L-R): Heather Hogan, Leslie Moulton, David Speer, J. Philip Bassett.

Second Row (L-R): Amber Wedin, Moira MacGregor-Conrad, John Senter, Brandon Rice.

Third Row (L-R): Christopher Kurtz, Alon Ben-David, Jamie Stewart, Brian Frankel.

Back Row (L-R): Steve Carver, Steve DeVerna, Jennifer Hohn, Brady Jarvis.

BAND
Front Row (L-R): Wilson Torres (Percussion), Manny Moreira (Guitar), Alex Lacamoire (Conductor/Music Director/Keyboard 1), Andres Patrick Forero (Drums), Irio O'Farrill (Bass), Raul Agraz (Lead Trumpet), Justin Hines (Percussion).

Back Row (L-R): Joe Fiedler (Horn), Dave Richards (Reeds), Ryan Keberle (Trombone), Dave Brandon (Reeds), Trevor Neumann (Trumpet), Zach Dietz (Keyboard 2/Associate Conductor).

Not Pictured: Doug Hinrichs (Percussion), Kristy Norter (Reeds)

FRONT OF HOUSE STAFF
Front Row (L-R): Jordany Sanchez, Thomas Davies, Robert Rea, Carmen Frank, Dorothy Darby

Second Row (L-R): Timothy Pettolina, Rose Santiago, Maureen Dabreo, Beverly Thornton, Joseph Melchiorre, Florence Coulter

Back Row (L-R): Richard Dahlia, Joan Heller, Roseanne Kelly

In The Heights

(L-R): Andréa Burns and Janet Dacal.

Photo by Joan Marcus

In The Heights
SCRAPBOOK

Correspondent: Mandy Gonzalez, "Nina."

Memorable Fan Letters: After our student matinees we received beautiful letters and drawings from the students to tell us how much the show meant to them.

Opening Night Gifts: We all received great gifts for opening night. Baseball caps with "In The Heights" written on them (graffiti style) from Janet Dacal. Keychains from the Rosarios. A beautiful drawing from the producers.

Most Exciting Celebrity Visitor And What They Did: Leonardo DiCaprio loved the show and came back after to meet the cast.

"Easter Bonnet" Sketch: Lin wrote it and Bill Sherman did the track. We did "Un Día Más" the Spanish version of "One Day More" from *Les Misérables*. Most of the cast participated and Priscilla wore the Bonnet. We won Third Place.

Actor Who Performed the Most Roles in This Show: Michael Balderrama is the master.

Special Backstage Ritual: We always hold hands for a prayer circle before the show.

Favorite Moments During Each Performance: When I first see Abuela on the stoop and when I first look at Benny after we sing "When You're Home."

Favorite In-Theatre Gathering Place: Doing Pilates and watching movies in Janet and Andrea's dressing room. It is the ultimate hangout.

Favorite Off-Site Hangout: Bar Centrale or the yogurt place Red Mango or any pizza joint that is still open.

Favorite Snack Foods: Does anyone have any nuts!?

Mascot: Plo.

Memorable Ad-Lib: One time the grate of the bodega wouldn't come down at the end of the show. It displays a picture of Abuela and is the deciding factor for Usnavi to stay in the community. So Lin started jumping up and trying to get the rope that pulls the grate down and while he was doing it he said to Graffiti Pete "What did you do?" It finally came down and we could end the show.

Audience Distraction: Not a lot of cell phones but a lot of ice crunching from the audience.

Memorable Press Encounter: When Diane Sawyer said congratulations to us after we performed on "Good Morning America" and we found out we were nominated for 13 Tony Awards.

Memorable Stage Door Fan Encounter: I remember after one of our student matinees this young girl jumped up when Robin DeJesús came on stage and said, "I love you, Sonny."

Fastest Costume Change: Josh Henry has to change during the blackout from his white jeans into black sweatpants.

Who Wore the Heaviest/Hottest Costume: Josh Henry has to wear many layers during "Paciencia Y Fe."

Who Wore the Least: Nina Lafarga...hey it's the summer in New York.

Nickname: "The Beast."

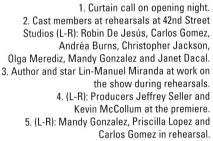

1. Curtain call on opening night.
2. Cast members at rehearsals at 42nd Street Studios (L-R): Robin De Jesús, Carlos Gomez, Andréa Burns, Christopher Jackson, Olga Merediz, Mandy Gonzalez and Janet Dacal.
3. Author and star Lin-Manuel Miranda at work on the show during rehearsals.
4. (L-R): Producers Jeffrey Seller and Kevin McCollum at the premiere.
5. (L-R): Mandy Gonzalez, Priscilla Lopez and Carlos Gomez in rehearsal.

Catchphrase Only the Company Would Recognize: No Pare Sigue Sigue.

Musical Note: Our band is out of this world and a huge part of our energy on stage.

Embarrassing Moment: When I tripped onstage and yelped loudly before a big love song.

Superstition That Turned Out To Be True: The Secret works!!!!

Ghostly Encounter: One time we were having a meeting in the balcony and the exit door opened on its own.

Coolest Thing About Being in This Show: That we all made it together and we get to perform it every night.

Is He Dead?

First Preview: November 8, 2007. Opened: December 9, 2007.
Closed March 9, 2008 after 13 Previews and 105 Performances.

PLAYBILL

CAST

(in order of appearance)

Agamemnon Buckner
  ("Chicago") .... MICHAEL McGRATH
Hans von Bismarck
  ("Dutchy") .... TOM ALAN ROBBINS
Papa Leroux .... JOHN McMARTIN
Marie Leroux .... JENN GAMBATESE
Cecile Leroux .... BRIDGET REGAN
Jean-François Millet .... NORBERT LEO BUTZ
Bastien André .... BYRON JENNINGS
Madame Bathilde .... PATRICIA CONOLLY
Madame Caron ....MARYLOUISE BURKE
Phelim O'Shaughnessy .... JEREMY BOBB
Basil Thorpe, Claude Rivière, Charlie,
  The King of France .... DAVID PITTU

TIME & PLACE

ACT ONE
Scene 1: An afternoon in Spring, 1846,
at Barbizon, near Paris.
The studio of Jean-François Millet.
Scene 2: The same, the next afternoon.

ACT TWO
The Widow's palatial drawing room in Paris,
three months later. Afternoon.

Continued on next page

Continued on next page

⊛ LYCEUM THEATRE
149 West 45th Street
A Shubert Organization Theatre
Gerald Schoenfeld, *Chairman*   Philip J. Smith, *President*

Robert E. Wankel, *Executive Vice President*

Bob Boyett   Roger Berlind   Daryl Roth   Jane Bergère
E. Morten/P. Robbins   J. O'Boyle-R. Stevens   Roy Miller
Sonia Friedman Productions/Ambassador Theatre Group   Tim Levy

in association with
Shelley Fisher Fishkin

present

IS HE DEAD?
A NEW COMEDY
BY MARK TWAIN

Adapted by
David Ives

Starring
Norbert Leo Butz

Michael McGrath   Jenn Gambatese   Tom Alan Robbins   Bridget Regan

with
Jeremy Bobb   Marylouise Burke   Patricia Conolly   David Pittu

also starring
Byron Jennings

and
John McMartin

Set Design	Costume Design	Lighting Design	Music & Sound Design
Peter J. Davison	**Martin Pakledinaz**	**Peter Kaczorowski**	**David Van Tieghem**
Hair & Wig Design		Casting	Associate Producer
Paul Huntley		**Jay Binder/Jack Bowdan**	**Jacki Barlia Florin** **Robert G. Bartner**
Press Representative		Marketing	Dance Sequences
Boneau/Bryan-Brown		**HHC Marketing**	**Pamela Remler**
General Management/Executive Producers		Production Supervisor	Technical Supervisor
101 Productions, Ltd.		**Steven Beckler**	**Aurora Productions**

Directed by
Michael Blakemore

LIVE BROADWAY

12/9/07

(L-R): John McMartin and Norbert Leo Butz (in drag).

Photo by Joan Marcus

Is He Dead?

MARK TWAIN'S *IS HE DEAD?*

In 1898, Mark Twain celebrated his emergence from bankruptcy by writing this high-spirited romp of a play. *The London Times* reported that *Is He Dead?* would be produced simultaneously in London and New York. But a combination of bad timing, bad luck and, perhaps, the irreverence of placing one of France's greatest painters at the center of a zany, cross-dressing farce conspired to foil Twain's plans. When I came across the manuscript in the Mark Twain Papers at UC-Berkeley's Bancroft Library in 2002, I decided that this delightfully ebullient play – from a period when Twain was known for much darker work – deserved to be rescued from the obscurity in which it had languished for more than a century. A mutual friend urged me to contact producer Bob Boyett, with whom I have worked ever since to bring the play to the stage. My edition of the play was published in 2003 (University of California Press). With help from Bob Boyett, David Ives, Michael Blakemore and the truly stellar cast and team they have assembled, Mark Twain is finally getting the first-rate production he deserves – in a theatre where Twain himself saw an insouciant comedy 99 years ago. Enjoy!

Shelley Fisher Fishkin
Stanford University

Cast Continued

UNDERSTUDIES

For Jean-François Millet, Agamemnon Buckner, Phelim O'Shaughnessy and Basil Thorpe:
SHEFFIELD CHASTAIN
For Papa Leroux, Bastien André
and Hans von Bismarck:
WILBUR EDWIN HENRY
For Marie Leroux and Cecile Leroux:
LIV ROOTH
For Madame Caron and Madame Bathilde:
PEGGY J. SCOTT

Norbert Leo Butz
Jean-François Millet

Byron Jennings
Bastien André

John McMartin
Papa Leroux

Michael McGrath
*Agamemnon
Buckner ["Chicago"]*

Jenn Gambatese
Marie Leroux

Tom Alan Robbins
*Hans von Bismarck
["Dutchy"]*

Bridget Regan
Cecile Leroux

Jeremy Bobb
*Phelim
O'Shaughnessy*

Marylouise Burke
Madame Caron

Patricia Conolly
Madame Bathilde

David Pittu
*Basil Thorpe,
Claude Rivière,
Charlie,
The King of France*

Sheffield Chastain
Understudy

Wilbur Edwin Henry
Understudy

Liv Rooth
Understudy

Peggy J. Scott
Understudy

Mark Twain
Playwright

David Ives
Adapter

Michael Blakemore
Director

Peter J. Davison
Set Design

Martin Pakledinaz
Costume Design

Peter Kaczorowski
Lighting Design

Is He Dead?

Paul Huntley
Hair & Wig Design

Pamela Remler
Dance Sequences

Jay Binder C.S.A.
Casting

Jack Bowdan C.S.A.
Casting

Bob Boyett
Producer

Roger Berlind
Producer

Daryl Roth
Producer

Jane Bergère
Producer

John O'Boyle
Producer

Ricky Stevens
Producer

Roy Miller
Producer

Sonia Friedman
Producer

Photos by Ben Strothmann

PROPS ASSISTANT
Alan C. Edwards

FRONT OF HOUSE STAFF
Front Row (L-R): Joann Swanson (Theatre Manager), Rose Ann Cipriano (Ticket Taker),
Merida Colon (Chief Usher), Bernadine Davis (Usher)

Back Row (L-R): Victor Beaulieu (Sound Associates Infrared Div.), Carmen Sanchez
(Assistant Porter), Elsie Grosvenor (Director), Sonia Moreno (Usher), Pamela Shelton
(Usher), Gerry Belitsis (Usher)

HAIR
(L-R): John McMartin, Robin Day (Hair
Supervisor), Taurance Williams (Assistant
Hair Supervisor), Jenn Gambatese

CREW
Front Row (L-R): Bill Colgan (Carpenter), Patrick O'Connor (Props), Leah Nelson (House Head Props),
Rebecca Heroff (Props)

Back Row (L-R): Jonathan Cohen (House Head Electrician), Joanna L. Staub (Sound), Reg Vessey (Props
Supervisor), Graeme McDonnell (Electrician)

STAGE AND COMPANY MANAGEMENT
(L-R): Alex Libby (Stage Manager),
Steve Beckler (Production Supervisor),
Gregg Arst (Company Manager)

Is He Dead?

STAGE DOORPERSON
John Donovan

Photos by Ben Strothmann

DRESSERS
(L-R): Vivienne Crawford, Jack Scott

STAFF FOR *IS HE DEAD?*

GENERAL MANAGEMENT
101 PRODUCTIONS, LTD.
Wendy Orshan   Jeffrey M. Wilson
David Auster

COMPANY MANAGER
Gregg Arst

GENERAL PRESS REPRESENTATIVE
BONEAU/BRYAN-BROWN
Adrian Bryan-Brown   Steven Padla
Heath Schwartz

PRODUCTION MANAGEMENT
AURORA PRODUCTIONS
Gene O'Donovan
W. Benjamin Heller II   Bethany Weinstein
John Horsman   Melissa Mazdra   Asia Evans

CASTING
BINDER CASTING
Jay Binder, CSA
Jack Bowdan, CSA, Mark Brandon, Sara Schatz
Assistants: Nikole Vallins, Allison Estrin

Makeup Design ....Angelina Avallone

Production Supervisor ....Steven Beckler
Stage Manager ....Alexander Libby
Associate Director ....Kim Weild
Associate Scenic Designer ....Bryan Johnson
Assistant Costume Designer ....Katie Irish
Assistant to Mr. Pakledinaz .... Tescia A. Seufferlein
London Costume Supervisor ....Lynette Mauro
Assistant Lighting Designers ....Aaron Sporer,
Aaron Spivey
Associate Sound Designer ....Jill DuBoff
Sound System Design ....TJ McEvoy

Production Props Supervisor ....Peter Sarafin
Production Electrician ....Michael Pitzer
Head Carpenter ....Adam Braunstein
Head Properties ....Reg Vessey
Assistant Properties ....Rebecca Heroff
Head Electrician ....Kevin Greene
Production Sound ....Tucker Howard
Wardrobe Supervisor ....Kay Grunder
Mr. Butz's Dresser ....Jack Scott
Dressers ....Vivienne Crawford,
Moira MacGregor-Conrad
Hair & Makeup Supervisor ....Robin Maginsky Day

Production Assistants ....Julie DeRossi,
Candace Potempa

Legal Counsel ....Lazarus & Harris LLP/
Scott Lazarus, Esq., Robert C. Harris, Esq.
Andrew Farber, Esq.
Assistants to Mr. Boyett ....Diane Murphy,
Michael Mandell
Assistant to Mr. Berlind ....Jeffrey Hillock
Assistant to Ms. Roth ....Greg Raby
Assistant to Ms. Bergère ....Amanda Woods
Assistant to Mr. Levy ....Evan Storey
Accountant ......Rosenberg, Neuwirth, & Kushner, CPAs,/
Chris Cacace, Jana Jevnikar
Advertising ....SPOTCO/
Drew Hodges, Jim Edwards,
Jim Aquino, Kyle Hall
Marketing ....HHC Marketing/
Hugh Hysell, Jaime Roberts,
Nicole Pardo, Michael Redman,
Matt Sicoli, Kayla Kuzbel,
Candice Beckman, James Hewson
101 Productions Dir. Finance/Mktg. ....Elie Landau
Assistant to the General Managers ....John Vennema
101 Productions, Ltd. Staff ....Denys Baker,
Ashley Berman, Katharine Croke,
Heidi Neven, Julie Ann Nolan,
Robert Parkison, Mary Six Rupert
Press Associates ....Chris Boneau, Brandi Cornwell,
Linnae Petruzzelli, Jim Byk,
Jackie Green, Joe Perrotta,
Steven Padla, Matt Polk,
Juliana Hannett, Jessica Johnson,
Aaron Meier, Danielle Crinnion,
Amy Kass, Christine Olver,
Matt Ross, Kevin Jones, Ian Bjorklund
Banking ....City National Bank/
Anne McSweeney
Insurance ....DeWitt Stern, Inc./
Peter Shoemaker
Immigration ....Traffic Control Group, Inc./
David King
Theatre Displays ....King Displays, Inc.
Merchandising ....Max Merchandising, LLC/
Randi Grossman
Payroll Services ....Castellana Services, Inc.
Website Design ....Situation Marketing/
Damian Bazadona, John Lanasa,
Jimmy Lee, Kristen Butler
Physical Therapist ....Rhonda M. Barkow, P.T., M.S.
Production Photographer ....Joan Marcus
Group Sales ....Telecharge.com Group Sales/
(212) 239-6262

CREDITS
Scenery by Hudson Scenic Studio, Inc., and Proof Productions, Inc. Lighting equipment from PRG Lighting. Sound equipment from Masque Sound. Costumes by Cosprop, London. Costumes for Mr. Butz and World Leaders by Eric Winterling, Inc. Additional millinery by Lynne Mackey. Dyeing by Gene Mignola, Inc. Costume painting by Izquierdo Studio. Custom footwear by Fred Longtin and La Pluma. Gloves by LaCrasia. Props fabricated by Peter Sarafin, Alan Edwards, Craig Grigg, Dominick Posillico and The Spoon Group. Upholstery by Roy Ruden. Oil painting reproduction by LIGiclee. Portrait and dachshund paintings by Max Miller. Special thanks to Early Halloween, Helen Uffner and Odds Costumes, Custom Jewelry by Larry Vrba.

To learn more about the production, please visit
www.IsHeDead.com

Is He Dead?
Rehearsed at New 42nd Street Studios

THE SHUBERT ORGANIZATION, INC.
Board of Directors

Gerald Schoenfeld	**Philip J. Smith**
Chairman	President
Wyche Fowler, Jr.	**John W. Kluge**
Lee J. Seidler	**Michael I. Sovern**

Stuart Subotnick

Robert E. Wankel
Executive Vice President

Peter Entin	**Elliot Greene**
Vice President –	Vice President –
Theatre Operations	Finance
David Andrews	**John Darby**
Vice President –	Vice President –
Shubert Ticketing Services	Facilities

D.S. Moynihan
Vice President – Creative Projects

House Manager ....Joann Swanson

Is He Dead?
SCRAPBOOK

Correspondent: Jeremy Bobb, "Phelim O'Shaughnessy"

Memorable Opening Night Letter, Fax or Note: Michael Blakemore wrote a nice opening night note on the inside cover of "The Portable Mark Twain," his gift to us. A keepsake, for sure.

Opening Night Gifts: My girlfriend, Allison, gave me a digital camera... which was awesome. As a result, I got socks for Christmas. But I think opening night is a much bigger deal than the birth of Christ...

Most Exciting Celebrity Visitor and What They Did/Said: Jerry Stiller and Anne Meara came backstage to congratulate everyone...and when I shook hands with Jerry Stiller he had a huge smile on his face and he said something like "Great, you were just great. Really great." It was all very sweet. I tried to see if he was wearing a "manssiere," but I couldn't tell.

Which Actor Performed the Most Roles in This Show: David Pittu. By a long shot. He plays four roles... one of whom is playing a role of his own. So, four and a half, I guess.

Who Has Done the Most Shows in Their Career: I think it's safe to say John McMartin and Patricia Conolly have done the most. Hell, McMartin gets his own applause every night and Trish always has someone impressive backstage to see her. They're quite a pair.

Special Backstage Ritual: I haven't seen anything, but sometimes I hear the theme music from *The Omen* coming from Jenn Gambatese's dressing room.

Favorite Moment During Each Performance (On Stage or Off): Byron Jennings, Michael McGrath, and David Pittu having arguments to provide the scripted "voices offstage" in the second act. There's singing, improvised lines, and even slapping. It's as entertaining as anything in the show.

Favorite In-Theatre Gathering Place: Producer Bob Boyett and the ad company came up with a new campaign using photos of the cast. They wanted a very candid look, like in photo booths at the mall. So, for a few days we had an actual photo booth sitting backstage at the Lyceum. That was definitely the favorite gathering place while it was there. You can imagine...11 actors and free photos. Enough said.

Favorite Off-Site Hangout: Cafe Un Deux Trois was a good time. They treated us really well and totally loved our show.

Favorite Snack Food: By the time this run is over I'll probably have spent five grand at Europa on 46th. I love the pita chips and Rice Crispies treats.

Mascot: We don't really have one. Maybe Dutchy's (Tom Robbins) sausage (an actual sausage, not his member).

Favorite Therapy: My favorite one to keep around is AirBorne. Is it therapy? I don't know. But in a theatre during winter, it's close enough.

Most Memorable Ad-Lib: In the first act we play a game with dice to fool an art buyer into buying a painting. One night the cup that holds the dice got stuck and we couldn't get the lid off. So we had to improvise a little. Rock-Paper-Scissors was the first thing that came to mind. But about halfway through the best of three, David Pittu said "Fuck it, I'm buying the painting" and threw the cup over his shoulder. You can't get that at the movies.

Record Number of Cell Phone Rings: We've

Curtain call on opening night.

been very fortunate on that front. I don't recall hearing a cell phone during this show. But people are laughing most of the way through, so even if there was a ring or two, we may not hear it.

Memorable Press Encounter: Usually opening night press happens when you arrive at the party...but because of the strike our plans had to be shifted a bit. So we did our press before the party in the old smoking lobby downstairs at the Lyceum. I'm not sure that room has been used in about 50 years.

Memorable Stage Door Fan Encounter: One guy made posters of the cast. When he gave David Pittu and I our copies David said, "I'm not in this." I noticed that I wasn't either. So a few nights later the guy was back with new posters in which David and I had been squeezed into a couple of the paintings in the background of the set. It looked like we had died and all the people on stage were having fun without us. But I still hung it in my dressing room.

Fastest Costume Change: Norbert changes out of the dress pretty quickly. But I think Marylouise, Patricia and David changing into the kings' costumes takes the cake.

Busiest Day at the Box Office: There was a day in late December where there were only three empty seats. So far that's the best.

Who Wore the Heaviest/Hottest Costume: Norbert. Easily. Wig, layers of dress, and all that makeup. Being a lady sucks.

Who Wore the Least: Probably me, McGrath, and Robbins. Our clothes were pretty simple. Though beautifully designed (thank you, Martin).

Catchphrases Only the Company Would Recognize: "Curtain."

Memorable Directorial Note: "Well, we got away with it."

Company In-Jokes: A certain cast member who

has a talent for scoping out the house... both for recognizable faces as well as good looking women.

Company Legends: Mark Twain actually saw a play at the Lyceum in 1908. According to Shelley Fisher Fishkin, the scholar who discovered our play, he sat in one of the boxes and was even considering the theatre for a project he was working on. As we're doing his long lost and newly found work, it's been suggested that his ghost is present.

Understudy Anecdote: Liv, who covers Bridget and Jenn, broke her nose playing football during the strike. A couple of weeks later she had to go on for Bridget, which she did with only a partially healed nose. What a bad-ass!!!

Embarrassing Moments: Learning to dance my jig. Sucking in front of Pam, our hot choreographer, never got easy.

Ghostly Encounters Backstage: When you first go into the Lyceum you hear about the "peep-hole" that Daniel Frohman had in his apartment upstairs. He could actually watch shows through it from his desk. For the first couple of days I kept looking up there with a bit of an eerie feeling.

Coolest Thing About Being in This Show: Originating my first Broadway role with such an accomplished group of actors, Michael Blakemore, David Ives, and of course, Mark Twain. There's a lesson around every corner and I feel very fortunate to be among these people.

Fan Club Info: www.ishedead.com.

Also: It's worth noting that our show, and many others, made it through a three week stagehand strike. In our case, we did two previews, had a great momentum going, and then the plug got pulled. Every day we gathered outside our theatre and signed in. It was one of the most frustrating periods of time I can remember.

Jersey Boys

First Preview: October 4, 2005. Opened: November 6, 2005.
Still running as of May 31, 2008.

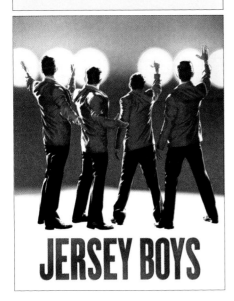

PLAYBILL

JERSEY BOYS

CAST

Tommy DeVito	CHRISTIAN HOFF
Bob Gaudio	SEBASTIAN ARCELUS
Nick Massi	J. ROBERT SPENCER
Frankie Valli	MICHAEL LONGORIA
Frankie Valli (Wed. & Sat. matinees)	CORY GRANT
Bob Crewe (and others)	PETER GREGUS
Gyp DeCarlo (and others)	MARK LOTITO

French Rap Star, Detective One, Hal Miller,
Barry Belson, Police Officer,
Davis (and others) ....KRIS COLEMAN
Stanley, Hank Majewski, Crewe's PA,
Joe Long (and others) ....ERIC GUTMAN
Nick DeVito, Stosh, Billy Dixon,
Norman Waxman,
Charlie Calello (and others) .....DONNIE KEHR
Joey, Recording Studio Engineer
(and others) ....TRAVIS CLOER
Mary Delgado,
Angel (and others) ....JENNIFER NAIMO
Church Lady, Miss Frankie Nolan,
Bob's Party Girl, Angel,
Lorraine (and others) ....ERICA PICCININNI
Frankie's Mother, Nick's Date, Angel,
Francine (and others) ....SARA SCHMIDT

Thugs..................................KEN DOW, JOE
PAYNE

Continued on next page

♪ AUGUST WILSON THEATRE

A JUJAMCYN THEATRE

ROCCO LANDESMAN
President

PAUL LIBIN	JACK VIERTEL	JORDAN ROTH
Producing Director	Creative Director	Vice President

Dodger Theatricals   Joseph J. Grano   Tamara and Kevin Kinsella   Pelican Group
in association with Latitude Link   Rick Steiner/Osher/Staton/Bell/Mayerson Group

present

JERSEY BOYS

The Story of Frankie Valli & The Four Seasons

Book by	Music by	Lyrics by
Marshall Brickman & Rick Elice	**Bob Gaudio**	**Bob Crewe**

with

Sebastian Arcelus   Christian Hoff   J. Robert Spencer and Michael Longoria

Travis Cloer   Kris Coleman   Ken Dow   Heather Ferguson   Cory Grant
Eric Gutman   Donnie Kehr   John Leone   Jennifer Naimo   Dominic Nolfi   Joe Payne
Erica Piccininni   Sara Schmidt   Eric Schneider   with Peter Gregus and Mark Lotito

Scenic Design	Costume Design	Lighting Design	Sound Design
Klara Zieglerova	Jess Goldstein	Howell Binkley	Steve Canyon Kennedy
Projection Design	Wig and Hair Design	Fight Director	Production Supervisor
Michael Clark	Charles LaPointe	Steve Rankin	Richard Hester
Orchestrations	Music Coordinator	Conductor	Production Stage Manager
Steve Orich	John Miller	Adam Ben-David	Michelle Bosch
Technical Supervisor	East Coast Casting	West Coast Casting	Company Manager
Peter Fulbright	Tara Rubin Casting	Sharon Bialy C.S.A. Sherry Thomas C.S.A.	Sandra Carlson
Associate Producers	Executive Producer	Promotions	Press Representative
Lauren Mitchell Rhoda Mayerson Stage Entertainment	Sally Campbell Morse	HHC Marketing	Boneau/Bryan-Brown

Music Direction, Vocal Arrangements & Incidental Music
Ron Melrose

Choreography
Sergio Trujillo

Directed by
Des McAnuff

World Premiere Produced by La Jolla Playhouse, La Jolla, CA
Christopher Ashley, Artistic Director-designate & Steven B. Libman, Managing Director

The producers wish to thank Theatre Development Fund for its support of this production.

LIVE BROADWAY

1/14/08

(L-R): J. Robert Spencer, Michael Longoria, Sebastian Arcelus and Christian Hoff.

Photo by Joan Marcus

Jersey Boys

MUSICAL NUMBERS

ACT ONE

"Ces Soirées-La (Oh What a Night)" – Paris, 2000	French Rap Star, Backup Group
"Silhouettes"	Tommy DeVito, Nick Massi, Nick DeVito, Frankie Castelluccio
"You're the Apple of My Eye"	Tommy DeVito, Nick Massi, Nick DeVito
"I Can't Give You Anything But Love"	Frankie Castelluccio
"Earth Angel"	Tommy DeVito, Full Company
"Sunday Kind of Love"	Frankie Valli, Tommy DeVito, Nick Massi, Nick's Date
"My Mother's Eyes"	Frankie Valli
"I Go Ape"	The Four Lovers
"(Who Wears) Short Shorts"	The Royal Teens
"I'm in the Mood for Love/Moody's Mood for Love"	Frankie Valli
"Cry for Me"	Bob Gaudio, Frankie Valli, Tommy DeVito, Nick Massi
"An Angel Cried"	Hal Miller and The Rays
"I Still Care"	Miss Frankie Nolan and The Romans
"Trance"	Billy Dixon and The Topix
"Sherry"	The Four Seasons
"Big Girls Don't Cry"	The Four Seasons
"Walk Like a Man"	The Four Seasons
"December, 1963 (Oh What a Night)"	Bob Gaudio, Full Company
"My Boyfriend's Back"	The Angels
"My Eyes Adored You"	Frankie Valli, Mary Delgado, The Four Seasons
"Dawn (Go Away)"	The Four Seasons
"Walk Like a Man" (reprise)	Full Company

ACT TWO

"Big Man in Town"	The Four Seasons
"Beggin'"	The Four Seasons
"Stay"	Bob Gaudio, Frankie Valli, Nick Massi
"Let's Hang On (To What We've Got)"	Bob Gaudio, Frankie Valli
"Opus 17 (Don't You Worry 'Bout Me)"	Bob Gaudio, Frankie Valli and The New Seasons
"Bye Bye Baby"	Frankie Valli and The Four Seasons
"C'mon Marianne"	Frankie Valli and The Four Seasons
"Can't Take My Eyes Off You"	Frankie Valli
"Working My Way Back to You"	Frankie Valli and The Four Seasons
"Fallen Angel"	Frankie Valli
"Rag Doll"	The Four Seasons
"Who Loves You"	The Four Seasons, Full Company

Cast Continued

SWINGS
HEATHER FERGUSON, JOHN LEONE,
DOMINIC NOLFI, ERIC SCHNEIDER

Dance Captain:
PETER GREGUS

Assistant Dance Captain:
DOMINIC NOLFI

UNDERSTUDIES
For Tommy Devito:
DONNIE KEHR, JOHN LEONE,
DOMINIC NOLFI
For Nick Massi:
ERIC GUTMAN, JOHN LEONE
For Frankie Valli:
TRAVIS CLOER, CORY GRANT,
ERIC SCHNEIDER
For Bob Gaudio:
ERIC GUTMAN, DOMINIC NOLFI
For Gyp DeCarlo and Bob Crewe:
DONNIE KEHR, JOHN LEONE

ORCHESTRA
Conductor:
ADAM BEN-DAVID
Associate Conductor:
DEBORAH N. HURWITZ
Keyboards:
DEBORAH N. HURWITZ, RON MELROSE,
STEPHEN "HOOPS" SNYDER
Guitars:
STEVE GIBB
Bass:
KEN DOW
Drums:
KEVIN DOW
Reeds:
MATT HONG, BEN KONO
Trumpet:
DAVID SPIER

Music Coordinator:
JOHN MILLER

Photo by Joan Marcus

(L-R): Sebastian Arcelus,
Michael Longoria,
Christian Hoff and
J. Robert Spencer.

Jersey Boys

Sebastian Arcelus
Bob Gaudio

Christian Hoff
Tommy DeVito

J. Robert Spencer
Nick Massi

Michael Longoria
Frankie Valli

Peter Gregus
Bob Crewe and others

Mark Lotito
Gyp DeCarlo and others

Travis Cloer
Joey, Recording Studio Engineer and others

Kris Coleman
Hal Miller and others

Ken Dow
Thug, Bass

Heather Ferguson
Swing

Cory Grant
Frankie Valli on Wed. & Sat. mats.

Eric Gutman
Hank Majewski and others

Donnie Kehr
Norm Waxman and others

John Leone
Swing

Jennifer Naimo
Mary Delgado and others

Dominic Nolfi
Swing

Joe Payne
Thug, Guitars

Erica Piccininni
Lorraine and others

Sara Schmidt
Francine and others

Eric Schneider
Swing

Marshall Brickman
Book

Rick Elice
Book

Bob Gaudio
Composer

Bob Crewe
Lyricist

Des McAnuff
Director

Sergio Trujillo
Choreographer

Ron Melrose
Music Direction, Vocal Arrangements and Incidental Music

Klara Zieglerova
Scenic Design

Jess Goldstein
Costume Design

Howell Binkley
Lighting Design

Steve Canyon Kennedy
Sound Design

Steve Rankin
Fight Director

Steve Orich
Orchestrations

John Miller
Music Coordinator

Adam Ben-David
Conductor

Jersey Boys

Sharon Bialy and Sherry Thomas
West Coast Casting

Stephen Gabis
Dialect Coach

Michael David,
Dodger Theatricals
Producer

Edward Strong,
Dodger Theatricals
Producer

Rocco Landesman,
Dodger Theatricals
Producer

Ivor Royston,
The Pelican Group
Producer

Kevin and Tamara Kinsella
Producer

Ralph Bryan,
Latitude Link
Producer

Rick Steiner
Producer

John and Bonnie
Osher
Producers

Dan Staton
Producer

Marc Bell
Producer

Frederic H.
Mayerson
Producer

Lauren Mitchell
Associate Producer

Rhoda Mayerson
Associate Producer

Joop van den Ende,
Stage Entertainment
Associate Producer

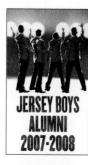
JERSEY BOYS
ALUMNI
2007-2008

Colin Donnell
*Stanley,
Hank Majewski,
Crewe's PA,
Joe Long
(and others)*

Graham Fenton
Swing

Steve Gibb
Thug

Jonathan Hadley
*Bob Crewe
(and others)*

Daniel Reichard
Bob Gaudio

Matthew Scott
Swing

John Lloyd Young
Frankie Valli

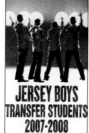
JERSEY BOYS
TRANSFER STUDENTS
2007-2008

Bridget Berger
*Mary Delgado,
Angel (and others)*

Rebecca Kupka
Swing

Jersey Boys

DOORMAN
Gustavo Catuy

STAGE MANAGEMENT
Michelle Reupert, Michelle Bosch, Robbie Young.

Not Pictured: Jason Brouillard and Richard Hester (Production Supervisor).

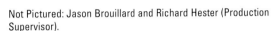

THEATRE MANAGEMENT
(L-R): Matt Fox (Theatre Manager), Stephanie Wallis (Associate Theatre Manager).

Photos by Ben Strothmann

ELECTRICS
Front Row (L-R): Robert Fehribach, Brian Aman, Andrew Dean.

Back Row (L-R): Patrick Ainge, Michael Lyons, Kevin Fedigan.

Not pictured: Sean Fedigan.

PROPS
(L-R): Emiliano Pares, Scott Mulrain, John Tomson.

Not pictured: Ken Harris.

FRONT OF HOUSE STAFF
Front Row (L-R): Carmella Galante (Ticket taker), Rose Balsamo (Chief), Gail Worthman (Usher).

Second Row (L-R): Joann Mariani (Sub Usher), Barbara Hill (Usher), Amy Marquez (Usher), Stephanie Zurich (Usher).

Back Row (L-R): Russell Saylor (Usher), Robert Fowler (Usher), Anne Cavanaugh (Ticket taker), Sally Lettieri (Usher).

ORCHESTRA
Standing (L-R): Kevin Dow, Ken Dow, Stephen (Hoops) Snyder.

Crouching: Joe Payne.

Sitting on Stairs (Top-Bottom): Adam Ben-David, Debra Barsha, Ben Kono, Steve Gibb, David Spier.

CARPENTRY
Front Row: Daniel Dour.

Middle Row: Cathy Prager.

Back Row (L-R): Ronald Fucarino, Joel Brandwine, Greg Burton, Alex Guiterres.

Not pictured: Peter Wright.

Jersey Boys

Scrapbook

Correspondent: Michael Longoria, "Frankie Valli"

Most Exciting Celebrity Visitors: It's a tie between Jack Nicholson and Bette Midler. I pointed to Jack at curtain call as if to say, "I see you!" He was all smiles with sunglasses on. Luckily I didn't know he was at the show until my bow. Bette came backstage looking absolutely stunning, gave me a hug and was very nice. I told her I was a huge fan.

"Gypsy of the Year" Sketch: I actually wrote a gypsy sketch, but we never got around to putting it together...Wah, Wahhhh! It was a spoof on reality tv shows that cast Broadway leads called, "So You Think You Can Frankie."

Special Backstage Ritual: Making tea in the stage management office while discussing politics at half hour call.

Favorite Moment During Each Performance: When the Four Seasons take their bow at the end of "Dawn" in Act I. If you open your eyes, look past your right leg, you can see the entire audience upside down and fully lit by the lights on stage at the height of their applause. It's an awesome sight.

Favorite In-Theatre Gathering Place: The swing boys dressing room. They have a TV and a microwave! The guys are fun, too.

Favorite Off-Site Hangout: World Wide Plaza in the spring/summer also known as "The Dance Belt" among us Jersey Boys. It's an outdoor public seating area where you are likely to run into performers you know passing time between shows on a two-show day.

Favorite Snack Food: Stage management always has the best homemade baked goods.

Mascot: Paco: El Shubert Alley Cat

Favorite Therapy: Acupuncture

Memorable Ad-Lib: One night, on my entrance as Joey in the original Broadway cast, I slipped on the cuff of my jeans. It looked like I was sliding to home plate screaming, "Tommy! I got your fourth guy!! Ahhhhh!!!" Christian Hoff helped me up, ad-libbing, "Have a nice trip?" To which I replied, "I did...thanks." The audience laughed.

Cell Phone Rings, Cell Phone Photos or Texting Incidents During a Performance: Never counted, but every now and then I hear a cell phone ring in the silence after Valli receives the news about his daughter.

Memorable Press Encounter: Singing a doo-wop version of "All I Ask of You" from *Phantom of the Opera* at "Broadway Under The Stars." It was an outdoor concert in Central Park honoring Hal Prince that aired on CBS.

Memorable Stage Door Fan Encounter: We have a few super-fans, but only one has been daring enough to bring me a pair of boxer-briefs and knew my size.

Latest Audience Arrival: I've seen people come in during the pizza scene.

Fastest Costume Change: Out of the kitchen scene into "Sherry." The four guys have to rip off shirts, change into blue shirts and red jackets, grab a swig of water and run out by the end of Barry Belson's speech to sing the number.

Busiest Day at the Box Office: The day after we won the Tony Award for Best Musical.

Who Wore the Heaviest/Hottest Costume: Eric Gutman has to wear the "I Go Ape" mask and I hear it gets pretty hot.

Who Wore the Least: Sara Schmidt in "Oh What a Night!"

Catchphrases Only the Company Would Recognize: "Every day in the school yard, yeah, yeah" (sung in an annoying pop voice).

Sweethearts Within the Company: I know who they are, but I think they are still on the DL, so I can't put them on blast.

Best In-House Parody Lyrics: There was once a version of Moody's Mood we sang at a rehearsal that is too dirty for publication ;)

Memorable Directorial Note: When the show was on the eve of opening night, Des gave us the "Bullseye," which meant we had finally reached the vision of the show and were ready to be received by the public.

Company In-Jokes: The Jersey Girls make up funny rap songs that we sing at the "places" call on Saturday nights as we come down to the stage.

Company Legends: There are tales of a midnight skinny-dipping venture at a beach in La Jolla when the show was first being workshopped. This was before my time.

Understudy Anecdote: Before I took over the role of Frankie Valli, there was one show where the audience saw me play Joe Pesci, and then step into the Valli role nine minutes later. Live theater.

Nicknames: I call Erica Piccininni "Chalissa."

Embarrassing Moment: One night during "Can't Take My Eyes," I grabbed the microphone stand a little more passionately than normal and sent the stand flying into the first row. I caught it before anyone got hurt.

Ghostly Encounter Backstage: There is a light cue in "Oh What a Night!" where, if you are watching the over-the-stage monitor backstage, you can see what appears to be a face on the screen.

Coolest Thing About Being in This Show: Playing a real life rock star who is still alive.

Fan Club Information: For *Jersey Boys*, there is a podcast (www.jerseyboyspodcast.com) and a blog (www.jerseyboysblog.com). Mine is www.michaellongoria.com.

STAFF FOR *JERSEY BOYS*

GENERAL PRESS REPRESENTATION
BONEAU/BRYAN-BROWN
Adrian Bryan-Brown   Susanne Tighe
Heath Schwartz

COMPANY MANAGER
Sandra Carlson

PRODUCTION SUPERVISOR	RICHARD HESTER
Production Stage Manager	Michelle Bosch
Stage Manager	Jason Brouillard
Assistant Stage Manager	Michelle Reupert
Associate General Manager	Jennifer F. Vaughan
Assistant General Manager	Dean A. Carpenter
Technical Supervision	Tech Production Services/ Peter Fulbright, Mary Duffe, Colleen Houlehen, Lauren A. Duffy
Music Technical Design	Deborah N. Hurwitz
Musician Swing	Steve Gibb
Assistant Directors	Holly-Anne Ruggiero, West Hyler, Daisy Walker
Second Assistant Director	Alex Timbers
Associate Choreographer	Kelly Devine

Assistant Choreographer	Danny Austin
Dialect Coach	Stephen Gabis
Assistant Company Manager	Tim Sulka
Fight Captain	Peter Gregus
Associate Scenic Designers	Nancy Thun, Todd Ivins
Assistant Scenic Designers	Sonoka Gozelski, Matthew Myhrum
Associate Costume Designer	Alejo Vietti
Assistant Costume Designers	China Lee, Elizabeth Flauto
Associate Lighting Designer	Patricia Nichols
Assistant Lighting Designer	Sarah E. C. Maines
Associate Sound Designer	Andrew Keister
Assistant Projection Designers	Jason Thompson, Chris Kateff
Story Board Artist	Don Hudson
Casting Directors	Tara Rubin, CSA; Merri Sugarman, CSA
Casting Associates	Eric Woodall, CSA; Laura Schutzel, CSA
Casting Assistants	Rebecca Carfagna, Paige Blansfield, Dale Brown
Automated Lighting Programmer	Hillary Knox
Projection Programming	Paul Vershbow
Set Model Builder	Anne Goelz
Costume Intern	Jessica Reed

Production Carpenter	Michael W. Kelly
Deck Automation	Greg Burton
Fly Automation	Ron Fucarino
Flyman	Peter Wright
Production Electrician	James Fedigan
Head Electrician	Brian Aman
Assistant Electrician	Patrick Ainge
Follow Spot Operator	Sean Fedigan
Production Sound Engineer	Andrew Keister
Head Sound Engineer	Julie M. Randolph
Production Props	Emiliano Pares
Assistant Props	Kenneth Harris Jr.
Production Wardrobe Supervisor	Lee J. Austin
Assistant Wardrobe Supervisor	Nancy Ronan
Wardrobe Department	Davis Duffield, Kelly Kinsella, Shaun Ozminski, Michelle Sesco, Nicholas Staub, Ricky Yates
Hair Supervisor	Amy Neswald
Hair Assistant	Frederick G. Waggoner
Hair Department	Hazel Higgins
Assistant to John Miller	Charles Butler
Synthesizer Programming	Deborah N. Hurwitz, Steve Orich
Music Copying	Anixter Rice Music Service
Music Production Assistant	Alexandra Melrose

Jersey Boys

Production Assistants ....Kerry McGrath,
    Michelle Reupert, Bryan Rountree,
    Deborah Wolfson
Dramaturg ....Allison Horsley
Associates to Messrs. Michael David
  and Ed Strong.................Pamela Lloyd, James Love
Advertising.............................Serino Coyne, Inc./
    Scott Johnson, Sandy Block, Jean Leonard
Marketing...............................Dodger Marketing/
    Gordon Kelly, Jessica Ludwig
Press Assistant ....Danielle Crinnion
Promotions ....HHC Marketing/
    Hugh Hysell, Michael Redman
Banking ....Commerce Bank/Barbara von Borstel
Payroll...............................Castellana Services Inc./
    Lance Castellana, Norman Seawell, James Castellana
Accountants...................Schall and Ashenfarb, C.P.A.
Finance Director ....Paula Maldonado
Insurance ......AON/Albert G. Ruben Insurance Services/
    George Walden, Claudia Kaufman
Counsel ....Nan Bases, Esq.
Special Events ....John L. Haber
Travel Arrangements.........The "A" Team at Tzell Travel/
    Andi Henig
MIS Services ....Rivera Technics: Sam Rivera
Web Design ....Curious Minds Media, Inc.
Production Photographer ....Joan Marcus
Theatre Displays ....King Displays

DODGERS

DODGER THEATRICALS

Michael Bolgar, Sandra Carlson, Dean A. Carpenter, Michael David, Flora Johnstone, John L. Haber, Gordon Kelly, Jennifer Hindman Kemp, Abigail Kornet, Pamela Lloyd, James Elliot Love, Jessica Ludwig, Paula Maldonado, Lauren Mitchell, Sally Campbell Morse, Jessica K. Phillips, Samuel Rivera, R. Doug Rodgers, Maureen Rooney, Bill Schaeffer, Andrew Serna, Edward Strong, Tim Sulka, Jennifer F. Vaughan, Nefertiti Warren, Laurinda Wilson, Ashley Zimmerman

LA JOLLA PLAYHOUSE

Artistic Director ....Christopher Ashley
Managing Director ....Steven B. Libman
Associate Artistic Director ....Shirley Fishman
Director Emeritus...............................Des McAnuff
General Manager ....Debby Buchholz
Associate General Manager ....Jenny Case
Director of Marketing ....Joan Cumming
Director of Development ....Ellen Kulik
Director of Finance ....John T. O'Dea
Director of Education & Outreach ....Steve McCormick
Production Manager ....Peter J. Davis
Associate Production Manager ....Linda S. Cooper
Technical Director ....Brian Busch
Associate Technical Directors ....Chris Borreson,
    Chris Kennedy
Costume Shop Manager ....Susan Makkoo
Sound Supervisor ....Peter Hashagen
Lighting Supervisor ....Mike Doyle
Prop Master ....Debra Hatch
Charge Scenic Artist ....Mark Jensen
Theatre Operations Manager ....Ned Collins

Dodger Group Sales 1-877-5DODGER
Exclusive Tour Direction ....Steven Schnepp/
    Broadway Booking Office NYC

CREDITS

Scenery, show control and automation by ShowMotion, Inc., Norwalk, CT. Lighting equipment from PRG Lighting. Sound equipment by Masque Sound. Projection equipment by Sound Associates. Selected men's clothing custom made by Saint Laurie Merchant Tailors, New York City. Costumes executed by Carelli Costumes, Studio Rouge, Carmen Gee, John Kristiansen New York, Inc. Selected menswear by Carlos Campos. Props provided by The Spoon Group, Downtime Productions, Tessa Dunning. Select guitars provided by Gibson Guitars. Laundry services provided by Ernest Winzer Theatrical Cleaners. Additional set and hand props courtesy of George Fenmore, Inc. Rosebud matches by Diamond Brands, Inc., Zippo lighters used. Rehearsed at the New 42nd Street Studios. Natural herb cough drops courtesy of Ricola USA, Inc. Emergen-C by Alacer Corporation. PLAYBILL® cover photo by Chris Callis.

---

www.jerseyboysinfo.com

Scenic drops adapted from *George Tice: Urban Landscapes*/W.W. Norton. Other photographs featured are from *George Tice: Selected Photographs 1953–1999*/David R. Godine. (Photographs courtesy of the Peter Fetterman Gallery/Santa Monica.)

SONG CREDITS

"Ces Soirees-La ("Oh What a Night")" (Bob Gaudio, Judy Parker, Yannick Zolo, Edmond David Bacri). Jobete Music Company Inc., Seasons Music Company (ASCAP). **"Silhouettes"** (Bob Crewe, Frank Slay, Jr.), Regent Music Corporation (BMI). **"You're the Apple of My Eye"** (Otis Blackwell), EMI Unart Catalog Inc. (BMI). **"I Can't Give You Anything But Love"** (Dorothy Fields, Jimmy McHugh), EMI April Music Inc., Aldi Music Company, Cotton Club Publishing (ASCAP). **"Earth Angel"** (Jesse Belvin, Curtis Williams, Gaynel Hodge), Embassy Music Corporation (BMI). **"Sunday Kind of Love"** (Barbara Belle, Anita Leanord Nye, Stan Rhodes, Louis Prima), LGL Music Inc./Larry Spier, Inc. (ASCAP). **"My Mother's Eyes"** (Abel Baer, L. Wolfe Gilbert), Abel Baer Music Company, EMI Feist Catalog Inc. (ASCAP). **"I Go Ape"** (Bob Crewe, Frank Slay, Jr.), MPL Music Publishing Inc. (ASCAP). **"(Who Wears) Short Shorts"** (Bob Gaudio, Bill Crandall, Tom Austin, Bill Dalton), EMI Longitude Music, Admiration Music Inc., Third Story Music Inc., and New Seasons Music (BMI). **"I'm in the Mood for Love"** (Dorothy Fields, Jimmy McHugh), Famous Music Corporation (ASCAP). **"Moody's Mood for Love"** (James Moody, Dorothy Fields, Jimmy McHugh), Famous Music Corporation (ASCAP). **"Cry for Me"** (Bob Gaudio), EMI Longitude Music, Seasons Four Music (BMI). **"An Angel Cried"** (Bob Gaudio), EMI Longitude Music (BMI). **"I Still Care"** (Bob Gaudio), Hearts Delight Music, Seasons Four Music (BMI). **"Trance"** (Bob Gaudio), Hearts Delight Music, Seasons Four Music (BMI). **"Sherry"** (Bob Gaudio), MPL Music Publishing Inc. (ASCAP). **"Big Girls Don't Cry"** (Bob Gaudio, Bob Crewe), MPL Music Publishing Inc. (ASCAP). **"Walk Like a Man"** (Bob Crewe, Bob Gaudio), Gavadima Music, MPL Communications Inc. (ASCAP). **"December, 1963 (Oh What a Night)"** (Bob Gaudio, Judy Parker), Jobete Music Company Inc, Seasons Music Company (ASCAP). **"My Boyfriend's Back"** (Robert Feldman, Gerald Goldstein, Richard Gottehrer), EMI Blackwood Music Inc. (BMI). **"My Eyes Adored You"** (Bob Crewe, Kenny Nolan), Jobete Music Company Inc,

Kenny Nolan Publishing (ASCAP), Stone Diamond Music Corporation, Tannyboy Music (BMI). **"Dawn, Go Away"** (Bob Gaudio, Sandy Linzer), EMI Full Keel Music, Gavadima Music, Stebojen Music Company (ASCAP). **"Big Man in Town"** (Bob Gaudio), EMI Longitude Music (BMI), Gavadima Music (ASCAP). **"Beggin'"** (Bob Gaudio, Peggy Farina), EMI Longitude Music, Seasons Four Music (BMI). **"Stay"** (Maurice Williams), Cherio Corporation (BMI). **"Let's Hang On (To What We've Got)"** (Bob Crewe, Denny Randell, Sandy Linzer), EMI Longitude Music, Screen Gems-EMI Music Inc., Seasons Four Music (BMI). **"Opus 17 (Don't You Worry 'Bout Me)"** (Denny Randell, Sandy Linzer) Screen Gems-EMI Music Inc, Seasons Four Music (BMI). **"Everybody Knows My Name"** (Bob Gaudio, Bob Crewe), EMI Longitude Music, Seasons Four Music (BMI). **"Bye Bye Baby"** (Bob Crewe, Bob Gaudio), EMI Longitude Music, Seasons Four Music (BMI). **"C'mon Marianne"** (L. Russell Brown, Ray Bloodworth), EMI Longitude Music and Seasons Four Music (BMI). **"Can't Take My Eyes Off You"** (Bob Gaudio, Bob Crewe), EMI Longitude Music, Seasons Four Music (BMI). **"Working My Way Back to You"** (Denny Randell, Sandy Linzer), Screen Gems–EMI Music Inc, Seasons Four Music (BMI). **"Fallen Angel"** (Guy Fletcher, Doug Flett), Chrysalis Music (ASCAP). **"Rag Doll"** (Bob Crewe, Bob Gaudio), EMI Longitude Music (BMI), Gavadima Music (ASCAP). **"Who Loves You?"** (Bob Gaudio, Judy Parker), Jobete Music Company Inc, Seasons Music Company (ASCAP).

SPECIAL THANKS

Peter Bennett, Elliot Groffman, Karen Pals, Janine Smalls, Chad Woerner of La Jolla Playhouse, Alma Malabanan-McGrath and Edward Stallsworth of the New 42nd Street Studios, David Solomon of the Roundabout Theatre Company, Dan Whitten. The authors, director, cast and company of *Jersey Boys* would like to express their love and thanks to Jordan Ressler.

IN MEMORY

It is difficult to imagine producing anything without the presence of beloved Dodger producing associate James Elliot Love. Friend to everyone he met, James stood at the heart of all that is good about the theatrical community. He will be missed, but his spirit abides.

Grammy Award-winning cast album now available on Rhino Records.

🎭 JUJAMCYN THEATERS

ROCCO LANDESMAN
President

PAUL LIBIN   **JACK VIERTEL**   **JORDAN ROTH**
Producing Director Creative Director   Vice President
DANIEL ADAMIAN   **JENNIFER HERSHEY**
General Manager   Director of Operations
MEREDITH VILLATORE   **JERRY ZAKS**
Chief Financial Officer   Resident Director

STAFF FOR THE AUGUST WILSON THEATRE

Manager ....Matt Fox
Treasurer ....Nick Russo
Assistant Manager........................Stephanie Wallis
Carpenter ....Dan Dour
Propertyman ....Scott Mulrain
Electrician ....Robert Fehribach
Engineer ....Ralph Santos

Journey's End

First Preview: February 8, 2007. Opened: February 22, 2007.
Closed June 10, 2007 after 15 Previews and 125 Performances.

CAST

(in order of appearance)

Captain Hardy ....JOHN CURLESS
Lieutenant Osborne ....BOYD GAINES
Private Mason ....JEFFERSON MAYS
2nd Lieutenant Raleigh ....STARK SANDS
Captain Stanhope ....HUGH DANCY
2nd Lieutenant Trotter ....JOHN AHLIN
Private Albert Brown ....JOHN BEHLMANN
2nd Lieutenant Hibbert ....JUSTIN BLANCHARD
Sergeant Major ....JOHN CURLESS
Colonel ....RICHARD POE
German Soldier.................KIERAN CAMPION
Lance Corporal Broughton ..NICK BERG BARNES

THE SCENE

A dugout in the British trenches near
St. Quentin, France

ACT I

Evening on Monday, March 18, 1918

ACT II

Scene 1: Tuesday morning
Scene 2: Tuesday afternoon

ACT III

Scene 1: Wednesday afternoon
Scene 2: Wednesday night
Scene 3: Thursday, towards dawn

Continued on next page

Continued on next page

BELASCO THEATRE

111 West 44th Street
A Shubert Organization Theatre

Gerald Schoenfeld, *Chairman*   Philip J. Smith, *President*

Robert E. Wankel, *Executive Vice President*

BOYETT OSTAR PRODUCTIONS

| STEPHANIE P. McCLELLAND | BILL ROLLNICK | JAMES D'ORTA | PHILIP GEIER |

present

HUGH DANCY   BOYD GAINES   JEFFERSON MAYS

in

JOURNEY'S END

By R.C. SHERRIFF

Featuring

| JOHN AHLIN | NICK BERG BARNES | JOHN BEHLMANN |

| JUSTIN BLANCHARD | KIERAN CAMPION | JOHN CURLESS | RICHARD POE |

and **STARK SANDS** as Raleigh

| Casting by JAY BINDER JACK BOWDAN | Production Stage Manager ARTHUR GAFFIN | Technical Supervisor LARRY MORLEY |

| Marketing HHC MARKETING | Press Representation THE PETE SANDERS GROUP | General Management ALAN WASSER ALLAN WILLIAMS |

| Scenic & Costume Design JONATHAN FENSOM | Lighting Design JASON TAYLOR | Sound Design GREGORY CLARKE |

Directed by
DAVID GRINDLEY

Originally produced in London by Background Productions
The producers wish to express their appreciation to Theatre Development Fund for its support of this production.

LIVE BROADWAY

6/4/07

(L-R): Stark Sands, John Ahlin and Boyd Gaines

Photo by Paul Kolnik

Journey's End

Cast Continued

UNDERSTUDIES

For Stanhope, German Soldier, Broughton:
JOHN BEHLMANN
For Osborne:
RICHARD POE
For Mason, Colonel:
JOHN CURLESS
For Raleigh, Hibbert, Albert, Broughton:
KIERAN CAMPION
For Hardy, Sergeant Major, Trotter:
NICK BERG BARNES

Hugh Dancy is appearing with the permission of
Actors' Equity Association pursuant to an exchange
program between American Equity and UK Equity.

Hugh Dancy
Captain Stanhope

Boyd Gaines
Lieutenant Osborne

Jefferson Mays
Private Mason

Stark Sands
2nd Lieutenant Raleigh

John Ahlin
2nd Lieutenant Trotter

Nick Berg Barnes
Lance Corporal Broughton

John Behlmann
Private Albert Brown

Justin Blanchard
Hibbert

Kieran Campion
German Soldier

John Curless
Captain Hardy, Sergeant Major

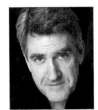
Richard Poe
Colonel

David Grindley
Director

Jonathan Fensom
Set and Costume Designer

Jay Binder C.S.A.
Casting

Jack Bowdan C.S.A.
Casting

Alan Wasser Associates
General Manager

The Pete Sanders Group
Press Representative

Hugh Hysell, HHC Marketing
Marketing

Bill Haber, OSTAR Enterprises
Producer

Bob Boyett
Producer

Stephanie P. McClelland
Producer

STAGE CREW
Front Row (L-R): Penelope Daulton (Company Manager), Arthur Gaffin (Production Stage Manager).

Second Row (L-R): Joe Moritz (House Flyman), Kay Grunder (Wardrobe Supervisor), David Sugarman (Stage Manager).

Third Row (L-R): Susan Goulet (House Electrician), Jeff McGovney (Dresser), Eric Castaldo (Production Props).

Back Row (L-R): Tucker Howard (Production Sound), Heidi Brown (House Props), George Dummitt (House Carpenter).

Journey's End

Photos by Ben Strothmann

FRONT OF HOUSE STAFF
Front Row (L-R): Dexter Luke, David Josephson, Elisabel Ascensio.

Back Row (L-R): Eugenia Raines, Meaghan McElroy, Marissa Gioffre, Gwen Coley, Eileen Kinberg, Kathy Dunn.

STAGE MANAGERS & COMPANY MANAGER
(L-R): David Sugarman (Stage Manager), Penelope Daulton (Company Manager), Arthur Gaffin (Production Stage Manager).

STAFF FOR *JOURNEY'S END*

GENERAL MANAGEMENT
ALAN WASSER ASSOCIATES
Alan Wasser   Allan Williams
Aaron Lustbader   Connie Chong

GENERAL PRESS REPRESENTATIVE
BLUE CURRENT PUBLIC RELATIONS
Pete Sanders
Andrew Snyder

CASTING
JAY BINDER CASTING
Jay Binder CSA
Jack Bowdan CSA, Mark Brandon, Megan Larche
Assistants: Nikole Vallins, Allison Estrin

COMPANY MANAGER
PENELOPE DAULTON

PRODUCTION STAGE MANAGER
ARTHUR GAFFIN

U.S. TECHNICAL SUPERVISOR
Larry Morley

UK TECHNICAL SUPERVISOR
THE PRODUCTION DESK, LTD.
Paul Hennessy

Stage Manager ....David Sugarman
Dialect Coach ....Majella Hurley
Fight Director ....Thomas Schall
Fight Captain ....John Behlmann
Scenic Artist.................................James Rowse at
Decorative Arts Project, Ltd.
Scenic Drop Artwork ....Alasdair Oliver
House Carpenter ....George Dummitt
House Flyman................................Joe Moritz
House Electrician ....Susan Goulet
Electrician ....Neil McShane
House Props ....Heidi Brown
Production Props ....Eric J. Castaldo
UK Props Supervisor ....Fahmida Bakht
Production Sound ....Tucker Howard
Sound ....Brien Brannigan

UK Wardrobe Consultant ....Charlotte Bird
US Wardrobe Consultant ....Patrick Bevilacqua
Wardrobe Supervisor ....Kay Grunder
Dresser ....Jeff McGovney

Production Photographer ....Paul Kolnik
Logo & Artwork Design ....Frank "Fraver" Verlizzo
Advertising ....Eltran Murphy Group Ltd./
Jon Bierman, Frank Verlizzo
Marketing..........................HHC Communications
Hugh Hysell, Michael Redman
Website Design ....Carrie Schoenfeld
Legal Counsel ....Lazarus & Harris LLP/
Scott Lazarus, Esq.,
Robert C. Harris, Esq.
Accounting ....Rosenberg, Neuwirth & Kuchner/
Chris Cacace, Pat Pedersen
Assistants to Mr. Haber ....Theresa Pisanelli,
Andrew Cleghorn
Associate Producer for
Ostar Productions ....Rachel Neuburger
Assistant to Mr. Boyett ....Diane Murphy
General Management Office ....Christopher Betz,
Jason Hewitt, Jake Hirzel,
Patty Montesi, Jennifer Mudge
Press Assistant ....Katie Kirby
Production Assistant ....Mary Kathryn Flynt
Insurance ....Ventura Insurance Brokerage/
Janice Brown
Banking ....City National Bank/
Anne McSweeney
Payroll ....Castellana Services, Inc.
Merchandising ....Max Merchandising/
Randi Grossman
Travel Services ....Road Rebel
Entertainment Touring
Housing Services ....Premier Relocation Services/
Christine Sodikoff
Opening Night
Coordination ....Tobak Lawrence Company/
Suzanne Tobak,
Michael P. Lawrence
Group Sales ....Telecharge.com Group Sales
(212) 239-6262

www.journeysendonbroadway.com

CREDITS AND ACKNOWLEDGEMENTS
Set built by Set-up Scenery Ltd. Automation by Hudson Scenic Studios. Lighting equipment provided by PRG Lighting. Sound equipment provided by PRG Audio. Period uniforms and hand props by Khaki Devil Ltd. and Western Costume Company. Yarn supplied by Andrea at Seaport Yarn, NYC and Portland, ME. Knitting by Margiann Flanagan, Phillip Rolfe, Penny Daulton and Susan Lyons. Moustaches by Ryan P. McWilliams. Select military accessories provided by Kaufman's Army & Navy. Weaponry provided by Weapons Specialist. Natural herb cough drops courtesy of Ricola USA, Inc. Emergen-C super energy booster provided by Alacer Corp.

Special thanks to Max Arthur,
Author of "Forgotten Voices of the Great War."

THE SHUBERT ORGANIZATION, INC.
Board of Directors

Gerald Schoenfeld	**Philip J. Smith**
Chairman	President
Wyche Fowler, Jr.	**John W. Kluge**
Lee J. Seidler	**Michael I. Sovern**

Stuart Subotnick

Robert E. Wankel
Executive Vice President

Peter Entin	**Elliot Greene**
Vice President –	Vice President –
Theatre Operations	Finance
David Andrews	**John Darby**
Vice President –	Vice President –
Shubert Ticketing Services	Facilities

D.S. Moynihan
Vice President – Creative Projects

House Manager ....Carol Flemming

Legally Blonde

First Preview: April 3, 2007. Opened: April 29, 2007.
Still running as of May 31, 2008.

CAST

Elle Woods	LAURA BELL BUNDY
Warner Huntington III	RICHARD H. BLAKE
Vivienne Kensington	KATE SHINDLE
Emmett Forrest	CHRISTIAN BORLE
Professor Callahan	MICHAEL RUPERT
Paulette	ORFEH
Serena	TRACY JAI EDWARDS
Margot	HAVEN BURTON
Pilar	ASMERET GHEBREMICHAEL
Shandi/Brooke Wyndham	NIKKI SNELSON
Kate/Chutney	KATE WETHERHEAD
Leilani	BECKY GULSVIG
Cece/District Attorney	MICHELLE KITTRELL
Kristine	APRIL BERRY
Gabby/Stenographer	BETH CURRY
Veronica/Enid	NATALIE JOY JOHNSON
Store Manager/Judge	AMBER EFÉ
Courtney/Mom/Whitney	GAELEN GILLILAND
Grandmaster Chad/Dewey/Kyle	ANDY KARL
Dad/Winthrop/Reporter	KEVIN PARISEAU
Pforzheimer	JASON GILLMAN
Lowell/Carlos	MATTHEW RISCH
Padamadan/Nikos	MANUEL HERRERA
Aaron	NOAH WEISBERG
Bruiser	CHICO
Rufus	CHLOE
Beer Bash Dancers	MANUEL HERRERA, NICK KENKEL
Harvard Students, Marching Band, Cheerleaders, Inmates, Salespeople	NATHAN BALSER, APRIL BERRY, PAUL CANAAN,

Continued on next page

PALACE THEATRE

UNDER THE DIRECTION OF
STEWART F. LANE, JAMES M. NEDERLANDER AND JAMES L. NEDERLANDER

Hal Luftig   Fox Theatricals   Dori Berinstein

James L. Nederlander   Independent Presenters Network   Roy Furman   Amanda Lipitz
Broadway Asia   Barbara Whitman   FWPM Group   Hendel/Wiesenfeld
Goldberg/Binder   Stern/Meyer   Lane/Comley   Bartner-Jenkins/Nocciolino
and Warren Trepp

In Association with MGM ON STAGE   Darcie Denkert and Dean Stolber

Present

LEGALLY BLONDE
The Musical™

Music and Lyrics by
LAURENCE O'KEEFE and NELL BENJAMIN   Book by HEATHER HACH

BASED UPON THE NOVEL BY AMANDA BROWN
and THE METRO-GOLDWYN-MAYER MOTION PICTURE

Starring

LAURA BELL BUNDY

CHRISTIAN BORLE   ORFEH

RICHARD H. BLAKE   KATE SHINDLE   NIKKI SNELSON

and MICHAEL RUPERT

With

HAVEN BURTON   TRACY JAI EDWARDS   ASMERET GHEBREMICHAEL   NATALIE JOY JOHNSON
NATHAN BALSER   APRIL BERRY   PAUL CANAAN   LINDSAY NICOLE CHAMBERS   CARA COOPER
BETH CURRY   AMBER EFÉ   GAELEN GILLILAND   JASON GILLMAN   BECKY GULSVIG   ROD HARRELSON
MANUEL HERRERA   ANDY KARL   NICK KENKEL   MICHELLE KITTRELL   RUSTY MOWERY
KEVIN PARISEAU   MATTHEW RISCH   NOAH WEISBERG   KATE WETHERHEAD

Produced for Fox Theatricals by
KRISTIN CASKEY and MIKE ISAACSON

Scenic Design	Costume Design	Lighting Design	Sound Design
DAVID ROCKWELL	GREGG BARNES	KEN POSNER & PAUL MILLER	ACME SOUND PARTNERS

Casting	Hair Design	Associate Director	Associate Choreographer
TELSEY + COMPANY	DAVID BRIAN BROWN	MARC BRUNI	DENIS JONES

Technical Supervisor	Animal Trainer	Production Stage Manager
SMITTY/ THEATERSMITH, INC.	WILLIAM BERLONI	BONNIE L. BECKER

Press Representative	Associate Producers	General Management
BARLOW•HARTMAN	PMC PRODUCTIONS YASUHIRO KAWANA ANDREW ASNES/ADAM ZOTOVICH	NLA/MAGGIE BROHN

Music Director/Conductor	Orchestrations	Arrangements	Music Contractor
JAMES SAMPLINER	CHRISTOPHER JAHNKE	LAURENCE O'KEEFE & JAMES SAMPLINER	MICHAEL KELLER

Directed and Choreographed by

JERRY MITCHELL

10/1/07

(L-R): Laura Bell Bundy, Orfeh and Andy Karl.

Photo by Paul Kolnik

Legally Blonde

SCENES AND MUSICAL NUMBERS

ACT I

Scene 1: UCLA Delta Nu Sorority House/Mall/Elle's Door
"Omigod You Guys" ....Margot, Serena, Pilar, Delta Nu's, Elle, Shopgirl, Manager
Scene 2: Restaurant
"Serious" ....Warner, Elle
Scene 3: Delta Nu Sorority House/Golf Course/Harvard Law School Admissions Office
"Daughter of Delta Nu" ....Margot, Serena, Pilar, Kate, Delta Nu's
"What You Want" ......Elle, Margot, Serena, Pilar, Kate, Mom, Dad, Grandmaster Chad, Winthrop,
Pforzheimer, Lowell, Delta Nu's and Company
Scene 4: Harvard Yard
"The Harvard Variations" ....Emmett, Aaron, Enid, Padamadan and Harvard Students
Scene 5: Callahan's Classroom
"Blood in the Water" ....Callahan and Company
Scene 6: Harvard Yard
"Positive" ....Elle, Margot, Serena, Pilar, Greek Chorus
Scene 7: The Hair Affair
"Ireland" ....Paulette
"Ireland" (Reprise) ....Paulette
Scene 8: Harvard Party
"Serious" (Reprise) ....Elle, Warner
Scene 9: Harvard Yard/Elle's Room/Callahan's Classroom
"Chip on My Shoulder" ....Emmett, Elle, Greek Chorus, Company
Scene 10: Dewey's Trailer
Scene 11: Harvard Hallway
"So Much Better" ....Elle, Greek Chorus and Company

ACT II

Scene 1: Conference Room of Stidwell, Zyskowski, Fox & Callahan/Women's Prison
"Whipped Into Shape" ....Brooke, Callahan and Company
Scene 2: Hansen-Harkness Department Store
"Take It Like a Man" ....Elle, Emmett, Salespersons
Scene 3: The Hair Affair
"Bend and Snap" ....Elle, Paulette, Serena, Margot, Pilar, Salonfolk
Scene 4: Courtroom
"There! Right There!" ....Elle, Callahan, Emmett, Brooke, Vivienne, Warner,
Enid, Judge, Nikos, Carlos and Company
Scene 5: Callahan's Office/Elle's Door
"Legally Blonde" ....Elle, Emmett
Scene 6: The Hair Affair
"Legally Blonde Remix" ....Vivienne, Enid, Elle, Company
Scene 7: Courtroom/Bathroom of the Wyndham Mansion
"Omigod You Guys" (Reprise) ....Elle and Company
Scene 8: Harvard Law Graduation
"Find My Way/Finale" ....Elle, Paulette and Company

Cast Continued

BETH CURRY, AMBER EFÉ,
GAELEN GILLILAND, JASON GILLMAN,
BECKY GULSVIG, MANUEL HERRERA,
NATALIE JOY JOHNSON, ANDY KARL,
NICK KENKEL, MICHELLE KITTRELL,
KEVIN PARISEAU, MATTHEW RISCH,
NOAH WEISBERG, KATE WETHERHEAD

UNDERSTUDIES

For Elle Woods:
HAVEN BURTON, BECKY GULSVIG
For Emmett Forrest:
ANDY KARL, NOAH WEISBERG
For Professor Callahan:
ANDY KARL, KEVIN PARISEAU
For Paulette:
AMBER EFÉ, GAELEN GILLILAND
For Warner Huntington III:
JASON GILLMAN, MATTHEW RISCH
For Vivienne Kensington:
TRACY JAI EDWARDS, GAELEN GILLILAND
For Brooke Wyndham/Shandi:
BETH CURRY, MICHELLE KITTRELL
For Serena:
CARA COOPER, BECKY GULSVIG
For Margot:
BETH CURRY, BECKY GULSVIG
For Pilar:
BETH CURRY, MICHELLE KITTRELL
For Enid:
LINDSAY NICOLE CHAMBERS,
GAELEN GILLILAND

SWINGS

LINDSAY NICOLE CHAMBERS,
CARA COOPER,
RUSTY MOWERY, ROD HARRELSON

DANCE CAPTAINS

RUSTY MOWERY, MICHELLE KITTRELL

SETTING

In and around the Delta Nu house,
Southern California.
In and around the Harvard Law campus,
Cambridge, Massachusetts.

ORCHESTRA

Conductor: JAMES SAMPLINER
Associate Conductor: JASON DeBORD
Concertmaster: ANTOINE SILVERMAN
Viola: JONATHAN DINKLAGE
Cello: PETER SACHON
Lead Trumpet: DAVE TRIGG
Trumpet: BUD BURRIDGE
Trombone: KEITH O'QUINN

Reed 1: VINCENT DELLAROCCA
Reed 2: DAN WILLIS
Reed 3: CHAD SMITH
French Horn: ROGER WENDT
Drums: GREG JOSEPH
Bass: MARK VANDERPOEL
Keyboard 1: JAMES SAMPLINER
Keyboards: JASON DeBORD,
MATT GALLAGHER

Guitars: JOHN PUTNAM, KENNY BRESCIA
Percussion: PABLO RIEPPI
Music Coordinator: MICHAEL KELLER

Copyist: EMILY GRISHMAN
MUSIC PREPARATION —
EMILY GRISHMAN/
KATHARINE EDMONDS
Synthesizer Programming: LELAND MUSIC CO.

Legally Blonde

Laura Bell Bundy
Elle Woods

Christian Borle
Emmett Forrest

Orfeh
Paulette

Michael Rupert
Professor Callahan

Richard H. Blake
Warner Huntington III

Kate Shindle
Vivienne Kensington

Nikki Snelson
Brooke Wyndham

Nathan Balser
Ensemble

April Berry
Ensemble

Haven Burton
Margot

Paul Canaan
Ensemble

Lindsay Nicole
Chambers
Swing

Cara Cooper
Swing

Beth Curry
Ensemble

Tracy Jai Edwards
Serena

Amber Efé
Judge/Ensemble

Asmeret
Ghebremichael
Pilar

Gaelen Gilliland
Ensemble

Jason Gillman
Pforzheimer

Becky Gulsvig
Ensemble

Rod Harrelson
Swing

Manuel Herrera
Nikos/Padamadan

Natalie Joy Johnson
Enid

Andy Karl
*Kyle/Dewey/
Grandmaster Chad*

Nick Kenkel
*Ensemble/Assistant
Choreographer*

Michelle Kittrell
*DA Joyce Riley/
Ensemble/
Co-Dance Captain*

Rusty Mowery
*Dance Captain/
Swing*

Kevin Pariseau
Ensemble

Matthew Risch
Carlos/Lowell

Noah Weisberg
Aaron/ Ensemble

Kate Wetherhead
Kate/Chutney

Heather Hach
Book Writer

Laurence O'Keefe and Nell Benjamin
Music and Lyrics

Jerry Mitchell
*Director/
Choreographer*

Legally Blonde

David Rockwell
Scenic Designer

Gregg Barnes
Costume Design

Kenneth Posner
Lighting Designer

Paul Miller
Lighting Designer

Tom Clark, Mark Menard and Nevin Steinberg,
Acme Sound Partners
Sound Design

David Brian Brown
Wig/Hair Design

Justen M. Brosnan
Makeup Design

Bernard Telsey,
Telsey + Company
Casting

James Sampliner
*Music Director/
Conductor/
Co-Arranger*

Christopher Jahnke
Orchestrations

Michael Keller
Music Coordinator

Smitty/
Theatersmith, Inc./
Christopher C. Smith
Technical Supervisor

William Berloni
Animal Trainer

Marc Bruni
Associate Director

Denis Jones
*Associate
Choreographer*

Hal Luftig
Producer

Dori Berinstein
Producer

James L.
Nederlander
Producer

Roy Furman
Producer

Amanda Lipitz
Producer

Marc Routh,
Broadway Asia
Producer

Barbara Whitman
Producer

Barbara Freitag,
FWPM Group
Producer

Jennifer Maloney,
FWPM Group
Producer

Ruth Hendel,
Hendel/Wiesenfeld
Producer

Hal Goldberg,
Goldberg/Binder
Producer

Douglas L. Meyer,
Stern/Meyer
Producer

Stewart F. Lane and
Bonnie Comley
Producers

Michael A. Jenkins,
Bartner-Jenkins/
Nocciolino
Producer

Yasuhiro Kawana
Associate Producer

Adam Zotovitch
Associate Producer

Andrew Asnes
Associate Producer

2007-2008 AWARD

Actors' Equity ACCA Award for
Outstanding Broadway Chorus

Legally Blonde

Annaleigh Ashford
Margot

Leslie Kritzer
Serena

DeQuina Moore
Pilar

Jason Patrick Sands
Ensemble

Tiffany Engen
Swing

Stephanie Fittro
Kate/Chutney

Nicolette Hart
*Shandi/
Brooke Wyndham*

Kate Rockwell
Margot

Bryce Ryness
Aaron

Dani Spieler
*Courtney/Mom/
Whitney, Kristine,
Store Manager/
Judge, Swing*

Casey Leigh
Thompson
*Gabby/Stenographer,
Swing*

Photo by Ben Strothmann

FRONT OF HOUSE STAFF
Front Row (L-R): Estello Genesoni, Verne Shayne, Kelly Collins

Second Row (L-R): Rebecca Segarra, Ani Kehr, Robert Collins, Colleen Keenan

Third Row (L-R): Sandy Darbasie, Adriana Casablanca, Lynette Meyers, Bill Mullen, Gloria Hill, Dixon Rosario, Disting Birona, Lorraine O'Sullivan

Back Row (L-R): Val Ramos, Juliar Pazmino, Rachel Bentley, Scott Muso, Jennifer Butt

Legally Blonde

MERCHANDISING
(L-R): Jen Zappola, Vic Romero.

CONCESSIONS
(L-R): Shrondia Curry, Shantell Cargle, Christina Weathersby, Rohan Redwood.

CREW
Front Row (L-R): Fred Castner, Dolly Williams, Jack Scott, Chastity Neutze.

Second Row (L-R): Jeff Johnson, Pam Sorenson, Jeff McGovney, Marcia McIntosh, Laura Bell Bundy.

Third Row (L-R): Eugene Nicks, Grant Barrett, Tasha Cowd, Michael Harrell, John Cooper.

Back Row (L-R): Ken Keneally, Seth Sklar-Heyn, Christel Murdock, Tina Clifton, Joel Hawkins, Melanie McClintock, Gina Gornick, Joe Whitmeyer, Veneda Truesdale, Enrique Vega.

Photos by Ben Strothmann

Legally Blonde

STAFF FOR *LEGALLY BLONDE*

GENERAL MANAGER
NINA LANNAN ASSOCIATES
Maggie Brohn

Company Manager
Kimberly Kelley
Associate Company Manager ....Nathan Gehan

GENERAL PRESS REPRESENTATIVE
Barlow•Hartman

Michael Hartman	John Barlow
Leslie Baden	Kevin Robak

CASTING
TELSEY + COMPANY
Bernie Telsey, Will Cantler, David Vaccari, Bethany Knox,
Craig Burns, Tiffany Little Canfield,
Rachel Hoffman, Stephanie Yankwitt, Carrie Rosson,
Justin Huff, Joe Langworth, Bess Fifer

Associate Director ....Marc Bruni
Associate Choreographer ....Denis Jones
Assistant Choreographer ....Nick Kenkel
PRODUCTION STAGE MANAGER ..Bonnie L. Becker
Stage Manager ....Kimberly Russell
Assistant Stage Managers ....Scott Rowen,
Seth Sklar-Heyn
Dance Captains ....Rusty Mowery, Michelle Kittrell
Assistant to David Rockwell ....Barry Richards
Associate Designer ....Richard Jaris
Assistant Designers ....Todd Ivins, Gaetane Bertol,
Brian Drucker, Rob Bissinger,
Larry Brown, Corrine Merrill
Modelmakers ....Joannie Schlaffer,
Rachael Short-Janocko, Morgan Moore,
Tomo Tanaka
Set Design Graphics......................Alexi Logothetis,
Charles Rush, Jerry Sabatini,
Matthew Goodrich
Associate Costume Designer ....Sky Switser
Assistant Costume Designer ....Matthew R. Pachtman
Costume Assistants ....Sarah Sophia Turner,
Jeriana Hochberg
Costume Interns ....Nina Damato, Sydney Gallas
Assistant Lighting Designer ....Jonathan Spencer
Advance Sound ....Dan Robillard
Assistant Sound Designer ....Jeffrey Yoshi Lee
Automated Lighting Programmer ....Timothy F. Rogers
Dialect Coach ....Stephen Gabis
Fight Director ....Thomas Schall

MAKEUP DESIGN ....JUSTEN M. BROSNAN

Production Carpenter ....Donald J. Oberpriller
Fly Automation Carpenter ....Robert M. Hentze
Production Flyman ....Robert W. Kelly
Carpenters ....Jeff Lunsford, Ian Michaud
Production Electricians ....James J. Fedigan,
Randall Zaibek
Head Electrician ....Dan Coey
Assistant Electricians ....Eric Abbott, Ron Martin
Production Sound ....Robert Biasetti
Production Properties ....Timothy M. Abel
Head Properties ....Robert N. Valli
Assistant Properties ....Ken Keneally

Wardrobe Supervisors ......Jessica Scoblick, Dolly Williams
Star Dresser ....Laura Ellington
Dressers ....Grant Barrett, Larry Callahan,
Fred Castner, Tasha Cowd,
Gina Gornik, Michael Harrell,
James Hodun, Jeff Johnson,
Melanie McClintock, Marcia McIntosh,
Jack Scott, Pamela Sorensen,
Veneda Truesdale
Hair Supervisor ....Carole Morales
Assistant Hair Supervisor ....Joseph Whitmeyer
Hair Dressers ....Joel Hawkins, Enrique Vega
Additional Arrangements ....Alex Lacamoire
Rehearsal Musicians ....Jason DeBord, Greg Joseph
Production Assistants ....Caroline Andersen,
Christopher Munnell
Dog Trainer ....William Berloni
Dog Handler ....Rob Cox
Assistant Trainer ....Dorothy Berloni
Company Physical Therapist ....Sean Gallagher, PAPT

Advertising ....Serino Coyne, Inc./
Sandy Block, Jill Jefferson,
Roger Micone, Omar Reyes
Website Design/
Online Marketing Strategy ...Situation Marketing LLC/
Damian Bazadona, Chris Powers,
Ian Bennett, Jimmy Lee
Marketing Director ....Adam Jay
Comptroller....................................Sarah Galbraith/
Sarah Galbraith Company
Accountants ....Robert Fried CPA,
Fried & Kowgios CPAs LLP
General Management Associates ......Katherine McNamee,
Roseanna Sharrow
General Management Interns ....Dana Chie,
Rebecca Hinkson, Danielle Saks
Press Associates ....Michelle Bergmann,
Dennis Crowley, Tom D'Ambrosio,
Ryan Ratelle, Wayne Wolfe
Press Office Manager ....Bethany Larsen
Production Photographer ....Paul Kolnik
Insurance ....Albert G. Ruben Company Inc./
Claudia Kauffman
Banking ....City National Bank, Gregg Santos
Payroll ....Castellana Services, Inc.
Merchandising ....Max Merchandising,
Randi Grossman
Travel Agent ....Tzell Travel/The "A" Team,
Andi Henig
Legal Counsel ..Franklin, Weinrib, Rudell & Vassallo, P.C./
Elliot H. Brown, Daniel M. Wasser,
Matthew C. Lefferts
Associate to Mr. Luftig ....Shannon Morrison
Assistant to Ms. Caskey ....Megan Larche
Assistant to Mr. Isaacson ....Jamie Griser
SSDC Observer ....Christine O'Grady
Music Intern ....Evan Jay Newman

GROUP SALES
Theatre Direct/Showtix
1-800-BROADWAY

www.legallyblondethemusical.com

ACKNOWLEDGEMENTS
The producers wish to thank the following partners for their
generous support: VISA, TIFFANY & CO., VAVOOM
PROFESSIONAL HAIRCARE and ELLE MAGAZINE.
Other products graciously provided by the following
partners: Puma, Juicy Couture, UPS, Manhattan Portage,
Nanette Lepore. Handbags provided by Lana Marks; Mobile
phones provided by Verizon Wireless; iPods and Elle Woods'
computer provided by Apple; Sound effects by Tivo, Inc.;
some jeans provided by Rich & Skinny Jeans; and Elle's
dorm room furnished by Pottery Barn Teen.

CREDITS
Scenery constructed and automation equipment provided
by Showmotion Inc. Scenic drops painted by Scenic Arts
Studio. Costumes constructed by Barbara Matera Ltd.,
Carelli Costumes, Donna Langman, John David Ridge,
Tricorne and D.D. Dolan. Custom millinery by Lynne
Mackey Studio, Killer. Custom shoes by Capri Shoes, J.C.
Theatrical, LaDuca Productions and T.O. Dey. Custom
painting by Jeff Fender, screenprinting by Steven Gillespie
and knitting by C.C. Wei. Undergarments provided by
Bra*Tenders. Lighting Equipment by PRG Lighting. Sound
equipment supplied by Sound Associates. Props provided by
Spoon Group, Beyond Imagination, Jennie
Marino/Moonboots. Special assistant with hand prop
construction Meghan Abel. Receptors provided by Muse
Research. Guitar amps by Mega Boogie. Pianos provided by
Yamaha Musical Theatre Corp. Dogs adopted from
Associated Humane Society of New Jersey, Four Paws
Rescue of New Jersey, the Connecticut Humane Society and
Bulldog Rescue of Connecticut. Rehearsed at the New 42nd
Street Studios. Natural herb cough drops supplied by Ricola
USA Inc. Makeup provided by M•A•C Cosmetics.

SPECIAL THANKS
Michael Harrell, Rosemary Phelps, Cory Ching, Dr. Wayne
Goldberg, Rachel Pachtman, Tom LaMere, Stephanie
Steele, Stewart Adelson, Joe Ortmeyer, Marc Platt, Karen
McCullah, Kirsten Smith, Gail Cannold, Sue Spiegel, Ken
Marsolais, Mitchell Cannold, Bairbre Finn. San Francisco
Business Agent FX Crowley. Our production team would
like to thank the San Francisco crew for their terrific work.

NEDERLANDER

Chairman ....**James M. Nederlander**	
President ....**James L. Nederlander**	

Executive Vice President
Nick Scandalios

Vice President	Senior Vice President
Corporate Development	Labor Relations
Charlene S. Nederlander	**Herschel Waxman**

Vice President	Chief Financial Officer
Jim Boese	**Freida Sawyer Belviso**

STAFF FOR THE PALACE THEATRE
Theatre Manager ....Dixon Rosario
Treasurer ....Cissy Caspare
Assistant Treasurer ....Anne T. Wilson
Carpenter ....Thomas K. Phillips
Flyman ....Robert W. Kelly
Electrician ....Eddie Webber
Propertymaster ....Steve Camus
Chief Usher ....Gloria Hill

Legally Blonde
SCRAPBOOK

Ensemble members (including Yearbook Correspondent Orfeh, second from left in back row) take part in "Broadway on Broadway 2007" in Times Square.

Correspondent: Orfeh, "Paulette"

Memorable Note, Fax or Fan Letter: One grandmother wrote to say she was very, very upset that no one told her it was such a scandalous show. She said she had to take her granddaughter out in the middle of the first act, and how could nobody have warned her. Actually, I can't think of a less scandalous show on Broadway right now. Laura Bell thought it was very funny and put it on her dressing room door. Most of our mail runs along the lines of "Dear Cast of Legally Blonde, This was my favorite show ever."

Most Exciting Celebrity Visitors: We were very excited when Katharine McPhee showed up. I got to take a picture with her. Bette Midler came and Laura Bell got to meet her.

"Gypsy of the Year" Sketch: The majority of it was written by my husband Andy Karl, who plays Dewey, making fun of the "Hills" girls.

Actors Who Performed the Most Roles in This Show: Other than those who play three roles all the time, our two swings have had to play any number of different roles, including crossing gender lines. Roderick Harrelson has had to go on as Amber Efé and play the Judge as a man. Lindsay Nicole Chambers had to go on as Aaron Schultz. They made her "Erin Schultz." Roderick brought the house down!

Who Has Done the Most Shows: I imagine Michael Rupert or Michelle Kittrell, but a lot of our dance captains have done a lot of shows.

Special Backstage Rituals: Everybody warms up on stage. For me, I listen to music and work out in my dressing room. Richard Blake sings at the top of his lungs to warm up. I knock on a certain block of wood every night on the way to stage right, where most of my entrances are.

Favorite Moment During Each Performance (On Stage or Off): I look forward to our dog trainers bringing Boo to my dressing room each day.

Favorite In-Theatre Gathering Place: We all gather in the quad outside the stage management office. It's warm up there; it's the water cooler of our theatre.

Favorite Off-Site Hangout: Everybody goes different places, some go to Bar Centrale, others got to QT, and a group of us go to Tony's DiNapoli.

Favorite Snack Foods: This is a big candy cast. No limits!

Mascot: Boo is our mascot!!!

Favorite Therapies: Everyone fights for the Saturday physical therapy spots. We only get six PT spots a week and everyone puts their name in. We're also big on throat sprays and we're big on Ricola. We go through tubs and tubs of it.

Memorable Ad-Lib: One of the most responsive moments in the show is where Laura Bell calls Christian a doofus. One night, Laura Bell called him a "Butt Head." When he replied "No one calls me a Butt Head!" a kid in the audience also called him a "butt-head" Laura Bell said, "Well, he thinks you are! He agrees with me!" The audience went insane!

Record Number of Cell Phone Rings or Texting Incidents During a Performance: Our show is not exactly a quiet show, so if there are cell phone rings, we might not always hear them. But I can tell you there is text-messaging going on 24/7. It's shocking! It's just a big text-messaging show. There's no hiding the lights. We can see the lights from the stage.

Memorable Fan Encounters: Those could fill a book. On Halloween someone dressed up as me in a very detailed manner. A group of drag queens dressed up as Elle Woods and all sat in a row. There was a sea of pink in a specific section. And they were big girls, ya know.

Latest Audience Arrival: We can only see the section with the "rush" tickets—and those kids are always on time.

Fastest Costume Change: I have a 20-second costume change, but there's also the onstage Elle change in the department store, in which she goes from the white dress into the pink dress. An onstage costume change wins.

Who Wore the Heaviest/Hottest Costume: The band outfits are heavy and intricate. My pregnancy pad isn't all that comfortable, either.

Who Wore The Least: Laura Bell, when she wears the bunny costume.

Catchphrase Only The Company Would Recognize: "Boots."

Sweethearts Within the Company: The famous sweethearts are me and Andy, the married couple.

Memorable Directorial Note: "Let me be you." That was Jerry Mitchell's way: he would act it out.

Nicknames: I'm "Orph" or "O." Andy and I call each other "Sam." Laura Bell is "LBB." Natalie Joy Johnson is "NJJ." Michelle Kittrell is "Kitty." Rod, I call "Gerard." Amber is "Hombre." April Berry is "Berries." Jason Gillman is always "Gillman." "TJ" is what we call Tracy Jai Edwards. Richard Blake is "Blakemore." Asmeret is "Esmeralda." Michael Rupert is called "Mr. Michael Rupert," in its entirety.

Embarrassing Moments: Laura Bell has lost her shoe a couple of times. Once it hit somebody in the audience and we had to get it back!

Ghostly Encounters Backstage: On nights when things get wacky at the theatre we say, "Oh, Judy [Garland]'s angry." Things tend to happen in a cluster on one show. Things get stuck, things get lost. How could it be happening? It's either Judy or the gremlins having fun.

Coolest Thing About Being in This Show: Getting to have those big freaking live audiences every night. I love those cavernous theatres. The Palace is such a legendary theatre. I think everybody wants to play the Palace once in their career.

Not-So-Shaggy-Dog Story: No one will forget the night the dog puked onstage. It happened in early previews in San Francisco. Chloe, the bulldog who plays Rufus, is the only "person" in the cast who never missed a show. The trainer, Bill Berloni, told us that when bulldogs get excited or happy they throw up. It's a reflex in that breed. The first time we were in front of a huge audience at the Golden Gate, when Chloe came on in Act II, she threw up all over the stage. It's live theatre—what are you gonna do? I ad-libbed that I did that a lot when I left Dewey, too. I said, "It's time for your manicure and some Pepto." The crew had to soak it all up and clean off the stage because there's a big number right after that. The Golden Gate was not so golden after that.

Memorable Event: Recording the show for MTV—live! We'll always be the first show that ever got to do that for such a big freaking mainstream channel. They didn't try to make it more movielike; they wanted it to really feel like a live performance with a lot of audience reaction. I find that fascinating. I think it's something that every one of us will forever and ever remember. And so many more people got to see it than just the theatergoing public, people all over the country. MTV also made it so there would be only a limited time they could run it. So it hasn't hurt us at the box office at all. If anything, more people want to see us live. And it looks great; crisp and gorgeous. They did a really nice job. All of us will forever have that piece of film to look back on and enjoy.

Fan Club Info: LegallyBlondeonBroadway.com.

Les Liaisons Dangereuses

First Preview: April 11, 2008. Opened: May 1, 2008.
Still running as of May 31, 2008.

PLAYBILL

AMERICAN AIRLINES THEATRE

ROUNDABOUT THEATRE COMPANY

Todd Haimes, Artistic Director
Harold Wolpert, Managing Director
Julia C. Levy, Executive Director

Present

Laura Linney   Ben Daniels

By Christopher Hampton
From the novel by Choderlos de Laclos

with

Siân Phillips
Jessica Collins   Mamie Gummer   Kristine Nielsen   Benjamin Walker
Rosie Benton   Derek Cecil
Kevin Duda   Delphi Harrington   Tim McGeever   Nicole Orth-Pallavicini   Jane Pfitsch

Set Design Scott Pask	*Costume Design* Katrina Lindsay	*Lighting Design* Donald Holder	*Sound Design* Paul Arditti
Hair & Wig Design Paul Huntley	*Voice and Speech Coach* Deborah Hecht	*Fight Director* Rick Sordelet	*Production Stage Manager* Arthur Gaffin
Casting Jim Carnahan C.S.A. & Carrie Gardner	*General Manager* Sydney Beers	*Technical Supervisor* Steve Beers	*Press Representative* Boneau/Bryan-Brown
Director of Marketing & *Sales Promotion* David B. Steffen	*Director of Development* Jeffory Lawson	*Founding Director* Gene Feist	*Associate Artistic Director* Scott Ellis

Directed by
Rufus Norris

Roundabout Theatre Company is a member of the League of Resident Theatres.
www.roundabouttheatre.org

5/1/08

CAST

(in order of appearance)

La Marquise de Merteuil ....LAURA LINNEY
Madame de Volanges ....KRISTINE NIELSEN
Cécile Volanges ....MAMIE GUMMER
Major-domo ....TIM McGEEVER
Le Vicomte de Valmont ....BEN DANIELS
Azolan ....DEREK CECIL
Madame de Rosemonde.............SIÂN PHILLIPS
La Présidente de Tourvel ....JESSICA COLLINS
Émilie ....ROSIE BENTON
Le Chevalier Danceny ....BENJAMIN WALKER
Footman/Tenor ....KEVIN DUDA
Maid/Soprano ....JANE PFITSCH
Servants...................DELPHI HARRINGTON,
NICOLE ORTH-PALLAVICINI

TIME & PLACE

ACT I

Scene 1: An August evening.
Madame la Marquise de Merteuil's salon.

Scene 2: Three weeks later, early evening.
The principal salon in Madame de
Rosemonde's château in the country.

Scene 3: A couple of days later, the middle
of the night. Émilie's bedroom in her
house on the outskirts of Paris.

Scene 4: Ten days later, a September afternoon.
The grand salon of La Marquise
de Merteuil.

Scene 5: A week later, after lunch. The salon in
Madame de Rosemonde's château.

Continued on next page

(L-R): Ben Daniels and Laura Linney.

Photo by Joan Marcus

The Playbill Broadway Yearbook 2007-2008

Les Liaisons Dangereuses

Cast Continued

Scene 6: A fortnight later, the middle of the night. Cécile's bedroom in the château.

Scene 7: The following day, 1st October; afternoon. The salon in Madame de Rosemonde's château.

Scene 8: Two nights later, Valmont's bedroom in the château.

Scene 9: Late the following evening, the salon in the château.

ACT II

Scene 1: Late October, the principal salon in Valmont's Paris house.

Scene 2: Two days later, six pm. The salon in Madame de Tourvel's house.

Scene 3: The following evening, Merteuil's salon.

Scene 4: A fortnight later, afternoon. The salon in Valmont's house.

Scene 5: Ten days later, evening. Madame de Merteuil's salon.

Scene 6: The following afternoon. The salon in Madame de Tourvel's house.

Scene 7: About a week later. A December evening in Madame de Merteuil's salon.

Scene 8: A December dawn in the Bois de Vincennes.

Scene 9: New Year's Eve, Madame de Merteuil's salon.

The action takes place in various salons and bedrooms in a number of houses and châteaux in and around Paris, and in the Bois de Vincennes, one autumn and winter in the 1780s.

UNDERSTUDIES

For La Marquise de Merteuil, Madame de Volanges: NICOLE ORTH-PALLAVICINI

For Cécile Volanges, Émilie: JANE PFITSCH

For Major-domo, Le Chevalier Danceny: KEVIN DUDA

For Le Vicomte de Valmont, Azolan: TIM McGEEVER

For Madame de Rosemonde: DELPHI HARRINGTON

For La Présidente de Tourvel: ROSIE BENTON

Production Stage Manager: ARTHUR GAFFIN

Stage Manager: JAMIE GREATHOUSE

Laura Linney
La Marquise de Merteuil

Ben Daniels
Le Vicomte de Valmont

Siân Phillips
Madame de Rosemonde

Jessica Collins
La Présidente de Tourvel

Mamie Gummer
Cécile Volanges

Kristine Nielsen
Madame de Volanges

Benjamin Walker
Le Chevalier Danceny

Rosie Benton
Émilie

Derek Cecil
Azolan

Kevin Duda
Footman/Tenor

Delphi Harrington
Servant

Tim McGeever
Major-domo

Nicole Orth-Pallavicini
Servant

Jane Pfitsch
Soprano

Christopher Hampton
Playwright

Rufus Norris
Director

Scott Pask
Set Designer

Katrina Lindsay
Costume Designer

Donald Holder
Lighting Designer

Paul Huntley
Hair & Wig Design

Les Liaisons Dangereuses

Rick Sordelet
Fight Director

Jim Carnahan
Casting

Gene Feist
*Founding Director,
Roundabout Theatre
Company*

Todd Haimes
*Artistic Director,
Roundabout Theatre
Company*

Photos by Ben Strothmann

FRONT OF HOUSE STAFF
Front Row (L-R): Anne Ezell, Elsie Jamin Maguire, Kristin Asher.

Back Row (L-R): Ilia Diaz, Jacklyn Rivera, Victoria Tjoelker, Zipporah Aguasvivas.

STAGE AND COMPANY MANAGEMENT
(L-R): Jamie Greathouse, Arthur Gaffin, Carly DiFulvio.

WARDROBE
Front Row (L-R): Brittany Jones-Pugh, Vangeli Kaseluris.

Back Row (L-R): Susan Fallon, Susan Kroeter, James Strunk, Luana Michaels.

Les Liaisons Dangereuses

CREW
Front Row (L-R): Brian Maiuri, Glenn Merwede, Abigail Nemec-Merwede, Carmel Sheehan.

Back Row (L-R): Jason Bowles, Chris Mattingly, Barb Bartel, Jill Anania, Liz Coleman, Andrew Forste.

Photos by Ben Strothmann

HAIR & WIG
(L-R): Yolanda Ramsay, Nellie LaPorte.

DOORMAN
Adolf Torres

BOX OFFICE
(L-R): Robert Morgan, Heather Siebert.

ROUNDABOUT THEATRE COMPANY STAFF
ARTISTIC DIRECTOR ....TODD HAIMES
MANAGING DIRECTOR ....HAROLD WOLPERT
EXECUTIVE DIRECTOR ....JULIA C. LEVY
ASSOCIATE ARTISTIC DIRECTOR ...SCOTT ELLIS

ARTISTIC STAFF
DIRECTOR OF ARTISTIC DEVELOPMENT/
DIRECTOR OF CASTING ....**Jim Carnahan**
Artistic Consultant ....Robyn Goodman
Resident Director ....Doug Hughes
Associate Artists ....Scott Elliott, Bill Irwin, Joe Mantello, Mark Brokaw, Kathleen Marshall
Artistic Associate ....Jill Rafson
Casting Director ....Carrie Gardner
Casting Associate ....Kate Schwabe
Casting Associate ....Stephen Kopel
Artistic Assistant ....Erica Rotstein
Literary Associate ....Josh Fiedler
Casting Interns ....Kerry Ann Minchinton, Kyle Bosley

EDUCATION STAFF
EDUCATION DIRECTOR ....**David A. Miller**
Director of Instruction and
    Curriculum Development ....Reneé Flemings
Education Program Manager ....Jennifer DiBella
Program Associate for
    School-Based Programs ....Amanda Hinkle
Education Associate
    for Theatre-Based Programs ....Jay Gerlach
Education Assistant ....Aliza Greenberg
Education Dramaturg ....Ted Sod
Teaching Artists ....Phil Alexander, Cynthia Babak, Victor Barbella, LaTonya Borsay, Rob Bronstein, Lori Brown-Niang, Miss Stella, Hamilton Clancy, Joe Doran, Katie Down, Amy Fortoul, Tony Freeman, Sheri Graubert, Matthew Gregory, Adam Gwon, Karla Hendrick, Jim Jack, Lisa Renee Jordan, Alvin Keith, Jonathan Lang, Rebecca Lord, Tami Mansfield, Erin McCready,

Jordana Oberman, Evan O'Brient, Deirdre O'Connor, Andrew Ondrecjak, Laura Poe, Alexa Polmer-Spencer, Nicole Press, Jennifer Rathbone, Leah Reddy, Amanda Rehbein, Taylor Ruckel, Chris Rummel, Cassy Rush, Drew Sachs, Nick Simone, Derek Straat, Daniel Robert Sullivan, Vickie Tanner, Olivia Tsang, Cristina Vaccaro, Jennifer Varbalow, Leese Walker, Eric Wallach, Gail Winar
Education Interns ....Sara Curtin, Steven Tarca

ADMINISTRATIVE STAFF
GENERAL MANAGER ....**Sydney Beers**
Associate Managing Director ....Greg Backstrom
General Manager, Steinberg Center ....Rebecca Habel
General Counsel ....Nancy Hirschmann
Human Resources Manager ....Stephen Deutsch
MIS Director ....Jeff Goodman
Assistant General Manager ....Maggie Cantrick

Les Liaisons Dangereuses

Management Associate ....Tania Camargo
Office Manager ....Scott Kelly
MIS Database Administrator ....Micah Kraybill
MIS Associate ....Dylan Norden
Receptionists ....Dee Beider, Raquel Castillo,
    Elisa Papa, Allison Patrick,
    Monica Sidorchuk
Messenger ....Darnell Franklin
Management Interns ....Michael Crowley,
    Jessica Segal

FINANCE STAFF
DIRECTOR OF FINANCE...............**Susan Neiman**
Assistant Controller.........................John LaBarbera
Accounts Payable Administrator ....Frank Surdi
Financial Associate ....Yonit Kafka
Business Office Assistant ....Joshua Cohen
Business Interns ....Jeffrey Darland, Jaclyn Verbitski

DEVELOPMENT STAFF
DIRECTOR OF DEVELOPMENT .....**Jeffory Lawson**
Director, Institutional Giving ....Julie K. D'Andrea
Director, Special Events ....Steve Schaeffer
Director, Major Gifts ....Joy Pak
Director, Patron Programs ....Amber Jo Manuel
Manager, Donor Information Systems ....Lise Speidel
Manager, Individual Giving ....Kara Kandel
Telefundraising Manager ....Gavin Brown
Manager, Corporate Relations ....Corey Young
Individual Giving Associate ....Kate Bartoldus
Patrons Services Assistant ....John Haynes
Development Assistants ....Joshua Poole, Daniel Curley
Special Events Assistant ....Ashley Firestone
Institutional Giving Assistant ....Nick Nolte
Assistant to the Executive Director ....Allyson Stewart
Development Interns...................Kaitlin Cherichello,
    Victoria Pardo-Posse

MARKETING STAFF
DIRECTOR OF MARKETING
  AND SALES PROMOTION ....**David B. Steffen**
Associate Director of Marketing ....Wendy Hutton
Marketing/Publications Manager .....Margaret Casagrande
Marketing Manager ....Stefanie Schussel
Marketing Assistant ....Shannon Marcotte
Website Consultant ....Keith Powell Beyland
DIRECTOR OF TELESALES
  SPECIAL PROMOTIONS ....**Daniel Weiss**
Telesales Manager ....Michael Pace
Telesales Office Coordinator ....Anthony Merced
Marketing Intern ....Dragica Dabo

TICKET SERVICES STAFF
DIRECTOR OF
  SALES OPERATIONS ....**Charlie Garbowski, Jr.**
Ticket Services Manager ....Ellen Holt
Subscription Manager ....Ethan Ubell
Box Office Managers ....Edward P. Osborne,
    Andrew Clements
Group Sales Manager ....Jeff Monteith
Assistant Box Office Managers ....Krystin MacRitchie,
    Robert Morgan, Nicole Nicholson
Customer Services Coordinator ....Thomas Walsh
Assistant Ticket Services Managers ....Robert Kane,
    Bill Klemm, Carlos Morris
Ticket Services ....Solangel Bido,
    Lauren Cartelli, David Carson,

Joseph Clark, Barbara Dente,
Nisha Dhruna, Adam Elsberry,
Lindsay Ericson, Scott Falkowski,
Catherine Fitzpatrick,
James Graham, Tova Heller,
Nicki Ishmael, Kate Longosky, Elisa Mala,
Mead Margulies, Chuck Migliaccio,
Adam Owens, Kayrose Pagan, Ethan Paulini,
David Pittman, Thomas Protulipac,
Kaia Rafoss, DeeAnna Row,
Benjamin Schneider, Heather Siebert,
Nalene Singh, Lillian Soto, DJ Thacker,
Pam Unger
Ticket Services Intern ....Andrea Finlayson

SERVICES
Counsel ....Paul, Weiss,
  Rifkind, Wharton and Garrison LLP,
  John Breglio, Deborah Hartnett
Counsel ....Rosenberg & Estis
Counsel ....Andrew Lance,
  Gibson, Dunn, & Crutcher, LLP
Counsel ....Harry H. Weintraub,
  Glick and Weintraub, P.C.
Immigration Counsel ....Mark D. Koestler and
  Theodore Ruthizer
Government
  Relations ....Law Offices of Claudia Wagner LLC
House Physicians ....Dr. Theodore Tyberg,
  Dr. Lawrence Katz
House Dentist ....Neil Kanner, D.M.D.
Insurance ....DeWitt Stern Group, Inc.
Accountant ....Lutz & Carr CPAs, LLP
Advertising ....SpotCo/
  Drew Hodges, Jim Edwards,
  Tom Greenwald, Y. Darius Suyama,
  Beth Watson
Sponsorship ....Allied Live/
  Tanya Grubich, Laura Matalon,
  William Critzman
Interactive Marketing ....Situation Marketing/
  Damian Bazadona, John Lanasa,
  Ryan Klink, Joey Oliva
Events Photography ....Anita and Steve Shevett
Production Photographer ....Joan Marcus
Theatre Displays.............King Displays, Wayne Sapper
Lobby Refreshments ....Sweet Concessions
Merchandising ....Marquee Merchandise, LLC/
  Matt Murphy

MANAGING DIRECTOR
  EMERITUS ....Ellen Richard

Roundabout Theatre Company
231 West 39th Street, New York, NY 10018
(212) 719-9393.

GENERAL PRESS REPRESENTATIVES
BONEAU/BRYAN-BROWN
Adrian Bryan-Brown
Matt Polk   Jessica Johnson   Amy Kass

STAFF FOR *LES LIAISONS DANGEREUSES*
GENERAL MANAGER ....Sydney Beers
Company Manager ....Nichole Jennino
Assistant Company Manager ....Carly DiFulvio
Production Stage Manager ....Arthur Gaffin

Stage Manager ....Jamie Greathouse
Assistant Director ....Wes Grantom
Associate Scenic Designer ....Jeff Hinchee
Associate Lighting Designer ....Caroline Chao
Associate Costume Designer ....Mitchell Bloom
Associate Sound Designer ....David Stephen Baker
Assistant to the Costume Designer ....Daryl Stone
Production Carpenter ....Glenn Merwede
Production Electrician ....Brian Maiuri
Deck Electrician ....Barb Bartel
Properties ....Andrew Forste
Flyman ....Chris Mattingly
Production Properties ....Kathy Fabian
Wardrobe Supervisor ....Susan J. Fallon
Sound Operator ....Jill Anania
Local One IATSE Apprentice ....Carmel Sheehan
Rehearsal Pianist ....Chris Fenwick
Wardrobe Daywork ....Jesse Galvan
Make-Up Design ....Angelina Avallone
Dressers ....Brittany Jones-Pugh, Vangeli Kaseluris,
  Susan Kroeter, Luana Michaels
Hair & Wig Supervisor ....Manuela LaPorte
Hair & Wig Assistant ....Yolanda Ramsay
Production Assistants ....Kelly Glasow, Chris Kateff
Scenery Constructed by ....PRG Scenic Technologies
Sound Equipment provided by ....Sound Associates
Lighting Equipment provided by ....PRG
Deck and Automation Construction
  provided by ....PRG Scenic Technologies
Costumes constructed by ....Eric Winterling, Inc.,
  Euro Co Costumes,
  Barbara Matera, LTD
Custom Embroidery by ....Penn & Fletcher
Drapery and Soft Goods by ....I. Weiss, New York
Card Shark Consultant ....Laura Linney
Theatrical Equipment ...is transported on a carbon neutral
  basis by Clark Transfer
  in partnership with NativeEnergy
Special Thanks to ....The Metropolitan Opera
  Costume Shop; Period Corset,
  Angels the Costumiers and CosProp

Make-up provided by M•A•C

AMERICAN AIRLINES THEATRE STAFF
Company Manager ....Nichole Jennino
Assistant Company Manager ....Carly DiFulvio
House Carpenter ....Glenn Merwede
House Electrician ....Brian Maiuri
House Properties ....Andrew Forste
House Sound ....Dann Wojnar
IA Apprentice ....Carmel Sheehan
Wardrobe Supervisor ....Susan J. Fallon
Box Office Manager ....Ted Osborne
Assistant Box Office Manager ....Robert Morgan
House Manager ....Steve Ryan
Associate House Manager ....Zipporah Aguasvivas
Head Usher ....Jacklyn Rivera
House Staff ....Ilia Diaz, Anne Ezell, Adam Wier,
  Elsie Jamin Maguire, Idair Melendez,
  Rebecca Knell, James Watanachaiyot,
  Victoria Tjoelker, Kristin Asher,
  Joaquin Melendez
Security ....Julious Russell
Additional Security Provided by ....Gotham Security
Maintenance ....Jerry Hobbs, Willie Philips,
  Daniel Pellew, Magali Western

Les Liaisons Dangereuses
SCRAPBOOK

Correspondents: Artie Gaffin, PSM. Jamie Greathouse, SM. Ben Walker, "Danceny."

Memorable Opening Night Faxes: We got a bunch of faxes from other shows. We love the ones that get personalized to various members of the company from other actors they have worked with.

Opening Night Gifts: Laura Linney made a mixed CD for everybody, with each song dedicated to a different person in the company. She dedicated "Love Fool" to Artie, "Sexy Mother F---er" to Ben Daniels—all sort of sex puns. The stage managers found a place that sold stuffed animals of various microbes, and we gave the cast adorable stuffed "Clap," "Gonorrhea" and "Chlamydia." Ben Walker also made t-shirts with Artie Gaffin's face.

Most Exciting Celebrity Visitors and What They Said: Meryl Streep came to see her daughter, Mamie Gummer. She told us to be careful during the sword fights. There is nudity in the show and Ben Walker's mother told him to put his pants on.

Who Has Done the Most Shows in Their Career: Siân Phillips, definitely.

Special Backstage Rituals: There's a fight call before every show. Ben Walker, the fight captain, manages to make it completely fun and also to get the work done. Everyone speaks aloud their inner monologue—what their character is thinking when he's doing the fighting, which they don't do during the show. It's very amusing.

Also, there's the legendary Sunday brunch at the Roundabout, provided by wardrobe supervisor Susan Fallon (but everyone calls her Fallon). There is a weekly menu—it can be pancakes, or waffles, or French toast, or omelets with rosemary potatoes, et cetera. It's unlike any other brunch. She claims you can tell the quality of a cast by the quantity of bacon they eat at the brunch, and last week we went through six pounds of it, which is pretty good. I think people audition for Roundabout shows just so they can work with Fallon! She also decorates the dressing rooms so you feel like you're living in the best studio apartment in New York. And she is a fantastic baker so we try to have as many birthdays during a run as possible.

Favorite Moment During Each Performance: The fart joke.

Favorite In-Theatre Gathering Place: Artie generously brings tons of food and chips and candy so we're always congregating in the stage managers' office.

Favorite Off-Site Hangout: Bond 45.

Favorite Snack Food: Mini chocolates, pretzel rods, Twizzlers, Skittles, Gold Fish and wasabi peas.

Mascot: Artie (Ben said that!).

Favorite Therapy: Artie hugs. Ben Daniels does yoga before the show. The Ricola company generously gives us their throat lozenges, so they're always tastefully presented stage right and stage left.

1. Curtain call on opening night.
2. Cast member Mamie Gummer at the opening night cast party at Hilton New York.

Memorable Ad-Lib: Sometimes the names get twisted a bit. Volanges gets called Tourvel. It's all French to a lot of people. One time during the fight Ben said "Son of a...," but then caught himself.

Memorable Press Encounter: The press has been pretty classy.

Memorable Fan Encounters: The American Airlines Theatre is set up in an odd way; there's not a traditional exterior stage door. We exit through the theatre and sometimes people wait out front. Laura Linney said she got a fan letter from somebody in Hungary who enclosed a photo and said, "You're my favorite star, please sign this." But it wasn't a photo of Laura. Laura is really good at responding to fan mail. But one time somebody wrote to her requesting a signed PLAYBILL or a photograph. She sent the PLAYBILL, but then the person wrote back complaining that they "were a little disappointed" they didn't get the photo too!

Fastest Costume Change: Ben Daniels has quick changes from clothing to clothing, and from clothing to naked for the seduction scenes. The Wardrobe Department has commented on how calm he is during the changes.

Who Wore the Heaviest Costume: All the women wear corsets and panniers (they look like cages) under their dresses. They've learned that they basically can't breathe, eat, lounge or sit in them but they all have adjusted beautifully.

Who Wore the Least: The two Bens are naked at various points in the show.

The Worst Thing About Doing a Show in Late Spring: It's the awards season and though everyone deserves an award, realistically that never happens. The best time to do a show is in November and December when the only thing to complain about is working on Thanksgiving and Christmas.

Coolest Thing About Being in This Show: It's a fantastic company; the crew is great; Roundabout has been sensational. We feel surrounded by a loving atmosphere from everyone.

Les Misérables

First Preview: October 24, 2006. Opened: November 9, 2006.
Closed January 6, 2008 after 17 Previews and 463 Performances.

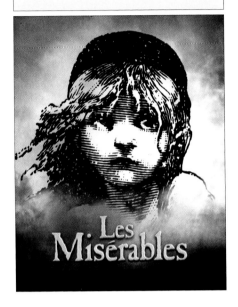

PLAYBILL

CAST

(in order of appearance)

Jean Valjean	DREW SARICH
Javert	ROBERT HUNT
Farmer	DOUG KREEGER
Innkeeper	MICHAEL MINARIK
Innkeeper's Wife	KAREN ELLIOTT
Laborer	MIKE EVARISTE
The Bishop of Digne	JAMES CHIP LEONARD
Constables	ANDERSON DAVIS, JEFF KREADY
Factory Foreman	BEN CRAWFORD
Fantine	LEA SALONGA
Factory Girl	HAVILAND STILLWELL
Factory Workers	BECCA AYERS, DANIEL BOGART, DON BREWER, ANDERSON DAVIS, KAREN ELLIOTT, MIKE EVARISTE, RONA FIGUEROA, BLAKE GINTHER, MARYA GRANDY, JEFF KREADY, DOUG KREEGER, JAMES CHIP LEONARD, MICHAEL MINARIK, LUCIA SPINA, KEVIN DAVID THOMAS, IDARA VICTOR, CORTNEY WOLFSON
Sailors	DON BREWER, ANDERSON DAVIS, KEVIN DAVID THOMAS
Pimp	MIKE EVARISTE
Madame	LUCIA SPINA
Whores	BECCA AYERS, ALI EWOLDT, RONA FIGUEROA, MEGAN McGINNIS, HAVILAND STILLWELL, IDARA VICTOR, CORTNEY WOLFSON

Continued on next page

⊛ BROADHURST THEATRE

235 West 44th Street
A Shubert Organization Theatre

Gerald Schoenfeld, *Chairman*   **Philip J. Smith,** *President*

Robert E. Wankel, *Executive Vice President*

CAMERON MACKINTOSH
presents

Les Misérables

By ALAIN BOUBLIL and CLAUDE-MICHEL SCHÖNBERG
Based on the novel by VICTOR HUGO

Music by CLAUDE-MICHEL SCHÖNBERG
Lyrics by HERBERT KRETZMER

Original French text by ALAIN BOUBLIL and JEAN-MARC NATEL
Additional material by JAMES FENTON

New Orchestrations by CHRISTOPHER JAHNKE
Co-Orchestrator STEPHEN METCALFE
Original Orchestrations by JOHN CAMERON
Orchestral Adaptation and Musical Supervision STEPHEN BROOKER
Music Director KEVIN STITES
Sound Design by JON WESTON

Associate Lighting Designer TED MATHER
Executive Producers NICHOLAS ALLOTT, MATTHEW DALCO
Executive Producer/Associate Director FRED HANSON
Casting by TARA RUBIN CASTING, C.S.A.
General Management ALAN WASSER ASSOCIATES

Designed by JOHN NAPIER
Lighting by DAVID HERSEY
Original Sound Design by ANDREW BRUCE
Costumes by ANDRÉANE NEOFITOU

Associate Director SHAUN KERRISON
Directed and Adapted by JOHN CAIRD & TREVOR NUNN

**Is there not in every human soul, and
was there not in the soul of Jean
Valjean, an essential spark, an element
of the divine; indestructible in this
world and immortal in the next, which
goodness can preserve, nourish and
fan into glorious flame, and which
evil can never quite extinguish?**

VICTOR HUGO

Original London production by
CAMERON MACKINTOSH and THE ROYAL SHAKESPEARE COMPANY

LIVE ⊛
BROADWAY

10/1/07

(L-R): Ann Harada and Gary Beach as The Thénardiers.

Lea Salonga as Fantine.

Photos by Joan Marcus

Les Misérables

MUSICAL NUMBERS

<table>
<tr><td colspan="2" align="center">PROLOGUE: 1815, DIGNE</td></tr>
<tr><td>Prologue</td><td>The Company</td></tr>
<tr><td>"Soliloquy"</td><td>Valjean</td></tr>
<tr><td colspan="2" align="center">PROLOGUE: 1823, MONTREUIL-SUR-MER</td></tr>
<tr><td>"At the End of the Day"</td><td>Unemployed and factory workers</td></tr>
<tr><td>"I Dreamed a Dream"</td><td>Fantine</td></tr>
<tr><td>"Lovely Ladies"</td><td>Ladies and clients</td></tr>
<tr><td>"Who Am I?"</td><td>Valjean</td></tr>
<tr><td>"Come to Me"</td><td>Fantine and Valjean</td></tr>
<tr><td>"Castle on a Cloud"</td><td>Young Cosette</td></tr>
<tr><td colspan="2" align="center">1823, MONTFERMEIL</td></tr>
<tr><td>"Master of the House"</td><td>Thénardier, Mme. Thénardier and customers</td></tr>
<tr><td>"Thénardier Waltz"</td><td>M. and Mme. Thénardier and Valjean</td></tr>
<tr><td colspan="2" align="center">1832, PARIS</td></tr>
<tr><td>"Look Down"</td><td>Gavroche and the beggars</td></tr>
<tr><td>"Stars"</td><td>Javert</td></tr>
<tr><td>"Red and Black"</td><td>Enjolras, Marius and the students</td></tr>
<tr><td>"Do You Hear the People Sing?"</td><td>Enjolras, the students and the citizens</td></tr>
<tr><td>"In My Life"</td><td>Cosette, Valjean, Marius and Eponine</td></tr>
<tr><td>"A Heart Full of Love"</td><td>Cosette, Marius and Eponine</td></tr>
<tr><td>"One Day More"</td><td>The Company</td></tr>
<tr><td>"On My Own"</td><td>Eponine</td></tr>
<tr><td>"A Little Fall of Rain"</td><td>Eponine and Marius</td></tr>
<tr><td>"Drink With Me to Days Gone By"</td><td>Grantaire, students and women</td></tr>
<tr><td>"Bring Him Home"</td><td>Valjean</td></tr>
<tr><td>"Dog Eats Dog"</td><td>Thénardier</td></tr>
<tr><td>"Soliloquy"</td><td>Javert</td></tr>
<tr><td>"Empty Chairs at Empty Tables"</td><td>Marius</td></tr>
<tr><td>"Wedding Chorale"</td><td>Guests</td></tr>
<tr><td>"Beggars at the Feast"</td><td>M. and Mme. Thénardier</td></tr>
<tr><td>Finale</td><td>The Company</td></tr>
</table>

Cast Continued

Old Woman	KAREN ELLIOTT
Crone	MARYA GRANDY
Bamatabois	DANIEL BOGART
Fauchelevant	JEFF KREADY
Champmathieu	BEN CRAWFORD
Young Cosette	KYLIE LIYA GOLDSTEIN, KAYLIE RUBINACCIO, CARLY ROSE SONENCLAR
Thénardier	GARY BEACH
Madame Thénardier	ANN HARADA
Young Eponine	KYLIE LIYA GOLDSTEIN, KAYLIE RUBINACCIO, CARLY ROSE SONENCLAR
Old Beggar Woman	KAREN ELLIOTT
Madeleine	RONA FIGUEROA
Gavroche	BRIAN D'ADDARIO, ZACH RAND
Eponine	MEGAN McGINNIS
Cosette	ALI EWOLDT
Major Domo	KEVIN DAVID THOMAS

THÉNARDIER'S GANG

Montparnasse	MIKE EVARISTE
Babet	JEFF KREADY
Brujon	BEN CRAWFORD
Claquesous	JAMES CHIP LEONARD

STUDENTS

Enjolras	MAX von ESSEN
Marius	ADAM JACOBS
Combeferre	DANIEL BOGART
Feuilly	BLAKE GINTHER
Courfeyrac	DON BREWER
Joly	KEVIN DAVID THOMAS
Grantaire	MICHAEL MINARIK
Lesgles	ANDERSON DAVIS
Jean Prouvaire	DOUG KREEGER

Swings	MATT CLEMENS, MARISSA McGOWAN, Q. SMITH, STEPHEN TRAFTON
Dance Captain	MATT CLEMENS

Chain Gang, The Poor, Factory Workers, Sailors,
Whores, Pimps and Wedding Guests
will be played by members of the Ensemble.

Movement Consultant	Kate Flatt

UNDERSTUDIES

For Jean Valjean:
BEN CRAWFORD, JEFF KREADY
For Javert:
BEN CRAWFORD, MICHAEL MINARIK
For Thénardier:
JAMES CHIP LEONARD,
MICHAEL MINARIK
For Madame Thénardier:
BECCA AYERS, KAREN ELLIOTT,
MARYA GRANDY
For Fantine:
RONA FIGUEROA, HAVILAND STILLWELL
For Cosette:
MARISSA McGOWAN, IDARA VICTOR
For Marius:
DANIEL BOGART, DOUG KREEGER
For Eponine:
MARISSA McGOWAN, CORTNEY WOLFSON
For Enjolras:
DON BREWER, ANDERSON DAVIS

ORCHESTRA

Conductor: KEVIN STITES
Associate Conductor: PAUL RAIMAN
Assistant Conductor: ANNBRITT duCHATEAU
Flute/Piccolo/Alto Flute/Alto Recorder: BOB BUSH
Oboe/English Horn: LAURA WALLIS
Clarinet/Bass Clarinet/Tenor Recorder:
    JONATHAN LEVINE
Trumpet/Flugel: TIM SCHADT
Bass Trombone/Tuba: CHRIS OLNESS
French Horns: MICHAEL ATKINSON,
    SARA CYRUS
Violin: MARTIN AGEE
Viola: DEBRA SHUFELT-DINE
Cello: LAURA BONTRAGER
Bass: DAVE PHILLIPS
Mallets/Timpani/Percussion:
    CHARLES DESCARFINO
Keyboards: PAUL RAIMAN,
    ANNBRITT duCHATEAU
Music Coordinator: JOHN MILLER

Les Misérables

Becca Ayers
Ensemble

Gary Beach
Thénardier

Daniel Bogart
Combeferre

Don Brewer
Courfeyrac

Matt Clemens
Swing

Ben Crawford
Brujon

Brian D'Addario
Gavroche

Anderson Davis
Lesgles

Karen Elliott
Ensemble

Mike Evariste
Montparnasse

Ali Ewoldt
Cosette

Rona Figueroa
Ensemble

Blake Ginther
Feuilly

Kylie Liya Goldstein
*Young Cosette/
Young Eponine*

Marya Grandy
Ensemble

Ann Harada
Madame Thénardier

Robert Hunt
Javert

Adam Jacobs
Marius

Jeff Kready
Babet

Doug Kreeger
Jean Prouvaire

James Chip Leonard
*Bishop of Digne/
Claquesous*

Megan McGinnis
Eponine

Marissa McGowan
Swing

Michael Minarik
Grantaire

Zach Rand
Gavroche

Kaylie Rubinaccio
*Young Cosette/
Young Eponine*

Lea Salonga
Fantine

Drew Sarich
Jean Valjean

Q. Smith
Swing

Carly Rose Sonenclar
*Young Cosette/
Young Eponine*

Lucia Spina
Ensemble

Haviland Stillwell
Ensemble

Kevin David Thomas
Joly

Stephen Trafton
Swing

Idara Victor
Ensemble

Les Misérables

Max von Essen
Enjolras

Cortney Wolfson
Ensemble

Alain Boublil
Conception, Book and Original French Lyrics

Claude-Michel Schönberg
Composer

Herbert Kretzmer
Lyricist

Cameron Mackintosh
Producer

John Caird
Direction and Adaptation

Trevor Nunn
Direction and Adaptation

John Napier
Production Designer

David Hersey
Lighting Designer

Andreane Neofitou
Costumes

Andrew Bruce
Sound

Christopher Jahnke
New Orchestrations

Stephen Brooker
Orchestral Adaptation and Musical Supervision

Stephen Metcalfe
Co-Orchestrator

John Cameron
Original Orchestrations

Shaun Kerrison
Associate Director

Kate Flatt
Movement Consultant

Sue Jenkinson DiAmico
Associate Set Designer

Tom Watson
Hair Designer

Tara Rubin Casting
Casting

John Miller
Music Coordinator

Nick Allott
Executive Producer

Alan Wasser Associates
General Manager

Mandy Bruno
Eponine, Whore

Kate Chapman
Factory Worker, Madame

Nikki Renée Daniels
Factory Worker, Madeleine, Whore

Ben Davis
Javert

Christy Faber
Factory Worker, Innkeeper's Wife, Madeleine, Old Beggar Woman, Old Woman, Whore

Alexander Gemignani
Jean Valjean

Les Misérables

JD Goldblatt
*Factory Worker,
Laborer,
Montparnasse, Pimp*

Victor Hawks
*Brujon, Factory
Worker, Sailor*

Jeremy Hays
*Factory Worker,
Farmer, Jean
Prouvaire, Swing*

Nehal Joshi
*Constable, Factory
Worker, Lesgles,
Sailor*

Snara-Joye Ross
*Factory Worker,
Innkeeper's Wife,
Old Beggar Woman,
Old Woman*

Chip Zien
Thénardier

Carlos Encinias
*Factory Worker,
Feuilly*

Christy Faber
*Crone,
Factory Worker*

Jenny Galloway
Madame Thénardier

Sean Gilbert
Gavroche

Jeremy Hays
*Bamatabois,
Combeferre, Factory
Worker, Swing*

Leah Horowitz
Cosette, Whore

Judy Kuhn
Fantine

John Owen-Jones
Jean Valjean

Ivan Rutherford
Jean Valjean

2007-2008 AWARD

ACTORS' EQUITY ASSOCIATION AWARD
Extraordinary Excellence
in Diversity on Broadway

**WARDROBE SUPERVISOR/
ASSOCIATE COSTUME DESIGNER**
Rick Kelly

FRONT OF HOUSE
Front Row (L-R): Rose Ann Cipriano, Yenny Fernandez, Karen Diaz and Christian Leguia.

Back Row (L-R): Juan Lopez, Josh Rosier and Hugh Lynch.

Les Misérables

STAGEHANDS
Front Row (L-R): Joanna Staub, Steve "Woof" Callahan, Sandra Paradise, Steve Abbott, Rob Brenner and Ron Vitelli.

Middle Row (L-R): Dave Karlson, Brian McGarty.

Back Row (L-R): Charlie DeVerna, Patrick Pummill, Dan Novi, Jeremy Wahlers, Jonathan Cohen, William Rowland, Spencer Bell, Todd Frank, Brian "Boomer" Bullard, Chris Martin, William Garvey.

WARDROBE
Front Row (L-R): Stacia Williams, Mark Caine.

Back Row (L-R): Marisa Lerette and Francine Buryiak.

BOX OFFICE
(L-R): Clifford Cobb, Noreen Morgan and Mike Lynch.

Not Pictured: Al Crivelli, Gerard O'Brien.

Les Misérables

Photos by Ben Strothmann

STAGE MANAGEMENT
(L-R): Jim Athens (Stage Manager), Michael Passaro (Production Stage Manager) and Charles Underhill (Stage Manager).

COMPANY MANAGEMENT
(L-R): Steve Greer (Associate Company Manager) and Abra Stanley Leonard (Company Manager).

ORCHESTRA
Front Row (L-R): Sara Cyrus (French Horn), Kevin Stites (Conductor).
Second Row (L-R): Annbritt duChateau (Keyboard/Assistant Conductor), Laura Bontrager (Cello), Jonathan Levine (Clarinet/Recorder).
Third Row (L-R): Junah Chung (Viola), Charles Descarfino (Percussion), Laura Wallis (Oboe).
Fourth Row (L-R): Chris Olness (Trombone), Martin Agee (Violin).
Back Row (L-R): Bob Bush (Flute), Ray Kilday (Bass) and Tim Schadt (Trumpet).

Not Pictured: Michael Atkinson (French Horn), Debra Shufelt-Dine (Viola), Dave Phillips (Bass) and Paul Raiman (Keyboard/Associate Conductor).

WARDROBE
Front Row (L-R): Christina M. Ainge.

Second Row (L-R): Sarah Schaub (Asst. Wardrobe Supervisor), Kimberly Baird, Jason Heisey.

Third Row L-R): Mary Ann Lewis-Oberpriller, Julienne Schubert Blechman, Hiro Hosomizu.

Back Row (L-R): Bob Kwiatkowski and Alan Berkoski.

Les Misérables

Drew Sarich as Jean Valjean.

Photo by Joan Marcus

Les Misérables
SCRAPBOOK

Correspondent: Max von Essen, "Enjolras"
Opening Night Gifts: My favorite opening night gift was a life size chocolate leg.
Most Exciting Celebrity Visitors: I joined after the show had opened, so I missed the thrill and excitement of meeting David Hasselhoff. Although one day, Bernadette Peters was backstage. I was saddened to find out she was just there to pick up alterations from Rick, our head of wardrobe. LOL.
Actors Who Performed The Most Roles in This Show/Understudy Anecdote: Our unreal swings knew something like 10 roles each, which is insane. But I have to give props to the amazing Drew Sarich. He started the show as Grantaire, a fantastic featured role. He also covered Enjolras and Javert, and performed both those roles beautifully several times. THEN he auditioned to take over the role of Jean Valjean and HE BOOKED IT!!! And he was incredible in that role, too. Playing all of those roles must be a first in *Les Miz* history.
Special Backstage Rituals: We had all kinds. The main ritual for all the guys was to play hackysack for 15 or 20 minutes before the curtain went up. We even had some pretty amazing specialty moves...Sensai, Special Delivery, Left Nancy, Daniel Day, Neji, Gemignia-hoo-hoo, DS Al Fine, Cow F*%ker, Putting On Ayers, Jester, Lazarwolf. For a while, our neighbors in *A Chorus Line* used to visit and hack with us. It was quite a sight to see all of the opening scene prisoners covered in dirt and rags mixed in with all these dancers in '70s dance clothes. Also, I used to eat a banana every night before I entered as Enjolras. One night I tripped and knocked the banana into my eye (BEFORE I peeled it) and the stem scratched my eye. I couldn't see for almost 10 minutes and it got all red and swollen. Took me a while to live that one down. Whenever there was a banana around people would yell, "MAX...LOOK OUT!!!!!" My absolute favorite pastime was Ass Friday. Every Friday night, during the courtroom scene, myself and the other judges, who were only seen from the waist up, would go pantless and have our butts out. I just feel bad for the crew guys who had to stand behind us. I'm sort of convinced it's why they went on strike. But I'm just speculating. Then of course, some other faves were our "Saturday Night On Broadway" songs, mine and Doug Kreeger's rat song, Ben Crawford and Jeff Kready's own version of the confrontation, Adam riffing in the wings, sourdough song (I almost put in my notice over that one), the young Eponine and Cosette high fives to their older counterparts as one group would exit and the other would get ready to enter, Brian and Zach's spitball academy, Brian's rock concerts in the lower lobby, half hour joketime, Adam's amazing Tissue stories, booby trapping the judge's mallet, Idara's sexy nun dance, Ben and Carlos' amazing rap before the wedding, and basketball in my dressing area.
Favorite Moment During Each Performance (On Stage or Off): Lea Salonga's favorite moment was right after her death as Fantine, because it meant she could put on comfy clothes and relax. My favorite moment was definitely the ABC cafe scene. Just the greatest. Such an honor to perform all that material.
Favorite In-Theatre Gathering Place: Usually up in the men's dressing room on the fifth floor. It was so fun, even I'd walk up there sometimes.

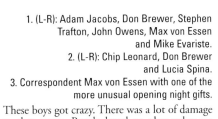

1. (L-R): Adam Jacobs, Don Brewer, Stephen Trafton, John Owens, Max von Essen and Mike Evariste.
2. (L-R): Chip Leonard, Don Brewer and Lucia Spina.
3. Correspondent Max von Essen with one of the more unusual opening night gifts.

These boys got crazy. There was a lot of damage to that room. People loved to play poker up there between shows, too.
Favorite Off-Site Hangout: In the summer, we did a lot of tequila-induced damage at Blockheads. Other times you could find us at Angus, Irish Rogue or Victor's apartment.
Favorite Snack Foods: The guys and dressers in my changing area would keep all kinds of candy stocked at all times. I can't tell you how many shows I got through just on Skittles! And the amount of doughnuts consumed by this cast was staggering.
Mascots: Tumor (AKA Burrito), the Paris baby. Brian's younger brother, Michael. And the inflatable woman in the guys' dressing room.
Favorite Therapies: Where to begin? When you sing for three hours, you learn all the tricks. Ricolas, Throat Coat tea, my inhaler, personal steamer, gargling with Alkolol, and when reflux would hit, I'd bring out the salt, baking soda and Karo syrup mix. And Lea enjoyed a nice massage on two-show days.
Memorable Ad-Lib: One night, Drew Sarich, as Valjean, was supposed to sing "I will pay in advance, I can sleep in a barn. You see how dark it is? I'm not some kind of dog!" He lost the lyrics completely and all he could manage was to yell out "You see how dark I am?" It was amazing. And I'll never forget Chip Zien's first night as Thénardier. He finds Valjean passed out in the sewers, runs to him, rolls him over and yells "Javert." Ooops. Once again, hilarious. Lea used to like to add a "f%*king bastard" as an ad-lib at one point. She got a note to cut it and wasn't too happy. Victor's "Eh, Caliope. Let's go!" was pretty genius, too. And sadly, Nehal's "You ass!" was also ultimately cut.
Memorable Stage Door Fan Encounter: I love the girls who used to show up with handmade dolls of all of our characters. Well, until they sent me photos of some of the dolls in slightly compromising positions. Or on Halloween, when I wanted a little air, and went and peeked out the stage door. There was someone there dressed as me! Amazing. Also, most of us remember, not fans exactly, but a couple sitting in the front row making out pretty much the entire show. I mean, going at it. Hands were involved. Are you catching on? I'm not sure if it was distracting or not, but all of us couldn't wait to get back onstage to see what they were up to each scene. Or what base they had reached.
Busiest Day at the Box Office: Probably the day they announced I was joining the show. ;-)
Catchphrases Only the Company Would Recognize: "Feuilly-dom," "Broadway weight," "Felty," and "Uranus" (enough said).
Sweethearts Within the Company: Chip Leonard married our Company Manager, Abra (they first met out on tour). They just had their first baby. Nikki Renee Daniels and Jeff Kready

Les Misérables

SCRAPBOOK

1. (L-R): Doug Kreeger, Idara Victor (in mirror) and Gary Beach backstage.
2. (L-R): Idara Victor, Nikki Renee Daniels, Soara Joye Ross, Becca Ayers and Megan McGinnis.
3. (L-R): Mike Minarik, Ben Crawford, Carlos Encinias, Jeremy Hays, Max von Essen and Jeff Kready.
4. (L-R): Kylie Goldstein, Ali Ewoldt, Carly Rose Sonenclar,, Megan McGinnis, Kaylie Rubinaccio and friends.

started dating during the show. And Ali Ewoldt and Kevin David Thomas got engaged before one of our matinees.

Onstage Mishaps: My favorite was the night the turntable broke down just as I was entering. We had to hold the show for about 15 minutes and then re-start from that point. It's amazing that only happened once. And another fave was when Gary Beach missed his entrance for "Master of the House." After about 32 bars of music, he ran on stage and picked up right at that point, like nothing had happened. Total pro! Then, one night when Lea Salonga had to spit at Valjean, she was so into it, she knocked Drew Sarich's contact out with a loogie. The girl could spit! Another time, Adam Jacobs was climbing over the gate to find Cosette and got caught on his crotch. Ouch. Anderson's pants splitting, a roach in Lucia's peasant shoe, my huge vocal crack in "One Day More," Lucia almost knocking out Marya with her huge wooden nun cross, Mandy Bruno slipping on stage and sliding right between Adam's leg when they see each other in Paris, several people exiting stage right and slamming their heads, Kevin David Thomas almost wiping out during "One Day More," Ann Harada biting it onstage during the curtain call, and the list goes on and on and on.

Nicknames: Big Sexy Ox, Dupes (because Jeff Kready knew what a duple was at rehearsal),

Bogie, Broadway Max, Baron von Twizzler Schmidt, Sensai, Laser, Nice-T, Merle, Goody, Chocolat, Idara One Note, Idara County Faira, Soupy and Soupy's Dad, Sharkbait.

Coolest Thing About Being in This Show: Lea Salonga said "It was such an honor to be doing the show with some of the most ridiculously talented people on Broadway, not to mention some of the funniest." Drew Sarich said "You crazy, crazy folks! Best cast ever! I miss you all like nuts!" I must agree. Best group of people I have ever worked with. I miss seeing them everyday and being a part of such a legendary musical.

Closing Night Story: All I know is I heard screams of excitement coming from the 5th floor. I later found out all the girls streaked through the guys' dressing room. Amazing! My favorite moment was when I held my high note for about three minutes, 'cause I knew they couldn't fire me. Other than that, I don't think any of us actually remembers the rest of the closing night. :-)

Other Stories: I will never forget the night I was heading up to my dressing room and stepped on a mouse. It must have been limping or on its last leg from the exterminator or something, but my foot definitely ended it all. I felt terrible. Next day I came to work and someone had taped out the outline of a mouse at the very spot, like it was a crime scene or something. It

was hilarious. I also loved the day we arrived at the theatre and there was what must have been a slightly mentally unstable lady out on my fire escape. How she got there, none of us could figure out. But she had rolling luggage (how did she get it up there??!!) and said she was a member of the cast and was just trying to get into the theatre. Amazing. Also, going down in history, is our six- hour brush up rehearsal held at the Alvin Ailey Studios. We were all dreading it so much that we knew we had to do something fun to help us get through. In honor of it being held at a dance studio, we all dressed up in our best '80s dancewear—jazz pants, leg warmers, sweat bands, you name it. We did it up! It was amazing. Also fun, was the day we reprised all our outfits and surprised the cast of *A Chorus Line* during their onstage warm up.

Which leads me to my fondest memory of my time at the Broadhurst Theatre. Our stage-left shared a door that connected to stage-right of the Schoenfeld Theatre. During breaks, I would run over there and watch their show from the wings. They used to do the same. It was just the most amazing thing. Two of the most beloved musicals of all time and cast members of each in the wings supporting each other and appreciating each other's work and gifts. Absolutely, one of the most special things I've ever experienced. I miss those guys as much as my own cast.

The Lion King

First Preview: October 15, 1997. Opened: November 13, 1997.
Still running as of May 31, 2008.

CAST

(in order of appearance)

RAFIKI ....Tshidi Manye
MUFASA ....Nathaniel Stampley
SARABI ....Jean Michelle Grier
ZAZU ....Jeff Binder
SCAR ....Dan Donohue
YOUNG SIMBA ....Guy V. Barfield II
    (Wed. Mat., Thurs., Sat. Eve., Sun. Eve.)
YOUNG SIMBA......................Shavar McIntosh
    (Wed. Eve., Fri., Sat. Mat., Sun. Mat.)
YOUNG NALA ....NicKayla Tucker
    (Wed. Mat., Fri., Sat. Eve., Sun. Mat.)
YOUNG NALA ....Halle Vargas Sullivan
    (Wed. Eve., Thurs., Sat. Mat., Sun. Eve.)
SHENZI ....Bonita J. Hamilton
BANZAI ....James Brown-Orleans
ED ....Enrique Segura
TIMON ....Danny Rutigliano
PUMBAA ....Blake Hammond
SIMBA ....Dashaun Young
NALA ....Kissy Simmons
ENSEMBLE SINGERS ....Alvin Crawford,
    Lindiwe Dlamini, Bongi Duma,
  Jean Michelle Grier, Michael Alexander Henry,
   Joel Karie, Ron Kunene, Sheryl McCallum,
    S'bu Ngema, Selloane A. Nkhela,
   Mpume Sikakane, Lisa Nicole Wilkerson,
    Kenny Redell Williams
ENSEMBLE
  DANCERS ....Kristina Michelle Bethel,
    Kylin Brady, Camille M. Brown,

Continued on next page

MINSKOFF THEATRE

UNDER THE DIRECTION OF
JAMES M. NEDERLANDER, JAMES L. NEDERLANDER,
SARA MINSKOFF ALLAN AND THE MINSKOFF FAMILY

Disney PRESENTS

THE LION KING

Music & Lyrics by
ELTON JOHN & TIM RICE

Additional Music & Lyrics by
LEBO M, MARK MANCINA, JAY RIFKIN, JULIE TAYMOR, HANS ZIMMER

Book by
ROGER ALLERS & IRENE MECCHI

Starring

DAN DONOHUE   NATHANIEL STAMPLEY   TSHIDI MANYE
JEFF BINDER   BLAKE HAMMOND   DANNY RUTIGLIANO
DASHAUN YOUNG   KISSY SIMMONS
JAMES BROWN-ORLEANS   BONITA J. HAMILTON   ENRIQUE SEGURA
GUY V. BARFIELD II   SHAVAR McINTOSH   HALLE VARGAS SULLIVAN   NicKayLa TUCKER

KRISTINA MICHELLE BETHEL   KYLIN BRADY   CAMILLE M. BROWN   MICHELLE AGUILAR CAMAYA   ALVIN CRAWFORD
GABRIEL A. CROOM   GARLAND DAYS   LINDIWE DLAMINI   BONGI DUMA   ANGELICA EDWARDS   JIM FERRIS
IAN YURI GARDNER   JEAN MICHELLE GRIER   MICHAEL ALEXANDER HENRY   TONY JAMES
NICOLE JOHNSON   DENNIS JOHNSTON   CORNELIUS JONES, JR.   JOEL KARIE   GREGORY A. KING   JACK KOENIG
RON KUNENE   SHERYL McCALLUM   RAY MERCER   JENNIFER HARRISON NEWMAN   S'BU NGEMA
SELLOANE A. NKHELA   BRANDON CHRISTOPHER O'NEAL   NATALIE RIDLEY   MPUME SIKAKANE   SOPHIA N. STEPHENS
RYAN BROOKE TAYLOR   TORYA   PHILLIP W. TURNER   LISA NICOLE WILKERSON   KENNY REDELL WILLIAMS

Adapted from the screenplay by
IRENE MECCHI & JONATHAN ROBERTS & LINDA WOOLVERTON

Produced by
PETER SCHNEIDER & THOMAS SCHUMACHER

Scenic Design	*Costume Design*	*Lighting Design*	*Mask & Puppet Design*
RICHARD HUDSON	JULIE TAYMOR	DONALD HOLDER	JULIE TAYMOR & MICHAEL CURRY

Sound Design	*Hair & Makeup Design*	*Associate Director*	*Production Dance Supervisor*
STEVE CANYON KENNEDY	MICHAEL WARD	JOHN STEFANIUK	MAREY GRIFFITH

Associate Producers	*Technical Director*	*Production Stage Manager*	*Production Supervisor*
AUBREY LYNCH II ANNE QUART	DAVID BENKEN	RON VODICKA	DOC ZORTHIAN

Music Supervisor	*Music Director*	*Associate Music Producer*	*Music Coordinator*	*Orchestrators*
CLEMENT ISHMAEL	KARL JURMAN	ROBERT ELHAI	MICHAEL KELLER	ROBERT ELHAI DAVID METZGER BRUCE FOWLER

Music Produced for the Stage & Additional Score by	*Additional Vocal Score, Vocal Arrangements & Choral Director*	*Casting*	*Press Representative*
MARK MANCINA	LEBO M	BINDER CASTING/ MARK BRANDON	BONEAU/ BRYAN-BROWN

Choreography by
GARTH FAGAN

Directed by
JULIE TAYMOR

Disney BROADWAY

© Disney

11/11/07

(L-R): Nathaniel Stampley, Tshidi Manye and Jean Michelle Grier in the finale.

Photo by Joan Marcus

The Lion King

SCENES AND MUSICAL NUMBERS

ACT ONE

Scene 1	Pride Rock	
	"Circle of Life" with "Nants' Ingonyama" ....Rafiki, Ensemble	
Scene 2	Scar's Cave	
Scene 3	Rafiki's Tree	
Scene 4	The Pridelands	
	"The Morning Report" ....Zazu, Young Simba, Mufasa	
Scene 5	Scar's Cave	
Scene 6	The Pridelands	
	"I Just Can't Wait to Be King" ....Young Simba, Young Nala, Zazu, Ensemble	
Scene 7	Elephant Graveyard	
	"Chow Down" ....Shenzi, Banzai, Ed	
Scene 8	Under the Stars	
	"They Live in You" ....Mufasa, Ensemble	
Scene 9	Elephant Graveyard	
	"Be Prepared" ....Scar, Shenzi, Banzai, Ed, Ensemble	
Scene 10	The Gorge	
Scene 11	Pride Rock	
	"Be Prepared" (Reprise) ....Scar, Ensemble	
Scene 12	Rafiki's Tree	
Scene 13	The Desert/The Jungle	
	"Hakuna Matata" ....Timon, Pumbaa, Young Simba, Simba, Ensemble	

ACT TWO

Entr'acte	"One by One" ....Ensemble	
Scene 1	Scar's Cave	
	"The Madness of King Scar" ....Scar, Zazu, Banzai, Shenzi, Ed, Nala	
Scene 2	The Pridelands	
	"Shadowland" ....Nala, Rafiki, Ensemble	
Scene 3	The Jungle	
Scene 4	Under the Stars	
	"Endless Night" ....Simba, Ensemble	
Scene 5	Rafiki's Tree	
Scene 6	The Jungle	
	"Can You Feel the Love Tonight" ....Timon, Pumbaa, Simba, Nala, Ensemble	
	"He Lives in You" (Reprise) ....Rafiki, Simba, Ensemble	
Scene 7	Pride Rock	
	"King of Pride Rock"/"Circle of Life" (Reprise) ....Ensemble	

SONG CREDITS

All songs by Elton John (music) and Tim Rice (lyrics) except as follows:

"Circle of Life" by Elton John (music) and Tim Rice (lyrics)
with **"Nants' Ingonyama"** by Hans Zimmer and Lebo M
"He Lives in You" (**"They Live in You"**): Music and lyrics by Mark Mancina, Jay Rifkin, and Lebo M
"One by One": Music and lyrics by Lebo M
"Shadowland": Music by Lebo M and Hans Zimmer, lyrics by Mark Mancina and Lebo M
"Endless Night": Music by Lebo M, Hans Zimmer, and Jay Rifkin, lyrics by Julie Taymor
"King of Pride Rock": Music by Hans Zimmer, lyrics by Lebo M

ADDITIONAL SCORE

Grasslands chant and Lioness chant by Lebo M; Rafiki's chants by Tsidii Le Loka.

Michelle Aguilar Camaya, Gabriel A. Croom, Nicole Johnson, Gregory A. King, Ray Mercer, Brandon Christopher O'Neal, Natalie Ridley, Ryan Brooke Taylor, Phillip W. Turner

SWINGS AND UNDERSTUDIES
RAFIKI: Angelica Edwards, Sheryl McCallum, Selloane A. Nkhela, Mpume Sikakane
MUFASA: Alvin Crawford, Michael Alexander Henry
SARABI: Camille M. Brown, Sheryl McCallum, Torya
ZAZU: Jim Ferris, Enrique Segura
SCAR: Jeff Binder, Jack Koenig
SHENZI: Angelica Edwards, Sophia N. Stephens
BANZAI: Garland Days, Ian Yuri Gardner, Cornelius Jones, Jr., Kenny Redell Williams
ED: Ian Yuri Gardner, Dennis Johnston, Cornelius Jones Jr.
TIMON: Jim Ferris, Enrique Segura
PUMBAA: Jim Ferris, Jack Koenig
SIMBA: Dennis Johnston, Cornelius Jones, Jr., Joel Karie
NALA: Kylin Brady, Selloane A. Nkhela, Sophia N. Stephens
SWINGS: Garland Days, Angelica Edwards, Ian Yuri Gardner, Tony James, Dennis Johnston, Cornelius Jones, Jr., Jennifer Harrison Newman, Sophia N. Stephens, Torya

DANCE CAPTAINS
Garland Days, Torya

SPECIALTIES
CIRCLE OF LIFE VOCALS: Bongi Duma, S'bu Ngema
MOUSE SHADOW PUPPET: Joel Karie
ANT HILL LADY: Kristina Michelle Bethel
GUINEA FOWL: Ryan Brooke Taylor
BUZZARD POLE: Gregory A. King
GAZELLE WHEEL: Michelle Aguilar Camaya
BUTTERFLIES: Michelle Aguilar Camaya
GAZELLE: Brandon Christopher O'Neal
LIONESS CHANT VOCAL: S'bu Ngema
ACROBATIC TRICKSTER: Ray Mercer
STILT GIRAFFE CROSS: Gabriel A. Croom
GIRAFFE SHADOW PUPPETS: Kenny Redell Williams, Brandon Christopher O'Neal
CHEETAH: Natalie Ridley
SCAR SHADOW PUPPETS: Brandon Christopher O'Neal, Ryan Brooke Taylor, Kenny Redell Williams
SIMBA SHADOW PUPPETS: Gregory A. King, Ray Mercer, Phillip W. Turner

The Lion King

Cast Continued

ONE BY ONE VOCAL: Bongi Duma,
   Selloane A. Nkhela
ONE BY ONE DANCE: Bongi Duma,
   Ron Kunene, S'bu Ngema
FIREFLIES: Camille M. Brown
PUMBAA POLE PUPPET: Kenny Redell Williams
NALA POLE PUPPET: Natalie Ridley
FLOOR DANCERS: Kristina Michelle Bethel,
   Ryan Brooke Taylor
FLYING DANCERS: Michelle Aguilar Camaya,
   Gabriel A. Croom, Brandon Christopher O'Neal,
   Natalie Ridley
LIONESS/HYENA SHADOW PUPPETS:
   Lindiwe Dlamini, Ron Kunene,
   Sheryl McCallum, Selloane A. Nkhela,
   Mpume Sikakane, Lisa Nicole Wilkerson

Bongi Duma, Tshidi Manye, S'bu Ngema,
Selloane A. Nkhela and Mpume Sikakane are
appearing with the permission of Actors' Equity
Association.

ORCHESTRA
CONDUCTOR: Karl Jurman
KEYBOARD SYNTHESIZER/
ASSOCIATE CONDUCTOR: Cherie Rosen
SYNTHESIZERS: Ted Baker, Paul Ascenzo
WOOD FLUTE SOLOIST/FLUTE/PICCOLO:
   David Weiss
CONCERTMASTER: Francisca Mendoza
VIOLINS: Krystof Witek, Avril Brown
VIOLIN/VIOLA: Ralph Farris
CELLOS: Eliana Mendoza, Bruce Wang
FLUTE/CLARINET/BASS CLARINET:
   Robert DeBellis
FRENCH HORNS: Alexandra Cook, Katie Dennis,
   Greg Smith
TROMBONE: Rock Ciccarone
BASS TROMBONE/TUBA: George Flynn
UPRIGHT AND ELECTRIC BASSES:
   Tom Barney
DRUMS/ASSISTANT CONDUCTOR:
   Tommy Igoe
GUITAR: Kevin Kuhn
PERCUSSION/ASSISTANT CONDUCTOR:
   Rolando Morales-Matos
MALLETS/PERCUSSION: Valerie Dee Naranjo,
   Tom Brett
PERCUSSION: Junior "Gabu" Wedderburn
MUSIC COORDINATOR: Michael Keller

Based on the Disney film *The Lion King*
Directed by Roger Allers and Rob Minkoff
Produced by Don Hahn
**Special thanks to all the artists and staff of
Walt Disney Feature Animation**

Dan Donohue
Scar

Nathaniel Stampley
Mufasa

Tshidi Manye
Rafiki

Jeff Binder
Zazu

Blake Hammond
Pumbaa

Danny Rutigliano
Timon

Dashaun Young
Simba

Kissy Simmons
Nala

James
Brown-Orleans
Banzai

Bonita J. Hamilton
Shenzi

Enrique Segura
Ed

Guy V. Barfield II
Young Simba

Shavar McIntosh
Young Simba

Halle Vargas Sullivan
Young Nala

NickKayla Tucker
Young Nala

Kristina Michelle
Bethel
Ensemble

Kylin Brady
Ensemble

Camille M. Brown
Ensemble

Michelle Aguilar
Camaya
Ensemble

Alvin Crawford
Ensemble

The Lion King

Gabriel A. Croom
Ensemble

Garland Days
*Swing,
Dance Captain*

Lindiwe Dlamini
Ensemble

Bongi Duma
Ensemble

Angelica Edwards
Swing

Jim Ferris
*Standby Timon,
Pumbaa, Zazu*

Ian Yuri Gardner
Swing

Jean Michelle Grier
Sarabi/Ensemble

Michael Alexander
Henry
Ensemble

Tony James
Swing

Nicole Johnson
Ensemble

Dennis Johnston
Swing

Cornelius Jones, Jr.
Swing

Joel Karie
Ensemble

Gregory A. King
Ensemble

Jack Koenig
*Standby for
Scar and Pumbaa*

Ron Kunene
Ensemble

Sheryl McCallum
Ensemble

Ray Mercer
*Ensemble,
Fight Captain*

Jennifer Harrison
Newman
Swing

S'bu Ngema
Ensemble

Selloane A. Nkhela
Ensemble

Brandon Christopher
O'Neal
Ensemble

Natalie Ridley
Ensemble

Mpume Sikakane
Ensemble

Sophia N. Stephens
Swing

Ryan Brooke Taylor
Ensemble

Torya
*Swing,
Dance Captain*

Phillip W. Turner
Ensemble

Lisa Nicole
Wilkerson
Ensemble

Kenny Redell
Williams
Ensemble

Sir Elton John
Music

Tim Rice
Lyrics

Roger Allers
Book

Irene Mecchi
Book

The Lion King

Julie Taymor
*Director,
Costume Design,
Mask/Puppet
Co-Design,
Additional Lyrics*

Garth Fagan
Choreographer

Lebo M
*Additional Music &
Lyrics, Additional
Vocal Score, Vocal
Arrangements,
Choral Director*

Mark Mancina
*Additional Music &
Lyrics, Music
Produced for the
Stage, Additional
Score*

Hans Zimmer
*Additional Music &
Lyics*

Jay Rifkin
*Additional Music &
Lyrics*

Richard Hudson
Scenic Design

Donald Holder
Lighting Design

Michael Curry
*Mask & Puppet
Design*

Steve Canyon
Kennedy
Sound Design

Mark Brandon,
Binder Casting
Casting

John Stefaniuk
Associate Director

Karl Jurman
*Music Director/
Conductor*

Jen Bender
Resident Director

Ruthlyn Salomons
*Resident Dance
Supervisor*

Robert Elhai
*Associate Music
Producer,
Orchestrator*

Michael Keller
Music Coordinator

Thomas
Schumacher,
Disney Theatrical
Productions

Kyle R. Banks
*Ensemble Singer,
Lioness/Hyena
Shadow Puppets,
One by One Dance*

John E. Brady
*Understudy for
Pumbaa, Timon, Zazu*

Rodrick Covington
Banzai

Alicia Fisher
Ensemble Dancer

Christopher Freeman
*Ensemble Dancer,
Floor Dancer,
Guinea Fowl, Scar
Shadow Puppets*

India Scandrick
Young Nala

Julian Ivey
Young Simba

Meena T. Jahi
*Sarabi,
Ensemble Singer*

Lisa Lewis
*Cheetah,
Ensemble Dancer,
Flying Dancer,
Nala Pole Puppet*

Willia-Noel
Montague
*Ant Hill Lady,
Ensemble Dancer,
Floor Dancer*

Patrick Page
Scar

Dawn Noel Pignuola
Ensemble Dancer

Angelo Rivera
*Ensemble Dancer,
Flying Dancer,
Stilt Giraffe Cross*

Tom Alan Robbins
Pumbaa

Derek Smith
Scar

Wallace Smith
Simba

The Lion King

Josh Tower
Simba

Steven Evan
Washington
*Ensemble Dancer,
Simba Shadow
Puppets*

Rema Webb
*Ensemble Singer,
Lioness/Hyena
Shadow Puppets*

Mucuy Bolles
*Fireflies,
Ensemble Dancer*

Sean Bradford
Swing

John E. Brady
*Understudy for
Pumbaa, Timon, Zazu*

Michelle Brugal
*Ant Hill Lady,
Ensemble Dancer,
Floor Dancer*

Meena T. Jahi
*Ensemble Singer,
Lioness/Hyena
Shadow Puppets*

Lisa Lewis
*Cheetah,
Ensemble Dancer,
Flying Dancer,
Nala Pole Puppet*

Willia-Noel
Montague
Ensemble Dancer

Theresa Nguyen
*Butterflies, Cheetah,
Ensemble Dancer,
Flying Dancer,
Gazelle Wheel,
Nala Pole Puppet*

Derek Smith
Scar

Wallace Smith
Simba

L. Steven Taylor
Ensemble Singer

Rema Webb
*Ensemble Singer,
Lioness/Hyena
Shadow Puppets*

Photos by Ben Strothmann

CREW

First Row: Elaine Healey (Usher)

Second Row (L-R): Michael Height (Assistant Company Manager), Thomas Schlenk (Company Manager)

Third Row (L-R): Jennie Andrea (Usher), Joanne Shannon (Usher), David Eschinger (Usher)

Fourth Row (L-R): Austin Branda (Usher), Maria Compton (Usher), Jing (Fanny) Zhang (Usher), Marion Mooney (Head Usher)

Fifth Row (L-R): D'Ambrose Boyd (Dresser), Kjeld Andersen (Wardrobe Supervisor), Walter Weiner (Dresser), Ron Vodicka (Production Stage Manager), Cheryl Budd (Usher)

DOORMAN
(L-R): Halle Vargas Sullivan ('Young Nala' at certain performances), Nathan Enebrami (Doorman)

The Lion King

THE LION KING...

...HAS WELCOMED 45 MILLION AUDIENCE MEMBERS WORLDWIDE

...HAS PLAYED IN 11 COUNTRIES,
VISITING MORE THAN 60 CITIES AROUND THE WORLD

...HAS BEEN TRANSLATED INTO 5 DIFFERENT LANGUAGES

...HAS RECEIVED OVER 70 MAJOR AWARDS WORLDWIDE

...HAS BECOME THE 9TH LONGEST-RUNNING MUSICAL ON BROADWAY

...HAS ASSISTED MEN, WOMEN AND CHILDREN LIVING WITH AIDS IN
SOUTH AFRICA BY PROVIDING OVER $2 MILLION TO 36 COMMUNITY
CENTERS, SERVICE PROVIDERS AND CHURCH KITCHENS
OVER THE LAST 10 YEARS

ROARING MILESTONES

BROADWAY November 13, 1997 – **THE LION KING** opens on Broadway at the New Amsterdam Theatre. Over 7 million theatergoers have seen the Broadway production to date.

BROADWAY June 1, 1998 – **THE LION KING** receives six 1998 Tony® Awards including Best Musical. Director Julie Taymor becomes the first woman in Broadway history to win the Tony Award® for Best Director of a Musical.

TOKYO December 20, 1998 – **THE LION KING** opens its first international production in Tokyo at the Shiki Haru Theatre (Theatre de Printemps). It is currently the longest-running show in Tokyo history, seen by over 3 million people.

BROADWAY February 24, 1999 – **THE LION KING** receives the 1998 GRAMMY® Award for Best Musical Show Album. It has since sold over 1 million copies.

LOS ANGELES October 19, 2000 – **THE LION KING** opens in Los Angeles. It remains the longest-running production ever to play at the Pantages Theatre. In 2006, **THE LION KING** returned to the Pantages for a second successful engagement.

US TOURS April 27, 2002 – **THE LION KING** kicks off its first national tour in Denver.

US TOURS May 3, 2003 – **THE LION KING** kicks off its second national tour in Chicago. Each domestic touring company of **THE LION KING** continues to sell out 7-10 markets a year and has been seen by more than 8 million people to date.

BROADWAY June 13, 2006 – **THE LION KING** moves the Broadway production in its entirety from the New Amsterdam Theatre to the Minskoff Theatre in the heart of Times Square.

CHINA July 18, 2006 – **THE LION KING** opens an English-language production in Shanghai. It becomes the longest-running Broadway show to be presented there.

JOHANNESBURG June 6, 2007 – **THE LION KING** celebrates 10 triumphant years on Broadway with a special anniversary production in Johannesburg, South Africa, the cultural inspiration for the show. Around the world, **THE LION KING** has featured nearly 100 South African actors in its productions.

PARIS October 4, 2007 – **THE LION KING** opens in France with 'Le Roi Lion,' its first French-language production at Le Mogador Theatre in Paris.

BROADWAY November 13, 2007 – **THE LION KING** celebrates 10 years on Broadway!

The Lion King

NEW YORK CITY CELEBRATES THE LION KING!

Ten years ago, **THE LION KING** roared onto Broadway and changed the theatre world forever. The landmark musical has been seen by 45 million guests in 63 cities across 11 countries and has received over 70 awards. The Broadway cast recording has sold over a million copies in North America. The show continues to be one of Broadway's most popular productions, thrilling audiences eight times a week in the heart of Times Square.

Meanwhile, the show continues to make its mark around the world. This year, **THE LION KING** opened new productions in Johannesburg, South Africa and in Paris, France, marking the first time the musical has been performed in French. *Le Monde* called *'Le Roi Lion'* a "magnificent visual showcase." Fox News said the French production is "an ebullient and authentic rendering of African music and dance... a joyous, moving experience."

Now, in celebration of our ten-year milestone, the city of New York recognizes the King of Broadway! This weekend, the following events were held in honor of this special occasion:

THE LION KING LIGHTS UP NEW YORK!
In honor of an entire decade of **THE LION KING**, one New York City landmark saluted another! Since Friday night, the Empire State Building has been illuminated in "Lion King Yellow" in recognition of the show. This marks the first time that the famous tower has saluted a Broadway production. Taking part in a once in a lifetime experience, Tshidi Manye, who plays Rafiki, was lucky enough to "flip the switch" in a special lighting ceremony held on Friday.

AN EVENT WORTHY OF THE MAYOR'S ROAR
Michael R. Bloomberg, Mayor of the City of New York, proclaimed Tuesday, November 13th, 2007 as "**THE LION KING** on Broadway Day" in recognition of "the important anniversary of one of the city's most successful musicals." This proclamation was made by the Mayor's Office during the special lighting ceremony at the Empire State Building on Friday.

JOINING THE STARS ON BROADWAY'S "WALL OF FAME"
Sardi's, the famous New York restaurant heralded as the "toast of Broadway," unveiled a new face on its wall of famous caricatures of Broadway stars. A special caricature of **THE LION KING**'s Rafiki was unveiled at a ceremony on Friday and will grace the walls of Sardi's for years to come.

Thank you for joining us in celebrating **THE LION KING**– still visually stunning, powerfully human, and emotionally unforgettable. Long live the KING!

Photo credits: All photos by Joan Marcus except #7 by Per Breiehagen.

1. Blake Hammond as Pumbaa and Danny Rutigliano as Timon.
2. Tshidi Manye as Rafiki.
3. Nathaniel Stampley as Mufasa, Tshidi Manye as Rafiki and Jean Michelle Greier as Sarabi.
4. Jeff Binder as Zazu.
5. Ensemble members S'Bu Ngema, Bongi Duma, and Original Broadway Company member Ron Kunene.

6. Tsidii Le Loka as Rafiki and ensemble members. Original Broadway Company.
7. Jason Raize as Simba and Heather Headley as Nala. Original Broadway Company.
8. John Vickery as Scar and Samuel Wright as Mufasa. Original Broadway Company.
9. Sam Wright as Mufasa, Gina Breedlove as Sarabi and ensemble members as Lionesses. Original Broadway Company.
10. John Vickery as Scar and Scott Irby-Ranniar as Young Simba. Original Broadway Company.

The Lion King
SCRAPBOOK

Above: Ensemble members at the September 2007 "Broadway on Broadway" event in Times Square.

Correspondent: Ron Vodicka, Production Stage Manager
Most Exciting Celebrity Visitor and What They Did/Said: Michael Jackson: "Come on Blanket say something."
Favorite Snack Food: Chocolate covered bacon!

Favorite Therapy: Human Growth Hormone.
Most Memorable Ad-Lib: "It was in Zulu but I am told it was hilarious."
Mascot: Harlem and Jade.
Who Wore the Least: The female dance ensemble at a cast member's birthday party.

Catchphrases Only the Company Would Recognize: "We have already called and asked them to warm it up."
Memorable Opening Night Letter, Fax or Note: "Please take all of your belongings out of the theater this evening in case The Nederlanders lock us out."

Staff for *THE LION KING* Worldwide

Associate Producer ....Aubrey Lynch II
Associate Producer...............................Anne Quart
Production Supervisor ....Doc Zorthian
Associate Director ....John Stefaniuk
Production Dance Supervisor ....Marey Griffith
Music Supervisor ....Clement Ishmael
Dance Supervisor ....Celise Hicks
Associate Scenic Designer ....Peter Eastman
Associate Costume Designer ....Mary Nemecek Peterson
Associate Mask & Puppet Designer ....Louis Troisi
Associate Sound Designer ....John Shivers
Associate Hair & Makeup Designer ....Carole Hancock
Associate Lighting Designer ....Jeanne Koenig
Assistant Lighting Designer ....Marty Vreeland
Creative Coordinator ....Suyin Chan
Management Assistant ....Tara Engler

GENERAL PRESS REPRESENTATIVES
BONEAU/BRYAN-BROWN

Chris Boneau   Matt Polk
Susanne Tighe   Aaron Meier   Christine Olver

Staff for *THE LION KING* New York

Company Manager ....THOMAS SCHLENK
Assistant Company Manager...............Michael Height
Production Stage Manager ....Ron Vodicka
Resident Director ....Jen Bender
Resident Dance Supervisor ....Ruthlyn Salomons
Musical Director/Conductor ....Karl Jurman

Stage Managers ....Carmen I. Abrazado,
Victoria Epstein, Antonia Gianino,
Arabella Powell
Fight Captain ....Ray Mercer
Assistant Choreographers ....Norwood J. Pennewell,
Natalie Rogers
Fight Consultant ....Rick Sordelet
South African Dialect Coach ....Ron Kunene
Casting Associates ....Jack Bowdan, C.S.A.;
Mark Brandon; Sara Schatz
Casting Assistants ....Allison Estrin, Nikole Vallins
Corporate Counsel ....Michael Rosenfeld
Physical Therapy............Neuro Tour Physical Therapy/
Kristin Walthers
Consulting Orthopedist ....Philip A. Bauman, M.D.
Child Wrangler ....Niki White
Executive Travel ....Robert Arnao, Patt McRory
Production Travel ....Jill Citron
Web Design Consultant ....Joshua Noah
Advertising ....Serino/Coyne Inc.

Production Carpenter ....Drew Siccardi
Head Carpenter ....Michael Trotto
House Carpenter ....Patrick Sullivan
Assistant Carpenters ....Kirk Bender, Michael Phillips
Automation Carpenters ....Aldo "Butch" Servilio,
George Zegarsky
Carpenters ....Joe Ianello, Daniel Macormack,
Terry McGarty, Duane Mirro
Flying Supervision ....Dave Hearn
Production Flymen ....Kraig Bender, Dylan Trotto
House Flyman ....Richard McQuail

Production Electrician ....James Maloney
House Electrician ....Michael Lynch
Board Operator ....Edward Greenberg
House Assistant Electrician ....Stephen Speer
Automated Lighting Technician ....Sean Strohmeyer
Key Spot Operator...............................Doug Graf
Assistant Electricians ....William Brennan,
David Holliman, Joseph P. Lynch,
Thomas Richards
Production Propman ....Victor Amerling
House Propman ....Frank Lavaia
Props ....Matthew Lavaia, Michael Lavaia,
Robert McCauley
Head Sound ....Alain Van Achte
Sound Assistants ....Donald McKennan, Scott Scheidt
Production Wardrobe Supervisor ....Kjeld Andersen
Assistant Wardrobe Supervisor ....Cynthia Boardman
Puppet Supervisor ....Anne Salt
Puppet Dayworkers....................Islah Abdul-Rahiim,
Ilya Vett
Mask/Puppet Studio ....Jeff Curry
Dressers ....Meredith Chase-Boyd,
Andy Cook, Tom Daniel, Donna Doiron,
April Fernandez-Taylor, Michelle Gore,
Douglas Hamilton, Mark Houston,
Sara Jablon, Kathy Karadza, Mark Lauer,
Paul Riner, Kathryn Rohe,
Sarah Stith, Sheila Little Terrell,
Dave Tisue, Walter Weiner
Stitcher ....Janeth Iverson
Production Hair Supervisor ....Monica Costea
Assistant Hair Supervisor ....Adenike Wright

The Lion King

Production Makeup Supervisor ....Elizabeth Cohen
Assistant Makeup Supervisor ....Milagros Medina-Cerdeira
Makeup Artist ....Marian Torre

Music Development ....Nick Glennie-Smith
Music Preparation ....Donald Oliver and Evan Morris/
　　　　　　　　　　　　　Chelsea Music Service, Inc.
Synthesizer Programmer ....Ted Baker
Orchestral Synthesizer Programmer ......Christopher Ward
Electronic Drum Programmer ....Tommy Igoe
Addt'l Percussion Arrangements ....Valerie Dee Naranjo
Music Assistant ....Elizabeth J. Falcone
Personal Assistant to Elton John ....Bob Halley
Assistant to Tim Rice ....Eileen Heinink
Assistant to Mark Mancina ....Chuck Choi

Associate Scenic Designer ....Jonathan Fensom
Assistant Scenic Designer ....Michael Fagin
Lighting Design Assistant ....Karen Spahn
Automated Lighting Tracker ....Lara Bohon
Projection Designer ....Geoff Puckett
Projection Art ....Caterina Bertolotto
Assistant Sound Designer ....Kai Harada
Assistant Costume Designer ....Tracy Dorman
Stunt Consultant ....Peter Moore
Children's Tutoring ....On Location Education
Production Photography ....Joan Marcus,
　　　　　　　　　　　　　　　　Marc Bryan-Brown
Associate Producer 1996–1998 ....Donald Frantz
Project Manager 1996–1998 ....Nina Essman
Associate Producer 1998–2002 ....Ken Denison
Associate Producer 2000-2003 ....Pam Young
Associate Producer 2002-2007 ....Todd Lacy
Original Music Director ....Joseph Church

Disney's *The Lion King* is a registered trademark owned by
The Walt Disney Company and used under special license
by Disney Theatrical Productions.

HOUSE STAFF FOR THE MINSKOFF THEATRE

House Manager ....Victor Irving
Treasurer ....Nicholas Loiacono
Assistant Treasurer ....Cheryl Loiacono

CREDITS

Scenery built and mechanized by Hudson Scenic Studio,
Inc. Additional scenery by Chicago Scenic Studios, Inc.;
Edge & Co., Inc.; Michael Hagen, Inc.; Piper Productions,
Inc.; Scenic Technologies, Inc.; I. Weiss & Sons, Inc.
Lighting by Westsun, vari*lite® automated lighting
provided by Vari-Lite, Inc. Props by John Creech Design &
Production. Sound equipment by Pro-Mix, Inc. Additional
sound equipment by Walt Disney Imagineering. Rehearsal
Scenery by Brooklyn Scenic & Theatrical. Costumes
executed by Barbara Matera Ltd., Parsons-Meares Ltd.,
Donna Langman, Eric Winterling, Danielle Gisiger, Suzie
Elder. Millinery by Rodney Gordon, Janet Linville, Arnold
Levine. Ricola provided by Ricola, Inc. Shibori dyeing by
Joan Morris. Custom dyeing and painting by Joni Johns,
Mary Macy, Parsons-Meares Ltd., Gene Mignola.
Additional Painting by J. Michelle Hill. Knitwear by Maria
Ficalora. Footwear by Sharlot Battin, Robert W. Jones,
Capezio, Vasilli Shoes. Costume Development by
Constance Hoffman. Special Projects by Angela M. Kahler.
Custom fabrics developed by Gary Graham and Helen
Quinn. Puppet Construction by Michael Curry Design, Inc.
and Vee Corporation. Shadow puppetry by Steven Kaplan.

Pumbaa Puppet Construction by Andrew Benepe. Flying by
Foy. Trucking by Clark Transfer. Wigs created by Wig
Workshop of London. Marimbas by De Morrow
Instruments, Ltd. Latin Percussion by LP Music Group.
Drumset by DrumWorkshop. Cymbals by Zildjian. Bass
equipment by Eden Electronics.

SONG EXCERPTS (used by permission):
"Supercalifragilisticexpialidocious" written by Richard M.
Sherman and Robert B. Sherman; "Five Foot Two, Eyes of
Blue" written by Sam Lewis, Joe Young, and
Ray Henderson; "The Lion Sleeps Tonight" written by
Hugo Peretti, George David Weiss, Luigi Creatore and
Solomon Linda.

NEDERLANDER

Chairman	**James M. Nederlander**
President	**James L. Nederlander**

Executive Vice President
Nick Scandalios

Vice President	Senior Vice President
Corporate Development	Labor Relations
Charlene S. Nederlander	**Herschel Waxman**

Vice President	Chief Financial Officer
Jim Boese	**Freida Sawyer Belviso**

DISNEY THEATRICAL PRODUCTIONS

President ....Thomas Schumacher
SVP & General Manager ....Alan Levey
SVP, Managing Director & CFO ....David Schrader

Senior Vice President, Creative Affairs .....Michele Steckler
Senior Vice President, International ....Ron Kollen
Vice President, Operations ....Dana Amendola
Vice President, Labor Relations ....Allan Frost
Vice President, Worldwide Publicity
　　& Communications ....Joe Quenqua
Vice President, Domestic Touring ....Jack Eldon
Director, Domestic Touring ....Michael Buchanan
Vice President, Theatrical Licensing ....Steve Fickinger
Director, Casting &
　　Development ....Jennifer Rudin Pearson
Director, Human Resources ....June Heindel
Manager, Labor Relations ....Stephanie Cheek
Manager, Human Resources ....Cynthia A. Young
Human Resources Representative ....Jewel Neal
Manager, Information Systems ....Scott Benedict
Senior Computer Support Analyst ....Kevin A. McGuire
Senior IT Support Analyst ....Andy Singh
IT/Business Analyst ....William Boudiette

Production

Executive Music Producer ....Chris Montan
Vice President, Physical Production ....John Tiggeloven
Senior Manager, International ....Michael Cassel
Senior Manager, Safety ....Canara Price
Manager, Physical Production ....Karl Chmielewski
Purchasing Manager ....Joseph Doughney
Staff Associate Designer ....Dennis W. Moyes
Dramaturg & Literary Manager ....Ken Cerniglia

Marketing

Vice President, Broadway ....Andrew Flatt
Vice President, International ....Fiona Thomas
Director, Broadway ....Kyle Young
Director, Education & Outreach ....Peter Avery
Senior Manager, Broadway ....Michele Groner
Website Manager ....Eric W. Kratzer
Media Asset Manager ....Cara L. Moccia
Assistant Manager, Communications ....Dana Torres
Assistant Manager, Promotions ....Craig Buckley

Sales

Director, National Sales ....Bryan Dockett
Manager,
　　New Business Development ....Jacob Lloyd Kimbro
Manager, Sales & Ticketing ....Nick Falzon
Manager, Group Sales ....Juil Kim

Business and Legal Affairs

Senior Vice President ....Jonathan Olson
Vice President ....Robbin Kelley
Executive Director ....Harry S. Gold
Senior Counsel ....Seth Stuhl
Paralegal/Contract Administration ....Colleen Lober

Finance

Director.................................Joe McClafferty
Senior Manager, Finance ....Dana James
Manager, Finance ....John Fajardo
Production Accountants ....Joy Brown, Nick Judge,
　　　　　　　　　　　　　　　　　Barbara Toben
Assistant Production Accountant ....Isander Rojas
Senior Financial Analyst ....Tatiana Bautista
Senior Sales Analyst ....Liz Jurist

Controllership

Director, Accounting ....Leena Mathew
Senior Analysts ....Stephanie Badie,
　　　　　　　　　　　　　　　　　　Mila Danilevich,
　　　　　　　　　　　　　　　　　Adrineh Ghoukassian
Analysts ....Bilda Donado, Ken Herrell

Administrative Staff

Dusty Bennett, Amy Caldamone, Lauren Daghini,
Jessica Doina, Cristi Finn, Cristina Fornaris, Dayle Gruet,
Gregory Hanoian, Jonathan Hanson, Jay Hollenback,
Connie Jasper, Tom Kingsley, Kerry McGrath,
Lisa Mitchell, Ryan Pears, Roberta Risafi, Colleen Rosati,
Kisha Santiago, David Scott, Benjy Shaw, Jason Zammit

BUENA VISTA THEATRICAL
MERCHANDISE, L.L.C.

Vice President ....Steven Downing
Operations Manager ....Shawn Baker
Merchandise Manager ....Neil Markman
Associate Buyer ....Violet Burlaza
Assistant Manager, Inventory ....Suzanne Jakel
Retail Supervisor ....Michael Giammatteo
On-Site Retail Manager ....Anjie Maraj
On-Site Assistant Retail Manager ....Jana Cristiano

Disney Theatrical Productions • 1450 Broadway
New York, NY 10018

guestmail@disneytheatrical.com

The Little Mermaid

First Preview: November 3, 2007. Opened: January 10, 2008.
Still running as of May 31, 2008.

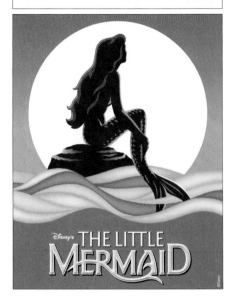

CAST OF CHARACTERS

(in order of appearance)

Pilot.....................................MERWIN FOARD
Prince Eric...........................SEAN PALMER
Grimsby...................JONATHAN FREEMAN
King Triton...........................NORM LEWIS
Sebastian........................TITUSS BURGESS
Ariel.................................SIERRA BOGGESS
Flounder.........................TREVOR BRAUN,
BRIAN D'ADDARIO,
CODY HANFORD, J.J. SINGLETON
Scuttle..............................EDDIE KORBICH
Gulls ...ROBERT CREIGHTON, TIM FEDERLE,
ARBENDER J. ROBINSON
Ursula.......................SHERIE RENE SCOTT
Flotsam ....TYLER MAYNARD
Jetsam ....DERRICK BASKIN
Carlotta...................HEIDI BLICKENSTAFF
Chef Louis.................JOHN TREACY EGAN

ENSEMBLE

ADRIAN BAILEY, CATHRYN BASILE,
HEIDI BLICKENSTAFF,
ROBERT CREIGHTON, CICILY DANIELS,
JOHN TREACY EGAN, TIM FEDERLE,
MERWIN FOARD, BEN HARTLEY,
MICHELLE LOOKADOO, ALAN MINGO, JR.,
ZAKIYA YOUNG MIZEN,
ARBENDER J. ROBINSON,
BAHIYAH SAYYED GAINES, BRET SHUFORD,
CHELSEA MORGAN STOCK, KAY TRINIDAD,
DANIEL J. WATTS

Continued on next page

Continued on next page

LUNT–FONTANNE THEATRE

UNDER THE DIRECTION OF
JAMES M. NEDERLANDER AND JAMES L. NEDERLANDER

Disney Theatrical Productions
under the direction of
Thomas Schumacher

presents

DISNEY's THE LITTLE MERMAID

Music	*Lyrics*	*Book*
ALAN MENKEN	HOWARD ASHMAN and GLENN SLATER	DOUG WRIGHT

Based on the Hans Christian Andersen story and the Disney film produced by Howard Ashman & John Musker
and written & directed by John Musker & Ron Clements.

Starring
SIERRA BOGGESS   SEAN PALMER
NORM LEWIS   TITUSS BURGESS   EDDIE KORBICH   JONATHAN FREEMAN
DERRICK BASKIN   TYLER MAYNARD
TREVOR BRAUN   BRIAN D'ADDARIO   CODY HANFORD   J.J. SINGLETON
and
SHERIE RENE SCOTT

ADRIAN BAILEY CATHRYN BASILE HEIDI BLICKENSTAFF JAMES BROWN III ROBERT CREIGHTON
CICILY DANIELS JOHN TREACY EGAN TIM FEDERLE MERWIN FOARD BEN HARTLEY
MEREDITH INGLESBY MICHELLE LOOKADOO JOANNE MANNING ALAN MINGO, JR. ZAKIYA YOUNG MIZEN
BETSY MORGAN ARBENDER J. ROBINSON BAHIYAH SAYYED GAINES BRET SHUFORD JASON SNOW
CHELSEA MORGAN STOCK KAY TRINIDAD PRICE WALDMAN DANIEL J. WATTS

Scenic Design	*Costume Design*	*Lighting Design*
GEORGE TSYPIN	TATIANA NOGINOVA	NATASHA KATZ

Sound Design	*Hair Design*	*Makeup Design*	*Projection & Video Design*
JOHN SHIVERS	DAVID BRIAN BROWN	ANGELINA AVALLONE	SVEN ORTEL

Dance Arrangements	*Music Coordinator*	*Fight Director*	*Casting*
DAVID CHASE	MICHAEL KELLER	RICK SORDELET	TARA RUBIN CASTING

Associate Producer	*Associate Director*	*Associate Choreographer*
TODD LACY	BRIAN HILL	TARA YOUNG

Technical Director	*Production Supervisor*	*Press Representative*
DAVID BENKEN	CLIFFORD SCHWARTZ	BONEAU/BRYAN-BROWN

Orchestrations by
DANNY TROOB

Music Director
Incidental Music & Vocal Arrangements by
MICHAEL KOSARIN

Choreography by
STEPHEN MEAR

Directed by
FRANCESCA ZAMBELLO

©Disney
Disney
BROADWAY

1/10/08

(L-R): Derrick Baskin watches as Sierra Boggess surrenders her voice to a magic shell offered by Sherie Rene Scott and Tyler Maynard.

Photo by Joan Marcus

The Little Mermaid

MUSICAL NUMBERS

ACT I

Overture

"Fathoms Below"† .... Pilot, Sailors, Prince Eric, Grimsby
"Daughters of Triton"* .... Mersisters
"The World Above" .... Ariel
"Human Stuff" .... Scuttle, Gulls
"I Want the Good Times Back" .... Ursula, Flotsam, Jetsam, Eels
"Part of Your World"* .... Ariel
"Storm at Sea"
"Part of Your World" (Reprise)* .... Ariel
"She's in Love" .... Mersisters, Flounder
"Her Voice" .... Prince Eric
"The World Above" (Reprise) .... King Triton
"Under the Sea"* .... Sebastian, Sea Creatures
"Sweet Child" .... Flotsam, Jetsam
"Poor Unfortunate Souls"* .... Ursula

ACT II

Entr'acte

"Positoovity" .... Scuttle, Gulls
"Beyond My Wildest Dreams" .... Ariel, Carlotta, Maids
"Les Poissons"* .... Chef Louis
"Les Poissons" (Reprise) .... Chef Louis, Chefs
"One Step Closer" .... Prince Eric
"I Want the Good Times Back" (Reprise) .... Ursula, Flotsam, Jetsam
"Kiss the Girl"* .... Sebastian, Animals
"Sweet Child" (Reprise) .... Flotsam, Jetsam
"If Only" .... Ariel, Prince Eric, Sebastian, King Triton
"The Contest" .... Grimsby, Princesses
"Poor Unfortunate Souls" (Reprise) .... Ursula
"If Only" (Reprise) .... King Triton, Ariel
"Finale"† .... Prince Eric, Ariel, Ensemble

Music by Alan Menken
* Lyrics by Howard Ashman
† Lyrics by Howard Ashman and Glenn Slater
All other lyrics by Glenn Slater

ORCHESTRA

Conductor: MICHAEL KOSARIN
Associate Conductor: GREG ANTHONY

Concertmaster: SUZANNE ORNSTEIN
Violin: MINEKO YAJIMA
Cello 1: ROGER SHELL
Cello 2: DEBORAH ASSAEL-MIGLIORE
Lead Trumpet: NICHOLAS MARCHIONE
Trumpet: FRANK GREENE
Trombone: GARY GRIMALDI
Bass Trombone/Tuba: JEFF CASWELL
Reed 1: STEVE KENYON

Reed 2: DAVID YOUNG
Reed 3: MARC PHANEUF
French Horn: ZOHAR SCHONDORF
Keyboard 1: ARON ACCURSO
Keyboard 2: GREG ANTHONY
Keyboard 3: ANDREW GROBENGIESER
Bass: RICHARD SARPOLA
Drums: JOHN REDSECKER
Percussion: JOE PASSARO

Electronic Music Design: ANDREW BARRETT
Music Coordinator: MICHAEL KELLER

Cast Continued

SWINGS
JAMES BROWN III, MEREDITH INGLESBY,
JOANNE MANNING, BETSY MORGAN,
JASON SNOW, PRICE WALDMAN

DANCE CAPTAIN
JOANNE MANNING

ASSISTANT DANCE CAPTAIN
JAMES BROWN III

UNDERSTUDIES
Ariel:
BETSY MORGAN,
CHELSEA MORGAN STOCK
Ursula:
HEIDI BLICKENSTAFF, CICILY DANIELS
Prince Eric:
ARBENDER J. ROBINSON, BRET SHUFORD
King Triton:
ADRIAN BAILEY, MERWIN FOARD
Sebastian:
DERRICK BASKIN, ALAN MINGO, JR.
Scuttle:
ROBERT CREIGHTON, TIM FEDERLE
Grimsby:
MERWIN FOARD, PRICE WALDMAN
Flotsam:
BRET SHUFORD, JASON SNOW,
PRICE WALDMAN
Jetsam:
TIM FEDERLE, PRICE WALDMAN

Sierra Boggess, as Ariel, spies on the human sailors.

Photo by Joan Marcus

The Little Mermaid

Sierra Boggess
Ariel

Sherie Rene Scott
Ursula

Sean Palmer
Prince Eric

Norm Lewis
King Triton

Tituss Burgess
Sebastian

Eddie Korbich
Scuttle

Jonathan Freeman
Grimsby

Derrick Baskin
Jetsam

Tyler Maynard
Flotsam

Trevor Braun
Flounder at certain performances

Brian D'Addario
Flounder at certain performances

Cody Hanford
Flounder at certain performances

J.J. Singleton
Flounder at certain performances

Adrian Bailey
Ensemble

Cathryn Basile
Ensemble

Heidi Blickenstaff
Carlotta/Ensemble

James Brown III
Swing/Assistant Dance Captain

Robert Creighton
Ensemble

Cicily Daniels
Ensemble

John Treacy Egan
Chef Louis/Ensemble

Tim Federle
Ensemble

Merwin Foard
Pilot/Ensemble

Ben Hartley
Ensemble

Meredith Inglesby
Swing

Michelle Lookadoo
Ensemble

Joanne Manning
Swing/ Dance Captain

Alan Mingo, Jr.
Ensemble

Zakiya Young Mizen
Ensemble

Betsy Morgan
Swing

Arbender J. Robinson
Ensemble

Bahiyah Sayyed Gaines
Ensemble

Bret Shuford
Ensemble

Jason Snow
Swing

Chelsea Morgan Stock
Ensemble

Kay Trinidad
Ensemble

The Little Mermaid

Price Waldman
Swing

Daniel J. Watts
Ensemble

Alan Menken
Composer

Howard Ashman
Lyrics

Glenn Slater
Lyrics

Doug Wright
Book

Francesca Zambello
Director

Stephen Mear
Choreographer

George Tsypin
Scenic Design

Tatiana Noginova
Costume Design

Natasha Katz
Lighting Design

John H. Shivers
Sound Design

Danny Troob
Orchestrator

Michael Kosarin
*Music Direction/
Vocal and Incidental
Music Arrangements*

David Brian Brown
Wig/Hair Design

Angelina Avallone
Make-up Design

Sven Ortel
*Projection &
Video Design*

Michael Keller
Music Coordinator

Rick Sordelet
Fight Director

Pichón Baldinu
Aerial Design

Tara Rubin Casting
Casting

Brian Hill
Associate Director

Tara Young
*Associate
Choreographer*

David Benken
Technical Director

Clifford Schwartz
*Production
Supervisor*

Andrew Barrett
*Electronic Music
Design*

Thomas Schumacher
*Disney Theatrical
Productions*

Julie Barnes
Carlotta, Swing

The Little Mermaid

ORCHESTRA
Front Row (L-R): Greg Anthony, Michael Kosarin, Aron Accurso, Andy Grobengieser.

Back Row (L-R): Roy Lewis, Deborah Assael Migliore, Dave Shank, David Young, John Redsecker, Dick Sarpola, Marc Phaneuf, Gary Grimaldi.

STAGE MANAGEMENT AND COMPANY MANAGEMENT
Front Row (L-R): Matthew Aaron Stern, Margie Freeswick, Sarah Tschirpke, Kenneth J. McGee.

Back Row (L-R): Clifford Schwartz, Randy Meyer, Theresa Bailey.

STAGE DOORMAN
Bobby Garner

FRONT OF HOUSE STAFF
Front Row (L-R): Carlo Mosarra, Adriana Casablanca, Honey Owens, Carmella Cambio, Angalic Cortes, Evelyn Fernandez.

Second Row (L-R): Lauren Banyai, Mildred Villano, Rosalind Joyce, Stephanie Martinez, Madeline Flores, Joseph Cintron.

Third Row (L-R): Roberto Calderon, Barry Jenkins, Paul Perez, Melody Rodriguez.

Back Row (L-R): Hector Aguilar, Charles Thompson, Joseph Smith, William Pacheco, Tracey Malinowski.

MERCHANDISING
(L-R): Thomas Bradfield, Jeff Knizner, Annemarie Rosano, Michael Crouch, Riley Rosenholtz, Stephen Hayhard, Mike Raymond.

MERCHANDISING
(L-R): Frank Sansone, Bridget Davidson, Stacey Rockwell, Ryan Makely.

The Little Mermaid

CREW

Front Row (L-R): Steven E. Wood, Michael L. Shepp Jr., Franklin Hollenbeck, Terry LaVada, Rachael Garrett, Damian Caza-Cleypool, Claire Verlaet, Joshua First, Pete Bentz, Freddy Mecionis and (Laying in Front) John Mara.

Middle Row (L-R): Lori Flwell, Mel Hansen, Rodd Sovar, Amelia Haywood, Kathleen Gallagher, Kirsten Mogg, Barbara Hladsky, Joseph Pearson, Anna Hoffman.

Back Row (L-R): Jeff Zink, Patrick Eviston, Jerry L. Marshall, Paul Riner, Jay Woods, Brendan Lynch, Dave Brickman, Jesse Hancox, George Huckins, Scott Anderson.

Staff for *THE LITTLE MERMAID*

COMPANY MANAGER ....RANDY MEYER
Production Associate ....Jane Abramson
Assistant Company Manager ....Margie Freeswick
Show Accountant ....Barbara Toben
Production Stage Manager ....Clifford Schwartz
Stage Manager ....Theresa Bailey
Assistant Stage Managers ....Kenneth J. McGee, Matthew Aaron Stern, Sarah Tschirpke
Dance Captain ....Joanne Manning
Assistant Dance Captain ....James Brown III
Fight Captain ....James Brown III
Assistant to the Associate Producer ....Kerry McGrath
Production Assistants ....Steven Malone, Jennifer Noterman, Thomas Recktenwald, Marielle Solan

GENERAL PRESS REPRESENTATIVE
BONEAU/BRYAN-BROWN
Chris Boneau   Matt Polk   Adriana Douzos
Juliana Hannett   Danielle Crinnion

Associate Scenic Designer ....Peter Eastman
Scenic Design Assistants .....Gaetane Bertol, Larry Brown, Kelly Hanson, Niki Hernandez-Adams, Nathan Heverin, Rachel Short Janocko, Jee an Jung, Mimi Lien, Frank McCullough, Arnulfo Maldonado, Robert Pyzocha, Chisato Uno
Sculptor ....Arturs Virtmanis
Associate Costume Designer ....Tracy Christensen
Assistant Costume Designers ...Brian J. Bustos, Amy Clark

Costume Shoppers ....Leon Dobkowski, Vanessa Leuck
Associate Lighting Designer ....Yael Lubetzky
Lighting Design Assistant ....Craig Stelzenmuller
Automated Lighting Programmer ....Aland Henderson
Automated Lighting Tracker ....Joel Shier
Assistant to the Lighting Designer ....Richard Swan
Associate Sound Designer ....David Patridge
Associate Hair Designer ....Jonathan Carter
Assistant Hair Designer ....Thomas Augustine
Projection Design Assistants ......Peter Acken, Katy Tucker
Associate Aerial Designer ....Angela Phillips
Magic/Illusion Designer ....Joe Eddie Fairchild
Associate to Technical Director ....Rose Palombo
Production Carpenter ....Stephen Detmer
Head Carpenter ....Patrick Eviston
Fly Automation ....Jeff Zink
Deck Automation ....Michael L. Shepp, Jr.
Rigger ....Rick Howard
Production Electrician ....Rick Baxter
Head Electrician ....Joseph Pearson
Assistant Electrician ....Damian Caza-Cleypool
Moving Light Technician ....Jesse Hancox
Production Props ....Jerry L. Marshall
Assistant Props ....Steven E. Wood
Production Sound Engineer ....David Patridge
Head Sound ....George Huckins
Deck Sound ....Scott Anderson
Wardrobe Supervisor ....Nancy Schaefer
Assistant Wardrobe Supervisor ....Edmund Harrison
Wardrobe Staff ....Vanessa Fernandez, Kathleen Gallagher, Rachael Garrett, Sue Hamilton, Melanie Hansen,

Amelia Haywood, Barbara Hladsky, Franklin Hollenbeck, Terry LaVada, Robert J. Malkmus III, Paul Riner, Eric Rudy, Rita Santi, Rodd Sovar, Claire Verlaet, Jay Woods
Hair Supervisor ....Thomas Augustine
Assistant Hair Supervisor ....Gary Arave
Hairdressers ....Joshua First, Shanah Kendall
Make-Up Supervisor ....Tiffany Hicks
Assistant Make-Up Supervisor ....Jorge Vargas
Associate Music Director ....Greg Anthony
Additional Orchestrations.................Larry Hochman, Michael Starobin
Music Preparation ....Anixter Rice Music Service
Electronic Music Design ....Andrew Barrett, for Lionella Productions, Ltd.
Electronic Music Design Assistant ....Jeff Marder
Associate to Mr. Menken ....Rick Kunis
Rehearsal Drummer ....John Redsecker
Rehearsal Pianists ....Aron Accurso, Matt Eisenstein, Andrew Grobengieser
Children's Vocal Coach ....Marianne Challis
Chaperone ....John Mara
Children's Tutoring ....On Location Education/ Serena Stanley

CASTING
TARA RUBIN CASTING
Tara Rubin, CSA, Eric Woodall, CSA
Laura Schutzel, CSA, Merri Sugarman, CSA
Rebecca Carfagna, Paige Blansfield, Dale Brown

The Little Mermaid

AERIAL DESIGNER ....PICHÓN BALDINU

DIALOGUE &
  VOCAL COACH ....DEBORAH HECHT

Advertising ....Serino Coyne, Inc.
Press Associates ....Adrian Bryan-Brown,
  Aaron Meier, Christine Olver, Susanne Tighe
Logo Art ....Scott Thornley + Company
Production Photography ....Joan Marcus
Acoustic Consultant ....Paul Scarbrough, A'Kustiks
Structural Engineering Consultant ....Bill Gorlin,
  McLaren, P.C.
Executive Travel ....Robert Arnao, Patricia McRory
Production Travel ....Jill L. Citron
Payroll Managers ....Anthony DeLuca, Cathy Guerra
Counsel – Immigration ....Michael Rosenfeld
Physical Therapy ....The Green Room P.T./
  Heidi Green
Consulting Orthopedic Surgeon ....Dr. Phillip Bauman

CREDITS

Scenery by Showman Fabricators, Inc.; Show Canada Industries; Adirondack Studios, Inc.; The Paragon Innovation Group, Inc.; Proof Productions. Automation of scenery and rigging by Showman Fabricators, Inc., Long Island City, NY featuring Raynok Motion Control. Lighting equipment by PRG Lighting. Projection equipment by PRG Lighting. Sound equipment by Sound Associates Inc. Costume construction by Parsons-Meares Ltd.; Barbara Matera, Ltd.; Eric Winterling, Inc.; Tricorne, Inc.; Martin Izquierdo Studio. Custom millinery provided by Lynne Mackey Studio; Rodney Gordon; Arnold S. Levine, Inc.; Marian Jean Hose. Custom fabric dyeing and printing by Gene Mignola, Hochi Asiatico, Martin Izquierdo Studio, Olympus Flag and Banner. Costume painting by Hochi Asiatico, Virginia Clow, Claudia Dzundza, Martin Izquierdo Studio, Mary Macy, Parmelee Welles Tolkan, Margaret Peot. Custom footwear by Capri Shoes by Oscar Navarro; Handmade Shoes by Fred Longtin; LaDuca Shoes; Pluma Shoes by Walter Raimundo; Capezio. Custom jewelry and crafts by Arnold S. Levine, Inc.; Marian Jean Hose; Martin Izquierdo Studios; Gaetane Bertol; Larry Vrba. Undergarments by Bra*Tenders; On Stage Dancewear. Ursula mechanics by Jon Gellman Effects. Mermaid tails by Michael Curry Design, Inc. Eel electrics by Birtek Specialty Lighting. Knitwear provided by Karen Eifert and Maria Ficalora Knitwear, Ltd. Wigs by Bob Kelly Wigs; Ray Marston Wigs; Victoria Wood. Props by Arnold S. Levine, Inc.; Jerard Studio; Michael Curry Design, Inc.; The Paragon Innovation Group, Inc.; Provost Displays; I.C.B.A; Puppet Heap; Rabbit's Choice; Vogue Too; Zoë Morsette. Ricola natural herb cough drops courtesy of Ricola USA, Inc. Emergen-C health and energy drink mix provided by Alacer Corp.

Make Up Provided By M•A•C.

Gliding By Heelys®.

THE LITTLE MERMAID originally premiered at the Ellie Caulkins Opera House, Denver Center for the Performing Arts, Colorado.

THE LITTLE MERMAID
rehearsed at the New 42nd Street Studios.

SPECIAL THANKS

Kate Boucher, Ian Galloway and Dan Murtha of Bolt Action Five, Michael Curry, Jackie Galloway, Helen Goddard, Michael Harrell of MHNY Wardrobe Services, Inc., Green Hippo, Nichol Hignite, Courtney Hoffman, Diana Kuriyama, Anna Ledwich, Roland Wolfe of Saks Fifth Avenue and the styling team at the Fifth Avenue Club, Larry Sonn, Georgia Stitt, Crystal Thompson, Walt Disney Imagineering R&D.

DISNEY THEATRICAL PRODUCTIONS

President ....Thomas Schumacher
SVP & General Manager ....Alan Levey
SVP, Managing Director & CFO ....David Schrader

Senior Vice President, Creative Affairs .....Michele Steckler
Senior Vice President, International ....Ron Kollen
Vice President, Operations ....Dana Amendola
Vice President, Labor Relations ....Allan Frost
Vice President, Worldwide Publicity
  & Communications ....Joe Quenqua
Vice President, Domestic Touring ....Jack Eldon
Director, Domestic Touring ....Michael Buchanan
Vice President, Theatrical Licensing ....Steve Fickinger

Director, Casting & Development ....Jennifer Rudin, CSA
Vice President, Human Resources ....June Heindel
Manager, Labor Relations ....Stephanie Cheek
Human Resources Representative ....Jewel Neal
Manager, Information Systems ....Scott Benedict
Senior Computer Support Analyst ....Kevin A. McGuire
Senior IT Support Analyst ....Andy Singh
IT/Business Analyst ....William Boudiette

Production

Executive Music Producer ....Chris Montan
Vice President, Physical Production ....John Tiggeloven
Senior Manager, International ....Michael Cassel
Senior Manager, Safety ....Canara Price
Manager, Physical Production ....Karl Chmielewski
Staff Associate Designer ....Dennis W. Moyes
Dramaturg & Literary Manager ....Ken Cerniglia

Marketing

Vice President, Broadway ....Andrew Flatt
Vice President, International ....Fiona Thomas
Director, Broadway ....Kyle Young
Director, Education & Outreach ....Peter Avery
Senior Manager, Broadway ....Michele Groner
Website Manager ....Eric W. Kratzer
Media Asset Manager ....Cara L. Moccia
Assistant Manager, Communications ....Dana Torres
Assistant Manager, Promotions ....Craig Buckley

Sales

Director, National Sales ....Bryan Dockett
Manager,
  New Business Development ....Jacob Lloyd Kimbro
Manager, Sales & Ticketing ....Nick Falzon
Manager, Group Sales ....Juil Kim

Business and Legal Affairs

Senior Vice President ....Jonathan Olson
Vice President ....Robbin Kelley
Executive Director ....Harry S. Gold
Senior Counsel ....Seth Stuhl
Paralegal/Contract Administration ....Colleen Lober

Finance

Director ....Joe McClafferty
Senior Manager, Finance ....Dana James
Manager, Finance ....John Fajardo
Manager, Production Accounting ....Liza Breslin
Production Accountants ....Joy Brown, Nick Judge,
  Barbara Toben
Assistant Production Accountant ....Isander Rojas
Senior Financial Analyst ....Tatiana Bautista
Senior Sales Analyst ....Liz Jurist Schwarzwalder

Administrative Staff

Dusty Bennett, Amy Caldamone, Lauren Daghini, Surayah Davis, Jessica Doina, Cristi Finn, Cristina Fowler, Dayle Gruet, Gregory Hanoian, Jonathan Hanson, Jay Hollenback, Connie Jasper, Tom Kingsley, Kerry McGrath, Lisa Mitchell, Melanie Montes, Ryan Pears, Jessica Powers, Roberta Risafi, Colleen Rosati, Kisha Santiago, David Scott, Benjy Shaw, Jason Zammit

BUENA VISTA THEATRICAL MERCHANDISE, L.L.C.

Vice President ....Steven Downing
Operations Manager ....Shawn Baker
Merchandise Manager ....Neil Markman
Associate Buyer ....Violet Burlaza
Assistant Manager, Inventory ....Suzanne Jakel
Retail Supervisor ....Michael Giammatteo
On-Site Retail Manager ....Jeff Knizner
On-Site Assistant Retail Manager ....Mark Murynec

Disney Theatrical Productions • 1450 Broadway
New York, NY 10018

guestmail@disneytheatrical.com

≋N≋
NEDERLANDER

Chairman ....**James M. Nederlander**
President ....**James L. Nederlander**

Executive Vice President
Nick Scandalios

Vice President	Senior Vice President
Corporate Development	Labor Relations
Charlene S. Nederlander	**Herschel Waxman**
Vice President	Chief Financial Officer
Jim Boese	**Freida Sawyer Belviso**

STAFF FOR THE LUNT-FONTANNE

House Manager ....Tracey Malinowski
Treasurer ....Joe Olcese
Assistant Treasurer ....Gregg Collichio
House Carpenter ....Terry Taylor
House Electrician ....Dennis Boyle
House Propertyman ....Scott Meciones
House Flyman ....Matt Walters
House Engineers ....Robert MacMahon,
  Joseph Riccio III

The Little Mermaid
SCRAPBOOK

1. Curtain call on opening night.
2. (L-R): Sierra Boggess and Jodi Benson, who voiced the animated film version of Ariel, at the opening night party at Roseland.
3. (L-R): Sierra Boggess and Tituss Burgess at the launch party for the original cast album.
4. Sherie Rene Scott (center) flanked by (L-R) Tyler Maynard and Derrick Baskin, who play her henchmen.

Correspondent: Eddie Korbich, "Scuttle"

Memorable Opening Night Fax: Sierra got an opening night fax from Barbra Streisand that said "Congratulations on your opening night—I remember my opening nights." Sierra is a big fan of Barbra, so this was HUGE!

Opening Night Gifts: A beautiful, large Murano glass conch shell—"whozits and whatzits galore." Also caps and mugs with the show logo. My partner and daughter got me a stuffed Scuttle and *Little Mermaid* figurines.

Most Exciting Visitors and What They Said: David Beckham and Posh Spice. I don't know what they said, but hearts were a-flutterin' (and not about Posh)!

Who Got the Gypsy Robe and What They Put on It: Adrian Bailey got the robe (12 shows) and we put the show logo and a big mermaid tail on the back of the robe.

Actor Who Performed the Most Roles in This Show: Ben Hartley (eight), though Michelle Lookadoo has the most costume changes. And swing Betsy Morgan—I don't know how many roles, but she covers almost every female role.

Who Has Done the Most Shows in Their Career: It's a toss-up between me and Jonathan Freeman, but I'll say Jonathan. Also, Clifford Schwartz, our PSM.

Special Backstage Rituals: In Denver, we had "Fast"ography: during the quick part of the overture, we'd be in a circle and one person was selected to ad-lib for us! In NYC—I annoy everyone by constantly singing orchestrations. Heidi does a Flamenco style rhythmic stomp

during "Fathoms Below." And Sierra kicks her fluffy slippers off of her feet right before Act II to her dresser Lori who catches them.

Favorite Moment During Each Performance: Twirling Ariel in to me and singing the high 'D' at the end of "Positoovity."

Favorite In-Theatre Gathering Place: Norm Lewis gets a lot of visitors.

Favorite Off-Site Hangout: Latitude on Eighth Avenue.

Favorite Snack Food: The #1 thing is Adrian Bailey's baking. He brings everything from cheese biscuits to so many cookies to bread pudding with custard sauce. He is amazing!

Mascots: Kay Trinidad has this rubber fish left over from "Flipper." And an old 'Chef Louis' prop. All the Mersisters kiss it before "She's in Love."

Favorite Therapies: Ricola-Ricola-Ricola. And Emergen-C.

Fastest Costume Change: Sierra into her bath attire from the beach scene.

Who Wore the Heaviest/Hottest Costume: All the Gulls in Denver—heavy, heavy tail coats made of thick white yarn. We looked like giant cotton balls!

Who Wore the Least: Sierra washed up on the beach—or Bahiyah's exotic fish-girl.

Catchphrases Only the Company Would Recognize: PhWhew! Sugar-Free Ricola! "Ambassadors!" (When anyone curses or does anything untoward.)

Memorable Directorial Notes: One person got, "Could you possibly base what you're doing

in some kind of reality?" Also, "Keep growing and keep discovering, but also keep editing!"

Nicknames: Derrick is the king of nicknames! He and I are "Sunshine," Tyler is "T," Cicily is "Ciss," Katie is "Boom Boom," Michelle is "Koodoo" and Bahiyah is "Heeya."

Embarrassing Moment: Me walking out on stage with my microphone gauze on my forehead.

Ghostly Encounter Backstage: To quote my dresser Jay, "There's not a damn thing in this building. Famous last words. And if there is, there's not enough negative energy around here to draw it out."

Coolest Thing About Being in This Show: It is fun to play for so many different types of audiences—women in groups who remember the movie, fathers that don't want to be there but end up crying by the end, and children laughing and cheering at their first Broadway show!

Also: The multi-cultural aspect of our company was something deliberately planned to reflect theatre today, but also to encompass the vast society of the sea—it's pretty great to be a part of that.

Other Memories: Opening Night in Denver—Sierra graciously dancing with five children (including my daughter) who were enchanted by getting to meet Ariel! Opening Night in NYC—Sierra meeting Jodi Benson and the two of them jumping up and down like schoolgirls. For me—meeting Pat Carroll—and Phil Collins.

LoveMusik

First Preview: April 12, 2007. Opened: May 3, 2007.
Closed June 24, 2007 after 24 Previews and 60 Performances.

PLAYBILL

CAST

Kurt Weill	MICHAEL CERVERIS
Lotte Lenya	DONNA MURPHY
Bertolt Brecht	DAVID PITTU
George Davis	JOHN SCHERER
Woman on Stairs	JUDITH BLAZER
Magistrate/Judge	HERNDON LACKEY
Court Secretary	RACHEL ULANET
Brecht's Women	JUDITH BLAZER, ANN MORRISON, RACHEL ULANET
Auditioners	HERNDON LACKEY, RACHEL ULANET
Interviewer	ERIK LIBERMAN
Otto	GRAHAM ROWAT
Photographer	ANN MORRISON
Allen Lake	GRAHAM ROWAT
Handyman	ERIK LIBERMAN
Stage Manager	MEGAN SCHNEID

UNDERSTUDIES

For Bertolt Brecht, Kurt Weill:
EDWIN CAHILL
For Bertolt Brecht:
ERIK LIBERMAN
For Lotte Lenya:
ANN MORRISON
For George Davis:
GRAHAM ROWAT

Continued on next page

BILTMORE THEATRE

MANHATTAN THEATRE CLUB

Artistic Director	Executive Producer
LYNNE MEADOW	BARRY GROVE

by special arrangement with

MARTY BELL   ALDO SCROFANI   BOYETT OSTAR PRODUCTIONS
TRACY ARON   ROGER BERLIND/DEBRA BLACK   CHASE MISHKIN   TED SNOWDON

Presents

LoveMusik

book by	music by
ALFRED UHRY	KURT WEILL

Suggested by the letters of Kurt Weill and Lotte Lenya

Lyrics by

MAXWELL ANDERSON   BERTOLT BRECHT   HOWARD DIETZ   ROGER FERNAY   IRA GERSHWIN   OSCAR HAMMERSTEIN II
LANGSTON HUGHES   ALAN JAY LERNER   MAURICE MAGRE   OGDEN NASH   ELMER RICE   KURT WEILL

with

MICHAEL CERVERIS   DONNA MURPHY   DAVID PITTU   JOHN SCHERER
JUDITH BLAZER   EDWIN CAHILL   HERNDON LACKEY   ERIK LIBERMAN   ANN MORRISON
GRAHAM ROWAT   RACHEL ULANET   JESSICA WRIGHT

Scenic Design	Costume Design	Lighting Design	Sound Design
BEOWULF BORITT	JUDITH DOLAN	HOWELL BINKLEY	DUNCAN ROBERT EDWARDS
Wig Design	Make-Up Design	Production Stage Manager	Casting
PAUL HUNTLEY	ANGELINA AVALLONE	JOSHUA HALPERIN	MARK SIMON

Orchestrations	Musical Supervisor
JONATHAN TUNICK	KRISTEN BLODGETTE

Music Coordinator	Additional Vocal Arrangements	Conductor
SEYMOUR RED PRESS	MILTON GRANGER	NICHOLAS ARCHER

Musical Staging by

PATRICIA BIRCH

Directed by

HAROLD PRINCE

Director of Artistic Operations	Production Manager
MANDY GREENFIELD	RYAN McMAHON
Director of Development	Director of Marketing	Press Representative
JILL TURNER LLOYD	DEBRA A. WAXMAN	BONEAU/BRYAN-BROWN
General Manager	Director of Artistic Development
FLORIE SEERY	PAIGE EVANS

Special funding thanks to the Harold and Mimi Steinberg Charitable Trust for supporting new American plays and musicals at Manhattan Theatre Club.
Manhattan Theatre Club wishes to express its appreciation to Theatre Development Fund for its support of this production.

6/24/07

(L-R): Michael Cerveris and David Pittu

Photo by Carol Rosegg

LoveMusik

MUSICAL NUMBERS

ACT I — EUROPE

Speak Low (lyrics by Ogden Nash) ....Weill, Lenya
Nanna's Lied (lyrics by Bertolt Brecht) ....Woman on Stairs
Kiddush ....Weill's Family
Song of the Rhineland (lyrics by Ira Gershwin) ....Lenya's Family
Klops Lied (Meatball Song) ....Weill
Berlin Im Licht (lyrics by Kurt Weill) ....Lenya
Wooden Wedding (lyrics by Ogden Nash) ....Weill, Lenya, Magistrate, Court Secretary
Tango Ballad (lyrics by Bertolt Brecht) ....Brecht, Brecht's Women
Alabama Song (lyrics by Bertolt Brecht) ....Auditioners, Lenya
Girl of the Moment (lyrics by Ira Gershwin) ....Ensemble
Moritat (lyrics by Bertolt Brecht) ....Brecht, Lenya, Otto, Ensemble
Schickelgruber (lyrics by Howard Dietz) ....Weill, Brecht
Come to Paris (lyrics by Ira Gershwin) ....Ensemble
I Don't Love You (lyrics by Maurice Magre) ....Weill, Lenya
Wouldn't You Like to Be on Broadway?
    (lyrics by Langston Hughes & Elmer Rice) ....Weill, Lenya
Alabama Song, Reprise (lyrics by Bertolt Brecht) ....Lenya, Weill, Brecht, Ensemble

ACT II — AMERICA

How Can You Tell an American? (lyrics by Maxwell Anderson) ....Ensemble
Very, Very, Very (lyrics by Ogden Nash) ....Weill
It's Never Too Late to Mendelssohn (lyrics by Ira Gershwin) ....Weill, Lenya, Stenographer, Judge
Surabaya Johnny (lyrics by Bertolt Brecht) ....Lenya
Youkali (lyrics by Roger Fernay) ....Brecht, Brecht's Women
Buddy on the Night Shift (lyrics by Oscar Hammerstein II) ....Allen
That's Him (lyrics by Ogden Nash) ....Weill
Hosannah Rockefeller (lyrics by Bertolt Brecht) ....Brecht, Brecht's Women
I Don't Love You, Reprise (lyrics by Maurice Magre) ....Lenya, Weill
The Illusion Wedding Show (lyrics by Alan Jay Lerner) ....Davis, Ensemble
It Never Was You (lyrics by Maxwell Anderson) ....Weill
A Bird of Passage (lyrics by Maxwell Anderson) ....Ensemble
September Song (lyrics by Maxwell Anderson) ....Lenya, Davis

Cast Continued

SWINGS
EDWIN CAHILL, JESSICA WRIGHT

Dance Captain:
JESSICA WRIGHT

ORCHESTRA

Conductor/Piano:
NICHOLAS ARCHER
Violins:
KATHERINE LIVOLSI-LANDAU,
SUZY PERELMAN
Viola:
DAVID BLINN
Cello:
MAIRI DORMAN
Woodwinds:
JAMES ERCOLE, JOHN WINDER

Trumpet:
CHRISTIAN JAUDES
Bass:
JEFFREY COOPER
Drums/Percussion:
BILLY MILLER
Associate Conductor:
STAN TUCKER

Music copying:
EMILY GRISHMAN MUSIC PREPARATION—
KATHARINE EDMONDS/EMILY GRISHMAN

Michael Cerveris
Kurt Weill

Donna Murphy
Lotte Lenya

David Pittu
Bertolt Brecht

John Scherer
George Davis

Judith Blazer
*Woman on Stairs,
Brecht's Woman*

Edwin Cahill
Swing

Herndon Lackey
*Magistrate/Judge,
Auditioner*

Erik Liberman
*Interviewer,
Handyman*

Ann Morrison
*Brecht's Woman,
Photographer*

Graham Rowat
Otto, Allen Lake

LoveMusik

Rachel Ulanet
*Court Secretary,
Brecht's Woman,
Auditioner*

Jessica Wright
Swing

Alfred Uhry
Book

Harold Prince
Director

Patricia Birch
Musical Staging

Beowulf Boritt
Scenic Design

Howell Binkley
Lighting Design

Paul Huntley
Wig Design

Angelina Avallone
Make-up Design

Jonathan Tunick
Orchestrations

Kristen Blodgette
Musical Supervisor

Seymour Red Press
Musical Coordinator

Lynne Meadow
*Artistic Director,
Manhattan Theatre
Club*

Barry Grove
*Executive Producer,
Manhattan Theatre
Club*

Marty Bell
Producer

Aldo Scrofani
Producer

**Bob Boyett,
Boyett OSTAR
Productions**
Producer

**Bill Haber,
Boyett OSTAR
Productions**
Producer

Tracy Aron
Producer

Roger Berlind
Producer

Debra Black
Producer

Chase Mishkin
Producer

Ted Snowdon
Producer

Photo by Carol Rosegg

(L-R): Rachel Ulanet,
David Pittu, Ann Morison
and Judith Blazer.

LoveMusik

Photos by Ben Strothmann

ORCHESTRA
Front Row (L-R): David Blinn (Viola), Nicholas Archer (Conductor), Katherine Livolsi-Landau (Concertmaster), Jeffrey Cooper (Bass).
Back Row (L-R): Stan Tucker (Associate Conductor), James Ercole (Reeds), Mairi Dorman (Cello), Billy Miller (Percussion) and John Winder (Reeds)

STAGE CREW
Front Row (L-R): Angie Simpson, Ryan Rossetto (with unicorn), Rachel Miller and Megan Schneid.
Middle Row (L-R): Jessica Dermody, Suzanne Williams, Tracey Boone, Sue Poulin, Rich Wichrowksi, Seth Shepsle.
Back Row (L-R): Gerard Fortunato, Taurance Williams, Josh Halperin, Andrew Sliwinski Lou Shapiro, Marc Grimshaw, Brandon Maloney, Matt Maloney, Jeff Dodson.

FRONT OF HOUSE STAFF
Front Row (L-R): Wendy Wright (Head Usher), Ed Brashear (Ticket Taker), Miranda Scopel (Assistant House Manager).
Middle Row (L-R): Jonathan Pate (Treasurer), Alana Samuels (Biltmore Intern), Taylor Holt (Usher), Quanda Johnson (Usher), Bru Dye (Usher), David Dillon (Head Treasurer).
Back Row (L-R): Russ Ramsey (Theatre Manager) and Jackson Ero (Usher).

LoveMusik

Angela Pietropinto, Alfonso Ramirez,
Carmen Rivera, Judy Tate,
Candido Tirado, Joe White
Theatre Management Interns .... Nicky Barton,
Laurel Bear, Joe Breed,
Stephanie Cowan, Ashley D'Angiolini,
Helen DeBuse, Tyler Ennis,
Randi Fields, Jason Fitzgerald,
Katie Murray, Alana Samuels,
Arhonda Thompson, Gabriel Weissman,
Amy Windle

The Paul A. Kaplan Theatre Management Program, MTC's internship program, is designed to train the next generation of theatre leaders.

Randy Carrig Casting Intern .... Shira Sandler
Production Manager .... **Ryan McMahon**
Associate Production Manager .... Bridget Markov
Assistant Production Manager .... Stephanie Madonna
Lights and Sound Supervisor .... **Matthew T. Gross**
Properties Supervisor .... **Scott Laule**
Assistant Properties Supervisor .... Julia Sandy
Props Carpenter .... Peter Grimes
Costume Supervisor .... **Erin Hennessy Dean**

GENERAL PRESS REPRESENTATION
BONEAU/BRYAN-BROWN
Chris Boneau   Jim Byk
Aaron Meier   Heath Schwartz   Christine Olver

Script Readers .... Erin Detrick, Liz Jones,
Asher Richelli, Michelle Tattenbaum,
Kathryn Walat, Ethan Youngerman
Musical Theatre Reader .... Emily King

SERVICES
Accountants .... ERE, LLP
Advertising .... SpotCo/
Drew Hodges, Jim Edwards,
Ben Downing, Laura Price
Web Design .... Pilla Marketing Communications
Legal Counsel .... John Breglio, Deborah Hartnett/
Paul, Weiss, Rifkind,
Wharton and Garrison LLP
Real Estate Counsel .... Marcus Attorneys
Labor Counsel .... Harry H. Weintraub/
Glick and Weintraub, P.C.
Immigration Counsel .... Theodore Ruthizer/
Kramer, Levin, Naftalis & Frankel, LLP
Special Projects .... Elaine H. Hirsch
Insurance .... Dewitt Stern Group, Inc./Anthony Pittari
Maintenance .... Reliable Cleaning
Production Photographer .... Carol Rosegg
Event Photography .... Bruce Glikas
Cover Photo .... Henry Leutwyler
Cover Design .... SpotCo
Theatre Displays .... King Display

PRODUCTION STAFF FOR *LOVEMUSIK*
Company Manager .... **Seth Shepsle**
Production Manager .... **Bridget Markov**
Production Stage Manager .... Joshua Halperin
Stage Manager .... Megan Schneid
Assistant to Mr. Prince .... Daniel Kutner
Assistant Choreographer .... Deanna Dys

Additional Incidental
Music Arrangements .... Nicholas Archer
Rehearsal Pianist .... Stan Tucker
Associate Scenic Designer .... Jo Winiarski
Assistant Scenic Designer .... Camille Connolly
Assistant Scenic Designer .... Jessie T. Moore
Assistant Scenic Designer .... Jason Lajka
Assistant Costume Designer .... Rebecca Lustig
Associate Lighting Designer .... Ryan O'Gara
Assistant Lighting Designer .... Brad King
Assistant Sound Designer .... Nathaniel Hare
Assistant to Paul Huntley .... Darlene Dannenfelser
Assistant Costume Supervisor .... Michelle Sesco
Dialect Consultant .... Stephen Gabis
Automation Operator .... Patrick Murray
Flymen .... John Fullum, Leomar Susana, Rich Wichrowski
Assistant Carpenter .... Gerard Fortunato
Assistant Propertyman .... Sue Poulin
Moving Light Programmer .... Hillary Knox
Conventional Light Programmer .... J. Day
Frontlight Operators ...... Timothy Coffey, Matt Maloney
Light Board Operator .... Suzanne Williams
Dressers .... Tracey Boone, Jessica Dermody,
Dolores Jones, Ryan Rossetto
Hair Supervisor .... Alice Ramos
Assistant Hair Supervisor .... Taurance Williams
Production Sound Engineer .... Jens Muehlhausen
Production Assistant .... Rachel Miller
Directing Intern .... Josh Halloway
Costume Intern .... Maggie Whitaker
SDCF Observer .... Andy Sandberg
Music Fellow .... Brian Scott Taylor

MARK SIMON CASTING
Casting Assistant: Selby Brown

LoveMusik is suggested by *Speak Low (When You Speak Love)*, edited and translated by Lys Symonette and Kim H. Kowalke (U. of California Press, 1996). Professor Kowalke has served as historical and musical consultant for this production.

MUSIC CREDITS
Use of the musical compositions in the play is by permission of European American Music Corporation.

Lyrics: "Speak Low" (from *One Touch of Venus*) used by permission from Curtis Brown, Ltd. Copyright ©1944; all rights reserved. "Nanna's Lied," translation by Michael Feingold, used by arrangement with European American Music Corporation. "Kiddush" used by arrangement with European American Music Corporation. "Klops Lied (Meatball Song)," translation by Milton Granger, used by arrangement with European American Music Corporation. "Berlin Im Licht," translation by Milton Granger, used by arrangement with European American Music Corporation. "Wooden Wedding" (from *One Touch of Venus*) by permission from Curtis Brown, Ltd. Copyright ©1944; all rights reserved. "Tango Ballad" (from *The Threepenny Opera*), translation by Marc Blitzstein, used by arrangement with European American Music Corporation. "Alabama Song" (from *Rise and Fall of the City of Mahagonny*) used by arrangement with European American Music Corporation. "Girl of the Moment" (from *Lady in the Dark*) used with permission. "Moritat" (from *The Threepenny Opera*), translation by Marc Blitzstein, used by arrangement with European American Music Corporation.

"Schickelgruber," adapted by Alfred Uhry, used by arrangement with European American Music Corporation. "Come to Paris" (from *The Firebrand of Florence*) used with permission. "I Don't Love You," translation by Michael Feingold, used by arrangement with European American Music Coporation on behalf of Heugel S. A. "Wouldn't You Like to Be on Broadway?" (from *Street Scene*), book by Elmer Rice; lyrics by Langston Hughes. "How Can You Tell an American?" (from *Knickerbocker Holiday*) used with permission. "Very, Very, Very" (from *One Touch of Venus*) used by permission from Curtis Brown, Ltd. Copyright ©1944; all rights reserved. "Surabaya Johnny" (from *Happy End*), translation by Michael Feingold, used by arrangement with European American Music Corporation. "Youkali," translation by Anne Cattaneo, used by arrangement with European American Music Corporation on behalf of Heugel S.A. "That's Him" (from *One Touch of Venus*) used by permission from Curtis Brown, Ltd. Copyright ©1944; all rights reserved. "Hosannah Rockefeller" (from *Happy End*), translation by Michael Feingold, used by arrangement with European American Music Corporation. "The Illusion Wedding Show" (from *Love Life*) used with permission of the Alan Jay Lerner Testamentary Trust. "It Never Was You" (from *Knickerbocker Holiday*) used with permission. "A Bird of Passage" (from *Lost in the Stars*) used with permission. "September Song" (from *Knickerbocker Holiday*) used with permission.

CREDITS
Show control and scenic motion control featuring Stage Command Systems® by PRG-Scenic Technologies, a division of Production Resource Group, LLC, New Windsor, NY. Scenery fabrication by PRG-Scenic Technologies and Great Lakes Scenic Studios. Additional hanging and deck scenery provided by Global Scenic Services. Lighting equipment by PRG Lighting. Projected imagery by Adam Larsen. Sound equipment by Masque Sound. Costume construction by Barbara Matera Limited, Carelli Costumes, Paul Chang and Tricorne, Inc. Millinery by Rodney Gordon, Inc. Piano provided by Steinway & Sons. Natural herbal cough drops courtesy of Ricola USA. MTC wishes to thank the TDF Costume Collection for its assistance in this production.

SPECIAL THANKS
Irish Repertory Theatre

For more information visit
www.ManhattanTheatreClub.com

MANHATTAN THEATRE CLUB/
BILTMORE THEATRE STAFF
Theatre Manager .... **Russ Ramsey**
Assistant House Manager .... Miranda Scopel
Box Office Treasurer .... **David Dillon**
Assistant Box Office Treasurers .... Tevy Bradley,
Jonathan Pate
Head Carpenter .... Chris Wiggins
Head Propertyman .... Timothy Walters
Sound Engineer .... Louis Shapiro
Master Electrician .... Jeff Dodson
Wardrobe Supervisor .... Angela Simpson
Apprentices .... Marc Grimshaw, Andrew Sliwinski
Engineers .... Robert Allen,
Richardo Deosarran, Byron Johnson
Security .... Initial Security
Lobby Refreshments .... Sweet Concessions

Macbeth

First Preview: March 28, 2008. Opened: April 8, 2008.
Closed May 24, 2008 after 11 Previews and 52 Performances.

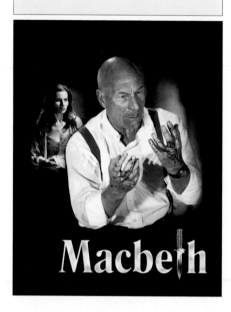

PLAYBILL

Macbeth

CAST

(in order of appearance)

Duncan, King of Scotland/	
A Doctor	BYRON JENNINGS
Malcolm	SCOTT HANDY
Bloody Sergeant/Murderer	HYWEL JOHN
Donalbain/Young Seyward	BEN CARPENTER
Witch	SOPHIE HUNTER
Witch/Gentlewoman	POLLY FRAME
Witch	NIAMH McGRADY
Macbeth	PATRICK STEWART
Banquo	MARTIN TURNER
Lennox	MARK RAWLINGS
Ross	TIM TRELOAR
Angus	BILL NASH
Lady Macbeth	KATE FLEETWOOD
Lady Macbeth's Servant	OLIVER BIRCH
Fleance	HENRY HODGES
	or EMMETT WHITE
Seyton,	
a Porter	CHRISTOPHER PATRICK NOLAN
Macduff	MICHAEL FEAST
Lady Macduff	RACHEL TICOTIN
Macduff Children	HENRY HODGES,
	GABRIELLE PIACENTILE,
	JACOB ROSENBAUM,
	PHOEBE KEELING VanDUSEN
Old Seyward/Murderer	CHRISTOPHER KNOTT

Continued on next page

⑤LYCEUM THEATRE

149 West 45th Street
A Shubert Organization Theatre

Gerald Schoenfeld, *Chairman*   Philip J. Smith, *President*

Robert E. Wankel, *Executive Vice President*

Duncan C. Weldon & Paul Elliott

Jeffrey Archer   Bill Ballard   Terri & Timothy Childs
Rodger Hess   David Mirvish   Adriana Mnuchin and Emanuel Azenberg

with

BAM

present

the Chichester Festival Theatre Production

of

Macbeth

by William Shakespeare

with

Oliver Birch   Ben Carpenter   Michael Feast   Kate Fleetwood
Polly Frame   Scott Handy   Henry Hodges   Sophie Hunter   Byron Jennings
Hywel John   Christopher Knott   Niamh McGrady   Bill Nash
Christopher Patrick Nolan   Gabrielle Piacentile   Mark Rawlings
Jacob Rosenbaum   Patrick Stewart   Rachel Ticotin   Tim Treloar
Martin Turner   Phoebe Keeling VanDusen   Emmett White

Directed by
Rupert Goold

Design by
Anthony Ward

Lighting Design by	Composer and Sound Design by	Video & Projection Design by
Howard Harrison	Adam Cork	Lorna Heavey

Associate Director	Movement Director	Fight Director	UK Production Manager
Steve Marmion	Georgina Lamb	Terry King	Dan Watkins
			The Production Desk

Technical Supervision	General Management	Press Representative	Production Stage Manager
Neil A. Mazzella	Abbie M. Strassler	Barlow • Hartman	Jane Pole

4/8/08

(L-R): Kate Fleetwood and Patrick Stewart.

Photo by Manuel Harlan

Macbeth

UNDERSTUDIES

For Ross, 2nd Murderer:
OLIVER BIRCH
For Malcolm, Bloody Sergeant/1st Murderer, Angus:
BEN CARPENTER
For Lady Macbeth, Witch, Servant:
POLLY FRAME
For Witches:
SOPHIE HUNTER, RACHEL TICOTIN
For Seyton a Porter, Young Seyward:
HYWEL JOHN
For Duncan/Doctor, Servant:
CHRISTOPHER KNOTT
For Lady Macduff, Witch/Gentlewoman:
NIAMH McGRADY
For Banquo/Old Seyward:
BILL NASH
For Lennox:
CHRISTOPHER PATRICK NOLAN
For Macduff:
MARK RAWLINGS
For Macbeth:
TIM TRELOAR

The actors in *Macbeth* are appearing with the permission of Actors' Equity Association.

Patrick Stewart as Macbeth.

Photo by Manuel Harlan

Oliver Birch
Lady Macbeth's Servant

Ben Carpenter
Donalbain/ Young Seyward

Michael Feast
Macduff

Kate Fleetwood
Lady Macbeth

Polly Frame
Witch/Gentlewoman

Scott Handy
Malcolm

Henry Hodges
Macduff's Son; Fleance at certain performances

Sophie Hunter
Witch

Byron Jennings
Duncan/A Doctor

Hywel John
Bloody Sergeant/ 1st Murderer

Christopher Knott
Old Seyward/ Murderer

Niamh McGrady
Witch

Bill Nash
Angus

Christopher Patrick Nolan
Seyton, a Porter

Gabrielle Piancentile
Macduff's Daughter

Mark Rawlings
Lennox

Jacob Rosenbaum
Macduff's Son at certain performances

Patrick Stewart
Macbeth

Rachel Ticotin
Lady Macduff

Tim Treloar
Ross

Macbeth

Martin Turner
Banquo

Phoebe Keeling VanDusen
Macduff's Daughter

Emmett White
Fleance at certain performances

Rupert Goold
Director

Anthony Ward
Set and Costume Design

Howard Harrison
Lighting Design

Adam Cork
Sound Design and Original Composition

Neil A. Mazzella/ Hudson Theatrical Associates
Technical Supervision

Emanuel Azenberg
Producer

2007-2008 AWARD

DRAMA LEAGUE AWARD
Distinguished Revival of a Play

**Opening Night BAM: February 12, 2008
Opening Night Gielgud Theatre,
London: September 21, 2007
Opening Night Chichester Festival Theatre:
May 25, 2007**

STAFF FOR *Macbeth*

GENERAL MANAGEMENT
Abbie M. Strassler

COMPANY MANAGER
John E. Gendron

GENERAL PRESS REPRESENTATIVE
Barlow•Hartman
Michael Hartman   John Barlow
Tom D'Ambrosio   Michelle Bergmann

Production Stage Manager ....Jane Pole
Stage Manager ....Lorna Seymour
Assistant Stage Managers ....Laura Levis, Sarah Coates
Technical Supervision ....Neil A. Mazzella, Sam Ellis
Production Stage Engineer ....Howard Woodliffe
Associate Lighting Design ....Paul Miller
Lighting Programmer ....Marc Polimeni
Associate Sound Design ....Christopher Cronin
Video Engineer ....Gareth Jeanne
Production Carpenter ....Adam Braunstein
Advance Carpenter ....Frank Illo
Production Electrician... ....Kevin Barry
Advance Electrician ....James Maloney
Production Sound Engineer ....Wallace Flores
Production Properties...........................Reg Vessey
Properties Assistant ....Augie Mericola
Wardrobe Supervisor ....Terri Purcell
Assistant Wardrobe Supervisor...............Joby Horrigan
Dresser to Mr. Stewart ....Zinda Williams

Dressers ....Shana Dunbar, Frances Myer,
Pat Sullivan
Makeup Artist ....Gina Leon
Child Wrangler ....Bridget Walders
Management Assistant ....Michael Salonia
Accountants ....Fried & Kowgios CPAs LLP/
Robert Fried, CPA
Comptroller ....Sarah Galbraith
Advertising ....Serino Coyne Inc./Angelo Desimini
Insurance ....Ventura Insurance Brokerage, Inc./
Janice Brown,
Robert Israel for Gordon & Co. (UK)
Legal Counsel ......The Law Offices of Noel L. Silverman/
Noel L. Silverman
Merchandising ....Max Merchandising
Banking ....JP Morgan Chase/Richard Callian
Payroll Service ....Castellana Services Inc./
Lance Castellana
Additional Casting......................Jay Binder C.S.A.,
Jack Bowdan C.S.A.
Displays ....King Displays

FOR TRIUMPH ENTERTAINMENT LTD.
Directors ....Paul Elliott, Duncan C. Weldon
General Manager ....David Bownes
Finance Director ....Dinesh Khanderia
Production Administrator ....Beth Eden

CHICHESTER FESTIVAL THEATRE
Chairman ......The Rt. Hon. Lord Young of Graffham DL
Artistic Director ....Jonathan Church
Executive Director ....Alan Finch

CREDITS AND ACKNOWLEDGEMENTS
Scenery by All Scene All Props. Scenic artwork by James Rowse. Stage engineering by Weld-Fab Stage Engineering Ltd. Lighting equipment from Hudson Sound and Light LLC. Video equipment supplied by Stage Sound Services.

Sound equipment by Sound Associates, Inc. Uniform and costume hires from Angels. Tailoring by William Baboo. Women's costumes by Kate Allen, Nicole Small, Roxanne Armstrong. Women's hats by Sian Barrett

SPECIAL THANKS
Housing for the artists is generously provided by Furnished Quarters.

THE SHUBERT ORGANIZATION, INC.
Board of Directors

Gerald Schoenfeld
Chairman

Philip J. Smith
President

Wyche Fowler, Jr.

John W. Kluge

Lee J. Seidler

Michael I. Sovern

Stuart Subotnick

Robert E. Wankel
Executive Vice President

Peter Entin
Vice President –
Theatre Operations

Elliot Greene
Vice President –
Finance

David Andrews
Vice President –
Shubert Ticketing Services

John Darby
Vice President –
Facilities

D.S. Moynihan
Vice President – Creative Projects

House Manager ....Joann Swanson

Mamma Mia!

First Preview: October 5, 2001. Opened: October 18, 2001.
Still running as of May 31, 2008.

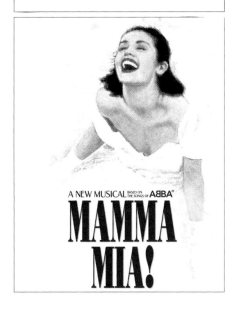

CAST

(in order of speaking)

Sophie Sheridan .... CAREY ANDERSON
Ali .... VERONICA J. KUEHN
Lisa .... SAMANTHA EGGERS
Tanya .... JUDY McLANE
Rosie .... GINA FERRALL
Donna Sheridan .... CAROLEE CARMELLO
Sky .... ANDY KELSO
Pepper .... BEN GETTINGER
Eddie .... RAYMOND J. LEE
Harry Bright .... BEN LIVINGSTON
Bill Austin .... PEARCE BUNTING
Sam Carmichael .... CHRISTOPHER SHYER
Father Alexandrios .... BRYAN SCOTT JOHNSON

THE ENSEMBLE

BRENT BLACK, TIMOTHY BOOTH,
ISAAC CALPITO, ALLYSON CARR,
MEGHANN DREYFUSS, LORI HALEY FOX,
FRANKIE JAMES GRANDE,
BRYAN SCOTT JOHNSON,
MONICA KAPOOR, CORINNE MELANÇON,
STEVE MORGAN, COURTNEY REED,
AMINA ROBINSON, GERARD SALVADOR,
LEAH ZEPEL

WINTER GARDEN

1634 Broadway
A Shubert Organization Theatre

Gerald Schoenfeld, *Chairman*   Philip J. Smith, *President*

Robert E. Wankel, *Executive Vice President*

JUDY CRAYMER, RICHARD EAST AND BJÖRN ULVAEUS
FOR LITTLESTAR IN ASSOCIATION WITH UNIVERSAL

PRESENT

MAMMA MIA!

MUSIC AND LYRICS BY
BENNY ANDERSSON
BJÖRN ULVAEUS

AND SOME SONGS WITH STIG ANDERSON

BOOK BY CATHERINE JOHNSON

PRODUCTION DESIGNED BY
MARK THOMPSON

LIGHTING DESIGNED BY
HOWARD HARRISON

SOUND DESIGNED BY
**ANDREW BRUCE &
BOBBY AITKEN**

MUSICAL SUPERVISOR, ADDITIONAL MATERIAL
& ARRANGEMENTS
MARTIN KOCH

CHOREOGRAPHY
ANTHONY VAN LAAST

DIRECTED BY
PHYLLIDA LLOYD

LIVE BROADWAY

10/1/07

Andy Kelso and Carey Anderson (center) perform with the Ensemble.

Photo by Joan Marcus

Continued on next page

Mamma Mia!

MUSICAL NUMBERS

(in alphabetical order)

CHIQUITITA
DANCING QUEEN
DOES YOUR MOTHER KNOW
GIMME! GIMME! GIMME!
HONEY, HONEY
I DO, I DO, I DO, I DO, I DO
I HAVE A DREAM
KNOWING ME, KNOWING YOU
LAY ALL YOUR LOVE ON ME
MAMMA MIA
MONEY, MONEY, MONEY
ONE OF US
OUR LAST SUMMER
SLIPPING THROUGH MY FINGERS
S.O.S.
SUPER TROUPER
TAKE A CHANCE ON ME
THANK YOU FOR THE MUSIC
THE NAME OF THE GAME
THE WINNER TAKES IT ALL
UNDER ATTACK
VOULEZ-VOUS

(L-R): Andy Kelso as Sky and Carey Anderson as Sophie.

Photos by Joan Marcus

THE BAND

Music Director/Conductor/Keyboard 1:
WENDY BOBBITT CAVETT
Associate Music Director/Keyboard 3:
ROB PREUSS
Keyboard 2:
STEVE MARZULLO
Keyboard 4:
MYLES CHASE
Guitar 1:
DOUG QUINN
Guitar 2:
JEFF CAMPBELL
Bass:
PAUL ADAMY
Drums:
RAY MARCHICA
Percussion:
DAVID NYBERG
Music Coordinator:
MICHAEL KELLER
Synthesizer Programmer:
NICHOLAS GILPIN

(L-R): Judy McLane, Carolee Carmello and Gina Ferrall.

UNDERSTUDIES
For Sophie Sheridan:
MEGHANN DREYFUSS,
SAMANTHA EGGERS, VERONICA J. KUEHN
For Ali:
COURTNEY REED, AMINA ROBINSON,
LEAH ZEPEL
For Lisa:
LANENE CHARTERS, MONICA KAPOOR,
LEAH ZEPEL
For Tanya:
LORI HALEY FOX, CORINNE MELANÇON
For Rosie:
LORI HALEY FOX
For Donna Sheridan:
LORI HALEY FOX, CORINNE MELANÇON
For Sky:
STEVE MORGAN, RYAN SANDER
For Pepper:
ISAAC CALPITO, GERARD SALVADOR
For Eddie:
MATTHEW FARVER,
FRANKIE JAMES GRANDE, RYAN SANDER
For Harry Bright:
TIMOTHY BOOTH, BRYAN SCOTT
JOHNSON
For Bill Austin:
BRENT BLACK, TIMOTHY BOOTH,
BRYAN SCOTT JOHNSON
For Sam Carmichael:
BRENT BLACK, TIMOTHY BOOTH
For Father Alexandrios:
BRENT BLACK, TIMOTHY BOOTH,
MATTHEW FARVER

SWINGS
LANENE CHARTERS, MATTHEW FARVER,
ERICA MANSFIELD, RYAN SANDER,
COLLETTE SIMMONS

DANCE CAPTAIN
JANET ROTHERMEL

On a Greek Island, a wedding is about to take place...

PROLOGUE
Three months before the wedding

ACT ONE
The day before the wedding

ACT TWO
The day of the wedding

Mamma Mia!

Carolee Carmello
Donna Sheridan

Carey Anderson
Sophie Sheridan

Gina Ferrall
Rosie

Judy McLane
Tanya

Christopher Shyer
Sam Carmichael

Pearce Bunting
Bill Austin

Ben Livingston
Harry Bright

Andy Kelso
Sky

Samantha Eggers
Lisa

Veronica J. Kuehn
Ali

Ben Gettinger
Pepper

Raymond J. Lee
Eddie

Brent Black
Ensemble

Timothy Booth
Ensemble

Isaac Calpito
Ensemble

Allyson Carr
Ensemble

Lanene Charters
Swing

Meghann Dreyfuss
Ensemble

Matthew Farver
Swing

Lori Haley Fox
Ensemble

Frankie James
Grande
Ensemble

Bryan Scott Johnson
*Father Alexandrios,
Ensemble*

Monica Kapoor
Ensemble

Erica Mansfield
Swing

Corinne Melançon
Ensemble

Steve Morgan
Ensemble

Courtney Reed
Ensemble

Amina Robinson
Ensemble

Janet Rothermel
Dance Captain

Gerard Salvador
Ensemble

Ryan Sander
*Assistant Dance
Captain, Swing*

Collette Simmons
Swing

Leah Zepel
Ensemble

Björn Ulvaeus
Music & Lyrics

Benny Andersson
Music & Lyrics

Mamma Mia!

Catherine Johnson
Book

Phyllida Lloyd
Director

Anthony Van Laast
Choreographer

Mark Thompson
Production Designer

Howard Harrison
Lighting Designer

Andrew Bruce
Sound Designer

Bobby Aitken
Sound Design

Martin Koch
*Musical Supervisor;
Additional Material;
Arrangements
Musical Supervisor*

David Holcenberg
*Associate Music
Supervisor*

Nichola Treherne
*Associate
Choreographer*

Martha Banta
Resident Director

Tara Rubin Casting
Casting

David Grindrod
Casting Consultant

Arthur Siccardi
Theatrical Services,
Inc.
Production Manager

Judy Craymer
Producer

Richard East
Producer

Jen Burleigh-Bentz
Ensemble

Joan Hess
Tanya

Michael Mastro
Harry Bright

David McDonald
Sam Carmichael

Sandy Rosenberg
Ensemble

Christopher Carl
Ensemble

Heidi Godt
Ensemble

Jon-Erik Goldberg
Swing

Robin Levine
Ensemble, Swing

Laurie Wells
Ensemble

Joi Danielle Price
Ensemble

Mamma Mia!

BAND
Front Row (L-R): Vince Fay,
Wendy Bobbitt Cavett, Steve Marzullo.

Back Row (L-R): Officer Steve Fabb,
Ray Marchica, David Nyberg,
Jeff Campbell, Doug Quinn.

FRONT OF HOUSE & CREW
Front Row (L-R): Felicia Robles,
Sabiel Almonte, Vickey Walker (Assistant
Hair Supervisor).

Second Row (L-R): Tim Young,
Paula Parente, Ken Costigan,
Jennifer Pendergraft, John Walsh.

Back Row (L-R): Officer Steve Fabb,
Robin Steinthal, Michael Cleary,
Craig Dawson, John Mitchell,
Mendy Levine (House Manager),
Michael Bosch.

Photos by Ben Strothmann

CREW
Front Row (L-R): Andy Sather,
Lauren Kievit, Irene Bunis, Carey Bertini,
Pitsch Karrer.

Middle Row (L-R): Aarne Lofgren,
Chad Heulitt, Art Soyk, Reginald Carter,
Michael Maloney.

Back Row (L-R): Officer Steve Fabb,
John Maloney, Don Lawrence,
Glenn Russo, Craig Cassidy.

Mamma Mia!

Photo by Ben Strothmann

CAST & MANAGEMENT

Front Row (L-R): Veronica J. Kuehn, Carolee Carmello, Corinne Melançon, Carey Anderson, Amina Robinson, Monica Kapoor.

Second Row (L-R): Andy Fenton, Ben Livingston, Sherry Cohen, Frankie James Grande, Allyson Carr, Lanene Charters, Heidi Godt, Isaac Calpito, Courtney Reed, Andy Kelso.

Third Row (L-R): Matt Farver, Sean Gallagher, Rina Saltzman, Raymond J. Lee, Judy McLane, Ryan Sander.

Back Row (L-R): Officer Steve Fabb, Liza Garcia, Dean R. Greer, Steve Morgan, Bryan Scott Johnson, Meghann Dreyfuss, Erica Mansfield, Pearce Bunting.

In loving memory of Daniel McDonald, cast member of the *Mamma Mia!* Broadway Company 2004-2005.

LITTLESTAR SERVICES LIMITED

Directors .... Judy Craymer
Richard East
Benny Andersson
Björn Ulvaeus
International Executive Producer .... Andrew Treagus
Business & Finance Director .... Ashley Grisdale
Administrator .... Peter Austin

PA to Judy Craymer .... Katie Wolfryd
Marketing & Communications Manager .... Claire Teare
Marketing & Communications
Coordinator .... Liz McGinity
Head of Accounts .... Jo Reedman
Accountant .... Sheila Egbujie
Accountant .... Kerri Jordan
Accounts Assistant .... Eleanor Booth
Administrative Assistant .... Matthew Willis
Legal Services .... Barry Shaw
Howard Jones at Sheridans
Production Insurance Services .... Walton & Parkinson Ltd.

Business Manager for
Benny Andersson and
Björn Ulvaeus & Scandinavian Press ...... Görel Hanser

NINA LANNAN ASSOCIATES

GENERAL MANAGERS .... DEVIN M. KEUDELL,
AMY JACOBS
ASSOCIATE GENERAL MANAGER/
COMPANY MANAGER .... RINA L. SALTZMAN
Assistant Company Manager .... Liza Garcia
Management Associate .... Katherine McNamee

Mamma Mia!

ANDREW TREAGUS ASSOCIATES LIMITED

GENERAL MANAGER .... JULIAN STONEMAN
Production Administrator .... Daniel Sparrow
PA to Andrew Treagus .... Jacki Harding
Production Coordinator &
  PA to Julian Stoneman .... Stella Warshaw
International Travel Manager .... Maria Persson

PRODUCTION TEAM

ASSOCIATE
  CHOREOGRAPHER ...... NICHOLA TREHERNE
DANCE SUPERVISOR .... JANET ROTHERMEL
RESIDENT DIRECTOR .... MARTHA BANTA
ASSOCIATE
  MUSIC SUPERVISOR ...... DAVID HOLCENBERG
ASSOCIATE
  SCENIC DESIGNER (US) .... NANCY THUN
ASSOCIATE
  SCENIC DESIGNER (UK) ..... JONATHAN ALLEN
ASSOCIATE
  COSTUME DESIGNERS .... LUCY GAIGER
                               SCOTT TRAUGOTT
ASSOCIATE HAIR DESIGNER .. JOSH MARQUETTE
ASSOCIATE
  LIGHTING DESIGNERS .... DAVID HOLMES
                             ED MCCARTHY
                           ANDREW VOLLER
ASSOCIATE
  SOUND DESIGNERS .... BRIAN BEASLEY
                          DAVID PATRIDGE
MUSICAL TRANSCRIPTION ..... ANDERS NEGLIN
CASTING CONSULTANT .... DAVID GRINDROD

CASTING
TARA RUBIN CASTING
Tara Rubin CSA
Eric Woodall, CSA; Laura Schutzel, CSA;
Merri Sugarman, CSA;
Rebecca Carfagna; Paige Blansfield; Dale Brown

PRESS REPRESENTATIVE
BONEAU/BRYAN-BROWN
Adrian Bryan-Brown   Joe Perrotta
Danielle Crinnion

MARKETING U.S.
TMG – THE MARKETING GROUP
TANYA GRUBICH   LAURA MATALON
Anne Rippey   Victoria Cairl

MUSIC PUBLISHED BY EMI GROVE PARK MUSIC, INC. AND EMI WATERFORD MUSIC, INC.

STAFF FOR *MAMMA MIA!*

PRODUCTION
  STAGE MANAGER .... ANDREW FENTON
Stage Managers .... Sherry Cohen, Dean R. Greer
Assistant Dance Captain .... Ryan Sander

PRODUCTION MANAGER ..... ARTHUR SICCARDI

Head Carpenter .... Chris Nass
Assistant Carpenters .... Stephen Burns,
                          Clark Middleton
Production Electrician .... Rick Baxter
Head Electrician .... Don Lawrence

Assistant Electrician .... Andy Sather
Vari*Lite Programmer .... Andrew Voller
Production Sound .... David Patridge
Head Sound .... Craig Cassidy
Assistant Sound .... Pitsch Karrer
Production Properties .... Simon E.R. Evans
Head Properties .... Gregory Martin
Wardrobe Supervisor .... Irene L. Bunis
Assistant Wardrobe .... Ron Glow
Dressers .... Carey Bertini, Jim Collum,
                Lauren Kievit, Trevor McGuiness,
                Elvia Pineda, Eric Pregent,
                Christine Richmond, I Wang
Hair Supervisor .... Josh Marquette
Assistant Hair Supervisor .... Vickey Walker
Assistant Lighting Designer .... Jeffrey Lowney
Assistant Costume Designer .... Angela Kahler
House Crew .... Richard Carney, Reginald Carter,
      Gregory Chabay, Mai-Linh Lofgren DeVirgilio,
           Meredith Kievit, Aarne Lofgren,
           Francis Lofgren, John Maloney,
           Glenn Russo, Dennis Wiener
Box Office .... Mary Cleary, Lee Cobb,
           Steve Cobb, James Drury, Sue Giebler,
           Bob McCaffrey, Ron Schroeder
Casting Directors .... Tara Rubin CSA, Eric Woodall
Casting Associates .... Laura Schutzel, Merri Sugarman
Casting Assistants .... Rebecca Carfagna, Jeff Siebert,
                    Paige Blansfield
Canadian Casting .... Stephanie Gorin Casting, C.D.C.
Associate to Casting Consultant .... Stephen Crockett
London Casting Assistant .... James Orange
Legal Counsel (U.S.) .... Lazarus & Harris LLP
                       Scott Lazarus, Esq.
                       Robert Harris, Esq.
Immigration Counsel .... Mark D. Koestler/
           Kramer Levin Naftalis & Frankel LLP
Accounting .... Rosenberg, Neuwirth and Kuchner/
                Chris Cacace, In Woo
Advertising .... Serino Coyne, Inc./
          Nancy Coyne, Greg Corradetti,
          Ryan Greer, Caroline Lenher,
          Ruth Rosenberg
Press Office Staff .... Chris Boneau, Ian Bjorklund,
          Jim Byk, Brandi Cornwell,
          Jackie Green, Juliana Hannett,
      Hector Hernandez, Jessica Johnson, Amy Kass,
      Kevin Jones, Aaron Meier, Christine Olver,
      Linnae Petruzelli, Matthew Polk, Matt Ross,
      Heath Schwartz, Susanne Tighe
Production Photographer .... Joan Marcus
Merchandising .... Max Merchandise, LLC/
           Randi Grossman, Victor Romero
Theater Displays .... King Display
Insurance .... Dewitt, Stern/
           Walton & Parkinson Ltd.
Orthopedic Consultant .... Dr. Philip Baumann
Banking .... J.P. Morgan Trust
Travel Agent .... Tzell Travel
Original Logo Design .... © Littlestar Services Limited

CREDITS AND ACKNOWLEDGMENTS
Scenery constructed and painted by Hudson Scenic Studio, Inc. and Hamilton Scenic Specialty. Computer motion control and automation by Feller Precision, Inc. SHOWTRAK computer motion control for scenery and rigging. Sound equipment supplied by Masque Sound.

Lighting equipment supplied by Fourth Phase and Vari*Lite, Inc. Soft goods by I. Weiss and Sons. Costumes by Barbara Matera, Ltd., Tricorne New York City and Carelli Costumes, Inc. Additional costume work by Allan Alberts Productions. Millinery by Lynn Mackey. Wet suits by Aquatic Fabricators of South Florida. Custom men's shirts by Cego. Custom knitting by C.C. Wei. Custom fabric printing and dyeing by Dye-namix and Gene Mignola. Shoes by Native Leather, Rilleau Leather and T. O. Dey. Gloves by Cornelia James - London. Hair color by Redken. Properties by Paragon Theme and Prop Fabrication. Cough drops provided by Ricola U.S.A. Physical therapy provided by Sean Gallagher.

Mamma Mia! was originally produced in London by LITTLESTAR SERVICES LIMITED on April 6, 1999.

Experience *Mamma Mia!* in these cities:
London/Prince of Wales Theatre/mamma-mia.com
Broadway/Winter Garden Theatre/telecharge.com
Las Vegas/Mandalay Bay Theatre/mandalaybay.com
North American Tour/ticketmaster.com
International Tour/mamma-mia.com

For more information on the above
and our other productions in
Berlin, Barcelona, Moscow and Essen
visit and book at:
www.mamma-mia.com

Mamma Mia! How Can I Resist You? The Inside Story of Mamma Mia! and the songs of ABBA available now. Order at: www.barnesandnoble.com

For more information and tour schedules visit:
www.mamma-mia.com

THE SHUBERT ORGANIZATION, INC.
Board of Directors

Gerald Schoenfeld	**Philip J. Smith**
Chairman	President
Wyche Fowler, Jr.	**John W. Kluge**
Lee J. Seidler	**Michael I. Sovern**

Stuart Subotnick

Robert E. Wankel
Executive Vice President

Peter Entin	**Elliot Greene**
Vice President –	Vice President –
Theatre Operations	Finance
David Andrews	**John Darby**
Vice President –	Vice President –
Shubert Ticketing Services	Facilities

D.S. Moynihan
Vice President – Creative Projects

House Manager .... Manuel Levine

Mamma Mia!

SCRAPBOOK

Correspondent: Carolee Carmello, "Donna Sheridan"

Celebrity Visitors: We've had lots of fun visitors this year including Mayor Michael Bloomberg and Colin Powell. Pierce Brosnan (preparing for his role as "Sam" in the film of *Mamma Mia!*) stopped by...don't know if he got any tips about his character, but 'the cast and crew definitely enjoyed him...especially when he got on the loud speaker to make the 5-minute call! Another stand out: Miley Cyrus (a.k.a. Hannah Montana) came to see the show with her friends and family. Everyone in the building who had children (including me!) brought them backstage to meet her. She was very sweet and signed lots of autographs and took photos with every kid within miles. Of course, the moms all went crazy over her dreamy dad, Billy Ray!

"Gypsy of the Year": This year's sketch was written by Gerard Salvador (who also performed the role of "Telemundo Sam") and was about all the absurd possibilities for "*Mamma Mia!*, the TV Show"! The cast included Allyson Carr, Meghann Dreyfuss, Samantha Eggers, Heidi Godt, Frankie James Grande, Monica Kapoor, Raymond J. Lee, Matthew Marks, Paul McGill, Brian Patrick Murphy, Courtney Reed, Christopher Shyer, Collette Simmons, Matthew Steffens and the unforgettable performance as "Madonna" by our own Tim Booth.

"Easter Bonnet": Cast members sang a song called "I'll Walk With You" (by Sean Altman and Billy Straus) in memory of a beloved cast member who passed away this year, Daniel McDonald. Daniel played "Sam" in 2004/2005 and was an amazing talent, a loving husband, a wonderful daddy, and a great friend. We all miss him so much.

"Carols For a Cure" Carol: "My Gift" (by Dan Ponce)

Favorite Moment On Stage: I love holding out that last note of "The Winner Takes It All." It's fun and challenging and sometimes makes me light-headed! The cast used to time me to see if I could break my record. Now I think they're just tired and want to go home already! One crew member told me he could go out for a cigarette and come back before the note was over. (Maybe a *slight* exaggeration.)

Favorite Moment Off Stage: We sometimes play what we call "Mia Roller Derby" Several cast members (including Judy McLane, Gina Ferrall, Ben Livingston, Chris Shyer and Yours Truly) and occasionally a crew member, too, will pretend to beat each other up in the style of the old Roller Derby or the new W.W.E. to entertain the girls who are in a "freeze" on the stage, but facing the stage-right wing. We take turns punching, slapping, falling, kicking, all in our very fancy "Voulez-Vous" costumes. (Don't tell the Wardrobe Department!)

Favorite In-Theater Gathering Place: We are lucky to have a little greenroom upstairs at the Winter Garden where people love to hang out, eat dinner, nap, play games, etc. It's also where we celebrate birthdays in the company. Apparently, it's a pretty fun place, because my son informed me that he wanted to celebrate his 7th birthday there, just like all the other cool *Mamma Mia!* types. Of course, everyone was happy to oblige!

Favorite Off-Site Hangout: The most popular neighborhood joint for the *Mamma Mia!* cast has to be Harmony View (recently renamed Emmett

At the post-strike event at the Marriott Marquis Hotel (L-R): Max Crumm and Laura Osnes of *Grease*, Stephanie J. Block of *Wicked* and Carolee Carmello of *Mamma Mia!*

O'Lunney's Irish Pub). Emmett is a great host and makes us feel very welcome. We love it there.

Favorite Snack Food: Doughnuts, doughnuts and more doughnuts!!! (That's my fault 'cause I tend to bring them in a lot, along with some occasional "munchkins.")

Favorite Therapy: The big foam rollers are still very popular at *Mamma Mia!*. They seem to be the best way to counteract the effects of the steep rake on stage, which takes a toll on everyone's knees and backs.

Memorable Ad-Lib: This award has to go to Judy McLane, who recently had some microphone problems during a costume change and was very late for her next entrance. She decided not to make a secret of her presence when she finally got on stage, so she yelled out "For Cryin' Out Cranberries!" and got a big laugh. (Lots of people thought she should keep it in.)

Fastest Costume Change: My fastest change has to be during the wedding scene at the end of the show when I get out of my pink dress and into a white version of same, and add a wedding veil and bouquet all in about 13 seconds. (It helps that my dresser is hiding behind the set, waiting for me and that "Tanya" and "Rosie" help, too!)

Best In-House Parody Lyric: Stage manager Andy Fenton has a very interesting version of "Waterloo." It starts off something like this: "Watery-poo! I need Imodium right away!"

Memorable Note on My Performance: When I first joined the cast, I got word that our brilliant, beautiful, (and very witty) producer, Judy Craymer, was in the audience. I was very excited to meet her and hear her thoughts. The next day I was told that, during my first scene, she was heard saying "Well, of course Donna is exhausted, she's been styling her hair all day!" Needless to say I had to make some adjustments to my hairdo.

Nicknames: Judy McLane and I call each other by our first names backwards. So she's YDUJ (pronounced "EE-Duje") and I'm EELORAC (pronounced "EE-low-rack"). It makes us feel like we're 8 years old, which is about the way we act most of the time.

Embarrassing Moments: My first happened during my very first performance. I was in the middle of that very quick quick-change in the wedding, and my zipper broke! I had no time to do anything about it (not even a safety pin!) so I went out on stage with my back open all the way down to my thong and whispered to Daniel McDonald (my "Sam") "Don't turn me around,

what ever you do!" We proceeded to re-choreograph the entire wedding dance and scene for ourselves so as to feature ONLY my front half!

Ghostly Encounters: The Winter Garden Theater is a very old building. Its bones go back to The American Horse Exchange (1885). The Shuberts converted it to a theater around 1910. Al Jolson made his Broadway debut there. This is all to say that there are lots of spirits from days gone by in that building! Glenn Russo, who has worked on the crew at the Winter Garden for 29 years, says that he once saw a pipe fall (and nearly kill him) up in the cat walk when no one else was around. Another time, he felt "something" pass by him on stage...he's convinced it's ghosts. House cleaning staff report toilets flushing and voices heard in one particular restroom that they believe is haunted! I just wish we could get all the mice out of the building. You'd think *Cats* would have cleared that up for good !

Most Trying Time: The strike by the Stagehands' Union (Local 1) which shut down most Broadway shows for about three weeks during the Thanksgiving season. Lots of losses on both sides, but theatergoers lost out more than anyone. When the strike ended, there was a press event at the Marriott Marquis where lots of Broadway performers gathered to celebrate the reopening of their various shows. We had a great time, but it was a bit surreal seeing "The Grinch" stand next to "The Frankenstein Monster" and "Sandy and Danny." What an amazing feeling to get back to work and be so grateful...we all appreciated our jobs so much after that.

Coolest Thing About Playing This Role: I love pretending to be a rock star—even a has-been rock star.

Best Thing About Being in This Show: It sounds corny, but it really is a family at *Mamma Mia*. Everyone gets along well. We really do have fun and I think that comes from the top. The producers make us feel valuable and important, the musical staff really cares about the integrity of the show on a daily basis, the crew like the cast and vice versa, and we all know how hard everyone works. And our stage managers (headed by the incomparable Andy Fenton) are great camp counselors. There are always activities to pass the time: scavenger hunts backstage, social events, a softball team, a bowling team, parties...everything a good camp (or Broadway show) needs! Wait...we could use a shuffleboard court.

Mary Poppins

First Preview: October 14, 2006. Opened: November 16, 2006.
Still running as of May 31, 2008.

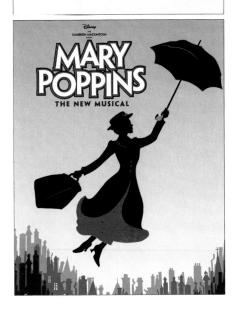

PLAYBILL

CAST OF CHARACTERS
(in order of appearance)

Bert	GAVIN LEE
George Banks	DANIEL JENKINS
Winifred Banks	REBECCA LUKER
Jane Banks	NICOLE BOCCHI, KATHRYN FAUGHNAN or DEVYNN PEDELL
Michael Banks	MATTHEW GUMLEY, HENRY HODGES or JACOB LEVINE
Katie Nanna	MEGAN OSTERHAUS
Policeman	COREY SKAGGS
Miss Lark	ANN ARVIA
Admiral Boom	MICHAEL McCARTY
Mrs. Brill	JANE CARR
Robertson Ay	MARK PRICE
Mary Poppins	ASHLEY BROWN
Park Keeper	JAMES HINDMAN
Neleus	BRIAN LETENDRE
Queen Victoria	RUTH GOTTSCHALL
Bank Chairman	MICHAEL McCARTY
Miss Smythe	RUTH GOTTSCHALL
Von Hussler	SEAN McCOURT
Northbrook	MATT LOEHR
Bird Woman	CASS MORGAN
Mrs. Corry	JANELLE ANNE ROBINSON
Fannie	VASTHY E. MOMPOINT
Annie	MEGAN OSTERHAUS
Valentine	DOMINIC ROBERTS
William	T. OLIVER REID
Mr. Punch	JAMES HINDMAN

Continued on next page

The Playbill Broadway Yearbook 2007-2008

NEW AMSTERDAM THEATRE

Disney
and
CAMERON MACKINTOSH
present

MARY POPPINS

A MUSICAL BASED ON THE STORIES OF P.L. TRAVERS AND THE WALT DISNEY FILM

With

ASHLEY BROWN   GAVIN LEE

DANIEL JENKINS   REBECCA LUKER

CASS MORGAN   MARK PRICE   RUTH GOTTSCHALL   MICHAEL McCARTY

and

JANE CARR

NICOLE BOCCHI   KATHRYN FAUGHNAN   MATTHEW GUMLEY   HENRY HODGES   JACOB LEVINE   DEVYNN PEDELL
ANN ARVIA   JAMES HINDMAN   BRIAN LETENDRE   MATT LOEHR   SEAN McCOURT   JANELLE ANNE ROBINSON   COREY SKAGGS

PAM BRADLEY   KRISTIN CARBONE   BRIAN COLLIER   NICOLAS DROMARD
ERIC HATCH   SUZANNE HYLENSKI   TONY MANSKER   JEFF METZLER   VASTHY E. MOMPOINT
KATHLEEN NANNI   MEGAN OSTERHAUS   T. OLIVER REID   DOMINIC ROBERTS   NICK SANCHEZ
ROMMY SANDHU   LAURA SCHUTTER   SARAH SOLIE   SHEKITRA STARKE   CATHERINE WALKER   KEVIN SAMUAL YEE

Original Music and Lyrics by
RICHARD M. SHERMAN and ROBERT B. SHERMAN

Book by
JULIAN FELLOWES

New Songs and Additional Music and Lyrics by
GEORGE STILES and ANTHONY DREWE

Co-created by
CAMERON MACKINTOSH

Produced for Disney Theatrical Productions by
THOMAS SCHUMACHER

Music Supervisor	Music Director
DAVID CADDICK	BRAD HAAK

Orchestrations by
WILLIAM DAVID BROHN

Broadway Sound Design	Dance and Vocal Arrangements
STEVE CANYON KENNEDY	GEORGE STILES

Associate Choreographer	Associate Director	Associate Producer	Makeup Design	Casting
GEOFFREY GARRATT	ANTHONY LYN	JAMES THANE	NAOMI DONNE	TARA RUBIN CASTING

Technical Director	Production Stage Manager	Resident Choreographer	Press Representative
DAVID BENKEN	MARK DOBROW	TOM KOSIS	BONEAU/BRYAN-BROWN

Co-choreographer	Lighting Design
STEPHEN MEAR	HOWARD HARRISON

Scenic and Costume Design
BOB CROWLEY

Co-direction and Choreography
MATTHEW BOURNE

Directed by
RICHARD EYRE

Disney
BROADWAY

©Disney/CML

10/1/07

The original Broadway company performs "Supercalifragilisticexpialidocious."

Photo by Joan Marcus

251

Mary Poppins

MUSICAL NUMBERS

Mary Poppins takes place in and around the Banks' household
somewhere in London at the turn of the last century.

ACT I

"Chim Chim Cher-ee" † ....Bert
"Cherry Tree Lane" (Part 1)* ....George and Winifred Banks,
Jane and Michael, Mrs. Brill, and Robertson Ay
"The Perfect Nanny" ....Jane and Michael
"Cherry Tree Lane" (Part 2) ....George and Winifred Banks, Jane, and Michael,
Mrs. Brill, and Robertson Ay
"Practically Perfect"* ....Mary Poppins, Jane, and Michael
"Jolly Holiday" † ....Bert, Mary Poppins, Jane, Michael, Neleus, and the Statues
"Cherry Tree Lane" (Reprise),
    "Being Mrs. Banks,"*
    "Jolly Holiday" (Reprise) ....George, Winifred, Jane, and Michael
"A Spoonful of Sugar" ....Mary Poppins, Jane, Michael, Robertson Ay, and Winifred
"Precision and Order"* ....Bank Chairman and the Bank Clerks
"A Man Has Dreams" † ....George Banks
"Feed the Birds" ....Bird Woman and Mary Poppins
"Supercalifragilisticexpialidocious" † ....Mary Poppins, Mrs. Corry, Bert, Jane,
Michael, Fannie, Annie, and Customers
"Temper, Temper"* ....Valentine, William, Mr. Punch, the Glamorous Doll, and other Toys
"Chim Chim Cher-ee" (Reprise) ....Bert and Mary Poppins

ACT II

"Cherry Tree Lane" (Reprise) ....Mrs. Brill, Michael, Jane, Winifred, Robertson Ay, and George
"Brimstone and Treacle" (Part 1)* ....Miss Andrew
"Let's Go Fly a Kite" ....Bert, Park Keeper, Jane, and Michael
"Cherry Tree Lane" (Reprise),
    "Being Mrs. Banks" (Reprise) ....George and Winifred
"Brimstone and Treacle" (Part 2) ....Mary Poppins and Miss Andrew
"Practically Perfect" (Reprise) ....Jane, Michael, and Mary Poppins
"Chim Chim Cher-ee" (Reprise) ....Bert
"Step in Time" † ....Bert, Mary Poppins, Jane, Michael, and the Sweeps
"A Man Has Dreams,"
    "A Spoonful of Sugar" (Reprise) ....George and Bert
"Anything Can Happen"* ....Jane, Michael, Mary Poppins, and the Company
"A Spoonful of Sugar" (Reprise) ....Mary Poppins
"A Shooting Star" † ....Orchestra

* New Songs   † Adapted Songs

SONG CREDITS

"The Perfect Nanny," "A Spoonful of Sugar," "Feed the Birds," "Let's Go Fly a Kite"
— written by Richard M. Sherman and Robert B. Sherman.

"Chim Chim Cher-ee," "Jolly Holiday," "A Man Has Dreams," "Supercalifragilisticexpialidocious,"
"Step in Time" — written by Richard M. Sherman and Robert B. Sherman,
with new material by George Stiles and Anthony Drewe.

"Cherry Tree Lane," "Practically Perfect," "Being Mrs. Banks," "Precision and Order," "Temper, Temper,"
"Brimstone and Treacle," "Anything Can Happen" — written by George Stiles and Anthony Drewe.

Glamorous Doll ....CATHERINE WALKER
Jack-In-A-Box ....SEAN McCOURT
Miss Andrew.................RUTH GOTTSCHALL

ENSEMBLE

ANN ARVIA, KRISTIN CARBONE,
ERIC HATCH, JAMES HINDMAN,
BRIAN LETENDRE, MATT LOEHR,
TONY MANSKER, SEAN McCOURT,
JEFF METZLER, VASTHY E. MOMPOINT,
KATHLEEN NANNI, MEGAN OSTERHAUS,
T. OLIVER REID, DOMINIC ROBERTS,
JANELLE ANNE ROBINSON,
NICK SANCHEZ, LAURA SCHUTTER,
COREY SKAGGS, SHEKITRA STARKE,
CATHERINE WALKER, KEVIN SAMUAL YEE

SWINGS

PAM BRADLEY, BRIAN COLLIER,
NICOLAS DROMARD, SUZANNE HYLENSKI,
ROMMY SANDHU, SARAH SOLIE

Statues, bank clerks, customers, toys, chimney
sweeps, lamp lighters and inhabitants of
Cherry Tree Lane played by members of the
company.

UNDERSTUDIES

Mary Poppins: KRISTIN CARBONE,
    MEGAN OSTERHAUS,
    CATHERINE WALKER
Bert: NICOLAS DROMARD, MATT LOEHR
George Banks: JAMES HINDMAN,
    SEAN McCOURT
Winifred Banks: KRISTIN CARBONE,
    MEGAN OSTERHAUS
Mrs. Brill: ANN ARVIA, PAM BRADLEY
Robertson Ay: BRIAN COLLIER,
    DOMINIC ROBERTS
Bird Woman: ANN ARVIA,
    JANELLE ANNE ROBINSON
Miss Andrew/Queen Victoria/Miss Smythe:
    ANN ARVIA, JANELLE ANNE ROBINSON
Admiral Boom/Bank Chairman:
    JAMES HINDMAN, SEAN McCOURT,
    COREY SKAGGS
Mrs. Corry: MEGAN OSTERHAUS, SARAH
    SOLIE
Katie Nanna: PAM BRADLEY,
    SUZANNE HYLENSKI, SARAH SOLIE
Miss Lark: PAM BRADLEY, LAURA SCHUTTER,
    SARAH SOLIE
Neleus: BRIAN COLLIER,
    NICOLAS DROMARD, ERIC HATCH,
    KEVIN SAMUAL YEE

Mary Poppins

Cast Continued

Von Hussler/Jack-in-a-Box:
  NICOLAS DROMARD, ROMMY SANDHU,
  COREY SKAGGS
Northbrook: NICOLAS DROMARD,
  JAMES HINDMAN
Policeman/Mr. Punch: NICOLAS DROMARD,
  SEAN McCOURT, ROMMY SANDHU
Park Keeper: NICOLAS DROMARD,
  TONY MANSKER, COREY SKAGGS
William: BRIAN COLLIER,
  NICOLAS DROMARD, ROMMY SANDHU
Valentine: BRIAN COLLIER,
  NICOLAS DROMARD
Glamorous Doll: SUZANNE HYLENSKI,
  SARAH SOLIE

DANCE CAPTAIN
ROMMY SANDHU
ASSISTANT DANCE CAPTAIN
SUZANNE HYLENSKI

ORCHESTRA
Conductor: BRAD HAAK
Associate Conductor/2nd Keyboard:
  KRISTEN BLODGETTE
Piano: MILTON GRANGER
Bass: PETER DONOVAN
Drums: DAVE RATAJCZAK
Percussion: DANIEL HASKINS
Guitar/Banjo/E-Bow: NATE BROWN
Horns: RUSSELL RIZNER,
  LAWRENCE DiBELLO
Trumpets: JOHN SHEPPARD, LOUIS HANZLIK
Trombone/Euphonium: MARC DONATELLE
Bass Trombone/Tuba: RANDY ANDOS
Clarinet: PAUL GARMENT
Oboe/English Horn: ALEXANDRA KNOLL
Flutes: BRIAN MILLER
Cello: STEPHANIE CUMMINS
Music Contractor: DAVID LAI

Ashley Brown as
Mary Poppins.

Photo by Joan Marcus

Ashley Brown
Mary Poppins

Gavin Lee
Bert

Daniel Jenkins
George Banks

Rebecca Luker
Winifred Banks

Jane Carr
Mrs. Brill

Cass Morgan
Bird Woman

Mark Price
Robertson Ay

Ruth Gottschall
*Miss Andrew,
Queen Victoria,
Miss Smythe*

Michael McCarty
*Admiral Boom,
Bank Chairman*

Nicole Bocchi
*Jane Banks
at certain
performances*

Kathryn Faughnan
*Jane Banks
at certain
performances*

Matthew Gumley
*Michael Banks
at certain
performances*

Henry Hodges
*Michael Banks
at certain
performances*

Jacob Levine
*Michael Banks
at certain
performances*

Devynn Pedell
*Jane Banks
at certain
performances*

Ann Arvia
Miss Lark, Ensemble

James Hindman
*Park Keeper,
Mr. Punch, Ensemble*

Brian Letendre
Neleus, Ensemble

Matt Loehr
*Northbrook,
Ensemble*

Sean McCourt
*Von Hussler,
Ensemble*

Mary Poppins

Janelle Anne
Robinson
*Mrs. Corry,
Ensemble*

Corey Skaggs
*Policeman,
Ensemble*

Pam Bradley
Swing

Kristin Carbone
Ensemble

Brian Collier
William, Swing

Nicolas Dromard
Swing

Eric Hatch
Ensemble

Suzanne Hylenski
*Swing, Assistant
Dance Captain*

Tony Mansker
Ensemble

Jeff Metzler
Swing

Vasthy E. Mompoint
Fannie, Ensemble

Kathleen Nanni
Ensemble

Megan Osterhaus
*Katie Nanna, Annie,
Ensemble*

T. Oliver Reid
William, Ensemble

Dominic Roberts
Valentine, Ensemble

Nick Sanchez
Ensemble

Rommy Sandhu
*Swing,
Dance Captain*

Laura Schutter
Ensemble

Sarah Solie
Swing

Shekitra Starke
Ensemble

Catherine Walker
*Glamorous Doll,
Ensemble*

Kevin Samual Yee
Ensemble

P.L. Travers
*Author of the
Mary Poppins
stories*

Cameron Mackintosh
*Producer &
Co-Creator*

Thomas Schumacher
Producer

Richard M. Sherman and Robert B. Sherman
Original Music & Lyrics

Julian Fellowes
Book

George Stiles
*New Songs,
Additional Music,
Dance & Vocal
Arrangements*

Anthony Drewe
*New Songs &
Additional Lyrics*

Richard Eyre
Director

Matthew Bourne
*Co-Director &
Choreographer*

Bob Crowley
*Scenic and Costume
Design*

Stephen Mear
Co-Choreographer

Howard Harrison
Lighting Designer

Mary Poppins

Steve Canyon
Kennedy
*Broadway Sound
Designer*

William David Brohn
Orchestrations

David Caddick
Music Supervisor

Brad Haak
Music Director

Naomi Donne
Makeup Designer

Angela Cobbin
Wig Creator

Geoffrey Garratt
*Associate
Choreographer*

Anthony Lyn
Associate Director

Tom Kosis
*Resident
Choreographer*

David Benken
Technical Director

Tara Rubin Casting
Casting

Eric B. Anthony
William, Ensemble

Nick Corley
*Park Keeper,
Ensemble*

Case Dillard
Ensemble

Regan Kays
Swing

Stephanie Kurtzuba
Swing

Mark Ledbetter
*Policeman,
Ensemble*

Melissa Lone
Ensemble

Jesse Nager
Ensemble

Alexandra Berro
Jane Banks

Lila Coogan
Jane Banks

Stephanie Kurtzuba
Swing

Daniel Marconi
Michael Banks

Jayne Paterson
Ensemble

Chad Seib
Swing

Jeff Steitzer
*Admiral Bloom,
Bank Chairman*

Mary Poppins

CREW

Front Row (L-R): Kevin Strohmeyer (Electrician), Joe Bivone (Props), Gary Wilner (Props), Joe Garvey (Electrician).

Second Row (L-R): Steven Stackle (Carpenter), Kurt Fischer (Sound), Bill Romanello (Sound), Marie Renee Foucher (Sound), Karen Zabinski (Sound).

Third Row (L-R): Gary Siebert (Wardrobe), Ginny Hounsell (Wardrobe), David Helck (Carpenter), Danny Caruso (Carpenter), Cody Siccardi (Carpenter).

Fourth Row (L-R): Michael Wilhoite (Assistant Stage Manager), Terry Alexander (Assistant Stage Manager), Alexis R. Prussack (Assistant Stage Manager), Valerie Lau-Kee Lai (Assistant Stage Manager), Jason Trubitt (Stage Manager), Mark Dobrow (Production Stage Manager).

Back Row (L-R): Carlos Martinez (Electrician), James Maloney (Production Electrician), Andy Catron (Electrician), Brad Robertson (Electrician), Al Manganaro (Electrician).

FRONT OF HOUSE STAFF

Front Row (L-R): Alex Metzler, Naomi Genece & son Brandon, Kenneth Miller (Guest Relations Manager).

Second Row (L-R): Carla Dawson, Cliff Herbst, Petol Weekes, Jeryl Costello.

Third Row (L-R): Alisa Schneider, Audrey Terrell, Bryan Lynch, Michael Gilbert.

Back Row (L-R): Kelli Bragdon, Jason Blanche, Kelly Flynn, Melissa Cabarcas.

SECURITY OFFICER
Belvin Williams

THE ORIGINAL FILM SCREENPLAY
FOR WALT DISNEY'S MARY POPPINS
BY BILL WALSH * DON DA GRADI

DESIGN CONSULTANT
TONY WALTON

STAFF FOR *MARY POPPINS*

COMPANY MANAGER ....DAVE EHLE
Production Associate ....Jeff Parvin
Assistant Company Manager ....Laura Eichholz
Show Accountant ....Joy Brown
Production Stage Manager ....Mark Dobrow
Stage Manager ....Jason Trubitt
Assistant Stage Managers ....Valerie Lau-Kee Lai,
Terence Orleans Alexander,
Michael Wilhoite
Dance Captain ....Rommy Sandhu
Assistant Dance Captain ....Suzanne Hylenski
Production Assistants ....Sarah Bierenbaum,
Will O'Hare, Thomas Recktenwald,
Verity Van Tassel

GENERAL PRESS REPRESENTATIVE
BONEAU/BRYAN-BROWN
Chris Boneau   Matt Polk   Susanne Tighe
Aaron Meier   Christine Olver

Associate Scenic Designer ....Bryan Johnson
Scenic Design Associate ....Rosalind Coombes
US Scenic Assistants ....Dan Kuchar,
Rachel Short Janocko,
Frank McCullough
UK Scenic Assistants ....Al Turner, Charles Quiggin,
Adam Wiltshire
Associate Costume Designer ....Christine Rowland
Associate Costume Designer .... Mitchell Bloom
Assistant Costume Designer ....Patrick Wiley
Assistant Costume Designer .... Rick Kelly
Associate Lighting Designer ....Daniel Walker
Assistant Lighting Designer .... Kristina Kloss
Lighting Programmer .... Rob Halliday
Associate Sound Designer ....John Shivers
Wig Creator ....Angela Cobbin
Illusions Designer ....Jim Steinmeyer
Technical Director .... David Benken
Scenic Production Supervisor ....Patrick Eviston
Assistant Technical Supervisor ....Rosemarie Palombo
Production Carpenter ....Drew Siccardi
Production Flyman .... Michael Corbett
Foy Flying Operator ....Raymond King
Automation ....Steve Stackle, David Helck
Carpenters ....Edward Ackerman, Frank Alter,
Fudie Carriocia, Tony Goncalves,
Raymond Ranellone, Brett Daley
Production Electrician ....James Maloney
Key Spot Operator........................Joseph P. Garvey
Lighting Console Operator ....Kevin Barry
Pyro Operator .... Kevin Strohmeyer
Automated Lighting Technician .... Andy Catron
Assistant Electricians .... Gregory Dunkin,
Carlos Martinez, Al Manganaro
Production Propman ....Victor Amerling
Assistant Propman .... Tim Abel
Props ....Joe Bivone, John Saye,
John Taccone, Gary Wilner

Mary Poppins

Production Sound Engineer .... Andrew Keister
Sound Engineer .... Kurt Fischer
Sound Engineer .... Marie Renee Foucher
Sound Assistant .... Bill Romanello, Karen Zabinski
Production Wardrobe Supervisor .... Helen Toth
Assistant Wardrobe Supervisor .... Abbey Rayburn
Dressers .... Richard Byron, Catherine Dee,
 Marjorie Denton, Russell Easley, Ron Fleming,
 Maya Hardin, Ginny Hounsell, Kyle LaColla,
 Janet Netzke, Tom Reiter, Elisa Richards,
 Erin Roth, Gary Seibert, Jean Steinline
Production Hair Supervisor .... Gary Martori
Hair Dept Assistants .... Chris Calabrese,
 Wanda Gregory, Kelly Reed
Production Makeup Supervisor .... Angela Johnson
UK Prop Coordinators .... Kathy Anders, Lisa Buckley
UK Wig Shop Assistant .... Beatrix Archer

Music Copyist .... Emily Grishman Music Preparation –
 Emily Grishman/Katharine Edmonds
Keyboard Programming .... Stuart Andrews

MUSIC COORDINATOR .... DAVID LAI

DIALECT & VOCAL COACH ... DEBORAH HECHT

Associate General Manager .... Alan Wasser
Production Co-Counsel .... F. Richard Pappas
Casting Directors .... Tara Rubin, Eric Woodall
Child Guardians .... Christina Huschle, Rick Plaugher
Children's Tutoring .... On Location Education,
 Muriel Kester
Physical Therapy .... Physioarts
Press Associates .... Adrian Bryan-Brown,
 Susanne Tighe, Jim Byk, Stephen Padla,
 Ian Bjorklund, Allison Houseworth,
 Brandi Cornwell, Linnae Petruzzelli,
 Adriana Douzos, Joe Perrotta, Juliana Hannett,
 Jessica Johnson, Heath Schwartz,
 Hector Hernandez, Kevin Jones, Amy Kass,
 Christine Olver, Danielle Crinnion
Advertising .... Serino Coyne, Inc
Web Design Consultant .... Joshua Noah
Production Photography .... Joan Marcus
Production Travel .... Jill L. Citron
Payroll Managers .... Cathy Guerra, Johnson West
Corporate Counsel .... Michael Rosenfeld

CREDITS

Scenery by Hudson Scenic, Inc.; Adirondack Studios, Inc.; Proof Productions, Inc.; Scenic Technologies, a division of Production Resource Group, LLC, New Windsor NY. Drops by Scenic Arts. Automation by Hudson Scenic, Inc. Lighting equipment by Hudson Sound & Light, LLC. Lighting truss by Showman Fabricators, Inc. Sound Equipment by Masque Sound. Projection equipment by Sound Associates Inc. Magic props by William Kennedy of Magic Effects. Props by The Spoon Group, LLC; Moonboots Productions Inc.; Russell Beck Studio Ltd. Costumes by Barbara Matera Ltd.; Parsons-Meares, Ltd.; Eric Winterling; Werner Russold; Studio Rouge; Seamless Costumes. Millinery by Rodney Gordon, Arnold Levine, Lynne Mackey Studio. Shoes by T.O. Dey. Shirts by Cego. Puppets by Puppet Heap. Flying by Foy. Ricola cough drops courtesy of Ricola USA, Inc. Emergen-C super energy booster provided by Alcer Corp. Makeup provided by M•A•C.

THANKS

Thanks to Marcus Hall Props, Claire Sanderson, James Ince and Sons, Great British Lighting, Bed Bazaar, The Wakefield Brush Company, Heron and Driver, Ivo and Kay Covney, Mike and Rosi Compton, Bebe Barrett, Charles Quiggin, Nicola Kileen Textiles, Carl Roberts Shaw, David Scotcher Interiors, Original Club Fenders Ltd., Lauren Pattison, Robert Tatad.

FOR CAMERON MACKINTOSH LIMITED

Directors .... Nicholas Allott
 Matthew Dalco
Associate Producer and Casting Director .... Trevor Jackson
Technical Director .... Nicolas Harris
Financial Controller .... Richard Knibb
General Manager .... Robert Noble
Production Administrator .... Darinka Nenadovic
Head of Marketing and Press .... Kendra Reid
Head of Musical Development .... Stephen Metcalfe
Production Associate .... Shidan Majidi

DISNEY THEATRICAL PRODUCTIONS

President .... Thomas Schumacher
SVP & General Manager .... Alan Levey
SVP, Managing Director & CFO .... David Schrader

Senior Vice President, Creative Affairs ..... Michele Steckler
Senior Vice President, International .... Ron Kollen
Vice President, Operations .... Dana Amendola
Vice President, Labor Relations .... Allan Frost
Vice President, Worldwide Publicity .... Joe Quenqua
Vice President, Domestic Touring .... Jack Eldon
Director, Domestic Touring .... Michael Buchanan
Vice President, Theatrical Licensing .... Steve Fickinger
Director, Casting & Development .. Jennifer Rudin Pearson
Director, Human Resources .... June Heindel
Manager, Labor Relations .... Stephanie Cheek
Manager, Human Resources .... Cynthia A. Young
Human Resources Representative .... Jewel Neal
Manager, Information Systems .... Scott Benedict
Senior Computer Support Analyst .... Kevin A. McGuire
Senior IT Support Analyst .... Andy Singh
IT/Business Analyst .... William Boudiette

Production

Executive Music Producer .... Chris Montan
Vice President, Physical Production .... John Tiggeloven
Senior Manager, Safety .... Canara Price
Manager, Physical Production .... Karl Chmielewski
Purchasing Manager .... Joseph Doughney
Staff Associate Designer .... Dennis W. Moyes
Dramaturg & Literary Manager .... Ken Cerniglia

Marketing

Vice President, Broadway .... Andrew Flatt
Vice President, International .... Fiona Thomas
Director, Broadway .... Kyle Young
Director, Education & Outreach .... Peter Avery
Senior Manager, Broadway .... Michele Groner
Website Manager .... Eric W. Kratzer
Media Asset Manager .... Cara L. Moccia
Assistant Manager, Communications .... Dana Torres
Assistant Manager, Promotions .... Craig Buckley

Sales

Director, National Sales .... Bryan Dockett
Manager, Group Sales .... Jacob Lloyd Kimbro
Manager, Sales & Ticketing .... Nick Falzon
Assistant Manager, Group Sales .... Juil Kim

Business and Legal Affairs

Senior Vice President .... Jonathan Olson
Vice President .... Robbin Kelley
Executive Director .... Harry S. Gold
Senior Counsel .... Seth Stuhl
Paralegal/Contract Administration .... Colleen Lober

Finance

Director .... Joe McClafferty
Senior Manager, Finance .... Dana James
Manager, Finance .... John Fajardo
Production Accountants .... Joy Brown, Nick Judge
Assistant Production Accountant .... Isander Rojas
Senior Financial Analyst .... Tatiana Bautista
Senior Analyst .... Liz Jurist

Controllership

Director, Accounting .... Leena Mathew
Senior Analysts .... Stephanie Badie,
 Mila Danilevich,
 Adrineh Ghoukassian
Analyst .... Ken Herrell

Administrative Staff

Dusty Bennett, Amy Caldamone, Lauren Daghini, Jessica Doina, Cristi Finn, Cristina Fornaris, Dayle Gruet, Gregory Hanoian, Jonathan Hanson, Jay Hollenback, Connie Jasper, Tom Kingsley, Kerry McGrath, Lisa Mitchell, Ryan Pears, Roberta Risafi, Colleen Rosati, Bridget Ruane, Kisha Santiago, David Scott, Jason Zammit

---

BUENA VISTA THEATRICAL
MERCHANDISE, L.L.C.

Vice President .... Steven Downing
Operations Manager .... Shawn Baker
Merchandise Manager .... Neil Markman
Associate Buyer .... Violet Burlaza
Assistant Manager, Inventory .... Suzanne Jakel
Retail Supervisor .... Michael Giammatteo
On-Site Retail Manager .... Keith Guralchuck
On-Site Assistant Retail Manager .... Scott Koonce

Disney Theatrical Productions • 1450 Broadway
New York, NY 10018

guestmail@disneytheatrical.com

STAFF FOR THE NEW AMSTERDAM THEATRE

Theatre Manager .... John M. Loiacono
Guest Services Manager .... Christopher Berger
Box Office Treasurer .... Helen Cullen
Assistant Treasurer .... Andrew Grennan
Chief Engineer .... Frank Gibbons
Engineer .... Dan Milan
Security Manager .... Carl Lembo
Head Usher .... Susan Linder
Lobby Refreshments .... Sweet Concessions
Special thanks .... Sgt. Arthur J. Smarsch,
 Det. Adam D'Amico

Mary Poppins
SCRAPBOOK

Correspondent: Cass Morgan, "Bird Woman"
Special Backstage Rituals: We are well into our second year here at The Poppins, and before this year's book goes to press, we will have said goodbye to fifteen original cast members, including all six of our original Banks children. We will have welcomed twenty new cast members (and we've already said goodbye to nine of them). Many tears have been shed and shaky farewell speeches given, to the strains of "Happy Trails," as the exiting actor signed the ceremonial umbrella. Each departure from the fourth-floor nursery has been especially hard. Our practically perfect child-wrangler Christina Huschle anticipated this and created the following text, accompanied by a very moving ceremony, to help celebrate the children's powerful connection to the show.

"Dearly Beloved, we are gathered here today to witness the final performance of (CHILD'S NAME) as "Jane/Michael" Banks in *Mary Poppins*. We will now honor the time you have spent here on the 4th Floor Nursery by retiring your headshot from the Cast Clock. This ceremony has been witnessed by Ashley Brown, our very own "Mary Poppins!" Have a practically perfect show! We won't forget you, (CHILD'S NAME)! We'll never forget!"

Christina came to NYC six years ago to work in journalism after graduating from the University of North Texas at Denton. She had a friend who was wrangling at *The Lion King* and so she began subbing there. She found she loved experiencing theatre from that perspective: "...like an actor but entrenched in backstage." Her mom was a grade school teacher, so she was comfortable around children. When she heard about the *Mary Poppins* gig, she jumped at the chance.

Shortly before each kid's final performance, as many of us as can fit cram ourselves into the fourth floor hallway. The departing child's picture is removed from the clock and pasted to a poster. The poster is signed, the script read by their counterpart sibling, and finally they are knighted with the Parrot umbrella by Mary Poppins herself. "I wanted to give them something beautiful on their last day, something they could all share, but also acknowledge the sadness."

A Family Show: Three babies have been born to company members: Calvin, Lillianna, and Rowan.

Extracurricular Activites: We added both a bowling team and a book club to our extracurricular activities this year, both of which were headed up by our Resident Principal Nerd, Dan Jenkins. So far we've read and discussed "Great Expectations," "Uncle Tom's Cabin," "Sense And Sensibility," "Dr. Jekyll And Mr. Hyde," "The Age Of Innocence," "East Of Eden," "Time And Again" and "The Brief and The Wondrous Life Of Oscar Wao." About the bowling team Dan said, "We have shirts and everything."

"Easter Bonnet" Sketch: Katie Nanni choreographed our skit, titled "Lazy River," and danced it with Brian Letendre.

1. (L-R): Kyle, Dan, Tom, Rebecca, Russell, Ron and Mark play the daily Uno game backstage. "There might be blood!"
2. Matthew Gumley (center) reads the farewell script as Kathryn Faughnan tries not to cry.
3. Child wrangler Christina Huschle.
4. Gavin Lee and Ashley Brown at the 2007 "Broadway Barks 9!" event.

Favorite Off-Site Gathering Place: Metro Marche is still packed with *Poppins* People on Sundays between shows.
Also: Jane is still having tea in her dressing room. Erin is still baking birthday cakes. The Uno game still rages in the bunker during "Step in Time" (see photo). The Candy Bag is ever-refilled.

Mauritius

First Preview: September 13, 2007. Opened: October 4, 2007.
Closed November 25, 2007 after 24 Previews and 61 Performances.

PLAYBILL

CAST
(in order of appearance)

Jackie ....ALISON PILL
Philip ....DYLAN BAKER
Dennis ....BOBBY CANNAVALE
Sterling ....F. MURRAY ABRAHAM
Mary ....KATIE FINNERAN

Stage Manager .... ELIZABETH MOLONEY

UNDERSTUDIES

For Dennis:
ROD BROGAN

For Jackie, Mary:
KATYA CAMPBELL

For Philip, Sterling:
ROBERT EMMET LUNNEY

BILTMORE THEATRE

Manhattan Theatre Club

Artistic Director
Lynne Meadow

Executive Producer
Barry Grove

Huntington Theatre Company

Artistic Director
Nicholas Martin

Managing Director
Michael Maso

Acting Artistic Director
2007-08 Season
Daniel Sullivan

Present

MAURITIUS

by
Theresa Rebeck

with

F. Murray Abraham   Dylan Baker   Bobby Cannavale
Katie Finneran   Alison Pill

Scenic Design
John Lee Beatty

Costume Design
Catherine Zuber

Lighting Design
Paul Gallo

Original Music & Sound Design
David Van Tieghem

Fight Director
Rick Sordelet

Production Stage Manager
Charles Means

Casting
David Caparelliotis

Directed by
Doug Hughes

General Manager
Florie Seery

Associate
Artistic Director/Programming
Paige Evans

Associate
Artistic Director/Production
Mandy Greenfield

Director of Marketing
Debra A. Waxman

Press Representatives
Boneau/Bryan-Brown

Production Manager
Kurt Gardner

Director of Casting
Nancy Piccione

Director of Development
Jill Turner Lloyd

Mauritius was developed at the Lark Play Development Center, New York City.
Mauritius was originally produced by the Huntington Theatre Company, Boston, Nicholas Martin, Artistic Director / Michael Maso, Managing Director.
Special thanks to the Harold and Mimi Steinberg Charitable Trust for supporting new American plays and musicals at Manhattan Theatre Club.
Special funding for this production was provided by The Blanche and Irving Laurie Foundation.
Manhattan Theatre Club wishes to express its appreciation to the Theatre Development Fund for its support of this production.

10/4/07

(L-R): Bobby Cannavale, Alison Pill and Dylan Baker.

Photo by Joan Marcus

Mauritius

F. Murray Abraham
Sterling

Dylan Baker
Philip

Bobby Cannavale
Dennis

Katie Finneran
Mary

Alison Pill
Jackie

Rod Brogan
u/s Dennis

Katya Campbell
u/s Jackie, Mary

Robert Emmet
Lunney
u/s Philip, Sterling

Theresa Rebeck
Playwright

Doug Hughes
Director

John Lee Beatty
Scenic Design

Catherine Zuber
Costume Design

Paul Gallo
Lighting Design

Rick Sordelet
Fight Director

Nicholas Martin
Artistic Director, Huntington Theatre Company

Michael Maso
Managing Director, Huntington Theatre Company

Lynne Meadow
Artistic Director, Manhattan Theatre Club, Inc.

Barry Grove
Executive Director, Manhattan Theatre Club, Inc.

Daniel Sullivan
Acting Artistic Director 2007-2008 Season, Manhattan Theatre Club, Inc.

FRONT OF HOUSE STAFF
Seated on Deck (L-R):
John Wyffels (Sweet Concessions Manager), Eric Dreier (Usher), Robert Allen (Engineer).

Seated at Desk:
Wendy Wright (Head Usher).

Standing First Row (L-R):
Patricia Polhill (Usher), Catherine Burke (Usher), Dinah Glorioso (Usher), James Clark (Sweet Concessions).

Standing Back Row (L-R):
Ed Brashear (Ticket Taker), Miranda Scopel (Asst. House Manager), Russ Ramsey (Theatre Manager), Jackson Ero (Usher), Lauren Frazer (MTC Intern).

Photo by Ben Strothmann

Mauritius

STAGE AND COMPANY MANAGEMENT
(L-R): Andrea Beukema (Production Assistant), Elizabeth Moloney (Stage Manager), Charles Means (Production Stage Manager), Seth Shepsle (Company Manager).

BOX OFFICE
(L-R): David Dillon (Box Office Treasurer) and Tevy Bradley (Assistant Box Office Treasurer).

CREW
Front Row (L-R): Charles Means (Production Stage Manager), Angie Simpson (Wardrobe Supervisor).

Second Row (L-R): Andrea Beukema (Production Assistant), Elizabeth Moloney (Stage Manager), Tracey Boone (Dresser), Seth Shepsle (Company Manager), Jane Masterson (Electrician).

Third Row (L-R): Tim Walters (Props), Marc Grimshaw (Apprentice), Lou Shapiro (Sound), Pat Murray (Automation).

Back Row (L-R): Jeff Dodson (Master Electrician), Andrew Sliwinski (Apprentice), Chris Wiggins (Head Carpenter).

Mauritius

Mauritius
SCRAPBOOK

Photos by Aubrey Reuben

1. Playwright Theresa Rebeck conducts an interview at the Biltmore Theatre on opening night.
2. (L-R): Co-stars Alison Pill and Bobby Cannavale at the opening night party at Bryant Park Grill.
3. Actor Dylan Baker at the party.
4. Outside the Biltmore Theatre for the premiere (L-R): guests Jerry Stiller, Ben Gazzara, Elke Gazzara and Gerald Schoenfeld.

Correspondent: Dylan Baker, "Philip"

Favorite Opening Night Gift: Mini-Photo albums from Mark (our Associate Director) documenting the entire rehearsal and tech process.

Most Exciting Celebrity Visitor: Murray's Oscar.

Which Actor Performed the Most Roles in This Show: Our hard-working understudies.

Actor Who Has Done the Most Shows in Their Career: F. Murray Abraham.

Special Backstage Rituals: Singing "Mauritius" to the tune of "Tradition." Preshow Pushups. Sundays in Fantasy Football Land in Bobby's & Dylan's dressing room.

Favorite In-Theatre Gathering Place: The house during fight call.

Favorite Off-Site Hangout: West Bank Cafe.

Favorite Snack Food: Goldfish, Dark Chocolate M&M's.

Mascot: Wally the Green Monster.

Memorable Ad-Lib: "Touching another person commits you."

Record Number of Cell Phone Rings: Three separate phones ringing during Act II.

Memorable Stage Door Fan Encounter: All the fans who think Andrea (our PA) is part of the cast.

Latest Audience Arrival: Final Scene in Act I (about five minutes until intermission) in the front row.

Catchphrases Only the Company Would Recognize: "There's no panties like show panties." "Schtamps!"

Favorite Moment During a Performance: One night, a special light for F. Murray Abraham wasn't on. It was supposed to illuminate his looking at the stamps for the first time. He paused, looked up as if to beseech God for a bit of help, (God of course being Chuck Means our SM) and God listened, the light shone, Murray nodded and went on.

Memorable Directorial Note(s): Our Harvard educated director, Doug Hughes, said to Alison Pill one afternoon: "Grab that verb out of his mouth and transmogrify!!" He also said: "I want to hear you throw around those philatelic phrases like Frisbees," "Are we having a Mandarin tea ceremony here?" and "If fisticuffs are your game, I'm your man!"

Company In-Jokes: "Walrus cloudy—now it's clear." Company Manager Free Zone. Let Bartlet Be Bartlet. Katie's One-Woman *Sweeney Todd*.

Nicknames: Bobby Valuables. Leo, Bartlet and Stockard. Wallace and Sherman. Bridgeeet.

Sweethearts within the Company: Alison and Beth and the 2007 Boston Red Sox.

Coolest Thing About Being in this Show: Working on Theresa Rebeck's Broadway debut.

Monty Python's Spamalot

First Preview: February 14, 2005. Opened: March 17, 2005.
Still running as of May 31, 2008.

PLAYBILL®

CAST OF CHARACTERS

(in order of appearance)

Historian, Not Dead Fred, French Guard,
   Minstrel, Prince Herbert ......TOM DECKMAN
Mayor, Patsy, Guard 2 ....DAVID HIBBARD
King Arthur...................JONATHAN HADARY
Sir Robin, Guard 1,
   Brother Maynard ....CLAY AIKEN
Sir Lancelot, The French Taunter, Knight of Ni,
   Tim the Enchanter ....RICK HOLMES
Sir Dennis Galahad, The Black Knight,
   Prince Herbert's
   Father...................CHRISTOPHER SIEBER
Dennis's Mother, Sir Bedevere,
   Concorde ....BRAD OSCAR
The Lady
   of the Lake ....HANNAH WADDINGHAM
Sir Not Appearing, Monk.........KEVIN COVERT
Nun ....MATTHEW CROWLE
God ....JOHN CLEESE
French Guards ....THOMAS CANNIZZARO,
                     GREG REUTER
Minstrels ....BRAD BRADLEY, EMILY HSU,
                     GREG REUTER
Sir Bors ....BRAD BRADLEY

ENSEMBLE

BRAD BRADLEY, THOMAS CANNIZZARO,
KEVIN COVERT, MATTHEW CROWLE,
JENNY HILL, EMILY HSU,
BRIAN J. MARCUM, ABBEY O'BRIEN,
ARIEL REID, GREG REUTER,
VANESSA SONON, BRANDI WOOTEN

Continued on next page

⑤ SAM S. SHUBERT THEATRE
225 West 44th Street
A Shubert Organization Theatre
Gerald Schoenfeld, *Chairman*   Philip J. Smith, *President*

Robert E. Wankel, *Executive Vice President*

Boyett Ostar Productions The Shubert Organization
Arielle Tepper Stephanie McClelland/Lawrence Horowitz Elan V. McAllister/Allan S. Gordon
Independent Presenters Network Roy Furman GRS Associates
Jam Theatricals TGA Entertainment Live Nation

present

Monty Python's

SPAMALOT

Book & Lyrics by   Music by
Eric Idle   **John Du Prez & Eric Idle**

A new musical lovingly *ripped off from the motion picture*
"Monty Python and the Holy Grail"
from the original screenplay by
Graham Chapman, John Cleese, Terry Gilliam, Eric Idle, Terry Jones, Michael Palin

starring

Jonathan Hadary   Hannah Waddingham

Clay Aiken

also starring

Tom Deckman   Rick Holmes   David Hibbard   Brad Oscar

with

Brad Bradley Thomas Cannizzaro Callie Carter Kevin Covert Matthew Crowle
Jenny Hill Anthony Holds Emily Hsu Beth Johnson James Ludwig Brian J. Marcum Abbey O'Brien
Ariel Reid Pamela Remler Greg Reuter Vanessa Sonon Rick Spaans Lee A. Wilkins Brandi Wooten

and

Christopher Sieber

Set & Costume Design by	Lighting Design by
Tim Hatley	Hugh Vanstone

Sound Design by	Hair & Wig Design by	Special Effects Design by	Projection Design by
Acme Sound Partners	David Brian Brown	Gregory Meeh	Elaine J. McCarthy

Music Director/Vocal Arrangements	Orchestrations by	Music Arrangements by	Music Coordinator
Todd Ellison	Larry Hochman	Glen Kelly	Michael Keller

Associate Director	Associate Choreographer	Production Stage Manager
Peter Lawrence	Darlene Wilson	Mahlon Kruse

Casting	Press Representative	Marketing
Tara Rubin Casting	Boneau/Bryan-Brown	HHC Marketing

General Management	Production Management	Associate Producers
101 Productions, Ltd.	Gene O'Donovan	Randi Grossman Tisch/Avnet Financial

Choreography by
Casey Nicholaw

Directed by
Mike Nichols

GRAMMY® - WINNING CAST ALBUM
AVAILABLE ON DECCA BROADWAY

LIVE BROADWAY

1/18/08

Clay Aiken as Sir Robin.

Photo by Joan Marcus

(L-R): Christopher Sieber and Hannah Waddingham.

Photo by Catherine Ashmore

Monty Python's Spamalot

SCENES & MUSICAL NUMBERS

ACT I

Overture
Scene 1: The Mighty Portcullis
Scene 2: Moose Village
"Fisch Schlapping Song" ....Historian, Mayor, Villagers
Scene 3: Mud Castle
"King Arthur's Song" ....King Arthur, Patsy
Scene 4: Plague Village
"I Am Not Dead Yet" ....Not Dead Fred, Lance, Robin and Bodies
Scene 5: Mud Village
Scene 6: The Lady of the Lake and The Laker Girls
"Come With Me" ....King Arthur, Lady of the Lake and Laker Girls
"The Song That Goes Like This" ....Sir Galahad and Lady of the Lake
Scene 7: The Knights
"All for One" ....King Arthur, Patsy, Sir Robin, Sir Lancelot,
Sir Galahad and Sir Bedevere
Scene 8: Camelot
"Knights of the Round Table" ....Lady of the Lake, King Arthur, Patsy,
Sir Robin, Sir Lancelot, Sir Galahad,
Sir Bedevere and The Camelot Dancers
"The Song That Goes Like This (Reprise)" ....Lady of the Lake
Scene 9: The Feet of God
Scene 10: Find Your Grail
"Find Your Grail" ....Lady of the Lake, King Arthur, Patsy, Sir Robin,
Sir Lancelot, Sir Galahad, Sir Bedevere,
Knights and Grail Girls
Scene 11: The French Castle
"Run Away" ....French Taunters, King Arthur, Patsy, Sir Robin,
Sir Lancelot, Sir Galahad, Sir Bedevere,
French Guards and French Citizens

ACT II

Scene 1: The Mighty Portcullis
Scene 2: A Very Expensive Forest
"Always Look on the Bright Side of Life" ....Patsy, King Arthur, Knights
and The Knights of Ni
Scene 3: Sir Robin and His Minstrels
"Brave Sir Robin" ....Sir Robin and Minstrels
Scene 4: The Black Knight
Scene 5: Another Part of the Very Expensive Forest
"You Won't Succeed on Broadway" ....Sir Robin and Ensemble
Scene 6: A Hole in the Universe
"The Diva's Lament" ....Lady of the Lake
Scene 7: Prince Herbert's Chamber
"Where Are You?" ....Prince Herbert
"Here Are You" ....Prince Herbert
"His Name Is Lancelot" ....Sir Lancelot, Prince Herbert and Ensemble
Scene 8: Yet Another Part of the Very Expensive Forest
"I'm All Alone" ....King Arthur, Patsy and Knights
"The Song That Goes Like This (Reprise)" ....Lady of the Lake and King Arthur
Scene 9: The Killer Rabbit
"The Holy Grail" ....King Arthur, Patsy, Sir Robin, Sir Lancelot,
Sir Galahad, Sir Bedevere and Knights
Finale
"Find Your Grail Finale - Medley" ....The Company

Cast Continued

STANDBYS
JAMES LUDWIG
ANTHONY HOLDS

UNDERSTUDIES
BRAD BRADLEY, THOMAS CANNIZZARO,
MATTHEW CROWLE, JENNY HILL,
EMILY HSU, GREG REUTER, LEE A. WILKINS

SWINGS
CALLIE CARTER, BETH JOHNSON,
PAMELA REMLER, RICK SPAANS,
LEE A. WILKINS

DANCE CAPTAINS
PAMELA REMLER, LEE A. WILKINS

Hannah Waddingham is appearing with the
permission of Actors' Equity Association
pursuant to an exchange program between American
Equity and UK Equity. The producers gratefully
acknowledge Actors' Equity Association for its
assistance of this production.

ORCHESTRA
Conductor: TODD ELLISON
Associate Conductor: ETHYL WILL
Assistant Conductor: ANTONY GERALIS
Concertmaster: ANN LABIN
Violins: MAURA GIANNINI, MING YEH
Viola: RICHARD BRICE
Cello: DIANE BARERE
Reeds: KEN DYBISZ, ALDEN BANTA
Lead Trumpet: CRAIG JOHNSON
Trumpet: ANTHONY GORRUSO
Trombone: MARK PATTERSON
French Horn: ZOHAR SCHONDORF
Keyboard 1: ETHYL WILL
Keyboard 2 and Accordion: ANTONY GERALIS
Guitars: SCOTT KUNEY
Bass: DAVE KUHN
Drums: SEAN McDANIEL
Percussion: DAVE MANCUSO

Music Coordinator: MICHAEL KELLER
Music Copying:
EMILY GRISHMAN MUSIC PREPARATION/
EMILY GRISHMAN, KATHARINE EDMONDS

Monty Python's Spamalot

Jonathan Hadary
King Arthur

Hannah Waddingham
The Lady of the Lake

Clay Aiken
Sir Robin, Guard 1, Brother Maynard

Christopher Sieber
Sir Dennis Galahad, The Black Knight, Prince Herbert's Father

Tom Deckman
Historian, Not Dead Fred, French Guard, Minstrel, Prince Herbert

Rick Holmes
Sir Lancelot, The French Taunter, Knight of Ni, Tim the Enchanter

David Hibbard
Mayor, Patsy, Guard 2

Brad Oscar
Dennis's Mother, Sir Bedevere, Concorde

Brad Bradley
Minstrel, Sir Bors, Ensemble

Thomas Cannizzaro
French Guard, Ensemble

Callie Carter
Swing

John Cleese
God

Kevin Covert
Sir Not Appearing, Monk, Ensemble

Matthew Crowle
Nun, Ensemble

Jenny Hill
Ensemble

Anthony Holds
Standby

Emily Hsu
Minstrel, Ensemble

Beth Johnson
Swing

James Ludwig
Standby

Brian J. Marcum
Ensemble

Abbey O'Brien
Ensemble

Ariel Reid
Ensemble

Pamela Remler
Swing, Dance Captain

Greg Reuter
French Guard, Minstrel, Ensemble, Fight Captain

Vanessa Sonon
Ensemble

Rick Spaans
Swing

Lee A. Wilkins
Swing, Assistant Dance Captain

Brandi Wooten
Ensemble

Eric Idle and John Du Prez
Book, Lyrics and Music; Composer

Mike Nichols
Director

Casey Nicholaw
Choreographer

Tim Hatley
Set & Costume Design

Hugh Vanstone
Lighting Design

Monty Python's Spamalot

Tom Clark, Mark Menard and Nevin Steinberg,
Acme Sound Partners
Sound Design

David Brian Brown
Wig & Hair Design

Gregory Meeh
Special Effects Design

Todd Ellison
Musical Director/ Vocal Arranger

Larry Hochman
Orchestrations

Michael Keller
Music Coordinator

Peter Lawrence
Associate Director

Tara Rubin Casting
Casting

Bill Haber,
OSTAR Enterprises
Producer

Bob Boyett
Producer

Gerald G. Schoenfeld,
Chairman,
The Shubert Organization
Producer

Philip J. Smith,
President,
The Shubert Organization
Producer

Arielle Tepper
Producer

Stephanie P. McClelland
Producer

Lawrence Horowitz, M.D.
Producer

Elan V. McAllister
Producer

Allan S. Gordon
Producer

Roy Furman
Producer

Morton Swinsky,
GRS Associates
Producer

Arny Granat,
Jam Theatricals
Producer

Steve Traxler,
Jam Theatricals
Producer

Steve Tisch,
Tisch-Avnet Financial
Associate Producer

Jon Avnet,
Tisch-Avnet Financial
Associate Producer

Lewis Cleale
Sir Dennis Galahad, The Black Knight, Prince Herbert's Father

Jennifer Frankel
Ensemble

Napiera Groves
Standby

Chris Hoch
Standby

Kristie Kerwin
Swing

Jeffrey Kuhn
Dennis's Mother, Sir Bedevere, Concorde

Gavin Lodge
Sir Not Appearing, Monk, Ensemble

Marin Mazzie
The Lady of the Lake

Michael McGrath
Mayor, Patsy, Guard 2

Martin Moran
Sir Robin, Guard 1, Brother Maynard

Monty Python's Spamalot

Robert Petkoff
Sir Robin, Guard 1,
Brother Maynard

Scott Taylor
Ensemble,
Dance Captain

Jonathan Brody
French Guard,
Ensemble

Bradley Dean
Sir Dennis Galahad,
The Black Knight,
Prince Herbert's
Father

Andrew Fitch
Ensemble

Kristie Kerwin
Swing

Gavin Lodge
French Guard,
Minstrel

Michael O'Donnell
Standby

Robert Petkoff
Sir Robin, Guard 1,
Brother Maynard

Photo by Ben Strothmann

CREW

Front Row (Seated, L-R): Rick Caroto, Mary Kay Yezerski-Bondoc, Sheri K. Turner, Chad Lewis, Frank Lombardi, Theresa MacDonnell, Sonya Wysocki, Jenny Barnes, Randy Morrison, Gary Fernandez, Rose Alaio

Second Row (Kneeling, L-R): Craig Johnson, Ron Mack, Mike LoBue, Shannon D. Quinones, Jim Woolley, Meredith Benson, Shannon MacDowell, Antony Geralis, Carli Beardsley, Douglas Eark, James A. Roy, Linda Lee, Tim Altman

Third Row (L-R): Anthony Gurrouso, Alden Banta, John Cullen, Carl Keator, Ann Labin, Dave Kuhn, Tim Albright, Ken Dybisz, Scott Kuney, John Dory, John Kenny, James Spradling

Back Row (L-R): Bones Malone, Jeremy Wahlers, James Cariot, Tommy Manoy, Joe Manoy, Robert Miller, Hank Hale, Cavan Jones, Andrea Roberts, Roy Franks, Adam Bair

Monty Python's Spamalot

FRONT OF HOUSE STAFF
Front Row (L-R): Kathleen Benoit, Nathaniel Wright, Paul Rodriguez, Erin O'Donnell

Second Row (L-R): Giovanni LaDuke, Delia Pozo, Joanne Blessington, Maura Gaynor

Third Row (L-R): Michael Harris, Tommy Vance, Tomas Ortiz, Luis Rodriguez, Alexis Stewart

Fourth Row (L-R): Melvin Caban, Elvis Caban, Aspacia Savas, Susan Maxwell

Back Row (L-R): Matt Bosco, Lee Leaseburge, Stephen Ivelja

BOX OFFICE
Craig Bowley

STAFF FOR *SPAMALOT*

GENERAL MANAGEMENT
101 PRODUCTIONS, LTD.
Wendy Orshan Jeffrey M. Wilson
David Auster

COMPANY MANAGER
Edward Nelson

GENERAL PRESS REPRESENTATIVE
BONEAU/BRYAN-BROWN
Adrian Bryan-Brown   Jackie Green
Aaron Meier   Juliana Hannett
Christine Olver

CASTING
TARA RUBIN CASTING
Tara Rubin, CSA, Eric Woodall, CSA
Laura Schutzel, CSA, Merri Sugarman, CSA
Rebecca Carfagna, Paige Blansfield, Dale Brown

PRODUCTION MANAGEMENT
AURORA PRODUCTIONS, INC.
Gene O'Donovan
W. Benjamin Heller II   Bethany Weinstein
Melissa Mazdra   Hilary Austin

Fight Director ....**David DeBesse**

Make-Up Designer ....**Joseph A. Campayno**

Production Stage Manager ....Frank Lombardi
Stage Manager ....Sheri K. Turner

Stage Managers ....Chad Lewis, Allison Lee
Associate Company Manager ....Katharine Croke
Dance Supervisor ....Scott Taylor
Dance Captain ....Pamela Remler
Assistant Dance Captain ....Lee A. Wilkins
Fight Captain ....Greg Reuter
Assistant to Mike Nichols ....Colleen O'Donnell
Associate Scenic Designer ....Paul Weimer
Assistant Scenic Designers ....Raul Abrego,
Derek Stenborg
UK Assistant Designer ....Andy Edwards
Associate Costume Designer ....Scott Traugott
Costume Associate ....Ilona Somogyi
Assistant Costume Designers ....Cory Ching,
Robert J. Martin
Costume Assistant ....Jessica Wegener
Magic Consultant ....Marshall Magoon
Puppetry Consultant ....Michael Curry
Associate Lighting Designer ....Philip S. Rosenberg
Assistant Lighting Designer ....John Viesta
Moving Light Programmer ....Laura Frank
Assistant Sound Designer ....Sten Severson
Associate Special Effects Designer ....Vivien Leone
Associate Projection Designer ....Gareth Smith
Assistant Projection Designers ....Ariel Sachter-Zeltzer,
Jake Pinholster
Projection Programmers ....Randy Briggs,
Paul Vershbow
Projection Illustrator ....Juliann E. Kroboth
Production Carpenter ....Michael Martinez
Assistant Carpenters ....Adam Bair, Bill Partello
Production Electrician ....Michael S. LoBue
Head Electrician ....Michael Hyman
Assistant Electricians ....Roy Frank, Karen Z. Hyman

Production Props Supervisor ....Will Sweeney
Assistant Props ....James Cariot
Props Shopper ....Maggie Kuypers
Production Sound Supervisor ....Bones Malone
Assistant Sound ....John Dory
Wardrobe Supervisor ....Linda Lee
Assistant Wardrobe Supervisor ....Sonya Wysocki
Dressers ....Carli Beardsley, Meredith Benson,
Douglas Earl, Ginene Licata, Nesreen Mahmoud,
Shannon McDowell, Shannon D. Quinones,
Andrea Roberts, James A. Roy, Keith Shaw
Hair Supervisor ....Susan Corrado
Assistant Hair Supervisor ....Ron Mack
Hairdresser ....Mary Kay Yezerski
Hair and Makeup Stylist ....Lisa Weiss
Vocal Coach ....Kate Wilson
Rehearsal Pianists....................Glen Kelly, Ethyl Will,
Antony Geralis
Rehearsal Drummer ....Sean McDaniel
Electronic Music Programming ....James Abbott
Production Associate ....Lisa Gilbar
Production Assistants ....Chad Lewis,
Mary Kathryn Flynt
Associate Producer
for Ostar Enterprises ....Rachel Neuburger
Executive Assistant to Mr. Haber ....Theresa Pisanelli
Assistant to Mr. Haber ....Kristen Jackson
Assistant to Mr. Boyett ....Diane Murphy
Assistant to Messrs. Granat & Traxler ....Katrine Heintz
Legal Counsel ....Lazarus & Harris LLP
Scott Lazarus, Esq.
Robert C. Harris, Esq.

Monty Python's Spamalot

SCRAPBOOK

Correspondent: Hannah Waddingham, "Lady of the Lake."

Memorable Fan Letter: When I played the show in London I got a fan letter that was very gushing and complimentary. "I loved you, you were so good, I loved 'Find Your Grail,' blah blah blah." I thought, oh, isn't that nice! I didn't think to question the last line where it said, "And I particularly like it when you fly out over the audience." But then I started to think, "Wait, I don't fly out over the audience." I realized she must have sent the same letter to *Mary Poppins*, with a few references changed. She made a template, cheeky woman!

Most Exciting Celebrity Visitor and What They Did/Said: Glenn Close. She didn't come to see me, she came to see Clay Aiken. I had just joined the show and I didn't realize she was there until I came out to the water cooler for a drink.

When I saw her I did a quadruple take and spilled my water all over the floor. She came over to me and said, "I hear you're the new Lady of the Lake. I'm sure everybody will love you. Have a wonderful time in New York." I felt like I'd been ordained!

"Easter Bonnet" Sketch: Ours consisted of Clay Aiken and I singing "The Prayer" one night; Bradley Dean and I the next. We sang it very seriously while Lee Wilkins, dressed as The Flying Nun, rolled around us on roller skates.

Actor Who Performs the Most Roles in This Show: Rick Holmes plays four: Lancelot, French Taunter, Tim the Enchanter, The Knight of Ni.

Special Backstage Rituals: Every night before "Finland," Lee Wilkins (the flying nun) knocks on the floor. At the end of the show, during curtain calls, he knocks again. Also, Jenny Hill will not open the quick-change curtain

backstage. She and Ariel Reid come off together and Ariel opens it for her. The one time she didn't, Jenny fell over on stage.

Favorite Moment During Each Performance: Mine is "Bright Side." The boys are extraordinary dancers, both here and in London. It's proper musical theatre, taking you somewhere and making you smile. If I'm feeling tired or anything, I watch it from the wings and it always makes me feel better.

Favorite Therapies: I do a lot of Pilates. Vocally, we don't have Mucinex in London so I'll be bringing a case of that back with me. A doctor here recommended putting a little bit of Gatorade or Smart Water in my water bottle to keep up the electrolytes. When my voice is feeling raw my dresser puts a teaspoon of Manuka honey in a bottle of warm water and it works wonders.

Accountant ....Rosenberg, Neuwirth, &
Kuchner, CPAs
Christopher Cacace
Comptroller ....Jana Jevnikar
Advertising ....Serino Coyne
Angelo Desimini, Tom Callahan,
Steve Knight
Marketing ....HHC Marketing
Hugh Hysell, Matt Sicoli, Michael Redman,
Chris Hall, Amanda Pekoe, Caitlin Strype
Marketing Interns ....Mandy Messina,
Alyssa Provenzano, Jennifer Scherer
101 Productions Director of Finance/
Marketing ....Elie Landau
Assistant to the General Manager ....John Vennema
101 Productions, Ltd. Staff ....Denys Baker,
Ashley Berman, Katharine Croke,
Sherra Johnston, Emily Lawson,
Heidi Neven, Kyle Pickles,
Mary Six Rupert
Press Associates ....Chris Boneau, Jim Byk,
Brandi Cornwell, Jackie Green,
Steven Padla, Matt Polk,
Susanne Tighe
Press Assistants ....Ian Bjorklund, Danielle Crinnion,
Adriana Douzos, Juliana Hannett,
Jessica Johnson, Kevin Jones,
Amy Kass, Joe Perrotta,
Linnae Petruzzelli, Matt Ross,
Heath Schwartz
Banking ....City National Bank/Anne McSweeney
Insurance ....DeWitt Stern, Inc./Jennifer Brown
Travel ....Altour International, Inc./Melissa Casal
Housing ....Road Rebel Entertainment Touring
Alison Muffitt
Opening Night Coordinator ....Tobak-Dantchik
Suzanne Tobak, Michael Lawrence
Physical Therapy ....PhysioArts/Jennifer Green
Orthopedist ....David S. Weiss, M.D.
Immigration ....Traffic Control Group, Inc./
David King
Theatre Displays ....King Displays, Inc.
Merchandising ....Max Merchandising, LLC/
Shopalot, LLC
Merchandise Manager.......................David Eck

Production Photographer ....Joan Marcus
Payroll Services ....Castellana Services, Inc.

Finnish program by Michael Palin

---

www.MontyPythonsSpamalot.com

CREDITS

Scenery and scenic automation by Hudson Scenic Studio, Inc. Additional scenery by Scenic Art Studios, Inc., Chicago Scenic Studios, Hawkeye Scenic Studios. Lighting equipment from Fourth Phase. Sound equipment from PRG Audio. Costumes executed by Barbara Matera Ltd.; Carelli Costumes; Euro Co Costumes; Parsons-Meares, Ltd.; Tricorne, Inc. Additional costumes by Costume Armour, Inc., John Kristiansen; Western Costumes. Shoes by T.O. Dey; LaDuca Shoes NYC; Capri Shoes; Capezio. Millinery by Lynne Mackey Studio, Rodney Gordon. Hair by Ray Marston Wig Studio Ltd., Bob Kelly Wig Creations. Selected makeup furnished by M•A•C. Props by The Spoon Group LLC; The Rabbit's Choice; Cigar Box Studios, Inc.; Costume Armour, Inc.; Jerard Studio; Gilbert Center; Margaret Cusack; Elizabeth Debbout; Erin Edmister; George Fenmore. Some specialty props and costumes furnished by Museum Replicas Inc. Piano from Ortigara's Musicville, Inc. Spamahorn created and provided by Dominic Derasse. Video projection system provided by Scharff-Weisberg, Inc. Video projection services by Vermillion Border Productions. Flying by Foy. Black Knight illusion executed by Entertainment Design & Fabrication. Spam cam and film furnished by Polaroid. Lozenges by Ricola.

SPAM® is a registered trademark of
Hormel Foods LLC.

Air travel consideration furnished by Orbitz®.

Housing consideration in NYC furnished by
Millennium Broadway, 145 W. 44th St., NYC.
Diarmaid O'Sullivan, Bernadette D'Arcy

All songs published by Rutsongs Music & Ocean Music Ltd., ©2004. All rights Reserved, except songs from Monty Python & the Holy Grail, published by EMI/Python

(Monty) Pictures as follows: "Finland," music and lyrics by Michael Palin; "Knights of the Round Table," music by Neil Innes, lyrics by Graham Chapman and John Cleese; "Brave Sir Robin," music by Neil Innes, lyrics by Eric Idle; and "Always Look on the Bright Side of Life," music and lyrics by Eric Idle from Life of Brian, published by Python (Monty) Pictures.

SPAMALOT
rehearsed at New 42nd Street Studios

SPECIAL THANKS
Bill Link, Devin Burgess,
Veronica DeMartini, John Malakoff

 THE SHUBERT ORGANIZATION, INC.
Board of Directors

Gerald Schoenfeld	**Philip J. Smith**
Chairman	President
Wyche Fowler, Jr.	**John W. Kluge**
Lee J. Seidler	**Michael I. Sovern**

Stuart Subotnick

Robert E. Wankel
Executive Vice President

Peter Entin	**Elliot Greene**
Vice President –	Vice President –
Theatre Operations	Finance
David Andrews	**John Darby**
Vice President –	Vice President –
Shubert Ticketing Services	Facilities

D.S. Moynihan
Vice President – Creative Projects

House Manager ....Brian Gaynair

Monty Python's Spamalot
SCRAPBOOK

Favorite In-Theatre Gathering Place: There's really no place backstage at the Shubert. It's quite crowded. While Clay was here my dressing room became the hangout place. We would sit and gossip to each other. It's the first one on the main level and it gets a lot of traffic. Jim Woolley redecorated it like a Barbie caravan home: pink curtains, lots of greenery and flowers, It's absolutely revolting—but I love it. It's like a 12-year-old's bedroom.

Favorite Off-Site Hangout: The Westway Diner on Ninth Avenue. Everyone goes there between shows because they have really good food.

Favorite Snack Foods: I'm completely addicted to lime Tostitos.

Mascot: We don't have one here in New York, but in London it was the cow and the company had a voting ceremony and named it Brian.

Memorable Ad-Libs: Rick Holmes plays the Knight of Ni and when he says, "We are no longer the knights who say 'Ni,' we are now the knights who say…," he makes up some marvelous new nonsense every night. During the time they were trying to get pop singer Amy Winehouse to go to rehab, he would go into a whole monologue as her: "They tried to make me go into rehab but I said no. They tried to make me sing at the Grammys and I said, 'Oh, all right then'." He would say it in her voice and it always made me laugh.

Technical Problem: In London, in the scene where I ride in the giant grail, I once got stuck when the grail was at the same height as the dress circle—you'd say the mezzanine. Everyone left the stage and there I was stuck up there with the audience looking at me. I said, "Hmm, hmm, hello! Talk amongst yourselves." Finally Chris Sieber, who was reprising his Broadway role in London, came out with some stagehands. They brought a ladder and Chris carried me down! In my next scene, which was "Diva's Lament," I milked it for all it was worth.

Memorable Press Encounter: The show asked Clay Aiken, Jonathan Hadary and I to take pictures of us in full costumes—but for some reason wearing 3D glasses. And I just thought, "Christ!"

Memorable Stage Door Fan Encounters: Clay Aiken's fans were very full-on but lovely. They were so embracing of the rest of us as well. Even after he left the show, I still get flowers and cookies from them, saying they liked me in the show as well.

Latest Audience Arrival: Somebody walked down front while I was singing. I stopped but she gestured with her hand as if to say, "Carry on," like your mum would do. Rude cow!

Fastest Costume Change: Clay, out of Robin into Brother Maynard in the space of just a few lines.

Busiest Day at the Box Office: Clay Aiken's opening and closing nights. I would liken them to Wembley Arena with Elvis in the building.

Memorable Directorial Note/Tale from a Put-In: During the put-in for Clay and me, Mike

Original cast member Michael McGrath (center) tries bravely to look happy as he and fellow cast members (L-R) Ariel Reid and Jennifer Frankel prepare to give away ice cream in Shubert Alley to celebrate the 1000th performance at the Shubert Theatre, August 9, 2007.

Nichols said, "Don't try to get laughs on every line. It's very cheap and it's like paying for sex: ultimately unsatisfying." There was slight hiatus and then all of us wet ourselves.

Another Tale from a Put-In: The next put-in was for Bradley Dean as Galahad. The only person who has to wear a costume during a put-in is the new person and Bradley was so embarrassed. So, to help, all of us dressed up in 1980s outfits: The boys all looked like something from *Flashdance* and the girls were all in leg warmers and hideously big dangly earrings. Great fun.

Who Wore the Heaviest/Hottest Costume: Without a doubt, I do. Every one is done in hand-beaded glass beads, so every one weighs a ton.

Who Wore the Least: Probably me as well, along with the girls in the Camelot scene. We have to wear see-through body stockings with sparkles. When I came to my first fitting they told me the girls usually wear a corset and underwear under it, but they wanted me not to wear anything but a bra and underpants—"a sparkly g-string" I believe they called it. I heard that and I knew I wouldn't be eating anything the whole time I'd be here.

Sweethearts Within the Company: In London two ensemble members are getting married.

Ghostly Encounters Backstage: There is a strange kind of slippery-slick spot on the floor upstage right. Jenny Hill, my understudy, told me that it's been there since somebody slipped and fell there years ago and nothing anybody does can get rid of it. In London we played at the Palace Theatre which has catacombs that go down into the earth four or five floor levels until

it comes to a small river. It seems the stage was raised several feet at one point and there is a ghost of a ballerina who appears on the stage—but you can only see her from the waist up because she's dancing on the old stage! Also at the Palace there is a ladder that goes up to the fly space. If you stand below it you feel a strange pressure, as if somebody doesn't want you standing near that ladder.

Superstitions That Turned Out To Be True: I've got a "Scottish Play" story. We were doing a production at the National Theatre in London and somebody said the name of the play while we were taking production photos. Well, when the photos came back not one person's face was visible! There was either a thumb over the person or a blurred spot or the picture was completely black.

Company Catchphrases: "Once upon a shime." In London, Chris Sieber and I were making our entrance on the boat to sing "The Song That Goes Like This" and he had a brain freeze. Instead of singing "Once in every show" he sang "Once upon a shime." He squeezed me so tightly that all the air came out of my body and we couldn't even look at each other for the rest of the song. Afterward we posted a sign on the level where his dressing room is, saying, "Once upon a shime."

Coolest Thing About Being in This Show: One of the wig people said the coolest thing is that we get out at a quarter past ten. Audiences get high satisfaction because it's so funny, but it's actually a comparatively short show. People start laughing from two seconds into the overture (when the trumpet player gets shot) all the way to the end because it's written so well.

A Moon for the Misbegotten

First Preview: March 29, 2007. Opened: April 9, 2007.
Closed June 10, 2007 after 13 Previews and 71 Performances.

PLAYBILL

CAST

(in order of appearance)

Josie Hogan ....EVE BEST
Mike Hogan ....EUGENE O'HARE
Phil Hogan ....COLM MEANEY
Jim Tyrone ....KEVIN SPACEY
T Stedman Harder ....BILLY CARTER

The action takes place in Connecticut,
September 1923.

UNDERSTUDIES

For Josie:
KATI BRAZDA

For Phil Hogan:
BILLY CARTER

For Mike, T Stedman Harder:
NICK WESTRATE

Eve Best, Billy Carter and Eugene O'Hare are appearing with the permission of Actors' Equity Association pursuant to an exchange program between American Equity and UK Equity.

⇥N⇤ BROOKS ATKINSON THEATRE
UNDER THE DIRECTION OF JAMES M. NEDERLANDER AND JAMES L. NEDERLANDER

Elliot Martin   Max Cooper   Ben Sprecher
Nica Burns   Max Weitzenhoffer   The Old Vic
Spring Sirkin   Wendy Federman   Louise Forlenza
Ian Osborne   Thomas Steven Perakos   James L. Nederlander

present

Eve Best   Kevin Spacey

in

The Old Vic Theatre Company
production of

A MOON FOR THE MISBEGOTTEN

by
Eugene O'Neill

also starring

Colm Meaney

with
Billy Carter and Eugene O'Hare

Costume Design Lynette Mauro	Lighting Design Mark Henderson	Sound Design Christopher Shutt	Sound System Design T. Richard Fitzgerald & Carl Casella
Original Music Dominic Muldowney	Casting Maggie Lunn	American Casting Stuart Howard Associates	Production Manager Brian Lynch
Production Stage Manager Bruce A. Hoover	Press Representative Barlow Hartman	General Manager Peter Bogyo	

Set Design
Bob Crowley

Directed by
Howard Davies

This production first performed at the Old Vic London on September 15, 2006, produced by The Old Vic, Elliot Martin, Nica Burns, Max Weitzenhoffer

6/10/07

(L-R): Eve Best and Kevin Spacey.

Photo by Simon Annand

A Moon for the Misbegotten

Eve Best
Josie Hogan

Kevin Spacey
*Jim Tyrone/
Artistic Director,
The Old Vic*

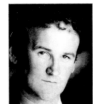
Colm Meaney
Phil Hogan

Billy Carter
T Stedman Harder

Eugene O'Hare
Mike Hogan

Kati Brazda
u/s Josie

Nick Westrate
u/s Mike, Harder

Eugene O'Neill
Playwright

Bob Crowley
Scenic Design

Mark Henderson
Lighting Design

Carl Casella
*Sound System
Design*

Brian Lynch/
Theatretech, Inc.
*Technical
Management*

Peter Bogyo
General Manager

Max Cooper
Producer

Ben Sprecher
Producer

Spring Sirkin
Producer

James L.
Nederlander
Producer

CREW
Front Row (L-R): Cyrille Blackburn (Production Assistant), Bernita Robinson (Stage Manager).
Back Row (L-R): Manuel Becker (Production Electrician), Joseph DePaulo (Production Properties), Yvonne Jensen (Dresser), Joseph Maher (Production Flyman), Kathleen Gallagher (Wardrobe Supervisor) and Wallace Flores (Production Sound).

A Moon for the Misbegotten

USHERS
Front theatre row (L-R): Barbara Carrellas (Theatre Manager) and Kimberlee Imperato (Usher).
Next theatre row (Seated, L-R): Marie Gonzalez (Usher), Michelle Gonzalez (Usher), Barbara Hart (Usher), Arlene Reilly (Usher).
Standing in the back row of the theatre (L-R): Diana Vidaic (Matron), Khadija Dib (Usher), Alexandra Kinter (Usher).

BOX OFFICE STAFF
(L-R): William O'Brien and Elaine Amplo.

STAFF LISTING FOR
A MOON FOR THE MISBEGOTTEN

GENERAL MANAGER
Peter Bogyo

GENERAL PRESS REPRESENTATIVE
BARLOW•HARTMAN, INC.

John Barlow   Michael Hartman
Dennis Crowley   Michelle Bergmann

COMPANY MANAGER
Mary Miller

PRODUCTION MANAGER
THEATRETECH, INC.
Brian Lynch

ORIGINAL LONDON LIGHTING DESIGN
Paule Constable

PRODUCTION STAGE MANAGER ...Bruce A. Hoover
Stage Manager ....Bernita Robinson
Production Assistant ....Cyrille Blackburn
Assistant Director ....Nathan Curry
Production Assistant to Elliot Martin ....Kristin Scafuri
Assistant to Ben Sprecher ....Michael Moss
Associate UK Set Designers ....Paul Atkinson,
                                           Alistair Turner
Associate U.S. Set Designer ....Bryan Johnson
Assistant Lighting Designer ....Daniel Walker
Associate Sound Designer ....Colin Pink
Production Carpenter ....Thomas A. LaVaia
Production Electrician ....Manuel Becker
Production Properties ....Joseph DePaulo
Production Sound ....Wallace Flores
Wardrobe Supervisor ....Kathleen Gallagher
Dresser ....Yvonne Jensen
Production
    Legal Counsel ....Robinson, Brog, Leinwand et al./
                                      Richard Ticktin, Esq.

Immigration Attorney ....Fragomen, Del Rey,
                                Bernsen & Loewy, LLP/
                          Freddi Weintraub, Susanah Wade
Insurance ....DeWitt Stern/Peter Shoemaker
Accountant ....Fried & Kowigos CPA's LLP/
                                           Robert Fried, CPA
Controller ....Galbraith & Company, Inc./
                                           Sarah Galbraith
Casting Consultant ....Marjorie Martin
Advertising ....Spotco/
                                  Drew Hodges, Jim Edwards,
                                 Dale Edwards, Peter Duffy
Production Photography ....Lorenzo Agius
Press Office Associates ....Leslie Baden,
                             Tom D'Ambrosio, Steve Dow,
                        Carol Fineman, Bethany Larsen, Ryan Ratelle,
                        Wayne Wolfe, Kevin Robak, Tom Prudenti
Theatre Displays ....BAM Signs, Inc./Adam Miller
Opening Night Coordination ....Broadway Parties/
                                Wendy Federman, Lisa Rice
Banking ....JP Morgan Chase/Michele Gibbons
Payroll Service ....CSI, Castellana Services Inc.
Car Service ....Broadway Trans, Inc./Ralph Taliercio
Rehearsal Space ....Manhattan Theatre Club

CREDITS
Scenery built and painted by Hudson Scenic Studios, Inc. Lighting equipment supplied by GSD Production Services, Inc., West Hempstead, NY. Sound equipment from Sound Associates, Inc. Costumes rented from Cosprop. Special thanks to Bra*Tenders for hosiery and undergarments.

THE
OLD VIC

Chief Executive ....Sally Greene
Artistic Director ....Kevin Spacey
Assistant Producer ....Simon Fliegner
Production Manager ....Dominic Fraser
Production Assistant ....Hamish Jenkinson
Finance Director ....Helen O'Donnell
Producer ....Kate Pakenham

Marketing Director ....Fiona Richards
Producer ....John Richardson
Managing Director ....Ann Samuel
New Voices Manager ....Rachael Stevens
Events Manager ....Tina Temple-Morris
Development Director ....Vivien Wallace
General Manager ....Dagmar Walz
Education Manager...........................Steve Winter
Associates ....Edward Hall, David Liddiment,
                            Anthony Page, Matthew Warchus

For Old Vic Productions plc
Administrator ....Becky Barber
Associate Producer ....Ros Povey
Producer ....Joseph Smith

For Nica Burns and Max Weitzenhoffer
Commercial Director ....Laurence Miller
Production Assistants ....Stephanie Creed,
                                           Jennie Jacques
U.S. Legal Counsel ....Nan Bases

Thanks to The Old Vic production team: Louise Askins, Annabel Bolton, Tracey Clarke, Stuart Crane, Alex Fox, PJ Holloway, Tom Humphrey, Olivia Kerslake, Fiona Lehmann, Claire Murphy, Jane Semark

≥N≤
NEDERLANDER

Chairman ....**James M. Nederlander**
President ....**James L. Nederlander**

Executive Vice President
Nick Scandalios

Vice President   Senior Vice President
Corporate Development   Labor Relations
Charlene S. Nederlander   **Herschel Waxman**

Vice President   Chief Financial Officer
Jim Boese   **Freida Sawyer Belviso**

November

First Preview: December 20, 2007. Opened: January 17, 2008.
Still running as of May 31, 2008.

CAST

(in order of appearance)

Charles Smith ....NATHAN LANE
Archer Brown ....DYLAN BAKER
A Representative of the National Association
   of Turkey By-Products
   Manufacturers ....ETHAN PHILLIPS
Clarice Bernstein ....LAURIE METCALF
Dwight Grackle ....MICHAEL NICHOLS

TIME
Morning, Night, Morning

SETTING
An Office

STANDBYS
Standby for Charles Smith:
RICHARD KLINE
Standby for Clarice Bernstein:
AMY HOHN
Standby for Archer Brown, Turkey Guy:
GREG STUHR
Standby for Dwight Grackle:
VICTOR TALMADGE

⑤ ETHEL BARRYMORE THEATRE
243 West 47th Street
A Shubert Organization Theatre
Gerald Schoenfeld, *Chairman*   **Philip J. Smith,** *President*

Robert E. Wankel, *Executive Vice President*

Jeffrey Richards   Jerry Frankel   Jam Theatricals

Bat-Barry Productions Michael Cohl Ergo Entertainment Michael Filerman
Ronald Frankel Barbara & Buddy Freitag James Fuld Jr. Roy Furman
JK Productions   Harold Thau   Jamie deRoy/Ted Snowdon

Present

Nathan Lane

Laurie Metcalf   Dylan Baker

In

NOVEMBER

By

David Mamet

With

Michael Nichols and **Ethan Phillips**

Scenic Design	Costume Design	Lighting Design
Scott Pask	**Laura Bauer**	**Paul Gallo**

Casting	Production Stage Manager	Technical Supervision
Telsey+Company	**Jill Cordle**	**Hudson Theatrical Associates**

General Management	Marketing Services	Company Manager
Richards/Climan, Inc.	**TMG The Marketing Group**	**Bruce Klinger**

Directed by

Joe Mantello

1/17/08

(L-R): Nathan Lane, Ethan Phillips and Dylan Baker.

Photo by Scott Landis

November

A MESSAGE FROM PRESIDENT SMITH

Laurie Metcalf as Clarice Bernstein.

Photo by Scott Landis

My Fellow Americans: It is with an understandable excess of those feelings associated with occasions of this kind that I address you today.

This country functions not only because of, but *in spite of* every man, woman and child legally within its borders. Those borders stretch from Canada, "Snow-Covered Landmass" to the North, down to "The Sleeping Giant on our Doorstep," Central and South America. Which were and continue to function not only as a "buffer," but, in many ways, as countries in their own right, shielding us from the incursions of a hostile world.

We must go forward, as part of a heritage of Faith which brought the pilgrims to our shore, fleeing oppression in the only way open to them at the time: ships.

Are we not equal in the sight of God?

If so, let petty differences disappear, in full-hearted endorsement of whatever programs I have been graced to envision. For "one hand full, with quietness," is, as we read in The Bible, better not only than "two hands full with strife," but than the benefits of so-called "free and fair elections."

A little child in Oregon said to me: "Mister President, be good to us...be kind," and pressed into my hand a crayon drawing of an ostrich. That drawing, today, rests in a place of honor on my desk – encased in Lucite, next to the coin which the *first* President threw across a river.

We *will* not be defeated. We must press on, looking neither to the right nor to the left, but looking forward – toward that day which even the most cynical among us must realize is The Future. Listen to your heart. That organ which we all share. There is a New Day dawning in America. Seven days a week.

Join with me and embrace it.

God bless you.
Charles H.P. Smith

Nathan Lane
Charles Smith

Laurie Metcalf
Clarice Bernstein

Dylan Baker
Archer Brown

Michael Nichols
Dwight Grackle

Ethan Phillips
Turkey Guy

Richard Kline
*Standby for
Charles Smith*

Amy Hohn
*Standby for
Clarice Bernstein*

Greg Stuhr
*Standby for
Archer Brown,
Turkey Guy*

Victor Talmadge
*Standby for
Dwight Grackle*

David Mamet
Playwright

Joe Mantello
Director

Scott Pask
Scenic Design

Laura Bauer
Costume Design

Paul Gallo
Lighting Design

November

Bernard Telsey,
Telsey + Company
Casting

Neil A. Mazzella,
Hudson Theatrical
Associates
*Technical
Supervision*

David R. Richards and Tamar Haimes,
Richards/Climan, Inc.
General Manager

Jeffrey Richards
Producer

Jerry Frankel
Producer

Arny Granat,
Jam Theatricals
Producer

Steve Traxler,
Jam Theatricals
Producer

Robert Masterson,
Bat-Barry
Productions
Producer

Donny Epstein,
Ergo Entertainment
Producer

Yeeshai Gross,
Ergo Entertainment
Producer

Elie Landau,
Ergo Entertainment
Producer

Michael Filerman
Producer

Barbara Freitag
Producer

James Fuld, Jr.
Producer

Roy Furman
Producer

Harold Thau
Producer

Jamie deRoy
Producer

Ted Snowdon
Producer

2007-2008 AWARD

OUTER CRITICS CIRCLE AWARD
Outstanding Featured Actress in a Play
(Laurie Metcalf)

CREW
Seated (L-R): Alejandro C. Galvez (Flyman), Jill Cordle (Production Stage
Manager)

Standing (L-R): Philip Feller (House Propertyman), Manny Diaz (House
Electrician), Rose Marie Cappelluti (Dresser), Ken Brown (Mr. Lane's
Dresser), Peter Condos (Doorman), Victor Verdejo (House Carpenter),
Neil Krasnow (Stage Manager), Erin Kennedy Lunsford (Hair Supervisor)

BARRYMORE THEATRE STAFF
Front Row (L-R): John Barbaretti (Ticket Taker), Alicia Califano, Dan Landon
(Manager), Dennis Scanlon, Aileen Kilburn

Back Row (L-R): Sandy Califano (Head Usher), John Cashman,
Sharon Moran, John Dancy, Michael Reilly

Photos by Ben Strothmann

November

MANAGEMENT
(L-R): Neil Krasnow (Stage Manager), Jill Cordle (Production Stage Manager), Bruce Klinger (Company Manager)

BOX OFFICE STAFF
(L-R): Robert Kelly, Bill Friendly

STAFF FOR *NOVEMBER*

GENERAL MANAGEMENT
RICHARDS/CLIMAN, INC.
David R. Richards   Tamar Haimes
Laura Janik Cronin

COMPANY MANAGER
BRUCE KLINGER

GENERAL PRESS REPRESENTATIVE
JEFFREY RICHARDS ASSOCIATES
IRENE GANDY / ELON RUTBERG

CASTING
TELSEY + COMPANY, C.S.A.
Bernie Telsey, Will Cantler, David Vaccari,
Bethany Knox, Craig Burns,
Tiffany Little Canfield, Rachel Hoffman,
Carrie Rosson, Justin Huff, Joe Langworth,
Bess Fifer, Patrick Goodwin

ASSISTANT PRODUCER
Noah Himmelstein

PRODUCTION STAGE MANAGER ....JILL CORDLE
TECHNICAL
    SUPERVISOR ....Hudson Theatrical Associates/
              Neil A. Mazzella, Sam Ellis, Irene Wang
Stage Manager ....Neil Krasnow
Assistant Director ....Stephanie Yankwitt
Assistant Set Designers ....Jeffrey Hinchee, Orit Carroll
Assistant Costume Designer ....Bobby Tilley
Associate Lighting Designer ....Phillip Rosenberg
Consultant ....Darron L. West
Assistant to Mr. West ....Matt Hubbs
Ladies' Wigs ....Paul Huntley
Men's Wigs ....Martial Corneville
General Management Associate ....Jeromy Smith
Production Assistant ....Nathan K. Claus

Production Carpenter ....Frank Illo
Production Electrician ....Jimmy Maloney
Production Props ....Denise J. Grillo
Wardrobe Supervisor ....Kristine Bellerud
Mr. Lane's Dresser ....Ken Brown
Dresser ....Rose Marie Cappelluti
Hair Supervisor ....Erin Kennedy Lunsford
Assistant to Mr. Lane ....Andrea Wolfson
Assistant to Mr. Mamet ....Pam Susemiehl
Assistant to Mr. Richards ....Noah Himmelstein
Assistant to Mr. Traxler ....Brandi Preston
Advertising ....Serino Coyne, Inc./
              Greg Corradetti, Tom Callahan
              Andrea Prince, Robert Jones
Marketing ....TMG – The Marketing Group/
              Tanya Grubich, Laura Matalon
              Victoria Cairl, Meghan Zaneski
Website Design/
    Internet Marketing ....Situation Marketing/
              Damian Bazadona, Chris Powers,
              Lisa Donnelly
Banking ................................J.P. Morgan Chase/
              Richard Callian, Margaret Wong
Accountants ....Fried & Kowgios, CPA's LLP,
              Robert Fried, CPA
Comptroller ....Elliott Aronstam, CPA
Legal Counsel ....Lazarus & Harris, LLP/
              Robert C. Harris, Esq.,
              Scott R. Lazarus, Esq.
Payroll ....CSI/Lance Castellana
Production Photographer ....Scott Landis
Merchandising ....George Fenmore/
             More Merchandising International
Company Mascots ....Lottie, Skye, Mabel,
              Maud and Bob

CREDITS
Scenery constructed by Hudson Scenic Studio Inc. Lighting equipment from PRG Lighting. *November* rehearsed at the New 42nd Street Studios. Natural herb cough drops courtesy of Ricola USA, Inc. Cellphone courtesy of Nokia. Desk accessories by Star Desk Pad Co., Inc. Johnny Walker Scotch used. Additional set and hand props courtesy of George Fenmore, Inc.

SPECIAL THANKS
David Hume Kennerly

---

www.NovemberThePlay.com

 THE SHUBERT ORGANIZATION, INC.
Board of Directors

Gerald Schoenfeld	**Philip J. Smith**
Chairman	President
Wyche Fowler, Jr.	**John W. Kluge**
Lee J. Seidler	**Michael I. Sovern**

Stuart Subotnick

Robert E. Wankel
Executive Vice President

Peter Entin	**Elliot Greene**
Vice President –	Vice President –
Theatre Operations	Finance
David Andrews	**John Darby**
Vice President –	Vice President –
Shubert Ticketing Services	Facilities

D.S. Moynihan
Vice President – Creative Projects

House Manager ....Dan Landon

November
SCRAPBOOK

Correspondent: Jill Cordle, Production Stage Manager

Opening Night Gifts: Lucite covered vintage "patriotic turkey" postcards.

Most Exciting Celebrity Visitor: Don Rickles

Who Has Done the Most Shows in Their Career: Nathan Lane

Favorite In-Theatre Gathering Place: Stage management office.

Favorite Snack Food: Chocolate.

Busiest Day at the Box Office: The week we broke the house record for a straight play at our theatre (Barrymore).

Nicknames: Daddy, Lloyd, Gidget

Coolest Thing About Being in This Show: We are a very happy company!!

An Amazing Fan Letter: This was not a fan letter, but it made us laugh!! "Dear Mr. Lane, Did you ever consider renaming your show F_ _ _? You use the word so much that your dialogue and humor is lost. You denigrate the office of President and make prejudicial remarks. Hopefully your next production will be on a par with your earlier ones. Sincerely, (name withheld)."

Photos by Aubrey Reuben

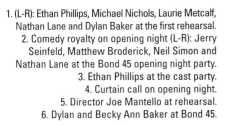

1. (L-R): Ethan Phillips, Michael Nichols, Laurie Metcalf, Nathan Lane and Dylan Baker at the first rehearsal.
2. Comedy royalty on opening night (L-R): Jerry Seinfeld, Matthew Broderick, Neil Simon and Nathan Lane at the Bond 45 opening night party.
3. Ethan Phillips at the cast party.
4. Curtain call on opening night.
5. Director Joe Mantello at rehearsal.
6. Dylan and Becky Ann Baker at Bond 45.

Old Acquaintance

First Preview: June 1, 2007. Opened: June 28, 2007.
Closed: August 19, 2007 after 31 previews and 61 performances.

PLAYBILL

CAST
(in order of appearance)

Katherine Markham	MARGARET COLIN
Rudd Kendall	COREY STOLL
Deirdre Drake	DIANE DAVIS
Karina	GORDANA RASHOVICH
Mildred Watson Drake	HARRIET HARRIS
Susan	CYNTHIA DARLOW
Preston Drake	STEPHEN BOGARDUS

TIME & PLACE

November-December 1940, New York City

Act 1
Katherine Markham's apartment in
Washington Square, November, 1940

Act 2
An apartment on Park Avenue, a month later

Act 3
Katherine Markham's apartment,
the following afternoon

UNDERSTUDIES

For Katherine: GORDANA RASHOVICH
For Mildred: CYNTHIA DARLOW
For Preston Drake, Rudd Kendall: TONY CARLIN
For Deirdre Drake, Karina, Susan: VIRGINIA KULL

Production Stage Manager: ROY HARRIS
Stage Manager: DENISE YANEY

AMERICAN AIRLINES THEATRE

ROUNDABOUT THEATRE COMPANY

Todd Haimes, Artistic Director
Harold Wolpert, Managing Director
Julia C. Levy, Executive Director

Presents

Margaret Colin   Harriet Harris

in

by

John van Druten

Stephen Bogardus   Diane Davis   Corey Stoll
Cynthia Darlow   Gordana Rashovich

Set Design Alexander Dodge	*Costume Design* David C. Woolard	*Lighting Design* Rui Rita	*Original Music & Sound Design* John Gromada

Hair & Wig Design Paul Huntley	*Dialect Coach* Deborah Hecht	*Production Stage Manager* Roy Harris

Casting Jim Carnahan, C.S.A.	*Technical Supervisor* Steve Beers	*General Manager* Sydney Beers	*Press Representative* Boneau/Bryan-Brown

Director of Marketing & *Sales Promotion* David B. Steffen	*Director of Development* Jeffory Lawson	*Founding Director* Gene Feist	*Associate Artistic Director* Scott Ellis

Directed by
Michael Wilson

Roundabout Theatre Company is a member of the League of Resident Theatres.
www.roundabouttheatre.org

6/28/07

(L-R): Harriet Harris and Margaret Colin.

Photo by Joan Marcus

Old Acquaintance

Margaret Colin
Katherine Markham

Harriet Harris
Mildred Watson Drake

Stephen Bogardus
Preston Drake

Diane Davis
Deirdre Drake

Corey Stoll
Rudd Kendall

Cynthia Darlow
Susan

Gordana Rashovich
Karina

Tony Carlin
u/s Preston Drake, Rudd Kendall

Virginia Kull
u/s Deirdre Drake, Karina, Susan

Alexander Dodge
Set Design

David C. Woolard
Costume Design

John Gromada
Original Music and Sound Design

Paul Huntley
Hair and Wig Design

Jim Carnahan
Casting

Gene Feist
Founding Director, Roundabout Theatre Company

Todd Haimes
Artistic Director, Roundabout Theatre Company

Photos by Ben Strothmann

CREW
Front Row (L-R): Melissa Crawford (Day Worker), Julie Hilimire (Dresser), Susan Fallon (Wardrobe Supervisor), Carmel Sheehan

Back Row (L-R): Andrew Forste (Running Properties/House Properties), Ben Barnes, Nichole Jennino (Company Manager), Victoria Grecki (Dresser), Dann Wojnar (Sound Engineer/Assistant Electrician), Glenn Merwede (Production Carpenter/House Carpenter), Brian Maiuri (Production Electrician/House Electrician), Barb Bartel (Moving Light Technician), Chris Mattingly (Flyman).

Not pictured: Brian Shumway (Deck Carpenter) and Nelson Vaughn (Deck Properties)

TICKET SERVICES
(L-R): Heather Siebert and Solangel Bido.

Old Acquaintance
SCRAPBOOK

Correspondent: Diane Davis, "Deirdre Drake"

Opening Night Gifts: I made a little storybook called "Deirdre Has Two Mommies" with pictures of the cast and gave copies to everyone. Director Michael Wilson gave us a little speech from John van Druten, quoting J.C. Squire's book "Playwright at Work": "Now I am a tin whistle, through which God blows. But I wish to God I were a trumpet. And why, God only knows." As gifts, we also got bottles of Champagne. Gordana Rashovich got us some great Marc Jacobs shirts.

Most Exciting Celebrity Visitor: Joan Rivers. She said she really liked it.

Who Has Done the Most Shows in Their Career: Either Harriet or Margaret, though I'm not sure which. They'd have to duke it out.

Special Backstage Rituals: Lots and lots of crosswords puzzles. Everyone from the stagehands to the actors does the *New York Times* crossword. Stage Manager Denise Yaney can do them all in the blink of an eye. We're pretty fierce about the Sundays; Corey Stoll and I work on them together.

Favorite In-Theatre Gathering Place: Corey's dressing room for the post-show cocktail when we are so inclined.

Favorite Off-Site Hangout: Angus McIndoe's is the spot.

Favorite Snack Food: Anything that Susan J. Fallon cooks, especially her birthday cakes. She made two incredible birthday cakes for Margaret. Denise makes some good deviled eggs. I make banana pudding. And Margaret keeps a supply of jelly beans.

Mascot: Corey's dog, a Shiba Inu named Iowa.

Favorite Therapy: Licorice Altoids.

Most Memorable Ad-Lib: Margaret was supposed to say, "You and Lucian," but she went up and it came out "Loo aloo baloo and loo."

Who Wore the Hottest Costume: We're all going crazy, considering that we're dressing for the winter in the middle of July. We all have to wear wool coats and hats and gloves.

1. (L-R): Stephen Bogardus, Diane Davis and director Michael Wilson at the American Airlines Theatre on opening night.
2. Curtain call at the premiere (L-R): Margaret Colin, Harriet Harris, Stephen Bogardus and Cynthia Darlow.

Who Wore the Least: Margaret wears a robe in one scene.

Catchphrase Only the Company Would Recognize: The Baby Panda Meter.

Memorable Directorial Note: Michael was giving Corey a note to react to my crying. He got up on stage and did some of the worst acting ever, wringing his hands and wiping his brow and going "Uh-uh-uh-uh-uh." We made a lot of fun of him for that. He also said at one point that Margaret had to "put her finger in the dike," meaning she had to stop the torrent. When we all laughed he said, "That's not what this play is about!"

Coolest Thing About Being in This Show: Just being on stage with those people.

Old Acquaintance

ADMINISTRATIVE STAFF

GENERAL MANAGER .... **Sydney Beers**

Associate Managing Director ....Greg Backstrom
General Manager, Steinberg Center ....Rebecca Habel
General Counsel ....Nancy Hirschmann
Human Resources Manager ....Stephen Deutsch
MIS Director ....Jeff Goodman
Assistant General Manager ....Maggie Cantrick
Management Associate ....Tania Camargo
Facilities Manager ....Abraham David
Manager of Corporate and Party Rentals ....Jetaun Dobbs
Office Manager ....Scott Kelly
Database Manager ....Dollye Evans
MIS Assistant ....Micah Kraybill
Receptionists ....Dena Beider, Raquel Castillo,
Elisa Papa, Allison Patrick,
Monica Sidorchuk
Messenger ....Darnell Franklin
Management Intern ....Erica Ruff

FINANCE STAFF

DIRECTOR OF FINANCE .... **Susan Neiman**

Assistant Controller ....John LaBarbera
Accounts Payable Administrator ....Frank Surdi
Financial Associate ....Yonit Kafka
Business Office Assistant ....Joshua Cohen
Business Interns ....Li Shen, Richard Patterson

DEVELOPMENT STAFF

DIRECTOR OF DEVELOPMENT ...... **Jeffory Lawson**

Director, Institutional Giving ....Julie K. D'Andrea
Director, Individual Giving ....Julia Lazarus
Director, Special Events ....Steve Schaeffer
Manager, Donor Information Systems ....Tina Mae Bishko
Corporate Relations Manager ....Sara Bensman
Manager, Individual Giving ....Kara Kandel
Telefundraising Manager ....Douglas Sutcliffe
External Affairs Associate ....Robert Weinstein
Institutional Giving Associate ....Sarah Krasnow
Individual Giving Associate ....Kate Bartoldus
Patrons Services Assistant ....John Haynes
Development Assistants ....Jillian Brewster,
Christopher Taggart
Special Events Assistant ....Ashley Firestone
Individual Giving Intern ....Ashley Turner

MARKETING STAFF

DIRECTOR OF MARKETING
AND SALES PROMOTION .... **David B. Steffen**

Marketing/Publications Manager .....Margaret Casagrande
Assistant Director of Marketing ....Sunil Ayyagari
Marketing Assistant ....Stefanie Schussel
Website Consultant ....Keith Powell Beyland

DIRECTOR OF TELESALES
SPECIAL PROMOTIONS .... **Daniel Weiss**

Telesales Manager ....Anton Borissov
Telesales Office Coordinator ...................J.W. Griffin
Marketing Intern ....Sari Abraham

TICKET SERVICES STAFF

DIRECTOR OF SALES OPERATIONS ..**Jim Seggelink**

Ticket Services Manager ....Ellen Holt
Subscription Manager ....Charlie Garbowski, Jr.
Box Office Managers ....Edward P. Osborne,
Andrew Clements
Group Sales Manager ....Jeff Monteith

Assistant Box Office Managers Krystin MacRitchie, Robert
Morgan, Nicole Nicholson
Assistant Ticket Services Managers ....Robert Kane,
Ethan Ubell, Carlos Morris
Customer Services Coordinator ....Trina Cox
Ticket Services ....Rachel Bauder, Solangel Bido,
Jacob Burstein-Stern, Lauren Cartelli,
David Carson, Joseph Clark,
Mike DePope, Nisha Dhruna,
Adam Elsberry, Lindsay Ericson,
Scott Falkowski, Catherine Fitzpatrick,
Katrina Foy, Daniel Gabriel,
James Graham, Tova Heller,
Nicki Ishmael, Bill Klemm,
Elisa Mala, Mead Margulies,
Chuck Migliaccio, Bekah Nutt,
Adam Owens, Ethan Paulini,
David Pittman, DeEanna Row,
Heather Siebert, Nalene Singh,
Lillian Soto, DJ Thacker,
Pam Unger, Thomas Walsh
Ticket Services Intern ....Hannah Weitzman

SERVICES

Counsel ....Paul, Weiss/Rifkind,
Wharton and Garrison LLP,
John Breglio, Deborah Hartnett
Counsel ....Rosenberg & Estis
Counsel ....Andrew Lance,
Gibson, Dunn, & Crutcher, LLP
Counsel ....Harry H. Weintraub,
Glick and Weintraub, P.C.
Immigration Counsel ....Mark D. Koestler and
Theodore Ruthizer
House Physicians ....Dr. Theodore Tyberg,
Dr. Lawrence Katz
House Dentist ....Neil Kanner, D.M.D.
Insurance ....DeWitt Stern Group, Inc.
Accountant ....Lutz & Carr CPAs, LLP
Sponsorship ....The Marketing Group/,
Tanya Grubich, Laura Matalon,
Anne Rippey, Erik Gensler
Advertising ....Eliran Murphy Group/
Denise Ganjou, Kara Eldridge
Events Photography ....Anita and Steve Shevett
Production Photographer ....Joan Marcus
Theatre Displays ....King Displays, Wayne Sapper

MANAGING DIRECTOR
EMERITUS ....Ellen Richard

Roundabout Theatre Company
231 West 39th Street, New York, NY 10018
(212) 719-9393.

GENERAL PRESS REPRESENTATIVES
Adrian Bryan-Brown
Matt Polk   Jessica Johnson   Amy Kass

STAFF FOR *OLD ACQUAINTANCE*
Company Manager ....Nichole Jennino
Production Stage Manager ....Roy Harris
Stage Manager ....Denise Yaney
Assistant Director ....Max Williams
Assistant Director/Dramaturg ....Ben West
Associate Scenic Designer ....Kevin Judge
Assistant Scenic Designer ....Robin Vest

Assistants to the Scenic Designer .... Kenichi Takahashi,
Andrew Layton
Assistant Sound Designers .... Daniel Baker,
David Stephen Baker
Assistant Lighting Designer ....Stephen Boulmetis
Assistant to the Lighting Designer ....Jake DeGroot
Assistant Costume Designer ....Daniele Hollywood
Assistant to the Costume Designer ....Angela Harner
Assistant Technical Supervisor ....Elisa Kuhar
Fight Coordinator ....Mark Olsen
Production Carpenter .... Glenn Merwede
Production Electrician .... Brian Maiuri
Running Properties ....Andrew Forste
Sound Engineer ....Dann Wojnar
Flyman ....Chris Mattingly
Deck Properties ....Nelson Vaughn
Deck Carpenters ....Brian Shumway, Jill Anania
Moving Light Technician ....Barb Bartel
Deck Electrician ....Jeff Rowland
Production Properties ....Kathy Fabian
Assistant Production Props
Coordinators ....Carrie Hash, Carrie Mossman
Wardrobe Supervisor ....Susan J. Fallon
Day Worker ....Melissa Crawford
Dressers ....Victoria Grecki, Julie Hilimire
Hair and Wig Supervisor ....Manuela LaPorte
Production Assistant ....Molly Eustis
Scenery Constructed by ....Global Scenic Services Inc.
and PRG Scenic Technologies,
a division of Production Resource Group, LLC,
New Windsor, NY
Lighting Equipment Provided by ....PRG Lighting
Costumes Constructed by ....Eric Winterling,
Studio Rouge,
Giliberto and Fur and Furgery
Millinery by ....Arnold Levine
Soft Goods and
Custom Drapery ....Mary Wilson, Anne Guay
Prop Fabricators ....Jen Lutz, Rose Howard
and Plumb Square
Flame Treatment Provided by ....Turning Star
Upholstery Provided by ....Joe's Fabric Warehouse
Special Thanks to ....Nadine Hettel,
Betty Hong Yiu Tung, Sara Sahin

AMERICAN AIRLINES THEATRE STAFF
House Carpenter ....Glenn Merwede
House Electrician ....Brian Maiuri
Assistant Electrician ....Dann Wojnar
House Properties..............................Andrew Forste
IA Apprentice ....Jill Anania
Wardrobe Supervisor ....Susan J. Fallon
Box Office Manager ....Ted Osborne
House Manager .... Steve Ryan
Associate House Manager .... Zipporah Aguasvivas
Head Usher .... Edwin Camacho
House Staff ....Ashley Blenman, Peter Breaden,
Ilia Diaz, Anne Ezell, Stephen Fontana,
Elsie Jamin-Maguire, Rebecca Knell,
Idair Melendez, Kimberly Oliver,
Jacklyn Rivera, Joe Vazquez
Security .... Julious Russell
Additional Security Provided by ....Gotham Security
Maintenance .... Willie Philips, John Sainz,
Madala Western
Lobby Refreshments .... Sweet Concessions

110 in the Shade

First Preview: April 13, 2007. Opened: May 9, 2007.
Closed July 29, 2007 after 27 Previews and 94 Performances.

CAST
(in order of appearance)

File ....CHRISTOPHER INNVAR
H.C. Curry ....JOHN CULLUM
Noah Curry ....CHRIS BUTLER
Jimmy Curry ....BOBBY STEGGERT
Lizzie Curry ....AUDRA McDONALD
Snookie ....CARLA DUREN
Starbuck ....STEVE KAZEE
Little Girl ....VALISIA LEKAE LITTLE
Clarence ....DARIUS NICHOLS
Townspeople
  Odetta Clark ....COLLEEN FITZPATRICK
  Vivian Lorraine
    Taylor ....VALISIA LEKAE LITTLE
  Clarence J. Taylor ....DARIUS NICHOLS
  Curjith (Curt)
    McGlaughlin ....DEVIN RICHARDS
  Reverend Clark ....MICHAEL SCOTT
  Cody Bridger ....WILL SWENSON
  Lily Ann Beasley ....ELISA VAN DUYNE
  Katheryn Brawner ....BETSY WOLFE

STUDIO 54

ROUNDABOUT THEATRE COMPANY

Todd Haimes, Artistic Director
Harold Wolpert, Managing Director
Julia C. Levy, Executive Director

Present

Audra McDonald

John Cullum   *in*   Steve Kazee

110 IN THE SHADE

Book by
N. Richard Nash

Music by
Harvey Schmidt

Lyrics by
Tom Jones

Based on a play by N. Richard Nash

Chris Butler Carla Duren Christopher Innvar Bobby Steggert
Elisa Van Duyne Colleen Fitzpatrick Valisia Lekae Little
Darius Nichols Mamie Parris Devin Richards
Michael Scott Will Swenson Matt Wall Betsy Wolfe

Set & Costume Design Santo Loquasto	*Lighting Design* Christopher Akerlind	*Sound Design* Dan Moses Schreier	*Hair and Wig Design* Tom Watson
Dance Music Arranged by David Krane	*Dialect Coach* Stephen Gabis	*Production Stage Manager* Peter Hanson	*Fight Director* Rick Sordelet
Casting Jim Carnahan, C.S.A.	*Technical Supervisor* Steve Beers	*General Manager* Sydney Beers	*Press Representative* Boneau/Bryan-Brown
Director of Marketing & *Sales Promotion* David B. Steffen	*Director of Development* Jeffory Lawson	*Founding Director* Gene Feist	*Associate Artistic Director* Scott Ellis

Orchestrations by Jonathan Tunick
Music Direction by Paul Gemignani
Choreographed by Dan Knechtges

Directed by Lonny Price

Lead support provided by Roundabout's Musical Theatre Fund partners:
Perry and Marty Granoff, The Kaplen Foundation, John and Gilda McGarry, Tom and Diane Tuft
Major support provided by JPMorgan Chase and The Blanche and Irving Laurie Foundation
Additional support provided by the National Endowment for the Arts

Roundabout Theatre Company is a member of the League of Resident Theatres. www.roundabouttheatre.org

7/29/07

(L-R): Steve Kazee and Audra McDonald.

Photo by Joan Marcus

Continued on next page

110 in the Shade

MUSICAL NUMBERS

Time: July 4, 1936
Place: Texas Panhandle

ACT I

Scene 1: Outside on the Prairie
"Another Hot Day"..File and Townspeople
Scene 2: The Curry Ranch
"Lizzie's Comin' Home"...H.C., Noah, Jimmy
"Love, Don't Turn Away"...Lizzie
Scene 3: File's Office
"Poker Polka"..File, H.C., Noah, Jimmy
Scene 4: The Picnic Grounds
"The Hungry Men"..Lizzie and Townspeople
"The Rain Song"..Starbuck and Townspeople
"You're Not Fooling Me"...Starbuck and Lizzie
"Cinderella"...Little Girl
"Raunchy"..Lizzie
"A Man and a Woman"..File and Lizzie
"Old Maid"..Lizzie

ACT II

Scene 1: Outside, twilight
"Evenin' Star"...Starbuck
Scene 2: Picnic Area
"Everything Beautiful"...Lizzie and Townspeople
Scene 3: Near Starbuck's Wagon
"Melisande"...Starbuck
"Simple Little Things"...Lizzie
Scene 4: Picnic Area
"Little Red Hat"..Jimmy and Snookie
Scene 5: Starbuck's Lean-to
"Is It Really Me?"..Lizzie
Scene 6: Picnic Area
"Wonderful Music"..Starbuck, File and Lizzie
"The Rain Song (Reprise)"..Townspeople

ORCHESTRA

Conductor:
PAUL GEMIGNANI
Associate Conductor:
MARK MITCHELL
Violins:
SYLVIA D'AVANZO, SEAN CARNEY
Viola:
JOSEPH GOTTESMAN
Cello:
ROGER SHELL
Flute/Piccolo:
SUSAN ROTHOLZ
Woodwinds:
RICK HECKMAN, ERIC WEIDMAN,
DON McGEEN
Trumpets:
DOMINIC DERASSE, MIKE PONELLA

Trombone:
BRUCE EIDEM
Harp:
JENNIFER HOULT
Keyboard:
MARK MITCHELL
Bass:
JOHN BEAL
Drums/Percussion:
PAUL PIZZUTI
Music Associate:
PAUL FORD
Music Copying:
EMILY GRISHMAN MUSIC PREPARATION/
KATHARINE EDMONDS, EMILY GRISHMAN

Cast Continued

UNDERSTUDIES
For Lizzie:
COLLEEN FITZPATRICK
For Starbuck:
WILL SWENSON
For H.C. and File:
MICHAEL SCOTT
For Noah:
DEVIN RICHARDS
For Jimmy:
DARIUS NICHOLS
For Snookie:
VALISIA LEKAE LITTLE

Swings:
MATT WALL, MAMIE PARRIS
Dance Captain:
MATT WALL

Production Stage Manager:
PETER HANSON
Assistant Stage Manager:
DAN DA SILVA

Photo by Joan Marcus

(L-R): Audra McDonald and John Cullum

110 in the Shade

Audra McDonald
Lizzie Curry

John Cullum
H.C. Curry

Steve Kazee
Starbuck

Chris Butler
Noah Curry

Carla Duren
Snookie

Christopher Innvar
File

Bobby Steggert
Jimmy Curry

Elisa Van Duyne
Lily Ann Beasley

Colleen Fitzpatrick
Odetta Clark

Valisia Lekae Little
Vivian Lorraine Taylor, Little Girl

Darius Nichols
Clarence J. Taylor

Mamie Parris
Female Swing

Devin Richards
Curjith McGlaughlin

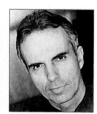
Michael Scott
Reverend Clark

Will Swenson
Cody Bridger

Matt Wall
Male Swing

Betsy Wolfe
Katheryn Brawner

Tom Jones
Lyrics

Harvey Schmidt
Music

Lonny Price
Director

Dan Knechtges
Choreographer

Paul Gemignani
Musical Director

Jonathan Tunick
Orchestration

Santo Loquasto
Set & Costume Design

Christopher Akerlind
Lighting Design

Dan Moses Schreier
Sound Design

Tom Watson
Hair and Wig Design

Stephen Gabis
Dialect Coach

Rick Sordelet
Fight Director

Jim Carnahan
Casting

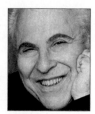
Gene Feist
Founding Director, Roundabout Theatre Company

Todd Haimes
Artistic Director, Roundabout Theatre Company

110 in the Shade

Photos by Ben Strothmann

COMPANY AND STAGE MANAGEMENT
(L-R): Dan da Silva, Nancy Mulliner and Peter Hanson.

ORCHESTRA
(L-R): Susan Rotholz, Dominic Derasse, Dennis Anderson, Don McGeen, Jennifer Hoult and John Beal.

WARDROBE
(L-R): Yleana Nunez, Steven R. Cozzi, Joe Godwin and Nadine Hettel.

110 in the Shade

BOX OFFICE
(L-R): David Carson (Ticket Services), Adam Owens (Ticket Services),
Krystin MacRitchie (Ticket Services), Scott Falkowski (Ticket Services), Jaime Perlman (Box Office Manager).

FRONT OF HOUSE STAFF
Front Row (L-R): Stella Varriale, LaConya Robinson (House Manager), Jonathan Martinez (House Staff),
Nicholas Wheatley (House Staff).

Back Row (L-R): Elicia Edwards (House Staff), Franco Roman (House Staff), Jose Cuello,
Katherine Longosky (House Staff) and Ana Bak-Kvapil.

STAGE CREW
Front Row (L-R): Dorian Fuchs, Rachel Bauder, Larry Jennino, Erin Delaney.

Middle Row (L-R): Josh Weitzman, Rob Manesman, Steve Jones, Bill Lombardi.

Back Row (L-R): John Wooding, Dan Schulteis, Dan Mendeloff, David Gotwald, Larry White,
and Dan Hoffman.

110 in the Shade

Office Manager	Scott Kelly
Database Manager	Dollye Evans
MIS Assistant	Micah Kraybill
Receptionists	Dena Beider, Raquel Castillo, Elisa Papa, Allison Patrick, Monica Sidorchuk
Messenger	Darnell Franklin
Management Intern	Erica Ruff

FINANCE STAFF
DIRECTOR OF FINANCE **Susan Neiman**

Assistant Controller	John LaBarbera
Accounts Payable Administrator	Frank Surdi
Financial Associate	Yonit Kafka
Business Office Assistant	Joshua Cohen
Business Interns	Li Shen, Richard Patterson

DEVELOPMENT STAFF
DIRECTOR OF DEVELOPMENT **Jeffory Lawson**

Director, Institutional Giving	Julie K. D'Andrea
Director, Individual Giving	Julia Lazarus
Director, Special Events	Steve Schaeffer
Manager, Donor Information Systems	Tina Mae Bishko
Corporate Relations Manager	Sara Bensman
Manager, Individual Giving	Kara Kandel
Telefundraising Manager	Douglas Sutcliffe
External Affairs Associate	Robert Weinstein
Institutional Giving Associate	Sarah Krasnow
Individual Giving Associate	Kate Bartoldus
Patrons Services Assistant	John Haynes
Development Assistants	Jillian Brewster, Christopher Taggart
Special Events Assistant	Ashley Firestone
Individual Giving Intern	Ashley Turner
Development Intern	Zachary Hollwedel

MARKETING STAFF
DIRECTOR OF MARKETING AND SALES PROMOTION **David B. Steffen**

Marketing/Publications Manager	Margaret Casagrande
Marketing Associate	Stefanie Schussel
Marketing Assistant	Stuart Goldman
Website Consultant	Keith Powell Beyland

DIRECTOR OF TELESALES SPECIAL PROMOTIONS **Daniel Weiss**

Telesales Manager	Michael Pace
Marketing Intern	Sari Abraham

TICKET SERVICES STAFF
DIRECTOR OF SALES OPERATIONS **Jim Seggelink**

Ticket Services Manager	Ellen Holt
Subscription Manager	Charlie Garbowski, Jr.
Box Office Managers	Edward P. Osborne, Andrew Clements
Group Sales Manager	Jeff Monteith
Assistant Box Office Managers	Krystin MacRitchie, Robert Morgan, Nicole Nicholson
Assistant Ticket Services Managers	Robert Kane, Ethan Ubell, Carlos Morris
Customer Services Coordinator	Trina Cox
Ticket Services	Rachel Bauder, Solangel Bido, Lauren Cartelli, David Carson, Joseph Clark, Mike DePope, Nisha Dhruna, Adam Elsberry, Lindsay Ericson, Scott Falkowski, Catherine Fitzpatrick, Daniel Gabriel, James Graham, Tova Heller,

	Nicki Ishmael, Bill Klemm, Elisa Mala, Mead Margulies, Chuck Migliaccio, Bekah Nutt, Adam Owens, Ethan Paulini, David Pittman, DeeAnna Row, Heather Siebert, Nalene Singh, Lillian Soto, DJ Thacker, Pam Unger, Thomas Walsh
Ticket Services Intern	Hannah Weitzman

SERVICES

Counsel	Paul, Weiss, Rifkind, Wharton and Garrison LLP, John Breglio, Deborah Hartnett
Counsel	Rosenberg & Estis
Counsel	Andrew Lance, Gibson, Dunn, & Crutcher, LLP
Counsel	Harry H. Weintraub, Glick and Weintraub, P.C.
Immigration Counsel	Mark D. Koestler and Theodore Ruthizer
House Physicians	Dr. Theodore Tyberg, Dr. Lawrence Katz
House Dentist	Neil Kanner, D.M.D.
Insurance	DeWitt Stern Group, Inc.
Accountant	Lutz & Carr CPAs, LLP
Sponsorship	The Marketing Group, Tanya Grubich, Laura Matalon, Anne Rippey, Erik Gensler
Advertising	Eliran Murphy Group/ Denise Ganjou, Kara Eldridge
Events Photography	Anita and Steve Shevett
Production Photographer	Joan Marcus
Theatre Displays	King Displays, Wayne Sapper

MANAGING DIRECTOR EMERITUS	Ellen Richard

Roundabout Theatre Company
231 West 39th Street, New York, NY 10018
(212) 719-9393.

GENERAL PRESS REPRESENTATIVES
Adrian Bryan-Brown
Matt Polk   Jessica Johnson   Amy Kass

CREDITS FOR *110 IN THE SHADE*

Company Manager	Nancy Mulliner
Production Stage Manager	Peter Hanson
Assistant Stage Manager	Dan da Silva
Assistant Company Manager	Dave Solomon
Assistant Director	Matt Cowart
Assistant to the Director	Will Nunziata
SSDC Observer	Kitt Lavoie
Assistant Choreographer	Caitlin Carter
Assistant Technical Supervisor	Elisa Kuhar
Associate Scenic Designer	Jenny Sawyers
Assistant Scenic Designer	Tobin Ost
Assistant to the Scenic Designer	Kanae Heike
Associate Costume Designer	Matthew Pachtman
Assistant to the Costume Designer	Sarah Sophia Turner
Associate Lighting Designer	Ben Krall
Assistant Lighting Designer	Caroline Chao
Associate Sound Designer	Phillip Scott Peglow
Synthesizer Programmer	Bruce Samuels
Production Carpenter	Dan Hoffman
Production Electrician	Josh Weitzman

Assistant Production Electrician	John Wooding
Production Properties Coordinator	Kathy Fabian, Propstar Inc.
Assistant Production Properties	Carrie Mossman, Carrie Hash
Wardrobe Supervisor	Nadine Hettel
Dressers	Steven R. Cozzi, Joe Godwin, Yleana Nunez
Hair and Wig Supervisor	Daryl Terry
Hair and Wig Stylist	Kat Ventura
Make-up Design	Angelina Avallone
Production Sound Engineer	Jesse Stevens
Automation Operator	Paul Ashton
Head Follow Spot Operator	John Wooding
Properties Running Crew	Erin Delaney, Daniel Mendeloff
Follow Spot Operators	Dorian Fuchs, Dan Schulteis
Flyman	Steve Jones
Moving Light Programmer	Victor Seastone
Conventional Light Programmer	Jessica Morton
Deck Sound	Larry White
Deck Electrician	Al Talbot
Local One IATSE Apprentice	Dan Schultheis
Production Assistants	Kathryn McKee, Rachel Bauder
Physical Therapy	Encore Physical Therapy P.C.
Orthopaedist	David S. Weiss, M.D.
Scenery Constructed, Automated, and Painted by	Hudson Scenic Studio, Inc.
Lighting Equipment Provided by	PRG, Production Resource Group
Sound Equipment Provided by	Sound Associates, Inc.
Specialty Prop Construction	Craig Grigg and Plumb Square
Rain Equipment by	Jauchem & Meeh
Costumes executed by	Euro Co Costumes, Barbara Matera, Ltd., Lynne Baccus, Luigi Custom Tailor, Arel Studios
Fabric Painting & Dyeing by	Jeff Fender
Custom Footwear by	T.O. Dey
Hosiery and Undergarments by	Bra*Tenders
Practical Lanterns	Jocelyn Smith
Natural herb cough drops courtesy of	Ricola USA Inc.
Rehearsed at	115 W. 45th Street and the New 42nd Street Studios

STUDIO 54 THEATRE STAFF

Theatre Manager	Matthew Armstrong
Box Office Manager	Jaime Perlman
House Manager	LaConya Robinson
Associate House Manager	Jack Watanachaiyot
House Staff	Elicia Edwards, Jason Fernandez, Jen Kneeland, Kate Longosky, Latiffa Marcus, Nicole Marino, Jonathan Martinez, Dana McCaw, Nicole Ramirez, Anthony Roman, Nick Wheatley, Stella Varriale
House Carpenter	Dan Hoffman
House Electrician	Josh Weitzman
House Properties	Lawrence Jennino
Security	Gotham Security
Maintenance	Ralph Mohan, Maman Garba
Lobby Refreshments by	Sweet Concessions
Merchandise	Marquee Merchandise LLC/ Matt Murphy

Passing Strange

First Preview: February 8, 2008. Opened: February 28, 2008.
Still running as of May 31, 2008.

CAST

(in order of appearance)

Narrator	STEW
Bass/Vocals	HEIDI RODEWALD
Keyboard/Guitar/Backing Vocals	JON SPURNEY
Drums	CHRISTIAN CASSAN
Guitar/Keyboard/ Backing Vocals	CHRISTIAN GIBBS

Los Angeles

Mother	EISA DAVIS
Youth	DANIEL BREAKER
Terry, a bad kid at church	CHAD GOODRIDGE
Sherry, another bad kid at church	REBECCA NAOMI JONES
Franklin, church pianist, youth choir director and the Reverend Jones' son	COLMAN DOMINGO
Edwina, a teenage goddess	DE'ADRE AZIZA

Amsterdam

Renata, an abstract artist and café waitress	REBECCA NAOMI JONES
Christophe, an academic who moonlights	CHAD GOODRIDGE
Joop, a body liberationist	COLMAN DOMINGO
Marianna, a neo-hippie	DE'ADRE AZIZA

Continued on next page

⊛ BELASCO THEATRE

111 West 44th Street
A Shubert Organization Theatre

Gerald Schoenfeld, *Chairman*   **Philip J. Smith**, *President*

Robert E. Wankel, *Executive Vice President*

The Shubert Organization   Elizabeth Ireland McCann LLC
Bill Kenwright   Chase Mishkin   Terry Allen Kramer   Barbara & Buddy Freitag
Broadway Across America   Emily Fisher Landau   Peter May   Boyett Ostar
Larry Hirschhorn   Janet Pailet/Steve Klein   Elie Hirschfeld/Jed Bernstein
Spring Sirkin/Ruth Hendel   Vasi Laurence/Pat Flicker Addiss   Wendy Federman/Jacki Barlia Florin
Joey Parnes Executive Producer

In Association with
The Public Theater
and
The Berkeley Repertory Theatre

Present

PASSING STRANGE

Book & Lyrics By	Music By
STEW	**STEW AND HEIDI RODEWALD**

Starring
STEW

with

DE'ADRE AZIZA	EISA DAVIS	COLMAN DOMINGO	CHAD GOODRIDGE	REBECCA NAOMI JONES

and
DANIEL BREAKER

Scenic Design	Costume Design	Lighting Design	Sound Design
DAVID KORINS	ELIZABETH HOPE CLANCY	KEVIN ADAMS	TOM MORSE

Music Supervision & Orchestrations	Music Coordinator
STEW & HEIDI RODEWALD	SEYMOUR RED PRESS

Casting	Production Stage Manager
JORDAN & HEIDI THALER GRIFFITHS	TRIPP PHILLIPS

Press Representative	Company Manager	Associate Producer
SAM RUDY MEDIA RELATIONS	KIM SELLON	S.D. WAGNER

Choreography By
KAROLE ARMITAGE

Directed by and Created in Collaboration with
ANNIE DORSEN

Originally Presented by Berkeley Repertory Theatre: Tony Taccone Artistic Director, Susan Medak Managing Director
and The Public Theater: Oskar Eustis Artistic Director, Mara Manus Executive Director.

The Producers wish to express their appreciation to Theatre Development Fund for its support of this production.

3/24/08

(L-R): Chad Goodridge, Daniel Breaker, Colman Domingo, Stew and Rebecca Naomi Jones.

Passing Strange

MUSICAL NUMBERS

ACT 1

Prologue ("We Might Play All Night")	Narrator, Heidi and the Band
"Baptist Fashion Show"	Narrator and Ensemble
"Blues Revelation/Freight Train"	Narrator and Ensemble
"Arlington Hill"	Narrator
"Sole Brother"	Youth, Terry and Sherry
"Must've Been High"	Narrator
"Mom Song"	Narrator, Mother and Ensemble
"Merci Beaucoup, M. Godard"	Narrator and Stewardesses
"Amsterdam"	Ensemble
"Keys"	Marianna, Youth and Narrator
"We Just Had Sex"	Youth, Marianna and Renata
"Stoned"	Youth and Narrator

ACT 2

"May Day"	Narrator and Ensemble
"Surface"	Mr. Venus
"Damage"	Narrator, Desi and Youth
"Identity"	Youth
"The Black One"	Narrator and Ensemble
"Come Down Now"	Heidi and Desi
"Work the Wound"	Youth and Narrator
"Passing Phase"	Youth and Narrator
"Love Like That"	Narrator and Heidi

Cast Continued

Berlin

Hugo, a militant essayist .....CHAD GOODRIDGE
Sudabey, an avant-garde filmmaker
    and writer ....DE'ADRE AZIZA
Desi, a den mother and
    social engineer ......REBECCA NAOMI JONES
Mr. Venus,
    a performance artist .....COLMAN DOMINGO

UNDERSTUDIES

For Mr. Franklin, Joop, Mr. Venus:
BILLY EUGENE JONES
For Edwina, Marianna, Sudabey & Sherry,
Renata, Desi:
KELLY McCREARY
For Mother:
KAREN PITTMAN
For Narrator:
DAVID RYAN SMITH
For Youth & Hugo, Christophe, Terry:
LAWRENCE STALLINGS

Dance Captain:
DAVID RYAN SMITH

Stew
*Book, Lyrics,
Co-Composer,
Co-Orchestrator,
Narrator*

Daniel Breaker
Youth

de'Adre Aziza
*Edwina, Marianna,
Sudabey*

Eisa Davis
Mother

Colman Domingo
*Mr. Franklin, Joop,
Mr. Venus*

Chad Goodridge
*Terry, Christophe,
Hugo*

Rebecca Naomi
Jones
Sherry, Renata, Desi

Billy Eugene Jones
*u/s for Mr. Franklin,
Joop, Mr. Venus*

Kelly McCreary
*u/s for Edwina,
Marianna, Sudabey,
Sherry, Renata, Desi*

Karen Pittman
u/s for Mother

David Ryan Smith
u/s for Narrator

Lawrence Stallings
*u/s for Youth, Hugo,
Christophe, Terry*

Heidi Rodewald
*Co-Composer,
Co-Orchestrator,
Bass, Vocals*

Christian Cassan
Drums

Passing Strange

Christian Gibbs
Guitar, Keyboards,
Backing Vocals

Jon Spurney
Keyboards, Guitar,
Backing Vocals

Annie Dorsen
Director

David Korins
Scenic Design

Kevin Adams
Lighting Design

Seymour Red Press
Music Coordinator

Heidi Griffiths and
Jordan Thaler
Casting

Gerald Schoenfeld,
Chairman,
The Shubert
Organization
Producer

Elizabeth Ireland
McCann
Producer

Bill Kenwright
Producer

Chase Mishkin
Producer

Terry Allen Kramer
Producer

Barbara Freitag
Producer

Larry Hirschhorn
Producer

Bob Boyett,
Boyett Ostar
Producer

Bill Haber,
Boyett Ostar
Producer

Wendy Federman
Producer

Spring Sirkin
Producer

Ruth Hendel
Producer

Pat Flicker Addiss
Producer

Oskar Eustis
Artistic Director,
The Public Theater

Mara Manus
Executive Director,
The Public Theater

Tony Taccone
Artistic Director,
Berkeley Repertory
Theatre

Joey Parnes
Executive Producer

Stew and Eisa Davis.

Photo by Carol Rosegg

Passing Strange

CREW
Front Row (L-R): Susan Goulet, Heidi Brown, Dylan Foley, Erika Wambrunn, Tommy Grasso.

Middle Row (L-R): Chris Fann, Celia Tackaberry, Julienne Shubert-Blechman.

Back Row (L-R): Craig Van Tassel, Bill Craven, Joe Moritz, Tucker Howard, George Dummitt, Greg Husinko, Dave Rogers.

FRONT OF HOUSE STAFF
Front Row (L-R): Pat Norton, Kathleen Powell, Tom Corcoran.

Second Row (L-R): Dexter Luke, Michelle Moyna, Eugenia Raines, Terry Lynch, Alyse Hyrnczyszyn.

Back Row (L-R): Lisa Maisonette, Joseph Pittman, Marissa Gioffre, Kathleen Dunn, Gwen Coley and William Phelan.

DOORMAN
Joe Trapasso

STAGE MANAGEMENT
(L-R): Jason Hindelang, Tripp Phillips, Cynthia "Cyd" Cahill.

BAND
(L-R): Jon Spurney, Christian Gibbs, Christian Cassan, Heidi Rodewald.

Passing Strange

Staff for *PASSING STRANGE*

GENERAL MANAGEMENT
JOEY PARNES

GENERAL PRESS REPRESENTATIVES
SAM RUDY MEDIA RELATIONS
Sam Rudy   Dale R. Heller
Robert Lasko   Charlie Siedenburg

ASSOCIATE PRODUCER
S.D. WAGNER

ASSISTANT PRODUCER
JOHN JOHNSON

For THE SHUBERT ORGANIZATION
Vice President, Creative Projects ........D.S. Moynihan
Director of Creative Projects ....Thomas Moynahan
Director of Audit &
    Production Finance ....Anthony S. LaMattina

For THE PUBLIC THEATER
Associate Producer ....Jenny Gersten
General Manager ....Nicki Genovese
Associate Artistic Director ....Mandy Hackett
Director of Production ....Ruth E. Sternberg

Production Stage Manager ....Tripp Phillips
Stage Manager ....Jason Hindelang
Assistant Stage Manager ....Cynthia Cahill
Management Associate ....Kit Ingui
Assistant Director ....Stephen Brackett
Assistant Choreographer ....William Isaac
Additional Casting ....Jay Binder, Jack Bowdan
Casting Associates ....Mark Brandon, Sara Schatz
Casting Assistants ....Nikole Vallins, Allison Estrin
Associate Set Designer ....Rod Lemmond
Assistants to the Set Designer ....Amanda Stephens,
                                    Nathan Koch
Assistant Lighting Designer ....Aaron Sporer
Assistant Costume Designer ....Chloe Chapin
Assistant Sound Designer ....Kevin Brubaker
Vocal Coach ....Barbara Maier
Dialect Coach ....Elizabeth Smith
Production Carpenter ....Larry Morley
Production Electrician ....Steve Cochrane
Production Prop Supervisor ....Mike Smanko
Production Sound Engineer ....Tucker Howard
Head Carpenter ....Bill Craven
Head Electrician ....Susan Goulet
Head Propertyman ....Dylan Foley
Sound Programmers ....Wally Flores, Mac Kerr
Rehearsal Monitor Mixers ....Craig Van Tassel,
                                    Tommy Grasso

Moving Light Programmer ....Rich Mortel
Wardrobe Supervisor ....Dave Olin Rogers
Dressers ....Francine Buryiak,
                            Julienne Shubert-Blechman
Hair Consultant ....Thelma L. Pollard
Costume Interns ....Jaime Torres,
                                    Natalie Sanabria
Production Assistant ....John Bantay
Assistant to Stew ....Mike James
Management Assistant ....Matt Farabee
Literary Manager ....Gaydon Phillips
Management Interns ....Amy Nowak, Dana Schmitt
Transcription & Music Consultant ....Matthew Henning
Music Copyist ......Emily Grishman Music Preparation/
                    Katharine Edmonds, Emily Grishman
Guitar Technician ....Mike Fornatale
Guitar Instructor ....Steve Bargonetti
Advertising ....Serino-Coyne/Nancy Coyne,
        Greg Corradetti, Ryan Greer, Kristina Curatolo
Interactive Marketing and Website
    Design .....Interactive Agency-Situation Marketing/
                Damian Bazadona, Ryan Klink, Joey Oliva,
                John Lanasa, Alex Bershaw, Jackie Bodley
Special Marketing ....Walk Tall Girl Productions/
                                    Marcia Pendelton
Legal Counsel ....Lowenstein Sandler PC/
                                Franklin R. Weissberg
Accountants ....Rosenberg, Neuwirth & Kuchner/
                                Mark A. D'Ambrosi,
                                Patricia M. Pedersen
Banking ....JP Morgan Chase Bank/
                    Stephanie Dalton, Richard Callian
Insurance ....Aon/Albert G. Ruben/
            George Walden, Claudia B. Kaufman,
            Stockbridge Group/Neil Goldstein
Payroll ....Castellana Services Inc./
            Lance Castellana, James Castellana,
                                    Norman Sewell
Production Physicians ....Dr. Karen Thornton,
                                    Dr. Barry Kohn
Physical Therapist ....Rhonda M. Barkow, P.T., M.S.
Opening Night Coordinator ....The Lawrence Company
Off-Broadway Photographer ....Michal Daniel
Pre-Production Photographer ....Steve Halin
Production Photographer ....Carol Rosegg

CREDITS
Scenery constructed by Hudson Scenic Studio Inc. Lighting equipment from PRG Lighting. Sound equipment from Sound Associates. In Ear monitors by Ultimate Ears. Car service by IBA Limousine. Furniture fabricated by Cigar Box Studios. Natural herb cough drops courtesy of Ricola USA. Emergen-C health and energy drink mix provided by Alacer Corporation.

Souvenir merchandise designed and created by The Araca Group.

Rehearsed at the New 42nd Street Studios.

GUITARS SUPPLIED BY GIBSON GUITARS.

SELECT MENSWEAR BY HUGO BOSS

Select women's wear by George Hudacko
Custom leather by David Menkes

Lyric use from "On the Street Where You Live" (copyright 1956, renewed) by permission of Alan Jay Lerner Testamentary Trust and Frederick Loewe Foundation, copyright owners, Warner Chappell Music publisher.

SPECIAL THANKS
Anne Wingate, Julian Christenberry,
Jane Pfeffer, Ed Stallsworth, Ana Perez,
Peter Dubois, Amy Carothers,
Christina Huschle, Greg Schanuel, Bill Bragin

www.PassingStrangeOnBroadway.com

Passing Strange
SCRAPBOOK

Correspondent: Eisa Davis, "Mother"

Memorable Fan Letter: To Chad Goodridge: "If this was long ago, I would sacrifice many goats to you." BTW: Chad is nearly vegan.

Opening Night Gifts: Engraved guitar picks.

Most Exciting Celebrity Visitors And What They Did/Said:

DIANA ROSS: Her daughters Rhonda and Tracee Ellis Ross are dear fans and recommended the show. Diana came during previews, rocked out, and said she wanted Eisa Davis's purple dress designed by Beth Clancy.

TONI MORRISON: Came twice.

ANGELA DAVIS: Hugged Stew in his underwear.

SPIKE LEE: Came three times, publicly endorsed the show and cast three people from the show in his newest movie.

DAVE CHAPPELLE: Said the Amsterdam scene made him want to smoke weed again.

MARIO VAN PEEBLES: Inspired us all with his environmental and social activism.

JAMES RADO: Loved the show

EDWARD ALBEE: Said it was fantastic.

Actor Who Performed The Most Roles in This Show: Chad Goodridge.

Special Backstage Rituals: Faux punches to the gonads.

Favorite Moments During Each Performance (On Stage or Off): Making each other break, "Arlington Hill," dancing in "Keys," Mom in dress, Rebecca Naomi Jones' "we listening" in church, beginning of show.

Favorite In-Theatre Gathering Place: The Berkeley greenroom.

Favorite Off-Site Hangout: Longevity Health Center.

Favorite Snack Food: Apple cider donuts from the Fort Greene farmers' market.

Mascot: Bibi.

Favorite Therapy: Screaming.

Memorable Ad-Lib: The whole show.

Record Number of Cell Phone Rings, Cell Phone Photos or Texting Incidents During a Performance: 5?

Memorable Press Encounter: Reporter: How do your parents feel about you being on Broadway? Colman Domingo: They're dead.

Memorable Stage Door Fan Encounter: A psychologist who demanded Stew and Rebecca speak with her alienated son as therapy for him.

Latest Audience Arrival: 53 minutes into the show, front row, then they ate loud snacks throughout.

Fastest Costume Change: Into Amsterdam.

Busiest Day at the Box Office: St. Patrick's Day.

Who Wore the Heaviest/Hottest Costume: Rebecca's leotard, minidress, leggings, striped socks, mary jane shoes, hippie skirt, apron, lacy top, vest, and hat in Act I, then a football jacket for the riot in Act II.

Who Wore the Least: Colman Domingo (kinda naked).

Catchphrases Only the Company Would Recognize: "Live...like I talk?" "We can't have nothin'." "Alterna-negroes."

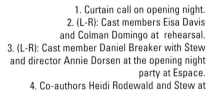

1. Curtain call on opening night.
2. (L-R): Cast members Eisa Davis and Colman Domingo at rehearsal.
3. (L-R): Cast member Daniel Breaker with Stew and director Annie Dorsen at the opening night party at Espace.
4. Co-authors Heidi Rodewald and Stew at rehearsal.

Sweethearts Within the Company: Me and my i-i-i-i-i-dentity

Which Orchestra Member Played the Most Instruments: We're a BAND!

Which Orchestra Member Played the Most Consecutive Performances Without a Sub: We're a BAND! We can't make it unless we make the band our life!

Best In-House Parody Lyrics: "Hamsterland." "We just ate Chex." "Get yo s#%t out of my squat." "Pay day, pay day, there's a check going down." "Why you got a weave? Right when it was starting to feel real...."

Company In-Jokes: The whole play.

Company Legends: Living in BERKELEY Cafe Gratitude (Stew never made it). Cesar. Fonda. Dance Breaks. Midday Break smoothies. Our hangout Downtown taking away our discount and consistently throwing us out. Our uncleaned apartments. De'Adre trying every flavor of gelato. Mr Venus of Berkeley at karaoke, etc. ...and the pretzel man is REAL.

Passing Strange
SCRAPBOOK

1. Recording the cast album live on the Belasco stage April 21, 2008.
2. Daniel Breaker and Rebecca Naomi Jones at rehearsal.
3. The cast poses for photographers at a Press Preview.
4. Stew (C) with guests Jerry Stiller and Anne Meara.
5. (L-R) de'Adre Aziza and Chad Goodridge at rehearsal.

Memorable Directorial Note: A notecard with just a heart drawn on it.
Understudy Anecdote: Where is the Ninja?
Nicknames:
Stew: Ebenezer Stooge, Stewage.
Colman: Coco, Hooker.
Daniel: DB, Deebs.
Chad: Chadly, Chaddeus, Chadwick.
de'Adre: de, yeah, son.
Rebecca: RJ, Jonesy.
Eisa: Eye-EEE-suh, ED, Erectile Dysfunction.

Spurney: Spurn.
Cynthia: Cyd.
Heidi: Rodewald.
Christian: Cassan.
Christian: Gibbs.
Annie: Dorsen.
Embarrassing Moments: When Colman fell. When Rebecca fell (with her chair). Spurney's ghost-in-the-machine keyboard malfunction in Berkeley.
Ghostly Encounters Backstage: A face in

Daniel's mirror that wasn't his. David Belasco touched Chad's leg. Christian Gibbs' pod rose without anyone flipping the switch
Superstitions That Turned Out To Be True: Said the name of the Scottish play accidentally backstage and then we went up on lines throughout the show.
Coolest Thing About Being in This Show: Being in THIS show.
Head of Our Fan Club: The woman who comes to the show every night.

The Phantom of the Opera

First Preview: January 9, 1988. Opened: January 26, 1988.
Still running as of May 31, 2008.

CAST

The Phantom of the Opera .HOWARD McGILLIN
Christine Daaé .... JENNIFER HOPE WILLS
Christine Daaé
    (at certain performances) .... SUSAN OWEN
Raoul, Vicomte
    de Chagny .... TIM MARTIN GLEASON
Carlotta Giudicelli .... KATIE BANKS
Monsieur André .... GEORGE LEE ANDREWS
Monsieur Firmin .... DAVID CRYER
Madame Giry .... MARILYN CASKEY
Ubaldo Piangi .... WAYNE HOBBS
Meg Giry .... KARA KLEIN
Monsieur Reyer/
    Hairdresser ("Il Muto") .... GEOFF PACKARD
Auctioneer .... JASON MILLS
Jeweler (Il Muto) .... FRANK MASTRONE
Monsieur Lefèvre/Firechief .. KENNETH KANTOR
Joseph Buquet .... RICHARD POOLE
Don Attilio ("Il
    Muto") .... GREGORY EMANUEL RAHMING
Passarino ("Don Juan Triumphant") JASON MILLS
Slave Master ("Hannibal") ...... DANIEL RYCHLEC
Flunky/Stage Hand/
    Solo Dancer ("Il Muto") .... JACK HAYES
Page ("Don Juan Triumphant") .... KRIS KOOP
Porter/Fireman .... CHRIS BOHANNON
Spanish Lady
    ("Don Juan Triumphant") ... SALLY WILLIAMS
Wardrobe Mistress/
    Confidante ("Il Muto") .... KATIE BANKS
Princess ("Hannibal") .... SUSAN OWEN

Madame Firmin .... MELODY RUBIE
Innkeeper's Wife ("Don Juan
    Triumphant") .WREN MARIE HARRINGTON
Marksman .... JIM WEITZER
The Ballet Chorus of
    the Opéra Populaire .... KARA KLEIN,
                GIANNA LOUNGWAY,
    MABEL MODRONO, JESSICA RADETSKY,
          CARLY BLAKE SEBOUHIAN,
               DIANNA WARREN
Ballet Swings ...DARA ADLER, HARRIET CLARK
Swings ....SCOTT MIKITA, JAMES ROMICK,
      JANET SAIA, JULIE SCHMIDT

Continued on next page

Continued on next page

---

⑤ MAJESTIC THEATRE
247 West 44th Street
A Shubert Organization Theatre

Gerald Schoenfeld, *Chairman*   **Philip J. Smith,** *President*

Robert E. Wankel, *Executive Vice President*

CAMERON MACKINTOSH and
THE REALLY USEFUL THEATRE COMPANY, INC.
present

The
PHANTOM
of the
OPERA.

starring

HOWARD McGILLIN
JENNIFER HOPE WILLS
TIM MARTIN GLEASON

GEORGE LEE ANDREWS DAVID CRYER PATRICIA PHILLIPS
MARILYN CASKEY WAYNE HOBBS HEATHER McFADDEN

At certain performances

JULIE HANSON

plays the role of 'Christine'

Music by

ANDREW LLOYD WEBBER

Lyrics by CHARLES HART

Additional lyrics by RICHARD STILGOE

Book by RICHARD STILGOE & ANDREW LLOYD WEBBER
Based on the novel 'Le Fantôme de L'Opéra' by GASTON LEROUX

Production Design by MARIA BJÖRNSON Lighting by ANDREW BRIDGE
Sound by MARTIN LEVAN Musical Supervision & Direction DAVID CADDICK
Musical Director DAVID LAI Production Supervisor PETER von MAYRHAUSER
Orchestrations by DAVID CULLEN & ANDREW LLOYD WEBBER
Casting by TARA RUBIN CASTING Original Casting by JOHNSON-LIFF ASSOCIATES
General Management ALAN WASSER

Musical Staging & Choreography by GILLIAN LYNNE

Directed by HAROLD PRINCE

LIVE
BROADWAY

10/1/07

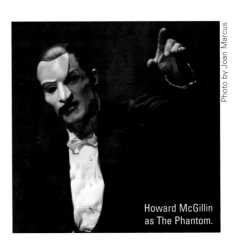

Howard McGillin
as The Phantom.

The Phantom of the Opera

SCENES & MUSICAL NUMBERS

PROLOGUE
The stage of the Paris Opéra House, 1911

OVERTURE

ACT ONE—PARIS 1881

Scene 1—The dress rehearsal of "Hannibal"
"Think of Me" ....Carlotta, Christine, Raoul
Scene 2—After the Gala
"Angel of Music" ....Christine and Meg
Scene 3—Christine's dressing room
"Little Lotte/The Mirror" (Angel of Music) ....Raoul, Christine, Phantom
Scene 4—The Labyrinth underground
"The Phantom of the Opera" ....Phantom and Christine
Scene 5—Beyond the lake
"The Music of the Night" ....Phantom
Scene 6—Beyond the lake, the next morning
"I Remember/Stranger Than You Dreamt It" ....Christine and Phantom
Scene 7—Backstage
"Magical Lasso" ....Buquet, Meg, Madame Giry and Ballet Girls
Scene 8—The Managers' office
"Notes/Prima Donna" ....Firmin, André, Raoul, Carlotta, Giry, Meg,
Piangi and Phantom
Scene 9—A performance of "Il Muto"
"Poor Fool, He Makes Me Laugh" ....Carlotta and Company
Scene 10—The roof of the Opéra House
"Why Have You Brought Me Here/Raoul, I've Been There" ....Raoul and Christine
"All I Ask of You" ....Raoul and Christine
"All I Ask of You" (Reprise) ....Phantom

ENTR'ACTE

ACT TWO—SIX MONTHS LATER

Scene 1—The staircase of the Opéra House, New Year's Eve
"Masquerade/Why So Silent" ....Full Company
Scene 2—Backstage
Scene 3—The Managers' office
"Notes/Twisted Every Way" ....André, Firmin, Carlotta, Piangi, Raoul,
Christine, Giry and Phantom
Scene 4—A rehearsal for "Don Juan Triumphant"
Scene 5—A graveyard in Peros
"Wishing You Were Somehow Here Again" ....Christine
"Wandering Child/Bravo, Bravo" ....Phantom, Christine and Raoul
Scene 6—The Opéra House stage before the Premiere
Scene 7—"Don Juan Triumphant"
"The Point of No Return" ....Phantom and Christine
Scene 8—The Labyrinth underground
"Down Once More/Track Down This Murderer" ....Full Company
Scene 9—Beyond the lake

Cast Continued

UNDERSTUDIES

For the Phantom: JASON MILLS,
    JAMES ROMICK, TIM MARTIN GLEASON
For Christine: KRIS KOOP, SUSAN OWEN
For Raoul: JASON MILLS, GEOFF PACKARD,
    JAMES ROMICK, JIM WEITZER
For Firmin: KENNETH KANTOR,
    GREGORY EMANUEL RAHMING,
    JAMES ROMICK
For André: SCOTT MIKITA, RICHARD POOLE,
    JAMES ROMICK
For Carlotta: KATIE BANKS,
    WREN MARIE HARRINGTON, KRIS KOOP,
    MELODY RUBIE, JULIE SCHMIDT
For Mme. Giry: KRIS KOOP, JANET SAIA,
    SALLY WILLIAMS
For Piangi: CHRIS BOHANNON,
    FRANK MASTRONE
For Meg Giry: AMANDA EDGE, KARA KLEIN,
    CARLY BLAKE SEBOUHIAN
For Slavemaster: JACK HAYES
For Solo Dancer ("Il Muto"): DANIEL RYCHLEC
Dance Captain: DARA ADLER
Assistant Dance Captain: HEATHER McFADDEN

ORCHESTRA

Conductors: DAVID CADDICK,
    KRISTEN BLODGETTE, DAVID LAI,
    TIM STELLA, NORMAN WEISS
Violins: JOYCE HAMMANN (Concert Master),
    ALVIN E. ROGERS, GAYLE DIXON,
    KURT COBLE, JAN MULLEN,
    KAREN MILNE
Violas: STEPHANIE FRICKER,
    VERONICA SALAS
Cellos: TED ACKERMAN, KARL BENNION
Bass: MELISSA SLOCUM
Harp: HENRY FANELLI
Flute: SHERYL HENZE
Flute/Clarinet: ED MATTHEW
Oboe: MELANIE FELD
Clarinet: MATTHEW GOODMAN
Bassoon: ATSUKO SATO
Trumpets: LOWELL HERSHEY,
    FRANCIS BONNY
Bass Trombone: WILLIAM WHITAKER
French Horns: DANIEL CULPEPPER,
    PETER REIT, DAVID SMITH
Percussion: ERIC COHEN, JAN HAGIWARA
Keyboards: TIM STELLA, NORMAN WEISS

The Phantom of the Opera

Howard McGillin
The Phantom of the Opera

Jennifer Hope Wills
Christine Daaé

Tim Martin Gleason
Raoul, Vicomte de Chagny

George Lee Andrews
Monsieur André

David Cryer
Monsieur Firmin

Patricia Phillips
Carlotta Giudicelli

Marilyn Caskey
Madame Giry

Wayne Hobbs
Ubaldo Piangi

Heather McFadden
Meg Giry

Dara Adler
Dance Captain/ Swing

Katie Banks
Wardrobe Mistress/ Confidante

Chris Bohannon
Porter/Fireman

Harriet Clark
Dance Captain/ Ballet Swing

Amanda Edge
Understudy for Meg Giry

Wren Marie Harrington
Innkeeper's Wife

Jack Hayes
Flunky/Stagehand

Kenneth Kantor
Monsieur Lefèvre/ Firechief

Kara Klein
Ballet Chorus

Kris Koop
Page

Gianna Loungway
Ballet Chorus

Frank Mastrone
Jeweler

Scott Mikita
Swing

Jason Mills
Auctioneer/ Passarino

Mabel Modrono
Ballet Chorus

Susan Owen
Princess & Christine Daaé at certain performances

Geoff Packard
Monsieur Reyer/ Hairdresser

Richard Poole
Joseph Buquet

Jessica Radetsky
Ballet Chorus

Gregory Emanuel Rahming
Don Attilio

James Romick
Swing

Melody Rubie
Madame Firmin

Daniel Rychlec
Slave Master

Janet Saia
Swing

Carly Blake Sebouhian
Ballet Chorus

Julie Schmidt
Swing

The Phantom of the Opera

Dianna Warren
Ballet Chorus

Jim Weitzer
Marksman

Sally Williams
Spanish Lady

Andrew Lloyd
Webber
*Composer/Book/
Co-Orchestrator*

Harold Prince
Director

Charles Hart
Lyrics

Richard Stilgoe
*Book and Additional
Lyrics*

Gillian Lynne
*Musical Staging and
Choreography*

Maria Björnson
(1949-2002)
Production Design

Andrew Bridge
Lighting Designer

Martin Levan
Sound Designer

David Caddick
*Musical Supervision
and Direction*

Kristen Blodgette
*Associate Musical
Supervisor*

David Cullen
Co-Orchestrator

Ruth Mitchell
(1919-2000)
*Assistant to
Mr. Prince*

Denny Berry
*Production Dance
Supervisor*

Craig Jacobs
*Production Stage
Manager*

Bethe Ward
*Stage Manager
from the beginning*

David Lai
Musical Director

Peter von
Mayrhauser
*Production
Supervisor*

Tara Rubin Casting
Casting

Vincent Liff and Geoffrey Johnson,
Johnson-Liff Associates
Original Casting

Alan Wasser
Associates
General Manager

Cameron Mackintosh
Producer

ALUMNI
2007-2008

Michael Babin
*Auctioneer,
Marksman,
Monsieur Reyer/
Hairdresser,
Passarino*

Sara Jean Ford
*Princess
("Hannibal")*

Julie Hanson
Christine Daaé

Rebecca Judd
Madame Giry

Michael Shawn
Lewis
*Raoul, Vicomte de
Chagny*

Fred Rose
*Marksman,
Porter/Fireman,
Swing*

Roland Rusinek
Ubaldo Piangi

Paul A. Schaefer
*Marksman; Raoul,
Vicomte de Chagny*

The Phantom of the Opera

Jimmy Smagula
Ubaldo Piangi

Carrington Vilmont
Auctioneer; Jeweler; Marksman; Monsieur Reyer/Hairdresser; Passarino; Raoul, Vicomte de Chagny

John Wasiniak
Porter/Fireman

Kimilee Bryant
Page ("Don Juan Triumphant")

John Cudia
The Phantom of the Opera

Kyle DesChamps
Flunky/Stage Hand/ Solo Dancer ("Il Muto")

David Gaschen
Ubaldo Piangi

Julie Hanson
Christine Daaé

Evan Harrington
Ubaldo Piangi

Rebecca Judd
Madame Giry

John Kuether
Auctioneer, Don Attilio ("Il Muto")

Elizabeth Loyacano
Christine Daaé

Janice Niggeling
The Ballet Chorus of the Opéra Populaire

Justin Peck
Slave Master ("Hannibal")

Marni Raab
Innkeeper's Wife ("Don Juan Triumphant"), Princess ("Hannibal")

Kristie Dale Sanders
Madame Firmin, Spanish Lady ("Don Juan Triumphant"), Swing

Paul A. Schaefer
Marksman

Kim Stengel
Carlotta Giudicelli

Jeremy Stolle
Auctioneer, Passarino ("Don Juan Triumphant")

**FRONT-OF-HOUSE STAFF
(USHERS, BAR, INFRA RED, SECURITY)**
Front Row (L-R): Lawrence Darden, Devin Harjes, Ron Raz, Cynthia Carlin, Dorothy Curich, Lucia Cappelletti.

Second Row (L-R): Angelique James, Matt Bosco, Danielle Bararducci, Maria Rodriguez, Joan Thorn, Luciana Lenihan, Sylvia Bailey.

Third Row (L-R): Georgina Villacorta, Vereita Austin, Denise Reich, Perry Dell'Aquila, James Muro, Ji Ming Zhu, Mattie Robinson, Darien Jones.

Back Row (L-R): Peter Kulok (House Manager), Emilio Benoit, Coco Fields, Stephanie Rivera, Keith Antone, Grace Price, Tony Stavick, Beren Willwerth.

Photo by Ben Strothmann

The Phantom of the Opera

STAGEHANDS
Front Row (L-R): Fred Smith, Brian Colonna, Alan Lampel, Ray Pesce, Joe Grillman, John Alban.

Back Row (L-R): Frank Dwyer, Matt Mezick, Rob Wallace, Jack Farmer, Jim Gallagher, John Hulbert.

Not Pictured: "Innumerable, and they were all working!"

ORCHESTRA
Front Row (L-R): Norman Weiss, Ted Ackerman, Larry Spivack, Al Rogers, Peter Reit.

Center (redhead): Karen Milne.

Back Row (L-R): Matthew Goodman, Sheryl Henze, Atsuko Sato, Lowell Hershey, Kurt Coble, Ed Matthew, Melanie Feld.

Not Pictured: David Lai (Musical Director), Tim Stella, Joyce Hammann, Alvin E. Rogers, Gayle Dixon, Jan Mullen, Stephanie Fricker, Veronica Salas, Francis Bonny, William Whitaker, Daniel Culpepper, David Smith, Eric Cohen, Jan Hagiwara.

WARDROBE, HAIR & MAKE-UP
First Row (L-R): Lisa Brownstein, Anna McDaniel, Erna Dias.

Second Row (L-R): Annette Lovece, Rosemary Taylor, Billy Hipkins, Shelley Friedman.

Third Row (L-R): Cara Sullivan, Katie Kurz, Thelma Pollard (Make-Up Supervisor), Marylou Rios, Elena Pellicciaro.

Back Row (L-R): Andrew Nelson, Peter McIver, Michael Jacobs, Bob Miller, Ron Blakely, Angie Finn.

Not Pictured: Julie Ratcliffe (Wardrobe Supervisor), Scott Westervelt (Wardrobe Supervisor), Leone Gagliardi (Hair Supervisor).

STAFF FOR *THE PHANTOM OF THE OPERA*

General Manager
ALAN WASSER

General Press Representative
THE PUBLICITY OFFICE
Marc Thibodeau   Michael S. Borowski
Jeremy Shaffer   Matthew Fasano

Assistant to Mr. Prince
RUTH MITCHELL

Production Supervisor
PETER von MAYRHAUSER

Production Dance Supervisor
DENNY BERRY

Associate Musical Supervisor
KRISTEN BLODGETTE

ASSOCIATE GENERAL
  MANAGER .... ALLAN WILLIAMS
TECHNICAL PRODUCTION
  MANAGERS ......JOHN H. PAULL III, JAKE BELL
COMPANY MANAGER ....ROBERT NOLAN
PRODUCTION STAGE
  MANAGER ....CRAIG JACOBS

The Phantom of the Opera

Stage Managers ....Bethe Ward, Brendan Smith

U.S. Design Staff
ASSOCIATE SCENIC DESIGNER ....DANA KENN
ASSOCIATE COSTUME
    DESIGNER ....SAM FLEMING
ASSOCIATE LIGHTING
    DESIGNER ....DEBRA DUMAS
ASSISTANT SOUND DESIGNER ......JON WESTON
Assistants to the Scenic Designer.................Paul Kelly,
    Paul Weimer, Steven Saklad
Assistants to the Costume Deslgner ......David Robinson,
    Marcy Froehlich
Assistant to the Lighting Designer ....Vivien Leone
Assistants to the Sound
    Designer ....James M. Bay, Joan Curcio

U.K. Design Staff
PRODUCTION TECHNICAL
    CONSULTANT ....MARTYN HAYES
    ASSOCIATES
ASSOCIATE SCENIC
    DESIGNER ....JONATHAN ALLEN
ASSOCIATE COSTUME
    DESIGNER ....SUE WILLMINGTON
ASSOCIATE LIGHTING
    DESIGNER ....HOWARD EATON
Automation Consultant ....Michael Barnet
Draperies Consultant ....Peter Everett
Sculptures Consultant ....Stephen Pyle
Sound Consultant ....Ralph Colhns

ASSISTANT TO
    GILLIAN LYNNE ....NAOMI SORKIN
Associate Manager ....Thom Mitchell
Associate Company Manager ....Steve Greer
Casting Directors ....Tara Rubin, Ron LaRosa,
    Jeff Siebert
Casting Associates ....Eric Woodall,
    Laura Schutzel, Merri Sugarman
Casting Assistants.......................Rebecca Carfagna,
    Paige Blansfield
Dance Captain ....Harriet Clark
Production Carpenter ....Joseph Patria
Production Electrician ....Robert Fehribach
Production Propertyman ....Timothy Abel
Production Sound Operator ....Steve Kennedy
Production Wig Supervisor ....Leone Gagliardi
Production Make-up Supervisor ....Thelma Pollard
Make-up Assistants ....Pearleta N. Price,
    Shazia J. Saleem
Head Carpenter ....Russell Tiberio III
Automation Carpenters ....Santos Sanchez,
    Michael Girman
Assistant Carpenter ....Giancarlo Cottignoli
Flyman ....Daryl Miller
Head Electrician ....Alan Lampel
Assistant Electrician ....JR Beket
Head Props ....Matthew Mezick
Asst. Props./Boat Captain ....Joe Caruso
Sound Operators........................Michael Eisenberg,
    Jason McKenna, Jason Strangfeld
Wardrobe Supervisor.....................Scott Westervelt
Assistant Wardrobe Supervisor ....Robert Strong Miller
Hair Supervisor ....Leone Gagliardi
Hairdressers ....Charise Champion, Lisa Harrell,
    Mary Mulligan, Erika Smith

Production Costume Design Assistant ..Cynthia Hamilton
Production Sound Design Assistant.........Larry Spurgeon

Associate Conductor ....Tim Stella
Assistant Conductor ....Norman Weiss
Musical Preparation
    Supervisor (U.S.) ....Chelsea Music Service, Inc
Synthesizer Consultant ....Brett Sommer
    Music Technologies Inc.

Assistants to the Gen. Mgr. ....Christopher Betz,
    Jake Hirzel, Bill Miller,
    Patty Montesi, Jennifer Mudge
Lighting Intern ....Wendy Bodzin

Legal Counsel ....S. Jean Ward,
    Frankfurt Garbus Kurnit Klein & Selz, P.C.
Legal Advisor to The Really
    Useful Company ....Brooks & Distler,
    Marsha Brooks
Accounting ....Rosenberg, Neuwirth and Kutchner
    Christopher A. Cacace
Logo Design and Graphics ....Dewynters Plc
    London
Merchandising ....Dewynters Advertising Inc.
Advertising ....Serino Coyne Inc.,
    Greg Corradetti, Andrea Prince,
    Natalie Serota
Marketing/Promotions ......Hugh Hysell Communications
    Hugh Hysell,
    Michael Redman, Matt Sicoli
Displays ....King Displays, Wayne Sapper
Insurance (U.S.) ....DeWitt Stern Group
    Peter K. Shoemaker
Insurance (U.K.) ....Walton & Parkinson Limited
    Richard Walton
Banklng ....Commerce Bank/Barbara von Borstel
Customs Broker
    (U.S.) ...............T.L. Customs House Brokers, Inc.
Customs Broker (U.K.) ....Theatours, Ltd.
Payroll Service ....Castellana Services, Inc.

Original Production Photographer ....Clive Barda
Additional Photography ....Joan Marcus
    Bob Marshak, Peter Cunningham
House Manager ....Peter Kulok

Special thanks to
McNABB & ASSOCIATES
Jim McNabb

CREDITS AND ACKNOWLEDGMENTS
Scenic construction and boat automation by
Hudson Scenic Studios.
Scenery automation by Jeremiah J. Harris Associates,
Inc./East Coast Theatre Supply, Inc. Scenery painted by
Nolan Scenery Studios. Set and hand properties by McHugh
Rollins Associates, Inc. Sculptural elements by Costume
Armour. "Opera Ball" newell post statues and elephant by
Nino Novellino of Costume Armour. Proscenium sculptures
by Stephen Pyle. Draperies by I. Weiss and Sons, Inc. Soft
goods provided by Quartet Theatrical Draperies. Safety
systems by Foy Lighting equipment and special lighting
effects by Four Star Lighting, Inc. Sound equipment and
technical service provided by Masque Sound and Recording
Corp. Special effects designed and executed by Theatre
Magic, Inc., Richard Huggins, President. Costumes

executed by Barbara Matera, Ltd. Costumes for "Hannibal"
and "Masquerade" executed by Parsons/Meares, Ltd. Men's
costumes by Vincent Costumes, Inc. Costume crafts for
"Hannibal" and "Masquerade" by Janet Harper and
Frederick Nihda. Fabric painting by Mary Macy. Additional
costumes by Carelli Costumes, Inc. Costume accessories by
Barak Stribling. Hats by Woody Shelp. Millinery and masks
by Rodney Gordon. Footwear by Sharlot Battin of Montana
Leatherworks, Ltd. Shoes by JC Theatrical and Costume
Footwear and Taffy's N.Y. Jewelry by Miriam Haskell Jewels.
Eyeglasses by H.L. Purdy. Wigs by The Wig Party. Garcia y
Vega cigars used. Makeup consultant Kris Evans. Emer'gen-
C super energy booster provided by Alacer Corp.

Champagne courtesy of
Champagne G.H. Mumm

Furs by Christie Bros.

Shoes supplied by Peter Fox Limlted

"The Phantom" character make-up created and
designed by Christopher Tucker

Magic Consultant—Paul Daniels

CAMERON MACKINTOSH, INC.
Joint Managing
    Directors ....Nicholas Allott & Matthew Dalco
Production Associate ....Shidan Majidi

THE REALLY USEFUL COMPANY INC
Public Relations ....BROWN LLOYD JAMES/
    PETER BROWN

THE REALLY USEFUL GROUP LIMITED
Directors ....THE LORD LLOYD-WEBBER
    WILLIAM TAYLOR
    JONATHAN HULL
    JONATHAN WHEELDON

 THE SHUBERT ORGANIZATION, INC.
Board of Directors

Gerald Schoenfeld	**Philip J. Smith**
Chairman	President
Wyche Fowler, Jr.	**John W. Kluge**
Lee J. Seidler	**Michael I. Sovern**

Stuart Subotnick

Robert E. Wankel
Executive Vice President

Peter Entin	**Elliot Greene**
Vice President –	Vice President –
Theatre Operations	Finance
David Andrews	**John Darby**
Vice President –	Vice President –
Shubert Ticketing Services	Facilities

D.S. Moynihan
Vice President – Creative Projects

The Phantom of the Opera

SCRAPBOOK

Correspondent: Kris Koop Ouellette, "Page"

Who Has Done the Most Performances: Without question, George Lee Andrews holds the performance record. George began his *Phantom* journey more than twenty years ago as an original cast member. He'd been acting, singing and dancing professionally for 24 years before THAT! Through this show's record-breaking run, George has taken brief leaves-of-absence to star in other productions, readings, workshops and seminars, but he's remained true to the *Phantom* company, graduating from starring role to starring role with aplomb. George relishes the steady work in this great show and the many friendships that he's formed with coworkers over the past twenty years…and counting.

Production Make-Up Supervisor Thelma L. Pollard has also been with the show from the very beginning, having started in the Wig Department and later covering for the original Make-Up Artist. Thelma hand-paints the gory Phantom mask pieces each night and glues them with great skill onto the tender skin of our title character. She also trains and supervises all of the *Phantom* make-up artists world-wide and treasures that this job allows her to work nightly on a craft she truly loves and serve as mentor to other artists. One of those artists is Thelma's sister, Pearleta Price, a treasured member of our company.

Gypsy of the Year Sketch: Stage Manager and playwright, Craig Jacobs, developed a skit titled "Broadway Ballerina Calendar Girl," a take-off on Lucille Ball's VitaMetaVegamin scene. Katie Banks, Shaun Colledge and I performed the piece in which they all got high from the spray used to take the glare off of the calendar. The audience started howling when the ingredients of the spray were read: alcohol and amyl nitrate, (a.k.a. "poppers"). Also, five cast members (Katie Banks, Susan Owen, Geoff Packard, Jim Weitzer and I) were honored to serve as pit singers in the opening and closing numbers of the show, providing back-up to the original cast of *West Side Story*! To sing that beautiful music alongside Broadway legends Chita Rivera and Carol Lawrence…to warble along with opera star Reri Grist…to shout "Mambo!" with the amazing dancers who made this material famous…it was a thrill from beginning to end.

"Easter Bonnet" Sketch: George Lee Andrews starred as "The Longest-Running Actor on Broadway," along with Jessica Radetsky, Carly Blake Sebouhian and Shaun Colledge. The Bonnet was designed and worn by Assistant Wardrobe Supervisor, Robert Strong Miller, a member of the *Phantom* company for 18 years. Based on a sketch by dresser Michael Jacobs titled "A Chandelier in Pizzas," the Bonnet took first place…we think the pepperoni made of sequins gave us the upper hand.

Special Backstage Rituals: 1.) At each intermission, George Lee Andrews and Frank Mastrone use the stage-right quick-change room as their forum to tell some of the raunchiest,

(L-R): Jennifer Hope Wills, Howard McGillin and Tim Martin Gleason at the show's 20th anniversary party at the Ava Lounge in the Dream Hotel.

silliest, oldest jokes known to man. Dressers Anna McDaniel and Rose Mary Taylor have been known to chip in a joke or two as well.

2.) Dresser Michael Jacobs creates a work of art each night with a Sharpie and his sharp wit. The best drawings and their accompanying captions decorate the hallways and restroom walls. This tradition began with Michael and actress Polly Baird animating silly sayings created by George Lee Andrews.

3.) We have, as a group, become addicted to Yahoo Games' "Text Twist" and play it constantly in the stage manager's office. One person acts as typist, and a group consisting of any cast or crew member who is not performing a cue…forms around the computer screen shouting out "Tee! Tees! Set! Tes! Isn't 'Tes' a word?" We have all admitted to spelling in our sleep and should probably check into some trendy detox ranch. Even our Actors' Fund Walk-On, Calvin Slater, admits that he is consumed with the game after spending only one performance with our cast!

Favorite Moment During Performance: Bob Miller LOVES, LOVES, LOVES when the two Wild Women characters accidentally get the wires in their wigs attached and struggle to disengage. Actor Chris Bohannon gets a giggle when Geoff Packard, in the role of Mssr. Reyer, plays the onstage piano as though he's wearing a baseball glove or "ham-hands." George Lee Andrews gets a thrill at each performance during the climax of the first Managers' scene, a.k.a. "Prima Donna." The voices are all at their grandest and the entire group on stage physically links up for the first time in the scene, presenting a united front against the threats made by the Phantom. Rebecca Judd adores the moment before her sneaky entrance into the first Manager's scene, where she stands in the wing and delights in watching George Lee and David Cryer working together. Ken Kantor enjoys the moment the play ends and he can FINALLY relax about getting all of his lines right. There's a good reason for this! Read ON! Dresser Billy Hipkins enjoys the adrenaline rush

of racing through the Carlotta quick-change behind the bed. There he stands, upstage center, working to remove the diva's three piece Prima Donna costume and replace it with her two-piece Il Muto dress. There are three dressers and two hairdressers, plus two stage-hands trapped behind that bed for the entire *Il Muto* scene each night! Michael Jacobs loves when the Marksman shoots the pistol and we all hear screams from the audience! Dresser Mary Lou Rios' favorite all-time *Phantom* moment was the exciting appearance of Michael Crawford during the finale of our record-breaking gala performance.

Favorite In-Theatre Gathering Places: There is not a lot of room backstage at the Majestic Theatre, even though the building went through major renovations to ready it for the installation of our show. But we are dedicated to the art of socializing, so we have carved out nooks where we can gather.

1.) The Stage Managers' Office is often crowded, boasting crazy-cold air conditioning and candy, candy, candy.

2.) The Greenroom (thus named for its high mold content and measuring approximately four square feet of space decorated with rotten furniture we've nipped from the trash over at the Milford Plaza) is the Act I hangout for Richard Poole, Paul A. Schaefer, Frank Mastrone, Wayne Hobbs, Chris Bohannon, Geoff Packard, John Galdieri, and me. This group is committed to keeping our conversation at least as clean as the furniture. 3.) Jennifer Hope Wills, Susan Owen, Geoff Packard, Jim Weitzer and Katie Banks frequent the Phantom's Dressing Room, sipping lattes and making sure our wonderful Howard McGillin feels the love.

4.) Patricia Phillips makes the Carlotta Dressing Room the ultimate hangout when we get visits from Lisa Harrell's son, Jalen, or Cara Hannah's daughter, Rachel! FUN!

5.) The Nook under the stage-left staircase leading to the chorus dressing rooms (a.k.a. "The Shtoop") has been cultivated into a living room by Sally Williams, and between shows, a large group gathers to share some laughs before preparing for the second show.

6.) Dick Miller's office is our favorite spot to gather to watch sports, which leads to an interesting story. During an AL Division Series game between the Cleveland Indians and the New York Yankees this past season, Jack Hayes, popped into Dick's office for a quick glance at the game before racing upstairs to go onstage. Jack saw a shot of the infield, covered in whirling white which he mistook for falling snow. (The flurries were actually 'midges'— little bugs that had swarmed the field.) When Jack asked "Is that SNOW?", a good-natured rib-fest between he and Dick Miller became the best game of all. Dick got on the P.A. system several times over the next few days and gave the snowy weather report in Cleveland, and Jack swore revenge. Jack is a man of his word! While Dick was away on vacation, Jack painted the interior of Dick's office PEPTO BISMOL

The Phantom of the Opera
SCRAPBOOK

PINK and detailed the work boxes with colorful names, like Big Dick's Little Pink Box, etc. We all anxiously awaited Dick's response: he was a good sport and fell into gales of laughter. To this day, his office remains PINK.

Favorite Off-Site Hangout: Our show has been around so long, some of our favorite hangouts are history! Fred Smith, Stage Carpenter, still longs for Barrymore's, formerly a beloved site just across the street from our Stage Door. Michael's Pub is another goner, missed by Dresser and Stitcher Margie Marchionni. Of course we still love our Sardi's, our Angus McIndoe, our Kodama, but most of us really just want to go HOME!

"Carols for a Cure" Track: Norman Weiss, our beloved pianist and Associate Conductor, is also an award-winning composer. He and his writing partner, William Squier, contributed their new piece titled "Following a Star," sung by Howard McGillin, George Lee Andrews, Kenneth Kantor, Scott Mikita and me, and accompanied brilliantly by Norman himself, and Larry Spivack. Lynn Pinto and her fantastic associates at Rock-It Science Records made the sessions a joy for our cast and for everybody on Broadway!

Favorite Snack Food: Everybody enjoys a different snacky-treat, but the theme seems to be sugar and/or caffeine. Chris Bohannon admits that "anything edible" will satisfy his tastes, while George Lee Andrews sustains his energy by eating nuts. Rebecca Judd combines apples, almonds and peanut butter for a healthy kick. Ken Kantor is our omnivore; Frank Mastrone and Wren Marie Harrington chomp on cookies. Susan Owen sips on Sour Straws, and Hair Dressers Cara Hannah and Katie Kurz go crazy for Vienna Fingers and ANYTHING CHOCOLATE! Paul Schaefer loves the famous blondies and brownies that Norman Weiss makes. The ever-sleeveless Billy Hipkins will munch on "whatever you've got"; Michael Jacobs enjoys pretzels, and Margie Marchionni will take a nibble of anything home-made. Mary Lou Rios isn't picky—bring on the cookies or the chocolate, and she's a happy gal!

Favorite Therapies: Most of us see a shrink—"like going to the gym for your head!" Here are our other favorite therapies. George Lee does Tai Chi and walks to relax; Jack Hayes enjoys Pilates so much, he's become a certified instructor and holds class for us between shows! Wren, Jennifer Arnold and Janet Saia go Salsa Dancing to relieve their stress, and Wren takes her son Trevor on trips to Italy as often as the show can give her time off. Richard Poole has honed the quickest meditation trick ever…close your eyes, count to ten and BREATHE! Paul Schaefer relishes coffee and a donut as his favorite therapeutic treat. Bob Miller works out at the gym and then enjoys a long massage, and Mary Lou relaxes in a hot bath.

Memorable Ad-Libs: This has got to be our favorite category. We don't screw up often, but when we do, we do it MEMORABLY! Here is a sampling of some classics—two old stories, and

The *Phantom* ballerinas obtained a special permit to shoot this photo in the Degas wing of the Metropolitan Museum for a fundraising calendar. Their costumes and wigs are fashioned after the famous Degas paintings and sculptures behind them.

one brand-new, from our frequent flier in this category: Kenneth M. Kantor. Sorry Andrew! Harriet Clark relishes one particular moment when the Marksman's pistol failed to fire. Raoul altered his line to say, "Why didn't you FIRE?", to which the Marksman replied (in his best Inspector Clouseau dialect): "But Monsieur! Z'ere were no boollets!"

Jim Weitzer recalls a desperate moment on stage in the role of Raoul. The Phantom was approaching him with the Punjab Lasso (the noose) when the trick-wire got caught on something and couldn't move forward any further. The quick-thinking Phantom started backing Jim upstage, but Jim wasn't sure what to make of the new blocking. Professional that he is, Jim found himself up against the great gate that creates the rear wall of the Phantom's Lair and decided that the way to save the scene was to shout "ELECTRIC PORTE COULISS!" and then proceeded to ACT AS IF ELECTRIFIED FOR THE DURATION OF THE SCENE! If you know the show at all, you know that Raoul gets caught in the Punjab Lasso—or in this case, electrically shocked—almost immediately after he enters the scene. There's a good five minutes to go. So there Jim stood, vibrating and shaking against the Porte Couliss. He sang on cue, still vibrating, still twitching against the current of the electric porte couliss. The Phantom and Christine couldn't watch—they altered their blocking to remain facing the audience for the rest of the scene. When the Phantom finally released Raoul from the electrified gate, all three actors had tears of

laughter running down their faces.

And, last but not least…the most recent contribution by Kenneth M. Kantor, Broadway veteran of something like twelve shows…a Broadway historian…a man who can quote almost any musical from almost any era at any given moment. Trouble starts when Ken has to deliver his OWN LINES. Ken plays the role of Mssr. LeFevre, the theatre manager who announces his retirement in the first scene of the show. But before Mssr. LeFevre can make that announcement and make his hasty exit, Ken must introduce EVERYONE ON STAGE to EVERYONE ELSE ON STAGE. It just so happened that on one night in the year 2007, prior to show time, Ken had seasoned himself a pork chop, cooked that seasoned pork chop and eaten it for dinner. Later that same, fateful evening, Ken—tummy full with the tasty pork chop—was just off center-stage at the Majestic Theatre, in Broadway's longest-running hit show, *The Phantom of the Opera*, in front of a full house. As Mssr. LeFevre, Ken had just begun to introduce the new theatre managers to the crowd on stage when a glaze came over his eyes. We've all learned Ken's "tell" when he's about to go up on his lines. He grows a little taller, he rocks backwards and forth on his heels, and his eyes go glassy. His nostrils flare and a silly grin spreads across his face. And so it was that night, just as he was about to introduce Ubaldo Piangi, the glorious tenor…We spotted the signs and everyone on stage also grew a little taller. We all tried to make eye-contact with the stricken actor who was beginning his search for the name

The Phantom of the Opera
SCRAPBOOK

Ubaldo Piangi…Ubaldo Piangi…Ubaldo Piangi. What came to Ken's mind INSTEAD of "Ubaldo Piangi" was the name of the seasoning he had sprinkled on his delicious pork chop dinner. Adobo. So he stuttered…"And Signor…Aaaaaa—aaaaa—Adobo. (Pause, pause, pause) Pasquale."

Yes, ladies and gentlemen, 19.5 years into the run, Ken introduced a new character, ADOBO PASQUALE. Well, we took that hit and ran with it. For the rest of that performance, we ALL referred to Ubaldo Piangi as "Adobo Pasquale," only later to be told by stage crew member Giancarlo, a native of Italy, the direct translation of "Adobo Pasquale" is "Easter Ornament." We can only assume the Easter Ornament resembles one helluva tasty pork chop.

Best Off-Stage Ad-lib: Honors go to almost anything Geoff Packard says, but the current favorite is: "I'm going to act the F#@K out of this scene, Boo!" right before making his entrance in the Travelator mob scene which leads into the final Lair scene. Geoff and the rest of us are onstage in near black-out lighting for no more than 20 seconds.

Best Excuse for Lateness: Scott Mikita had to call Stage Management to advise them of his delay due to a MOOSE ON THE HIGHWAY. In rural Maine, this is probably a run-of-the-mill excuse, but we are talking the areas surrounding New York City, baby!

Memorable Press Encounter: We were visited by a *New York Times* photographer who shot backstage throughout one entire performance. She captured the cast, crew and orchestra in preparation, performance, and restoration for another performance…and the vibrant energy required and exuded by all. Those pictures spoke volumes to us all about the work we all do and sometimes think mundane. Also, Margie Marchionni was interviewed about her job as dresser/stitcher for a different feature in the *New York Times*. We are all so grateful people are willing to hear about our crazy/wonderful jobs!

Catchphrases Only the Company Would Recognize: Richard Poole shouting "Caution!" Chris Bohannon speaking of the "Front Butt." Harriet Clark saying "Chickety, chickety BOOM!" Or "Second Beginning."

Who Wore the Least: Three people declared that Wren Marie Harrington wears the least—any time she's backstage between cues. And two people celebrated George Lee Andrews' "Birthday Suit"…he's truly a Broadway Baby!

Ghostly Encounters: Harriet Clark found a note on the floor by her desk, situated beneath the audience floor in the bowels of the theatre. The note, printed in italic writing, read, "Please perform again tonight when everyone has left. O.G." Rebecca Judd sees her own reflection as a ghostly encounter when she's applied Madame Giry's base and not yet the dark browns or shadow. And Katie Kurz felt spirits were in the room when she performed day-work in the Wig Room and hair pins kept mysteriously dropping from the shelves, as though being blown down

Eddie Griffenkranz 1955-2008

In Memoriam

Our cast, crew and orchestra were devastated by the sudden loss of our dear co-worker and friend, Eddie Griffenkranz. Eddie passed away in his prime, just 52 years old, the loving husband to Jeanette and devoted father of two-year-old Eddie, Jr. On the evening that he died, Marilyn Caskey witnessed Eddie chatting with some NYC tourists prior to show time, speaking in his friendly manner, proudly relating the details of his job on Broadway, and sharing his good nature and humor with these total strangers…people who likely will never know what a privileged moment they shared with this wonderful man in the last hours of his life. We will always miss his warm greeting, "How ya doin', Honey?" We will miss the way he worked to keep his troubles from stealing his—or our—joy. We will always remember how readily his arm shot into his coat-pocket to retrieve the latest photos of his beautiful son and wife; how Eddie kept his hand on the small of Jeanette's back when they were in a room together. We dedicate this Yearbook and all of the work we do on *Phantom* to Eddie, and to the others we have loved and lost: Wayne Hobbs, Sr.; Weldon Blodgette; Carol Hershey; Marion Aasland; Jennifer Alexander; Luz Marie Davila; Abigail H. Jacobs; Corvella Rosa; Mark Slavinsky; Philip Steele; Hedvig and Rowland Sturges; Robert James Williams; and always…our Barbara Mae Phillips, JC Sheets, Richard Warren Pugh and Bob Fennell.

by a sudden wind, all afternoon…very spooky!

Coolest Thing About Being in this Show: We get to make incredibly mad money for charity, and one of our favorite projects from this past year was the creation of the Phantom Calendar, a love-letter to New York City, featuring (and inspired and created by) our Phantom Ballerinas. Gorgeously shot by photographer

and Phantom dresser Andrew Nelson, this calendar is nothing short of a work of art. From beginning to end, the Calendar tells the story of our hard-working ballerinas escaping from the theatre, tired of rehearsal, and out on the town in NYC! The ballet corp was assisted heavily by the Wig Department who dressed and re-dressed spare wigs for each of the fifteen+ photo shoots. The Wardrobe Department pressed and re-pressed the retired "Degas" costumes that the girls wore for each scene in the calendar. The girls and Andrew gave generously—even to the point of pain—to create a visually stunning group of photos that celebrate New York's iconic sites. The Department of Tourism and Serino Coyne heightened the professional quality of the piece. We actually got to go on the field at Shea Stadium, guests of Jill Knee, the Mets Community Services Director. The girls were provided with actual batting helmets, official bats and balls, and team jerseys and hats, plus a bountiful buffet! An extraordinary treat, all around! At New York landmark Serendipity, the dancers shared a GIANT sundae. The beauties posed alongside our fantastic Heroic New York City Firemen, helmeted and ready to spring into action. Central Park played host to three shoots—on the lake, near Shepherd's Field, and on the antique merry-go-round. The calendar is almost as beautiful as these dancers, and the experience of creating it was extraordinary for all involved!

Understudy Anecdote: Jimmy Smagula appeared onstage, before a live audience, wearing his bedroom slippers instead of his Piangi boots. The slippers were a last-minute resort when his shoes went missing and his dresser could only shrug as to their where-abouts. The soft, puffy slippers looked black backstage in normal lighting, but onstage, the slippers seemed to glow an iridescent purple. Word passed amongst the ensemble like wild-fire, and we all gathered offstage to watch Jimmy finish the scene in his very bright purple shoes.

Memorable Directorial Quotes: Another favorite category… George Lee will never forget Hal Prince stating, before the entire company, "I give this note to George every five years or so…."

Working in a show where calipers are used to measure our spacing on stage has taught us a trick or two…Frank Mastrone was asked to move two inches to the left. He shifted his weight from his right foot to his left, but neither foot left the floor. "PERFECT!" was the dance supervisor's response.

Wayne Hobbs took a leave-of-absence from the Opera world to play with us Broadway folk. In a rehearsal, Production Supervisor Peter von Mayrhauser stopped the action and asked Wayne why he was looking downward so much. Wayne replied that in Opera, the singer's eyes are GLUED to the conductor. PvM gave him direction none of us will ever forget: "On Broadway, we ignore the Conductor—he's invisible."

The Pirate Queen

First Preview: March 6, 2007. Opened: April 5, 2007.
Closed: June 17, 2007 after 32 Previews and 85 Performances.

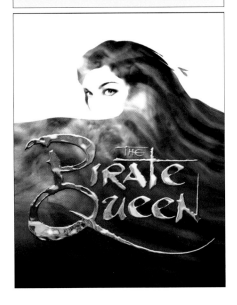

PLAYBILL

CAST

(in order of appearance)

Flute Player .... TROY EDWARD BOWLES
Grace (Grania) O'Malley ... STEPHANIE J. BLOCK
Tiernan .... HADLEY FRASER
Dubhdara .... JEFF McCARTHY
Evleen .... ÁINE UÍ CHEALLAIGH
Queen Elizabeth I .... LINDA BALGORD
Sir Richard Bingham .... WILLIAM YOUMANS
Donal O'Flaherty .... MARCUS CHAIT
Chieftain O'Flaherty .... JOSEPH MAHOWALD
Majella .... BROOKE ELLIOTT
Eoin ......(Wed. mat., Thurs., Sat. eve. & Sun. mat.)
CHRISTOPHER GREY MISA
Eoin ....(Tues., Wed. eve., Fri. & Sat. mat.)
STEVEN BARATH
Ensemble .... NICK ADAMS,
RICHARD TODD ADAMS, CAITLIN ALLEN,
SEAN BEGLAN, JERAD BORTZ,
TROY EDWARD BOWLES,
GRADY McLEOD BOWMAN,
ALEXIS ANN CARRA, NOELLE CURRAN,
BOBBIE ANN DUNN, BROOKE ELLIOTT,
CHRISTOPHER GARBRECHT, ERIC HATCH,
CRISTIN J. HUBBARD, DAVID KOCH,
TIMOTHY KOCHKA, JAMIE LAVERDIERE,
JOSEPH MAHOWALD, TOKIKO MASUDA,
PADRAIC MOYLES, BRIAN O'BRIEN,
KYLE JAMES O'CONNOR,
MICHAEL JAMES SCOTT, GREG STONE,
KATIE ERIN TOMLINSON, DANIEL TORRES,
JENNIFER WAISER, BRIANA YACAVONE

Continued on next page

HILTON THEATRE
A LIVE NATION VENUE

RIVERDREAM
UNDER THE DIRECTION OF
MOYA DOHERTY   JOHN McCOLGAN
PRESENTS
BOUBLIL & SCHÖNBERG'S

THE PIRATE QUEEN
A NEW MUSICAL

BOOK BY
ALAIN BOUBLIL   CLAUDE-MICHEL SCHÖNBERG
and RICHARD MALTBY, JR.

MUSIC BY
CLAUDE-MICHEL SCHÖNBERG

LYRICS BY
ALAIN BOUBLIL   RICHARD MALTBY, JR.   JOHN DEMPSEY

BASED UPON THE NOVEL, "GRANIA – SHE KING OF THE IRISH SEAS" BY MORGAN LLYWELYN

STARRING
Stephanie J. Block   Hadley Fraser
Linda Balgord   Marcus Chait   Jeff McCarthy   William Youmans

WITH

Nick Adams, Richard Todd Adams, Caitlin Allen, Steven Barath, Sean Beglan, Timothy W. Bish, Jerad Bortz, Troy Edward Bowles,
Grady McLeod Bowman, Rachel Bress, Don Brewer, Kimilee Bryant, Alexis Ann Carra, Cara Cooper, Noelle Curran,
Bobbie Ann Dunn, Brooke Elliott, Christopher Garbrecht, Eric Hatch, Cristin J. Hubbard, David Koch, Timothy Kochka, Jamie LaVerdiere,
Joseph Mahowald, Tokiko Masuda, Christopher Grey Misa, Padraic Moyles, Brian O'Brien, Kyle James O'Connor, Michael James Scott,
Greg Stone, Katie Erin Tomlinson, Daniel Torres, Áine Uí Cheallaigh, Kathy Voytko, Jennifer Waiser, Jeff Williams, Briana Yacavone

SCENIC DESIGN **EUGENE LEE**	COSTUME DESIGN **MARTIN PAKLEDINAZ**	LIGHTING DESIGN **KENNETH POSNER**	SOUND DESIGN **JONATHAN DEANS**
HAIR DESIGN **PAUL HUNTLEY**	SPECIAL EFFECTS DESIGN **GREGORY MEEH**	AERIAL SEQUENCE DESIGN **PAUL RUBIN**	MAKE-UP DESIGN **ANGELINA AVALLONE**
SCENIC DESIGN ASSOCIATE **EDWARD PIERCE**	FIGHT DIRECTOR **J. STEVEN WHITE**	ASSOCIATE DIRECTOR **TARA YOUNG**	ASSOCIATE CHOREOGRAPHER **RACHEL BRESS**
CASTING **TARA RUBIN CASTING**	PRODUCTION MANAGER **PETER W. LAMB**	PRODUCTION STAGE MANAGER **C. RANDALL WHITE**	MUSICAL COORDINATOR **MSI/SAM LUTFIYYA**

MARKETING   GENERAL PRESS REPRESENTATIVE   ASSOCIATE PRODUCER
TMG-THE MARKETING GROUP   **BONEAU BRYAN-BROWN**   **DANCAP PRODUCTIONS, INC.**

EXECUTIVE PRODUCER (DEVELOPMENT)   EXECUTIVE PRODUCER   GENERAL MANAGEMENT
RONAN SMITH   **EDGAR DOBIE**   **THEATRE PRODUCTION GROUP LLC**

ORCHESTRATIONS, VOCAL ARRANGEMENTS,
MUSICAL SUPERVISION & DIRECTION   ARTISTIC DIRECTOR   IRISH DANCE CHOREOGRAPHER
JULIAN KELLY   **JOHN McCOLGAN**   **CAROL LEAVY JOYCE**

MUSICAL STAGING
GRACIELA DANIELE

DIRECTED BY
FRANK GALATI

THE PRODUCERS WISH TO EXPRESS THEIR APPRECIATION TO THEATRE DEVELOPMENT FUND FOR ITS SUPPORT OF THIS PRODUCTION

LIVE BROADWAY

6/17/07

Hadley Fraser
and Company

Photo by Joan Marcus

The Pirate Queen

SCENES AND MUSICAL NUMBERS

Time: Late sixteen century
Place: Ireland and England

ACT 1

	Prologue	Grace, Tiernan
SCENE 1	"The Pirate Queen"	Dubhdara, Tiernan, Grace, Evleen, Oarsmen and Company
	"Woman"	Grace
SCENE 2	"The Storm"	Company
	"My Grace"	Dubhdara and Grace
SCENE 3	"Here on This Night"	Grace, Tiernan, Crew
SCENE 4	"The First Battle"	Grace, Tiernan, Dubhdara and Company
SCENE 5	"The Waking of the Queen"	Elizabeth, Ladies-in-Waiting
	"Rah-Rah, Tip-Top"	Elizabeth, Bingham, Lords and Ladies-in-Waiting
SCENE 6	"The Choice Is Mine"	Grace, Dubhdara, Chieftain O'Flaherty, Tiernan, Donal and Company
	"The Bride's Song"	Grace, Evleen, Women
SCENE 7	"Boys'll Be Boys"	Donal, Mates and Barmaids
SCENE 8	"The Wedding"	Grace, Tiernan, Donal, Dubhdara, Chieftain O'Flaherty, Evleen and Company
SCENE 9	"I'll Be There"	Tiernan
SCENE 10	"Boys'll Be Boys" (Reprise)	Donal and Mates, Grace, Chieftain O'Flaherty
SCENE 11	"Trouble at Rockfleet"	Grace, Tiernan, Donal, Bingham and Company
SCENE 12	"A Day Beyond Belclare"	Grace, Tiernan, Donal and Company
SCENE 13	"Go Serve Your Queen"	Elizabeth and Bingham
SCENE 14	"Dubhdara's Farewell"	Dubhdara and Grace
	"Sail to the Stars"	Grace, Tiernan, Donal, Evleen and Company

ACT 2

	Entr'Acte	
SCENE 1	"It's a Boy"	Grace, Tiernan, Donal, Evleen, Majella and Sailors
SCENE 2	"Enemy at Port Side"	Grace, Tiernan, Donal, Evleen, Majella and Sailors
	"I Dismiss You"	Grace, Donal and Sailors
SCENE 3	"If I Said I Loved You"	Tiernan and Grace
SCENE 4	"The Role of the Queen"	Elizabeth, Bingham, Lords and Ladies-in-Waiting
SCENE 5	"The Christening"	Evleen, Grace, Tiernan and Company
	"Let a Father Stand By His Son"	Donal, Grace, Bingham, Tiernan, Evleen and Company
SCENE 6	"Surrender"	Bingham, Tiernan, Elizabeth and Company
SCENE 7	"She Who Has All"	Elizabeth and Grace
SCENE 8	"Lament"	Grace, Majella, Eoin and Company
SCENE 9	"The Sea of Life"	Grace and Company
SCENE 10	"Terra Marique Potens"	Elizabeth, Grace, Bingham
	"Woman to Woman"	Elizabeth and Grace
	"Behind the Screen"	Company
	"Grace's Exit"	Elizabeth, Grace, Bingham and Company
SCENE 11	Finale	Grace, Tiernan and Company

Hadley Fraser and Áine Uí Cheallaigh are appearing with the permission of Actors' Equity Association. The producers gratefully acknowledge Actors' Equity Association for its assistance with this production.

Special thanks to Sean-nós singer and traditional Irish vocal and Irish language consultant, Áine Uí Cheallaigh

Cast Continued

UNDERSTUDIES

For Grace: KATIE ERIN TOMLINSON
For Tiernan: JAMIE LAVERDIERE, GREG STONE, DANIEL TORRES
For Queen Elizabeth I: KIMILEE BRYANT, CRISTIN J. HUBBARD
For Donal: RICHARD TODD ADAMS, DANIEL TORRES
For Bingham: RICHARD TODD ADAMS, JOSEPH MAHOWALD
For Dubhdara: CHRIS GARBRECHT, JOSEPH MAHOWALD
For Evleen: BROOKE ELLIOTT, CRISTIN J. HUBBARD
For Majella: KIMILEE BRYANT, CRISTIN J. HUBBARD
For Chieftain O'Flaherty: DON BREWER, BRIAN O'BRIEN, JEFF WILLIAMS
For Flute Player: TIMOTHY W. BISH

STANDBY

For Grace: KATHY VOYTKO

SWINGS

TIMOTHY W. BISH, RACHEL BRESS, DON BREWER, KIMILEE BRYANT, CARA COOPER, JEFF WILLIAMS

Dance Captain: RACHEL BRESS
Fight Captain, Assistant Dance Captain: TIMOTHY W. BISH
Assistant Dance Captain: PADRAIC MOYLES

Production Stage Manager: C. RANDALL WHITE
Stage Manager: KATHLEEN E. PURVIS

ORCHESTRA

Musical Director/Conductor: JULIAN KELLY
Associate Musical Director/Keyboard II/ Assistant Conductor: JOSHUA ROSENBLUM
Keyboard I: BRIAN CONNOR
Fiddle/Violin: LIZ KNOWLES
Uilleann Pipes/Whistles: KIERAN O'HARE
Soprano Sax/Clarinet: KENNETH EDGE
Horn: JEFF NELSEN
Harp/Gaelic Harp: KIRSTEN AGRESTA
Guitars/Banjo: STEVE ROBERTS
Electric Bass: MICHAEL PEARCE
Percussion: DAVE ROTH
Drums/Bodhran: FRANK PAGANO
Music Coordinator: SAM LUTFIYYA/ MUSIC SERVICES INTERNATIONAL

Additional choreography by MARK DENDY.

The Pirate Queen

Stephanie J. Block
Grace "Grania" O'Malley

Hadley Fraser
Tiernan

Linda Balgord
Queen Elizabeth I

Marcus Chait
Donal

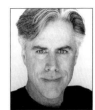

Jeff McCarthy
Dubhdara

William Youmans
Bingham

Nick Adams
Ensemble

Richard Todd Adams
Ensemble

Caitlin Allen
Ensemble

Steven Barath
Eoin

Sean Beglan
Ensemble

Timothy W. Bish
Assistant Fight Director, Fight Captain, Assistant Dance Captain, Swing

Jerad Bortz
Ensemble

Troy Edward Bowles
Flute Player, Ensemble

Grady McLeod Bowman
Ensemble

Rachel Bress
Associate Choreographer/ Dance Captain/ Swing

Don Brewer
Swing

Kimilee Bryant
Swing

Alexis Ann Carra
Ensemble

Cara Cooper
Swing

Noelle Curran
Ensemble

Bobbie Ann Dunn
Ensemble

Brooke Elliott
Ensemble, Majella

Christopher Garbrecht
Ensemble

Eric Hatch
Ensemble

Cristin J. Hubbard
Ensemble

David Koch
Ensemble

Timothy Kochka
Ensemble

Jamie LaVerdiere
Ensemble

Joseph Mahowald
Chieftan O'Flaherty, Ensemble

Tokiko Masuda
Ensemble

Christopher Grey
Misa Eoin

Padraic Moyles
Ensemble, Assistant Dance Captain

Brian O'Brien
Ensemble

Kyle James O'Connor
Ensemble

The Pirate Queen

Michael James Scott
Ensemble

Greg Stone
Ensemble

Katie Erin Tomlinson
Ensemble

Daniel Torres
Ensemble

Áine Uí Cheallaigh
Evleen

Kathy Voytko
Standby Grace

Jennifer Waiser
Ensemble

Jeff Williams
Swing

Briana Yacavone
Ensemble

Alain Boublil
Book and Lyrics

Claude-Michel
Schönberg
Book and Music

Richard Maltby, Jr.
Book and Lyrics

Frank Galati
Director

Graciela Daniele
Musical Staging

Carol Leavy Joyce
*Irish Dance
Choreographer*

Eugene Lee
Scenic Design

Martin Pakledinaz
Costume Design

Kenneth Posner
Lighting Design

Jonathan Deans
Sound Design

Paul Huntley
Wig Design

Paul Rubin
Aerial Effects Design

Angelina Avallone
Makeup Design

J. Steven White
Fight Director

Tara Young
Associate Director

Sam Lutfiyya
Musical Coordinator

Tara Rubin Casting
Casting

Ronan Smith
*Executive Producer,
Development*

Edgar Dobie
Executive Producer

Moya Doherty
Producer

John McColgan
*Producer and
Artistic Director*

The Pirate Queen

Photos by Ben Strothmann

FRONT OF HOUSE STAFF

Front Row (L-R): Kirssy Toribio (Head Usher), Errol Whittington (Head Usher), Edward Griggs (Usher), Mr. Kennedy (Usher), Denise Williams (Usher), Adam Sarsfield (Usher), D. Lloyd (Head Usher).

Second Row (L-R): Billy Pena (Usher), Lisa Lopez (Usher), D. Langenfield (Usher), Juana Rivas (Usher), Mike Chaves (Usher), S. Wilson (Usher), Alicia Wright (Usher), P. Fetini (Usher), Sharon Hawkins (Usher).

Back Row (L-R): Alan Toribio (Usher), J. Blaustein (Usher), K. Fuller (Usher), C. Kayser (Usher), M. Bell (Usher), K. Murry (Usher).

STAGE CREW

Seated (L-R): Steven Kirkham, Lair Max Paulsen, Bobbi Morse, Mickey Abbate, Billy Hipkins, Shannon Quinones, Tree Sarvay, Sandra M. Franck.

Second Row (L-R): Jillian Beglan, Michael Louis, Robin Cook, Shannon Munn, Vincent Berardi, Michael Wilhoite, Charlene Speyerer, Pam Hughes.

Standing (L-R): Arlene Watson, Kurt Kielmann, Danny Mura, Gregory Holtz, C. Randall White, Gary Seibert, Emily Ockenfels, Reginald Vessey, Donna Holland, Paul Verity, Vanessa Valeriano, Keith Caggiano, John Gibson, Chris Keene, Tommy McDonough, Dan C. Hochstine, Jeff Facinelli, Greg Fedigan, Mike Bernstein, Jimmy Harris, Walter Mazurek.

The Pirate Queen

Photo by Ben Strothmann

CAST AND CREW

Seated (L-R): Linda Balgord, Steven Kirkham, Cristin J. Hubbard, Briana Yacavone, Stephanie J. Block, Tara Young, Marcus Chait, Grady Bowman, Sandra M. Franck, Michael Wilhoite, William Youmans.

Second Row (L-R): Jason D. Shur, Bobbi Morse, John R. Gibson, Caitlin Allen, Tokiko Masuda, Michael James Scott, Noelle Curran, Kimilee Bryant, Timothy W. Bish, Jamie La Verdiere, Charlene Speyerer, Kathy Voytko, Alexis Ann Carra, Hadley Fraser, Jeff McCarthy, John McColgan.

Third Row (L-R): Sean Beglan, Brooke Elliott, Bobbie Ann Dunn, Nick Adams, Troy Edward Bowles, Joseph Mahowald, Kyle James O'Connor, Richard Todd Adams, Jeff Williams.

Fourth Row (L-R): Tonya Bodison, Therese Ducey, Padraic Moyles, Rachel Bress, Daniel Torres, Brian O'Brien, Jerad Bortz, Eric Hatch, Áine Uí Cheallaigh, Walter Mazurek, Jillian Beglan, Emily Ockenfels.

Fifth Row (L-R): Pam Hughes, Carrie Phillips, Gregory Holtz, Katie Erin Tomlinson, Lair Max Paulsen, Vanessa Valeriano, David Koch, Mickey Abbate, Shannon Munn, Tree Sarvay, Billy Hipkins, Shannon Quinones, Donna Holland, Gary Seibert, Paul Verity, Michael Bernstein, Dan C. Hochstine, Edgar Dobie.

Back Row (L-R): Elizabeth Talmadge, Keith Caggiano, Michael Louis, Danny Mura, Robin Cook, Kurt Kielmann (Hidden), Arlene Watson, Joshua Rosenblum, Christopher Garbrecht, Vincent Berardi, Jim Brandeberry (Hidden), Jeff Facinelli, Kris Keene, Tommy McDonough (Hidden), Jimmy Harris (Hidden), C. Randall White (Hidden).

STAFF FOR *THE PIRATE QUEEN*

RIVERDREAM
Moya Doherty, Managing Producer
John McColgan, Managing Producer
Edgar Dobie, Executive Producer (North America)
Ronan Smith, Executive Producer (Dublin)
Paula Burke, Executive Manager
Louise Byrne, Production Coordinator
Majella Cuttle, Executive Assistant
Wendy Mau, Assistant to Edgar Dobie

GENERAL MANAGEMENT
THEATRE PRODUCTION GROUP, LLC
Frank P. Scardino

COMPANY MANAGER
Jim Brandeberry

PRODUCTION MANAGER
Peter W. Lamb

GENERAL PRESS REPRESENTATIVE
BONEAU/BRYAN-BROWN
Adrian Bryan-Brown   Matt Polk
Adriana Douzos   Jessica Johnson   Amy Kass

PRODUCTION
STAGE MANAGER .... C. RANDALL WHITE
Stage Manager ....Kathleen E. Purvis

Assistant Stage Managers.................Sandra M. Franck,
Charlene Speyerer, Michael Wilhoite
Assistant Company Manager .... Elizabeth M. Talmadge
Associate Director .... Tara Young
Associate Choreographer .... Rachel Bress
Assistant to the General Manager .... Tegan Meyer
Associate Scenic Designer .... Edward Pierce
1st Assistant Scenic Designer .... Nick Francone
2nd Assistant Scenic Designer .... Jen Price
Scenic Design Studio Assistants .... Arielle Schiff,
Tristan Jeffers
Scenic Design Intern .... Iryna Clark
Associate Lighting Designers.............Philip Rosenberg,
Patricia Nichols
Assistant Lighting Designer ....Aaron Spivey

The Pirate Queen

Associate Costume Designer .... MaryAnn D. Smith
1st Assistant Costume Designer .... Courtney McClain
2nd Assistant Costume Designer .... Randall E. Klein
Assistant to the Costume Designer .... Erin Murphy
Costume Rendering Assistant .... William Beilke
Costume Student Intern .... Sarah Pauker
Assistant Sound Designer .... Brian Hsieh
Automated Lighting Programmer .... David Arch
Art Design Concept by ...The Apartment Creative Agency
Art Design Development
    and implementation by .... Zeus Creative Dublin
Special Effects Assistant .... Jeremy Chernick
Assistant Fight Director .... Timothy W. Bish
Electronic Music Programmer .... Brett Alan Sommer,
                                                    Jim Harp
Music Copying &
    Preparation .... Mark Cumberland for Hotstave LTD
Irish Music Consultant .... David Downes
Production Carpenter .... Don S. Gilmore
Head Carpenter .... Jim Kane
Assistant Carpenters .... Eric E. Smith,
                                            Scott "Gus" Poitras
Production Electrician .... Michael S. LoBue
Head Electrician .... Jon Mark Davidson
Advance Electrician .... Jody Durham
Automated Lighting Programmer
    (Chicago) .... Timothy F. Rogers
Assistant Electricians .... Adam Biscow,
                                            Andrew J. Bynum,
                                            Thomas Galinski Jr.
Production Sound .... Garth Helm
Head Sound .... Daniel C. Hochstine
Assistant Sound .... Keith Caggiano
Production Property Master .... Joseph P. Harris, Jr.
Head Property Man .... Michael Bernstein
Assistant Property Man .... Reginald Vessey
Wardrobe Supervisor........................... Robert Guy
Assistant Wardrobe Supervisor .... Michael Louis
Dressers .... Gilbert Aleman, Vincent Berardi,
                                Renee Borys, Bobby Condon,
                                Robin Cook, Donna Holland,
                                Gregory Holtz, Billy Hipkins,
                                Pam Hughes, Kurt Kielmann,
                                Estella Marie, Walter Mazurek,
                                Bobbi Morse, Shannon Munn,
                                Danny Mura, Emily Ockenfels,
                                Carrie Phillips, Shannon Quinones,
                                Tree Sarvay, Gary Seibert,
                                Vanessa Valeriano, Arlene Watson
Hair and Makeup Supervisor .... Edward J. Wilson
Assistant Hair and Makeup Supervisor .....Steven Kirkham
Hair Stylists .... Lair Max Paulsen, Therese Ducey,
                                Jason D. Shur, Tonya Bodison
Advertising .... SpotCo/Drew Hodges,
                                Jim Edwards, Jim Aquino, Darius Suyama
Marketing .... TMG - The Marketing Group/
                                Laura Matalon, Tanya Grubich,
                                Anne Rippey, Victoria Cairl,
                                Ronni Seif, Meghan Zaneski,
                                Allison Cabellon
Web Design/Internet Marketing ..... Situation Marketing/
                                Damian Bazadona, Chris Powers,
                                Joey Oliva
Souvenir Merchandise designed
    and created by .... The Araca Group
Castcom Producer .... Rachel O'Connor
Castcom Editor .... Andrew Robert Thomas

Casting .... Tara Rubin Casting
    Casting Directors: Tara Rubin, Dunja Vitolic
    Casting Associates: Eric Woodall, Laura Schutzel,
                                                    Merri Sugarman
    Casting Assistants: Rebecca Carfagna, Jeff Siebert,
                                                    Paige Blansfield
Production Assistants .... Christopher Munnell,
                                                    Eva L. Hare
SDCF Observer .... Selda Sahin
Legal Counsel .... Levine, Plotkin & Menin, LLP/
                                Loren H. Plotkin, Susan Mindell
Accountants .... Fried & Kowgios CPAs LLP/
                                Robert Fried, Sarah Galbraith
Banking .... Commerce Bank /
                                Barbara von Borstel, Ashley Elezi
Insurance .... AON Entertainment Insurance/
                                                    Claudia Kaufman
Payroll .... Castellana Services, Inc
Production Photographer .... Joan Marcus
Rehearsal Studio .... The New 42nd St. Studios
Travel Agent .... Protravel Incorporated, Beverly Hills
Housing Broker .... Marie-Claire Martineau,
                                Maison International, Ltd.
Hotel Accommodations .... Road Concierge Inc.
Ground Transportation .... Hollywood Limousine

Physical therapy provided by The Green Room PT
(Dr. Philip Bauman, MD, orthopedic consultant).

Makeup Provided by M.A.C Cosmetics

Scenery built by F&D Scene Changes; Show Control; and
Scenic Motion Control featuring Stage Command
Systems® by Scenic Technologies, a division of Production
Resource Group LLC, New Windsor, NY. Lighting equip-
ment and special lighting effects by PRG Lighting. Sound
equipment from PRG Audio. Special effects by Jauchem &
Meeh Inc. Faux-Fire by Technifex Inc. Costume Shops: Eric
Winterling, Inc.; Tricorne, Inc.; Euro Co. Costumes; Carelli
Costumes Inc.; Donna Langman Costumes; Seams
Unlimited, ltd. Armor by Costume Armour, Inc. Millinery
by Lynne Mackey Studio; Arnold S. Levine, Inc.; Rodney
Gordon, Inc. Queen Elizabeth's specialty collars by Killer
Theatrical Crafts. Printing and dyeing by Gene Mignola,
Inc. Dyeing and distressing by Izquierdo Studios, Ltd.; Dye-
namix Inc.; Asiatico Studio. Footwear by Handmade
Shoes/Fred Longtin; Pluma Handmade Dance Footwear;
J.C. Theatrical and Custom Footwear; Harr Theaterschuhe;
Capezio. Specialty jewelry by Lawrence Vrba. Celtic jewelry
by Christine McPartland. Celtic embroidery by Robert W.
Trump. Specialty gloves by Bionic Glove Technology. Props
constructed by Cigar Box Studios Inc., Paragon Innovation
Group Inc., The Spoon Group, John Creech Design &
Production, Peter Sarafin, Beyond Imagination, Portafiori
Flowers. Additional scenery built by Hawkeye Scenic
Studios, Inc. Throat lozenges provided by Ricola. Special
thanks to Ayotte Drums for building the drums, Axis
Percussion for supplying the drum hardware, Lyon-Healy
Harps for their generosity in coordinating the harps and
TOP HAT Amplification for building the guitar amps used
in this production. Additional music preparation by Anixter
Rice Music Service. Special thanks to BRA*TENDERS for
undergarments and hosiery.

Flying by Foy.

www.thepiratequeen.com

HILTON THEATRE STAFF

General Manager .... Micah Hollingworth
Assistant General Manager .... Teresa Ryno
House Manager .... Emily Fisher
Facility Manager .... Jeff Nuzzo
Assistant Facility Manager .... Alex Becerra
Box Office Treasurer .... Spencer Taustine
Assistant Box Office Treasurer .... Kenny Klein
Head Carpenter .... James C. Harris
Head Electrician .... Art J. Friedlander
Head of Properties .... Joseph P. Harris, Jr.
Head of Sound .... John R. Gibson
Staff Accountant .... Carmen Martinez
Payroll Administrator .... Tiyana Works
Shipping/Receiving .... Dinara Kratsch
Administrative Assistant .... Jenny Kirlin

Hilton Theatre – A Live Nation Venue

LIVE NATION

President and
    Chief Executive Officer .... Michael Rapino
Chief Executive Officer,
    North America Music .... Bruce Eskowitz
Chief Financial Officer .... Alan Ridgeway
Executive Vice President,
    North America Finance .... David Shuman
Vice-President, North America Finance .... Kathy Porter
Executive Vice President,
    North America Venues .... Ned Collett
Senior Vice President, NY and CT .... John Huff
Director of Labor Relations .... Chris Brockmeyer

LIVE NATION – THEATRICAL

Chairman, Global Theatre .... David Ian
CEO Theatrical, North America .... Steve Winton
President and COO, North America ..David M. Anderson
CFO, North America .... Paul Dietz
Senior Vice President, Producing .... Jennifer Costello
Executive Vice President/CMO .... Susie Krajsa
Senior Vice President, Operations .... Dan Swartz
Senior Vice President,
    Sales and Ticketing .... Courtney Pierce
Vice President, Programming .... Alison Spiriti

Live Nation is a leading live content and distribution company focused on creating superior experiences for artists,
performers, corporations and audiences. Live Nation owns,
operates or has booking rights for 150 venues worldwide
and has promoted or produced more than 20,000 events in
2005 and 2006. Producing credits include *Dr. Seuss' How the
Grinch Stole Christmas! The Musical, The Producers,
Hairspray, Dirty Rotten Scoundrels* and *Spamalot* on
Broadway; an all-new production of Andrew Lloyd Webber's
The Phantom of the Opera at the Venetian in Las Vegas; and
national tours of Dora the Explorer Live! and Barbie Live in
Fairytopia. The theatrical division also presents Broadway
Across America, www.BroadwayAcrossAmerica.com, an
annual subscription series of top Broadway shows and the-
atrical entertainment in more than 50 markets across North
America. Live Nation is listed on the New York Stock
Exchange, trading under the symbol "LYV." More information about Live Nation and its businesses is available at
www.LiveNation.com.

Pygmalion

First Preview: September 21, 2007. Opened: October 18, 2007.
Closed: December 16, 2007 after 31 previews and 69 performances.

PLAYBILL

CAST
(in order of speaking)

Miss Clara Eynsford Hill . . . . KERRY BISHÉ*
Mrs. Eynsford-Hill . . . . SANDRA SHIPLEY*
Bystander/Taxi Driver . . . . . . .DOUG STENDER*
Freddy Eynsford Hill . . . . . . .KIERAN CAMPION*
Liza Doolittle . . . . .CLAIRE DANES*
Colonel Pickering . . . . .BOYD GAINES*
Henry Higgins . . . . .JEFFERSON MAYS*
Sarcastic Bystander . . . . .TONY CARLIN*
Other Bystanders . . . . .JONATHAN FIELDING*,
ROBIN MOSELEY*,
JENNIFER ARMOUR, BRAD HEIKES,
CURTIS SHUMAKER
Mrs. Pearce . . . . .BRENDA WEHLE*
Alfred Doolittle . . . . .JAY O. SANDERS*
Mrs. Higgins . . . . .HELEN CAREY*
Parlor Maid . . . . .KAREN WALSH*

TIME & PLACE

London, 1913
Act I: Covent Garden, 11:15 pm
Act II: Higgins' laboratory on Wimpole Street,
11:00 am the next morning
Act III: Mrs. Higgins' drawing room,
Chelsea embankment,
between 4:00 and 5:00 pm some months later
Act IV: Higgins' laboratory, midnight
Act V: Mrs. Higgins' drawing room,
the next morning

Continued on next page

AMERICAN AIRLINES THEATRE

ROUNDABOUTTHEATRECOMPANY

Todd Haimes, Artistic Director
Harold Wolpert, Managing Director
Julia C. Levy, Executive Director

Presents

Claire Danes   Jefferson Mays

Boyd Gaines   Jay O. Sanders

in

PYGMALION

by

George Bernard Shaw

Helen Carey   Brenda Wehle

Kerry Bishé   Kieran Campion   Sandra Shipley

Tony Carlin   Jonathan Fielding   Robin Moseley   Doug Stender   Karen Walsh

Jennifer Armour   Brad Heikes   Curtis Shumaker

Set & Costume Design	Lighting Design	Sound Design
Jonathan Fensom	Jason Taylor	Gregory Clarke

Dialect Coach	Hair and Wig Design	Production Stage Manager
Majella Hurley	Richard Orton	Arthur Gaffin

Casting	Technical Supervisor	General Manager	Press Representative
Jim Carnahan, C.S.A.	Steve Beers	Sydney Beers	Boneau/Bryan-Brown

Director of Marketing & Sales Promotion	Director of Development	Founding Director	Associate Artistic Director
David B. Steffen	Jeffory Lawson	Gene Feist	Scott Ellis

Directed by

David Grindley

**Major support for this production provided by The Blanche and Irving
Laurie Foundation and the New York City Department of Cultural Affairs.**

Roundabout Theatre Company is a member of the League of Resident Theatres.
www.roundabouttheatre.org

10/18/07

(L-R): Jefferson Mays and Claire Danes.

Photo by Joan Marcus

Pygmalion

Cast Continued

UNDERSTUDIES

For Liza Doolittle, Clara Eynsford Hill:
   KAREN WALSH*
For Henry Higgins, Colonel Pickering:
   TONY CARLIN*
For Mrs. Eynsford Hill, Mrs. Pearce, Parlor Maid:
   ROBIN MOSELEY*
For Mrs. Higgins:
   SANDRA SHIPLEY*
For Freddy Eynsford Hill, Bystander, Taxi Driver,
Sarcastic Bystander:
   JONATHAN FIELDING*
For Alfred Doolittle:
   DOUG STENDER*

Production Stage Manager: ARTHUR GAFFIN*
Stage Manager: DAVID SUGARMAN*

*Members of Actors' Equity Association,
the union of professional actors and stage managers
in the United States.

(L-R): Claire Danes and Jefferson Mays.

Claire Danes
Liza Doolittle

Jefferson Mays
Henry Higgins

Boyd Gaines
Colonel Pickering

Jay O. Sanders
Doolittle

Helen Carey
Mrs. Higgins

Brenda Wehle
Mrs. Pearce

Kerry Bishé
Clara Eynsford Hill

Kieran Campion
Freddy Eynsford Hill

Sandra Shipley
Mrs. Eynsford Hill

Tony Carlin
Sarcastic Bystander

Jonathan Fielding
Bystander

Robin Moseley
Bystander

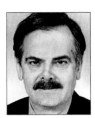
Doug Stender
Bystander, Taxi Driver

Karen Walsh
Parlour Maid

George Bernard Shaw
Playwright

David Grindley
Director

Jonathan Fensom
Set & Costume Designer

Jim Carnahan
Casting

Gene Feist
Founding Director, Roundabout Theatre Company

Todd Haimes
Artistic Director, Roundabout Theatre Company

Pygmalion

BOX OFFICE
(L-R): Robert Morgan, Heather Siebert, Mead Margulies

FRONT OF HOUSE STAFF
(L-R): Idair Melendez, Anne Ezell, Kristin Asher, Elsie Jamin-Maguire, Ilia Diaz, Jacklyn Rivera, Victoria Tjoelker

Photos by Ben Strothmann

CREW
Front Row (L-R): Kimberly Mark Sirota, Nelson Vaughn, Susan Fallon, Chris Mattingly

Second Row (L-R): Nichole Jennino, Jamie Greathouse, Julie Hilimire, David Sugarman

Back Row (L-R): Melissa Crawford, Victoria Grecki, Glenn Merwede, Nellie LaPorte, Carmel Sheehan, Andrew Forste, Artie Gaffin

DOORMAN
Adolf Torres

ROUNDABOUT THEATRE COMPANY STAFF
ARTISTIC DIRECTOR . . . .**TODD HAIMES**
MANAGING DIRECTOR . . . . .**HAROLD WOLPERT**
EXECUTIVE DIRECTOR . . . .**JULIA C. LEVY**
ASSOCIATE ARTISTIC DIRECTOR . .**SCOTT ELLIS**

ARTISTIC STAFF
DIRECTOR OF ARTISTIC DEVELOPMENT/
    DIRECTOR OF CASTING . . . .**Jim Carnahan**
Artistic Consultant . . . . .Robyn Goodman
Resident Director .Doug Hughes
Associate Artists . . . . .Scott Elliott, Bill Irwin,
                Joe Mantello, Mark Brokaw,
                Kathleen Marshall
Artistic Associate . . . . .Jill Rafson
Casting Director .Carrie Gardner
Casting Associate .Kate Schwabe
Casting Associate .Stephen Kopel
Artistic Assistant .Erica Rotstein
Literary Associate . . . . .Josh Fiedler
Casting Intern . . . . .Kerry Ann Minchinton

---

EDUCATION STAFF
EDUCATION DIRECTOR . . . .**David A. Miller**

Director of Instruction and
    Curriculum Development . . . . .Reneé Flemings
Education Program Manager . . . . .Jennifer DeBruin
Program Associate for
    School-Based Programs . . . . .Amanda Hinkle
Education Assistant . . . . .Allison Baucom
Education Dramaturg . . . . .Ted Sod
Teaching Artists . . . . .Phil Alexander, Cynthia Babak,
                Victor Barbella, LaTonya Borsay,
                Rob Bronstein, Lori Brown-Niang,
                Miss Stella, Hamilton Clancy,
                Joe Doran, Katie Down, Amy Fortoul,
                Tony Freeman, Sheri Graubert,
                Matthew Gregory, Adam Gwon,
                Karla Hendrick, Jim Jack, Lisa Renee Jordan,
                Alvin Keith, Jonathan Lang, Rebecca Lord,
                Tami Mansfield, Erin McCready,
                Jordana Oberman, Evan O'Brient,
                Deirdre O'Connor, Andrew Ondrecjak,
                Laura Poe, Alexa Polmer-Spencer,
                Nicole Press, Jennifer Rathbone,
                Leah Reddy, Amanda Rehbein,
                Taylor Ruckel, Chris Rummel,
                Cassy Rush, Drew Sachs, Nick Simone,

                Derek Straat, Daniel Robert Sullivan,
                Vickie Tanner, Olivia Tsang,
                Cristina Vaccaro, Jennifer Varbalow,
                Leese Walker, Eric Wallach, Gail Winar
Education Interns . . . . .Emily Holladay Anderson,
                Brent Stansell

ADMINISTRATIVE STAFF
GENERAL MANAGER . . . .**Sydney Beers**
Associate Managing Director . . . . .Greg Backstrom
General Manager, Steinberg Center . . . . . . .Rebecca Habel
General Counsel . . . . .Nancy Hirschmann
Human Resources Manager . . . . .Stephen Deutsch
MIS Director . . . . .Jeff Goodman
Assistant General Manager . . . . .Maggie Cantrick
Management Associate . . . . .Tania Camargo
Facilities Manager . . . . .Abraham David
Office Manager . . . . .Scott Kelly
MIS Assistant . . . . .Micah Kraybill
Receptionists . . . . .Dena Beider, Raquel Castillo,
                Elisa Papa, Allison Patrick,
                Monica Sidorchuk
Messenger . . . . .Darnell Franklin
Management Intern . . . . .Shoshanna Gross

Pygmalion

General Management Intern . . . . .Brent McCreary

FINANCE STAFF
DIRECTOR OF FINANCE . . . .**Susan Neiman**
Assistant Controller . . . . .John LaBarbera
Accounts Payable Administrator . . . . .Frank Surdi
Financial Associate . . . . .Yonit Kafka
Business Office Assistant . . . . .Joshua Cohen
Business Interns . . . . .Edgar Eguia, Nicholas Mustakas

---

DEVELOPMENT STAFF
DIRECTOR OF DEVELOPMENT . . . **Jeffory Lawson**
Director, Institutional Giving . . . . .Julie K. D'Andrea
Director, Special Events . . . . .Steve Schaeffer
Director, Major Gifts . . . . .Joy Pak
Manager, Donor Information Systems . . .Tina Mae Bishko
Manager, Individual Giving . . . . .Kara Kandel
Telefundraising Manager . . . . .Douglas Sutcliffe
Manager, Government &
    External Relations . . . . .Robert Weinstein
Institutional Giving Associate . . . . .Sarah Krasnow
Individual Giving Associate . . . . .Kate Bartoldus
Patrons Services Assistant . . . . .John Haynes
Development Assistant . . . . .Joshua Poole
Special Events Assistant . . . . .Ashley Firestone
Assistant Telefunding Manager . . . . .Gavin Brown
Special Events Interns . . .Michelle Dyer, Laurence Stepney

MARKETING STAFF
**DIRECTOR OF MARKETING
    AND SALES PROMOTION** . . . . . .**David B. Steffen**
Associate Director of Marketing . . . . .Wendy Hutton
Marketing/Publications Manager . . . .Margaret Casagrande
Marketing Associate . . . . .Stefanie Schussel
Marketing Assistant . . . . .Shannon Marcotte
Website Consultant . . . . .Keith Powell Beyland
**DIRECTOR OF TELESALES
    SPECIAL PROMOTIONS** . . . .**Daniel Weiss**
Telesales Manager . . . . .Michael Pace
Telesales Office Coordinator . . . . .Anthony Merced
Marketing Intern .Dragica Dabo

TICKET SERVICES STAFF
**DIRECTOR OF
    SALES OPERATIONS** . . . .**Jim Seggelink**
Ticket Services Manager . . . . .Ellen Holt
Subscription Manager . . . . .Charlie Garbowski, Jr.
Box Office Managers . . . . .Edward P. Osborne,
            Andrew Clements
Group Sales Manager . . . . .Jeff Monteith
Assistant Box Office Managers . . . . . .Krystin MacRitchie,
            Robert Morgan, Nicole Nicholson
Assistant Ticket Services Managers . . . . . . .Robert Kane,
            Ethan Ubell, Carlos Morris
Customer Services Coordinator . . . . .Trina Cox
Ticket Services . . . . .Rachel Bauder, Solangel Bido,
            Lauren Cartelli, David Carson,
            Joseph Clark, Mike DePope,
            Nisha Dhruna, Adam Elsberry,
            Lindsay Ericson, Scott Falkowski,
            Catherine Fitzpatrick, Daniel Gabriel,
            James Graham, Tova Heller,
            Nicki Ishmael, Bill Klemm,
            Elisa Mala, Mead Margulies,
            Chuck Migliaccio, Bekah Nutt,
            Adam Owens, Ethan Paulini,
            David Pittman, DeeAnna Row,

Heather Siebert, Nalene Singh,
            Lillian Soto, DJ Thacker,
            Pam Unger, Thomas Walsh
Ticket Services Intern . . . . .Kayrose Pagan

---

SERVICES
Counsel . . . . .Paul, Weiss, Rifkind, Wharton
            and Garrison LLP,
            John Breglio, Deborah Hartnett
Counsel . . . . .Rosenberg & Estis
Counsel . . . . .Andrew Lance,
            Gibson, Dunn, & Crutcher, LLP
Counsel . . . . .Harry H. Weintraub,
            Glick and Weintraub, P.C.
Immigration Counsel . . . . .Mark D. Koestler and
            Theodore Ruthizer
House Physicians . . . . .Dr. Theodore Tyberg,
            Dr. Lawrence Katz
House Dentist . . . . .Neil Kanner, D.M.D.
Insurance . . . . .DeWitt Stern Group, Inc.
Accountant . . . . .Lutz & Carr CPAs, LLP
Sponsorship . . . . .The Marketing Group,
            Tanya Grubich, Laura Matalon,
            Anna Rippey, Erik Gensler
Advertising . . . . .Eliran Murphy Group/
            Denise Ganjou, Kara Eldridge
Marketing . . . . .TMG-The Marketing Group/
            Laura Matalon, Tanya Grubich,
            William Critzman
Interactive Marketing . . . . .Situation Marketing/
            Damian Bazadona, John Lanasa,
            Ryan Klink, Joey Oliva
Events Photography . . . . .Anita and Steve Shevett
Production Photographer . . . . .Joan Marcus
Theatre Displays . . . . .King Displays, Wayne Sapper

---

MANAGING DIRECTOR EMERITUS . . .Ellen Richard

Roundabout Theatre Company
231 West 39th Street, New York, NY 10018
(212) 719-9393.

GENERAL PRESS REPRESENTATIVES
Adrian Bryan-Brown
Matt Polk   Jessica Johnson   Amy Kass

STAFF FOR *PYGMALION*
Company Manager . . . . Nichole Jennino
Production Stage Manager . . . . .Arthur Gaffin
Stage Manager . . . . David Sugarman
Fight Coordinator . . . . .Tom Schall
Voice Coach . . . . .Kate Maré
Production Properties Coordinator . . . . . . .Kathy Fabian
Associate Production
    Properties Coordinators . . . . Carrie Hash,
            Carrie Mossman
Assistant Production Properties . . . . . . .Melanie Mulder,
            Sid King
Assistant Director .Lori Wolter
Associate Scenic Designer . . . . Chad Owens
Associate Costume Designer . . . . Patrick Bevilacqua
Associate Lighting Designer . . . . .Hilary Manners
Associate Sound Designer . . . . . . .David Stephen Baker
Production Carpenter/Automation . . . . .Glenn Merwede
Production Electrician . . . . .Brian Maiuri
Running Properties . . . . .Andrew Forste
Sound Engineer . . . . Dann Wojnar

Deck Electrician . . . . .Carmel Sheehan
Flyman . . . . .Chris Mattingly
Props . . . . .Nelson Vaughn
Deck Electrician . . . . .Barb Bartel
Wardrobe Supervisor . . . . Susan J. Fallon
Dressers . . . . Victoria Grecki, Julie Hilimire,
            Kimberly Mark Sirota
Wardrobe Dayworker . . . . Melissa Crawford
Production Assistants . . . . Mary Kathryn Flynt,
            Jamie Greathouse
Press Assistant . . . . Jennifer Artesi
Scenery Constructed by . . . . . . .PRG Scenic Technologies,
            a division of Production Resource Group,
            LLC and Hudson Scenic Studio, Inc.
Stonework by . . . . .Dimensional Stone and Tile
Rain Special Effects
    Provided by . . . . .Jauchem and Meeh, Inc.
Sound Equipment Provided by . . . . . . .Sound Associates
Lighting Equipment Provided by . . . . .PRG Lighting,
            a division of Production Resource Group, LLC
Scenery Automation
    Provided by . . . . .PRG Scenic Technologies,
            a division of Production Resource Group, LLC
Costumes Constructed or
    Provided by . . . . .Jennifer Love Costumes,
            Carelli Costumes, Michael Harrell, Arel Studios,
            Giliberto Designs and Angels, The Costumiers
Millinery by . . . . Arnold S. Levine, Inc.
Shoes by . . . . .Peter Fox
Soft Goods Fabrication by . . . . .Ann Guay, Inc. and
            Mary Wilson
Upholstery provided by . . . . .Joe's Fabric Warehouse
Furniture Detailing by . . . . .Plumb Square
Flame Treatment provided by . . . . .Turning Star
Herbal Cough Drops courtesy of . . . . .Ricola USA
Emergen-C Health & Energy Drink mix
    provided by . . . . .Alacer Corp.
Special thanks to . . . .Connie Yung and Penelope Daulton,
            David Richenthal, Jay Binder,
            Jose Balverde and the staff at Southside Cafe

Make-up Provided by M•A•C

AMERICAN AIRLINES THEATRE STAFF
Company Manager . . . . .Nichole Jennino
House Carpenter . . . . .Glenn Merwede
House Electrician . . . . Brian Maiuri
House Properties . . . . Andrew Forste
House Sound . . . . .Dann Wojnar
IA Apprentice . . . . Carmel Sheehan
Wardrobe Supervisor . . . . Susan J. Fallon
Box Office Manager . . . . Ted Osborne
Assistant Box Office Manager . . . . Robert Morgan
House Manager . . . . Steve Ryan
Associate House Manager . . . . Zipporah Aguasvivas
Head Usher . . . . Edwin Camacho
House Staff . . . . Jacklyn Rivera, Ilia Diaz, Anne Ezell,
            Adam Wier, Elsie Jamin Maguire,
            Idair Melendez, Rich McNanna,
            Rebecca Knell, Stephen Fontana,
            Ashley Blenman, James Watanachaiyot
Additional Security Provided by . . . . Gotham Security
Maintenance . . . . Jerry Hobbs, Willie Philips,
            Daniel Pellew, Magali Western
Lobby Refreshments . . . . Sweet Concessions

Pygmalion
SCRAPBOOK

Correspondent: Karen Walsh, "Parlour Maid," understudy "Clara Eynsford Hill" and "Eliza Doolittle."

Memorable Opening Night Cards: Kieran superimposed David Grindley's head on Claire's body, using the poster design—scary!

Also, David's 4-year-old son made all of us cards—complete with feathers and stickers.

Opening Night Gifts: Handmade Shavian magnetic poetry from Kerry, William Morris print umbrellas from Helen, a variety of beautiful decoupage items from Claire, and Jonathan's handmade biscotti with tea.

Most Exciting Celebrity Visitors: Claire says it's the flowers she got from Tom and Katie, the rest of us say Hugh Dancy—he has many friends in this group (one lady friend in particular) and it's always nice when he comes by.

Most Broadway Shows: Artie Gaffin

Backstage Rituals: Many! Jogging whether the weather is cold. S.T. Society (Brenda, Doug, Robin and Sandra). Fridays on the Fourth. Jay rents his dressing room to me for seven minutes each day—he always leaves different music for me to enjoy and I always leave a note commenting on it. The downfall is paying him rent every week. Sports of any kind in Jonathan, Brad and Curt's "Pyg-pen"... there's an electronic dart board...(and hazelnut coffee). Scrabble with Kerry and Kieran.

Favorite Moments During the Show: Onstage—We all love the rain...and the tea scene is very fun for all involved.

Offstage—Personally, I love the few minutes I have with Claire and again with Helen every night before going on. Preshow gatherings on the truck. Also, a few of us really enjoy watching Jefferson and Boyd race behind the Act III truck to the other side of the stage, jumping over tracks, while everything is moving—a sight to behold!

Favorite In-Theatre Gathering Place: Sunday Brunch in the trap, courtesy of Fallon and Glenn. Kimberly thinks we should supply the Yearbook with a scratch and sniff for this.

Mascot: Two have been suggested...FOOD and Mr. Pearce (Brenda's fox stole for Act I).

Most Memorable Ad-lib: Claire once said "I know I am a book" instead of "I know I am a common, ignorant girl and you a book-learned gentleman."

Catchphrases: Boyd—"Am I in the way?" Artie—"It's Saturday night on BroadWAY."

Memorable Directorial Notes: David has a bag of notes he likes to give over and over. Sometimes we refer to them as "Oh yes, number 63?" These include "Notette," "Grace note," "Act better," "Tippity top" and "Trotty-trot." Helen really likes "Serve the tea to all five characters during this one sentence."

Understudy Anecdote: Tony Carlin covers both Pickering and Higgins, a very complicated assignment. I cover Eliza Doolittle. One rehearsal, Tony thought it would be fun to run the show with him playing both parts...one of the most confusing things I've ever done! He was wonderful but we were never totally sure who we were talking to. Tony now refers to this as one of his finest comic achievements :)

1. (L-R): Kerry Bishé, Claire Danes and Karen Walsh on opening night
2. *Pygmalion/Journey's End* send-off party for David Grindley.
3. Stage management team on Halloween.

Embarrassing Moments: Direct from Claire—"I tend to produce vast amounts of mucus in a rather emotional Act IV. The stream of green fluid emanating from my red nose slightly undermines the glamour of my ball gown." Couldn't have said it better.

Favorite Off-Site Hangouts: Bar Centrale, West Bank, Hilton "Above" and Green Symphony.

Other Stories: For Halloween Jennifer, Kerry and I (with Kimberly's help!) held a haunted house in our dressing room between shows. We stuck Jennifer under the bed to grab people's legs (she's the youngest), we had a costume contest where everyone had to make costumes out of things they found in their dressing rooms. We had apple bobbing, scary music, cobwebs and blood, and bowls with things like "eyeballs," "brains" and "mummified skin." We were very proud.

We also played *The Ritz* in Wiffleball, while David G was still here. The towel boys would like to think they beat us something like 28 to 11, but we believe we blew them out of the water with our athletic skill.

Coolest Thing About Being in This Show: Fantastic company in the truest spirit of the words. A real community for everyone.

Radio Golf

First Preview: April 20, 2007. Opened: May 8, 2007.
Closed July 1, 2007 after 17 Previews and 64 Performances.

PLAYBILL

AUGUST WILSON
1945 - 2005

CAST

(in order of appearance)

Mame Wilks ....TONYA PINKINS
Harmond Wilks ....HARRY LENNIX
Roosevelt Hicks ....JAMES A. WILLIAMS
Sterling Johnson ....JOHN EARL JELKS
Elder Joseph Barlow ......ANTHONY CHISHOLM

SETTING

The Hill District, Pittsburgh, Pennsylvania, 1997.
The office of Bedford Hills Redevelopment, Inc.,
in a storefront on Centre Avenue.

STANDBYS

Standby for Mame Wilks:
ROSALYN COLEMAN

Standby for Harmond Wilks and Roosevelt Hicks:
BILLY EUGENE JONES

Standby for Elder Joseph Barlow
and Sterling Johnson:
CEDRIC YOUNG

⊛ CORT THEATRE
138 West 48th Street
A Shubert Organization Theatre

Gerald Schoenfeld, *Chairman*   Philip J. Smith, *President*

Robert E. Wankel, *Executive Vice President*

JUJAMCYN   MARGO   JEFFREY / JERRY   TAMARA / WENDELL
THEATERS   LION   RICHARDS FRANKEL   TUNIE   PIERCE

FRAN   BUNTING MANAGEMENT   GEORGIA / OPEN
KIRMSER   GROUP   FRONTIERE   PICTURES

LAUREN / STEVEN &   THE AW   WONDER / TOWNSEND
DOLL   GREIL   GROUP   CITY, INC. TEAGUE

IN ASSOCIATION WITH

JACK VIERTEL and GORDON DAVIDSON

PRESENT

**HARRY LENNIX   TONYA PINKINS
ANTHONY CHISHOLM   JOHN EARL JELKS**

IN

AUGUST WILSON'S RADIO GOLF

AND INTRODUCING

JAMES A. WILLIAMS

AS ROOSEVELT HICKS

SCENIC DESIGN BY	COSTUME DESIGN BY	LIGHTING DESIGN BY	MUSIC COMPOSED & ARRANGED BY
DAVID GALLO	**SUSAN HILFERTY**	**DONALD HOLDER**	**DAN MOSES SCHREIER**

DRAMATURG   CASTING
TODD KREIDLER   **STANCZYK / CHERPAKOV CASTING**

PRODUCTION MANAGEMENT   PRODUCTION STAGE MANAGER   EXECUTIVE PRODUCER
AURORA PRODUCTIONS   **NARDA E. ALCORN**   **NICOLE KASTRINOS**

GENERAL MANAGEMENT   PRESS REPRESENTATIVE   MARKETING
101 PRODUCTIONS, LTD **BARLOW • HARTMAN**   **TMG
                                                     THE MARKETING GROUP**

DIRECTED BY

KENNY LEON

August Wilson's RADIO GOLF was first produced by Yale Repertory Theatre, New Haven, CT in April 2005.
It was subsequently produced at Mark Taper Forum in Los Angeles, CA; Seattle Repertory Theatre in Seattle, WA; Centerstage in Baltimore, MD;
Huntington Theatre in Boston, MA; Goodman Theatre in Chicago, IL; and McCarter Theatre in Princeton, NJ.
The Producers wish to express their appreciation to the Theatre Development Fund
for its support of this production.

LIVE
BROADWAY

7/1/07

(L-R): Anthony Chisholm and Harry Lennix

Photo by Carol Rosegg

Radio Golf

Harry Lennix
Harmond Wilks

Tonya Pinkins
Mame Wilks

Anthony Chisholm
Elder Joseph Barlow

John Earl Jelks
Sterling Johnson

James A. Williams
Roosevelt Hicks

Rosalyn Coleman
Standby Mame Wilks

Billy Eugene Jones
*Standby
Harmond Wilks,
Roosevelt Hicks*

Cedric Young
*Standby
Elder Joseph Barlow,
Sterling Johnson*

August Wilson
*Playwright,
1945-2005*

Kenny Leon
Director

David Gallo
Scenic Design

Susan Hilferty
Costume Design

Donald Holder
Lighting Design

Dan Moses Schreier
*Music Composition
and Arrangement*

Derrick Sanders
Assistant Director

Charlie Smith
*Associate Scenic
Designer*

Rocco Landesman,
President,
Jujamcyn Theaters
Producer

Margo Lion
Producer

Jeffrey Richards
Producer

Jerry Frankel
Producer

Tamara Tunie
Producer

Lauren Doll
Producer

John O'Boyle,
Wonder City, Inc.
Producer

Lauren Stevens,
Wonder City, Inc.
Producer

Ricky Stevens,
Wonder City, Inc.
Producer

Jack Viertel
Producer

Gordon Davidson
Producer

(L-R): Tonya Pinkins and Harry Lennix.

Photo by Carol Rosegg

Radio Golf

STAGE CREW
(L-R):
Dylan Foley (Production Props Supervisor),
Eileen Miller (Wardrobe Supervisor),
Lonnie Gaddy (Head Props),
Narda E. Alcorn (Production Stage Manager),
Marion Friedman (Stage Manager),
Scott DeVerna (Production Electrician),
Chris Morey (Company Manager),
David Ruble (Dresser)
and Phil Lojo (Head Sound Engineer).

USHER
Jeanine Buckley

FRONT OF HOUSE
(L-R): Miguel (Security Officer), Lea Lefler, William Denson (Chief Usher), Robert Evans, Shanette Santos and Danielle Smith.

BOX OFFICE
(L-R): Diane Heatherington (Head Treasurer), Joshua Skidmore (Assistant Treasurer).

HEAD PROPS
Lonnie Gaddy

Radio Golf

Rent

First Preview: April 16, 1996. Opened: April 29, 1996.
Still running as of May 31, 2008.

PLAYBILL

CAST

(in order of appearance)

Roger Davis ....Adam Pascal
Mark Cohen ....Anthony Rapp
Tom Collins ....Troy Horne
Benjamin Coffin III ....Rodney Hicks
Joanne Jefferson ....Tonya Dixon
Angel Schunard ....Justin Johnston
Mimi Marquez.............................Tamyra Gray
Maureen Johnson ....Nicolette Hart
Mark's mom and others ....Caren Lyn Manuel
Christmas caroler, Mr. Jefferson,
    a pastor, and others ....Marcus Paul James
Mrs. Jefferson, woman with bags,
    and others.....................Maia Nkenge Wilson
Gordon, the man,
    Mr. Grey, and others ....Luther Creek
Steve, man with squeegee,
    a waiter, and others......................Telly Leung
Paul, a cop, and others ....Shaun Earl
Alexi Darling, Roger's mom,
    and others............................Mayumi Ando

Standby for Mark Cohen ....Harley Jay
Standby for Mimi Marquez
    & Maureen Johnson ....Antonique Smith

Continued on next page

⇥N⇤ NEDERLANDER THEATRE

UNDER THE DIRECTION OF
JAMES M. NEDERLANDER AND JAMES L. NEDERLANDER

Jeffrey Seller   Kevin McCollum   Allan S. Gordon
and New York Theatre Workshop

present

Book, Music and Lyrics by
Jonathan Larson

with

Adam Pascal   Anthony Rapp
Tamyra Gray

Mayumi Ando Luther Creek Tonya Dixon Shaun Earl
Nicolette Hart Rodney Hicks Troy Horne Marcus Paul James
Justin Johnston Telly Leung Caren Lyn Manuel Maia Nkenge Wilson
Dana Dawson Crystal Monée Hall Harley Jay Trisha Jeffrey
Owen Johnston II Philip Dorian McAdoo Kyle Post Antonique Smith

Set Design	Costume Design	Lighting Design	Sound Design
Paul Clay	Angela Wendt	Blake Burba	Kurt Fischer

Original Concept/Additional Lyrics	Musical Arrangements	Dramaturg
Billy Aronson	Steve Skinner	Lynn M. Thomson

Casting	Publicity
Telsey + Company	Richard Kornberg/Don Summa

Music Director	Production Stage Manager
David Truskinoff	John Vivian

General Manager	Technical Supervision
John Corker	Unitech Productions, Inc.

Music Supervision and Additional Arrangements	Choreography
Tim Weil	Marlies Yearby

Director
Michael Greif

Original cast recording available on DreamWorks Records' CD's and cassettes

LIVE
BROADWAY

10/1/07

(L-R): Returning original cast members Anthony Rapp and Adam Pascal as Mark and Roger.

Photo by Joan Marcus

Rent

MUSICAL NUMBERS

ACT ONE

Tune Up/Voice Mail #1	Mark, Roger, Mrs. Cohen, Collins, Benny
Rent	The Company
You Okay Honey?...	Angel, Collins
One Song Glory	Roger
Light My Candle	Roger, Mimi
Voice Mail #2	Mr. & Mrs. Jefferson
Today 4 U	Angel
You'll See	Benny, Mark, Collins, Roger, Angel
Tango: Maureen	Mark, Joanne
Life Support	Paul, Gordon, The Company
Out Tonight	Mimi
Another Day	Roger, Mimi, The Company
Will I?	Steve, The Company
On the Street	The Company
Santa Fe	Collins and The Company
I'll Cover You	Angel, Collins
We're Okay	Joanne
Christmas Bells	The Company
Over the Moon	Maureen
La Vie Boheme/I Should Tell You	The Company

ACT TWO

Seasons of Love	The Company
Happy New Year/Voice Mail #3	Mimi, Roger, Mark, Maureen, Joanne, Collins, Angel, Mrs. Cohen, Alexi Darling, Benny, The man
Take Me or Leave Me	Maureen, Joanne
Without You	Roger, Mimi
Voice Mail #4	Alexi Darling
Contact	The Company
I'll Cover You: Reprise	Collins, The Company
Halloween	Mark
Goodbye, Love	Mark, Mimi, Roger, Maureen, Joanne, Collins, Benny
What You Own	Pastor, Mark, Collins, Benny, Roger
Voice Mail #5	Roger's Mom, Mimi's Mom, Mr. Jefferson, Mrs. Cohen
Your Eyes/Finale	Roger, The Company

The cast sings "La Vie Boheme."

Photo by Joan Marcus

UNDERSTUDIES

For Roger:
LUTHER CREEK, OWEN JOHNSTON II,
KYLE POST
For Mark:
LUTHER CREEK, KYLE POST
For Tom Collins and Benjamin:
MARCUS PAUL JAMES,
PHILIP DORIAN McADOO
For Joanne:
DANA DAWSON, CRYSTAL MONÉE HALL,
TRISHA JEFFREY, MAIA NKENGE WILSON
For Angel:
SHAUN EARL, OWEN JOHNSTON II,
TELLY LEUNG
For Mimi:
DANA DAWSON, TRISHA JEFFREY,
CAREN LYN MANUEL
For Maureen:
CAREN LYN MANUEL

SWINGS

DANA DAWSON, CRYSTAL MONÉE HALL,
TRISHA JEFFREY, OWEN JOHNSTON II,
PHILIP DORIAN McADOO, KYLE POST

DANCE CAPTAIN

OWEN JOHNSTON II

THE BAND

Conductor, Keyboards:
DAVID TRUSKINOFF
Bass:
STEVE MACK
Guitar:
BOBBY BAXMEYER
Drums:
JEFF POTTER
Keyboards, Guitar:
JOHN KORBA

Film by
TONY GERBER

Rent

Adam Pascal
Roger

Anthony Rapp
Mark

Tamyra Gray
Mimi

Mayumi Ando
Ensemble

Luther Creek
Ensemble

Tonya Dixon
Joanne

Shaun Earl
Ensemble

Nicolette Hart
Maureen

Rodney Hicks
Benny

Troy Horne
Collins

Marcus Paul James
Ensemble

Justin Johnston
Angel

Telly Leung
Ensemble

Caren Lyn Manuel
Ensemble

Maia Nkenge Wilson
Ensemble

Dana Dawson
Understudy

Crystal Monée Hall
Understudy

Harley Jay
Standby

Trisha Jeffrey
Understudy

Owen Johnston II
Understudy

Philip Dorian
McAdoo
Understudy

Kyle Post
Understudy

Antonique Smith
Standby

Jonathan Larson
Book, Music, Lyrics

Michael Greif
Director

Marlies Yearby
Choreography

David Truskinoff
*Music Director/
Conductor*

Billy Aronson
*Original Concept and
Additional Lyrics*

John Corker
General Manager

David Santana
*Wig, Hair and
Make-up Design*

Bernard Telsey,
Telsey + Company
Casting

Richard Kornberg &
Associates
Press Representative

Brian Lynch,
Unitech Productions,
Inc.
*Technical
Supervision*

Jeffrey Seller
Producer

Kevin McCollum
Producer

Rent

Allan S. Gordon
Producer

James C. Nicola,
Artistic Director,
New York Theatre
Workshop
Producer

Karmine Alers
Swing

Declan Bennett
*Standby for Roger
Davis*

Haven Burton
*Mark's mom and
others*

T.V. Carpio
*Alexi Darling,
Roger's Mom,
and others*

Merle Dandridge
Joanne Jefferson

D'Monroe
Benjamin Coffin III

Christopher J. Hanke
Mark Cohen

Tim Howar
Roger Davis

Kelly Karbacz
*Mark's mom and
others*

Moeisha McGill
Swing

Todd E. Pettiford
Swing

Andy Señor
*Angel Schunard;
Steve, Man with
squeegee, a waiter,
and others*

Yuka Takara
*Alexi Darling,
Roger's Mom,
and others*

Jay Wilkison
*Gordon, the man,
Mr. Grey, and others*

Karmine Alers
*Mimi Marquez,
Swing*

Declan Bennett
Roger Davis

Matt Caplan
*Gordon, the man,
Mr. Grey, and others*

Will Chase
Roger Davis

Merle Dandridge
Joanne Jefferson

Eden Espinosa
Maureen Johnson

Andrea Goss
*Alexi Darling,
Roger's Mom,
and others*

Adam Kantor
Mark Cohen

Tracy McDowell
*Mark's mom
and others*

Todd E. Pettiford
Swing

Kenna J. Ramsey
Joanne Jefferson

Andy Señor
*Steve, man with
squeegee, a waiter,
and others*

Jay Wilkison
*Gordon, the man,
Mr. Grey, and others*

Rent

BOX OFFICE
(L-R): Kelly Goode, Russ Hammel.

WIG AND MAKEUP
David Santana

MANAGEMENT
(L-R): Justin Scribner, John Vivian,
Crystal Huntington.

PROPS
Front Row (L-R): Mike Yannotti, Billy Wright.

Back Row (L-R): Joe Ferreri, Sr. (carpenter), Jan
Marasek, Joe Ferreri, Jr. (carpenter).

FRONT OF HOUSE STAFF
Front Row (L-R): Casey (dog),
Michael McDonoughe, Joaquin Quintana,
Bernard "Sonny" Curry.

Second Row (L-R): Toni Ostini,
Terrence Cummiskey, John Cuevas, Derek King,
Angel Serrano, Louise Angelino.

Third Row (L-R): Brandon Purves, Brian Baeza,
Kim Holmes, William Figueroa, Alverna Ivory,
Elena Mavoides.

Fourth Row (L-R): Whit Germano,
Renee Fleetwood, Junesse Cartagena, Trish Ryan.

Back Row (L-R): Ralph Hendrix, Edward Cuevas,
Kyle Luker.

ELECTRICS CREW
Jack Culver, Greg Freedman, Chaz Peek, Aaron
Straus, Susan Ash, Jason Penna.

Photos by Ben Strothmann

Rent

DOORMAN
Sonny Curry

WARDROBE
(L-R): Jackie Freeman, Karen Lloyd, Kurt Alger.

STAFF FOR *RENT*

GENERAL MANAGER
JOHN CORKER

GENERAL PRESS REPRESENTATIVE
RICHARD KORNBERG & ASSOCIATES
Richard Kornberg   Don Summa
Billy Zavelson   Laura Kaplow-Goldman
Alyssa Hart

CASTING
TELSEY + COMPANY, CSA
Bernie Telsey, Will Cantler, David Vaccari,
Bethany Knox, Craig Burns,
Tiffany Little Canfield, Rachel Hoffman,
Stephanie Yankwitt, Carrie Rosson,
Justin Huff, Joe Langworth, Bess Fifer

COMPANY MANAGER ....**NICK KALEDIN**

PRODUCTION STAGE
MANAGER ....**JOHN VIVIAN**
Stage Manager ....Crystal Huntington
Assistant Stage Manager ....Justin Scribner
Technical Supervision ....Unitech Productions, Inc.
Brian Lynch, Ken Keneally,
Manuel Becker & Jack Culver
Assistant Director ....Martha Banta
Resident Assistant Director ....Evan Ensign
Associate Conductor ....John Korba
Company Manager Associates ....Andrew Jones,
Ginger Montel
Wig, Hair and
Make-Up Designer ....David Santana
Assistant Costume Designer ....Lisa Zinni
Wardrobe Supervisors ....Karen Lloyd, Roberta Christy
Hair and Make-up Supervisor ....David Santana
House Manager ....Louise Angelino
Treasurer ....Gary Kenny
House Electrician ....Richard J. Beck
Head Electrician ....Jack Culver
Follow Spot Operators ....Tom O'Neill, Charles Peek
Sound Board Operators ....Susan Ash, Greg Freedman
Deck Electrician ....Aaron Straus
House Carpenter ....Joe Ferreri
Assistant House Carpenter ....Joe Ferreri, Jr.
House Prop Master ....Billy Wright
Prop Master ....Jan Marasek

Assistant House Prop Master ....William T. Wright
Dressers ....Jackie Freeman, Tamara Kopko,
Cleo Matheos
Wardrobe Daywork ....Paula Inocent
Costume Construction ....Marybeth Regan
Assistant to Messrs. Seller & McCollum ....Ryan Hill
Assistant to John Corker ....Kim Vasquez
Receptionist ....Nicholas Robideau
Office Intern ....Jennifer Collins
Dramaturg ....Lynn M. Thomson
Front of House/Lobby Creative Assistant ....Jamie Leo
Lobby Ceiling Murals ....Billy Miller
Music Preparation ....Eva Gianono
Marketing ....TMG-The Marketing Group/
Laura Matalon, Anne Rippey, Tanya Grubich,
Daya Wolterstorff, Allison Cabellon
Advertising ....Spotco
Lauren Hunter, Peter Milano
Education Program ....Students Live!/
Amy Weinstein, President
Allyson Morgan
Merchandising ....Max Merchandising, LLC/
Toni Ostini, Manager
Title Treatment Design ....Spot Design
Poster Artwork ....Amy Guip
Legal Counsel ....Levine Plotkin & Menin, LLP/
Loren H. Plotkin
Accounting ....Lutz & Carr
Insurance ....DeWitt Stern Group
Banking ....JP Morgan
Payroll Service ....ADP
Production Photographers ....Joan Marcus/
Carol Rosegg
Theatre Displays ....King Display
Product Placement ....George Fenmore/
More Merchandising Internat'l

New York Theatre Workshop
Artistic Director   Managing Director
James C. Nicola   Lynn Moffat

The Producing Office
Kevin McCollum   Jeffrey Seller
John Corker   Debra Nir

Allan S. Gordon Productions
Allan S. Gordon
Elan Vital McAllister
Anne Caruso

Credits
Scenery by Hudson Scenic Inc. Lighting equipment by PRG Lighting. Sound equipment by PRG Audio. Drums by Pearl Drums. Bed linens by Martex. Additional musical instruments courtesy of Sam Ash Music Stores. Motorcycle helmets courtesy of Bell Helmets. 16 mm Projectors by Elmo Mfg. Corp. Acrylic drinkware by US Acrylic, Inc. Candles courtesy of Will & Baumer, Inc. Diamond Brand matches used. Some skin care and hair products provided by Kiehl's. Guitar strings supplied by D'Addario & Co. Some denim wear by Lee Apparel and Rider. Make-up provided by Francois Nars. Tattoos by Temptu Marketing. Throat lozenges provided by Ricola, Inc. Plastic cups by Polar Plastic, Inc. Emer'gen-C Super Energy Booster provided by Alacer Corp.

Special Thanks to:
Allan and Nanette Larson; Julie Larson; Victoria Leacock.

"White Christmas" used by arrangement with the Irving Berlin Music Company. "Do You Know the Way to San Jose," written by Burt Bacharach and Hal David, used by permission of Casa David and New Hidden Valley Music. "The Christmas Song (Chestnuts Roasting on an Open Fire)" by Mel Torme and Robert Wells, used by permission of Edwin H. Morris & Company, a division of MPL Communications, Inc. "Rudolph the Red-Nosed Reindeer" written by Johnny Marks used by permission of St. Nicholas Music, Inc.

NEDERLANDER

Chairman ....**James M. Nederlander**
President ....**James L. Nederlander**

Executive Vice President
Nick Scandalios

Vice President   Senior Vice President
Corporate Development   Labor Relations
Charlene S. Nederlander   **Herschel Waxman**

Vice President   Chief Financial Officer
Jim Boese   **Freida Sawyer Belviso**

Rent
SCRAPBOOK

Correspondent: Rodney Hicks, "Benjamin Coffin III"

Memorable Fan Letter: It was a recent letter that was sent to us by a high school about a fatal car accident involving a beloved student named Allison. Her dream was to be on Broadway. The school came to see the show and we gave a very special and encouraging talk-back with them after the show.

Memorable Anniversary Celebration: This year to celebrate our 12th Anniversary on Broadway, company member Philip McAdoo (Swing) came up with an idea to do a fundraiser, in the vein of Oprah's Big Give, to support an organization called Ubuntu. All proceeds will help to build a theatre in South Africa for the children there.

Most Exciting Celebrity Visitors: Company member Kyle Post (Swing) remembers when Tyra Banks came to see the show and afterwards asked him to do "Light My Candle" with her onstage. They did it and not only did they do it but she knew EVERY word! Cast member Jay Wilkison (Gordon and Others) remembers when Dean Martin came to see the show and wrote on the *Rent* Alleyway, "Go you *Rent* folks!"

"Easter Bonnet" Sketch: It was truly a group effort! And we looked forward to presenting it this year, our final year on Broadway!

Actor Who Performed the Most Roles in This Show: Company member and Dance Captain Owen Johnston has performed the most roles in his eight years with the show—including female parts.

Actor Who Has Done the Most Shows: This year cast member Shaun Earl (Paul & Others) had the best attendance.

Special Backstage Ritual: Cast member Caren Lyn Manuel (Mark's Mom & Others) writes a letter to her eight-month-old daughter Raven before each show.

Favorite Moment During Each Performance: Cast Member Rodney Hicks (Benny) says it's singing "Seasons of Love."

Favorite In-Theatre Gathering Place: Cast member Telly Leung (Steve & Others) says our greenroom, in the basement under the stage, is our fave hangout spot. And we all concur!

Favorite Off-Site Hangout: Bar 41 of course!

Favorite Snack Foods: Pink birthday cake from Amy's Bread, frozen popsicles from the Asian Market in Little Korea.

Favorite Therapy: Cast member Nicolette Hart (Maureen) enjoys going to the gym and having a hardcore workout to keep her body tight and lean before a show.

Memorable Ad-Lib: Former cast member Chris Hanke (Mark) takes it hands down!! Once, he went up on the first verse of "Boheme" and instead danced the entire verse on top of the "La Vie Boheme" table.

Fastest Costume Change: Dresser Cleo says she remembers when the Alexi & Others track had a costume change from hell into "La Vie Boheme" transition.

Embarrassing Moment: Former cast member

1. (L-R): Adam Pascal, Gwen Stewart, Jesse L. Martin and Anthony Rapp at an Aug. 1, 2007 party welcoming original cast members back to the show.
2. (L-R): Cast members Nicolette Hart and Maia Nkenge Wilson at the party at 441/2 restaurant.
3. Tamyra Gray at the reception.

Harley Jay (Mark) accidentally flung the camera into the audience during the Happy New Year sequence and the audience kind of didn't want to give it back to him. All the while the scene was still going on.

Record Number of Cell Phone Rings, Cell Phone Photos or Texting Incidents During a Performance: Production Stage Manager John Vivian miraculously recalls only one time this year.

Busiest Days at the Box Office: Box office management says probably every day that Adam and Anthony—Roger and Mark respectively—were back in the summer and fall of 2007.

Memorable Directorial Note: Rent director Michael Greif joking at a note session, "Do anything that resembles *Wicked*. Their ticket sales are great!"

Catchphrase Only the Company Would

Recognize: Cast member Justin Johnston says, "Boo-Hiss!"

Understudy Anecdote: Company member Crystal Monée Hall (Swing) remembers Kyle Post getting a call from a rehearsal at Ripley-Grier Studios to get to the theatre and go right on as Mark. In the middle of the show. Wow!

Who Wore the Least: Wardrobe Supervisor Karen Lloyd says, hands down, Mimi in "Out Tonight." Others may say it's the Alexi & Others track in "La Vie Boheme."

Who Wore the Heaviest/Hottest Costume: Wardrobe Supervisor Karen Lloyd says the characters of Angel and Benny have the heaviest and hottest costumes.

Coolest Thing About Being in This Show: Cast member Adam Kantor (Mark) says "Being in the show!"

The Ritz

First Preview: September 15, 2007. Opened: October 11, 2007.
Closed December 9, 2007 after 30 Previews and 69 Performances.

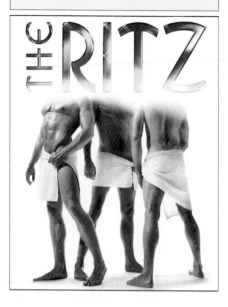

PLAYBILL

CAST

(in order of appearance)

Old Man Vespucci	TEDDY COLUCA
Carmine Vespucci	LENNY VENITO
Vivian Proclo	ASHLIE ATKINSON
Aunt Vera	ANGELA PIETROPINTO
Abe	ADAM SIETZ
Claude Perkins	PATRICK KERR
Gaetano Proclo	KEVIN CHAMBERLIN
Chris	BROOKS ASHMANSKAS
Michael Brick	TERRENCE RIORDAN
Googie Gomez	ROSIE PEREZ
Maurine	ANGELA PIETROPINTO
Tiger	LUCAS NEAR-VERBRUGGHE
Duff	DAVID TURNER

THE PATRONS

Patron in Chaps	MATTHEW MONTELONGO
Crisco Patron	RYAN IDOL
Chuck	TEDDY COLUCA
Snooty Patron	JEFFREY EVAN THOMAS
Sheldon Farenthold	SETH RUDETSKY
Other Patrons	JOSH BRECKENRIDGE, JUSTIN CLYNES, ANDREW R. COOKSEY, MARK LEYDORF, BILLY MAGNUSSEN, NICK MAYO, DILLON PORTER

Continued on next page

STUDIO 54

ROUNDABOUT THEATRE COMPANY

Todd Haimes, Artistic Director
Harold Wolpert, Managing Director
Julia C. Levy, Executive Director

Present

Rosie Perez   Kevin Chamberlin

in

THE RITZ

by

Terrence McNally

with

Brooks Ashmanskas

Ashlie Atkinson   Ryan Idol   Patrick Kerr   Lucas Near-Verbrugghe   Terrence Riordan
Seth Rudetsky   Adam Sietz   David Turner   Lenny Venito

Teddy Coluca   Mark Leydorf   Billy Magnussen   Matthew Montelongo
Angela Pietropinto   Jeffrey Evan Thomas

Josh Breckenridge   Justin Clynes   Andrew R. Cooksey   Nick Mayo   Dillon Porter

Set Design	*Costume Design*	*Lighting Design*	*Sound Design*
Scott Pask	William Ivey Long	Jules Fisher and Peggy Eisenhauer	Tony Meola

Hair and Wig Design	*Choreographer*	*Production Stage Manager*
Paul Huntley	Christopher Gattelli	Tripp Phillips

Casting	*Technical Supervisor*	*General Manager*	*Press Representative*
Jim Carnahan, C.S.A.	Steve Beers	Sydney Beers	Boneau/Bryan-Brown

Director of Marketing & Sales Promotion	*Director of Development*	*Founding Director*	*Associate Artistic Director*
David B. Steffen	Jeffory Lawson	Gene Feist	Scott Ellis

Directed by Joe Mantello

Roundabout Theatre Company is a member of the League of Resident Theatres.
www.roundabouttheatre.org

10/11/07

(L-R): Kevin Chamberlin, Rosie Perez, Terrence Riordan, Brooks Ashmanskas.

Photo by Joan Marcus

The Ritz

Cast Continued

UNDERSTUDIES/STANDBYS

For Gaetano Proclo, Carmine Vespucci:
ADAM SIETZ
For Chris:
SETH RUDETSKY
For Claude Perkins:
LUCAS NEAR-VERBRUGGHE
For Vivian Proclo:
ANGELA PIETROPINTO
For Michael Brick, Tiger, Duff:
BILLY MAGNUSSEN
For Abe:
TEDDY COLUCA
For Sheldon and Patrons:
MARK LEYDORF

Standby for Rosie Perez:
ANDRÉA BURNS

Production Stage Manager:
TRIPP PHILLIPS
Assistant Stage Manager:
JASON HINDELANG

Rosie Perez as
Googie Gomez

Photo by Joan Marcus

Rosie Perez
Googie Gomez

Kevin Chamberlin
Gaetano Proclo

Brooks Ashmanskas
Chris

Ashlie Atkinson
Vivian Proclo

Ryan Idol
Crisco Patron

Patrick Kerr
Claude Perkins

Lucas
Near-Verbrugghe
Tiger

Terrence Riordan
Michael Brick

Seth Rudetsky
Sheldon Farenthold

Adam Sietz
Abe

David Turner
Duff

Lenny Venito
Carmine Vespucci

Teddy Coluca
*Old Man Vespucci,
Chuck*

Mark Leydorf
Patron

Billy Magnussen
Patron

Matthew
Montelongo
Patron in Chaps

Angela Pietropinto
Aunt Vera, Maurine

Jeffrey Evan Thomas
Snooty Patron

Andréa Burns
Standby

Josh Breckenridge
Patron

The Ritz

Justin Clynes
Patron

Andrew R. Cooksey
Patron

Nick Mayo
Patron

Dillon Porter
Patron

Terrence McNally
Playwright

Joe Mantello
Director

Scott Pask
Set Design

William Ivey Long
Costume Design

Jules Fisher and Peggy Eisenhauer
Lighting Design

Tony Meola
Sound Design

Paul Huntley
Hair and Wig Design

Christopher Gattelli
Choreographer

Jim Carnahan
Casting

Gene Feist
*Founding Director,
Roundabout Theatre
Company*

Todd Haimes
*Artistic Director,
Roundabout Theatre
Company*

Caroline Aaron
Vivian Proclo

John Bantay
Other Patrons

Kevin Carolan
*Understudy for
Gaetano Proclo,
Carmine Vespucci,
Old Man Vespucci*

Photos by Ben Strothmann

PROPS ASSISTANT
Alan C. Edwards

MANAGEMENT AND ASSISTANTS
(L-R): Denise Cooper (Company Manager), Katie McKee (Production Assistant),
Jason Hindelang (Assistant Stage Manager), Tripp Phillips (Production Stage Manager),
David Solomon (Assistant Director)

BAR STAFF
(L-R): Ira Sargent, Brandi Vettenburg,
Darden Pitts

The Ritz

CREW

Front Row (L-R): Steven Cozzi, John Wooding, Joe Godwin, Nadine Hettel, Duane McKee.

Second Row (kneeling): Steve Jones

Back Row (L-R): Larry Jennino, Erin Mary Delaney, Peter Ruen, Vanessa Anderson, Vangeli Kaseluris, Susan Cook, Dan Schultheis, Jum Kim and Dorian Fuchs.

ROUNDABOUT THEATRE COMPANY STAFF
ARTISTIC DIRECTOR ....TODD HAIMES
MANAGING DIRECTOR ....HAROLD WOLPERT
EXECUTIVE DIRECTOR ....JULIA C. LEVY
ASSOCIATE ARTISTIC DIRECTOR ...SCOTT ELLIS

ARTISTIC STAFF
DIRECTOR OF ARTISTIC DEVELOPMENT/
DIRECTOR OF CASTING ....**Jim Carnahan**
Artistic Consultant ....Robyn Goodman
Resident Director ....Doug Hughes
Associate Artists ....Scott Elliott, Bill Irwin,
Joe Mantello, Mark Brokaw,
Kathleen Marshall
Artistic Associate ....Jill Rafson
Casting Director ....Carrie Gardner
Casting Associate ....Kate Schwabe
Casting Associate ....Stephen Kopel
Artistic Assistant ....Erica Rotstein
Literary Associate ....Josh Fiedler
Casting Intern ....Kerry Ann Minchinton

EDUCATION STAFF
EDUCATION DIRECTOR ....**David A. Miller**

Director of Instruction and
Curriculum Development ....Reneé Flemings
Education Program Manager ....Jennifer DeBruin
Program Associate for
School-Based Programs ....Amanda Hinkle
Education Assistant ....Allison Baucom
Education Dramaturg ....Ted Sod
Teaching Artists ....Phil Alexander, Cynthia Babak,
Victor Barbella, LaTonya Borsay,
Rob Bronstein, Lori Brown-Niang,
Miss Stella, Hamilton Clancy,
Joe Doran, Katie Down, Amy Fortoul,
Tony Freeman, Sheri Graubert,
Matthew Gregory, Adam Gwon,
Karla Hendrick, Jim Jack, Lisa Renee Jordan,
Alvin Keith, Jonathan Lang, Rebecca Lord,
Tami Mansfield, Erin McCready,
Jordana Oberman, Evan O'Brient,
Deirdre O'Connor, Andrew Ondrecjak,
Laura Poe, Alexa Polmer-Spencer,
Nicole Press, Jennifer Rathbone,
Leah Reddy, Amanda Rehbein,
Taylor Ruckel, Chris Rummel,
Cassy Rush, Drew Sachs, Nick Simone,

Derek Straat, Daniel Robert Sullivan,
Vickie Tanner, Olivia Tsang,
Cristina Vaccaro, Jennifer Varbalow,
Leese Walker, Eric Wallach, Gail Winar
Education Interns ....Emily Holladay Anderson,
Brent Stansell

ADMINISTRATIVE STAFF
GENERAL MANAGER ....**Sydney Beers**
Associate Managing Director ....Greg Backstrom
General Manager, Steinberg Center ....Rebecca Habel
General Counsel ....Nancy Hirschmann
Human Resources Manager ....Stephen Deutsch
MIS Director ....Jeff Goodman
Assistant General Manager ....Maggie Cantrick
Management Associate ....Tania Camargo
Facilities Manager ....Abraham David
Office Manager ....Scott Kelly
MIS Assistant ....Micah Kraybill
Receptionists ....Dena Beider, Raquel Castillo,
Elisa Papa, Allison Patrick,
Monica Sidorchuk
Messenger ....Darnell Franklin
Management Intern ....Shoshanna Gross

The Ritz

General Management Intern ....Brent McCreary

FINANCE STAFF
DIRECTOR OF FINANCE ....**Susan Neiman**
Assistant Controller ....John LaBarbera
Accounts Payable Administrator ....Frank Surdi
Financial Associate ....Yonit Kafka
Business Office Assistant ....Joshua Cohen
Business Intern ....Edgar Eguia, Nicholas Mustakas

DEVELOPMENT STAFF
DIRECTOR OF DEVELOPMENT ......**Jeffory Lawson**
Director, Institutional Giving ....Julie K. D'Andrea
Director, Special Events ....Steve Schaeffer
Director, Major Gifts ....Joy Pak
Manager, Donor Information Systems ....Tina Mae Bishko
Manager, Individual Giving ....Kara Kandel
Telefundraising Manager ....Douglas Sutcliffe
Manager, Government &
    External Relations ....Robert Weinstein
Institutional Giving Associate ....Sarah Krasnow
Individual Giving Associate ....Kate Bartoldus
Patrons Services Assistant ....John Haynes
Development Assistant ....Joshua Poole
Special Events Assistant ....Ashley Firestone
Assistant Telefunding Manager ....Gavin Brown
Special Events Interns   Michelle Dyer, Laurence Stepney

MARKETING STAFF
**DIRECTOR OF MARKETING
    AND SALES PROMOTION** ....**David B. Steffen**
Associate Director of Marketing ....Wendy Hutton
Marketing/Publications Manager ....Margaret Casagrande
Marketing Associate ....Stefanie Schussel
Marketing Assistant ....Shannon Marcotte
Website Consultant ....Keith Powell Beyland
**DIRECTOR OF TELESALES
    SPECIAL PROMOTIONS** ....**Daniel Weiss**
Telesales Manager ....Michael Pace
Telesales Office Coordinator ....Anthony Merced
Marketing Intern ....Dragica Dabo

TICKET SERVICES STAFF
DIRECTOR OF SALES OPERATIONS ..Jim Seggelink
Ticket Services Manager ....Ellen Holt
Subscription Manager ....Charlie Garbowski, Jr.
Box Office Managers ....Edward P. Osborne,
                                        Andrew Clements
Group Sales Manager ....Jeff Monteith
Assistant Box Office Managers ....Krystin MacRitchie,
                    Robert Morgan, Nicole Nicholson
Assistant Ticket Services Managers ....Robert Kane,
                    Ethan Ubell, Carlos Morris
Customer Services Coordinator ....Trina Cox
Ticket Services ....Rachel Bauder, Solangel Bido,
            Lauren Cartelli, David Carson,
            Joseph Clark, Mike DePope,
            Nisha Dhruna, Adam Elsberry,
            Lindsay Ericson, Scott Falkowski,
            Catherine Fitzpatrick, Daniel Gabriel,
            James Graham, Tova Heller,
            Nicki Ishmael, Bill Klemm,
            Elisa Mala, Mead Margulies,
            Chuck Migliaccio, Bekah Nutt,
            Adam Owens, Ethan Paulini,
            David Pittman, DeeAnna Row,
            Heather Siebert, Nalene Singh,

Lillian Soto, DJ Thacker,
Pam Unger, Thomas Walsh
Ticket Services Intern ....Kayrose Pagan

SERVICES
Counsel ....Paul, Weiss,
        Rifkind, Wharton and Garrison LLP,
        John Breglio, Deborah Hartnett
Counsel ....Rosenberg & Estis
Counsel ....Andrew Lance,
        Gibson, Dunn, & Crutcher, LLP
Counsel ....Harry H. Weintraub,
        Glick and Weintraub, P.C.
Immigration Counsel ....Mark D. Koestler and
        Theodore Ruthizer
House Physicians ....Dr. Theodore Tyberg,
        Dr. Lawrence Katz
House Dentist ....Neil Kanner, D.M.D.
Insurance ....DeWitt Stern Group, Inc.
Accountant ....Lutz & Carr CPAs, LLP
Sponsorship ....The Marketing Group,
        Tanya Grubich, Laura Matalon,
        Anne Rippey, Erik Gensler
Advertising ....Spotco/Drew Hodges, Jim Edwards,
        Tom Greenwald, Y. Darius Suyama,
        Beth Watson
Marketing ....TMG-The Marketing Group/
        Laura Matalon, Tanya Grubich,
        William Critzman
Interactive Marketing ....Situation Marketing/
        Damian Bazadona, John Lanasa,
        Ryan Klink, Joey Oliva
Events Photography ....Anita and Steve Shevett
Production Photographer ....Joan Marcus
Theatre Displays ....King Displays, Wayne Sapper

MANAGING DIRECTOR EMERITUS ....Ellen Richard

Roundabout Theatre Company
231 West 39th Street, New York, NY 10018
(212) 719-9393.

**GENERAL PRESS REPRESENTATIVES
BONEAU/BRYAN-BROWN**
Adrian Bryan-Brown
Matt Polk   Jessica Johnson   Amy Kass

CREDITS FOR *THE RITZ*
Company Manager ....Denise Cooper
Production Stage Manager ....Tripp Phillips
Assistant Stage Manager ....Jason Hindelang
Assistant Director ....Dave Solomon
Assistant to the Choreographer ....Michael Lee Scott
Googie's Musical Number Arranged by .....Seth Rudetsky
Googie's Musical Number Orchestrated by ....Jesse Vargas
Rehearsal Pianist ....Steve Marzullo
Associate Scenic Designer ....Frank McCullough
Assistant Scenic Designer ....Lauren Alvarez
Assistant Scenic Designer ....Jeff Hinchee
Scenic Design Intern ....Mary Charles Laird
Associate Costume Designer ....Tom Beall
Assistant to the Costume Designer ....Donald Sanders
Assistant Costume Designer ....Cathy Parrott
Assistant Lighting Designer ....David Leonard
Assistant Sound Designer ....Adam Rigby
Assistant Sound Designer ....Zach Williamson
Assistant Production Electrician ....John Wooding

Production Properties Supervisor ....Peter Sarafin
Properties Assistant ....Alan Edwards
Wardrobe Supervisor ....Nadine Hettel
Hair and Wig Supervisor ....Vanessa Anderson
Make-up Designer ....Angelina Avallone
Production Sound Engineer ....Duane McKee
House Properties ....Lawrence Jennino
Properties Running Crew ....Erin Mary Delaney
Automation Carpenter ....Paul Ashton
Flyman ....Steve Jones
Moving Light Programmer ....Richard Tyndall
Follow Spot Operator ....Dan Schultheis
Deck Sound ....Dorian Fuchs
Local One IATSE Apprentice ....Dan Schultheis
Dressers ....Susan Cook, Steven Cozzi,
        Joe Godwin, Vangeli Kaseluris
Hairdresser ....Jum Kim
Wardrobe Maintenance ....Barry Mazureck
Production Assistants ....John Bantay, Katie McKee,
        Elizabeth Olanoff
Press Assistant ....Jennifer Artesi
Scenery Constructed by ....PRG Scenic Technologies,
        a division of Production Resource Group, LLC,
        New Windsor, NY
Show Control and Scenic Motion Control
    Featuring Stage Command
    Systems by ....Scenic Technologies,
        a division of Production Resource Group, LLC
Lighting Equipment Provided by ....PRG Lighting,
        a division of Production Resource Group, LLC
Sound Equipment Provided by ....PRG Audio,
        a division of Production Resource Group, LLC
Costumes Constructed by ....Euro Co,
        Jennifer Love Costumes
Dance Shoes by ....La Duca
Vintage Costumes
    Supplied by ....Helen Uffner Vintage Clothing LLC,
        Dykeman-Young, Right to the Moon Alice,
        Goodspeed Opera House
Additional Prop Fabrication by ....Craig Grigg
Emergen-C Health and Energy Drink Mix
    Provided by ....Alacer Corp.
Natural Cough Drops Courtesy of ....Ricola USA Inc.
Special thanks to ....Zabar's

Make-up Provided by M•A•C

STUDIO 54 THEATRE STAFF
Theatre Manager ....Matthew Armstrong
Box Office Manager ....Jaime Perlman
House Manager ....LaConya Robinson
Associate House Manager ....Jack Watanachaiyot
House Staff................Elicia Edwards, Jason Fernandez,
        Jen Kneeland, Kate Longosky,
        Latiffa Marcus, Nicole Marino,
        Jonathan Martinez, Dana McCaw,
        Nicole Ramirez, Anthony Roman,
        Nick Wheatley, Stella Varriale
House Carpenter ....Dan Hoffman
House Electrician ....Josh Weitzman
House Properties ....Lawrence Jennino
Security ....Gotham Security
Maintenance ....Ralph Mohan, Maman Garba
Lobby Refreshments by ....Sweet Concessions

The Ritz
SCRAPBOOK

Correspondent: Seth Rudetsky, "Sheldon Farenthold"

Memorable Opening Night Gift: Someone got Kevin Chamberlin the British poster to the movie of *The Ritz*. He loved it and hung it up in the hallway leading to his dressing room. I, myself, have two special memories: During tech rehearsal I was regaling Jeffrey Evan Thomas with my favorite "Fame" (the TV show) episode. And by favorite, I mean the one that I made fun of the most. In it, the President of the United States is supposed to come to the school to see a performance and at the last minute has to cancel. A Secret Service man comes backstage to tell the English teacher played by Carol Mayo Jenkins.

Here is the dialogue I am obsessed with:

SECRET SERVICE GUY: The President can't come! I know all the kids were doing the show especially for him. I don't know what to say.

CAROL MAYO JENKINS There's only one thing to say. (Raising one eyebrow.) Places everyone…places.

Anyhoo, for opening night, Jeffrey gave me an 8x10 picture of Carol Mayo Jenkins (!) that she signed with "There's only one thing to say. Places everyone…places." Seriously! I don't know how he tracked her down but I love it so much! Also, Andrea Burns kept asking to take a picture of me in costume backstage all during previews. She finally took one…and turns out the reason she needed it is because she blew it up and put it in a frame that said "Congratulations, Seth. Broadway Debut, October 11th, 2007." So sweet!

Most Exciting Celebrity Visitor: Angela Lansbury came and sat right in front of my sister Nancy. Nancy said that around five people hit her in the head with their bags as they sat down. I don't think they knew it was her from the back!

Special Backstage Ritual: Rosie Perez played Googie Gomez, a singer with limited talent who performed in The Ritz bathhouse. She asked me to remind her that she had to unstrap her shoe in the middle of her end of Act I medley so it would be able to fly off at the end of the number when she kicked. Right at the end of scene one, we'd see each other in back of the bathhouse set and I'd say a rhyme to help her remember: (Pointing to myself) "I'm a Jew, (Pointing to her strap) don't forget your shoe." This turned into me just pointing to her strap saying "shoe" and her pointing to me saying "Jew." Then after a month we graduated to just pointing at each other without saying anything. And finally, the last eight weeks it became a contest to see who would point first. I'd sneak around the corner of the set before my first entrance and find her getting her wig adjusted with her finger already pointing at me. The only times I won were when she was distracted by talking to Lucas Near-Verbrugghe or when I once did my quick change super fast and got to the back of the bathhouse before she did. It

1. Curtain call on opening night.
2. Kevin Chamberlin at the press reception.
3. (L-R): Terrence McNally and Rosie Perez at Studio 54 for the premiere.

sounds moronic but I was obsessed with beating her to that finger point!

Favorite Moment During Each Performance: At the end of Act I Rosie sings this horribly inappropriate Broadway medley that Chris Gattelli, Joe Mantello and I put together. Joe blocked it so that all of the bathhouse patrons were in the box seats watching it. It was so fun to actually be in the audience to watch it every night and hear the audience go crazy. We put the whole medley together initially in my apartment. Chris said he wanted to do the "39 Lashes" from *Jesus Christ Superstar*, and I had said that I wanted to do "Sabbath Prayer" from *Fiddler on the Roof*. I suddenly said, "Why don't we combine them?" and I played the funky "Heaven on their Minds" vamp from *Superstar* while singing "Sabbath Prayer" above it. Then Chris and I decided that the back-up boys would punctuate the song by whipping Rosie

and counting, "39 Lashes"-style.

ROSIE: "May the Lord protect and defend you."

BOYS: (whip) One!

ROSIE: "May he always shield you from pain."

BOYS: (whip) Two!

That was always my favorite part to watch because it was so bizarre and the whip sounds were so loud!

Favorite In-Theatre Gathering Place: After the show, people would hang out in Ashlie/Andrea/Angela's dressing room which was on the top floor of Studio 54. Ashlie named it "The Top of the Ritz." During the show we all hung out in the 'greenroom' which is the Roundabout's tricky way of calling a hallway in front of the ensemble dressing rooms a 'room.' There were comfy couches and everybody would sit and chat and drink tea during intermission…and play with Kevin's doggie!

The Ritz
SCRAPBOOK

Seth Rudetsky backstage, demonstrating a prop he used to recreate Ben Vereen's "Magic to Do" number from *Pippin*.

Favorite Snack Food: The wig room always had big jars of candy (The Butterfingers always ran out first) and delish trail mix. I was offstage so much I was able to put on a good five pounds.

Mascot: Kevin Chamberlin would often bring his doggie Sammy backstage and she'd hang out with us in the greenroom before the show and during intermission. Cute! Also, Mark Leydorf would sometimes bring his doggie, Hamlet. I couldn't bring my Lab mix, Maggie, because I'm sure she'd come onstage looking for me during the show.

Most Memorable Ad-Lib: Brooks would sometimes ad-lib if he thought the audience needed perking up. One night, after he said the line to Kevin about his hairdresser friend, "He does Barbra Streisand's hair so they gave him the Gene Hersholt Humanitarian Award" there was silence. He started singing it as Judy Garland with lots of vibrato. "Gene Hersholt... Humanitarian...Award...Ba-a-a-a-a-a-a-b-y-y-y-y!" It literally took fifteen seconds. Also, Brooks' character Chris would get annoyed at Jeffrey Thomas who played Snooty Patron. Snooty would bend down to get a glass of water and Brooks would say "She is what is known as a famous face" and he would aim the word "face" into Jeffrey's butt and then make his voice echo (Face...ace...ace...ace). One night, the audience was not laughing at anything and Brooks started explaining his jokes. He said, "She is what is known as a famous face...ace...ace. (Silence) Because...people, it's like the Holland Tunnel down there." It got

nary a laugh from the audience but we loved it backstage.

Memorable Stage Door Fan Encounter: This wasn't the stage door...nor do I think it was a fan...but it sure was memorable. After the show, we'd raise money for BC/EFA by holding buckets in the lobby. Some man approached me and asked if I knew some woman I'd never heard of. He said that she went to school with me. I asked if she was my age and he said yes. He kept describing her and I finally wanted to clarify that she really was my age and wasn't a freshman when I was a junior.
ME: She really is my age?
HIM: Yes
ME: How old is she?
HIM: (nonplussed) Fifty.
I was mortified...and of course, Brooks heard the whole thing and was obsessed with the man's lack of affect. He didn't say 'fifty' apologetically, more like 'why are you making me clarify. You asked if she was your age, I said yes, now I'll spell it out: Fifty.' Devastating.

Fastest Costume Change: In the middle of her end of Act I Broadway medley, Rosie was in a blue pantsuit with a short red wig. At the end of "People" (which she pronounced "Peoples") she'd sing "...are the luckiest peoples in...the...world!" She'd back into a parting of the curtain and Tiger and Duff would enter dancing. Eight counts later she'd burst through the curtain singing "Some People" in a purple glitter dress with long, curly black hair. It was a full costume/wig change in seconds! (Tip o' the hat to "Heavy, Heavy" from *Dreamgirls*).

Who Wore the Heaviest Costume: Poor Kevin Chamberlin had to wear a full suit, mustache, afro wig and carry three suitcases up and down the three sets of stairs on the set. He lost around fifteen pounds doing the show!

Who Wore the Least: Wow. That's a hard one. Billy wore just a tight blue pair of underpants for most of the show and David Turner and Lucas Near-Verbrugghe wore crazy glitter matching thongs for a lot of Act II. I, however, was requested by William Ivey Long to make sure I always had a bathrobe on. Not cool.

Company In-Jokes: One of the reviews had the nerve to say that the cast was made up of hotties with six packs and trolls in towels. My friend Jeffrey and I noted that we do not have six-packs and by process of elimination were devastated. Right before our bow we'd count off the beats offstage: 1,2,3,4 Trolls in towels, take a bow!

Understudy Anecdote: Terrence Riordan threw his back out and Billy Magnussen had to go on. And at that point we had only had one understudy rehearsal...and only got through Act I! But Billy was on his gig and did a great job!

Embarrassing Moments: At one point in the show Brooks Ashmanskas who played Chris, is pretending to be Michael Brick. His line is "It's me, Bunny! Brick!" But the line before that got a bigger laugh than usual which threw Brooks' concentration and so he said "It's me, Bunny. Brooks!" He said his own name onstage! Right after he said 'Brooks', all the color drained from his face. It was, of course, hilarious.

Ghostly Encounters Backstage: I wouldn't say it was ghostly, but it was terrifying to run into me while I was wearing my Act II unitard. Scary.

Coolest Thing About Being in This Show: Every night we did our bows to the song "Last Dance." It was so much fun to be on the stage doing a Full Company disco line dance!

"Gypsy of the Year" Sketch: First of all, we raised the most money for any play and the most ever for any show at Studio 54: $139,514! I wrote a sketch called "Gypsy Lore" where we acted out stories that I feel all the young Gypsies on Broadway should be familiar with. My favorite is the classic story about *West Side Story*. Normally the show ends with Maria brandishing Chino's gun to the Sharks and the Jets. "How many bullets are left in the gun, Chino? Enough for you? All of you? I can kill now, too...because I hate." Well, supposedly one night Maria pointed the gun and said "How many bullets are left in this gun, Chino?" And the gun went off. Everyone looked at Chino who had been "shot" and he had no choice but to die onstage! Maria was mortified that her character just killed someone but she had to go on. When the gangs carried off Tony's body, nobody knew what to do with Chino's body so they just left it there. I'm sure the audience that night was like, "Why isn't anyone arresting Maria?" Our sketch wound up tying with *Xanadu/Stomp* for runner-up!

Rock 'n' Roll

First Preview: October 19, 2007. Opened: November 4, 2007.
Closed March 9, 2008 after 16 Previews and 123 Performances.

PLAYBILL

CAST

(in order of appearance)

The Piper/Policeman	SETH FISHER
Esme (Younger)/Alice	ALICE EVE
Jan	RUFUS SEWELL
Max	BRIAN COX
Eleanor/Esme (Older)	SINEAD CUSACK
Gillian/Magda	MARY BACON
Interrogator/Nigel	QUENTIN MARÉ
Ferdinand	STEPHEN KUNKEN
Milan/Waiter	KEN MARKS
Lenka	NICOLE ANSARI
Stephen	BRIAN AVERS
Candida	ALEXANDRA NEIL
Pupil	ANNA O'DONOGHUE

Continued on next page

⑤ BERNARD B. JACOBS THEATRE

242 West 45th Street
A Shubert Organization Theatre

Gerald Schoenfeld, *Chairman*   Philip J. Smith, *President*

Robert E. Wankel, *Executive Vice President*

Bob Boyett & Sonia Friedman Productions
Ostar Productions   Roger Berlind   Tulchin/Bartner
Douglas G. Smith   Dancap Productions   Jam Theatricals   The Weinstein Company

In association with
Lincoln Center Theater

Present

The Royal Court Theatre London Production of

ROCK 'N' ROLL

A new play by

TOM STOPPARD

Brian Cox   Sinead Cusack   Rufus Sewell

Nicole Ansari   Brian Avers   Mary Bacon   Alice Eve
Seth Fisher   Stephen Kunken   Quentin Maré
Ken Marks   Alexandra Neil   Anna O'Donoghue

Joseph Collins   Angela Reed   Joe Vincent

Set Designer	Costume Designer	Lighting Designer	Sound Designer
Robert Jones	**Emma Ryott**	**Howard Harrison**	**Ian Dickinson**
US Casting	UK Casting		Production Stage Manager
Tara Rubin Casting	**Lisa Makin**		**Rick Steiger**
Press Representative	Technical Supervisor		Associate Producer for RBT
Boneau/Bryan-Brown	**Aurora Productions**		**Tim Levy**
US General Management	UK General Management for SFP		Associate Producer
101 Productions, Ltd.	**Diane Benjamin & Matthew Gordon**		**Carole Shorenstein Hays**

Directed by

TREVOR NUNN

The Producers wish to express their appreciation to the Theatre Development Fund for its support of this production.

11/4/07

Rufus Sewell

(L-R): Sinead Cusack and Alice Eve.

Photos by Johan Persson

Rock 'n' Roll

Cast Continued

UNDERSTUDIES

For The Piper/Policeman:
BRIAN AVERS, JOSEPH COLLINS
For Esme (Younger)/Alice:
ANNA O'DONOGHUE
For Jan:
BRIAN AVERS, JOSEPH COLLINS
For Max:
KEN MARKS, JOE VINCENT
For Eleanor/Esme (Older):
ALEXANDRA NEIL, ANGELA REED
For Gillian/Magda:
ANNA O'DONOGHUE, ANGELA REED
For Interrogator/Nigel:
JOSEPH COLLINS, JOE VINCENT
For Ferdinand:
JOSEPH COLLINS, SETH FISHER
For Milan/Waiter:
JOE VINCENT
For Lenka.
MARY BACON, ANGELA REED
For Stephen:
JOSEPH COLLINS, SETH FISHER
For Candida:
MARY BACON, ANGELA REED
For Pupil:
SETH FISHER, ANGELA REED

Sinead Cusack and Rufus Sewell are appearing
with the permission of Actors' Equity Association.

Nicole Ansari is appearing with the permission of
Actors' Equity Association pursuant to an exchange
program between American Equity and UK Equity.

Photo by Johan Persson

(L-R): Nicole Ansari
and Brian Cox.

Brian Cox
Max

Sinead Cusack
Eleanor/Esme (Older)

Rufus Sewell
Jan

Nicole Ansari
Lenka

Brian Avers
Stephen

Mary Bacon
Gillian/Magda

Alice Eve
*Esme (Younger)/
Alice*

Seth Fisher
The Piper/Policeman

Stephen Kunken
Ferdinand

Quentin Maré
Interrogator/Nigel

Ken Marks
Milan/Waiter

Alexandra Neil
Candida

Anna O'Donoghue
Pupil

Joseph Collins
*u/s Jan, Ferdinand,
Piper/Policeman,
Interrogator/Nigel,
Stephen*

Angela Reed
*u/s Eleanor/
Esme (Older),
Gillian/Magda,
Lenka, Candida,
Pupil*

Joe Vincent
*u/s Max,
Interrogator/Nigel,
Milan/Waiter*

Tom Stoppard
Playwright

Trevor Nunn
Director

Howard Harrison
Lighting Designer

Tara Rubin Casting
U.S. Casting

Rock 'n' Roll

Ian Dickinson
*Sound Designer/
Projection*

Bob Boyett
Producer

Sonia Friedman
Productions Ltd
Producer

Bill Haber,
Ostar Productions
Producer

Roger Berlind
Producer

Steve Traxler,
Jam Theatricals
Producer

Bob Weinstein,
The Weinstein
Company
Producer

Harvey Weinstein,
The Weinstein
Company
Producer

André Bishop,
Artistic Director,
Lincoln Center
Theater
Producer

Bernard Gersten,
Executive Producer,
Lincoln Center
Theater
Producer

Carole Shorenstein
Hays
Associate Producer

Julie Jesneck
*Understudy for
Gillian/Magda, Pupil*

STAGE AND COMPANY MANAGEMENT
(L-R): Penny Daulton, Karen Evanouskas,
Rick Steiger, Timothy Eaker,
Alexis Shorter.

Photos by Ben Strothmann

BOX OFFICE
(L-R): Michael Kohlbrenner and Jules Ochao.

STAGE DOORMAN
Jerry Klein

Rock 'n' Roll

CREW
Front Row (L-R): Mickey Abbate, Jennifer Mooney

Second Row (L-R): Alfred Ricci, Kelly Saxon, Daniel E. Carpio

Back Row (L-R): John Alban, David Lawrence, Maeve Butler, Kevin Barry, Herbert Messing, David Cohen, Sarah Rochford, Andrew Meeker, Bill Lewis, Michael Van Praagh

FRONT OF HOUSE STAFF
Front Row (L-R): Annie Bree, Patanne McEvoy

Back Row (L-R): Eva Frances Laskow, Al Peay, Raisa Ramos, William Mitchell, Rosa Pesante, John Minore, Al Nazario

Photos by Ben Strothmann

STAFF FOR ROCK 'N' ROLL

GENERAL MANAGEMENT
101 PRODUCTIONS, LTD.
Wendy Orshan   Jeffrey M. Wilson
David Auster

COMPANY MANAGER
Penelope Daulton

GENERAL PRESS REPRESENTATIVE
BONEAU/BRYAN-BROWN
Adrian Bryan-Brown   Jim Byk
Matt Ross

U.S TECHNICAL SUPERVISION
AURORA PRODUCTIONS
Gene O'Donovan
W. Benjamin Heller II   Bethany Weinstein
John Horsman   Melissa Mazdra   Asia Evans

U.S. CASTING
TARA RUBIN CASTING
Tara Rubin, CSA, Eric Woodall, CSA
Laura Schutzel, CSA, Merri Sugarman, CSA
Rebecca Carfagna, Paige Blansfield, Dale Brown

Production Stage Manager ....Rick Steiger
Stage Manager ....Alexis Shorter
Assistant Director ....Seth Sklar-Heyn
U.S. Hair & Wig Designer ....David H. Lawrence

Rock 'n' Roll

Associate Set Designer ....Ted LeFevre
Associate Costume Designer ....Scott Traugott
Associate Lighting Designer ....Dan Walker
Moving Lights Programmer ....Marc Polimeni
Associate Sound Designer ....Chris Cronin
Dialect Coach ....Elizabeth Smith
Fight Director ....Tom Schall

Production Carpenter ....David Cohen
Assistant Carpenter ....Eric Smith
Production Electrician ....James Maloney, Jr.
Head Electrician ....Kevin Barry
Production Sound ....Bill Lewis
Production Props ....Andy Meeker
Wardrobe Supervisor ....Kelly Saxon
Dressers ....Mickey Abbate, Philip Heckman,
                                            Kyle LaColla
Hair & Makeup Supervisor ....David H. Lawrence
Hairdressers ....Jennifer Mooney,
                                       Jeannette Harrington
Production Assistants ....Timothy Eaker,
                                            Deanna Weiner

Legal Counsel ....Lazarus & Harris, LLP/
                                     Scott R. Lazarus, Esq.,
                                     Robert C. Harris, Esq.
Assistants to Mr. Boyett ....Diane Murphy,
                                         Michael Mandell
Assistant to Mr. Levy ....Evan Storey
Executive Assistant to Mr. Haber ....Theresa Pisanelli
Associate Producer for
   Ostar Enterprises ....Rachel Neuburger
Assistant to Mr. Haber ....Kristen Jackson
Assistant to Mr. Berlind ....Jeffrey Hillock
Assistant to Mssrs. Tulchin/Bartner ....Lauren Doll
Assistant to The Weinstein Company ....Ben Famiglietti
Accountant ......Rosenberg, Neuwirth, & Kushner, CPAs/
                     Chris Cacace, Patricia Pedersen
Advertising ....SPOTCO/
                                     Drew Hodges, Jim Edwards,
                                     Jim Aquino, Kyle Hall
101 Productions. Dir. Finance/Mktg ....Elie Landau
Assistant to the General Managers ....John Vennema
101 Productions, Ltd. Staff ....Denys Baker,
                     Ashley Berman, Katharine Croke,
                 Sherra Johnston, Emily Lawson, Heidi Neven,
                 Robert Parkison, Mary Six Rupert, Jeremy Scott
101 Productions, Ltd. Intern ....Julie Ann Nolan
Banking ....City National Bank/Anne McSweeney
Insurance ....Ventura Insurance/
                                           Janice Brown
Theatre Displays ....King Displays, Inc.
Merchandising ....Araca Merchandise L.P.
Payroll Services ....Castellana Services, Inc.
Music Rights ....BZ Rights and Permissions, Inc./
                                     Barbara Zimmerman
Housing ....Maison International/
                                     Marie Claire Martineau
Immigration ....Traffic Control Group, Inc./
                                           David King
Website Design ....Situation Marketing/
                 Damian Bazadona, John Lanasa, Jimmy Lee
Production Photographer ....Joan Marcus

FOR SONIA FRIEDMAN PRODUCTIONS
Producer ....Sonia Friedman
General Manager ....Diane Benjamin

Creative Producer ....Lisa Makin
Head of Production ....Pam Skinner
Associate Producer.........................Matthew Gordon
Literary Associate ....Jack Bradley
CEO-NY......................................David Lazar
Production Assistant ....Lucie Lovatt
Production Accountant ....Melissa Hay
SFP Board ....Helen Enright, Howard Panter,
                                           Rosemary Squire

FOR THE ROYAL COURT THEATRE
Artistic Director...........................Dominic Cooke
General Manager ....Diane Borger
Production Manager ....Paul Handley
Head of Communications ....Kym Bartlett

CREDITS
Scenery by Souvenir Scenic (UK) and Showman Fabricators (U.S.). Lighting equipment from PRG Lighting. Automation by Mountain Productions and Showman Fabricators. Sound and video equipment from Sound Associates, Inc. Props by Down Time Productions and The Spoon Group. Costumes executed by Angels. Special thanks to Bra*Tenders for hosiery and undergarments. Prosthetics by Millennium FX Ltd. Ricola and Emer'gen-C products used.

Makeup provided by M•A•C.

MUSIC RIGHTS
"**Wish You Were Here**" (Roger Waters, David Gilmour), ©1975 Muziekuitgeverij Artemis B.V. (Buma) and ©Pink Floyd Music Publishers, Inc. (BMI). All rights on behalf of Muziekuitgeverij Artemis B.V. (Buma) administered by Warner-Tamerlane Publishing Corp. (BMI). All rights reserved. Used by permission. "**Welcome to the Machine**" (Roger Waters), ©1975 Muziekuitgeverij Artemis B.V. (Buma). All rights on behalf of Muziekuitgeverij Artemis B.V. (Buma) administered by Warner-Tamerlane Publishing Corp. (BMI). All rights reserved. Used by permission. "**Vera**" (Roger Waters), ©1976 Muziekuitgeverij Artemis B.V. (Buma). All rights on behalf of Muziekuitgeverij Artemis B.V. (Buma) administered by Warner-Tamerlane Publishing Corp. (BMI). All rights reserved. Used by permission. "**Bring It on Home to Me**" written by Sam Cooke. Published by ABKCO Music, Inc. www.abkco.com. "**It's All Over Now**" written by Bobby Womack & Shirley Womack. Published by ABKCO Music, Inc. www.abkco.com. "**The Last Time**" written by Mick Jagger & Keith Richards. Published by ABKCO Music, Inc. www.abkco.com. "**Street Fighting Man**" written by Mick Jagger & Keith Richards. Published by ABKCO Music, Inc. www.abkco.com. "**Break on Through (to the Other Side)**" written by Jim Morrison, John Densmore, Ray Manzarek, Robby Krieger. Published by Doors Music Company (ASCAP). Used by permission. All rights reserved. "**I'll Be Your Baby Tonight**" written by Bob Dylan, ©1968; renewed 1996 Dwarf Music. "**I Still Haven't Found What I'm Looking For**" music by U2. Lyrics by Bono & The Edge. Published by Universal-Polygram Int. Publ., Inc. on behalf of Universal Music Publ. Int. B.V. "**Give Peace a Chance**" written by John Lennon. Published by Sony/ATV Tunes LLC (ASCAP). "**A Hard Day's Night**" written by John Lennon and Paul McCartney. Published by Sony/ATV Tunes LLC (ASCAP). "**Wouldn't It Be Nice**" written by Tony Asher, Mike Love and Brian Wilson. Published by Irving Music, Inc. "**Milk Cow Blues**" written by John Adam Estes. Published by Peer

International Corporation and Leric Music (administered by Bug Music). "**You Got Me Rocking**" written by Mick Jagger & Keith Richards. ©1994 Promopub B.V. "**I'm Waiting for the Man**" written by Lou Reed. Copyright ©1967 Oakfield Avenue Music, Ltd. (BMI). Rights for Oakfield Avenue Music, Ltd. (BMI) administered by Spirit One Music (BMI). All rights reserved. Used by permission. "**Venus in Furs**" written by Lou Reed. Copyright ©1967 Oakfield Avenue Music, Ltd. (BMI). Rights for Oakfield Avenue Music, Ltd. (BMI) administered by Spirit One Music (BMI). All rights reserved. Used by permission. "**Chinatown Shuffle**" written by Ron McKernan. Copyright ©1972 Ice Nine Publishing Company, Inc. (ASCAP). All rights reserved. Used by permission. "**Otce**" written by Milan Hlavsa and Vratislav Brabenec. "**It's Only Rock n Roll**" written by Mick Jagger & Keith Richards. "**Motherly Love**" written by Frank Zappa. All rights Munchkin Music.

To learn more about the production, please visit rocknrolltheplay.com

ROCK 'N' ROLL
Rehearsed at New 42nd Street Studios

SPECIAL THANKS
Jacky Matthews; Moragh Darby;
The Soho House; The London NYC;
Christine Sodikoff; Owen Kotler;
Martin Professional, Inc.

THE SHUBERT ORGANIZATION, INC.
Board of Directors

House Manager ....William Mitchell

The Seafarer

First Preview: October 30, 2007. Opened: December 6, 2007.
Closed March 30, 2008 after 19 Previews and 133 Performances.

PLAYBILL

BOOTH THEATRE
222 West 45th Street
A Shubert Organization Theatre

Gerald Schoenfeld, *Chairman* Philip J. Smith, *President*

Robert E. Wankel, *Executive Vice President*

Ostar Productions Bob Boyett Roy Furman Lawrence Horowitz
Jam Theatricals Bill Rollnick/Nancy Ellison Rollnick James D'Orta Thomas S. Murphy
Ralph Guild/Jon Avnet Philip Geier/Keough Partners Eric Falkenstein/Max OnStage

Present

NT The National Theatre of Great Britain's
production of

SEAFARER

A NEW PLAY WRITTEN AND DIRECTED BY
CONOR McPHERSON

with

Conleth Hill
Ciarán Hinds
Sean Mahon
David Morse
Jim Norton

Set and Costume Designer **Rae Smith**	Lighting Designer **Neil Austin**	Sound Designer **Mathew Smethurst-Evans**

Fight Director
Thomas Schall

Casting
Laura Stanczyk & Howie Cherpakov

Press Representative
Boneau / Bryan-Brown

Marketing
HHC Marketing

General Management
101 Productions, Ltd.

Production Stage Manager
Barclay Stiff

Technical Supervisor
David Benken

Directed by
Conor McPherson

The producers wish to express their appreciation to
Theatre Development Fund for its support of this production

LIVE BROADWAY

12/6/07

CAST
(in alphabetical order)

Ivan Curry .... CONLETH HILL
Mr. Lockhart .... CIARÁN HINDS
Nicky Giblin .... SEAN MAHON
James 'Sharky' Harkin .... DAVID MORSE
Richard Harkin .... JIM NORTON

SETTING

The action takes place in a house in Baldoyle, a coastal settlement north of Dublin city. It is an old area which could hardly be called a town these days. It is rather a suburb of the city with a church and a few pubs and shops at its heart. From the coast here, one is looking at the north side of the Howth peninsula. Howth Head (Binn Eadair) is a hill on the peninsula which marks the northern arm of Dublin Bay. Due to its prominence it has long been the focus of myths and legends.

Act One: Christmas Eve morning and late afternoon
Act Two: late on Christmas Eve night

In memory of Tom Murphy, winner of the 1998 Tony Award as Best Featured Actor in a Play for *The Beauty Queen of Leenane.*

UNDERSTUDIES

For Richard Harkin, Mr. Lockhart:
PETER ROGAN
For James "Sharky" Harkin, Ivan Curry,
Nicky Giblin:
DECLAN MOONEY

(L-R): Jim Norton, Sean Mahon, Conleth Hill, David Morse, Ciarán Hinds.

Photo by Joan Marcus

The Seafarer

Conleth Hill
Ivan Curry

Ciarán Hinds
Mr. Lockhart

Sean Mahon
Nicky Giblin

David Morse
James "Sharky" Harkin

Jim Norton
Richard Harkin

Declan Mooney
u/s James "Sharky" Harkin, Ivan Curry, Nicky Giblin

Peter Rogan
u/s Richard Harkin, Mr. Lockhart

Conor McPherson
Playwright/Director

David Benken
Technical Supervision

Nicholas Hytner,
Artistic Director,
National Theatre of
Great Britain
Producer

Bill Haber,
Ostar Enterprises
Producer

Bob Boyett
Producer

Roy Furman
Producer

Lawrence C.
Horowitz, M.D.
Producer

Arny Granat,
Jam Theatricals
Producer

Steve Traxler,
Jam Theatricals
Producer

Ralph Guild
Producer

Jon Avnet
Producer

Eric Falkenstein
Producer

2007-2008 AWARDS

TONY AWARD
Best Featured Actor in a Play
(Jim Norton)

DRAMA DESK AWARD
Outstanding Featured Actor in a Play
(Conleth Hill)

CREW
Front Row (L-R): Mary Kathryn Flynt, Ron Burns Sr., Patricia Sullivan

Standing (L-R): Steve Lukens, Barclay Stiff, Eileen Miller, Wayne E. Smith, Tom Lowrey, Jimmy Keane

FRONT OF HOUSE STAFF
Front Row (L-R): Chrissie Collins (Director), Teresa Aceves (Usher), Bernadette Bokun (Usher)

Back Row (L-R): Ken Weinstein (Concessionaire), Marco Malgiolio (Usher), Marjorie Glover (Usher), Daniel Rosario (Usher), Catherine Coscia (Chief Usher), Nadine Space (Usher), Timothy Wilhelm (Ticket Taker)

Photos by Aaron Meier & Christine Olver

The Seafarer

STAGE AND COMPANY MANAGEMENT
(L-R): Steve Lukens (Company Manager),
Mary Kathryn Flynt (Assistant Stage Manager),
Barclay Stiff (Production Stage Manager)

BOX OFFICE
(L-R): Vincent Whittaker, Ed Whittaker

STAFF FOR *THE SEAFARER*

GENERAL MANAGEMENT
101 PRODUCTIONS, LTD.
Wendy Orshan   Jeffrey M. Wilson
David Auster

COMPANY MANAGER
Thom Clay

GENERAL PRESS REPRESENTATIVE
BONEAU/BRYAN-BROWN
Adrian Bryan-Brown   Aaron Meier
Christine Olver

PRODUCTION MANAGEMENT
David Benken   Rose Palombo

CASTING
STANCZYK/CHERPAKOV CASTING
Laura Stanczyk   Howie Cherpakov

Production Stage Manager ....Barclay Stiff
Stage Manager ....Mary Kathryn Flynt
Assistant to the Director ....Mark Schneider
Assistant Costume Designer ....Barry Doss
Associate Lighting Designer ....Aaron Spivey
Scenic Coordinator ....Diane Willmott

Production Electrician ....Jon Lawson
Production Properties ....Denise J. Grillo
Production Sound ....Wayne Smith
Advance Carpenter ....Jack Anderson
Lighting Programmer ....Bobby Harrell
Wardrobe Supervisor ....Eileen Miller
Dresser ....Barry Doss
Production Assistants ....Ross Evans, Kyle Gates

Associate Producer
  for Ostar Enterprises ....Rachel Neuburger
Assistants to Mr. Haber ....Theresa Pisanelli,
                              Kristen Jackson
Assistants to Mr. Boyett ....Diane Murphy,
                             Michael Mandell
Assoc. Producer for
  Robert Boyett Theatricals ....Tim Levy
Assistant to Mr. Levy ....Evan Storey
Legal Counsel ....Lazarus & Harris, LLP/
      Scott Lazarus, Esq., Robert C. Harris, Esq.
Accountant .....Rosenberg, Neuwirth, & Kushner, CPAs,/
                   Chris Cacace, Jana Jevnikar

Advertising ....Serino Coyne, Inc./
         Nancy Coyne, Angelo Desimini,
         Steve Knight, Sunil Ayyagari
Marketing ....HHC Marketing/Hugh Hysell,
        Matt Sicoli, Candice Beckmann,
        Michael Redman, Jaime Roberts,
        James Hewson, Brandon Martin,
                     Nicole Pando
Immigration Processing ....Traffic Control Group/
                          David King
Dir. Finance/Marketing
  for 101 Productions ....Elie Landau
101 Productions, Ltd. Staff ....Denys Baker,
        Ashley Berman, Katherine Croke,
        Heidi Neven, Julie Anne Nolan,
        Robert Parkison, Mary Six Rupert,
                    John Vennema
Press Representative Staff ....Chris Boneau,
      Jackie Green, Jim Byk, Joe Perrotta,
      Matt Polk, Steven Padla, Susanne Tighe,
      Adriana Douzos, Jessica Johnson,
      Juliana Hannett, Heath Schwartz,
      Amy Kass, Danielle Crinnion, Matt Ross,
      Ian Bjorklund, Brandi Cornwell,
      Kevin Jones, Linnae Petruzzelli
Press Interns ....Jennifer Artesi, Elizabeth Griffin,
      Jennifer Guhl, Marissa Schwartz,
                  Nicole Truscinski
Banking ....City National Bank/Anne McSweeney
Insurance ....DeWitt Stern, Inc./Bethany Weise
Theatre Displays ....King Displays, Inc.
Merchandising ....Max Merchandising, LLC/
                     Randi Grossman
Payroll Services ....Castellana Services, Inc.
Website Design ....Situation Marketing/
        Damian Bazadona, John Lanasa
Additional Artwork Photography ....Catherine Ashmore

NATIONAL THEATRE, LONDON
Chairman of the Board ....Sir Hayden Phillips
Director ....Nicholas Hytner
Executive Director ....Nick Starr

CREDITS
Lighting equipment from Hudson Sound & Light, LLC. Sound equipment from Sound Associates. Mr. Hinds' suit and overcoat tailored by Saint Laurie Merchant Tailors. Natural herb cough drops courtesy of Ricola USA, Inc. Emergen-C super energy booster provided by Alacer Corp.

MUSIC CREDITS
"One World" and "Sweet Little Mystery" written by John Martyn. Used by permission of Universal-Songs of Polygram Int., Inc. (BMI). "Solid Air" written by John Martyn. ©Copyright Warlock Music Ltd./PRS, a division of EverGreen Copyrights (admin. by ICG). All rights reserved. Used by permission. "Don't Wanna Know Bout Evil" written by John Martyn. ©Copyright Warlock Music Ltd./PRS, a division of EverGreen Copyrights (admin. by ICG). All rights reserved. Used by permission. "Reach" written by Andrew Todd and Cathy Dennis. Published by Universal Music – MGB Songs/Universal Music Publishing MGB Ltd.; used by permission of COLGEMS-EMI Music Inc.

To learn more about the production, please visit SeafarerThePlay.com

---

THE SEAFARER
Rehearsed at New 42nd Street Studios

SPECIAL THANKS
Tom Richardson, Diane Willmott, Julia Wickham

THE SHUBERT ORGANIZATION, INC.
Board of Directors

House Manager ....Laurel Ann Wilson

The Seafarer
SCRAPBOOK

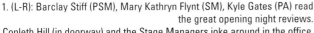

1. (L-R): Barclay Stiff (PSM), Mary Kathryn Flynt (SM), Kyle Gates (PA) read the great opening night reviews.
2. Conleth Hill (in doorway) and the Stage Managers joke around in the office.
3. (L-R): Sean Mahon, David Morse and Conleth Hill warm up before the show.
4. (L-R): Conleth Hill, David Morse catch up about their day before the show.

Correspondent: Barclay Stiff, Production Stage Manager

Special Backstage Ritual: The cast would arrive every night at the theatre an hour before the show. They would do a full cast vocal warm-up followed by running the lines for all three rounds of the intricate and very difficult card games played in Act II. This was a great time for the guys to say hello and catch up with each other. Often times the cast would choose a unique accent (Southern, cockney, etc.) to run the lines. This provided many great laughs before the show. Lots of fun!

Favorite Moment During Each Performance: This is an easy one to answer. Watching Conleth Hill's comedic performance every night was the highlight for everyone backstage. His interpretation on the character of Ivan was so fresh. His ability to instantly adjust his performance on the fly when he hits certain moments is the work of a master at the top of his game. You would always find the crew watching the backstage video monitors to see what Conleth had up his sleeve that night.

Favorite In-Theatre Gathering Place: The Stage Manger's office seemed to be the unofficial greenroom at the Booth. We had a unique baby blue leopard print couch that was left at the theatre (we often speculated what actor originally owned it). It no longer had its cushions, but people liked to relax on it and chat before the shows.

Favorite Snack Food: During rehearsal: Anything from the PAX deli downstairs from the New 42nd Street Studios. We did in the end grow so sick of eating there, but it was so convenient and they gave us a discount. Once we moved to the theatre the Starlite Deli and Junior's bakery became the favorite place to grab a snack before the show.

Mascot: Dusty the wonder dog.

Favorite Therapy: Hot tea seemed to be the therapy of choice with the guys. Irish Breakfast of course! Altoids and Ricola were certainly very popular also.

Busiest Day at the Box Office: The day after our opening night was incredible. Business was brisk. Amazing reviews and great word of mouth helped make the run of *Seafarer* so memorable.

Catchphrases Only the Company Would Recognize: "Nicky Touch and Walk Away." "Hey there Niffy."

Company In-Jokes: "Do you have Donuts in Ireland?" "Birth Ass Day." "Strikes and Spurs." "How High the hiiiigggh fdjdf."

Coolest Thing About Being on This Show: This was an incredible production to be involved with. The entire company came together during the stagehands strike and supported each other like a family. It was a great feeling. In many ways the play itself became even stronger after the strike. We came back to the theatre and knocked it out of the park. HOME RUN!

South Pacific

First Preview: March 1, 2008. Opened: April 3, 2008.
Still running as of May 31, 2008.

CAST OF CHARACTERS

Ensign Nellie Forbush	KELLI O'HARA
Emile de Becque	PAULO SZOT
Ngana, his daughter	LAURISSA ROMAIN
Jerome, his son	LUKA KAIN
Henry	HELMAR AUGUSTUS COOPER
Bloody Mary	LORETTA ABLES SAYRE
Liat, her daughter	LI JUN LI
Bloody Mary's Assistants	MARYANN HU, EMILY MORALES, KIMBER MONROE
Luther Billis	DANNY BURSTEIN
Stewpot (Carpenter's Mate Second Class, George Watts)	VICTOR HAWKS
Professor	NOAH WEISBERG
Lt. Joseph Cable, United States Marine Corps	MATTHEW MORRISON
Capt. George Brackett, United States Navy	SKIPP SUDDUTH
Cmdr. William Harbison, United States Navy	SEAN CULLEN
Lt. Buzz Adams	GEORGE MERRICK
Yeoman Herbert Quale, Sailor	CHRISTIAN DELCROIX
Radio Operator Bob McCaffrey, Sailor	MATT CAPLAN
Morton Wise, Seabee	GENSON BLIMLINE
Richard West, Seabee	NICK MAYO
Johnny Noonan, Seabee	JEREMY DAVIS
Billy Whitmore, Seabee	ROBERT LENZI
Tom O'Brien, Sailor	MIKE EVARISTE
James Hayes, Sailor	JEROLD E. SOLOMON
Kenneth Johnson, Sailor	CHRISTIAN CARTER

Continued on next page

PLAYBILL

LINCOLN CENTER THEATER AT THE VIVIAN BEAUMONT

under the direction of
ANDRÉ BISHOP and BERNARD GERSTEN
in association with
BOB BOYETT
presents

RODGERS & HAMMERSTEIN'S SOUTH PACIFIC

Music
RICHARD RODGERS

Lyrics
OSCAR HAMMERSTEIN II

Book OSCAR HAMMERSTEIN II and JOSHUA LOGAN
Adapted from the Pulitzer Prize-winning novel *Tales of the South Pacific* by JAMES A. MICHENER
Original stage production directed by JOSHUA LOGAN

with

KELLI O'HARA   PAULO SZOT

MATTHEW MORRISON   DANNY BURSTEIN   LORETTA ABLES SAYRE
SEAN CULLEN   VICTOR HAWKS   LUKA KAIN   LI JUN LI
LAURISSA ROMAIN   SKIPP SUDDUTH   NOAH WEISBERG

and

BECCA AYERS   WENDI BERGAMINI   GENSON BLIMLINE   GRADY McLEOD BOWMAN   CHARLIE BRADY
MATT CAPLAN   CHRISTIAN CARTER   HELMAR AUGUSTUS COOPER   JEREMY DAVIS
MARGOT DE LA BARRE   CHRISTIAN DELCROIX   LAURA BARRE DUNCAN   MIKE EVARISTE
LAURA GRIFFITH   LISA HOWARD   MARYANN HU   ZACHARY JAMES   ROBERT LENZI
GARRETT LONG   NICK MAYO   GEORGE MERRICK   WILLIAM MICHALS   KIMBER MONROE
EMILY MORALES   DARIUS NICHOLS   GEORGE PSOMAS   ANDREW SAMONSKY   JEROLD E. SOLOMON

Sets	Costumes	Lighting	Sound
MICHAEL YEARGAN	CATHERINE ZUBER	DONALD HOLDER	SCOTT LEHRER

Orchestrations
ROBERT RUSSELL BENNETT

Dance & Incidental Music Arrangments
TRUDE RITTMANN

Casting	Production Stage Manager	General Press Agent	Musical Theater Associate Producer
TELSEY + COMPANY	MICHAEL BRUNNER	PHILIP RINALDI	IRA WEITZMAN

General Manager	Production Manager	Director of Development	Director of Marketing
ADAM SIEGEL	JEFF HAMLIN	HATTIE K. JUTAGIR	LINDA MASON ROSS

Music Direction
TED SPERLING

Musical Staging
CHRISTOPHER GATTELLI

Directed by
BARTLETT SHER

LINCOLN CENTER THEATER GRATEFULLY ACKNOWLEDGES THE CONTRIBUTORS WHOSE EXTRAORDINARY GENEROSITY HAS MADE SOUTH PACIFIC POSSIBLE:
Debra and Leon Black • The Susan and Elihu Rose Foundation • Catherine and Ephraim Gildor
The Joseph and Joan Cullman Arts Foundation • The Blanche and Irving Laurie Foundation • WolfBlock
Sir Thomas Moore/Laurence Levine Charitable Fund • The Henry Nias Foundation courtesy of Dr. Stanley Edelman
The New York Community Trust - Mary P. Oenslager Foundation Fund • Leon Levy Foundation
Blanchette Hooker Rockefeller Fund • National Endowment for the Arts

American Airlines is the official airline of Lincoln Center Theater.
Merrill Lynch is a 2008 season sponsor of Lincoln Center Theater.

4/3/08

(L-R): Paulo Szot and Kelli O'Hara

Photo by Joan Marcus

South Pacific

MUSICAL NUMBERS AND SCENES

The action of the play takes place on two islands in the South Pacific during World War II.
There is one week's lapse of time between the two acts.

ACT I

OVERTURE
Scene 1: The Terrace of Emile de Becque's Plantation Home
DITES-MOI ....Ngana and Jerome
A COCKEYED OPTIMIST ....Nellie
TWIN SOLILOQUIES ....Nellie and Emile
SOME ENCHANTED EVENING ....Emile
Reprise: DITES-MOI ....Ngana, Jerome and Emile
Scene 2: Another Part of the Island
BLOODY MARY ....Seabees
THERE IS NOTHIN' LIKE A DAME ....Billis and Seabees
BALI HA'I ....Bloody Mary
Scene 3: The Company Street
Scene 4: Inside the Island Commander's Office
Scene 5: The Company Street
MY GIRL BACK HOME ....Cable and Nellie
Scene 6: The Beach
I'M GONNA WASH THAT MAN RIGHT OUTA MY HAIR ....Nellie and Nurses
Reprise: SOME ENCHANTED EVENING ....Emile and Nellie
A WONDERFUL GUY ....Nellie and Nurses
Scene 7: Inside the Island Commander's Office
Scene 8: On Bali Ha'i
Reprise: BALI HA'I ....Island Women
Scene 9: Inside a Hut on Bali Ha'i
YOUNGER THAN SPRINGTIME ....Cable
Scene 10: Near the Beach on Bali Ha'i
Scene 11: Emile's Terrace
FINALE ACT I ....Nellie and Emile

ACT II

ENTR'ACTE
Scene 1: A Performance of "The Thanksgiving Follies" ....Nellie, Nurses and G.I.'s
Scene 2: Backstage at "The Thanksgiving Follies"
HAPPY TALK ....Bloody Mary and Liat
Scene 3: The Stage
HONEY BUN ....Nellie, Billis and Ensemble
Scene 4: Backstage
YOU'VE GOT TO BE CAREFULLY TAUGHT ....Cable
THIS NEARLY WAS MINE ....Emile
Scene 5: The Radio Shack
Scene 6: The Beach
Reprise: SOME ENCHANTED EVENING ....Nellie
Scene 7: The Company Street
Scene 8: Emile's Terrace
FINALE ULTIMO ....Emile, Nellie, Ngana and Jerome

Cast Continued

Petty Officer Hamilton Steeves ..CHARLIE BRADY
Marine Staff
    Sgt. Thomas Hassinger ....ZACHARY JAMES
Lt. Eustis Carmichael,
    Shore Patrolman ....ANDREW SAMONSKY
Lt. Genevieve Marshall,
    lead nurse ....LISA HOWARD
Ensign Dinah Murphy .LAURA MARIE DUNCAN
Ensign Janet MacGregor ....LAURA GRIFFITH
Ensign
    Connie Walewska .....MARGOT DE LA BARRE
Ensign Sue Yaeger ....GARRETT LONG
Ensign Cora MacRae ....BECCA AYERS
Islanders, Sailors, Seabees,
    Party Guests ....BECCA AYERS,
        GENSON BLIMLINE, CHARLIE BRADY,
        MATT CAPLAN, CHRISTIAN CARTER,
            HELMAR AUGUSTUS COOPER,
        JEREMY DAVIS, MARGOT DE LA BARRE,
        MIKE EVARISTE, LAURA GRIFFITH,
            LISA HOWARD, MARYANN HU,
        ZACHARY JAMES, ROBERT LENZI,
        GARRETT LONG, NICK MAYO,
        GEORGE MERRICK, KIMBER MONROE,
        EMILY MORALES, ANDREW SAMONSKY,
            JEROLD E. SOLOMON

Assistant Stage Managers .....DAVID SUGARMAN,
                SAMANTHA GREENE

Dance Captain ....WENDI BERGAMINI
Asst. Dance
    Captain ....GRADY McLEOD BOWMAN
Swings.........................WENDI BERGAMINI,
            GRADY McLEOD BOWMAN,
    DARIUS NICHOLS, GEORGE PSOMAS

Paulo Szot is appearing with the permission of
Actors' Equity Association.

UNDERSTUDIES
For Nellie Forbush: LAURA MARIE DUNCAN,
GARRETT LONG
For Emile de Becque: WILLIAM MICHALS
For Ngana and Jerome: KIMBER MONROE
For Henry: CHRISTIAN CARTER,
MIKE EVARISTE
For Bloody Mary: MARYANN HU,
LISA HOWARD
For Liat: WENDI BERGAMINI,
EMILY MORALES
For Luther Billis: VICTOR HAWKS, NICK MAYO
For Stewpot: GENSON BLIMLINE,
JEREMY DAVIS

Continued on next page

South Pacific

Cast Continued

For Lt. Joseph Cable: ROBERT LENZI, ANDREW SAMONSKY
For Capt. George Brackett: VICTOR HAWKS, GENSON BLIMLINE
For Professor: MATT CAPLAN, GEORGE MERRICK
For Cmdr. William Harbison: GEORGE MERRICK, ANDREW SAMONSKY
For Bob McCaffrey and Yeoman Herbert Quale: GRADY McLEOD BOWMAN, GEORGE PSOMAS
For Ensign Dinah Murphy: WENDI BERGAMINI, LAURA GRIFFITH
For Lt. Eustis Carmichael and Lt. Buzz Adams: CHARLIE BRADY, NICK MAYO

ORCHESTRA

Conductor: TED SPERLING
Associate Conductor: FRED LASSEN

Violins: BELINDA WHITNEY (Concertmaster), ANTOINE SILVERMAN, KARL KAWAHARA, KATHERINE LIVOLSI-LANDAU, LISA MATRICARDI, JAMES TSAO, MICHAEL NICHOLAS, RENA ISBIN
Violas: DAVID BLINN, DAVID CRESWELL
Cellos: PETER SACHON, CARYL PAISNER, CHARLES DU CHATEAU (Assistant Conductor)
Bass: LISA STOKES-CHIN
Flute/Piccolo: LIZ MANN
Clarinet: TODD PALMER, SHARI HOFFMAN
Oboe/English Horn: MATT DINE
Bassoon: DAMIAN PRIMIS
French Horns: ROBERT CARLISLE, CHRIS KOMER, SHELAGH ABATE
Trumpets: DOMINIC DERASSE, GARETH FLOWERS, WAYNE DUMAINE
Trombones: MARK PATTERSON, MIKE BOSCHEN
Tuba: MARCUS ROJAS
Harp: GRACE PARADISE
Drums/Percussion: BILL LANHAM

Music Coordinator: DAVID LAI

Richard Rodgers' music is being presented in the 30-player orchestration created for the original production. The scores and orchestral parts were restored by The Rodgers & Hammerstein Organization using all existing material, including manuscripts (Rodgers, Trude Rittmann), the full orchestral scores (Robert Russell Bennett) and the individual instrumental parts played by the original orchestra.

Kelli O'Hara
Ensign Nellie Forbush

Paulo Szot
Emile de Becque

Matthew Morrison
Lt. Joseph Cable

Danny Burstein
Luther Billis

Loretta Ables Sayre
Bloody Mary

Sean Cullen
Cmdr. William Harbison

Victor Hawks
Stewpot

Luka Kain
Jerome

Li Jun Li
Liat

Laurissa Romain
Ngana

Skipp Sudduth
Capt. George Brackett

Noah Weisberg
Professor

Becca Ayers
Ensign Cora MacRae

Wendi Bergamini
Swing/ Dance Captain

Genson Blimline
Morton Wise

Grady McLeod Bowman
Swing/Assistant Dance Captain

Charlie Brady
Petty Officer Hamilton Steeves

Matt Caplan
Bob McCaffrey

Christian Carter
Kenneth Johnson

Helmar Augustus Cooper
Henry

South Pacific

Jeremy Davis
Johnny Noonan

Margot De La Barre
*Ensign Connie
Walewska*

Christian Delcroix
*Yeoman Herbert
Quale*

Laura Marie Duncan
*Ensign Dinah
Murphy*

Mike Evariste
Tom O'Brien

Laura Griffith
*Ensign Janet
MacGregor*

Lisa Howard
*Lt. Genevieve
Marshall*

MaryAnn Hu
*Bloody Mary's
Assistant*

Zachary James
Thomas Hassinger

Robert Lenzi
Billy Whitmore

Garrett Long
Ensign Sue Yaeger

Nick Mayo
Richard West

George Merrick
Lt. Buzz Adams

William Michals
*Understudy for
Emile de Becque*

Kimber Monroe
*Bloody Mary's
Assistant*

Emily Morales
*Bloody Mary's
Assistant*

Darius Nichols
Swing

George Psomas
Swing

Andrew Samonsky
Lt. Eustis Carmichael

Jerold E. Solomon
James Hayes

Joshua Logan
*Co-Author
(1908-1988)*

Richard Rodgers
*Music
(1902-1979)*

Oscar Hammerstein II
*Lyrics and Co-Author
(1895-1960)*

James A. Michener
*Author, Tales of the
South Pacific
(1907-1997)*

Bartlett Sher
Director

Christopher Gattelli
Musical Staging

Ted Sperling
Music Direction

Michael Yeargan
Sets

Catherine Zuber
Costumes

Donald Holder
Lighting

Scott Lehrer
Sound

Robert Russell
Bennett
*Orchestrations
(1894-1981)*

Trude Rittmann
*Dance and
Incidental Music
Arrangements
(1908-2005)*

David Lai
Music Coordinator

Bernard Telsey,
Telsey + Company
Casting

South Pacific

Bob Boyett

André Bishop and Bernard Gersten,
Lincoln Center Theater
Producer

RUNNING CREW

Front Row (L-R): Rudy Wood (Props), John Ross (Props), Pat Merryman (Production Electrician), Bruce Rubin (Electrician/Board Operator).

Second Row (L-R): Frank Linn (Electrician/Automation Tech), Andrew Belits (Carpenter), Julia Rubin (Sound Deck), Takuda Moody (Sound Deck), Mark Dignam (Props).

Third Row (L-R): Karl Rausenberger (Production Propman), Greg Cushna (Flyman), Kristina Clark (Electrics), Juan Bustamante (Deck Automation).

Fourth Row (L-R): John Weingart (Production Flyman), Nick Irons (Follow Spot), Joe Pizzuto (Follow Spot Operator), Bill Burke (Deck Electrician), Matt Altman (Follow Spot), Fred Bredenbeck (Carpenter), Jeff Ward (Follow Spot Operator).

Back Row (L-R): John Howie (Carpenter), Paul Gruen (Flyman), Ray Skillin (Deck Carpenter), Bill Nagle (Production Carpenter), Marc Saltzberg (Production Soundman).

Not pictured: Gary Simon (Sound Deck).

Photos by Ben Strothmann

STAGE MANAGEMENT
(L-R): David Sugarman (1st Asst. Stage Manager), Michael Brunner (Production Stage Manager), Brandon Kahn (Production Assistant), Samantha Greene (2nd Asst. Stage Manager).

South Pacific

FRONT OF HOUSE STAFF
First Row (L-R): Mim Pollock (Chief Usher), Jodi Gigliobianco, Susan Lehman, Jeff Goldstein, Rheba Flegelman (House Manager), Robert De Barros, Mildred Terrero, Judith Fanelli, Mike Murray, Connie DiGiovanni, Beatrice Gilliard.

Middle Row (L-R): Faeida Asencio, Nick Andors, Pat Jenkins, Barbara Hart, Eleanore Rooks.

Back Row (L-R): Margie Blair, Donna Zurich, Matt Barnaba, Lydia Tchornobai.

ORCHESTRA
Front Row (L-R): Liz Mann (Flute/Picolo), Rena Izbin (Violin), Fred Lassen (Assoc. Conductor), Grace Paradise (Harp), Ted Sperling (Conductor/ Music Direction), David Creswell (Viola), Shari Hoffman (Clarinet).

Middle Row (L-R): Peter Sachon (Cello), Gareth Flowers (Trumpet), Matt Dine (Oboe/ English Horn), Karl Kawahara (Violin), Caryl Paisner (Cello), David Blinn (Viola), Katherine Livolsi-Landau (Violin), Lisa Stokes-Chin (Bass), Todd Palmer (Clarinet), Mark Patterson (Trombone), Dominic Derasse (Trumpet), Antoine Silverman (Violin).

Back Row (L-R): Charles Du Chateau (Cello/Asst. Conductor), Wayne Dumaine (Trumpet), Michael Nicholas (Violin), Shelagh Abate (French Horn), Bill Lanham (Drums/Percussion), Damian Primis (Bassoon), Marcus Rojas (Tuba), Mike Boschen (Trombone), Belinda Whitney (Violin/ Concertmaster), Lisa Matricardi (Violin), Robert Carlisle (French Horn), James Tsao (Violin), Chris Komer (French Horn).

WARDROBE
(L-R): Stacia Williams, Leo Namba, Linda McAllister, Lynn Bowling (Wardrobe Supervisor) Patti Luther, Tammi Kopko, Mark Klein, Mark Caine.

Not pictured: James Nadeaux.

South Pacific

LINCOLN CENTER THEATER

ANDRÉ BISHOP	BERNARD GERSTEN
ARTISTIC DIRECTOR	EXECUTIVE PRODUCER

ADMINISTRATIVE STAFF

GENERAL MANAGER ....ADAM SIEGEL
  Associate General Manager ....Jessica Niebanck
  General Management Assistant ....Meghan Lantzy
  Facilities Manager ....Alex Mustelier
  Assistant Facilities Manager ....Michael Assalone
GENERAL PRESS AGENT ....PHILIP RINALDI
  Press Associate ....Barbara Carroll
PRODUCTION MANAGER ....JEFF HAMLIN
  Associate Production Manager ....Paul Smithyman
DIRECTOR OF
  DEVELOPMENT ....HATTIE K. JUTAGIR
  Associate Director of Development ......Rachel Norton
  Manager of Special Events and
    Young Patron Program ....Karin Schall
  Grants Writer ....Neal Brilliant
  Manager, Patron Program ....Sheilaja Rao
  Assistant to the
    Director of Development ....Marsha Martinez
  Development Assistant/
    Special Events ....Nicole Lindenbaum
  Development Associate ....Raelyn Richards
DIRECTOR OF FINANCE..........DAVID S. BROWN
  Controller ....Susan Knox
  Systems Manager ....Stacy Valentine
  Finance Assistant ....Megan Wildebour
DIRECTOR OF MARKETING .LINDA MASON ROSS
  Marketing Associate ....David Hatkoff
  Marketing Assistant ....Kristin Miller
DIRECTOR OF EDUCATION ....KATI KOERNER
  Associate Director of Education ....Dionne O'Dell
Assistant to the Executive Producer ......Barbara Hourigan
Office Assistant ....Kenneth Collins
Messenger ....Esau Burgess
Reception ....Terra Gillespie, Michelle Hamill

ARTISTIC STAFF

ASSOCIATE DIRECTORS ......GRACIELA DANIELE,
                    NICHOLAS HYTNER,
                    JACK O'BRIEN,
                    SUSAN STROMAN,
                    DANIEL SULLIVAN
DRAMATURG and DIRECTOR,
  LCT DIRECTORS LAB ....ANNE CATTANEO
CASTING DIRECTOR ....DANIEL SWEE, CSA
MUSICAL THEATER
  ASSOCIATE PRODUCER ....IRA WEITZMAN
DIRECTOR OF LCT3 ....PAIGE EVANS
Artistic Administrator ....Julia Judge
Casting Associate ....Camille Hickman
Education/Lab Assistant ....Jill MacLean

HOUSE STAFF

HOUSE MANAGER..............RHEBA FLEGELMAN
Production Carpenter ....William Nagle
Production Electrician ....Patrick Merryman
Production Propertyman ....Karl Rausenberger
Production Flyman ....John Weingart
House Technician ....Linda Heard
Chief Usher ...................................M.L. Pollock
Box Office Treasurer ....Fred Bonis
Assistant Treasurer ....Robert A. Belkin

SPECIAL SERVICES

Advertising ....Serino-Coyne/Jim Russek
              Roger Micone, Jill Jefferson
Principal Poster Artist ....James McMullan
Poster Art for *Rodgers & Hammerstein's*
  South Pacific ....James McMullan
Counsel ....Peter L. Felcher, Esq.;
              Charles H. Googe, Esq.;
        and Carol Kaplan, Esq. of
    Paul, Weiss, Rifkind, Wharton & Garrison
Immigration Counsel ....Theodore Ruthizer, Esq.;
              Mark D. Koestler, Esq.
    of Kramer, Levin, Naftalis & Frankel LLP
Labor Counsel ....Michael F. McGahan, Esq.
    of Epstein, Becker & Green, P.C.
Auditor ....Douglas Burack, C.P.A.
              Lutz & Carr, L.L.P.
Insurance ....Jennifer Brown of DeWitt Stern Group
Photographer ....Joan Marcus
Video Services ....Fresh Produce Productions/
                Frank Basile
Travel ....Tygon Tours
Consulting Architect ....Hugh Hardy,
      H3 Hardy Collaboration Architecture
Construction Manager ....Yorke Construction
Payroll Service ....Castellana Services, Inc.
Merchandising ....Marquee Merchandise, LLC/
               Matt Murphy

STAFF FOR
RODGERS & HAMMERSTEIN'S SOUTH PACIFIC

COMPANY MANAGER........MATTHEW MARKOFF
Assistant Company Manager ...Jessica Perlmeter Cochrane
Assistant Director ....Sarna Lapine
Associate Choreographer ....Joe Langworth
Associate Set Designer.......................Lawrence King
Assistant Set Designer ....Mikiko Suzuki
Assistant Costume Designers ....Holly Cain,
          David Newell, Court Watson
Associate Lighting Designer ....Karen Spahn
Assistant Lighting Designer ....Caroline Chao
Automated Light Programmer ....Victor Seastone
Associate Sound Designer ....Leon Rothenberg
Assistant Sound Designer ....Bridget O'Connor
Music Copyist ....Emily Grishman Music Preparation/
       Emily Grishman, Katharine Edmonds
Production Soundman ....Marc Salzberg
Wig and Hair Design ....Tom Watson
Make-up Designer ....Cookie Jordan
Properties Coordinator ....Kathy Fabian
Associate Props Coordinators ....Rose A.C. Howard,
     Carrie Mossman, and Propstar Associates
Prop Scenic Artist ....Curt Tomczyk
Wardrobe Supervisor ....Lynn Bowling
Dressers ....Mark Caine, David Caudle, Mark Klein,
    Tammi Kopko, Patti Luther, Linda McAllister,
    James Nadeaux, Leo Namba, Stacia Williams
Hair Supervisor ....Cindy Demand
Hair Assistants ....Gary Arave, Carrie Rohm
Casting Assistant ....Joe Langworth
Production Assistant ....Brandon Kahn
Children's Guardian ....Vanessa Brown
Children's Tutoring ....On Location Education
Costume Shopper ....Nicole Moody
Rehearsal Pianist ....Jonathan Rose

Vocal Coach ....Deborah Hecht

FOR THE RODGERS & HAMMERSTEIN
ORGANIZATION

President & Executive Director ....Ted Chapin
Senior Vice President &
  General Manager ....Bill Gaden
Senior Vice President &
  General Counsel ....Victoria G. Traube
Senior Vice President/Communications ....Bert Fink
Director of Music ....Bruce Pomahac

Performance rights to **South Pacific** are licensed by
R&H Theatricals: www.rnhtheatricals.com

For help with Michener matters, thanks to Selma Luttinger,
Shirley Soenksen at the University of Northern Colorado,
Alice Birney (Manuscript Division) and Mark Eden
Horowitz (Music Division) of the Library of Congress, and
the Vice President's Office at Swarthmore College.

The producers wish to thank the Naval Historical Center;
the Navy Medical Department; the CEC/Seabee Historical
Foundation; the Intrepid Sea, Air and Space Museum; the
New York City Marines; Major Seth Lapine, USMC; Dr.
Regina Anna Sekinger, Ph.D; and Katie McGerr for their
invaluable assistance with the military research for this
production.

CREDITS

Scenery construction by Hudson Scenic Studio, Inc. Show
control and scenic motion control featuring Stage
Command Systems® by PRG Scenic Technologies, a
division of Production Resource Group, LLC, New
Windsor, NY. Scenery fabrication by PRG Scenic
Technologies, a division of Production Resource Group,
LLC, New Windsor, NY. Costumes by Jennifer Love
Costumes; Angels the Costumiers; Parsons-Meares, Ltd.;
Euro Co. Costumes; and John Cowlesh. Men's tailoring by
Brian Hemesath and Edward Dawson. Millinery by Rodney
Gordon, Inc. and Arnold S. Levine, Inc. Fabric painting and
distressing by Jeffrey Fender. Fabric painting by Gene
Mignola, Inc. Undergarments and hosiery by Bra*Tenders.
Tattoos by Louie Zakarian. Sound equipment by Masque
Sound. Lighting equipment from PRG Lighting. Specialty
props construction by Costume Armour. Specific military
props and accessories provided by Jim Korn & Kaufman's
Army Navy. Special thanks to Frank Cwiklik at Metropolis
Collectibles, South Sea Rattan Collections and Carris Reels.
Cymbals provided courtesy of Paiste America Inc. Natural
herb cough drops courtesy of Ricola USA, Inc. Emergen-C
is the official health and energy drink of *South Pacific*.

For groups of 20 or more:
Caryl Goldsmith Group Sales, (212) 889-4300

Lobby refreshments by Sweet Concessions

(L-R): Li Jun Li and
Loretta Ables Sayre.

Photo by Joan Marcus

South Pacific
SCRAPBOOK

Correspondent: MaryAnn Hu, "Bloody Mary's Assistant."

Opening Night Gifts: My husband has worked at Lincoln Center several times and I was always jealous of the Tiffany key ring he got as an opening night gift. I need not be jealous anymore! I now have my own engraved Signature Tiffany key ring. The producers also gave us our own special version of the show poster signed by the artist, James McMullan. We also got leis - all the way from Hawaii from our Bloody Mary, Loretta Ables Sayre. The Rodgers and Hammerstein Organization gave us a beautiful book, "The *South Pacific* Companion," complete with a personalized book plate signed by Alice Hammerstein, Mary Rodgers and Ted Chapin. Kelli O'Hara gave us an awesome Matt Logan caricature of our show. We also have some very talented photographers, Matthew Morrison and Skipp Sudduth, who gave us candid photos they took themselves.

Most Exciting Celebrity Visitors: Stephen Sondheim, Steven Spielberg, Diane Keaton, Bette Midler, Whoopi Goldberg, Barbara Walters, Bernadette Peters, Nicole Kidman and the list keeps growing!

Who Got the Gypsy Robe: Laura Griffith got it and plans to add a grass skirt and an officer's hat signed by the cast and surrounded by orchids and shells (in keeping with an island theme.)

Actors Who Performed the Most Roles in This Show: Credit goes to our awesome Super Swings (as I like to call them): George Psomas, Darius Nichols, Grady McLeod Bowman, and most especially our Dance Captain Wendi Bergamini who knows everybody's track, including principals, and has performed every one of them at one time or another in rehearsals.

Who Has Done the Most Shows in Their Career: Paulo Szot, in the opera world, has done more than 50 productions. Next would be Danny Burstein, who has done like 12 Broadway shows.

Special Backstage Rituals: At "places" Samantha Greene, one of our stage managers, always comes to check on us and always wishes us a "GOOD SHOW." She also has a ritual where she says "pocket watch, pocket watch" at the same time every night, to remind herself of the prop she needs to give Matt Morrison. Before they make their entrance for "Bloody Mary," the Seabees get together in a circle, like a football huddle with hands together in the middle, and give a big Seabees cheer. Then the four Asians do our own mini version right afterward.

Favorite Moment During Each Performance: Every night I stand in the wings during the overture and I still get goosebumps when the stage pulls back to reveal the 30-piece orchestra.

Favorite In-Theatre Gathering Places: The green room in the middle where everybody eats their meals. Also, the boys' dressing room

1. (L-R): Correspondent MaryAnn Hu with Li Jun Li in their dressing room on opening night.
2. Danny Burstein and wife Rebecca Luker at the Tavern on the Green cast party.
3. MaryAnn Hu and Christopher Gattelli.
4. (L-R): Loretta Ables Sayre and MaryAnn Hu at the premiere.

downstairs where they play darts (and who knows what else goes on down there...).

Favorite Off-Site Hangouts: O'Neal's, Rosa Mexicano (for their frozen pomegranate margaritas), and between shows a lot of people like to go to the new Chipotle that just opened in the neighborhood.

Favorite Snack Foods: In a company this large: birthday cake! Magnolia bakery just opened a store on the Upper West Side and I find any excuse to go there.

Mascot: Loretta Ables Sayre has a shrunken head named "Harry" hanging in her dressing room. It was given to her by friends in Hawaii as a good luck charm on her audition and has stayed ever since. Has it worked? Well, 11 Tony nominations later (including hers for Best

Featured Actress in a Musical)...hmmm...I don't think Harry is going anywhere!

Favorite Therapies: Grether's Pastilles, Entertainer's Secret and Dr. Kessler's Vapors.

Most Memorable Ad-Lib: George Merrick has an ad-lib every night during "Honey Bun." My favorite one was, "Nice grass crack."

Memorable Flubs: Skipp Sudduth always has the best ones. 1. "You are causing an economic delerium on this island!" 2. "These planters can't find a native to pick a cow or milk a coconut." Which actually kind of made sense.

Fastest Costume Change: Matt Morrison, pretty quick, from his Marines jumpsuit and leather jacket into his officer's khakis.

Busiest Day at the Box Office: The day after opening I heard they sold a few tickets....

Photo courtesy MaryAnn Hu

Photo by Aubrey Reuben

Photo courtesy MaryAnn Hu

Photo courtesy MaryAnn Hu

South Pacific
SCRAPBOOK

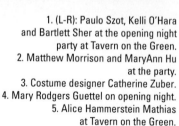

1. (L-R): Paulo Szot, Kelli O'Hara and Bartlett Sher at the opening night party at Tavern on the Green.
2. Matthew Morrison and MaryAnn Hu at the party.
3. Costume designer Catherine Zuber.
4. Mary Rodgers Guettel on opening night.
5. Alice Hammerstein Mathias at Tavern on the Green.

Who Wore the Heaviest/Hottest Costume: The men of the ensemble in the deployment scene where they have real military backpacks, rifles, helmets and flak jackets.

Who Wore the Least: Our lovely nurses have to wear bathing suits and they all look amazing in them!

Catchphrases Only the Company Would Recognize: "Hey, lookie lookie." "Joga." "I'm not sayin'...just sayin'...."

Which Orchestra Member Played the Most Instruments: Because our orchestra is so large, which is a very rare luxury on Broadway nowadays, they don't really have to double, except for the percussionist, who plays tympani and drums.

Which Orchestra Member Played the Most Consecutive Shows: That would be one of our cellists, Charles duChateau (who is also our assistant conductor).

Memorable Directorial Note: In an audition, one actress was reading the Head Nurse sides and Bart Sher kept asking her to be really stern. She wasn't getting it at first. He kept saying "Be rougher, be more stern, be harder on her." After a few attempts, in which her tone just kept getting louder and angrier, she finally turned and said, a little softly, "Do you mean more *butch*?" Bart kind of cracked a smile, gave a little chuckle and said, "Well, not in so many words" Needless to say she got the job and is quite brilliant in the show.

Understudy Anecdote: During previews, Andrew Samonsky and Laura Marie Duncan both went on for Lt. Cable and Nellie, respectively, without having any understudy rehearsals, and they were amazing. They set the bar really high for all of us understudies!

Coolest Things About Being in This Show: Being part of the first revival ever and a show that people have waited for over 50 years to see again on Broadway is quite exciting, I grew up on all the R&H musicals and in a world where pop musicals seem to be the norm, it's so nice to see a big, old-fashioned musical not only thrive, but be the hottest ticket on Broadway this season! The other cool thing is how well we are treated at Lincoln Center. They spoil us up here at Lincoln Center right down to the very fancy Japanese toilets that do...well...everything for you!

Spring Awakening

First Preview: November 16, 2006. Opened: December 10, 2006.
Still running as of May 31, 2008.

CAST
(in order of speaking)

Wendla ....LEA MICHELE
The Adult Women ....KATE BURTON
Martha ....LILLI COOPER
Ilse.............................LAUREN PRITCHARD
Anna ....PHOEBE STROLE
Thea.....................................REMY ZAKEN
The Adult Men ....GLENN FLESHLER
Otto ....BRIAN CHARLES JOHNSON
Hanschen ....JONATHAN B. WRIGHT
Ernst ....BLAKE DANIEL
Georg ....SKYLAR ASTIN
Moritz ....BLAKE BASHOFF
Melchior ....JONATHAN GROFF
Ensemble ....GERARD CANONICO,
MATT DOYLE,
ALEXANDRA SOCHA

TIME/PLACE

The play is set in a provincial German town
in the 1890s.

Continued on next page

✿ EUGENE O'NEILL THEATRE
A JUJAMCYN THEATRE
ROCCO LANDESMAN
President

PAUL LIBIN	JACK VIERTEL	JORDAN ROTH
Producing Director	Creative Director	Vice President

IRA PITTELMAN   TOM HULCE   JEFFREY RICHARDS   JERRY FRANKEL

ATLANTIC THEATER COMPANY
Jeffrey Sine   Freddy DeMann   Max Cooper

Mort Swinsky/Cindy and Jay Gutterman/Joe McGinnis/Judith Ann Abrams
ZenDog Productions/CarJac Productions
Aron Bergson Productions/Jennifer Manocherian/Ted Snowdon
Harold Thau/Terry Schnuck/Cold Spring Productions
Amanda Dubois/Elizabeth Eynon Wetherell
Jennifer Maloney/Tamara Tunie/Joe Cilibrasi/StyleFour Productions

present

Book & Lyrics by | Music by
Steven Sater | **Duncan Sheik**

Based on the play by
Frank Wedekind

with

Skylar Astin   Blake Bashoff   Kate Burton   Gerard Canonico   Tony Carlin
Lilli Cooper   Blake Daniel   Matt Doyle   Glenn Fleshler   Jonathan Groff
Brian Charles Johnson   Frances Mercanti-Anthony   Lea Michele   Eryn Murman   Lauren Pritchard
Alexandra Socha   Phoebe Strole   Jesse Swenson   Jonathan B. Wright   Remy Zaken

Scenic Design	Costume Design	Lighting Design	Sound Design
Christine Jones	Susan Hilferty	Kevin Adams	Brian Ronan
Orchestrations	Vocal Arrangements	String Orchestrations	Music Coordinator
Duncan Sheik	AnnMarie Milazzo	Simon Hale	Michael Keller
Casting	Fight Direction	Production Stage Manager	Associate Producers
Jim Carnahan, C.S.A.	J. David Brimmer	Bryan Landrine	Joan Cullman Productions
Carrie Gardner			Patricia Flicker Addiss
Technical Supervision	General Management	Press Representative	
Neil A. Mazzella	Abbie M. Strassler	Jeffrey Richards Associates	

Music Director
Kimberly Grigsby

Choreography
Bill T. Jones

Directed by
Michael Mayer

Originally produced by the Atlantic Theater Company by special arrangement with Tom Hulce & Ira Pittelman.
The producers wish to express their appreciation to the Theatre Development Fund for its support of this production.

12/24/07

(L-R): Lea Michele
and Jonathan Groff.

Photo by Joan Marcus

355

Spring Awakening

MUSICAL NUMBERS

ACT ONE

"Mama Who Bore Me" ....Wendla
"Mama Who Bore Me" (Reprise) ....Girls
"All That's Known" ....Melchior
"The Bitch of Living" ....Moritz with Boys
"My Junk" ....Girls and Boys
"Touch Me" ....Boys and Girls
"The Word of Your Body" ....Wendla, Melchior
"The Dark I Know Well" ....Martha, Ilse with Boys
"And Then There Were None" ....Moritz with Boys
"The Mirror-Blue Night" ....Melchior with Boys
"I Believe" ....Boys and Girls

ACT TWO

"The Guilty Ones" ....Wendla, Melchior with Boys and Girls
"Don't Do Sadness" ....Moritz
"Blue Wind" ....Ilse
"Left Behind" ....Melchior
"Totally Fucked" ....Melchior with Full Company
"The Word of Your Body" (Reprise) ....Hanschen, Ernst with Boys and Girls
"Whispering" ....Wendla
"Those You've Known" ....Moritz, Wendla, Melchior
"The Song of Purple Summer" ....Full Company

Cast Continued

UNDERSTUDIES

For Melchior:
MATT DOYLE, JESSE SWENSON
For Moritz:
GERARD CANONICO,
BRIAN CHARLES JOHNSON
For Georg:
GERARD CANONICO, MATT DOYLE,
BRIAN CHARLES JOHNSON,
JESSE SWENSON
For Hanschen, Otto:
GERARD CANONICO, MATT DOYLE,
JESSE SWENSON
For Ernst:
GERARD CANONICO, MATT DOYLE
For Wendla:
ERYN MURMAN, ALEXANDRA SOCHA,
PHOEBE STROLE
For Ilse:
ERYN MURMAN, PHOEBE STROLE
For Anna, Martha, Thea:
ERYN MURMAN, ALEXANDRA SOCHA
For the Adult Men:
TONY CARLIN
For The Adult Women:
FRANCES MERCANTI-ANTHONY

Swings:
FRANCES MERCANTI-ANTHONY,
ERYN MURMAN, JESSE SWENSON

Dance Captain:
LAUREN PRITCHARD

THE BAND

Conductor/Keyboards:
KIMBERLY GRIGSBY
Guitars:
THAD DeBROCK
Bass:
GEORGE FARMER
Associate Conductor/Drums:
TREY FILES
Cello:
BENJAMIN KALB
Violin/Guitar:
OLIVIER MANCHON
Viola:
HIROKO TAGUCHI

(L-R): Brian Johnson, Blake Daniel, Blake Bashoff, Matt Doyle, Gerard Canonico.

(L-R): Gerard Canonico and Kate Burton.

Photos by Doug Hamilton

Spring Awakening

Skylar Astin
Georg

Blake Bashoff
Moritz

Kate Burton
Adult Women

Gerard Canonico
Ensemble

Tony Carlin
u/s Adult Men

Lilli Cooper
Martha

Blake Daniel
Ernst

Matt Doyle
Ensemble

Glenn Fleshler
Adult Men

Jonathan Groff
Melchior

Brian Charles
Johnson
Otto

Frances Mercanti-
Anthony
u/s Adult Women

Lea Michele
Wendla

Eryn Murman
Swing

Lauren Pritchard
Ilse

Alexandra Socha
Ensemble

Phoebe Strole
Anna

Jesse Swenson
Swing

Jonathan B. Wright
Hanschen

Remy Zaken
Thea

Steven Sater
Book & Lyrics

Duncan Sheik
*Music,
Orchestrations*

Michael Mayer
Director

Bill T. Jones
Choreographer

Frank Wedekind
(1864-1918)
Author

Christine Jones
Set Designer

Susan Hilferty
Costume Designer

Kevin Adams
Lighting Designer

Kimberly Grigsby
Music Director

AnnMarie Milazzo
Vocal Arrangements

Simon Hale
String Orchestrations

Michael Keller
Music Coordinator

J. David Brimmer
Fight Director, SAFD

Neil A. Mazzella
*Technical
Supervision*

Jim Carnahan
Casting

Spring Awakening

Beatrice Terry
Associate Director

JoAnn M. Hunter
Dance Supervisor

Ira Pittelman
Producer

Tom Hulce
Producer

Jeffrey Richards
Producer

Jerry Frankel
Producer

Neil Pepe
*Artistic Director,
Atlantic Theater
Company*

Andrew D.
Hamingson
*Managing Director,
Atlantic Theater
Company*

Freddy DeMann
Producer

Max Cooper
Producer

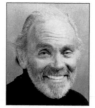
Morton Swinsky
Producer

Jay and Cindy Gutterman
Producers

Joe McGinnis
Producer

Judith Ann Abrams
Producer

Pun Bandhu,
ZenDog Productions
Producer

Marc Falato,
ZenDog Productions
Producer

Carl Moellenberg,
Carjac Productions
Producer

Jack M. Dalgleish,
Carjac Productions
Producer

Tracy Aron
Producer

Stefany Bergson
Producer

Jennifer
Manocherian
Producer

Ted Snowdon
Producer

Harold Thau
Producer

Terry E. Schnuck
Producer

Robert Bailenson
Producer

Amanda Dubois
Producer

Jennifer Maloney
Producer

Tamara Tunie
Producer

Joseph Cilibrasi
Producer

John Styles, Jr.
StylesFour
Productions
Producer

Pat Flicker Addiss
Associate Producer

Drew Tyler Bell
Hanschen

Jennifer Damiano
Ensemble

Spring Awakening

Rob Devaney
Swing

Christine Estabrook
The Adult Women

John Gallagher, Jr.
Moritz

Gideon Glick
Ernst

Robert Hager
Ensemble

Ken Marks
The Adult Men

Krysta Rodriguez
Ensemble

Stephen Spinella
The Adult Men

Christine Estabrook
The Adult Women

Emma Hunton
Ilse, Dance Captain

Alice Lee
Ensemble

Kristine Nielsen
The Adult Women

Kyle Riabko
Melchior

Matt Shingledecker
Ensemble, Swing

Jenna Ushkowitz
Swing

2007-2008 AWARD

GRAMMY AWARD
Best Musical Show album

PRODUCTION PROPERTIES
Christopher Beck

HAIR
(L-R): Heather Wright (Hair Dresser),
Jason Hayes (Hair Supervisor)

NIGHT DOORMAN
Dimitri Ponomarev

Photos by Ben Strothmann

Spring Awakening

CARPENTRY
(L-R): Donald Robinson (Head Carpenter), Anthony Menditto (Deck Automation), Kevin Maher (Fly Automation).

SOUND
(L-R): Francis Elers (Production Sound Engineer), Shannon Slaton (Deck Sound).

STAGE AND COMPANY MANAGEMENT
Front Row (L-R): Chris Recker (Assistant Company Manager), John Gendron (Company Manager).

Back Row (L-R): Gregg N. Kirsopp (Assistant Stage Manager), Bethany Russell (Stage Manager), Bryan Landrine (Production Stage Manager).

WARDROBE
Front Row (L-R): Vanessa Valeriano, Gayle Palmieri, Susan Checklick (Wardrobe Supervisor).

Back Row (L-R): Danny Paul, Cathy Cline.

Spring Awakening

BAND
(L-R): Rob Moose, Thad DeBrock, Pauline Kim, Jeff Lipstein, Alisa Horn, George Farmer.

ELECTRICS
Front Row (L-R): Todd D'Aiuto (Production Electrician), James Shea.

Back Row (L-R): Rocco Williams, James Gardner.

BOX OFFICE
(L-R): Stan Shaffer (Treasurer), Rusty Owen.

FRONT OF HOUSE STAFF
Front Row (L-R): Gillian Bell, Lorraine Wheeler, Cynthia Lopiano, Barbara Carroll, Verna Hobson, Charlotte Brauer.

Back Row (L-R): Andrea Sherman, Bruce Lucoff, Judy Jones, Saime Hodzic, Irene Vincent, Ross Crutchlow, Dorothy Lennon, Scott Rippe, James Cline, Bess Eckstein (House Manager).

Spring Awakening

STAFF FOR *SPRING AWAKENING*

GENERAL MANAGER
ABBIE M. STRASSLER

COMPANY MANAGER
JOHN E. GENDRON

GENERAL PRESS REPRESENTATIVE
JEFFREY RICHARDS ASSOCIATES/IRENE GANDY
Elon Rutberg   Noah Himmelstein   Judith Hansen

MARKETING AND PROMOTIONS
Situation Marketing
Damian Bazadona   Steve Tate

DIRECTOR OF MARKETING
TRG Promotions .... Nancy Richards

DANCE SUPERVISOR
JoAnn M. Hunter

Production Stage Manager	Bryan Landrine
Stage Manager	Bethany Russell
Assistant Stage Manager	Gregg Kirsopp
Assistant Company Manager	Christopher Recker
Dance Captain	Lauren Pritchard
Fight Captain	Brian Charles Johnson
National Marketing Consultants	Susan Blond, Simone Smalls, Liza Bychkov
National Press Consultants	Rubenstein Communications, Inc./ Amy Jacobs, Andy Shearer, Alice McGillion
Associate Technical Supervision	Sam Ellis
Associate Director	Beatrice Terry
Associate Set Designer	Edward Coco
Associate Costume Designer	Maiko Matsushima
Associate Lighting Designer	Aaron Sporer
Moving Light Programmer	Bobby Harrell
Conventional Light Programmer	Neil McShane
Assistant Sound Designer	David Stollings
Scenic Assistants	Tim McNath, Akiko Kosaka, Amy Rubin, Rob Monaco, Sarah Walsh
Costume Assistant	Marina Reti
Head Carpenter	Donald Robinson
Fly Automation	Kevin Maher
Deck Automation	Anthony Menditto
Production Electrician	Todd D'Aiuto
Head Electrician	James Gardner
Light Board Operator	James Shea
Front Light Operators	Michele Gutierrez, Albert Sayers
Properties Coordinator	Kathy Fabian/Propstar
Assistant Properties Coordinators	Peter Sarafin, Carrie Mossman, Carrie Hash
Production Properties	Christopher Beck
Production Sound Engineer	Francis Elers
Sound System Engineer	Mike Farfalla
Deck Sound	Craig Van Tassel
Wardrobe Supervisor	Susan Checklick
Dressers	Cathy Cline, Gayle Palmieri, Danny Paul, Vanessa Valeriano
Hair Supervisor	Nathaniel Hathaway
Hair Dresser	Heather Wright
Music Copyist	Steven M. Alper

Production Assistants	Maura Farver, Adam Grosswirth
Management Associate	Mike Salonia
Assistant to Mr. Hulce	Christopher Maring
Banking	JP Morgan Chase/Richard Callian
Payroll	Castellana Services, Inc./Lance Castellana
Accountant	Fried & Kowgios Partners CPA's LLP/ Robert Fried, CPA
Comptroller	Sarah Galbraith
Insurance	Tanenbaum Harber of Florida/ Carol Bressi-Cilona
Legal Counsel	Lazarus & Harris, LLP/ Scott R. Lazarus, Esq., Robert C. Harris, Esq.
Tutoring	On Location Education
Merchandising	Max Merchandising
Advertising	Serino Coyne, Inc.
Website Design/ Web Marketing	Situation Marketing/ Damian Bazadona, Steve Tate
Production Photographer	Joan Marcus
Additional Photography	Doug Hamilton
Travel Agency	Tzell Travel/The "A" Team
Opening Night Coordination	Tobak Lawrence Company/ Suzanne Tobak, Michael P. Lawrence
Mascots	Lottie and Skye

ATLANTIC THEATER COMPANY STAFF

Artistic Director	Neil Pepe
Managing Director	Andrew D. Hamingson
School Director	Mary McCann
General Manager	Melinda Berk
Associate Artistic Director	Christian Parker
Development Director	Erika Mallin
Development Associate	Rose Yndigoyen
Development Associate	Katherine Jaeger
Production Manager	Lester Grant
Marketing Director	Jodi Sheeler
Membership Coordinator	Sara Montgomery
Operations Manager	Anthony Francavilla
Company Manager	Nick Leavens
Executive Assistant	Laura Savia
Business Manager	Hilary O'Connor

CREDITS AND ACKNOWLEDGEMENTS
Scenery and automation by Hudson Scenic Studio, Inc. Lighting equipment from Hudson Sound and Light LLC. Sound equipment by Masque Sound. Costumes constructed by Eric Winterling Inc. Hosiery and undergarments provided by Bra*Tenders. Wigs by Paul Huntley. Specialty props construction by Tom Carroll Scenery Inc., Plumb Square, Ann Guay Inc. Custom framing by The Great Frame Up. Flame proofing by Turning Star. Piano provided by Beethoven Pianos. Guitars supplied courtesy of Lou Vito, Artist Relations East Coast Fender Musical Instruments. Natural herb cough drops courtesy of Ricola USA, Inc. Rehearsed at the New 42nd Street Studios. Special thanks to Brian McLane at www.program.tv.

Originally commissioned and developed by La Jolla Playhouse, *Spring Awakening* was further developed, in part, with the assistance of the Sundance Institute Theatre Lab, the Roundabout Theatre Company and the American Songbook Series at Lincoln Center for the Performing Arts. Special thanks to Anne Hamburger, Robert Blacker, Todd Haimes, Jon Nakagawa, the staff and crew of the Atlantic

Theater Company and Daniel Schmeder.

www.springawakening.com

STAFF FOR EUGENE O'NEILL THEATRE

Manager	Hal Goldberg
Treasurer	Stan Shaffer
Carpenter	Donald Robinson
Propertyman	Christopher Beck
Electrician	Todd D'Aiuto
Engineer	James Higgins

JUJAMCYN THEATERS

ROCCO LANDESMAN
President

PAUL LIBIN	**JACK VIERTEL**	**JORDAN ROTH**
Producing Director	Creative Director	Vice President

DANIEL ADAMIAN	**JENNIFER HERSHEY**
General Manager	Director of Operations

MEREDITH VILLATORE	**JERRY ZAKS**
Chief Financial Officer	Resident Director

1. Blake Bashoff as Moritz.
2. Kate Burton and Alexandra Socha.

Photos by Doug Hamilton

Spring Awakening
SCRAPBOOK

Correspondent: Bethany Russell, Stage Manager.

Memorable Art Project: Someone took the headshots from the Playbill and cut them in half horizontally. He then rearranged them to create new ones: Brian Charles Gallagher, Jr. and Skylar Estabrook.

Anniversary Parties and/or Gifts: We had a great one-year anniversary party. Everyone who works or worked on the show was there. Our producers gave us very cool show jackets for Christmas.

Most Exciting Celebrity Visitors: Tom Hanks, Bono, Demi Moore, Ashton Kutcher, Benjamin Netanyahu. Dr. Ruth said "If I had been there, that girl wouldn't have gotten pregnant."

Actor Who Performed the Most Roles in This Show: The Adult Man: 9 different people. Plus many more that are just in his head.

Who Has Done the Most Shows: Before he left, John Gallagher, Jr. In over a year he only missed six shows. Martyr.

Special Backstage Ritual: After "Guilty Ones," Jon Groff gives the calling stage manager a back massage.

Favorite Moment During Each Performance (On Stage or Off): For me, throwing the cue lights to start the show.

Favorite In-Theatre Gathering Place: Our dressing room area feels like a frat house; there's always a party and you never know where it will spring up.

Favorite Off-Site Hangout: Jon Groff's apartment to watch "Lost."

Favorite Snack Foods: Baked goods, pretzel sticks, and anything with sugar.

Favorite Therapies: Ricola, Emergen-C, peach tea.

Memorable Ad-Lib: "Conservatory, reformatory."

Cell Phone or Texting Incidents During a Performance: Two teenage girls, front row center, were on their Sidekicks for the first 25 minutes of the show until our house manager told them to stop. They never even looked at the stage until they turned their Sidekicks off.

Memorable Stage Door Fan Encounter: A young fan proposed to one of our actresses. The wedding is set for June, you will receive your invitation soon.

Latest Audience Arrival: A full week late.

Fastest Costume Change: Jonny B's change into his nightgown.

Busiest Day at the Box Office: The day after we won eight Tonys!

Who Wore the Heaviest/Hottest Costume: The Adult Woman. 20 pounds of dress, corset and bustle.

Who Wore the Least: Wendla at the top of the show.

Catchphrase Only the Company Would Recognize: Corn.

Sweethearts Within the Company: I can't keep up, and it will all have changed by the time this is printed.

Orchestra Member Who Played the Most Instruments: Thad DeBrock—six guitars. Most of them in tune.

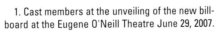

1. Cast members at the unveiling of the new billboard at the Eugene O'Neill Theatre June 29, 2007.
2. Lauren Pritchard (R) signs the new billboard.
3. (L-R): Lea Michele and Jonathan Groff with the portrait of "Spring Awakening" for the Broadway Wall of Fame at Tony's DiNapoli restaurant.

Orchestra Member Who Played the Most Consecutive Performances Without a Sub: Ben Kalb–cello. He sleeps in his locker and refuses to leave.

Best In-House Parody Lyrics: "With scallions that they ate" and "I'll make scrambled eggs and sometimes French toast."

Memorable Directorial Notes: "Bow, bow, acknowledge, bow, get off," "Too much dumbass," and "Don't clap for the audience, they didn't do anything."

Company In-Jokes: "Where's my necklace?"

Company Legend: Kate Burton

Nicknames: Mr. Cranky Pants, Crazy, EB.

Embarrassing Moment: The Adult Women understudy was on and at the end of "Totally Fucked" her bustle fell off. Another actor kicked it into the sand trap during the transition. She actually danced her butt off.

Ghostly Encounters Backstage: I'm told Kevin Maher's (our flyman) great-grandfather has been known to make an appearance, but he has not been spotted on this show.

Superstition That Turned Out To Be True: Klute. I've already said too much.

Coolest Thing About Being in This Show: Being in this show.

Fan Club: "The Guilty Ones" is our unofficial fansite. I don't know who runs it, but I'm sure they have seen our show a few times.

Sunday in the Park with George

First Preview: January 25, 2008. Opened: February 21, 2008.
Still running as of May 31, 2008.

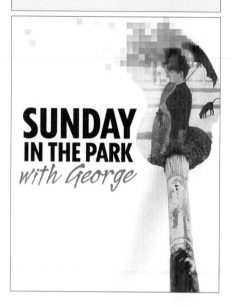

PLAYBILL

SUNDAY IN THE PARK with George

CAST

(in order of appearance)

ACT I

George, an artist	DANIEL EVANS
Dot, his mistress	JENNA RUSSELL
An Old Lady	MARY BETH PEIL
Her Nurse	ANNE L. NATHAN
Franz, a servant	DAVID TURNER
The Bathers	SANTINO FONTANA, DREW McVETY, KELSEY FOWLER*, ALISON HOROWITZ**
Jules, another artist	MICHAEL CUMPSTY
Yvonne, his wife	JESSICA MOLASKEY
A Boatman	ALEXANDER GEMIGNANI
Celeste #1	BRYNN O'MALLEY
Celeste #2	JESSICA GROVÉ
Louis, a baker	DREW McVETY
Louise, the daughter of Jules and Yvonne	KELSEY FOWLER*, ALISON HOROWITZ**
Frieda, a cook	STACIE MORGAIN LEWIS
A Soldier	SANTINO FONTANA
Mr.	ED DIXON
Mrs.	ANNE L. NATHAN

ACT II

George, an artist	DANIEL EVANS
Marie, his grandmother	JENNA RUSSELL
Dennis, a technician	ALEXANDER GEMIGNANI
Bob Greenberg, the museum director	MICHAEL CUMPSTY
Naomi Eisen, a composer	JESSICA MOLASKEY

Continued on next page

STUDIO 54

ROUNDABOUT THEATRE COMPANY

Todd Haimes, Artistic Director
Harold Wolpert, Managing Director
Julia C. Levy, Executive Director

in association with

Bob Boyett   Debra Black   Jam Theatricals   Stephanie P. McClelland
Stewart F. Lane/Bonnie Comley   Barbara Manocherian/Jennifer Manocherian   Ostar Productions

Presents

The Menier Chocolate Factory (David Babani, Artistic Director) production of

Daniel Evans   Jenna Russell
Michael Cumpsty   Alexander Gemignani   Jessica Molaskey

in

SUNDAY IN THE PARK with George

Music and Lyrics by Stephen Sondheim   Book by James Lapine

with

Mary Beth Peil

Ed Dixon   Santino Fontana   Kelsey Fowler   Jessica Grové   Alison Horowitz
Stacie Morgain Lewis   Drew McVety   Anne L. Nathan   Brynn O'Malley   David Turner
Colleen Fitzpatrick   Jeff Kready   Hayley Podschun   Andrew Varela

Set & Costume Design	Lighting Design	Sound Design	Projection Design
David Farley	Ken Billington	Sebastian Frost	Timothy Bird & The Knifedge Creative Network

Musical Supervisor	Orchestrations	Music Coordinator
Caroline Humphris	Jason Carr	John Miller

Production Stage Manager	Hair & Wig Design	Dialect Coach
Peter Hanson	Tom Watson	Kate Wilson

Casting	Technical Supervisor	Executive Producer	Press Representative
Jim Carnahan, C.S.A.	Steve Beers	Sydney Beers	Boneau/Bryan-Brown

Director of Marketing & Sales Promotion	Director of Development	Founding Director	Associate Artistic Director
David B. Steffen	Jeffory Lawson	Gene Feist	Scott Ellis

Musical Staging by Christopher Gattelli

Directed by Sam Buntrock

In association with Caro Newling for Neal Street Productions and Mark Rubinstein

**Lead support provided by Roundabout's Musical Theatre Fund partners:
Perry and Marty Granoff, GVA Williams, The Kaplen Foundation,
John and Gilda McGarry, The Shen Family Foundation, Tom and Diane Tuft.**

Playwrights Horizons produced the original production of *Sunday in the Park with George* in 1983
Originally directed on Broadway by James Lapine
Roundabout Theatre Company is a member of the League of Resident Theatres.
www.roundabouttheatre.org

2/21/08

(L-R): Alison Horowitz, Jessica Molaskey, Drew McVety, Brynn O'Malley, Jessica Grové, Daniel Evans, Michael Cumpsty, Jenna Russell.

Photo by Joan Marcus

Sunday in the Park with George

MUSICAL NUMBERS

ACT I

"Sunday in the Park With George"	Dot
"No Life"	Jules, Yvonne
"Color and Light"	Dot, George
"Gossip"	Celeste #1, Celeste #2, Boatman, Nurse, Old Lady, Jules, Yvonne
"The Day Off"	George, Nurse, Franz, Frieda, Boatman, Soldier, Celeste #1, Celeste #2, Yvonne, Louise, Jules, Louis
"Everybody Loves Louis"	Dot
"Finishing the Hat"	George
"We Do Not Belong Together"	Dot, George
"Beautiful"	Old Lady, George
"Sunday"	Company

ACT II

"It's Hot Up Here"	Company
"Chromolume #7"	Company
"Putting It Together"	George, Company
"Children and Art"	Marie
"Lesson #8"	George
"Move On"	George, Dot
"Sunday"	Company

2007-2008 AWARDS

Tony Award
Lifetime Achievement
(Stephen Sondheim)

Drama Desk Awards
Outstanding Orchestrations
(Jason Carr)
Outstanding Projection and Video Design
(Timothy Bird and
Knifedge Creative Network)

Outer Critics Circle Awards
Outstanding Lighting Design
(Ken Billington)
Outstanding Set Design
(David Farley and Timothy Bird)

Theatre World Award
First Major New York Stage Appearance
(Jenna Russell)

Cast Continued

Harriet Pawling,
a patron of the arts .... ANNE L. NATHAN
Billy Webster, her friend .... DREW McVETY
A Photographer .... JESSICA GROVÉ
Charles Redmond, a visiting curator ..... ED DIXON
Alex, an artist .... SANTINO FONTANA
Betty, an artist .... STACIE MORGAIN LEWIS
Lee Randolph,
the museum's publicist .... DAVID TURNER
Blair Daniels, an art critic .... MARY BETH PEIL
Elaine .... BRYNN O'MALLEY

UNDERSTUDIES

For Yvonne/Naomi Eisen, Old Lady/Blair Daniels, Nurse/Mrs./Harriet Pawling:
COLLEEN FITZPATRICK
For George:
SANTINO FONTANA
For Soldier/Alex, Louis/Billy Webster, Franz/ Lee Randolph:
JEFF KREADY
For Dot/Marie:
BRYNN O'MALLEY
For Celeste #1/Elaine, Celeste #2/A Photographer, Frieda/Betty:
HAYLEY PODSCHUN
Standby for Mr./Charles Redmond, Boatman/Dennis, Jules/Bob Greenberg:
ANDREW VARELA

Dance Captain: HAYLEY PODSCHUN

Production Stage Manager: PETER HANSON
Stage Manager: JON KRAUSE
Assistant Stage Manager: RACHEL ZACK

* Ms. Fowler appears on Tuesday, Wednesday and Friday evenings and Saturday matinees.
** Ms. Horowitz appears on Wednesday matinees, Thursday and Saturday evenings and Sunday matinees.

TIME AND PLACE

ACT I takes place on a series of Sundays from 1884 to 1886 and alternates between a park on an island in the Seine just outside of Paris, and George's studio.

ACT II takes place in 1984 at an American art museum and on the island.

Daniel Evans and Jenna Russell are appearing with the permission of Actors' Equity Association pursuant to an exchange program between American Equity and UK Equity.

ORCHESTRA

Conductor:
CAROLINE HUMPHRIS
Associate Conductor:
THOMAS MURRAY
Music Coordinator:
JOHN MILLER
Music Director/Piano:
CAROLINE HUMPHRIS
Keyboard:
THOMAS MURRAY
Violin/House Contractor:
MATTHEW LEHMANN
Cello:
MAIRI DORMAN-PHANEUF
Woodwinds:
TODD GROVES

Music Copying:
EMILY GRISHMAN MUSIC PREPARATION—KATHARINE EDMONDS/EMILY GRISHMAN

Sunday in the Park with George

Daniel Evans
George

Jenna Russell
Dot/Marie

Michael Cumpsty
Jules/
Bob Greenberg

Alexander
Gemignani
Boatman/Dennis

Jessica Molaskey
Yvonne/Naomi Eisen

Mary Beth Peil
Old Lady/
Blair Daniels

Ed Dixon
Mr./
Charles Redmond

Santino Fontana
Bather/Soldier/Alex

Kelsey Fowler
Louise

Jessica Grové
Celeste #2/
A Photographer

Alison Horowitz
Louise

Stacie Morgain
Lewis
Frieda/Betty

Drew McVety
Bather/Louis/
Billy Webster

Anne L. Nathan
Nurse/Mrs./
Harriet Pawling

Brynn O'Malley
Celeste #1/Elaine

David Turner
Franz/Lee Randolph

Colleen Fitzpatrick
u/s Yvonne/Naomi
Eisen, Old Lady/
Blair Daniels, Nurse/
Mrs./Harriet Pawling

Jeff Kready
u/s Soldier/Alex,
Louis/Billy Webster,
Franz/Lee Randolph

Hayley Podschun
u/s Celeste #1/Elaine,
Celeste #2/
A Photographer,
Frieda/Betty

Andrew Varela
Standby Mr./
Charles Redmond,
Boatman/
Dennis, Jules/
Bob Greenberg

Sam Buntrock
Director

Stephen Sondheim
Music & Lyrics

James Lapine
Book

Christopher Gattelli
Musical Staging

David Farley
Set and
Costume Design

Ken Billington
Lighting Design

Jason Carr
Orchestrations

Sebastian Frost
Sound Design

John Miller
Music Coordinator

Tom Watson
Hair and Wig Design

Dave Solomon
Assistant Director

Jim Carnahan
Casting

Bob Boyett
Producer

Debra Black
Producer

Timothy Bird
Projection Design

Sunday in the Park with George

Arny Granat,
Jam Theatricals
Producer

Steve Traxler,
Jam Theatricals
Producer

Stephanie P.
McClelland
Producer

Stewart F. Lane and Bonnie Comley
Producers

Barbara
Manocherian
Producer

Jennifer
Manocherian
Producer

Bill Haber,
Ostar Productions
Producer

Gene Feist
*Founding Director,
Roundabout Theatre
Company*

Todd Haimes
*Artistic Director,
Roundabout Theatre
Company*

STAGE AND COMPANY MANAGEMENT
Front Row (L-R): Denise Cooper, Brent McCreary.

Back Row (L-R): Peter Hanson, Rachel Zack, Jonny Krause.

CREW
Front Row (L-R): Dan Schultheis, Steve Jones, Dan Hoffman.

Middle Row (L-R): Erin Mary Delaney, Paul Ashton, Dorian Fuchs.

Back Row (L-R): Josh Weitzman, Lawrence Jennino, John Wooding.

FRONT OF HOUSE
Front Row (L-R): Hajjah Karriem, Jack Watanachaiyot, LaConya Robinson.

Middle Row (L-R): Nicole Ramirez, Essence Mason, Delilah Rivera.

Back Row (L-R): José Cuello, Justin Brown, Ana Bak-Kvapil,
Nicholas Wheatley.

Sunday in the Park with George

HAIR AND WARDROBE
Front Row (L-R): Victoria Grecki, Mary Ann Oberpiller, Nadine Hettel.

Back Row (L-R): Barry Ernst, Joe Godwin, Timothy Miller.

ORCHESTRA
(L-R): Thomas Murray, Mairi Dorman-Phaneuf.

BOX OFFICE
(L-R): Pam Unger, Scott Falkowski, Jamie Perlman.

Photos by Ben Strothmann

ROUNDABOUT THEATRE COMPANY STAFF
ARTISTIC DIRECTOR ....TODD HAIMES
MANAGING DIRECTOR.......HAROLD WOLPERT
EXECUTIVE DIRECTOR ....JULIA C. LEVY
ASSOCIATE ARTISTIC DIRECTOR ...SCOTT ELLIS

ARTISTIC STAFF
DIRECTOR OF ARTISTIC DEVELOPMENT/
   DIRECTOR OF CASTING ....**Jim Carnahan**
Artistic Consultant ....Robyn Goodman
Resident Director ....Doug Hughes
Associate Artists ....Scott Elliott, Bill Irwin,
                Joe Mantello, Mark Brokaw,
                Kathleen Marshall
Consulting Dramaturg ....Jerry Patch
Artistic Associate ....Jill Rafson
Casting Director ....Carrie Gardner
Casting Associate ....Kate Schwabe
Casting Associate ....Stephen Kopel
Artistic Assistant...............................Erica Rotstein
Literary Associate ....Josh Fiedler
Casting Interns ....Kerry Ann Minchinton, Kyle Bosley

EDUCATION STAFF
EDUCATION DIRECTOR ....**David A. Miller**
Director of Instruction and
   Curriculum Development ....Reneé Flemings
Education Program Manager ....Jennifer DiBella
Program Associate for
   School-Based Programs ....Amanda Hinkle
Education Associate for
   Theatre-Based Programs ....Jay Gerlach
Education Assistant ....Allison Figley
Education Dramaturg ....Ted Sod
Teaching Artists ....Phil Alexander, Cynthia Babak,

Victor Barbella, LaTonya Borsay,
Rob Bronstein, Lori Brown-Niang,
Miss Stella, Hamilton Clancy,
Joe Doran, Katie Down, Amy Fortoul,
Tony Freeman, Sheri Graubert,
Matthew Gregory, Adam Gwon,
Karla Hendrick, Jim Jack, Lisa Renee Jordan,
Alvin Keith, Jonathan Lang, Rebecca Lord,
Tami Mansfield, Erin McCready,
Jordana Oberman, Evan O'Brient,
Deirdre O'Connor, Andrew Ondrecjak,
Laura Poe, Alexa Polmer-Spencer,
Nicole Press, Jennifer Rathbone,
Leah Reddy, Amanda Rehbein,
Taylor Ruckel, Chris Rummel,
Cassy Rush, Drew Sachs, Nick Simone,
Derek Straat, Daniel Robert Sullivan,
Vickie Tanner, Olivia Tsang,
Cristina Vaccaro, Jennifer Varbalow,
Leese Walker, Eric Wallach, Gail Winar
Education Interns ....Sara Curtin, Steven Tarca

ADMINISTRATIVE STAFF
GENERAL MANAGER ....**Sydney Beers**
Associate Managing Director ....Greg Backstrom
General Manager, Steinberg Center ....Rebecca Habel
General Counsel..........................Nancy Hirschmann
Human Resources Manager ....Stephen Deutsch
MIS Director ....Jeff Goodman
Assistant General Manager ....Maggie Cantrick
Management Associate ....Tania Camargo
Facilities Manager ....Abraham David
Office Manager ....Scott Kelly
MIS Associates ....Micah Kraybill, Dylan Norden
Receptionists ....Dena Beider, Raquel Castillo,

Elisa Papa, Allison Patrick,
Monica Sidorchuk
Messenger ....Darnell Franklin
Management Intern ....Shoshanna Gross

FINANCE STAFF
DIRECTOR OF FINANCE...............**Susan Neiman**
Assistant Controller..........................John LaBarbera
Accounts Payable Administrator ....Frank Surdi
Financial Associate ....Yonit Kafka
Business Office Assistant ....Joshua Cohen
Business Interns ....Edgar Eguia, Nicholas Mustakas

DEVELOPMENT STAFF
DIRECTOR OF DEVELOPMENT ......**Jeffory Lawson**
Director, Institutional Giving ....Julie K. D'Andrea
Director, Special Events ....Steve Schaeffer
Director, Major Gifts ....Joy Pak
Manager, Donor Information Systems ....Lise Speidel
Manager, Individual Giving ....Kara Kandel
Telefundraising Manager ....Gavin Brown
Manager, Corporate Relations ....Corey Young
Individual Giving Associate ....Kate Bartoldus
Patrons Services Assistant ....John Haynes
Development Assistants ....Joshua Poole, Daniel Curley
Special Events Assistant ....Ashley Firestone
Institutional Giving Assistant ....Nick Nolte
Development Interns...................Kaitlin Cherichello,
                Victoria Pardo-Posse

MARKETING STAFF
DIRECTOR OF MARKETING
   AND SALES PROMOTION........**David B. Steffen**
Associate Director of Marketing ....Wendy Hutton
Marketing/Publications Manager .....Margaret Casagrande

Sunday in the Park with George

Marketing Associate ....Stefanie Schussel
Marketing Assistant ....Shannon Marcotte
Website Consultant ....Keith Powell Beyland

DIRECTOR OF TELESALES
SPECIAL PROMOTIONS ....**Daniel Weiss**
Telesales Manager ....Michael Pace
Telesales Office Coordinator ....Anthony Merced
Marketing Intern ....Dragica Dabo

TICKET SERVICES STAFF
DIRECTOR OF
SALES OPERATIONS ....**Charlie Garbowski, Jr.**
Ticket Services Manager ....Ellen Holt
Subscription Manager ....Ethan Ubell
Box Office Managers ....Edward P. Osborne,
Andrew Clements
Group Sales Manager ....Jeff Monteith
Assistant Box Office Managers ....Krystin MacRitchie,
Robert Morgan, Nicole Nicholson
Assistant Ticket Services Managers ....Robert Kane,
Bill Klemm, Carlos Morris
Ticket Services ....Solangel Bido,
Lauren Cartelli, David Carson,
Joseph Clark, Mike DePope,
Nisha Dhruna, Adam Elsberry,
Lindsay Ericson, Scott Falkowski,
Catherine Fitzpatrick, Daniel Gabriel,
James Graham, Tova Heller,
Nicki Ishmael, Kate Longosky, Elisa Mala,
Mead Margulies, Chuck Migliaccio,
Adam Owens, Ethan Paulini,
David Pittman, DeeAnna Row,
Benjamin Schneider, Heather Siebert,
Nalene Singh, Lillian Soto, DJ Thacker,
Pam Unger, Thomas Walsh
Ticket Services Intern ....Kayrose Pagan

SERVICES
Counsel ....Paul, Weiss,
Rifkind, Wharton and Garrison LLP,
John Breglio, Deborah Hartnett
Counsel ....Rosenberg & Estis
Counsel ....Andrew Lance,
Gibson, Dunn, & Crutcher, LLP
Counsel ....Harry H. Weintraub,
Glick and Weintraub, P.C.
Immigration Counsel ....'.......Mark D. Koestler and
Theodore Ruthizer, Esq.,
Matthew Dunn, Esq. of
Kramer Levin Naftalis & Frankel LLP
Government
Relations ....Law Offices of Claudia Wagner LLC
House Physicians ....Dr. Theodore Tyberg,
Dr. Lawrence Katz
House Dentist ....Neil Kanner, D.M.D.
Insurance ....DeWitt Stern Group, Inc.
Accountant ....Lutz & Carr CPAs, LLP
Advertising ....Spotco/
Drew Hodges, Jim Edwards,
Tom Greenwald, Y. Darius Suyama,
Beth Watson
Sponsorship ....TMG-The Marketing Group/
Laura Matalon, Tanya Grubich,
William Critzman
Interactive Marketing ....Situation Marketing/
Damian Bazadona, John Lanasa,
Ryan Klink, Joey Oliva

Events Photography ....Anita and Steve Shevett
Production Photographer ....Joan Marcus
Theatre Displays.............King Displays, Wayne Sapper
Lobby Refreshments ....Sweet Concessions

MANAGING DIRECTOR
EMERITUS ....Ellen Richard

Roundabout Theatre Company
231 West 39th Street, New York, NY 10018
(212) 719-9393.

GENERAL PRESS REPRESENTATIVES
Adrian Bryan-Brown

Matt Polk   Jessica Johnson   Amy Kass

CREDITS FOR
SUNDAY IN THE PARK WITH GEORGE
Company Manager .... Denise Cooper
Company Manager Assistant .... Brent McCreary
Production Stage Manager .... Peter Hanson
Stage Manager .... Jon Krause
Assistant Stage Manager .... Rachel Zack
Assistant Director ....Dave Solomon
Associate Director/Choreographer, UK .....Tara Wilkinson
Assistant to the Choreographer ....Lou Castro
SSDC Observer ....Michael Schwartz
Dance Captain ....Hayley Podschun
Associate Costume Designer .... Matthew Pachtman
Costume Assistant .... Cathy Parrott
Assistants to the Scenic/
Costume Designer, UK ....Julie Bowles, Sarah Cant,
Machiko Hombu
Associate Lighting Designer ....Paul Toben
Associate Sound Designer .... Nick Borisjuk
Assistant to the Music Coordinator ....Charles Butler
Dialect Coach ....Kate Wilson
Production Carpenter ....Dan Hoffman
Production Electrician ....Josh Weitzman
Assistant Production Electrician ....John Wooding
Production Projection Engineer .... Sam Hopkins
Media Programmer ....Sam Hopkins
Synthesizer Programmer ....Bruce Samuels
Production Properties ....Kathy Fabian, Propstar Inc.
Assistant Production Properties ....Rose Howard
Wardrobe Supervisor ....Nadine Hettel
Dressers ....Joe Godwin, Victoria Grecki,
Mary Ann Oberpiller
Hair and Wig Supervisor ....Barry Ernst
Hair Assistant ....Timothy Miller
Make-up Designer ....Angelina Avallone
Production Sound Engineer ....Brad Gyorgak
House Properties ....Lawrence Jennino
Properties Running Crew ....Erin Mary Delaney
Automation Carpenter ....Paul Ashton
Flyman ....Steve Jones
Moving Light Programmer ....David Arch
Obsession Programmer ....Jessica Morton
Follow Spot Operator ....Dorian Fuchs
Deck Sound ....Larry White
Local One IATSE Apprentice.............. Dan Schultheis
Production Assistant ....Rachel Bauder
Children's Tutoring Provided by ...On Location Education
Child Wrangler ....Lindsay Ericson
Dramatist's Guild Intern .... Andy Monroe
Scenery Constructed, Automated
and Painted by ....Hudson Scenic Studio, Inc.

Lighting Equipment
Provided by ....PRG, Production Resource Group
Sound Equipment
Provided by ....Masque Sound & Recording Corp.
Specialty Furniture Props ....Plumb Squares,
SPS Effects, Aardvark Interiors
Custom Parasols...................D.P. Birch and Company
Flame Treatment ....Turning Star
Projected Visual and
Animation Content ....Knifedge Creative Network
Projection equipment provided by ....XL Video

Animation & Visual Effects
Production ....Knifedge The Creative Network
Creative Director ....Timothy Bird
Previsualization &
Projection Strategy ....Sam Hopkins & his Light Studio
Team Leader/AFX Animator ....Nina Wilson
Rigging ....Raf Anzovin for Anzovin Studio
Content Librarian ....Ciara Fanning
Character Animator ....Shaun Freeman
Animator & Technical Director ....John Keates
Matte Artist ....Alex Laurent
3D Animator ....Andy McNamara
Animator ....Stephen Millingen
AFX Animator ....Aaron Trinder
With Additional Animation by ....Sam Buntrock
"Putting It Together" Visual Effects
Producer ....Amy DiPrima
"Putting It Together" Visual Effects
Videographer ....John Chimples for ImageMaintenance
Costumes by ....Euro Co. Costumes,
Giliberto Designs, Inc., Mardana,
Timberlake Studios, Inc., Tricorne, Inc.
Custom Fabric Painting and Dyeing ....Jeff Fender
Additional Fabric Dyeing ....Julianne Kroboth
Millinery by ....Leslie Norgate, Lynne Mackey, Inc.
Emergen-C health and energy drink mix
provided by ....Alacer Corp.
Natural cough drops courtesy of ....Ricola USA Inc.
Special Thanks to ....101 Productions, Ltd.,
Wendy Orshan, John Vennema,
Dave Auster
Associate Producer for Robert Theatrical ....Tim Levy
Assistant to Mr. Boyett ....Diane Murphy
Lazarus and Harris ....Scott Lazarus, Esq.

Make-up provided by M•A•C

STUDIO 54 THEATRE STAFF
Theatre Manager ....Matthew Armstrong
Box Office Manager ....Jaime Perlman
House Manager ....LaConya Robinson
Associate House Manager ....Jack Watanachaiyot
House Staff................Elicia Edwards, Jason Fernandez,
Jen Kneeland, Kate Longosky,
Latiffa Marcus, Nicole Marino,
Jonathan Martinez, Dana McCaw,
Nicole Ramirez, Anthony Roman,
Nick Wheatley, Stella Varriale
House Carpenter ....Dan Hoffman
House Electrician ....Josh Weitzman
House Properties ....Lawrence Jennino
Security ....Gotham Security
Maintenance ....Ralph Mohan, Maman Garba
Lobby Refreshments by ....Sweet Concessions

Sunday in the Park With George
SCRAPBOOK

1. Curtain call on opening night.
2. Jenna Russell and Daniel Evans with an original Seurat study at the Museum of Modern Art's Seurat exhibit.

Correspondent: Mary Beth Peil "Old Lady/Blair Daniels"

Opening Night Gifts: Two: First, Daniel Evans made each of us a photo album containing pictures he took, capturing little Kodak moments during rehearsals. They are very personal and very beautiful and they capture the color and vibrancy of the cast personality-wise.

Second, Stephen Sondheim and James Lapine made everyone a puzzle of the painting "Sunday Afternoon on the Island of La Grande Jatte." Stephen is known as a puzzle fanatic, so it had special resonance.

Most Exciting Celebrity Visitors: Original stars Mandy Patinkin and Bernadette Peters. Mandy came very quietly. He bought a ticket way up in the cheap seats and watched the show in a very private way. No one knew he was there except my daughter's friend who happened to be sitting next to him. Afterward he went to Daniel's dressing room and was very, very kind. When Bernadette came they made a press event of it. Having the two of them there was very meaningful for us. I think we "passed the test."

"Easter Bonnet" Sketch: No title. Written by James Lapine; directed by Alex Gemignani.

Actor Who Performs the Most Roles in This Show: Everyone has two roles, through Anne L. Nathan has three: Nurse, Mrs. and Harriet.

Who Has Done the Most Shows in Their Career: Hands down Ed Dixon. He has done ten Broadway shows, plus tons of regional and international stuff.

Special Backstage Ritual: There's something only a few of us are able to see at the top of the show. As they wait to make their entrances, Daniel and Jenna have an intimate moment where they pretend they're humping. It's sometimes hysterically funny—and sometimes a turn-on.

Favorite Moments During Each Performance: I don't know if "favorite" is the right description.

I come and go a lot, but I never leave the wings. I watch the entire show on the monitor so that when I make my entrance I can pick right up on the spirit and the tempo of that day's performance. I love so many moments in the show: "Moving On," the breakup scene, the end of Act I. I never get tired of watching them.

Memorable Ad-Lib: There's no room for ad-libbing in Sondheim.

Favorite In-Theatre Gathering Place: The Studio 54 greenroom is kind of odd—really just a hallway with sofas lining both walls; more of a plopping place than a gathering place per se. I am partial to the second-floor dressing room Anne Nathan and I share. It's become a kind of gossip corner. We've been known to have five or six people in there gossiping. It's not constant, but it's safe. It's become known as the DMZ.

Favorite Off-Site Hangout: We're on 54th Street so we're a little too far above the main hangout area in the 40s and too far below Lincoln Center. A bunch of us go out to Iguana down the block from our theatre. Sometimes we also go to The Divine Bar. My own personal favorite is Sosa Borella on Eighth Avenue between 50th and 51st Streets. It's an Argentinian restaurant that stays open late. I used to go there when I was appearing in *Nine*.

Favorite Snack Food: It's sort of "every man for himself." However we do have a lovely espresso maker.

Favorite Therapy: We probably go through more Ricola than any show in town.

Memorable Press Encounter: We had a press conference at an exhibition of Seurat prints and paintings at the Museum of Modern Art. It was so generous of the museum to allow us in there. The exhibit was so informative about Seurat's art, the kind of human being he was and what kind of artist he was.

Memorable Stage Door Fan Encounter: Jessica

Molaskey had some kid who said he wanted to take a picture of her on his cell phone. He started singing a song from one of her albums and she joined in with him. She didn't realize he was recording the whole thing and before you knew it, the clip was on YouTube.

Fastest Costume Change: Anne Nathan. She has to change from Mrs. to Nurse for an appearance on stage that lasts thirty seconds, then back into her Mrs. costume and then a few minutes later back to Nurse again. The change lasts longer than her time on stage.

Who Wore the Heaviest/Hottest Costume: I do! The Old Lady costume has a lot of layers and a train and a cape and gloves for goodness sake, plus a hat that covers my ears.

Who Wore the Least: Jenna in "Color and Light."

Catchphrase Only the Company Would Recognize: "It's an aural illusion."

Memorable Directorial Note: On the second day of rehearsal, Sam Buntrock whispered in my ear, "That's your grandchild she's carrying." He never told me what I should do with it, but that knowledge informed the rest of my work. It makes her whole backstory and journey so much more interesting.

Nicknames: The two young girls call Jenna "Mama Sausage" and she calls them "Baby Sausage."

Ghostly Encounters Backstage: We joke about the fact that ghosts or gremlins inhabit the sound system. Things seem to change every day and the sound system people swear they didn't touch any of the settings. There's also something unique to the show: Perhaps it's a combination of the backstage light and the costumes, but when you see a person sitting in a corner in costume, it looks like a ghost. Of course, at the end, we're all supposed to be ghosts except George.

Coolest Thing About Being in This Show: It's Sondheim!

Talk Radio

First Preview: February 15, 2007. Opened: March 11, 2007.
Closed June 24, 2007 after 29 Previews and 121 Performances.

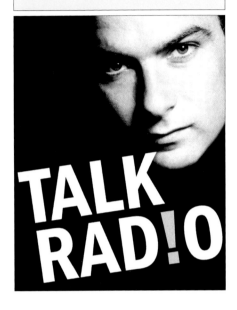

PLAYBILL

CAST

(in order of appearance)

Sid Greenberg .... ADAM SIETZ
Bernie .... CORNELL WOMACK
Spike .... KIT WILLIAMSON
Stu Noonan .... MICHAEL LAURENCE
Linda MacArthur .... STEPHANIE MARCH
Vince Farber .... MARC THOMPSON
Barry Champlain .... LIEV SCHREIBER
Dan Woodruff .... PETER HERMANN
Jordan Grant .... CHRISTY PUSZ
Kent .... SEBASTIAN STAN
Dr. Susan Fleming .... BARBARA ROSENBLAT
Rachael .... CHRISTINE PEDI
Callers' Voices .... CHRISTINE PEDI,
CHRISTY PUSZ, BARBARA ROSENBLAT,
ADAM SIETZ, MARC THOMPSON,
CORNELL WOMACK

TIME
Spring 1987

SETTING
Studio B of radio station WTLK in
Cleveland, Ohio

Continued on next page

ⓈLONGACRE THEATRE
220 West 48th Street
A Shubert Organization Theatre

Gerald Schoenfeld, *Chairman*   Philip J. Smith, *President*

Robert E. Wankel, *Executive Vice President*

JEFFREY RICHARDS   JERRY FRANKEL   JAM THEATRICALS
FRANCIS FINLAY   RONALD FRANKEL   JAMES FULD, JR.   STEVE GREEN   JUDITH HANSEN
PATTY ANN LACERTE   JAMES RILEY   MARY LU ROFFE/MORT SWINSKY
SHELDON STEIN   TERRI & TIMOTHY CHILDS/STYLEFOUR PRODUCTIONS
IRVING WELZER/HERB BLODGETT
present

LIEV SCHREIBER
in

TALK RAD!O

written by ERIC BOGOSIAN
created for the stage by ERIC BOGOSIAN and TAD SAVINAR

also starring

STEPHANIE MARCH   PETER HERMANN   MICHAEL LAURENCE
CHRISTINE PEDI   BARBARA ROSENBLAT   ADAM SIETZ
MARC THOMPSON   KIT WILLIAMSON   CORNELL WOMACK
and SEBASTIAN STAN

set design **MARK WENDLAND**	costume design **LAURA BAUER**	lighting design **CHRISTOPHER AKERLIND**
sound design **RICHARD WOODBURY**	casting **TELSEY + COMPANY**	production stage manager **JANE GREY**
press representative **JEFFREY RICHARDS ASSOC. IRENE GANDY**	general management **ALBERT POLAND**	technical supervisor **NEIL A. MAZZELLA**

directed by
ROBERT FALLS

Original New York Production by New York Shakespeare Festival Produced by Joseph Papp.
Originally produced at the Portland Center for Visual Arts through a grant from the
National Endowment for the Arts.

TALK RADIO is presented in association with the Atlantic Theater Company

The producers wish to express their appreciation to Theatre Development
Fund for its support of this production.

6/24/07

(L-R): Peter Hermann
and Liev Schreiber

Photo by Joan Marcus

Talk Radio

Cast Continued

UNDERSTUDIES/STANDBYS

Standby for Liev Schreiber:
MICHAEL LAURENCE
For Dan Woodruff:
MICHAEL LAURENCE, LEE SELLARS
For Stu Noonan:
LEE SELLARS, CORNELL WOMACK
For Linda MacArthur, Rachael:
CHRISTY PUSZ
For Kent:
KIT WILLIAMSON
For Spike:
LEE SELLARS
For Sid Greenberg, Bernie, Vince Farber:
OLIVER VAQUER
For Dr. Susan Fleming:
CHRISTINE PEDI
For Male Callers:
ADAM SIETZ, MARC THOMPSON,
OLIVER VAQUER, CORNELL WOMACK
For Female Callers:
CHRISTINE PEDI, CHRISTY PUSZ,
BARBARA ROSENBLAT

THIS PRODUCTION IS DEDICATED TO THE
MEMORY OF JOSEPH PAPP.

Photo by Joan Marcus

Stephanie March

Liev Schreiber
Barry Champlain

Stephanie March
Linda MacArthur

Peter Hermann
Dan Woodruff

Michael Laurence
Stu Noonan

Sebastian Stan
Kent

Christine Pedi
Rachael,
Female Callers

Barbara Rosenblat
Female Callers,
Dr. Susan Fleming

Adam Sietz
Sid Greenberg,
Male Callers

Marc Thompson
Vince Farber,
Male Callers

Kit Williamson
Spike

Cornell Womack
Bernie, Male Callers

Christy Pusz
Jordan Grant,
Female Caller

Lee Sellars
Understudy
Dan Woodruff,
Stu Noonan, Spike

Oliver Vaquer
Understudy
Sid Greenberg,
Bernie, Male Callers

Eric Bogosian
Playwright

Robert Falls
Director

Laura Bauer
Costume Designer

Christopher Akerlind
Lighting Designer

Richard Woodbury
Sound Designer

Bernard Telsey/
Telsey + Company
Casting

Talk Radio

Neil A. Mazzella
Technical Supervisor

Albert Poland
General Manager

Jeffrey Richards
Producer

Jerry Frankel
Producer

Steve Traxler,
Jam Theatricals
Producer

James Fuld Jr.
Producer

James Riley
Producer

Mort Swinsky
Producer

Sheldon Stein
Producer

Irving Welzer
Producer

Herb Blodgett
Producer

John Styles,
Stylefour
Productions
Producer

Dave Clemmons,
Stylefour
Productions
Producer

Neil Pepe
*Artistic Director,
Atlantic Theater
Company*

Andrew D.
Hamingson
*Managing Director,
Atlantic Theater
Company*

**THE *TALK RADIO*
FAMILY**

Standing (L-R):
Sebastian Stan,
Sandy Binion, Rose
Marie C. Cappelluti,
Brad Robertson,
Matthew Farrell,
Valerie Spradling,
Wilbur Graham,
Chris White,
John Lofgren.

Seated (L-R): Marc Thompson, Adam
Sietz, Michael Laurence, Barbara
Rosenblat, Jane Grey, Christine Pedi,
Stephanie March, Liev Schreiber, Michael
Altbaum, Oliver Vaquer.
Floor (L-R): Ben West and Christy Pusz.
Not Pictured: Kristine Bellerud, Peter
Hermann, Regan Kimmel, Daniel Kuney,
Bob Reilly, Richard F. Rogers, Lee Sellars,
Kit Williamson and Cornell Womack.

Photos by Melissa Merlo

STAGE MANAGEMENT
(L-R): Ben West (Production Assistant), Jane Grey (Production Stage
Manager) and Matthew Farrell (Stage Manager).

CREW
(L-R): Brad Robertson (Head Electrician), Valerie Spradling (Production
Sound), Sandy Binion (Dresser) and Richard F. Rogers (House Electrician).

Talk Radio

COMPANY MANAGER
Daniel Kuney

STAGE CREW
Standing (L-R): Richard F. Rogers (House Electrician), John Lofgren (House Prop Head), Wilbur Graham (Production Carpenter) and Brad Robertson (Head Electrician).
Seated: Valerie Spradling (Sound Engineer).

DOORMAN
Chris White

STAFF FOR *TALK RADIO*

GENERAL MANAGEMENT
ALBERT POLAND

GENERAL PRESS REPRESENTATIVE
JEFFREY RICHARDS ASSOCIATES
IRENE GANDY
Mark Barber   Elon Rutberg   Ben West

CASTING
TELSEY + COMPANY, C.S.A.
Bernie Telsey, Will Cantler, David Vaccari,
Bethany Knox, Craig Burns,
Tiffany Little Canfield, Rachel Hoffman,
Stephanie Yankwitt, Carrie Rosson,
Justin Huff, Joe Langworth, Bess Fifer

COMPANY MANAGER
DANIEL KUNEY

PRODUCTION STAGE MANAGER ...... JANE GREY
TECHNICAL SUPERVISOR ..... NEIL A. MAZZELLA
Stage Manager ....Matthew Farrell
Assistant Director ....José Zayas
Assistant Set Designer ....Rachel Nemec
Associate Costume Designer ....Bobby Tilley
Assistant Lighting Designer ....Ben Krall
Associate Sound Designer ....Jeremy Lee
Props Coordinator ....Kathy Fabian
Associate Props Coordinator ....Carrie Hash
Associate Properties
Coordinator .... Carrie Hash Propstar Associates/
Carrie Mossman, Melanie Mulder
Custom Prop Furniture .... Jason Gandy/
Aardvark Interiors
Prop Equipment .... Richard Fitzgerald/
Sound Associates
Custom Prop Equipment Engineers ....Robert Hale,
Lenny Will
Assistant to Mr. Schreiber .... Roger Mendoza
Assistant to Mr. Richards ....Mark Barber
Assistant to Mr. Bogosian .... Nikole Beckwith
Assistant to Mr. Falls ....Julie Massey
Assistant to Mr. Poland...................Michael Altbaum
Associate Technical Supervisor ....Sam Ellis

Production Assistant ....Ben West
Production Interns ....KathrynAnn Pierroz,
Jennifer Leigh Shipp
Sound Intern ....David Horowitz
Production Carpenter.................,,,,,,, Wilbur Graham Jr.
Production Electrician ....James Maloney
Head Electrician ....Brad Robertson
House Electrician ....Ric Rogers
Production Props ....John Lofgren
Production Sound ....Valerie Spradling
Sound Programmer ....Mark Fiore
Wardrobe Supervisor ....Kristine Bellerud
Mr. Schreiber's Dresser ....Rose Marie C. Cappelluti
Dresser ....Sandy Binion
Dialect Coach ....Kate Maré
Advertising ....Serino Coyne, Inc./
Greg Corradetti, Ruth Rosenberg,
Andrea Prince
Website Design/Web Marketing ......Situation Marketing/
Damian Bazadona, Steve Tate
Merchandising ....Max Merchandising
Banking ....JP Morgan Chase/
Richard Callian, Michele Gibbons
Accountants ....Rosenberg, Neuwirth & Kuchner/
Mark A. D'Ambrosi,
Jana M. Jevnikar
Insurance ....DeWitt Stern Group/
Peter Shoemaker, Stan Levine
Legal Counsel ....Lazarus & Harris, LLP/
Scott R. Lazarus, Esq.,
Robert C. Harris, Esq. Diane Viale
Payroll..............................Castellana Services, Inc.
Production Photographer ....Joan Marcus
Car Services ....Elegant Limousine/Joe Cox
Company Mascots ....Lottie, Skye and Buster

CREDITS
Scenery constructed by Hudson Scenic Studio Inc. Lighting equipment from Hudson Sound and Light LLC. Sound equipment from Sound Associates, Inc. Costumes executed by John Kristiansen New York Inc. Rehearsed at New 42nd Street Studios. Natural herb cough drops courtesy of Ricola USA, Inc. Emergen-C super energy booster provided by Alacer Corp. Vintage radio equipment provided by Georgie Talbert and Ron Erickson. Studio research by Alan Smith @ WNYC New York Public Radio.

THE AUTHOR WOULD LIKE TO THANK EDWARD PRESSMAN, OLIVER STONE AND FRED ZOLLO FOR THEIR INVALUABLE COLLABORATION ON *TALK RADIO*.

SPECIAL THANKS
Rick Sordelet,
Bra*Tenders for hosiery and undergarments

A special thanks to Bar Americain, a bright lively brasserie setting in midtown Manhattan, for *Talk Radio*'s opening night party.

www.talkradioonbroadway.com

 THE SHUBERT ORGANIZATION, INC.
Board of Directors

Gerald Schoenfeld	**Philip J. Smith**
Chairman	President
Wyche Fowler, Jr.	**John W. Kluge**
Lee J. Seidler	**Michael I. Sovern**

Stuart Subotnick

Robert E. Wankel
Executive Vice President

Peter Entin	**Elliot Greene**
Vice President –	Vice President –
Theatre Operations	Finance
David Andrews	**John Darby**
Vice President –	Vice President –
Shubert Ticketing Services	Facilities

D.S. Moynihan
Vice President – Creative Projects

House Manager ....Bob Reilly

Tarzan

First Preview: March 24, 2006. Opened: May 10, 2006.
Closed July 8, 2007 after 35 Previews and 486 Performances.

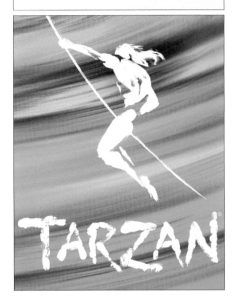

PLAYBILL

CAST

(in order of appearance)

Kerchak ....ROBERT EVAN
Kala ....MERLE DANDRIDGE
Young Tarzan ....J. BRADLEY BOWERS
(Tues., Thurs., Sat. Eve., Sun. Mat.)
ALEX RUTHERFORD
(Wed. Mat., Fri., Sat. Mat., Sun. Eve.)
Terk ....CHESTER GREGORY II
Tarzan ....JOSH STRICKLAND
Jane Porter ....JENN GAMBATESE
Professor Porter ....TIMOTHY JEROME
Mr. Clayton ....DONNIE KESHAWARZ
Snipes ....HORACE V. ROGERS

Ensemble ....CELINA CARVAJAL,
DWAYNE CLARK, VEN DANIEL,
VERONICA deSOYZA, ANDREA DORA,
GREGORY HANEY, MICHAEL HOLLICK,
JONATHAN JOHNSON, KARA MADRID,
ANASTACIA McCLESKEY,
JOHN ELLIOTT OYZON,
NICHOLAS RODRIGUEZ,
HORACE V. ROGERS,
KEPANI SALGADO-RAMOS,
SEAN SAMUELS, NIKI SCALERA

Continued on next page

RICHARD RODGERS THEATRE
UNDER THE DIRECTION OF JAMES M. NEDERLANDER AND JAMES L. NEDERLANDER

DISNEY THEATRICAL PRODUCTIONS
under the direction of
Thomas Schumacher

presents

TARZAN

Music and Lyrics by
PHIL COLLINS

Book by
DAVID HENRY HWANG

with

JOSH STRICKLAND   JENN GAMBATESE
MERLE DANDRIDGE   CHESTER GREGORY II   ROBERT EVAN
TIM JEROME   DONNIE KESHAWARZ
J. BRADLEY BOWERS   ALEX RUTHERFORD

CHRISTOPHER CARL CELINA CARVAJAL DWAYNE CLARK VEN DANIEL VERONICA deSOYZA ANDREA DORA
ALAYNA GALLO GREGORY HANEY MICHAEL HOLLICK JONATHAN JOHNSON JESLYN KELLY
JOSHUA KOBAK KARA MADRID ANASTACIA McCLESKEY MARLYN ORTIZ WHITNEY OSENTOSKI
JOHN ELLIOTT OYZON ANGELA PHILLIPS NICHOLAS RODRIGUEZ HORACE V. ROGERS KEPANI SALGADO-RAMOS
SEAN SAMUELS NICK SANCHEZ NIKI SCALERA NATALIE SILVERLIEB JD AUBREY SMITH

Based on the story *Tarzan of the Apes* by
EDGAR RICE BURROUGHS
and the Disney film *Tarzan®*
Screenplay by
TAB MURPHY, BOB TZUDIKER & NONI WHITE
Directed by
KEVIN LIMA & CHRIS BUCK

Scenic and Costume Design   Lighting Design
BOB CROWLEY   **NATASHA KATZ**

Sound Design   Hair Design   Make-Up Design
JOHN SHIVERS   **DAVID BRIAN BROWN**   **NAOMI DONNE**

Soundscape   Special Creatures   Fight Direction
LON BENDER   **IVO COVENEY**   **RICK SORDELET**

Vocal Arrangements   Dance Arrangements   Orchestrations
PAUL BOGAEV   **JIM ABBOTT**   **DOUG BESTERMAN**

Music Director   Music Coordinator   Casting
JIM ABBOTT   **MICHAEL KELLER**   **TELSEY + COMPANY**

Production Stage Manager   Technical Supervisor   Press Representative
FRANK LOMBARDI   **TOM SHANE BUSSEY**   **BONEAU/BRYAN-BROWN**

Associate Director   Associate Producer   Production Supervisor
JEFF LEE   **MARSHALL B. PURDY**   **CLIFFORD SCHWARTZ**

Aerial Design by
PICHÓN BALDINU

Music Produced by
PAUL BOGAEV

Choreography by
MERYL TANKARD

Direction by
BOB CROWLEY

7/8/07

(L-R): Jenn Gambatese and Josh Strickland.

Photo by Joan Marcus

Tarzan

MUSICAL NUMBERS

ACT I

"Two Worlds"	Voice of Tarzan, Ensemble
"You'll Be in My Heart"	Kala, Ensemble
"Jungle Funk"	Instrumental
"Who Better Than Me?"	Terk, Young Tarzan
"No Other Way"	Kerchak
"I Need to Know"	Young Tarzan
"Son of Man"	Terk, Tarzan, Ensemble
"Son of Man" (Reprise)	Terk, Tarzan, Ensemble
"Sure As Sun Turns to Moon"	Kala, Kerchak
"Waiting for This Moment"	Jane, Ensemble
"Different"	Tarzan

ACT II

"Trashin' the Camp"	Terk, Ensemble
"Like No Man I've Ever Seen"	Jane, Porter
"Strangers Like Me"	Tarzan, Jane, Ensemble
"For the First Time"	Jane, Tarzan
"Who Better Than Me?" (Reprise)	Terk, Tarzan
"Everything That I Am"	Voice of Young Tarzan, Tarzan, Kala, Ensemble
"You'll Be in My Heart" (Reprise)	Tarzan, Kala
"Sure As Sun Turns to Moon" (Reprise)	Kala
"Two Worlds" (Finale)	Ensemble

Instrumental score for "Two Worlds" and "Meeting the Family"
based on the original score by Mark Mancina, written for the Disney film TARZAN®.

ORCHESTRA

Conductor: JIM ABBOTT
Associate Conductor: ETHAN POPP
Synthesizer Programmer: ANDREW BARRETT

Keyboard 1: JIM ABBOTT
Keyboard 2: ETHAN POPP
Keyboard 3: MARTYN AXE
Drums: GARY SELIGSON
Percussion: ROGER SQUITERO, JAVIER DIAZ
Bass: HUGH MASON
Guitar: JJ McGEEHAN
Cello: JEANNE LeBLANC
Flutes: ANDERS BOSTRÖM
Reeds: CHARLES PILLOW
Trumpet: ANTHONY KADLECK
Trombone: BRUCE EIDEM
French Horn: THERESA MacDONNELL

Music Coordinator: MICHAEL KELLER

(L-R): Jenn Gambatese and Josh Strickland.

Photo by Joan Marcus

Cast Continued

SWINGS

ALAYNA GALLO,
JESLYN KELLY,
JOSHUA KOBAK,
MARLYN ORTIZ,
WHITNEY OSENTOSKI,
ANGELA PHILLIPS,
NICK SANCHEZ,
NATALIE SILVERLIEB,
JD AUBREY SMITH

Dance Captain .... MARLYN ORTIZ

STANDBYS AND UNDERSTUDIES

Standby for Kerchak, Porter and Clayton:
CHRISTOPHER CARL
Understudies:
Tarzan:
JOSHUA KOBAK,
NICHOLAS RODRIGUEZ
Jane:
CELINA CARVAJAL,
NIKI SCALERA,
NATALIE SILVERLIEB
Kerchak:
MICHAEL HOLLICK,
HORACE V. ROGERS
Kala:
ANDREA DORA,
NATALIE SILVERLIEB
Terk:
DWAYNE CLARK,
NICK SANCHEZ
Clayton:
MICHAEL HOLLICK,
JOSHUA KOBAK
Porter:
MICHAEL HOLLICK

SPECIALTIES

Waterfall Ribbon Dancer:
KARA MADRID
Lead Son of Man Vocals:
HORACE V. ROGERS
Moth:
JONATHAN JOHNSON

Tarzan

Josh Strickland
Tarzan

Jenn Gambatese
Jane

Merle Dandridge
Kala

Chester Gregory II
Terk

Robert Evan
Kerchak

Timothy Jerome
Professor Porter

Donnie Keshawarz
Clayton

J. Bradley Bowers
Young Tarzan

Alex Rutherford
Young Tarzan

Christopher Carl
Standby for Kerchak, Porter and Clayton

Celina Carvajal
Ensemble

Dwayne Clark
Ensemble

Ven Daniel
Ensemble

Veronica deSoyza
Ensemble

Andrea Dora
Ensemble

Alayna Gallo
Swing

Gregory Haney
Ensemble

Michael Hollick
Ensemble

Jonathan Johnson
Ensemble

Jeslyn Kelly
Swing

Joshua Kobak
Swing

Kara Madrid
Ensemble

Anastacia McCleskey
Ensemble

Marlyn Ortiz
Swing

Whitney Osentoski
Swing

John Elliott Oyzon
Ensemble

Angela Phillips
Swing/Assistant Aerial Designer

Nicholas Rodriguez
Ensemble

Horace V. Rogers
Snipes/Ensemble

Kepani Salgado-Ramos
Ensemble

Sean Samuels
Ensemble

Nick Sanchez
Swing

Niki Scalera
Ensemble

Natalie Silverlieb
Swing

JD Aubrey Smith
Swing

Tarzan

Phil Collins
Music/Lyrics

David Henry Hwang
Book

Bob Crowley
Director/Scenic and Costume Design

Meryl Tankard
Choreography

Pichón Baldinu
Aerial Design

Natasha Katz
Lighting Design

John Shivers
Sound Design

David Brian Brown
Hair Design

Naomi Donne
Makeup Design

Lon Bender
Soundscape

Ivo Coveney
Special Creatures

Rick Sordelet
Fight Director

Paul Bogaev
Music Producer/ Vocal Arrangements

Jim Abbott
Music Director, Dance Arrangements

Doug Besterman
Orchestrator

Michael Keller
Music Coordinator

Andrew Barrett
Synthesizer Programmer

Bernard Telsey, Telsey + Company
Casting

Jeff Lee
Associate Director

Clifford Schwartz
Production Supervisor

Thomas Schumacher, Director Disney Theatrical Productions
Producer

Kevin Massey
Swing

Rika Okamoto
Ensemble

Stefan Raulston
Ensemble

Dylan Riley Snyder
Young Tarzan

Tarzan

STAGE MANAGEMENT
Front Row: Tanya Gillette (Assistant Stage Manager).

Back Row (L-R): Allison A. Lee (Assistant Stage Manager), Kenneth J. McGee (Assistant Stage Manager), Robert M. Armitage (Assistant Stage Manager), Frank Lombardi (Production Stage Manager).

COMPANY MANAGEMENT
(L-R): Eduardo Castro (Company Manager) and Francesca Panagopoulos (Associate Company Manager).

BOX OFFICE
(L-R): Ken Klein and Corinne Parker-Dorso.

FRONT OF HOUSE STAFF
Front Row (L-R): Nadia Earle, Frances Eppy, Carmen Frank, Rafael Ortiz, Roseanne Kelly, William Phelan.

Middle Row (L-R): Jose Rivera, Wayne Cameron, Dorothy Darby, Dianne Hosang, Beverly Thornton, Joseph Melchiorre, Maureen Babreo.

Back Row (L-R): Timothy Pettolina (House Manager), Jamie Sponcil, Robert Rea, Frank Almiron, Nicole Pasquale, Lucy Horton, Julia McDarris and Michael Stalling.

Tarzan

STAGE CREW

Front Row (L-R): Charlene Belmond (Assistant Hair Supervisor), Margo Lawless (Dresser), Mike Kearns (Assistant Carpenter), Sonia Rivera (Hair Supervisor), Franklin Hollenbeck, Dan Tramontozzi (Sound Engineer), Eric Nahaczewski.

Second Row (L-R): Paul Curran (Assistant Carpenter), Denise Grillo (Production Props), Nanette Golia (Wardrobe Supervisor), Melanie McClintock (Dresser), Beth Frank (Physical Therapy), Dawn Reynolds, Margaret Kurz (Assistant Wardrobe Supervisor).

Third Row (L-R): Vivienne Crawford (Dresser), Denise Ozker, Christina Grant (Makeup Supervisor), Jorge Vargas (Assistant Makeup Supervisor), Theresa Distasi, Kevin Crawford (Assistant Props), Lisa Preston (Dresser), Don McCarty, David Dignazio.

Back Row (L-R): Robert Terrill Jr., Andrew Trotto, Randy Zaibek (Head Electrician/Light Board Operator), Hugh Mason, Frank Illo, Walter Bullard, Joseph De Paulo, Ronald Knox, Thomas Maher, Robert Kelly.

STAFF FOR _TARZAN_ ®

COMPANY MANAGER ....EDUARDO CASTRO
Assistant Company Manager ....Francesca Panagopoulos
Assistant to the Associate Producer ....Janine McGuire
Show Accountant ....Isander Rojas

Assistant Choreographer.................Leonora Stapleton
Assistant Aerial Designer ....Angela Phillips

"Son of Man" Animated
    Sequence ....**Little Airplane Productions, Inc.**

GENERAL PRESS REPRESENTATIVE
BONEAU/BRYAN-BROWN
Chris Boneau
Jim Byk   Matt Polk   Juliana Hannett

Production Stage Manager ....Frank Lombardi
Stage Manager............................Kenneth J. McGee
Assistant Stage Managers ....Robert M. Armitage,
                Tanya Gillette, Allison A. Lee
Dance Captain ....Marlyn Ortiz
Assistant Dance Captain ....JD Aubrey Smith
Fight Captain ....Robert M. Armitage
Production Assistants ....Ryan J. Bell, Sara Bierenbaum

Associate Scenic Designer ....Brian Webb
Scenic Design Associate ....Rosalind Coombes
Assistant Scenic Designer...............Frank McCullough
Associate Costume Designer ....Mary Peterson
Assistant Costume Designer ....Daryl Stone
Associate Lighting Designer ....Yael Lubetzky
Assistant Lighting Designer ....Aaron Spivey
Automated Lighting Programmer ....Aland Henderson
Automated Lighting Tracker ....Jesse Belsky
Assistant to Lighting Designer ....Richard Swan
Associate Sound Designer ....David Patridge
Assistant Sound Designer ....Jeremy Lee
LCS Sound System Programmer ....Garth Hemphill
"Son of Man" Visual Development ....Kevin Harkey
Hand Lettering of
    Show Scrim ....Harriet Rose Calligraphy & Design

Technical Supervisor ....Tom Shane Bussey
Associate Technical Supervisor ....Rich Cocchiara
Assistant Technical Supervisor ....Matt Richman
Technical Production Assistant ....Noelle Font
Production Carpenter ....Jeff Goodman
Assistant Carpenter ....Mike Kearns
Assistant Carpenter/Foy Operator ....Richard Force
Scenic Automation ....Dave Brown
Deck Automation ....Thomas Maher

Assistant Carpenter ....Kirk Aengenheyster
Assistant Carpenter.............................Paul Curran
Assistant Carpenter ....Michael Cimino
Assistant Carpenter ....Brent Nyland
Harness Construction ....Dany Conde
Production Electrician ....Jimmy Fedigan
Head Electrician/Light Board Operator ....Mike Ward
Lead Follow Spot Operator ....Andrew Dean
Moving Light Technician ....Derek Healy
Pyrotechnician ....Norman Ballard
Production Props ....Denise J. Grillo
Assistant Props ....Kevin Crawford
Props Shopper ....Kate Foster
Production Sound ....David Patridge
Sound Engineer............................Dan Tramontozzi
Atmospheric Effects ....Chic Silber
Associate to Mr. Silber ....Aaron Waitz
Wardrobe Supervisor ....Nanette Golia
Assistant Wardrobe Supervisor ....Margaret Kurz
Dressers ....Vivienne Crawford, Jay Gill,
                Margo Lawless, Lisa Preston,
             Tina Marie Clifton, David Turk
Hair Supervisor ....Sonia Rivera
Assistant Hair Supervisor ....Charlene Belmond
Hairdresser ....Enrique Vega
Makeup Supervisor ....Christina Grant

Tarzan

Assistant Makeup Supervisor ....Jorge Vargas

Music Copyist ....Russell Anixter, Donald Rice/
                                           Anixter Rice Music Service
Synthesizer Programming ....Andrew Barrett
Synthesizer Programming Assistant ....Anders Boström
Electronic Drum Arrangements ....Gary Seligson
Rehearsal Drummer ....Gary Seligson
Rehearsal Pianist ....Ethan Popp
Music Production Assistant ....Brian Allan Hobbs

CASTING
TELSEY + COMPANY, C.S.A.
Bernie Telsey, Will Cantler, David Vaccari,
Bethany Knox, Craig Burns, Tiffany Little Canfield,
Rachel Hoffman, Stephanie Yankwitt, Carrie Rosson,
Justin Huff, Joe Langworth, Bess Fifer

DIALOGUE & VOCAL COACH ...DEBORAH HECHT

Web Design Consultant ....Joshua Noah
Advertising ....Serino Coyne, Inc.
Production Photography ....Joan Marcus
Acoustic Consultant ....Paul Scarbrough/a.'ku.stiks
Structural Engineering
   Consultant ....Bill Gorlin, McLaren, P.C.
Production Travel ....Jill L. Citron
Payroll Manager ....Cathy Guerra, Johnson West
Children's Tutoring ....On Location Education/
                                     Maryanne Keller
Physical Therapy ....Neuro Tour Physical Therapy, Inc./
                               Lindsey Facciolo, DPT
Medical Consultant ....Neil S. Roth, MD
Chaperone ....Robert Wilson
Assistant to Phil Collins ....Danny Gillen
Assistant to Bob Crowley ....Fred Hemminger
Press Assistant ....Matt Ross

TARZAN® owned by Edgar Rice Burroughs, Inc. and used by permission. TARZAN® cover artwork ©2006 Edgar Rice Burroughs, Inc. and Disney Enterprises, Inc. All rights reserved.

CREDITS
Scenery by Hudson Scenic Studio, Inc., Scenic Technologies, a division of Production Resource Group, LLC, New Windsor, NY; Dazian Fabrics; CMEANN Productions, Inc.; Stone Pro Rigging, Inc. Automation by Foy Inventerprise, Inc.; Hudson Scenic Studio, Inc., Show control and scenic motion control featuring Stage Command Systems® by Scenic Technologies, a division of Production Resource Group, LLC, New Windsor, NY. Lighting equipment by PRG Lighting. Sound equipment by Masque Sound. Costumes by Donna Langman Costumes; Tricorne, Inc.; DerDau; G! Willikers!; Pluma; Hochi Asiatico; Gene Mignola. Millinery provided by Rodney Gordon. Wigs provided by Ray Marston Wig Studio Ltd. Props by Paragon; Rabbit's Choice; Jauchem and Meeh; Randy Carfagno; ICBA, Inc.; John Creech Design & Production; Camille Casaretti, Inc.; Steve Johnson; Jerard Studios, Trashin' the Camp furniture fabric by Old World Weavers, division of Stark Carpet. Special effects equipment by Jauchem & Meeh, Inc. Firearms by Boland Production Supply, Inc. Soundscape by Soundelux. Atmospheric effects equipment provided by Sunshine Scenic Studios and Aztec Stage Lighting. Acoustic drums by Pearl Drums. Rehearsal catering by Mojito Cuban Cuisine. Ricola natural herb cough drops courtesy of Ricola

USA, Inc. Emergen-C super energy booster provided by Alacer Corp. Special event clothing provided by Calvin Klein.

Makeup provided by M•A•C

TARZAN® rehearsed at Studio 2, Steiner Studios Brooklyn Navy Yard and New 42nd Street Studios.

SPECIAL THANKS
James M. Nederlander; James L. Nederlander; Nick Scandalios; Herschel Waxman; Jim Boese; David Perry of the Nederlander Organization and Ojala Producciones, S. A.; Siam Productions, LLC

⊁N⊱
NEDERLANDER
Chairman ....James M. Nederlander
President ....James L. Nederlander

Executive Vice President
Nick Scandalios

Vice President   Senior Vice President
Corporate Development   Labor Relations
Charlene S. Nederlander   **Herschel Waxman**

Vice President   Chief Financial Officer
Jim Boese   **Freida Sawyer Belviso**

HOUSE STAFF FOR
THE RICHARD RODGERS THEATRE
House Manager ....Timothy Pettolina
Box Office Treasurer ....Fred Santore Jr.
Assistant Treasurer ....Daniel Nitopi
Electrician ....Steve Carver
Carpenter ....Kevin Camus
Propertymaster ....Steve DeVerna
Engineer ....Sean Quinn

Theatre insurance provided by Emar Group.

DISNEY THEATRICAL PRODUCTIONS
President ....Thomas Schumacher
SVP & General Manager ....Alan Levey
SVP, Managing Director & CFO ....David Schrader

Senior Vice President, Creative Affairs .....Michele Steckler
Senior Vice President, International ....Ron Kollen
Vice President, Operations ....Dana Amendola
Vice President, Labor Relations ....Allan Frost
Vice President, Domestic Touring ....Jack Eldon
Director, Domestic Touring ....Michael Buchanan
Vice President, Theatrical Licensing ....Steve Fickinger
Director, Casting & Development ....Jennifer Rudin
Director, Human Resources ....June Heindel
Manager, Labor Relations ....Stephanie Cheek
Manager, Human Resources ....Cynthia A. Young
Human Resources Representative................Jewel Neal
Manager, Information Systems ....Scott Benedict
Senior Computer Support Analyst ......Kevin A. McGuire

Production
Executive Music Producer ....Chris Montan
Vice President, Physical Production ....John Tiggeloven
Senior Manager, Safety ....Canara Price
Manager, Physical Production ....Karl Chmielewski
Purchasing Manager ....Joseph Doughney

Staff Associate Designer ....Dennis W. Moyes
Dramaturg and Literary Manager ....Ken Cerniglia

Marketing
Vice President, Broadway ....Andrew Flatt
Vice President, International ....Fiona Thomas
Director, Broadway ....Kyle Young
Director, Education and Outreach ....Peter Avery
Senior Manager, Broadway ....Michele Groner
Website Manager ....Eric W. Kratzer
Online Marketing Manager ....Roseann Warren
Media Asset Manager ....Cara L. Moccia
Assistant Manager, Communications ....Dana Torres
Assistant Manager, Promotions ....Craig Buckley

Sales
Director, National Sales ....Bryan Dockett
Manager, Group Sales ....Jacob Lloyd Kimbro
Manager, Sales & Ticketing ....Nick Falzon
Assistant Manager, Group Sales ....Juil Kim

Business and Legal Affairs
Senior Vice President ....Jonathan Olson
Vice President ....Robbin Kelley
Executive Director ....Harry S. Gold
Senior Counsel ....Seth Stuhl
Paralegal/Contract Administration ....Colleen Lober

Finance
Director..Joe McClafferty
Senior Manager, Finance ....Dana James
Manager, Finance ....Justin Gee
Manager, Finance ....John Fajardo
Production Accountants ....Joy Brown, Nick Judge,
                                      Barbara Toben
Assistant Production Accountant ....Isander Rojas
Senior Financial Analyst ....Tatiana Bautista
Analyst ....Liz Jurist

Controllership
Director, Accounting ....Leena Mathew
Senior Analysts ....Stephanie Badie, Mila Danilevich,
                                  Adrineh Ghoukassian
Analysts ....Ken Herrell, Bilda Donado

Administrative Staff
Dusty Bennett, Amy Caldamone, Lauren Daghini, Jessica Doina, Cristi Finn, Cristina Fornaris, Dayle Gruet, Lance Gutterman, Gregory Hanoian, Jonathan Hanson, Jay Hollenback, Connie Jasper, Tom Kingsley, Tivon Marcus, Kerry McGrath, Lisa Mitchell, Ryan Pears, Roberta Risafi, Kisha Santiago, David Scott, Andy Singh, Jason Zammit

BUENA VISTA THEATRICAL
MERCHANDISE, L.L.C.
Vice President ....Steven Downing
Operations Manager ....Shawn Baker
Assistant Manager, Inventory ....Suzanne Jakel
Associate Buyer ....Violet Burlaza
On-site Retail Manager ....Jamie Sponcil
On-site Assistant Retail Manager ....Seth Augspurger
Retail Supervision ....Michael Giammatteo

Disney Theatrical Productions • 1450 Broadway
New York, NY 10018

guestmail@disneytheatrical.com

The 39 Steps

First Preview: January 4, 2008. Opened: January 15, 2008.
Still running as of May 31, 2008.

PLAYBILL

CAST

(in order of appearance)

Man #1 ....CLIFF SAUNDERS
Man #2 ....ARNIE BURTON
Richard Hannay ....CHARLES EDWARDS
Annabella Schmidt/Pamela/
Margaret ....JENNIFER FERRIN

UNDERSTUDIES

For Annabella Schmidt/Pamela/Margaret:
CLAIRE BROWNELL
For Man #1 & #2:
CAMERON FOLMAR
For Richard Hannay:
MARK SHANAHAN

Production Stage Manager: NEVIN HEDLEY
Stage Manager: JANET TAKAMI

Charles Edwards is appearing with the permission of
Actors' Equity Association pursuant to an exchange
program between American Equity and UK equity.

AMERICAN AIRLINES THEATRE

ROUNDABOUTTHEATRECOMPANY

Todd Haimes, Artistic Director
Harold Wolpert, Managing Director
Julia C. Levy, Executive Director

In association with
Bob Boyett, Harriet Newman Leve/Ron Nicynski, Stewart F. Lane/Bonnie Comley,
Manocherian Golden Prods., Olympus Theatricals/Douglas Denoff, Marek J. Cantor/Pat Addiss
and
Huntington Theatre Company (Nicholas Martin, Artistic Director; Michael Maso, Managing Director)
and Edward Snape for Fiery Angel Ltd.
Present

Adapted by Patrick Barlow

Based on an original concept by Simon Corble & Nobby Dimon
Based on the book by John Buchan

with

Arnie Burton, Charles Edwards, Jennifer Ferrin, Cliff Saunders

Set & Costume Design Peter McKintosh	*Lighting Design* Kevin Adams	*Sound Design* Mic Pool	*Dialect Coach* Stephen Gabis
Original Movement Created by Toby Sedgwick	*Additional Movement Created by* Christopher Bayes	*Production Management* Aurora Productions	*Production Stage Manager* Nevin Hedley
Casting Jay Binder/Jack Bowdan	*General Manager* Rebecca Habel Roy Gabay	*Associate Producer* Sydney Beers	*Press Representative* Boneau/Bryan-Brown
Director of Marketing & *Sales Promotion* David B. Steffen	*Director of Development* Jeffory Lawson	*Founding Director* Gene Feist	*Associate Artistic Director* Scott Ellis

Directed by
Maria Aitken

Roundabout Theatre Company is a member of the League of Resident Theatres.
www.roundabouttheatre.org

1/15/08

(L-R): Arnie Burton, Cliff Saunders and Charles Edwards.

Photo by Charles Erickson

The 39 Steps

Arnie Burton
Man #2

Charles Edwards
Richard Hannay

Jennifer Ferrin
*Annabella Schmidt/
Pamela/Margaret*

Cliff Saunders
Man #1

Cameron Folmar
u/s Man #1 & #2

Mark Shanahan
u/s Richard Hannay

Claire Brownell
*u/s Annabella
Schmidt/Pamela/
Margaret*

Maria Aitken
Director

Patrick Barlow
Adaptor

Peter McKintosh
*Set & Costume
Design*

Kevin Adams
Lighting Design

Mic Pool
Sound Design

Stephen Gabis
Dialect Coach

Jay Binder C.S.A.
Casting

Jack Bowdan C.S.A.
Casting

Bob Boyett
Producer

Harriet Newman Leve
Producer

Ron Nicynski
Producer

Stewart F. Lane and Bonnie Comley
Producers

Jennifer
Manocherian
Producer

Barbara
Manocherian
Producer

Douglas Denoff
Producer

Pat Flicker Addiss
Producer

Nicholas Martin
*Artistic Director,
Huntington Theatre
Company*

Michael Maso
*Managing Director,
Huntington Theatre
Company*

Gene Feist
*Founding Director,
Roundabout Theatre
Company*

Todd Haimes
*Artistic Director,
Roundabout Theatre
Company*

2007-2008 AWARDS

TONY AWARDS
Best Lighting Design of a Play
(Kevin Adams)
Best Sound Design of a Play
(Mic Pool)

DRAMA DESK AWARDS
Unique Theatrical Experience
Best Lighting Design of a Play
(Kevin Adams)

The 39 Steps

FRONT OF HOUSE STAFF
(L-R): Ilia Diaz, Zipporah Aguasvivas.

BOX OFFICE STAFF
(L-R): Robert Morgan, Heather Siebert, Mead Margulies.

CREW
First Row (L-R): Brittany Jones-Pugh, Janet Takami, Peggy Donovan, Rosy Garner, Susan Fallon, Carly DiFulvio.

Second Row (L-R): Renee Mariotti, Barb Bartel, Nellie LaPorte, Carmel Sheehan, Nelson Vaughn.

Back Row (L-R): Nevin Hedley, Brian Maiuri, Andrew Forste, Dann Wojnar, Glenn Merwede.

Photos by Ben Strothmann

ROUNDABOUT THEATRE COMPANY STAFF
ARTISTIC DIRECTOR .... **TODD HAIMES**
MANAGING DIRECTOR .... **HAROLD WOLPERT**
EXECUTIVE DIRECTOR .... **JULIA C. LEVY**
ASSOCIATE ARTISTIC DIRECTOR ...**SCOTT ELLIS**

ARTISTIC STAFF
DIRECTOR OF ARTISTIC DEVELOPMENT/
  DIRECTOR OF CASTING .... **Jim Carnahan**
Artistic Consultant ....Robyn Goodman
Resident Director ....Doug Hughes
Associate Artists ....Scott Elliott, Bill Irwin,
        Joe Mantello, Mark Brokaw, Kathleen Marshall
Consulting Dramaturg ....Jerry Patch
Artistic Associate ....Jill Rafson
Casting Director ....Carrie Gardner
Casting Associate ....Kate Schwabe
Casting Associate ....Stephen Kopel
Artistic Assistant...............................Erica Rotstein
Literary Associate ....Josh Fiedler
Casting Interns ....Kerry Ann Minchinton, Kyle Bosley

EDUCATION STAFF
EDUCATION DIRECTOR .... **David A. Miller**
Director of Instruction and
    Curriculum Development ....Renee Flemings
Education Program Manager ....Jennifer DiBella
Program Associate for
    School-Based Programs ....Amanda Hinkle
Education Assistant ....Allison Baucom
Education Dramaturg ....Ted Sod
Teaching Artists.....................Phil Alexander, Cynthia
                                          Babak,
            Victor Barbella, LaTonya Borsay,
            Rob Bronstein, Lori Brown-Niang,
            Miss Stella, Hamilton Clancy,
        Joe Doran, Katie Down, Amy Fortoul,
            Tony Freeman, Sheri Graubert,
        Matthew Gregory, Adam Gwon,
    Karla Hendrick, Jim Jack, Lisa Renee Jordan,
    Alvin Keith, Jonathan Lang, Rebecca Lord,
        Tami Mansfield, Erin McCready,
        Jordana Oberman, Evan O'Brient,
        Deirdre O'Connor, Andrew Ondrecjak,
        Laura Poe, Alexa Polmer-Spencer,
        Nicole Press, Jennifer Rathbone,
        Leah Reddy, Amanda Rehbein,
        Taylor Ruckel, Chris Rummel,
    Cassy Rush, Drew Sachs, Nick Simone,
        Derek Straat, Daniel Robert Sullivan,
        Vickie Tanner, Olivia Tsang,
        Cristina Vaccaro, Jennifer Varbalow,
    Leese Walker, Eric Wallach, Gail Winar
Education Interns................Emily Holladay Anderson,
                                    Brent Stansell

ADMINISTRATIVE STAFF
GENERAL MANAGER ....**Sydney Beers**
Associate Managing Director ....Greg Backstrom
General Manager, Steinberg Center ....Rebecca Habel
General Counsel ....Nancy Hirschmann
Human Resources Manager ....Stephen Deutsch
MIS Director ....Jeff Goodman
Assistant General Manager ....Maggie Cantrick
Management Associate ....Tania Camargo
Facilities Manager ....Abraham David
Office Manager ....Scott Kelly

The 39 Steps

MIS Associate ....Micah Kraybill
Receptionists ....Dena Beider, Raquel Castillo,
Elisa Papa, Allison Patrick,
Monica Sidorchuk
Messenger ....Darnell Franklin
Management Intern ....Shoshanna Gross

FINANCE STAFF
DIRECTOR OF FINANCE ....**Susan Neiman**
Assistant Controller ....John LaBarbera
Accounts Payable Administrator ....Frank Surdi
Financial Associate ....Yonit Kafka
Business Office Assistant ....Joshua Cohen
Business Interns ....Edgar Eguia, Nicholas Mustakas

DEVELOPMENT STAFF
DIRECTOR OF DEVELOPMENT .....**Jeffory Lawson**
Director, Institutional Giving ....Julie K. D'Andrea
Director, Special Events ....Steve Schaeffer
Director, Major Gifts ....Joy Pak
Manager, Donor Information Systems ....Lise Speidel
Manager, Individual Giving ....Kara Kandel
Telefundraising Manager ....Gavin Brown
Manager, Corporation Relations ....Corey Young
Individual Giving Associate ....Kate Bartoldus
Patrons Services Assistant ....John Haynes
Development Assistants ....Joshua Poole, Daniel Curley
Special Events Assistant ....Ashley Firestone
Assistant to the Executive Director ....Dan Fingerman
Institutional Giving Assistant ....Nick Nolte
Special Events Interns ....Michell Dyer,
Laurence Stepney

MARKETING STAFF
**DIRECTOR OF MARKETING
AND SALES PROMOTION** ....**David B. Steffen**
Associate Director of Marketing ....Wendy Hutton
Marketing/Publications Manager ....Margaret Casagrande
Marketing Associate ....Stefanie Schussel
Marketing Assistant ....Shannon Marcotte
Website Consultant ....Keith Powell Beyland
**DIRECTOR OF TELESALES
SPECIAL PROMOTIONS** ....**Daniel Weiss**
Telesales Manager ....Michael Pace
Telesales Office Coordinator ....Anthony Merced
Marketing Intern ....Dragica Dabo

TICKET SERVICES STAFF
**DIRECTOR OF
SALES OPERATIONS** ....**Charlie Garbowski, Jr.**
Ticket Services Manager ....Ellen Holt
Subscription Manager ....Ethan Ubell
Box Office Managers ....Edward P. Osborne,
Andrew Clements
Group Sales Manager ....Jeff Monteith
Assistant Box Office Managers ....Krystin MacRitchie,
Robert Morgan, Nicole Nicholson
Assistant Ticket Services Managers ....Robert Kane,
Bill Klemm, Carlos Morris
Ticket Services ....Solangel Bido,
Lauren Cartelli, David Carson,
Joseph Clark, Mike DePope,
Nisha Dhruna, Adam Elsberry,
Lindsay Ericson, Scott Falkowski,
Catherine Fitzpatrick, Daniel Gabriel,
James Graham, Tova Heller,
Nicki Ishmael, Kate Longosky, Elisa Mala,

Mead Margulies, Chuck Migliaccio,
Adam Owens, Ethan Paulini,
David Pittman, DeeAnna Row,
Benjamin Schneider, Heather Siebert,
Nalene Singh, Lillian Soto, DJ Thacker,
Pam Unger, Thomas Walsh
Ticket Services Intern ....Kayrose Pagan

SERVICES
Counsel ....Paul, Weiss, Rifkind,
Wharton and Garrison LLP,
John Breglio, Deborah Hartnett
Counsel ....Rosenberg & Estis
Counsel ....Andrew Lance,
Gibson, Dunn, & Crutcher, LLP
Counsel ....Harry H. Weintraub,
Glick and Weintraub, P.C.
Immigration Counsel ....Mark D. Koestler and
Theodore Ruthizer
Government
Relations ....Law Offices of Claudia Wagner LLC
House Physicians ....Dr. Theodore Tyberg,
Dr. Lawrence Katz
House Dentist ....Neil Kanner, D.M.D.
Insurance ....DeWitt Stern Group, Inc.
Accountant ....Lutz & Carr CPAs, LLP
Advertising ....Spotco/
Drew Hodges, Jim Edwards,
Tom Greenwald, Y. Darius Suyama,
Beth Watson
Sponsorship ....TMG–The Marketing Group/
Laura Matalon, Tanya Grubich,
William Critzman
Interactive Marketing ....Situation Marketing/
Damian Bazadona, John Lanasa,
Ryan Klink, Joey Oliva
Events Photography ....Anita and Steve Shevett
Production Photographer ....Joan Marcus
Theatre Displays ....King Displays, Wayne Sapper
Lobby Refreshments ....Sweet Concessions

MANAGING DIRECTOR EMERITUS ....Ellen Richard

Roundabout Theatre Company
231 West 39th Street, New York, NY 10018
(212) 719-9393.

GENERAL PRESS REPRESENTATIVES
Adrian Bryan-Brown
Matt Polk   Jessica Johnson   Amy Kass

STAFF FOR *THE 39 STEPS*
Company Manager ....Nichole Jennino
Assistant Company Manager ....Carly DiFulvio
Production Stage Manager ....Nevin Hedley
Stage Manager ....Janet Takami
Production Management by ....Aurora Productions/
Gene O'Donovan, W. Benjamin Heller II,
Bethany Weinstein, John Horsman,
Melissa Mazdra, Asia Evans
Movement Director ....Christopher Bayes
Wig Design ....Jason Allen
Assistant Director ....Kevin Bigger
Assistant Scenic Designer ....Josh Zangen
Assistant Lighting Designer ....Aaron Sporer
Assistant Sound Designer ....Drew Levy
Production Properties ....Peter Sarafin

Production Carpenter ....Glenn Merwede
Production Electrician ....Brian Maiuri
Running Properties ....Andrew Forste
Sound Engineer ....Dann Wojnar
Props ....Nelson Vaughn, Carmel Sheehan
Deck Electrician ....Barb Bartel
Wardrobe Supervisor ....Susan J. Fallon
Hair and Wig Supervisor ....Manuela LaPorte
Dressers ....Renee Mariotti, Margaret M. Donovan
Wardrobe Dayworker ....Melissa Crawford
Production Assistant ....Rosy Garner
Scenery
Constructed by ....Huntington Theatre Company
and Hudson Scenic Studios, Inc.
Sound Equipment provided by ....Sound Associates
Lighting Equipment provided by ....PRG Lighting,
a division of Production Resource Group, LLC
Costumes
Constructed by ....Huntington Theatre Company
Additional Costume Alterations ....Carmen Gee
Casting Associates ....Jack Bowdan, Mark Brandon,
Sara Schatz
Casting Assistants ....Nikole Vallins, Allison Estrin
39 Steps L.P. Legal Counsel ....Lazarus & Harris LLP/
Scott Lazarus, Robert C. Harris
Special thanks to ....Steve Beers and Simon Jones

Make-up Provided by M•A•C

AMERICAN AIRLINES THEATRE STAFF
Company Manager ....Nichole Jennino
House Carpenter ....Glenn Merwede
House Electrician ....Brian Maiuri
House Properties ....Andrew Forste
House Sound ....Dann Wojnar
IA Apprentice ....Carmel Sheehan
Wardrobe Supervisor ....Susan J. Fallon
Box Office Manager ....Ted Osborne
Assistant Box Office Manager ....Robert Morgan
House Manager ....Steve Ryan
Associate House Manager ....Zipporah Aguasvivas
Head Usher ....Jacklyn Rivera
House Staff ....Ilia Diaz, Anne Ezell, Adam Wier,
Elsie Jamin Maguire, Idair Melendez,
Rich McNanna, Rebecca Knell,
Stephen Fontana, Ashley Blenman,
James Watanachaiyot
Security ....Julious Russell
Additional Security Provided by ....Gotham Security
Maintenance .... Jerry Hobbs, Willie Philips,
Daniel Pellew, Magali Western

THE 39 STEPS was first produced on stage by North
Country Theatre in April 1996 at the Georgian Theatre,
Richmond, North Yorkshire. This latest version, adapted by
Patrick Barlow and based on an original concept by Simon
Corble and Nobby Dimon, was first performed at the West
Yorkshire Playhouse, directed by Fiona Buffini, on June 17,
2005. This new production, directed by Maria Aitken,
opened at the Tricycle Theatre on August 14, 2006, and
transferred to the Criterion Theater on September 14, 2006.

The 39 Steps
SCRAPBOOK

Curtain call on opening night (L-R): Arnie Burton, Charles Edwards, Jennifer Ferrin and Cliff Saunders.

Correspondent: Nevin Hedley, Production Stage Manager

Memorable Opening Night Letter, Fax or Note: We got a nice fax from the London company; each person wrote their best wishes on it.

Opening Night Gifts: The best gift was the *New York Times* review. Edward Snape, our producer, had our names put on the original poster.

Most Exciting Celebrity Visitors: Sarah Jessica Parker and Matthew Broderick came backstage and spoke to us in the greenroom.

Actors Who Performed the Most Roles in This Show: It's got to be between Cliff and Arnie. They say that our four actors do 150 parts. We've counted up to 39, but it may be more than that if you count the scene where they play bogs and clefts and trees.

Who Has Done the Most Shows in Their Career: Our director, Maria Aitken, who also is an actress, has performed endlessly in the UK and around the world. She is the most superb director.

Special Backstage Rituals: At the top of the show, Charlie and Arnie always wave across the stage to Cliff. He's stage-left for his entrance and the rest of the cast is stage-right and always do a wave. At the top of Act II, Charlie rings the offstage bell in the McGarricle Hotel. Cliff always does headstands and flips backstage. I can always tell when he's in place by the noise. I go up 15 minutes minutes early and practice my Spanish vocabulary up there. One of our electricians is learning Italian the same way.

Favorite Moments During Each Performance (On Stage and Off): I love the character of Mrs. McGarricle. She's so loopy and looney and fun. I also love the Act II marching band sequence where Charlie gets lost in a band of people. Fallon, who is our wardrobe mistress, and Glenn, our head carpenter, run around the stage to get stuff into place and to catch things thrown by the actors. They race each other through the crossover. At one point Cliff does a hat throw and tries to get the hat to land right on the wardrobe sign. He misses most of the time, but the thing about Cliff is that he never gives up. He'll do it until he gets it perfect.

Favorite Off-Site Hangout: We go to O'Flaherty's, Un Deux Trois and Bar Centrale. We go to Sardi's on Wednesday for the actors' matinee lunch.

Favorite Snack Food: Susan J. Fallon, our wardrobe mistress, is legendary. She bakes these amazing cakes and, of course, there is the famous Sunday brunch. The menu goes up on Saturday and everyone comes, crew, cast, family and friends.

Mascot: Walter, who's Arnie's dog.

Favorite Therapy: Most non-musicals don't have a physical therapist, but we do: Rhonda Barkow comes and gives us a workout.

Most Memorable Ad-Lib: Things hardly ever go wrong, but Arnie once went up in the opening Mr. Memory scene. Cliff tried to prompt him. Arnie said something happened in 1943, when the play takes place in 1937. Cliff had to repeat it, which he thought was funny. Cliff gave his normal answer, but put 1943 in it.

Cell Phone Rings, Cell Phone Photos or Texting Incidents During a Performance: Never! People just don't do it at our show. However I did once notice on one of my monitors that shows the first two rows that a woman was playing with the footlights. They are specially focused so we had to send someone down to check them.

Memorable Press Encounters: We had the New York Times backstage twice, shooting the quick changes. We had a press photographer backstage at our invited dress rehearsal and the shutter on the camera made a noise that was audible the entire evening. Afterward a patron came up to Maria to compliment her on the concept of having a typewriter going throughout the show, to suggest a novel of the story being written!

Memorable Fan Encounters: Some wait outside for us, and people write in from all over the country. During intermission and before the show begins we play 1930s British dance hall music over the sound system and the house manager says sometimes people get up and dance to it.

Fastest Costume Changes: Our show is full of fast changes. In the train scene where Arnie and Cliff exchange hats, the changes are instantaneous. But that's more choreography than quick-change. The actor with the fastest series of complete changes would have to be Arnie near the end of the play when he starts as Mr. Memory, then goes through a curtain and instantly becomes Professor Jordan for five seconds, then slips away and comes back immediately in his Inspector outfit.

Who Wore the Heaviest/Hottest Costume: Charlie wears a heavy wool suit throughout. By intermission it's completely soaked from his running constantly, so he changes at intermission. The backstage life of this play is just blurs of people racing around. If he stops backstage for an instant, his dresser mops him down. It's hot work. It doesn't look like a hot costume, but it is.

Who Wore the Least: We don't know what Jennifer wears under her nightgown.

Catchphrases Only the Company Would Recognize: "Sorry!" "Let us see, let us see. Let us see."

Memorable Directorial Note: "In the scenes between Jennifer and Charlie, remember the erotic thread."

Understudy Anecdote: Cameron understudies both Cliff and Arnie, which makes understudy rehearsals kind of frenetic and schizophrenic. But the understudies have never gone on.

Nicknames: Arnie is "Arnica."

Ghostly Encounter Backstage: At the Huntington Theatre in Boston we had an appalling first preview. The technical people there blamed it on the fact that we didn't have the resident ghost's mascot. The mascot, it seems, makes the ghost happy. So we put a stuffed toy in the fire bucket on stage and we never had a problem again!

Coolest Thing About Being in This Show: The people. It's a wonderful group. It's kind of funny: we get along so well we're always saying, "It can't last. Something's going to happen." But everyone gets on. It's really lovely.

386   The Playbill Broadway Yearbook 2007-2008

Photo by Aubrey Reuben

Thurgood

First Preview: April 12, 2008. Opened: April 30, 2008.
Still running as of May 31, 2008.

PLAYBILL

THURGOOD

CAST

Thurgood Marshall ......LAURENCE FISHBURNE

PLACE

Howard University Law School Auditorium,
Washington, D.C.

Laurence Fishburne as
Thurgood Marshall

Photo by Carol Rosegg

VERNON JORDAN   THE SHUBERT ORGANIZATION   BILL ROLLNICK / NANCY ELLISON ROLLNICK   MATT MURPHY
DARYL ROTH / DEBRA BLACK   ROY FURMAN   JAM THEATRICALS   LAWRENCE HOROWITZ
ERIC FALKENSTEIN   MAX ONSTAGE   JAMES D'ORTA   JAMIE deROY   AMY NEDERLANDER

in association with

OSTAR PRODUCTIONS and THE WESTPORT COUNTRY PLAYHOUSE

present

LAURENCE FISHBURNE
THURGOOD

A Play by

GEORGE STEVENS, JR.

Scenic Design by	Costume Design by	Lighting Design by
ALLEN MOYER	**JANE GREENWOOD**	**BRIAN NASON**

Projection Design by	Sound Design by	Production Stage Manager
ELAINE J. McCARTHY	**RYAN RUMERY**	**MARTI McINTOSH**

Production Manager	Press Representative	General Management
JUNIPER STREET PRODUCTIONS	**PETE SANDERS FIFTEEN MINUTES PR**	**ALAN WASSER ALLAN WILLIAMS**

Directed by

LEONARD FOGLIA

The producers wish to express their appreciation to Theatre Development Fund
for its support of this production.

Originally produced at the Westport Country Playhouse in Westport, CT

4/30/08

Laurence Fishburne
Thurgood Marshall

George Stevens, Jr.
Playwright

Leonard Foglia
Director

Allen Moyer
Scenic Design

Thurgood

Jane Greenwood
Costume Design

Brian Nason
Lighting Design

Alan Wasser
General Manager

Pete Sanders/
Fifteen Minutes
*Press
Representative*

Guy Kwan, John Paull III, Hillary Blanken,
Kevin Broomell, Ana Rose Greene,
Juniper Street Productions
Production Manager

Gerald Schoenfeld,
Chairman,
The Shubert
Organization
Producer

Philip J. Smith,
President,
The Shubert
Organization
Producer

Daryl Roth
Producer

Debra Black
Producer

Roy Furman
Producer

Arny Granat,
Jam Theatricals
Producer

Steve Traxler,
Jam Theatricals
Producer

Lawrence C.
Horowitz, M.D.
Producer

Eric Falkenstein
Producer

Jamie deRoy
Producer

Bill Haber,
OSTAR Enterprises
Producer

Photos by Ben Strothmann

CREW
Front Row (L-R): Bill Lewis, Bernita Robinson, Marti McIntosh, Valerie Gladstone,
James Keane.

Back Row (L-R): Jon Lawson, Kenny McDonough, Lee Iwanski, Billy Staples.

FRONT OF HOUSE STAFF
Front Row (L-R): Melissa Maniglia, Nadine Space,
Bernadette Bokun.

Back Row (L-R): Marjorie Glover, Bill Vitale, Catherine Coscia,
Daniel Rosario, Chrissie Collins.

Thurgood

Laurence Fishburne as
Thurgood Marshall.

Photo by Carol Rosegg

Top Girls

First Preview: April 15, 2008. Opened: May 7, 2008.
Still running as of May 31, 2008.

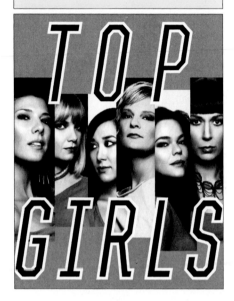

PLAYBILL

TOP GIRLS

CAST
(in alphabetical order)

Patient Griselda/Kit/Jeanine/
   Shona . . . . . . MARY CATHERINE GARRISON
Waitress/Louise . . . . MARY BETH HURT
Lady Nijo/Win . . . . .JENNIFER IKEDA
Marlene . . . . .ELIZABETH MARVEL
Pope Joan/Angie . . . . .MARTHA PLIMPTON
Dull Gret/Nell . . . . .ANA REEDER
Isabella Bird/Joyce/Mrs. Kidd . . . MARISA TOMEI

The play takes place in England in the early 1980s.

Act I   A restaurant, London. Saturday.
Act II Scene 1: Joyce's back yard in Suffolk. Sunday.
          Scene 2: "Top Girls" Employment Agency,
            London. Monday.
Act III Joyce's kitchen. Sunday, a year earlier.

Stage Manager . . . . .AMY McCRANEY

UNDERSTUDIES

For Marlene, Pope Joan/Angie:
TINA BENKO

For Patient Griselda/Kit/Jeanine/Shona,
Lady Nijo/Win:
ANGELA LIN

For Waitress/Louise, Dull Gret/Nell,
Isabella Bird/Joyce/Mrs. Kidd:
ANNE TORSIGLIERI

BILTMORE THEATRE

MANHATTAN THEATRE CLUB

Artistic Director
LYNNE MEADOW

Executive Producer
BARRY GROVE

Acting Artistic Director 2007-08 Season
DANIEL SULLIVAN

Presents

TOP GIRLS

By
CARYL CHURCHILL

with

MARY CATHERINE GARRISON   **MARY BETH HURT**
JENNIFER IKEDA   **ELIZABETH MARVEL**   **MARTHA PLIMPTON**
ANA REEDER   **MARISA TOMEI**

Scenic Design
TOM PYE

Costume Design
LAURA BAUER

Lighting Design
CHRISTOPHER AKERLIND

Sound Design
DARRON L WEST

Original Music
MATTHEW HERBERT

Hair & Wig Design
PAUL HUNTLEY

Dialect Consultant
ELIZABETH SMITH

Production Stage Manager
MARTHA DONALDSON

Directed By
JAMES MACDONALD

General Manager
FLORIE SEERY

Associate Artistic
Director/Production
MANDY GREENFIELD

Director of Marketing
DEBRA A. WAXMAN

Press Representative
BONEAU/BRYAN-BROWN

Production Manager
KURT GARDNER

Director of Casting
NANCY PICCIONE

Director of Development
JILL TURNER LLOYD

Top Girls was first performed at the Royal Court Theatre, London on August 28, 1982
and transferred to the Joseph Papp Public Theatre, New York on December 29, 1982.

Funding for Healthy Choice food items provided by ConAgra Foods.

Manhattan Theatre Club wishes to express its appreciation to Theatre Development Fund
for its support of this production.

5/7/08

(L-R): Ana Reeder, Jennifer Ikeda, Elizabeth Marvel, Marisa Tomei, Mary Catherine Garrison, Mary Beth Hurt and Martha Plimpton in Act I.

Photo by Joan Marcus

Top Girls

Mary Catherine
Garrison
*Patient Griselda/Kit/
Jeanine/Shona*

Mary Beth Hurt
Waitress/Louise

Jennifer Ikeda
Lady Nijo/Win

Elizabeth Marvel
Marlene

Martha Plimpton
Pope Joan/Angie

Ana Reeder
Dull Gret/Nell

Marisa Tomei
*Isabella Bird/Joyce/
Mrs. Kidd*

Tina Benko
*Understudy for
Marlene, Pope Joan/
Angie*

Angela Lin
*Understudy for
Patient Griselda/Kit/
Jeanine/Shona,
Lady Nijo/Win*

Anne Torsiglieri
*Understudy for
Waitress/Louise,
Dull Gret/Nell,
Isabella Bird/Joyce/
Mrs. Kidd*

Caryl Churchill
Playwright

James Macdonald
Director

Tom Pye
Scenic Design

Laura Bauer
Costume Design

Christopher Akerlind
Lighting Design

Paul Huntley
Hair & Wig Design

Elizabeth Smith
Dialect Consultant

Lynne Meadow
*Artistic Director,
Manhattan Theatre
Club, Inc.*

Barry Grove
*Executive Producer,
Manhattan Theatre
Club, Inc.*

Daniel Sullivan
*Acting Artistic
Director 2007-2008
Season, Manhattan
Theatre Club, Inc.*

FRONT OF HOUSE STAFF
Front Row (L-R): Miranda Scopel
(Assistant House Manager), John Wyffels
(Sweet Concessions), Ramon Pesante
(Usher), Ed Brashear (Ticket Taker),
Russ Ramsey (Theatre Manager)

Back Row (L-R): Tom Jarus (Usher),
William Branham (Usher), Jorge Sarante
(Biltmore Theatre Intern),
Dinah Glorioso (Usher), Evan Weinstein
(Sweet Concessions), Wendy Wright
(Head Usher)

Photo by Ben Strothmann

Top Girls

SECURITY
Marcos Paez and Olanrewaju Ayinde.

BOX OFFICE
(L-R): Jeffrey Davis (Assistant Box Office Treasurer), Dave Dillon (Box Office Treasurer).

CREW
Front Row (L-R): Sue Poulin (in sunglasses), Jon Jordan, Jeff Dodson.

Middle Row (L-R): La Sonya Gunter, Angie Simpson, Amy McCraney, Martha Donaldson, Christina Elefante.

Back Row (L-R): Lou Shapiro, Tim Walters, Andrew Sliwinski, Marc Grimshaw, Chris Wiggins, John Fullum, Patrick Murray.

Top Girls

MANHATTAN THEATRE CLUB STAFF

Artistic Director	**Lynne Meadow**
Executive Producer	**Barry Grove**
Acting Artistic Director	
2007-08 Season	Daniel Sullivan
General Manager	**Florie Seery**
Associate Artistic Director/	
Production	Mandy Greenfield
Director of Artistic Administration/	
Assistant to the Artistic Director	Amy Gilkes Loe
Associate Director of Artistic Operations	Lisa McNulty
Artistic Assistant	Kevin Emrick
Administrative Assistant	Rebecca Stang
Director of Casting	**Nancy Piccione**
Casting Associate	Kelly Gillespie
Casting Assistant	Kristin Svenningsen
Literary Manager	**Raphael Martin**
Play Development Associate/	
Sloan Project Manager	Annie MacRae
Play Development Assistant	Alex Barron
Director of Musical	
Development	Clifford Lee Johnson III
Director of Development	**Jill Turner Lloyd**
Director, Institutional Giving	Josh Jacobson
Director, Individual Giving	Jon Haddorff
Director, Special Events	Antonello Di Benedetto
Manager, Institutional Giving	Andrea Gorzell
Manager, Institutional Giving	Jessica Sadowski Comas
Development Associate/Special Events	Darra Messing
Development Associate/Institutional Giving	Laurel Bear
Development Associate/Individual Giving	Sage Young
Development Associate/	
Database Coordinator	Kelly Haydon
Patrons' Liaison	Samantha Mascali
Director of Marketing	**Debra A. Waxman**
Marketing Manager	Tom O'Connor
Marketing Associate	Andrea D. Paul
Director of Finance	**Jeffrey Bledsoe**
Business Manager	Holly Kinney
Human Resources Manager	Darren Robertson
Business & HR Associate	Adam Cook
Business Assistant	Charles Graytok
Receptionist/Studio Coordinator	Christina Prints
IT Manager	Mendy Sudranski
Systems Administrator	Dilshan Keregala
Associate General Manager	**Lindsey Brooks Sag**
Company Manager/NY City Center	Erin Moeller
General Management Assistant	Ann Mundorff
Assistant to the Executive Producer	Ashley Dunn
Director of Subscriber Services	**Robert Allenberg**
Associate Subscriber Services Manager	Andrew Taylor
Subscriber Services Representatives	Mark Bowers,
	Rebekah Dewald, Eric Gerdts,
	Matthew Praet, Rosanna Consalva Sarto
Director of Telesales and Telefunding	**George Tetlow**
Assistant Manager	Terrence Burnett
Director of Education	**David Shookhoff**
Asst. Director of Education/	
Coordinator, Paul A. Kaplan Theatre	
ManagementProgram	Amy Harris
Education Assistants	Sarah Ryndak,
	Kelli Bragdon
MTC Teaching Artists	David Auburn,
	Michael Bernard, Carl Capotorto,
	Chris Ceraso, Charlotte Colavin,
	Dominic Colon, Gilbert Girion,
	Andy Goldberg, Elise Hernandez,

Jeffrey Joseph, Julie Leedes,
Kate Long, Louis D. Moreno,
Andres Munar, Melissa Murray,
Angela Pietropinto, Alexa Polmer,
Alfonso Ramirez, Carmen Rivera,
Judy Tate, Candido Tirado, Joe White

Theatre Management Interns	Caitlin Baird,
	Julia Davis, Stephen Ferrell,
	Emily Gasser, Ryan Hudec, Caryn Morrow,
	Erin Ozer, Flora Pei, Jorge Sarante,
	Miranda Shutte, Rachel Slaven
Randy Carrig Casting Intern	Emily Hammond

Production Manager	**Kurt Gardner**
Associate Production Manager	Philip Naudé
Assistant Production Manager	Kelsey Martinez
Lighting and Sound Supervisor	**Matthew T. Gross**
Properties Supervisor	**Scott Laule**
Assistant Properties Supervisor	Julia Sandy
Props Carpenter	Peter Grimes
Costume Supervisor	**Erin Hennessy Dean**

GENERAL PRESS REPRESENTATION
BONEAU/BRYAN-BROWN

Chris Boneau	Aaron Meier
Heath Schwartz	Christine Olver

Script Readers	Kyle Frisina, Liz Jones,
	Portia Krieger, Aaron Leichter,
	Stephan Sanders, Kathryn Walat

SERVICES

Accountants	ERE, LLP
Advertising	SpotCo/Drew Hodges,
	Jim Edwards, Laura Price, Kristen Rathbun
Web Design	Pilla Marketing Communications
Legal Counsel	John Breglio, Deborah Hartnett/
	Paul, Weiss, Rifkind,
	Wharton and Garrison LLP
Real Estate Counsel	Marcus Attorneys
Labor Counsel	Harry H. Weintraub/
	Glick and Weintraub, P.C.
Immigration Counsel	Theodore Ruthizer/
	Kramer, Levin, Naftalis & Frankel, LLP
Sponsorship Consultant	Above the Title Entertainment/
	Jed Bernstein
Technical Supervisor	
Consultant	Aurora Productions, Inc./
	Gene O'Donovan
Special Projects	Elaine H. Hirsch
Insurance	Dewitt Stern Group, Inc./
	Anthony Pittari
Maintenance	Reliable Cleaning
Production Photographer	Joan Marcus
Event Photography	Bruce Glikas
Cover Photo	Henry Leutwyler
Cover Design	SpotCo
Theatre Displays	King Display

PRODUCTION STAFF FOR *TOP GIRLS*

Company Manager	**Seth Shepsle**
Production Stage Manager	**Martha Donaldson**
Stage Manager	Amy McCraney
Assistant Director	Gaye Taylor Upchurch
Associate Scenic Designer	Frank McCullough
Associate Costume Designer	Bobby F. Tilley
Associate Lighting Designer	Ben Krall

Associate Sound Designer	Matthew Hubbs
Assistant Sound Designer	Bray Poor
Etiquette Consultant	Frank Ventura
Hair/Make-Up Supervisor	Jon Jordan
Assistant Hair Supervisor	La Sonya Gunter
Flymen	John Fullum, Patrick Murray,
	Leomar Susana
Assistant Propertyman	Sue Poulin
Lighting Programmer	Marc Polimeni
Dressers	Jackeva Hill, Virginia Neininger
Production Assistant	Christina Elefante

CREDITS
Scenery by Showman Fabricators, Inc. Softgoods and digital prints by I. Weiss, LLC NY. Lighting equipment provided by PRG Lighting. Sound equipment provided by Masque Sound. Costume construction by Jeffrey Fender; John Kristiansen; Arnold S. Levine, Inc.; and Schneeman Studio, Limited. Makeup provided by M•A•C Cosmetics. Natural herbal cough drops courtesy of Ricola USA.

SPECIAL THANKS
Aurora Productions, Inc.;
Electronic Theatre Controls, Inc.

For more information visit
www.ManhattanTheatreClub.org

MANHATTAN THEATRE CLUB BILTMORE THEATRE STAFF

Theatre Manager	**Russ Ramsey**
Assistant House Manager	Miranda Scopel
Box Office Treasurer	**David Dillon**
Assistant Box Office	
Treasurers	Tevy Bradley, Jeffrey Davis
Head Carpenter	Chris Wiggins
Head Propertyman	Timothy Walters
Sound Engineer	Louis Shapiro
Master Electrician	Jeff Dodson
Wardrobe Supervisor	Angela Simpson
Apprentices	Marc Grimshaw,
	Andrew Sliwinski
Chief Engineer	Dino Deosarran
Maintenance Engineers	Robert Allen,
	Ricky Deosarran, Maximo Perez
Security	Initial Security
Lobby Refreshments	Sweet Concessions

(L-R): Mary Catherine Garrison and Ana Reeder.

The 25th Annual Putnam County Spelling Bee

First Preview: April 15, 2005. Opened: May 2, 2005.
Closed January 20, 2008 after 21 Previews and 1136 Performances.

PLAYBILL®

CAST
(in alphabetical order)

Chip Tolentino ....AARON J. ALBANO
Leaf Coneybear ....STANLEY BAHOREK
Olive Ostrovsky ....JENNI BARBER
William Barfee ....JARED GERTNER
Mitch Mahoney ....JAMES MONROE IGLEHART
Logainne Schwartzandgrubenierre .....SARA INBAR
Marcy Park ....GRETA LEE
Douglas Panch ....DANIEL PEARCE
Rona Lisa Peretti ....JENNIFER SIMARD

UNDERSTUDIES

For William Barfee:
BRIAN GONZALES
For Mitch Mahoney and Chip Tolentino:
MAURICE MURPHY
For Leaf Coneybear and Douglas Panch:
BRIAN GONZALES, MAURICE MURPHY
For Marcy Park:
ANGELICA-LEE ASPIRAS, JACQUI POLK
For Rona Lisa Peretti:
ANGELICA-LEE ASPIRAS
For Olive Ostrovsky and
Logainne Schwartzandgrubenierre:
JACQUI POLK

Dance Captain: JACQUI POLK

CIRCLE IN THE SQUARE
UNDER THE DIRECTION OF
THEODORE MANN and PAUL LIBIN

David Stone   James L. Nederlander   Barbara Whitman   Patrick Catullo
Barrington Stage Company   Second Stage Theatre

Present

The 25th Annual Putnam County

SPELLING BEE

Music & Lyrics by
WILLIAM FINN

Book By
RACHEL SHEINKIN

Conceived by
REBECCA FELDMAN

Additional Material by
JAY REISS

With

AARON J. ALBANO, STANLEY BAHOREK, JENNI BARBER, JARED GERTNER,
JAMES MONROE IGLEHART, SARA INBAR, GRETA LEE, DANIEL PEARCE, JENNIFER SIMARD
ANGELICA-LEE ASPIRAS, BRIAN GONZALES, MAURICE MURPHY, JACQUI POLK

Set Design by
BEOWULF BORITT

Costume Design by
JENNIFER CAPRIO

Lighting Design by
NATASHA KATZ

Sound Design by
DAN MOSES SCHREIER

Orchestrations by
MICHAEL STAROBIN

Music Director &
Dance Arrangements by
VADIM FEICHTNER

Vocal Arrangements by
CARMEL DEAN

Music Coordinator
MICHAEL KELLER

Press
BARLOW • HARTMAN

Casting
TARA RUBIN CASTING

Production Stage Manager
ANDREA "SPOOK" TESTANI

Production Manager
KAI BROTHERS

General Management
321 THEATRICAL MANAGEMENT

Choreographed by
DAN KNECHTGES

Directed by
JAMES LAPINE

Based on C-R-E-P-U-S-C-U-L-E, an original play by THE FARM.
Original Broadway Cast Recording on GHOSTLIGHT RECORDS.

10/1/07

(L-R): Sara Inbar, Aaron J. Albano,
Greta Lee (Bottom), Jared Gertner (Top),
Stanley Bahorek and Jenni Barber.

Photo by Joan Marcus

Continued on next page

The 25th Annual Putnam County Spelling Bee

Stanley Bahorek as Leaf Coneybear.

Photo by Joan Marcus

Aaron J. Albano
Chip Tolentino

Stanley Bahorek
Leaf Coneybear

Jenni Barber
Olive Ostrovsky

Jared Gertner
William Barfee

James Monroe
Iglehart
Mitch Mahoney

Sara Inbar
*Logainne
Schwartzandgrubenierre*

Greta Lee
Marcy Park

Daniel Pearce
*Vice Principal
Douglas Panch*

Jennifer Simard
Rona Lisa Peretti

Angelica-Lee
Aspiras
*Understudy for
Marcy, Rona Lisa
Peretti*

Brian Gonzales
*Understudy for
Barfee, Coneybear,
Panch*

Maurice Murphy
*Understudy for
Mitch, Chip, Panch,
Coneybear*

Jacqui Polk
*Understudy for
Marcy, Olive,
Logainne;
Dance Captain*

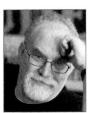
William Finn
Music/Lyrics

Rachel Sheinkin
Book

Rebecca Feldman
Conceiver

Jay Reiss
Additional Material

James Lapine
Director

Dan Knechtges
Choreographer

Darren Katz
Resident Director

The 25th Annual Putnam County Spelling Bee

Beowulf Boritt
Set Designer

Jennifer Caprio
Costume Designer

Natasha Katz
Lighting Designer

Dan Moses Schreier
Sound Designer

Michael Starobin
Orchestrations

Vadim Feichtner
*Musical Director/
Dance Arrangements*

Carmel Dean
*Vocal Arranger/
Associate
Conductor/
Synthesizer*

Michael Keller
Music Coordinator

Tara Rubin Casting
Casting

Marty Kopulsky
*Hair and Wig
Designer*

Marcia Goldberg, Nancy Nagel Gibbs and
Nina Essman,
321 Theatrical Management
General Management

David Stone
Producer

James L.
Nederlander
Producer

Barbara Whitman
Producer

Carole Rothman,
Artistic Director,
Second Stage
Theatre
Producer

Brian Gonzales
*Understudy for
Chip Tolentino*

Darrell Hammond
Douglas Panch

Carly Hughes
*Understudy for
Marcy Park and
Rona Lisa Peretti*

Mo Rocca
Douglas Panch

Greta Lee (front)
as Marcy Park.

Photo by Joan Marcus

The 25th Annual Putnam County Spelling Bee

WARDROBE
(L-R): Maggie Dominic (Sub Dresser),
Cleon Byerly (Dresser) and
Yvonna Balfour (Wardrobe Supervisor).

Not Pictured: Susan Sigrist (Dresser).

BOX OFFICE
(L-R):
Thomas Motylenski (Assistant Box Office
Treasurer)
and Ilene Towell
(Box Office Treasurer).

Photos by Ben Strothmann

ORCHESTRA
Top Row (L-R):
Sarah Carter (Sub Cello), Dennis Anderson (Sub
Reeds), Carmel Dean (Associate
Conductor/Synthesizer).

Bottom Row (L-R):
Vadim Feichtner (Conductor/Piano)
and Glenn Rhian (Drums/Percussion).

Not Pictured: Amy Ralske (Cello) and
Rick Heckman (Reeds).

The 25th Annual Putnam County Spelling Bee

STAGE CREW
Front Row (L-R): Robert S. Lindsay (F.O.H. Sound Engineer), Bill Seelig (Flyman), Stephanie Vetter (Monitor Engineer), Stewart Wagner (Head Electrician).

Back Row (L-R):
Owen E. Parmele (Prop Master) and Robert Gordon (Head Carpenter).

COMPANY & STAGE MANAGERS
(Top-Bottom): Dan Shaheen (Sub Stage Manager), Lisa Koch Rao (Company Manager) and Kelly Hance (Stage Manager).

Not Pictured: Spook Testani (Production Stage Manager).

VOLUNTEER SPELLER WRANGLERS
Bottom Row (L-R): Dana Wickens, Irene Pastuszek.

Top Row (L-R): Jen Norton and Aaron Glick.

FRONT OF HOUSE STAFF
Front Row (L-R): Sophie Koufakis (Usher), Allyson Ansel (Porter), Stephen Winterhalter (Merchandise), Margarita Caban (Usher), Xavier Young (Usher).

Back Row (L-R): Shawn Fertitta (House Manager), Georgia Keghlian (Usher), Tammy Cummiskey (Usher), Michael Trupia (Usher) and Barbara Zavilowicz (Usher).

The 25th Annual Putnam County Spelling Bee

The 25th Annual Putnam County Spelling Bee
SCRAPBOOK

Correspondent: Jared Gertner, "William Barfee"

Anniversary Parties and/or Gifts: We celebrated our 1000th show with a fun party and a cake. We also had a rocking closing night party at The Harmony View.

"Gypsy of the Year" Sketch: Jared Gertner wrote it with some help from Jenni Barber, Greta Lee, James Monroe Iglehart, and Jennifer Simard. It was a spoof on "The Bitch of Living" from *Spring Awakening* called "The Bitch of Aging." It was all about us being young looking actors who can play kids....but the cast of *Spring Awakening* are actually kids, which makes us worry about our future as adults. Performers were Jared Gertner, Jenni Barber, Stanley Bahorek, Greta Lee, Aaron Albano, Angelica-Lee Aspiras, and James Monroe Iglehart.

Actor Who Performed The Most Roles in This Show: Todd Buonopane went on as Chip, Barfee, Coneybear, and Panch.

Favorite Moment: We always loved hearing the descriptions that Rona and Panch would come up with to describe the audience volunteers. It was always a test of will to try not to break when they would get a really good one.

In-Theatre Gathering Place: The green room. Some weekends we would agree to get take out food and all meet back in the green room. We would laugh a lot and be totally wiped out by the time the evening half hour call would be given.

Off-Site Hangout: Emmett O'Lunney's Harmony View And/Or The Palm. Both places would treat us like gold and we loved the people there.

Favorite Snack Food: Animal Crackers that our A2 would bring in, and just about anything else....we really liked to eat.

Mascot: The mice that live in Circle in the Square.

Favorite Therapy: We really liked Throat Coat, and some of us would steam sometimes. Also...Emergen-C.

Memorable Ad-Lib: Everything Panch and Rona said. One time two people were making out the whole show, and during the Chip/Barfee fight scene, Jennifer Simard said "...You two...stop making out! And Chip go apologize!"

Record Number of Cell Phone Rings: We had one woman whose cell phone rang three separate times...THE SAME WOMAN!!! On two different occasions, a phone rang right at the quietest moment of the show during the Second Act after Barfee says "YOU!" to Olive.

Memorable Stage Door Fan Encounter: We were a very short cast, and one guy came to the show and waited to meet all of us. He was probably 6' 7." He took a picture with each one of us and we all marveled at the height difference.

Fastest Costume Change: We didn't have too many of those...but James Iglehart had a cou-

The cast and crew greet visitors Bill Clinton (3rd from left in back row) and Chelsea Clinton (2nd from right).

Group photo backstage at the Circle in the Square Theatre.

ple really quick ones.

Busiest Day at the Box Office: Every day during the stagehands' strike was busy. We were one of the eight Broadway shows that stayed open, so we were SRO every night.

Who Wore the Heaviest/Hottest Costume: Probably Stanley Bahorek. He wears a sweatshirt and corduroy pants and a helmet.

Who Wore the Least: Probably Jared Gertner. His shirt was short sleeved and he had shorts on.

Orchestra Member Who Played the Most Instruments: Our reeds player.

Catchphrases Only the Company Would Recognize: "Meow." "Valuables." "Pink or Blue."

Company In-Jokes: Colin Farrell. Feta. Holding our nose and breathing out. "James make me tea," "You're a (blank)."

Coolest Thing About Being in This Show: Improvising, working with the audience, never having to wear make-up.

Wicked

First Preview: October 8, 2003. Opened: October 30, 2003.
Still running as of May 31, 2008.

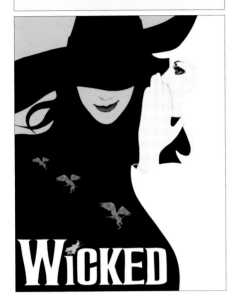

THE CAST
(in order of appearance)

Glinda ....ANNALEIGH ASHFORD
Witch's Father ....MICHAEL DeVRIES
Witch's Mother ....KATIE WEBBER
Midwife ....KATHY SANTEN
Elphaba ....STEPHANIE J. BLOCK
Nessarose ....CRISTY CANDLER
Boq ....LOGAN LIPTON
Madame Morrible................CAROLE SHELLEY
Doctor Dillamond ....STEVEN SKYBELL
Fiyero ....SEBASTIAN ARCELUS
Ozian Official ....MICHAEL DeVRIES
The Wonderful Wizard of Oz .....LENNY WOLPE
Chistery..............................BRENDAN KING
Monkeys, Students, Denizens of the Emerald City,
    Palace Guards and
    Other Citizens of Oz.........IOANA ALFONSO,
      SONSHINE ALLEN, BRAD BASS,
      JERAD BORTZ, KATHY DEITCH,
      MICHAEL DeVRIES, LORI ANN FERRERI,
      LAUREN GIBBS, TODD HANEBRINK,
      REED KELLY, RYAN PATRICK KELLY,
      BRENDAN KING, CHELSEA KROMBACH,
      KENWAY HON WAI K. KUA,
      LINDSAY K. NORTHEN,
      EDDIE PENDERGRAFT,
      ALEXANDER QUIROGA, NOAH RIVERA,
      KATHY SANTEN, HEATHER SPORE,
      CJ TYSON, KATIE WEBBER

Continued on next page

❧N❧ GERSHWIN THEATRE
UNDER THE DIRECTION OF
JAMES M. NEDERLANDER AND JAMES L. NEDERLANDER

Marc Platt
Universal Pictures
The Araca Group and Jon B. Platt
David Stone

present

Stephanie J. Block   Annaleigh Ashford

WICKED

Music and Lyrics   Book
Stephen Schwartz   **Winnie Holzman**

Based on the novel by Gregory Maguire

with

Sebastian Arcelus

Cristy Candler   Logan Lipton   Steven Skybell

Ioana Alfonso Sonshine Allen Clyde Alves Brad Bass Jerad Bortz Kathy Deitch Michael DeVries
Kristina Fernandez Lori Ann Ferreri Anthony Galde Lauren Gibbs Kristen Leigh Gorski Todd Hanebrink
Reed Kelly Ryan Patrick Kelly Brendan King Chelsea Krombach Kenway Hon Wai K. Kua
Lindsay K. Northen Eddie Pendergraft Alexander Quiroga Noah Rivera Kathy Santen
Heather Spore CJ Tyson Katie Webber Briana Yacavone

and

Carole Shelley   Lenny Wolpe

Settings	Costumes	Lighting	Sound
Eugene Lee	**Susan Hilferty**	**Kenneth Posner**	**Tony Meola**

Projections	Wigs & Hair	Technical Supervisor	
Elaine J. McCarthy	**Tom Watson**	**Jake Bell**	

Music Arrangements	Music Director	Dance Arrangements	Music Coordinator
Alex Lacamoire &	**Dominick Amendum**	**James Lynn Abbott**	**Michael Keller**
Stephen Oremus			

Associate Set Designer	Special Effects	Production Supervisor	Dance Supervisor	Associate Director
Edward Pierce	**Chic Silber**	**Thom Widmann**	**Mark Myars**	**Lisa Leguillou**

Casting	Production Stage Manager	General Management	Press	Executive Producers
Telsey + Company	**Chris Jamros**	**321 Theatrical Management**	**Barlow • Hartman**	**Marcia Goldberg & Nina Essman**

Orchestrations
William David Brohn

Music Supervisor
Stephen Oremus

Musical Staging by
Wayne Cilento

Directed by
Joe Mantello

Grammy Award-winning Original Cast Recording on DECCA BROADWAY

LIVE BROADWAY

12/3/07

(L-R): Annaleigh Ashford and Stephanie J. Block.

Photo by Joan Marcus

401

Wicked

MUSICAL NUMBERS

ACT I

"No One Mourns the Wicked"	Glinda and Citizens of Oz
"Dear Old Shiz"	Students
"The Wizard and I"	Morrible, Elphaba
"What Is This Feeling?"	Galinda, Elphaba and Students
"Something Bad"	Dr. Dillamond and Elphaba
"Dancing Through Life"	Fiyero, Galinda, Boq, Nessarose, Elphaba and Students
"Popular"	Galinda
"I'm Not That Girl"	Elphaba
"One Short Day"	Elphaba, Glinda and Denizens of the Emerald City
"A Sentimental Man"	The Wizard
"Defying Gravity"	Elphaba, Glinda, Guards and Citizens of Oz

ACT II

"No One Mourns the Wicked" (reprise)	Citizens of Oz
"Thank Goodness"	Glinda, Morrible and Citizens of Oz
"The Wicked Witch of the East"	Elphaba, Nessarose and Boq
"Wonderful"	The Wizard and Elphaba
"I'm Not That Girl" (reprise)	Glinda
"As Long As You're Mine"	Elphaba and Fiyero
"No Good Deed"	Elphaba
"March of the Witch Hunters"	Boq and Citizens of Oz
"For Good"	Glinda and Elphaba
"Finale"	All

ORCHESTRA

Conductor: DOMINICK AMENDUM
Associate Conductor: DAVID EVANS
Assistant Conductor: BEN COHN

Concertmaster: CHRISTIAN HEBEL
Violin: VICTOR SCHULTZ
Viola: KEVIN ROY
Cello: DANNY MILLER
Harp: LAURA SHERMAN
Lead Trumpet: JON OWENS
Trumpet: TOM HOYT
Trombones: DALE KIRKLAND,
    DOUGLAS PURVIANCE
Flute: HELEN CAMPO
Oboe: TUCK LEE
Clarinet/Soprano Sax: JOHN MOSES
Bassoon/Baritone Sax/Clarinets: JOHN CAMPO
French Horns: THEO PRIMIS,
    CHAD YARBROUGH
Drums: MATT VANDERENDE
Bass: KONRAD ADDERLEY
Piano/Synthesizer: BEN COHN
Keyboards: PAUL LOESEL, DAVID EVANS
Guitars: RIC MOLINA, GREG SKAFF
Percussion: ANDY JONES

Music Coordinator: MICHAEL KELLER

Lenny Wolpe as The Wonderful Wizard of Oz.

Photo by Joan Marcus

Cast Continued

UNDERSTUDIES and STANDBYS

Standby for Elphaba:
LISA BRESCIA
Standby for Glinda:
KATIE ADAMS

Understudy for Elphaba:
CHELSEA KROMBACH
For Glinda:
LINDSAY K. NORTHEN, HEATHER SPORE
For Fiyero:
BRAD BASS, JERAD BORTZ,
ANTHONY GALDE
For the Wizard and Dr. Dillamond:
MICHAEL DeVRIES, ANTHONY GALDE
For Madame Morrible:
KATHY DEITCH, KATHY SANTEN
For Boq:
CLYDE ALVES, NOAH RIVERA
For Nessarose and Midwife:
LORI ANN FERRERI, BRIANA YACAVONE
For Chistery:
CLYDE ALVES, REED KELLY,
RYAN PATRICK KELLY, CJ TYSON
For Witch's Father and Ozian Official:
BRAD BASS, ANTHONY GALDE,
ALEXANDER QUIROGA
For Witch's Mother:
LORI ANN FERRERI, KRISTINA
FERNANDEZ, KRISTEN LEIGH GORSKI.

Swings:
ANTHONY GALDE,
KRISTEN LEIGH GORSKI,
BRIANA YACAVONE

Dance Captains/Swings:
CLYDE ALVES, KRISTINA FERNANDEZ

Wicked

Stephanie J. Block
Elphaba

Annaleigh Ashford
Glinda

Carole Shelley
Madame Morrible

Lenny Wolpe
The Wizard

Sebastian Arcelus
Fiyero

Cristy Candler
Nessarose

Logan Lipton
Boq

Steven Skybell
Dr. Dillamond

Katie Adams
Standby for Glinda

Ioana Alfonso
Ensemble

Sonshine Allen
Ensemble

Clyde Alves
*Swing;
Dance Captain*

Brad Bass
Ensemble

Jerad Bortz
Ensemble

Lisa Brescia
Standby for Elphaba

Kathy Deitch
Ensemble

Michael DeVries
*Witch's Father/
Ozian Official*

Lori Ann Ferreri
Ensemble

Kristina Fernandez
*Swing;
Ass't Dance Captain*

Anthony Galde
Swing

Lauren Gibbs
Ensemble

Kristen Leigh Gorski
Swing

Todd Hanebrink
Ensemble

Reed Kelly
Ensemble

Ryan Patrick Kelly
Ensemble

Brendan King
Chistery

Chelsea Krombach
Ensemble

Kenway Hon Wai K.
Kua
Ensemble

Lindsay K. Northen
Ensemble

Eddie Pendergraft
Ensemble

Alexander Quiroga
Ensemble

Noah Rivera
Ensemble

Kathy Santen
Midwife

Heather Spore
Ensemble

CJ Tyson
Ensemble

Wicked

Katie Webber
Ensemble,
Witch's Mother

Briana Yacavone
Swing

Stephen Schwartz
Music and Lyrics

Winnie Holzman
Book

Joe Mantello
Director

Wayne Cilento
Musical Staging

Eugene Lee
Scenic Designer

Susan Hilferty
Costume Designer

Kenneth Posner
Lighting Designer

Tony Meola
Sound Designer

Tom Watson
Wig and Hair
Designer

Joe Dulude II
Makeup Designer

Stephen Oremus
Music Supervisor;
Music Arrangements

William David Brohn
Orchestrations

Alex Lacamoire
Music Arrangements

James Lynn Abbott
Dance Arrangements

Michael Keller
Music Coordinator

Chic Silber
Special Effects

Thom Widmann
Production
Supervisor

Bernard Telsey,
Telsey + Company
Casting

Gregory Maguire
Author of the
Original Novel

Marcia Goldberg, Nancy Nagel Gibbs and
Nina Essman,
321 Theatrical Management
General Management

Marc Platt
Producer

Jon B. Platt
Producer

David Stone
Producer

Stephen Lee
Anderson
Swing

Kevin Aubin
Swing

Meggie Cansler
Swing

Jason Davies
Chistery, Ensemble,
Swing

David Garrison
The Wonderful
Wizard of Oz

Wicked

Tiffany Haas
Swing

Jayne Houdyshell
Madame Morrible

Kendra Kassebaum
Glinda

Allison Leo
Swing

Caissie Levy
Ensemble

Alli Mauzey
Standby for Glinda

Julia Murney
Elphaba

Jan Neuberger
Midwife, Ensemble

Brandon Christopher
O'Neal
Ensemble

Robert Pendilla
Swing

Adam Perry
Swing

Carson Reide
Swing

Adam Sanford
Swing

Michael Seelbach
Ensemble

Brian Slaman
Ensemble

Charlie Sutton
Ensemble

Lorna Ventura
Swing

Jennifer Waldman
Ensemble

Jonathan Warren
Chistery, Ensemble

Ryan Weiss
Swing

Samantha Zack
Ensemble

TRANSFER
STUDENTS
2007-2008

David Burnham
Fiyero

Sam Cahn
Chistery, Ensemble

Jason Davies
Swing

Lauren Haughton
Swing

Lindsay Janisse
*Assistant Dance
Captain/Swing*

Kendra Kassebaum
Glinda

Ben Liebert
Boq

Miriam Margolyes
Madame Morrible

Brian Munn
Swing

Robert Pendilla
Swing

Julie Reiber
Standby for Elphaba

Jonathan Richard
Sandler
Chistery, Swing

Wicked

Brian Wanee
Ensemble

Jonathan Warren
*Chistery, Ensemble,
Co-Dance Captain,
Swing*

Ryan Weiss
Swing

Derrick Williams
Fiyero

Samantha Zack
Swing

STAGE DOORMAN
Carlos Borja

CREW
First Row (L-R): Val Gilmore, Tim Shea, Mark Overton, John Curvan, Nick Garcia.

Second Row (L-R): Joe Schwarz, Jordan Pankin, Terry McGuarty, Danny Gadreau, Sean Kane.

Third Row (L-R): Ralph Perez, Wally Bullard, Brendan Quigley, Jeff Hahn and Jeff Schepis.

WARDROBE DEPARTMENT
Seated (L-R): Bobbye Sue Albrecht, Kathe Mull, Alyce Gilbert

Standing (L-R): Kevin Hucke, Randy Witherspoon, Barbara Rosenthal, James Byrne, Michael Michalski, Teri Pruitt, Jason Viarengo, Dianne Hylton, Laurel Parrish, Michelle Reisch, Robin Cook

Not pictured: Trent Armstrong, Christina Cocchiara, Nancy Lawson

HAIR AND MAKE-UP DEPARTMENT
Front Row (L-R): Chris Clark, Beverly Belletieri, Nora Martin

Back Row (L-R): Jimmy Cortes, Ryan P. McWilliams

Wicked

ORCHESTRA
Front Row (L-R): Victor Schultz, Danny Miller, Greg Skatt, Tuck Lee, Christian Hebel.

Second Row (L-R): Eric Weidman, Janet Axelrod, Theo Primis, David Evans, Jon Owens, Dale Kirkland.

Third Row (L-R): Ben Cohn, Andy Jones, Dominick Amendum (Conductor), Matt vanderEnde, Laura Sherman, Barry Nudelman, Kevin Roy, Ric Molina, Chad Yarbrough, Douglas Purviance, Tom Hoyt.

Back Row (L-R): Brian Hamm, Paul Loesel.

FRONT OF HOUSE STAFF
Front Row (L-R): Eileen Ruig, Peggy Boyles, Martha Boniface, Rick Kaye, James Gunn, Elizabeth Reed.

Second Row (L-R): Edda Sorrentino, Carmen Rodriguez, Philippa Koopman, Siobhan Dunne, Sharon Nelson, Penny Bonacci.

Back Row (L-R): Marianna Casanova, Jacob Korder, Albert Cruz, Lary Ann Williams, Gregory Woolard, Maria Szymanski, Brenda Denaris, Michele Belmond.

Photos by Ben Strothmann

COMPANY AND STAGE MANAGERS
Front Row (L-R): Mark Gordon, Jason Daunter, Bob Brinkerhoff.

Back Row (L-R): Susan Sampliner, Marybeth Abel, Jennifer Marik.

STAGE MANAGERS
(L-R): Chris Zaccardi, Christy Ney.

Wicked

Wicked
SCRAPBOOK

Correspondent: Jason Viarengo, Dresser to "The Wizard."

Milestones: On August 30, 2007 *Wicked* celebrated its 1,600th performance with a chocolate sheet cake for the entire company.

On October 7 we held a benefit performance for the New York Restoration Project to create a *Wicked*-themed garden in one of New York's under-served neighborhoods.

On October 28 *Wicked* celebrated its fourth anniversary on Broadway with the opening of The Friendship Garden in upper Manhattan. The garden was designed by Associate Scenic Designer Edward Pierce. The opening ceremony included a performance by members of the cast, as well as a free block party for the community and fans, featuring ways for the community and fans to join us in our effort to go "Green. For Good."

Also on October 28 the cast and crew celebrated our fourth year on Broadway at Serafina at The Time Hotel. To do something, "Green. For Good." the producers gave everyone a reusable bag and water bottle with the *Wicked* Day logo. On December 1, the producers threw the company a catered dinner and a champagne toast in between shows to celebrate the re-opening of Broadway after the stagehands' strike. On December 2 we had an Actors' Fund performance.

On December 12 the stage managers threw a pizza party in the greenroom to thank the company for all their hard work helping out with BC/EFA Gypsy Fundraising.

On December 16, the producers threw the company a holiday party at the Time Lounge in The Time Hotel.

The cast also threw a surprise gathering in the greenroom celebrating Ben Liebert, who portrays Boq, on his Broadway debut. Ben not only made his Broadway debut in a principal part with *Wicked* but he also received his Actors' Equity card by joining our company.

The seven productions of the musical *Wicked* broke worldwide box office records for the week ending December 30. *Wicked* set a new record for the highest grossing eight-performance week in Broadway history with a gross of $1,839,950. The show also broke records as the highest grossing show in Los Angeles history ($1,949,968), the highest grossing show in Chicago history ($1,418,363) and the highest grossing show in North American touring history ($2,291,608 in St. Louis, MO). *Wicked* was the previous record-holder in each market. When combined with the weekly grosses for the musical's three international productions (in London, Stuttgart, and Tokyo), *Wicked* cumulatively grossed $11.2 million, breaking box office records around the world.

On April 27, 2008 *Wicked* became the 31st longest running show in Broadway history, passing *Aida*. On the way, we recently passed *Ain't Misbehavin', Dancin', Harvey, Deathtrap* and *Gemini*.

Also on April 27 the stage management team threw the company a brunch in the men's ensemble dressing room to thank everyone for their hard work collecting for BC/EFA.

Celebrity Visitors: Actresses Hayley Mills,

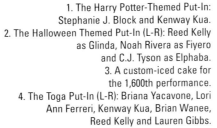

1. The Harry Potter-Themed Put-In: Stephanie J. Block and Kenway Kua.
2. The Halloween Themed Put-In (L-R): Reed Kelly as Glinda, Noah Rivera as Fiyero and C.J. Tyson as Elphaba.
3. A custom-iced cake for the 1,600th performance.
4. The Toga Put-In (L-R): Briana Yacavone, Lori Ann Ferreri, Kenway Kua, Brian Wanee, Reed Kelly and Lauren Gibbs.

Drew Barrymore and Kate Winslet; actor Clive Owen; opera singer Placido Domingo; and celebrity couple Tony Parker and Eva Longoria Parker.

Fundraising: For the 19th annual Gypsy of the Year contest, *Wicked* raised $208,406 to benefit BC/EFA.

For the Easter Bonnet Competition *Wicked* won second runner up in the Broadway fundraising with $197,890. This brings the *Wicked* Broadway Easter Bonnet / Gypsy fundraising total since 2004 to $1,955,802.

"Gypsy of the Year": "Dear Mr. President" was conceived, directed & choreographed by ensemble member Kenway Kua.

"Carols for a Cure" Carol: "Jingle Bells."

Special Backstage Rituals: "*Wicked* Broadway Campaign for Fun" is a program that was created by Stage Managers Chris Zaccardi and Christy Ney for when new cast members join the show and have their put-in rehearsal before they begin performing in the show. Someone in the ensemble or stage management comes up with a theme and then (with the exception of the put-in member), the rest of the company dresses up for that particular theme, with the person wearing the best costume winning a prize. Past themes have included: '70s and '80s dance wear, "The Role you think you'll never play," Toga, Halloween, Pajamas, Luau, Harry Potter for Miriam Margolyes' put-in and Blonde/Pirate for Stephanie Block and Annaleigh Ashford's put-in. Steven Skybell who plays Dr. Dillamond keeps a

toy turtle at his dressing room table, which he received in 1979 when he played Tevye in a production of *Fiddler on the Roof*. The turtle has been with him in every single dressing room since then. Mementos from many of his previous shows are attached to the turtle.

David Burnham who plays Fiyero keeps a little pair of Ruby Slippers on his dressing room table. They were a gift from composer Stephen Schwartz when David appeared in the very first workshop of *Wicked* in 2000.

Annaleigh Ashford who plays Glinda always stops by the Elphaba dressing room to say hello before she heads out to the stage.

Marybeth Abel, our Production Stage Manager, always has a quiet moment to herself before the show.

Lenny Wolpe who plays The Wizard loves penguins and keeps a few ceramic penguins on his dressing table.

Fun Fact: Stephanie J. Block (Elphaba), David Burnham (Fiyero), and Lenny Wolpe (The Wizard) all appeared in the very first *Wicked* workshop in 2000. Eight years later they are all appearing on Broadway together.

Favorite In-Theatre Place: Male ensemble member Eddie Pendergraft designed and painted a *Wicked*-themed mural in the stage right stairwell, which is the most used stairwell in the theatre. The mural goes up three flights and at the top of the staircase is a section labeled Citizens of Oz, where members who have left the company can sign their name.

Xanadu

First Preview: May 23, 2007. Opened: July 10, 2007.
Still running as of May 31, 2008.

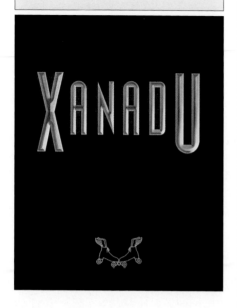

PLAYBILL

XANADU

CAST

(in order of appearance)

Sonny	CHEYENNE JACKSON
Thalia, Siren, Young Danny, '80s Singer, Cyclops	CURTIS HOLBROOK
Euterpe, Siren, '40s Singer, Thetis	ANIKA LARSEN
Erato, Siren, '40s Singer, Eros, Hera	KENITA MILLER
Melpomene, Medusa	MARY TESTA
Calliope, Aphrodite	JACKIE HOFFMAN
Terpsicore, Siren, '80s Singer, Hermes, Centaur	ANDRÉ WARD
Clio/Kira	KERRY BUTLER
Danny Maguire, Zeus	TONY ROBERTS
Featured Skater	MARTY THOMAS
Featured Skater #2	DAVID TANKERSLEY

UNDERSTUDIES

For Clio/Kira:
ANIKA LARSEN, KENITA MILLER,
PATTI MURIN
For Sonny:
CURTIS HOLBROOK, ANDRÉ WARD
For Danny Maguire:
PETER SAMUEL
For Melpomene and Calliope:
ANNIE GOLDEN, ANIKA LARSEN,
ANDRÉ WARD

Swings: MARTY THOMAS, PATTI MURIN
Dance Captain: MARTY THOMAS

THE HELEN HAYES THEATRE

MARTIN MARKINSON   DONALD TICK

ROBERT AHRENS   DAN VICKERY   TARA SMITH/B. SWIBEL   SARAH MURCHISON/DALE SMITH
present

KERRY BUTLER   **JAMES CARPINELLO**
and
TONY ROBERTS

in

XANADU

Book by
DOUGLAS CARTER BEANE

Music & Lyrics by
JEFF LYNNE & JOHN FARRAR

Based on the Universal Pictures Film Screenplay by
RICHARD DANUS & MARC RUBEL

Also Starring

JACKIE HOFFMAN   **MARY TESTA**

with

CURTIS HOLBROOK   **ANIKA LARSEN**

KENITA MILLER   **MARTY THOMAS**   **ANDRÉ WARD**

Scenic Design	Lighting Design	Costume Design
DAVID GALLO	HOWELL BINKLEY	DAVID ZINN

Sound Design	Projection Design	Wig & Hair Design
T. RICHARD FITZGERALD CARL CASELLA	ZACHARY BOROVAY	CHARLES G. LAPOINTE

Press Representative	Marketing	Technical Supervision
PETE SANDERS BLUE CURRENT PUBLIC RELATIONS	HHC MARKETING	JUNIPER STREET PRODUCTIONS

Music Coordinator	Casting
JOHN MILLER	CINDY TOLAN

Associate Producers
CARI SMULYAN   MARC RUBEL   ALLISON BIBICOFF   CHRISTOPHER R. WEBSTER III/MAGGIE FINE

Production Stage Manager	General Manager
ARTURO E. PORAZZI	LAURA HELLER

Music Direction and Arrangements by
ERIC STERN

Choreographed by
DAN KNECHTGES

Directed by
CHRISTOPHER ASHLEY

7/10/07

Kerry Butler (center) and the Muses.

Photo by Paul Kolnik

Xanadu

Kerry Butler
Clio/Kira

Cheyenne Jackson
Sonny

MUSICAL NUMBERS

Time: 1980   Place: Los Angeles and Mount Olympus

Scene 1: Venice Beach
"I'm Alive" ....Muses and Clio/Kira
Scene 2: Santa Monica Pier
"Magic" ....Sonny, Kira and Muses
"Evil Woman" ....Melpomene, Calliope and Sirens
Scene 3: Outside the Auditorium
"Suddenly" ....Sonny and Kira
Scene 4: Danny Maguire's Office
"Whenever You're Away From Me" ....Danny Maguire, Kira and Young Danny
Scene 5: Inside Auditorium
"Dancin'" ....'40s and '80s Singers, Kira, Sonny and Danny
"Strange Magic" ....Sonny and Kira, Melpomene, Calliope and Eros
"All Over the World" ....Full Company
"Don't Walk Away" ....Sonny, Kira and Muses
Scene 6: Venice Beach
"Fool" ....Kira, Melpomene and Calliope
"The Fall" ....Sonny and Muses
"Suspended in Time" ....Kira and Sonny
Scene 7: Mount Olympus
"Have You Never Been Mellow?" ....Zeus, Hera, Aphrodite, Thetis, Cyclops, Medusa, Centaur
Scene 8: Club Xanadu
"Xanadu" ....Full Company

Tony Roberts
Danny, Zeus

Jackie Hoffman
Calliope, Aphrodite

BAND

Music Director:
ERIC STERN
Associate Music Director:
KARL MANSFIELD
Synths:
ERIC STERN, KARL MANSFIELD
Guitar:
CHRIS BIESTERFELDT
Drums:
ERIC HALVORSON

Music Coordinator:
JOHN MILLER

Music Copying:
ANNE KAYE, DOUG HOUSTON
(KAYE-HOUSTON MUSIC)

(L-R): Cheyenne Jackson and Kerry Butler.

Photo by Peter Lueders/Paul Kolnik Studio

Mary Testa
Melpomene, Medusa

Curtis Holbrook
Thalia, '80s Singer, Cyclops, Young Danny

Anika Larsen
Euterpe, '40s Singer, Thetis

Kenita Miller
Erato, '40s Singer, Eros, Hera

2007-2008 AWARDS

DRAMA DESK AWARD
Outstanding Book of a Musical
(Douglas Carter Beane)

OUTER CRITICS CIRCLE AWARD
Outstanding New Broadway Musical

BROADWAY BEAUTY PAGEANT
"Mr. Broadway"
(Marty Thomas)

André Ward
Terpsicore, '80s Singer, Hermes, Centaur

Marty Thomas
Featured Skater, Male Swing, Dance Captain

Xanadu

Annie Golden
u/s Melpomene and Calliope

Peter Samuel
u/s Danny Maguire

Patti Murin
Female Swing, u/s Clio/Kira

Douglas Carter Beane
Bookwriter

Christopher Ashley
Director

Dan Knechtges
Choreographer

David Gallo
Scenic Design

Howell Binkley
Lighting Director

John Miller
Music Coordinator

Pete Sanders/ Blue Current PR
Press Representative

Hugh Hysell, HHC Marketing
Marketing

Guy Kwan, John Paull III, Hillary Blanken, Kevin Broomell, Ana Rose Greene, Juniper Street Productions
Production Manager

Tara Smith
Producer

Dana Iris Harrel
Associate Director

James Carpinello
Sonny

Shannon Antalan
Erato, Siren, '40s Singer, Eros, Hera

Kate Loprest
Swing

Stuart Marland
Understudy for Danny Maguire

Kyle Dean Massey
Thalia, Siren, Young Danny, '80s Singer, Cyclops

Ken Nelson
Swing

FRONT OF HOUSE STAFF
Front Row (center): Alan Markinson (House Manager Helen Hayes Theatre).

Second Row (L-R): Robert LoBiondo (Usher), Natasha Thomas (Usher), Linda Maley (Usher/Swing), Rita Sussman (Usher), Kiki Lenoue (Box Office Assistant Treasurer), Berd Vaval (Ticket Taker).

Back Row (L-R): Margaret Flanagan (Usher), Ron Johnson (Usher) and Maley-Biancamano (Usher).

Ryan Watkinson
Featured Skater, Swing

Xanadu

STAGE MANAGEMENT
(L-R): Peter Samuel (Assistant Stage Manager), Arturo E. Porazzi (Production Stage Manager), John M. Atherlay (Stage Manager)

HAIR AND WARDROBE
Front Row (L-R): Amy Kitzhaber (Dresser), Ryan Oslak (Wardrobe Supervisor), Cherie Cunningham (Dresser)

Back Row: Nicholas Carbonaro (Hair Supervisor)

STAGE CREW
Front Row (L-R): Joseph Beck (Head Electrician), Emile LaFargue (Deck Sound), Bob Etter (Deck Sound), Ann Cavanaugh (Flyman), Roger Keller (Head Properties).

Back Row (L-R): Michael Cennamo (Sub Flyman), Douglas Purcell (Head Carpenter), Scott Silvian (Sound Engineer) and Joseph Redmond (Follow Spot Operator).

BAND
Front Row (L-R): Eric Stern (Music Director), Eric Halvorson (Drums).

Back Row (L-R): Chris Biesterfeldt (Guitarist), Karl Mansfield (Keyboards/Assistant Conductor).

Xanadu

FLYMAN
Ann Cavanaugh

The *Xanadu* Playbill: August 2007

The *Xanadu* Playbill: April 2008

STAFF FOR *XANADU*

GENERAL MANAGEMENT
LAURA HELLER

GENERAL PRESS REPRESENTATION
BLUE CURRENT PUBLIC RELATIONS
Pete Sanders Andrew Snyder

COMPANY MANAGER
Jolie Gabler

PRODUCTION MANAGEMENT
JUNIPER STREET PRODUCTIONS
Hillary Blanken Guy Kwan
Kevin Broomell Ana Rose Greene

PRODUCTION
    STAGE MANAGER ....ARTURO E. PORAZZI
Stage Manager ....John M. Atherlay
Assistant Stage Manager ....Peter Samuel
Associate to Mr. Ahrens ....Eric Sanders
Associate Director ....Dana Iris Harrel
Associate Choreographer ....DJ Gray
Dance Captain ....Marty Thomas
Makeup and Wig Designer ....,,,,,,........Jon Carter
Associate Scenic Designer ....Frank McCullough
Associate Lighting Designer ....Ryan O'Gara
Associate Costume Designers ....Amelia Dombrowski,
                                  Sarah Laux
Associate Projection Designer ....Austin Switser
Associate Sound Designer ....David Bullard
Casting Associate ....Adam Caldwell
Assistant Choreographer ....Allison Bibicoff
Skating Coach/Dance Assistant/
    Specialty Skater ....David Tankersley
Assistant Lighting Designer ....Bradley King
Design Studio Assistant ....Mary Hamrick
Production Carpenter ....Fred Gallo
Production Electrician ....Joseph Beck
Production Properties Supervisor ....Peter Sarafin
Head Carpenter ....Doug Purcell
Production Flyman ....Joseph Maher
Flyman ....Ann Cavanaugh
Head Electrician ....Joseph Beck
Followspot Operator ....Joseph Redmond
Automated Lights Programmer ....Hillary Knox
Sound Engineer ....Scott Silvian
Deck Sound ....Emile LaFargue
Head Properties ....Roger Keller
Production Wardrobe Supervisor ....Sabado Lam
Assistant Wardrobe
    Supervisors................Nicholas Lawson Carbonaro,
                            Cherie Cunningham
Associate Conductor/
    Synthesizer Programmer ....Karl Mansfield
Assistant to John Miller......................Charles Butler
Production Assistants ....Kerry Whigham, Elise Hanley
Production Intern ....Ning Yap
Press Assistant ....Clifton Guterman
Legal Counsel ....Cowan, DeBaets, Abrahams &
                                Sheppard LLP/
    Frederick P. Bimbler, Esq.; M. Kilburg Reedy, Esq.
Insurance .........................D.R. Reiff & Associates/
                      Dennis Reiff, Regina Newsom
Banking................................Commerce Bank/
              Barbara Von Borstel, Ashley Elezi

Accounting ....Fried & Kowgios Partners CPA's LLP/
                           Robert Fried, CPA
Controller ....Galbraith & Company, Inc./
              Sarah Galbraith, Tabitha Falcone
Payroll Service ....Castellana Services Inc./
                        Lance Castellana
Advertising ....Eliran Murphy Group Ltd./
              Jon Bierman, Sasha DeFazio
Logo Design ....Jeronimo Sochaczewski
Marketing ....HHC Marketing;
            Hugh Hysell, Michael Redman,
                       Mandi Messina
General Management Office ....Michael Moss
Merchandising ....Karen Davidov
Website Design ....The Buddy Group/
                Pete Lim, Pete Deutschman
Additional Website Design/Animation ......Steve Channon
Theatre Displays ....King Displays, Inc.
Car Service ....Harry Duhl/dba Harry Trans
Rehearsal Space ....Chelsea Studios,
                   New 42nd Street Studios
Original Artwork ....Mac and Retna

MUSIC CREDITS

"Magic," "Suddenly," "Dancin'," "Suspended in Time," "Whenever You're Away From Me," "Fool" and "Have You Never Been Mellow" written by John Farrar, published by John Farrar Music. "Xanadu," "All Over the World," "The Fall," "I'm Alive," "Evil Woman," "Don't Walk Away" and "Strange Magic" written by Jeff Lynne, published by EMI Blackwood Music Inc.

ACKNOWLEDGEMENTS

Rollerblade USA; American Apparel; Scenery and scenic effects built and electrified by PRG Scenic Technologies, New Windsor, NY. Show control and scenic motion control featuring Stage Command Systems® by PRG Scenic Technologies. Lighting equipment provided by GSD Production Services, Inc. West Hempstead, NY. Sound equipment provided by Sound Associates, Inc. Video equipment provided by Scharff Weisberg Inc., Long Island City, NY. Synthesizer rentals supplied by Randy Cohen. Costumes executed by John Kristiansen NY, Inc.; Marc Happel; Brian Hemesuth; and Izquierdo Studios. Props designed and fabricated by Pete Sarafin. Additional props by the Spoon Group and Craig Grigg. Additional skating lessons by Lezly Skate School. Makeup by M•A•C Cosmetics. Natural herb cough drops courtesy of Ricola USA, Inc.

SPECIAL THANKS

Special thanks to Bra*Tenders for hosiery and undergarments; PRG Project Managers: Mark Peterson and Troy Atkinson; David Schweizer; Mikael Eliasen; Mike Klimis; Adam at Capezio; Allison at LaDuca Shoes

THE HELEN HAYES THEATRE

Owned and operated by Little Theatre Group LLC
MARTIN MARKINSON and DONALD TICK
General Manager ....SUSAN S. MYERBERG
House Manager ....ALAN R. MARKINSON
Associate General Manager ....SHARON FALLON
Engineer ....HECTOR ANGULO
Treasurer ....DAVID HEVERAN
Assistant Treasurer ....Chuck Stuis
Head Usher ....John Biancamano
Stage Door ....Robert Seymour, Jon Angulo
Accountant ....Chen-Win Hsu, CPA, PC

Xanadu
Scrapbook

Correspondent: Curtis Holbrook, "Thalia," "Siren," "Young Danny," "'80s Singer," "Cyclops"

Opening Night Gifts: Olivia Newton-John (who looks flawless in person) along with John Farrar gave each member of the cast a beautiful engraved glass X!!!!!

Most Exciting Celebrity Visitor: We've had a plethora of celebs come to see the show, including Michelle Pfeiffer, Nathan Lane, Sarah Jessica Parker, Whoopi Goldberg and Joan Rivers. But I think Olivia coming to our opening night was the most exciting. She said in an interview that she laughed hysterically through the whole show, that our cast was first-class and that Kerry was brilliant and had all of her awkward mannerisms down perfectly!

Who Got the Gypsy Robe and What Did They Put on It: Well it's funny you should ask...cuz it was me!!! I was so psyched to receive the robe, especially with this show, and I loooooooove to work on artsy fartsy things (in fact I'm a bit anal about it). I spent five hours bedazzling a logo from one of our t-shirts. It was pretty brilliant, I must admit!

Which Actor Performed the Most Roles in This Show: Our fantastic swing Patti Murin! She's played four roles in the show.

Who Has Done the Most Shows in Their Career: Peter Samuel, our multi-talented and multi-tasking Standby. He has been in thirteen Broadway shows.

Backstage Rituals: At the fifteen minute call Cheyenne sings "Oh My God I'll Never Be Ready" in country music stylings. And the boys (André, Marty and I) respond with a big "Thank you!" Before the Muses enter for "I'm Alive" we have a prayer circle every night.

Favorite Moment During Each Performance (On Stage or Off): Every night there is a specific moment when Jackie Hoffman throws in an ad-lib. She is so freakin hysterical that she has every person in the building waiting to hear what she will say. She's always tormenting the onstage audience. It's great!

Favorite In-Theatre Gathering Place: You'll never believe this but in our tiny little theater we actually have a greenroom! So we all gather there. We have two comfy couches, an overstuffed chair and a TV!

Favorite Off-Site Hangout: Sardi's for sure! Annie Golden always has a sign-up on the call board for a table at Sardi's. Keepin' the tradition alive!

Favorite Snack Food: We always have lots of baked goods around. But in particular Arturo (our PSM) regularly brings delicious homemade banana bread!

Favorite Therapy: Ricolas go very, very quickly at our show. We are always running out.

Best In-House Parody Lyrics: Instead of "Suddenly the wheels are in motion..." we sing, "Suddenly my butt needs some lotion!"

1. Curtain call (L-R): Original film Clio Olivia Newton-John, Broadway Clio Kerry Butler and leading man Cheyenne Jackson.
2. (L-R) Director Christopher Ashley, librettist Douglas Carter Beane and guest Cynthia Nixon arrive at the Helen Hayes Theatre for the premiere.

Most Memorable Ad-Lib: Cheyenne's first performance he went up on his lines (he only had two days of rehearsal) and he said "I need the muse of forgotten lines!" The audience ate it up!

Who Wore the Heaviest/Hottest Costume: André Ward wins with the Centaur costume. He hauls around a huge horse's butt during "Mellow."

Who Wore the Least: Kenita Miller as Eros. Hot!!!!!

Memorable Press Encounter: When we received rave reviews!

Memorable Stage Door Fan Encounter: I didn't witness this, but apparently one day there was a fan at the show with a tattoo of Kerry's face on their arm!

Catchphrases Only the Company Would Recognize: "No one cares!"

Nicknames: André's are "Scoopy" and "Crop Top." Mine are "Curtie" and "Curtriss."

Superstitions That Turned Out To Be True: That bad things happen in three's. James broke his foot, then Kenita, then Marty.

Coolest Thing About Being in This Show: Working with this kick-ass cast!

The Year of Magical Thinking

First Preview: March 6, 2007. Opened: March 29, 2007.
Closed August 25, 2007 after 23 Previews and 144 Performances.

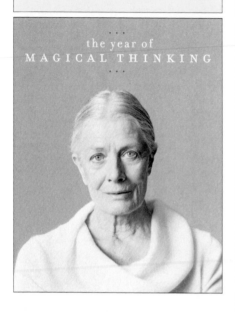

CAST

Joan Didion .... VANESSA REDGRAVE

STANDBY

MAUREEN ANDERMAN

Vanessa Redgrave is appearing with the permission of Actors' Equity Association.

Vanessa Redgrave as Joan Didion.

Photo by Brigitte Lacombe

⊛ BOOTH THEATRE
222 West 45th Street
A Shubert Organization Theatre
Gerald Schoenfeld, *Chairman*   **Philip J. Smith,** *President*

Robert E. Wankel, *Executive Vice President*

SCOTT RUDIN

ROGER BERLIND   DEBRA BLACK   DARYL ROTH

THE SHUBERT ORGANIZATION

Executive Producers

STUART THOMPSON   JOHN BARLOW

present

VANESSA REDGRAVE

· · ·

the year of
MAGICAL THINKING

· · ·

a play by

JOAN DIDION

based on her memoir

Scenic Design BOB CROWLEY	*Costume Design* ANN ROTH	*Lighting Design* JEAN KALMAN
Sound Design PAUL ARDITTI	*Production Stage Manager* KAREN ARMSTRONG	*Associate Director* BT McNICHOLL
Press Representative BONEAU/BRYAN-BROWN		*Marketing* ERIC SCHNALL
Production Management AURORA PRODUCTIONS		*General Management* STP/JAMES TRINER

Directed by

DAVID HARE

8/25/07

Vanessa Redgrave
Joan Didion

Joan Didion
Playwright

David Hare
Director

Bob Crowley
Scenic Design

The Year of Magical Thinking

Ann Roth
Costume Design

Jean Kalman
Lighting Design

Naomi Donne
*Hair & Makeup
Design*

Maureen Anderman
*Standby for
Ms. Redgrave*

James Triner
General Manager

BT McNicholl
Associate Director

Scott Rudin
Producer

Roger Berlind
Producer

Daryl Roth
Producer

Debra Black
Producer

Gerald Schoenfeld,
Chairman,
The Shubert
Organization
Producer

Stuart Thompson
Executive Producer

John Barlow
Executive Producer

DOORPERSON
Amanda Tramontozzi

STAGE CREW
Front Row (L-R): Tim McDonough (Carpenter), Aleksandra Nesterchuk (Hairdresser),
Maureen Anderman (Standby for Ms. Redgrave), R.J. Burns Sr. (House Electrician).

Middle Row (L-R): Ronald Fogel (Head Electrician), Laura Beattie (Wardrobe Supervisor),
Martha Donaldson (Stage Manager).

Back Row (L-R): Kenny McDonough (House Carpenter), Jimmy Keane (House Properties) and
Bill Lewis (Production Sound Operator).

The Year of Magical Thinking

HAIR AND WARDROBE
(L-R): Aleksandra Nesterchuk (Hairdresser) and Laura Beattie (Wardrobe Supervisor/Dresser).

BOX OFFICE
(L-R): Eddie Whittaker and Vinnie Whittaker.

STAFF FOR *THE YEAR OF MAGICAL THINKING*

GENERAL MANAGEMENT
STUART THOMPSON PRODUCTIONS
Stuart Thompson Caroline Prugh James Triner

COMPANY MANAGER
Cassidy J. Briggs

PRODUCTION MANAGEMENT
AURORA PRODUCTIONS INC.
Gene O'Donovan   W. Benjamin Heller II
Bethany Weinstein   Melissa Mazdra

GENERAL PRESS REPRESENTATION
BONEAU/BRYAN-BROWN
Chris Boneau Steven Padla Heath Schwartz

CASTING
Daniel Swee, C.S.A.

HAIR & MAKEUP DESIGN
Naomi Donne

COVER PHOTO & PRODUCTION PHOTOGRAPHY
Brigitte Lacombe

DIALECT COACH
Deborah Hecht

Production Stage Manager ....Karen Armstrong
Stage Manager ....Martha Donaldson
Associate Scenic Designer ....Bryan Johnson
Associate Scenic Designer ....Jeffrey Hinchee
Associate Costume Designer ....Michelle Matland
Associate Lighting Designer ....Bobby Harrell
Associate Sound Designers ....Walter Trarbach,
Tony Smolenski IV
Production Electrician ....Michael Pitzer
Head Electrician ....Ronald Fogel
Production Sound Operator ....Bill Lewis

Wardrobe Supervisor/Dresser ....Laura Beattie
Hairdresser/Make-up ....Aleksandra Nesterchuk
Production Carpenter ....Kenneth McDonough
Assistant Carpenter ....Ed White
Production Properties ....Jimmy Keane
House Electrician ....Ronnie Burns, Sr.
Props Fabrication ....Craig Grigg
Production Assistant ....Johanna Karlin
Assistants to Mr. Rudin ....Mark Rothman,
Nathan Kelly
Assistant to Mr. Berlind ....Jeffrey Hillock
Assistant to Ms. Black ....Ana Pilar Camacho
Assistant to Ms. Roth ....Greg Raby
Assistant to Ms. Didion ....Sharon Lieberman
Assistant to Mr. Hare ....Erica Lipez
Assistant to Ms. Redgrave ....Eamonn Burke
General Management
Assistants ....Megan Curren, Aaron Thompson
Press Representative
Staff ....Adrian Bryan-Brown, Ian Bjorklund,
Jim Byk, Brandi Cornwell,
Danielle Crinnion, Adriana Douzos,
Jackie Green, Juliana Hannett,
Hector Hernandez, Allison Houseworth,
Jessica Johnson, Kevin Jones, Amy Kass,
Aaron Meier, Christine Olver, Joe Perrotta,
Linnae Petruzzelli, Matt Polk, Matt Ross,
Susanne Tighe
Banking ....JP Morgan Chase/Michele Gibbons
Payroll ....Castellana Services, Inc.
Accountant ....Fried & Kowgios CPA's LLP/
Robert Fried, CPA
Controller ....Anne Stewart FitzRoy
Insurance ....DeWitt Stern Group
Legal Counsel ....Loeb & Loeb Inc./
Seth Gelblum, Esq.
Advertising ....SPOTCO/
Drew Hodges, Jim Edwards,
Jim Aquino, Y. Darius Suyama
Immigration ....Traffic Control Group, Inc./
David King
Theatre Displays ....King Displays, Inc.

CREDITS

Scenery and automation from Hudson Scenic Studio, Inc. Soft goods by I. Weiss. Lighting equipment from PRG Lighting. Sound equipment from PRG Audio. Natural herb cough drops courtesy of Ricola USA, Inc. Rehearsed at the New 42nd Street Studios.

The producers would like to express their thanks to Michael Weber for his contribution to this production.

---

www.MagicalThinkingonBroadway.com

 THE SHUBERT ORGANIZATION, INC.
Board of Directors

Gerald Schoenfeld
Chairman

Philip J. Smith
President

Wyche Fowler, Jr.

John W. Kluge

Lee J. Seidler

Michael I. Sovern

Stuart Subotnick

Robert E. Wankel
Executive Vice President

Peter Entin
Vice President –
Theatre Operations

Elliot Greene
Vice President –
Finance

David Andrews
Vice President –
Shubert Ticketing Services

John Darby
Vice President –
Facilities

D.S. Moynihan
Vice President – Creative Projects

House Manager ....Laurel Ann Wilson

Young Frankenstein

First Preview: October 11, 2007. Opened: November 8, 2007.
Still running as of May 31, 2008.

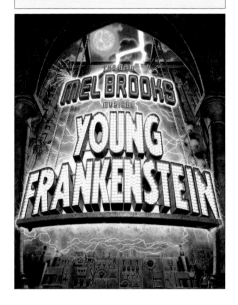

CAST

(in order of appearance)

Herald	PAUL CASTREE
Ziggy	JIM BORSTELMANN
Inspector Kemp	FRED APPLEGATE
Medical Students	JUSTIN PATTERSON, MATTHEW LaBANCA, KEVIN LIGON
Frederick Frankenstein	ROGER BART
Mr. Hilltop	JACK DOYLE
Telegraph Boy	BRIAN SHEPARD
Elizabeth	MEGAN MULLALLY
Shoeshine Man	JIM BORSTELMANN
Igor	CHRISTOPHER FITZGERALD
Equines	ERIC JACKSON, JUSTIN PATTERSON
Inga	SUTTON FOSTER
Lawrence	JIM BORSTELMANN
Frau Blucher	ANDREA MARTIN
Victor	KEVIN LIGON
The Monster	SHULER HENSLEY
Transylvania Quartet	PAUL CASTREE, JACK DOYLE, KEVIN LIGON, BRIAN SHEPARD
Hermit	FRED APPLEGATE
Sasha	ERIC JACKSON
Masha	HEATHER AYERS
Basha	CHRISTINA MARIE NORRUP
Tasha	LINDA MUGLESTON
Bob	PAUL CASTREE
Ritz Specialty	ERIC JACKSON
The Count	MATTHEW LaBANCA

Continued on next page

HILTON THEATRE
A LIVE NATION VENUE

ROBERT F.X. SILLERMAN and MEL BROOKS
in association with
THE R/F/B/V GROUP
Present

THE NEW
MEL BROOKS
MUSICAL
YOUNG
FRANKENSTEIN

Book by MEL BROOKS and THOMAS MEEHAN   Music and Lyrics by MEL BROOKS

Based on the story and screenplay by GENE WILDER and MEL BROOKS and on the original motion picture by special arrangement with TWENTIETH CENTURY FOX

Starring

ROGER BART   MEGAN MULLALLY
SUTTON FOSTER   SHULER HENSLEY   ANDREA MARTIN
FRED APPLEGATE   CHRISTOPHER FITZGERALD

With

HEATHER AYERS   JIM BORSTELMANN   PAUL CASTREE
JACK DOYLE   KEVIN LIGON   LINDA MUGLESTON

JENNIFER LEE CROWL   RENÉE FEDER   JAMES GRAY   AMY HEGGINS   ERIC JACKSON
KRISTIN MARIE JOHNSON   MATTHEW LABANCA   BARRETT MARTIN   CHRISTINA MARIE NORRUP   JUSTIN PATTERSON
BRIAN SHEPARD   SARRAH STRIMEL   CRAIG WALETZKO   COURTNEY YOUNG

Scenery Designed by	Costumes Designed by	Lighting Designed by
ROBIN WAGNER	WILLIAM IVEY LONG	PETER KACZOROWSKI

Sound Designed by	Special Effects Designed by
JONATHAN DEANS	MARC BRICKMAN

Wigs & Hair Designed by	Make Up Designed by
PAUL HUNTLEY	ANGELINA AVALLONE

Casting by	Associate Director	Associate Choreographer
TARA RUBIN CASTING	STEVEN ZWEIGBAUM	CHRIS PETERSON

Music Direction and Vocal Arrangements by	Orchestrations by	Music Coordination by
PATRICK S. BRADY	DOUG BESTERMAN	JOHN MILLER

General Management	Technical Supervision	Press Representative	Associate Producer
RICHARD FRANKEL PRODUCTIONS LAURA GREEN	HUDSON THEATRICAL ASSOCIATES	BARLOW · HARTMAN	ONE VIKING PRODUCTIONS CARL PASBJERG

Music Arrangements & Supervision by
GLEN KELLY

Direction & Choreography by
SUSAN STROMAN

Proudly Sponsored by Fidelity Investments

11/8/07

(L-R): Sutton Foster, Christopher Fitzgerald and Roger Bart go for a "Roll in the Hay."

Photo by Paul Kolnik

Young Frankenstein

MUSICAL NUMBERS

ACT ONE

Scene 1: A Village in Transylvania, 1934
"The Happiest Town" ....Villagers
Scene 2: Medical School, New York City
"The Brain" ....Frederick, Students
Scene 3: Hudson River, Pier 57
"Please Don't Touch Me" ....Elizabeth and Voyagers
Scene 4: A Railroad Station in Transylvania
"Together Again" ....Frederick, Igor
Scene 5: A Hay Wagon
"Roll in the Hay" ....Inga, Frederick, Igor
Scene 6: Castle Frankenstein
Scene 7: The Grand Hall of Castle Frankenstein
"Join the Family Business" ....Victor, Frederick, Ancestors
Scene 8: The Laboratory
"He Vas My Boyfriend" ....Frau Blucher
Scene 9: The Town Hall
"The Law" ....Kemp and Villagers
Scene 10: The Laboratory
"Life, Life" ....Frederick
Scene 11: The Courtyard of Castle Frankenstein
"Welcome to Transylvania" ....Transylvania Quartet
"Transylvania Mania" ....Igor, Frederick, Inga, Kemp and Villagers

ACT TWO

Scene 1: The Forest
"He's Loose" ....Kemp and Villagers
Scene 2: The Laboratory
"Listen to Your Heart" ....Inga
"Surprise" ....Elizabeth, Igor, Frau Blucher, Sasha, Masha, Basha, Tasha and Bob
Scene 3: A Remote Cottage in the Forest
"Please Send Me Someone" ....Hermit
Scene 4: The Dungeon of Castle Frankenstein
"Man About Town" ....Frederick
Scene 5: A Theatre in Transylvania
"Puttin' on the Ritz"
Music and Lyrics by Irving Berlin ....Frederick, The Monster, Inga, Igor, Frau Blucher, Ensemble
Scene 6: A Cave in the Forest
"Deep Love" ....Elizabeth
Scene 7: The Laboratory
Scene 8: The Village Square
Frederick's Soliloquy ....Frederick
"Deep Love" (Reprise) ....The Monster
Finale Ultimo ....The Company

ORCHESTRA

Conductor: PATRICK S. BRADY
Associate Conductor: GREGORY J. DLUGOS
Assistant Conductor: DAVID GURSKY

Woodwinds: VINCENT DELLA-ROCCA,
  STEVEN J. GREENFIELD,
  CHARLES PILLOW, FRANK SANTAGATA
Trumpets: DON DOWNS, GLENN DREWES,
  SCOTT HARRELL

Tenor Trombone: TIMOTHY SESSIONS
Bass Trombone: MIKE CHRISTIANSON
French Horns: PATRICK PRIDEMORE,
  JUDY YIN-CHI LEE
Concert Master: RICK DOLAN
Violins: ASHLEY D. HORNE, HELEN H. KIM
Violas: MAXINE ROACH,
  DEBRA SHUFELT-DINE
Celli: LAURA BONTRAGER, CHUNGSUN KIM

String Bass: BOB RENINO
Drums: PERRY CAVARI
Percussion: CHARLIE DESCARFINO
Keyboard 1: GREGORY J. DLUGOS
Keyboard 2: DAVID GURSKY
Keyboard 3: PATRICK S. BRADY

Synthesizer Programming: RANDY COHEN
Music Coordinator: JOHN MILLER

Cast Continued

THE ENSEMBLE

HEATHER AYERS, JIM BORSTELMANN,
PAUL CASTREE, JENNIFER LEE CROWL,
JACK DOYLE, RENÉE FEDER,
AMY HEGGINS, ERIC JACKSON,
MATTHEW LABANCA, KEVIN LIGON,
BARRETT MARTIN, LINDA MUGLESTON,
CHRISTINA MARIE NORRUP,
JUSTIN PATTERSON, BRIAN SHEPARD,
SARRAH STRIMEL

UNDERSTUDIES

Inspector Kemp/Hermit:
JIM BORSTELMANN, KEVIN LIGON
Frederick Frankenstein:
PAUL CASTREE, MATTHEW LABANCA
Elizabeth:
HEATHER AYERS, LINDA MUGLESTON
Igor:
JAMES GRAY, BRIAN SHEPARD
Inga:
RENÉE FEDER, CHRISTINA MARIE NORRUP
Frau Blucher:
HEATHER AYERS, LINDA MUGLESTON
The Monster:
JIM BORSTELMANN, JUSTIN PATTERSON

SWINGS

JAMES GRAY, KRISTIN MARIE JOHNSON,
CRAIG WALETZKO, COURTNEY YOUNG

DANCE CAPTAINS

JAMES GRAY, COURTNEY YOUNG

(L-R): Shuler Hensley and Fred Applegate.
Photo by Paul Kolnik

Young Frankenstein

Roger Bart
*Frederick
Frankenstein*

Megan Mullally
Elizabeth

Sutton Foster
Inga

Shuler Hensley
The Monster

Andrea Martin
Frau Blucher

Fred Applegate
*Inspector Kemp/
Hermit*

Christopher
Fitzgerald
Igor

Heather Ayers
Ensemble

Jim Borstelmann
Ensemble

Paul Castree
Ensemble

Jack Doyle
Ensemble

Kevin Ligon
Ensemble

Linda Mugleston
Ensemble

Jennifer Lee Crowl
Ensemble

Renée Feder
Ensemble

James Gray
*Swing/
Dance Captain*

Amy Heggins
Ensemble

Eric Jackson
Ensemble

Kristin Marie
Johnson
Swing

Matthew LaBanca
Ensemble

Barrett Martin
Ensemble

Christina Marie
Norrup
Ensemble

Justin Patterson
Ensemble

Brian Shepard
Ensemble

Sarrah Strimel
Ensemble

Craig Waletzko
Swing

Courtney Young
*Swing/
Dance Captain*

Mel Brooks
*Book, Composer &
Lyricist, Producer*

Thomas Meehan
Book

Susan Stroman
*Director/
Choreographer*

Robin Wagner
Set Designer

William Ivey Long
Costume Designer

Peter Kaczorowski
Lighting Designer

Jonathan Deans
Sound Designer

Paul Huntley
Hair and Wig Design

Young Frankenstein

Angelina Avallone
Make-up Design

Tara Rubin Casting
Casting

Scott Bishop
Assistant Director

Jeff Whiting
*Assistant
Choreographer*

Doug Besterman
Orchestrations

John Miller
Music Coordinator

Laura Green,
Richard Frankel
Productions
*General
Management*

Neil A. Mazzella,
Hudson Theatrical
Associates
*Technical
Supervision*

Robert F.X. Sillerman
Producer

Marc Routh,
The R/F/B/V Group
Producer

Richard Frankel,
The R/F/B/V Group
Producer

Steven Baruch,
The R/F/B/V Group
Producer

Tom Viertel,
The R/F/B/V Group
Producer

Angie Schworer
Ensemble

Jon Patrick Walker
*Understudy for
Frederick
Frankenstein, Igor*

DOORMAN
Bill Blackstock

FRONT OF HOUSE STAFF
Front Row (L-R): Juana Rivas,
Delilah Lloyd, Kirssy Toribio,
Eddie Camacho, Adrian Zambrano,
Emily Fisher

Second Row (L-R): Katie Proctor,
Eroll Whittington, Denise Williams

Third Row (L-R): Howard Emanuel,
Mike Chavez, Kaitlin Becker,
Edward Griggs, Bengey Asse,
Meghann Early, Danielle Doherty

Fourth Row (L-R): Peter Adamson,
Clinton Kennedy, Whitney Spears,
Jennifer Coolbaugh

Back Row (L-R): Adam Sarsfield,
Robert Parkinson, Karen Murray,
Sharon Hawkins, Stephanie Wilson

Color Photos by Ben Strothmann

Young Frankenstein

STAGE MANAGEMENT, DANCE DEPARTMENT, STAGEHANDS, WARDROBE, HAIR, MAKE-UP

Front Row (L-R): Brian Dawson, Adam Girardet, Charlene Belmond, Steve Kirkham, Therese Ducey, Lair Paulsen, Jameson Eaton, Ed Wilson, Tom Sherman, Julia P. Jones, Juliet White, Mark Diaz, Ira Mont, Geoff Vaughn, Thomas Ford, Douglas Petitjean, Steven Zweigbaum, Mark Trezza

Middle Row (L-R): Scotty Cain, Dorothy DiComo, Jessica Dermody, Steve Pulgliese, John VanBuskirk, Norm Ballard

Back Row (L-R): Yanushka Kasabova, Maura Clifford, Roy Seiler, John Rinaldi, Barry Hoff, Deirdre LaBarre, Tom Galinski, John Gibson, Tom McDonough, Eric Castaldo, James Harris, John Warburton, Laura Beattie, Sean Jones, John Sibley, Mark Davidson, Chris Peterson, Simon Matthews

---

STAFF FOR *YOUNG FRANKENSTEIN*

GENERAL MANAGEMENT
RICHARD FRANKEL PRODUCTIONS
Richard Frankel   Marc Routh   Laura Green
Rod Kaats   Joe Watson

COMPANY MANAGER
Kathy Lowe
Associate Company Manager ....Bobby Driggers

GENERAL PRESS REPRESENTATIVE
BARLOW•HARTMAN
John Barlow   Michael Hartman
Dennis Crowley   Michelle Bergmann

CASTING
TARA RUBIN CASTING
Tara Rubin, CSA, Eric Woodall, CSA
Laura Schutzel, CSA, Merri Sugarman, CSA
Rebecca Carfagna, Paige Blansfield, Dale Brown

Production Stage Manager ....Steven Zweigbaum
Stage Manager ....Ira Mont
Assistant Stage Manager ....Àra Marx
Associate Choreographer ....Chris Peterson
Assistant Director ....Scott Bishop
Assistant Choreographer ....Jeff Whiting
Dance Captains ....James Gray, Courtney Young
Dance Assistant ....Christina Marie Norrup
SSDC Observer ....Jennifer DiDonato
Technical Supervisor ....Neil Mazzella,
                                        Hudson Theatrical Associates
Associate Technical Supervisor ....Sam Ellis,
                                        Hudson Theatrical Associates
Associate Set Designer ....David Peterson
Assistant Set Designers ....Atkin Pace,
                          Thomas Peter Sarr, Robert F. Wolin
Associate Costume Designer ....Scott Traugott
Assistant to William Ivey Long ....Donald Sanders
Assistant Costume Designer ....Robert Martin
Assistants to the
      Costume Designer ....Brenda Abbandandalo,
                                        Cathy Parrott

Associate Lighting Designer ....John Viesta
Assistant Lighting Designers ....Joel E. Silver,
                          Chris Reay, Keri Thibodeau
Assistant Sound Designer/Programmer ....Brian Hsieh
Assistant to the Wig Designer ....Giovanna Calabretta
Management Associate ....Ed Brooks
Management Assistant ....Annie L. Grappone

Animations Designer ....Joshua Frankel

Frankenstein Puppet ....Michael Curry Design

Prosthetic Designer ....John Dods

Production Carpenter ....Todd Frank
Automation Carpenters ......Mark Diaz, Thomas Sherman
Assistant Carpenter ....Geoffrey Vaughn
Production Electrician ....Richard Mortell
Head Electrician ....Brian Dawson
Assistant Electricians ....Thomas Ford, Tom Galinski
Moving Light Programmer ....Josh Weitzman
GrandMa/Hippotizer Programmer ....Thomas Hague

Young Frankenstein

Production Sound Engineer ....Simon Matthews
Assistant Sound Engineer ....John Sibley
Advance Sound Engineer ....David Dignazio
Production Properties Supervisor ....Laura Koch
Head Properties Supervisor ....Eric Castaldo
Props Production Assistants ....Dorothy DiComo,
                                Eugene McGuinness
Wardrobe Supervisor ....Douglas Petitjean
Assistant Wardrobe Supervisor ....Deirdre LaBarre
Dressers ....Jessica Dermody, Mark Trezza
                      Laura Beattie, Dennis Birchall,
                      Scotty Cain, Maura Clifford,
                      Dorothy DiComo, Adam Girardet,
                      Tim Greer, Julien Havard, Barry Hoff,
                      Herb Ouelette, John Rinaldi, Roy Seiler
Hair/Wig Supervisor ....Edward J. Wilson
Hair Stylists ....Charlene Belmond, Therese Ducey,
                      Jameson Eaton, Steven Kirkham,
                      Lair Paulsen
Makeup Supervisor ....Juliet White
Assistant Makeup Supervisor ....Yanushka Kasabova
Dialect Coach ....Deborah Hecht
Production Assistants ....Emily Andres, Jarrod Carland,
                      Emma Tammi
Physical Therapy Services ....PhysioArts

Additional Orchestrations ....Michael Starobin
Music Coordinator ....John Miller
Assistants to John Miller ....Kelly M. Rach, Joel Rieke
Associate Conductor ....Gregory J. Dlugos
Assistant Conductor ....David Gursky
Synthesizer Programming ....Randy Cohen
Rehearsal Drummer ....Perry Cavari
Music Preparation ....Anixter-Rice Services
Music Department Assistant ....Seth Sikes

Associate to Mr. Brooks ....Leah Zappy
Asst. to Mr. Brooks ....Shelby Van Vliet
Assts. to Mr. Sillerman ....Gini Smythe,
                      Kyra Wiedenkeller
Asst. to Mr. Baruch ....Sonja Soper
Asst. to Mr. Viertel ....Tania Senewiratne
Asst. to Ms. Mullally ....Erin Cass
Advertising ....Spotco, Inc./
                      Drew Hodges, Jim Edwards,
                      Tom McCann, Tom Greenwald,
                      Steve Sosnowski
Press Associates ....Leslie Baden, Melissa Bixler,
                      Tom D'Ambrosio, Bethany Larsen,
                      Ryan Ratelle, Kevin Robak,
                      Wayne Wolfe
Promotions/Marketing ....Broadway Print and Mail
Photographers ....Paul Kolnik
Insurance ....De Witt Stern Group
Legal Counsel ....Elliot Brown, Dan Wasser/
                    Franklin, Weinrib, Rudell & Vassallo, P.C.;
                    Alan U. Schwartz; Greenberg Traurig, LLP
Banking ....Deutsche Bank
Payroll Service ....Castellana Service, Inc.
Accounting ....Fried and Kowgios Partners, LLP
Travel Agencies ....JMC Travel, Road Rebel,
                      Road Concierge
Merchandising ....Dewynters
Rehearsals ....New 42nd Street Studios
Opening Night Party
    Coordination ....The Lawrence Company Events,
                      Michael P. Lawrence

Group Sales ....Theater Direct International
                      (800)-BROADWAY

RICHARD FRANKEL PRODUCTIONS STAFF
Finance Director ....**Michael Naumann**
Assistant to Mr. Frankel ....Heidi Libby
Assistant to Mr. Routh ....Katie Adams
Assistant to Ms. Green ....Joshua A. Saletnik
Development Manager ....Myriah Perkins
Assistant Finance Director ....Susan Bartelt
Information Technology Manager ....Roddy Pimentel
Accounting Assistant ....Heather Allen
Accounting Assistant ....Nicole O'Bleanis
National Sales and Marketing Director ..**Ronni Mandell**
Marketing Manager ....Melissa Marano
Director of Business Affairs ....**Michael Sinder**
Office Manager ....**Lori Steiger-Perry**
Assistant Office Manager ....Taryn Cagnina
Receptionists ....Christina Cataldo, Jasmine Torres
Interns ....Amanda Axelrod, Tova Bomzer,
                  Laurice Farrel, Emily Gasser, Ekaterina Goujova,
                  Kelly Guiod, Melissa Heller, LeeAnn Kelley,
                  Amaryllis Rivera, Reena Rosenthal,
                  Danielle Russo, Theo Salter, Emily Wright

Makeup provided by M•A•C Cosmetics.

CREDITS AND ACKNOWLEDGEMENTS
Scenery, special effects and automation provided by Hudson Scenic Studio. Additional scenery and automation provided by Showmotion, Inc. Additional scenery provided by Showman Fabricators. Painted drops provided by Scenic Art Studios. Lighting equipment provided by PRG Lighting. Sound equipment provided by PRG Audio. Stage properties provided by Cigar Box Studios, Rabbit's Choice and Costume Armour. Frankenstein puppet provided by Michael Curry Design. Hand props by Moon Boots - Jennie Marino. 3D visualization by Chris Nyfield/Hindsight Studios. Costumes by Carelli Costumes, Inc.; David Quinn; EuroCo Costumes, Inc.; Jennifer Love Costumes, Inc.; John David Ridge, Inc.; Scafati Tailoring, Inc.; Tricorne, Inc. Shoes by T.O. Dey, J.C. Theatrical, Kapri Shoes. Millinery by Carelli Costumes, Inc.; Rodney Gordon; Inc. Lozenges provided by Ricola, Inc. Umbrellas courtesy of TOTES.

World premiere at the Paramount Theatre,
Seattle, Washington, August 23, 2007.

HILTON THEATRE STAFF
General Manager ....Micah Hollingworth
Assistant General Manager ....Teresa Ryno
House Manager ....Emily Fisher
Facility Manager ....Jeff Nuzzo
Assistant Facility Manager ....Alex Becerra
Box Office Treasurer ....Spencer Taustine
Assistant Box Office Treasurer ....Kenny Klein
Head Carpenter ....James C. Harris
Head Electrician ....Art J. Friedlander
Head of Properties ....Joseph P. Harris Jr.
Head of Sound ....John R. Gibson
Staff Accountant ....Carmen Martinez
Payroll Administrator ....Tiyana Works
Shipping/Receiving ....Dinara Kratsch
Administrative Assistant ....Jenny Kirlin

Hilton Theatre — A Live Nation Venue

Megan Mullally (top) with Andrea Martin and Christopher Fitzgerald.

Young Frankenstein
SCRAPBOOK

1. Author Mel Brooks at an autograph session at the Hilton Theatre.
2. Curtain call on opening night.
3. A teaser poster that appeared in Times Square in spring 2007 promoting the first day of ticket sales.
4. Line at the box office the day tickets went on sale.
5. (L-R): Shuler Hensley, original film star Gene Wilder and Mel Brooks on opening night.
6. (L-R): New York State First Lady Tilda Spitzer and costume designer William Ivey Long at the premiere.

Correspondent: Heather Ayers, "Masha"
Memorable Opening Night Gifts: Our producers gave us a cruise around Manhattan. Our writer Tom Meehan gave us a dish with ceramic eyeballs in it, complete with tongs. Megan Mullally had all the ensemble dressing rooms carpeted for opening night.
Exciting Visitor: Original Dr. Frankenstein Gene Wilder surprised us by coming up on stage opening night.
Who Got the Gypsy Robe: Amy Heggins, who has been in more than 10 Broadway shows.
Most and Fastest Costume Changes: Paul Castree has 14 changes, the fastest being seven seconds. The fastest on-stage costume change is Fred Applegate going from Kemp into the Hermit in two seconds during curtain call.
Heaviest Total Costume: Linda Mugleston—21 lbs.
Heaviest Single Costume Piece: Paul Castree's mania coat—10 lbs.
Backstage Activities: Sutton & Julian's Wednesday Shot Night, Dollar Friday, Sutton's Bagel Saturday, and planning four weddings.
Favorite Hangouts: Trailer park, Shuler's pool, Cheetah's (Megan's birthday).
Favorite Snacks: Stage Manager Ára Marx brings vegan treats every payday and·understudy rehearsal. There are always treats in the wig room.
Favorite Therapies: Tiger Balm, Wednesday Night Shots.
Catchphrases Only the Company Would Recognize: "Less get beck to ze heppiness"—Heather Ayers' line that was cut in rehearsal. The song "Family Business" has become "Biscuits."
Nickname: Jimmy Borstelmann is known as GOM (a.k.a. Gypsy of the Month).
Memorable Director Note: Stro: "So let's say that went well."
Crazy On-Stage Moments: Megan's lift came up halfway during curtain call, and Eric Jackson singlehandedly pulled her out. The dance bar didn't come up for the Russian dance section of "Biscuits" and we had eleven dancers fall to the ground on their backs like little turtles. Eric Jackson's pole broke during the monster puppet in "Biscuit" so the monster was headless.

Autographs

Events

Events

Stars in the Alley
June 6, 2007 in Shubert Alley

The 21st Annual "Stars in the Alley" concert gave fans a chance to get an up-close and free look at favorite performers from nearly every current Broadway musical and many plays.

Among those appearing on the Shubert Alley stage this year: Vanessa Redgrave, Julie White, Kerry Butler, Swoosie Kurtz, Kevin Spacey, Ashley Parker Angel, Tamyra Gray, Joey Lawrence, Jerry Mathers and Lea Salonga.

Grease stars Max Crumm and Laura Osnes announced the first "Fan Favorite" play and musical, as voted by visitors to the StarsintheAlley.com website. Winners were *Spring Awakening* as Favorite Musical and *Coram Boy* as Favorite Play.

This year's Star Award, which "recognizes an individual in public or government service who has demonstrated significant support for Broadway," was presented to The Actors' Fund of America in recognition of the organization's 125th anniversary. Actors' Fund president Brian Stokes Mitchell and executive director Joe Benincasa accepted the award from Redgrave.

1. (L-R): Julie White (*The Little Dog Laughed*), James Carpinello and Kerry Butler (*Xanadu*) getting ready to go on.
2. (L-R): Martha Plimpton and Jennifer Ehle of *The Coast of Utopia.*
3. (L-R): Marin Mazzie and Carolee Carmello (*Mamma Mia!*).
4. (L-R): Charlotte St. Martin (Executive Director of the League of American Theatres and Producers) with Vanessa Redgrave (*The Year of Magical Thinking*).
5. (L-R): *The Drowsy Chaperone*'s John Glover and Beth Leavel.
6. Lea Salonga of *Les Misérables* on stage.

American Theatre Wing's Spring Gala

June 4, 2007 at Cipriani

The American Theatre Wing held its annual fundraising Spring Gala at Cipriani restaurant. Guests of honor at the event were Broadway stars Carol Channing, James Earl Jones and Tommy Tune.

1. James Earl Jones at the Spring Gala.

2. (L-R): Doug Leeds, Carol Channing, Sondra Gilman and Tommy Tune at Cipriani.

A Memorial Tribute to Betty Comden

September 18, 2007 at the Majestic Theatre

Tony- and Oscar-winning Broadway lyricist and librettist Betty Comden, who died November 23, 2006, was remembered with a starry concert tribute featuring songs from her many musicals (co-written with lifelong partner Adolph Green) sung by women Broadway stars.

Among the participants were Lauren Bacall, Phyllis Newman, Carolee Carmello, Barbara Cook, Leslie Uggams, Beth Leavel, Karen Ziemba, Stephanie J. Block, Ann Hampton Callaway and Liz Callaway. Comden's classic works included *Peter Pan, On The Town, Wonderful Town, Bells Are Ringing, Singin' in the Rain, The Will Rogers Follies*, and many more.

1. Broadway veterans Celeste Holm (original cast of *Oklahoma!*) and George S. Irving (original cast of *Gentlemen Prefer Blondes*) in the audience at the Majestic.
2. (L-R): Stephanie J. Block, Karen Ziemba, Beth Leavel perform Comden's "New York, New York."

Events

Broadway Bares XVII: Myth Behavior

June 17, 2007 at the Roseland Ballroom

The 17th annual "Broadway Bares" fundraising event, held June 17 at Roseland Ballroom, was another record-breaker, raising $743,787 for Broadway Cares/Equity Fights AIDS. For the tenth year the burlesque-style event was sponsored by the M•A•C AIDS Fund, which presented a check for $115,000, helping the event reach its record-breaking amount.

This year's event, titled "Broadway Bares XVII: Myth Behavior," featured the work of 17 choreographers and 240 of Broadway's sexiest chorus members in production numbers celebrating Greek mythology with a signature skin-baring twist.

Denis Jones directed the evening starring Leslie Kritzer (*Legally Blonde*), who rocked the house with an opening number penned by Gary Adler of *Altar Boyz*. Also featured in the cast were Ashley Brown (*Mary Poppins*), Laura Bell Bundy (*Legally Blonde*), Harvey Fierstein (*A Catered Affair*), Deidre Goodwin (*A Chorus Line*), Capathia Jenkins (*Martin Short: Fame Becomes Me*), David Hyde Pierce (*Curtains*), Bebe Neuwirth (*Chicago*) and Daphne Rubin-Vega (*Jack Goes Boating*).

1. Nancy Anderson (center L), John Salvatore (center) and Daria Lynn Scatton (center R) in the opening number.
2. (L-R): Heather Lang, Emily Loftiss and Brittany Marcin backstage at Roseland.
3. Leslie Kritzer as Frustracia.
4. Harvey Fierstein as Pandora.
4. Ven Daniel as Cupid.

Broadway Barks 9!

July 14, 2007 in Shubert Alley

Award-winning actresses, friends and animal activists Bernadette Peters and Mary Tyler Moore hosted the ninth annual "Broadway Barks" fundraiser and pet adopt-a-thon July 14, 2007 in Shubert Alley. The event benefits New York City animal shelters and adoption agencies. Produced by Broadway Cares/Equity Fights AIDS, the afternoon included celebrity presentations of pets from animal shelters throughout New York City.

Celebrity presenters included Audra McDonald (*110 in the Shade*); Marin Mazzie (*Spamalot*); Lea Michele (*Spring Awakening*); David Hyde Pierce, Jason Danieley, Edward Hibbert, Michael McCormick, Debra Monk and Karen Ziemba (*Curtains*); Jerry Mathers and Paul Vogt (*Hairspray*), Priscilla Lopez and Mandy Gonzalez (*In the Heights*); Cheyenne Jackson, Mary Testa, Jackie Hoffman and Kerry Butler (*Xanadu*); Michael Cerveris (*LoveMusik*); Jo Anne Worley, John Glover and Beth Leavel (*The Drowsy Chaperone*); Ashley Brown, Daniel Jenkins and Gavin Lee (*Mary Poppins*); Christine Ebersole, John McMartin and Mary Louise Wilson (*Grey Gardens*); Charlotte d'Amboise and Michael Berresse (*A Chorus Line*); John Earl Jelks (*Radio Golf*), Angela Lansbury and Michael Mulheren (*Deuce*), Orfeh, Andy Karl, Laura Bell Bundy and their canine co-stars, Bruiser and Rufus (*Legally Blonde*).

1. (L-R): Co-host Mary Tyler Moore, Angela Lansbury (*Deuce*) and co-host Bernadette Peters in Shubert Alley.
2. (L-R): Michael Cerveris (*LoveMusik*) and Xanthe Elbrick (*Coram Boy*).
3. Orfeh (*Legally Blonde*).
4. (L-R): Mary Testa (*Xanadu*), Michael Berresse (*A Chorus Line*) and Jackie Hoffman (*Xanadu*).
5. (L-R): *Curtains* stars Jason Danieley, Michael McCormick, Karen Ziemba and Debra Monk.

Photos by Aubrey Reuben

Broadway Show League Softball Championship

August 16, 2007 at Heckscher Ball Fields, Central Park

Broadway's best softball teams battled for the annual championship August 16, 2007, and when the dust settled, the team from *The Lion King* had clobbered *Wicked/Spelling Bee* by a score of 6-1.

It was the first championship for the *Lion King* team.

The Broadway Show League consists of about three dozen teams that play Thursday afternoon games on the Heckscher Fields in Central Park.

The 2007 show championship contenders:

The Lion King
Billy Brennan *Outfield*
John Brady *Infield/Pitcher*
April Fernandez-Taylor *Catcher*
Gabe Harris *Third Base*
Joann Hunter *Catcher*
Joe Iannello *Outfield*
Matt Lavaia *First Base*
Jack Mansager *Pitcher*
Tim McDonough Sr. *Pitcher*
Tim McDonough Jr. *Shortstop*
Ryan McDonough *Outfield*
Sean McDonough *Second Base*
Courtney McDonough *Outfield*
Richard McQuail *First Base*
Danny Rutigliano *First Base*
Patrick Sullivan *Outfield/Mngmt.*
Rueven Weissberg *Infield*

Wicked/Spelling Bee
Jack Babin *Pitcher/Mngmt.*
Tom Ciaccio *Base Coach*
Albert Cruz *Left Field*
Tina Cruz *Second Base*
Michael Devries *First Base*
Ephraim Dunsky *Base Coach*
Frankie Feliciano *Center Field*
Melanie Ganim *Catcher*
Kendra Kassebaum *Catcher*
Danny Mendoza *Center Field*
Teri Pruitt *Catcher*
Brendan Quigley *First Base*
Noah Rivera *Right Field*
Gene Ruda *Shortstop*
Rob Sheridan *Right Field*
"Spook" Testani *Catcher*
Peter Ventura *Third Base*

1. Championship winners, the *Lion King* team (with lion mascot, center).
2. (L-R): *Jersey Boys'* John Lloyd Young, Christian Hoff, Daniel Reichard and J. Robert Spencer sing the National Anthem on opening day.
3. Team *Lion King* (right) high-fives second-place team *Wicked/Bee* after the championship game.

Broadway on Broadway

September 16, 2007 in Times Square

Photos by Aubrey Reuben

Broadway on Broadway," the annual concert celebrating the new theatre season, rolled out on a huge stage set up in Times Square.

Lance Bass, the former *NSYNC star who was making his Broadway debut as Corny Collins in *Hairspray*, hosted the free event.

The concert featured performances by Lea Salonga, Chazz Palminteri, Sierra Boggess, Debra Monk, Laura Osnes, Max Crumm, Adriane Lenox, Julia Murney, Beth Leavel, Carolee Carmello, Ashley Brown, Gavin Lee and Orfeh as well as 200 other Broadway actors from productions including *Avenue Q, Chicago, A Chorus Line, The Color Purple, Curtains, The Drowsy Chaperone, Grease, Hairspray, Jersey Boys, Legally Blonde: The Musical, Les Misérables, The Lion King, Mamma Mia!, Mary Poppins, Monty Python's Spamalot, The Phantom of the Opera, Rent, The Little Mermaid, The 25th Annual Putnam County Spelling Bee* and *Wicked*.

An estimated 50,000 fans attended the concert which was presented by The League of American Theatres and Producers and the Times Square Alliance.

1. Gypsies of *Mamma Mia!* get ready to go on.
2. Marin Mazzie of *Spamalot*.
3. (L-R): League Executive Director Charlotte St. Martin, host Lance Bass and President of the Times Square Alliance Tim Tompkins.
4. Ladies of *Grease*.
5. (L-R): Jennifer Hope Wills and Tim Martin Gleason of *The Phantom of the Opera* with Lea Salonga of *Les Misérables*.

The 2007 Tony Honors for Excellence in Theatre

October 30, 2007 at Tavern on the Green

Tommy Tune hosted the 2007 Tony Honors for Excellence in Theatre ceremony October 30, 2007 at Tavern on the Green. The Tony Honors recognize contributions to the field of theatre by individuals and organizations that are not eligible in any of the established Tony categories. Honors were presented to:

* Choreographer Gemze De Lappe, who danced in the original production of *Carousel,* and who has been the go-to person to recreate much of the choreography of the great Agnes de Mille, mounting productions of *Oklahoma!,* *Brigadoon* and *Carousel,* as well as staging many of the de Mille ballets.

* Alyce Gilbert, a longtime wardrobe supervisor who has worked both on and Off-Broadway for nearly 40 years. She is currently the wardrobe supervisor on *Wicked.*

* Neil Mazzella, proprietor of Hudson Scenic Studios, which has built scenery for more than 200 Broadway and touring productions. He has been an unsung hero to many producers, directors and designers over the past two decades.

* Seymour "Red" Press, who began his career 50 years ago in the orchestra of the Broadway musical *The Body Beautiful,* and has gone on to serve as musical coordinator or contractor in approximately 60 Broadway productions.

Clockwise from upper left: Tommy Tune (host), Alyce Gilbert (honoree), Neil Mazzella (honoree), Doug Leeds (American Theatre Wing), Sondra Gilman (American Theatre Wing), Gemze de Lappe (honoree), Seymour "Red" Press (honoree) and Charlotte St. Martin (The Broadway League).

Leading Men III

April 21, 2008 at Birdland

The Leading Men III"—a benefit concert for Broadway Cares/Equity Fights AIDS—was hosted by John Tartaglia (*Avenue Q, Shrek the Musical*).

Directed by Alan Muraoka (*Pacific Overtures, Miss Saigon*) with musical direction by Seth Rudetsky, the event was produced by Wayman Wong.

The roster of leading men who performed included Tom Andersen, Skylar Astin, David Burnham, Jim Caruso, Jonathan Groff, Aaron Lazar, Norm Lewis, Michael McElroy, Skie Ocasio, Aaron Ramey, Robb Sapp, Benjamin Schrader, Christopher Sieber, Marcus Simeone, Bobby Steggert and Jim Walton.

The evening featured an eclectic set list that included show tunes, cabaret standards, original songs and parodies.

(L-R): Norm Lewis of *The Little Mermaid* and David Burnham of *Wicked.*

Jonthan Groff of *Spring Awakening* performs at the concert.

Broadway Flea Market and Grand Auction

September 23, 2007 in Shubert Alley

The photos credit runs vertically: Photos by Aubrey Reuben

The 21st Annual Broadway Flea Market & Grand Auction, which was held in Shubert Alley September 23, raised $559,810 for Broadway Cares/Equity Fights AIDS, according to a spokesperson for the organization.

That's a ten percent increase over the 2006 Flea Market, which raised $505,832.

The outdoor theatrical extravaganza featured several fundraising events, including a Celebrity Table, a Silent Auction, a Grand Auction, a VIP Photo Booth and more than 50 tables manned by theatre performers and theatre lovers.

The tables that raised the most money included Broadway Beat ($15,016) and United Scenic Artists ($10,510). The show table that took in the most money was *Xanadu* ($10,138). Tyne Daly's table brought in $6,370, while the PLAYBILL table raised $6,331 for the charitable organization.

At the silent auction, a fragment of the score for *Jersey Boys'* "Can't Take My Eyes Off of You" brought in $2,200, while the grand auction took in $12,000 for a walk-on role in *Rent* with co-stars Adam Pascal and Anthony Rapp.

1. Autographed PLAYBILL posters were available for collectors.
2. Kerry Butler of *Xanadu* and Julia Murney of *Wicked* are ready to sign autographs.
3. The sign at the entrance to Shubert Alley.
4. (L-R): Angie Schworer and Chris Sieber.
5. (L-R): *Spring Awakening* stars Lea Michele and John Gallagher Jr. pose with Sir Ian McKellen.

Brian Stokes Mitchell at Carnegie Hall

October 15, 2007 at Carnegie Hall

(L-R): Brian Stokes Mitchell with his wife, Allyson, arriving at the Russian Tea Room reception.

Tony-winning Broadway star Brian Stokes Mitchell made his solo concert debut at Carnegie Hall to benefit the Actors Fund of America (celebrating its 125th year), of which he is president. Mitchell offered highlights from his award-winning career and his self-titled solo CD, as well as other pop and stage music he has always wanted to perform.

Mitchell was joined on the Carnegie Hall stage by several of his past leading ladies as well as stars from the worlds of opera, Broadway and the concert stage, including Reba McEntire, Phylicia Rashad, Heather Headley, Nikki Renée Daniels and the Broadway Inspirational Voices.

A reception at the Russian Tea Room followed the concert.

(L-R): Mitchell with Ernie Sabella, who played Sancho in his *Man of La Mancha*.

Duran Duran: *Red Carpet Massacre*

November 1-9, 2007 at the Ethel Barrymore Theatre

The Grammy-winning British pop group Duran Duran launched its latest album, "Red Carpet Massacre," with a Broadway concert of the same title. Originally scheduled through November 13 and then extended, the run was cut short by the stagehands' strike November 10, and did not resume when the strike was over. The band's Broadway-debut engagement featured hits from the past 29 years as well as all the tunes on the new recording.

Duran Duran: Simon LeBon, Nick Rhodes, John Taylor and Roger Taylor.

Broadway Beauty Pageant

April 28, 2008 at New World Stages

Xanadu's Marty Thomas was named winner of the "Broadway Beauty Pageant" (formerly titled "Mr. Broadway") after a competition at New World Stages. *Hairspray*'s Daniel Robinson was named runner-up.

Original *Rent* star Anthony Rapp hosted the evening, which benefited the Ali Forney Center; $15,000 was raised for the organization. Contestants competed for the crown through talent, interview and swimsuit competitions.

Celebrity judges included *The Ritz*'s Seth Rudetsky and *[title of show]*'s Hunter Bell and Susan Blackwell.

Marty Thomas (center), Mr. *Xanadu* and winner of the pageant, performing "Proud Marty" with backup dancers.

Gypsy of the Year

December 17-18, 2007 at the New Amsterdam Theatre

The Color Purple presented the best skit, and the national tour of Jersey Boys raised the most money for a single show at the 19th annual Gypsy of the Year Competition. But Broadway's generosity was the real star, with a last-minute outpouring of checks pushing the total to a new record, $3,927,110, despite a 19-day stagehands strike that virtually blacked out the peak of the charity's fundraising season.

The theme of the event was the 50th anniversary of the musical West Side Story. More than two dozen original cast members were on hand, including Carol Lawrence, the original Maria; and Chita Rivera, the original Anita, who were received with standing ovations by the sold-out crowd.

Among skits, songs and dances, the company of The Color Purple impressed the judges with an interpretative dance about seeking relief from the pressures of the world, winning the coveted "Gypsy of the Year" award for best stage presentation.

1. Chita Rivera (center) leads a group of dancers in a recreation of "The Dance at the Gym" from West Side Story.
2. Cast members of The Color Purple perform their winning skit.
3. Surviving West Side Story original 1957 cast members reunite for the 50th anniversary of their show.
4. (L-R): Carol Lawrence (the original Maria), Reri Grist (original soloist in "Somewhere") and Rivera in a tribute to West Side Story.
5. The cast of Spelling Bee.
6. The cast of Avenue Q.

37th Annual Theater Hall of Fame Induction

January 28, 2008 at the Gershwin Theatre and Sardi's

Nine-time Tony Award winner Tommy Tune hosted the 37th annual Theater Hall of Fame ceremony, inducting actors John Cullum, Harvey Fierstein, Dana Ivey and Lois Smith; director Jack O'Brien; playwright Peter Shaffer; and librettist Joseph Stein. The late theatre critic Mel Gussow was inducted posthumously.

Presenters for the evening included directors Harold Prince and Mike Nichols, lyricist Sheldon Harnick, LaMama ETC founder Ellen Stewart, playwright Alfred Uhry and Shubert Organization Chairman Gerald Schoenfeld.

The sold-out evening, which included the ceremony at the Gershwin and a dinner at Sardi's, also featured the presentation of the 2007 Founders Award for Outstanding Contribution to the American Theater to Broadway manager-producer Roy Somlyo. Somlyo managed and produced more than 40 Broadway shows and was president of the American Theater Wing 1998-2003.

Eligible nominees for the Theater Hall of Fame must have had a minimum of five major credits and 25 years in the Broadway theatre. The inductees are elected by the American Theater Critics Association and the members of the Theater Hall of Fame.

1. (L-R): Broadcaster Pia Lindstrom with Founders Award winner Roy Somlyo at Sardi's.
2. (L-R): Honoree Dana Ivey with Frances Sternhagen.
3. (L-R): Honoree Harvey Fierstein with Matthew Broderick.
4. (L-R): Honoree John Cullum and Paige Price.
5. (L-R): Honoree Lois Smith.
6. (L-R): Honoree Joseph Stein and lyricist Sheldon Harnick.
7. (L-R): Scott Wittman and honoree Jack O'Brien.

Photos by Aubrey Reuben

Broadway Bears XI

February 17, 2008 at B.B. King Blues Club & Grill

The *Spamalot* bear, signed by Clay Aiken and David Hyde Pierce, raised the most money—$17,000—at the annual Broadway Bears fundraiser, which benefits Broadway Cares/Equity Fights AIDS. Hosted by Bryan Batt, "Broadway Bears XI" earned a total of $130,878. Other top money-makers were the *Lion King* bear ($9,000), the *Cyrano de Bergerac* bear ($8,000), the *Little Mermaid* bear ($5,000) and the *Wicked* bear ($5,000). The event features an auction of teddy bears dressed as famous Broadway characters, many autographed by the original stars.

1. Gavin Lee with the "Bert Bear" from *Mary Poppins.*
2. (L-R): Jose Llana and Peter Gregus with the "Chip Bear" from *Spelling Bee.*
3. André Ward with the "Centaur Bear" from *Xanadu.*

12th Annual Kids' Night on Broadway

February 5-13, 2008 at Madame Tussauds, and Around Times Square

Rosie O'Donnell and her "Broadway Kids" helped kick off the 12th Annual Kids' Night on Broadway with a concert as part of a three-hour "Fan Festival" at Madame Tussauds on 42nd Street. The afternoon activities with the casts and crews of participating Broadway shows, were a prelude to the first of fours evenings of theatregoing (February 5, 6, 12 and 13), on which grownups who bought a full-price Broadway ticket could bring along a youngster for free.

"Rosie's Broadway Kids" perform for the 12th Annual Kids' Night on Broadway at Madame Tussauds.

Sherie Rene Scott: *You May Now Worship Me*

March 31, 2008 at the Eugene O'Neill Theatre

Sherie Rene Scott raised $200,000 for the Phyllis Newman Women's Health Initiative with her concert of songs and autobiographical stories, *You May Now Worship Me*. The evening was presented in lieu of the annual "Nothin' Like a Dame" fundraiser.

You May Now Worship Me was conceived and written by Scott and Tony nominee Dick Scanlan. Scott recalled growing up in Topeka, Kansas and how she was influenced by such icons as Judy Garland, Rickie Lee Jones, Tom Waits, and Mr. Rogers.

(L-R): Phyllis Newman (far left) accepts a check from Sherie Rene Scott (far right) and her backup singers on the stage of the O'Neill Theatre.

Pamela's First Musical

May 18, 2008 at Town Hall

Pamela's First Musical, a musical left unfinished by Cy Coleman and Wendy Wasserstein at their untimely deaths, got its world-premiere presentation as a starry fundraiser for Broadway Cares/Equity Fights AIDS and TDF's Open Doors Program, which was founded by Wasserstein. The event was supervised by lyricist David Zippel.

Based on Wasserstein's children's book of the same title, about a girl introduced to Broadway by her aunt, the concert staging starred Donna Murphy as Aunt Louise and Lila Coogan as Pamela, with guest appeaances by Carolee Carmello, Lillias White, Donna McKechnie, Lynn Ahrens & Stephen Flaherty, Tommy Tune, Gregg Edelman, Christian Borle, David Garrison, Kathie Lee Gifford and *New York Post* theatre columnist Michael Riedel as a waspish critic.

Curtain call for *Pamela's First Musical* including Christian Borle (far left), David Garrison (fourth from right) and Donna Murphy (second from right).

(L-R): Joel Grey and Tommy Tune at the Sardi's afterparty for *Pamela's First Musical,* in which they played their own Sardi's caricatures who come to life.

Mandy Patinkin on Broadway

May 19, 2008 at the Gerald Schoenfeld Theatre

Tony Award winner Mandy Patinkin performed a one-night-only concert May 19 to benefit the Off-Broadway theatre company Classic Stage Company. Titled *Mandy Patinkin on Broadway*, the event was presented at the Gerald Schoenfeld Theatre. Patinkin was backed by long-time musical director Paul Ford on piano.

Under the leadership of artistic director Brian Kulick and executive director Jessica R. Jenen, Classic Stage Company was celebrating its 40th anniversary this season.

Mandy Patinkin

The 22nd Annual Easter Bonnet Competition

April 28-29, 2008 at the Minskoff Theatre

The Broadway musical *Rent*, which is set to close in September 2008, said farewell to the annual Broadway Cares/Equity Fights AIDS Easter Bonnet Competition by rallying to win the top prize in the competition, raising a record $277,739 in support of people facing HIV/AIDS, toward a grand total of $3,734,129 for the 22nd annual event, also a record.

The prize for best bonnet presentation went to *Sunday in the Park With George*, which presented two of the child members of the company, Kelsey Fowler and Alison Horowitz, performing "We Do Not Belong Together" in costume as George and Dot. The show's Easter Bonnet used a plasma lamp to create a mini lightning bolt under a small umbrella.

The $3.7 million total was raised by more than 50 participating Broadway, Off-Broadway and touring shows in six weeks of post-show appeals from their respective stages. The previous record was set in 2004 when $3,435,997 was raised.

Special guests Harvey Fierstein and Faith Prince (*A Catered Affair*) and David Hyde Pierce (*Curtains*) presented the awards.

1. *Gypsy* cast members sent up their critically-reviled lamb puppet both with a marionette and with a flaming barbecue.
2. Anika Noni Rose of *Cat on a Hot Tin Roof* sings "Help Is On the Way" in the finale.
3. Clay Aiken (right) introduces *Spamalot's* bonnet, a giant grail full of Easter blooms.
4. Award presenters Harvey Fierstein and David Hyde Pierce.
5. The opening number, a parody of TV's "Project Runway."
6. Perennial "Easter Bonnet" highlight, 104-year-old original Ziegfeld girl Doris Eaton Travis.

Photos by Aubrey Reuben

The Tony Awards

June 15, 2008 at Radio City Music Hall

*I*n *The Heights, August: Osage County, South Pacific* and *Boeing-Boeing* won the major production categories at the 2008 Tony Awards.

The 62nd annual awards, representing excellence in Broadway theatre for the 2007-08 season, were presented at Radio City Music Hall.

The Latin-flavored musical *In The Heights* beat back a strong challenge from *Passing Strange* to win the Tony as Best Musical, joining hands with Tracy Letts' family drama *August: Osage County*, which was honored as Best Play. Deanna Dunagan won the Tony as Best Actress in a Play for her performance as *August: Osage County*'s raging matriarch. Her *August: Osage County* co-star, Rondi Reed, was named Best Featured Actress in a Play.

In The Heights won the most awards of any new show, including Best Score for its composer and star Lin-Manuel Miranda. It was his first try at writing a musical, which he conceived when he was still a teenager.

Patti LuPone was named Best Actress in a Musical for her performance as Madame Rose in *Gypsy*. It was her first Tony since *Evita* 28 years ago. Laura Benanti won the Tony as Best Featured Actress in a Musical for her turn in that same show as Gypsy Rose Lee. Boyd Gaines won Best Featured Actor in a Musical for playing Herbie. It was his fourth Tony win.

However, *Gypsy* lost the Best Revival of a Musical prize to Lincoln Center Theatre's *South Pacific*, the classic musical's first-ever Broadway revival. The Rodgers and Hammerstein classic won the most Tony Awards of any show, seven. Its leading man, Brazilian opera singer and matinee idol Paulo Szot, won the Tony as Best Actor in a Musical.

Once again, the supposedly cursed Shakespearean drama *Macbeth* failed to win Best Revival of a Play, which went to the stylish revival of the British sex farce *Boeing-Boeing*. Also following history, the actor playing the Shakespearean antihero, Patrick Stewart, lost the Best Actor in a Play Tony Award—to *Boeing-Boeing* star Mark Rylance.

The 2008 Tonys were the first at which awards were given for Best Sound Design. The inaugural awards went to Mic Pool of *The 39 Steps* (play) and Scott Lehrer of *South Pacific* (musical).

The Tonys were hosted for the first time by Whoopi Goldberg, who amused the crowd at

1. Winners (L-R): Paulo Szot of *South Pacific*, Patti LuPone of *Gypsy*, Deanna Dunagan of *August: Osage County* and Mark Rylance of *Boeing-Boeing*.
2. *Gypsy* featured actors (L-R): Laura Benanti and Boyd Gaines.
3. Rondi Reed of *August: Osage County*.
4. *In The Heights* producers and star (L-R) Kevin McCollum, Lin-Manuel Miranda, Jeffrey Seller and Jill Furman.

The Tony Awards

Radio City Music Hall by inserting herself into scenes from long-running musicals including *Spring Awakening* and *Mary Poppins*.

The nominees and recipients of the 62nd Annual Antoinette Perry "Tony" Awards follow. Winners are listed in **boldface**, with an asterisk (*).

Best Musical
Cry-Baby
In The Heights*
Passing Strange
Xanadu

Best Play:
August: Osage County*
Rock 'n' Roll
The Seafarer
The 39 Steps

Best Revival of a Musical
Grease
Gypsy
Rodgers and Hammerstein's South Pacific*
Sunday in the Park With George

Best Revival of a Play
Boeing-Boeing*
The Homecoming
Les Liaisons Dangereuses
Macbeth

Best Original Score
Cry-Baby, Music & Lyrics: David Javerbaum & Adam Schlesinger
In The Heights*, **Music & Lyrics: Lin-Manuel Miranda**
The Little Mermaid, Music: Alan Menken; Lyrics: Howard Ashman and Glenn Slater
Passing Strange, Music: Stew and Heidi Rodewald; Lyrics: Stew

Best Book of a Musical
Cry-Baby, Mark O'Donnell and Thomas Meehan
In The Heights, Quiara Alegría Hudes
Passing Strange*, **Stew**
Xanadu, Douglas Carter Beane

Best Performance By a Leading Actress in a Musical
Kerry Butler, *Xanadu*
Patti LuPone*, ***Gypsy***
Kelli O'Hara, *Rodgers and Hammerstein's South Pacific*
Faith Prince, *A Catered Affair*
Jenna Russell, *Sunday in the Park With George*

Best Performance By a Leading Actor in a Musical
Daniel Evans, *Sunday in the Park With George*
Lin-Manuel Miranda, *In The Heights*
Stew, *Passing Strange*
Paulo Szot, Rodgers and Hammerstein's South Pacific*
Tom Wopat, *A Catered Affair*

Best Performance By a Leading Actress in a Play
Eve Best, *The Homecoming*
Deanna Dunagan, August: Osage County*
Kate Fleetwood, *Macbeth*
S. Epatha Merkerson, *Come Back, Little Sheba*
Amy Morton, *August: Osage County*

Best Performance By a Leading Actor in a Play
Ben Daniels, *Les Liaisons Dangereuses*
Laurence Fishburne, *Thurgood*
Mark Rylance, Boeing-Boeing*
Rufus Sewell, *Rock 'n' Roll*
Patrick Stewart, *Macbeth*

Best Performance By a Featured Actor in a

Musical
Daniel Breaker, *Passing Strange*
Danny Burstein, *Rodgers & Hammerstein's South Pacific*
Robin De Jesús, *In The Heights*
Christopher Fitzgerald, *The New Mel Brooks Musical Young Frankenstein*
Boyd Gaines, Gypsy*

Best Performance By a Featured Actress in a Musical
de'Adre Aziza, *Passing Strange*
Laura Benanti, Gypsy*
Andrea Martin, *The New Mel Brooks Musical Young Frankenstein*
Olga Merediz, *In The Heights*

1. Kerri Butler of *Xanadu*.
2. Stew, with his Tony for Best Book of a Musical for *Passing Strange*.
3. Creators of *Xanadu* on the red carpet (L-R): Lewsi Flinn, Douglas Carter Beane, Christopher Ashley and Dan Knechtges.
4. (L-R): Loretta Ables Sayre and Kelli O'Hara of *South Pacific*.

The Tony Awards

Loretta Ables Sayre, *Rodgers and Hammerstein's South Pacific*

Best Performance By a Featured Actor in a Play
Bobby Cannavale, *Mauritius*
Raúl Esparza, *The Homecoming*
Conleth Hill, *The Seafarer*
*__Jim Norton, The Seafarer__
David Pittu, *Is He Dead?*

Best Performance By a Featured Actress in a Play
Sinead Cusack, *Rock 'n' Roll*
Mary McCormack, *Boeing-Boeing*
Laurie Metcalf, *November*
Martha Plimpton, *Top Girls*
*__Rondi Reed, August: Osage County__

Best Direction of a Musical
Sam Buntrock, *Sunday in the Park With George*
Thomas Kail, *In The Heights*
Arthur Laurents, *Gypsy*
*__Bartlett Sher, Rodgers and Hammerstein's South Pacific__

Best Direction of a Play
Maria Aitken, *The 39 Steps*
Conor McPherson, *The Seafarer*
*__Anna D. Shapiro, August: Osage County__
Matthew Warchus, *Boeing-Boeing*

Best Choreography
Rob Ashford, *Cry-Baby*
*__Andy Blankenbuehler, In The Heights__
Christopher Gattelli, *Rodgers and Hammerstein's South Pacific*
Dan Knechtges, *Xanadu*

Best Scenic Design of a Musical
David Farley and Timothy Bird & The Knifedge Creative Network, *Sunday in the Park With George*
Anna Louizos, *In The Heights*
Robin Wagner, *The New Mel Brooks Musical Young Frankenstein*
*__Michael Yeargan, Rodgers and Hammerstein's South Pacific__

Best Scenic Design of a Play
Peter McKintosh, *The 39 Steps*
Scott Pask, *Les Liaisons Dangereuses*
*__Todd Rosenthal, August: Osage County__
Anthony Ward, *Macbeth*

Best Costume Design of a Musical
David Farley, *Sunday in the Park With George*
Martin Pakledinaz, *Gypsy*
Paul Tazewell, *In The Heights*
*__Catherine Zuber, Rodgers and Hammerstein's South Pacific__

Best Costume Design of a Play
Gregory Gale, *Cyrano de Bergerac*
Rob Howell, *Boeing-Boeing*
*__Katrina Lindsay, Les Liaisons Dangereuses__
Peter McKintosh, *The 39 Steps*

1. The supporting cast of *In The Heights* on their way to a win for Best Musical (L-R): Christopher Jackson, Janet Dacal, Seth Stewart, Andrea Burns, Karen Ulivo, Priscilla Lopez, Mandy Gonzalez and Carlos Gomez.
2. *South Pacific's* Catherine Zuber won a Best Costume Design Tony for the fourth year in a row.

Best Lighting Design of a Musical
Ken Billington, *Sunday in the Park With George*
Howell Binkley, *In The Heights*
*__Donald Holder, Rodgers and Hammerstein's South Pacific__
Natasha Katz, *The Little Mermaid*

Best Lighting Design of a Play
*__Kevin Adams, The 39 Steps__
Howard Harrison, *Macbeth*
Donald Holder, *Les Liaisons Dangereuses*
Ann G. Wrightson, *August: Osage County*

Best Orchestrations
Jason Carr, *Sunday in the Park with George*
*__Alex Lacamoire & Bill Sherman, In The Heights__
Stew & Heidi Rodewald, *Passing Strange*
Jonathan Tunick, *A Catered Affair*

Best Sound Design of a Musical
Acme Sound Partners, *In The Heights*
Sebastian Frost, *Sunday in the Park with George*
*__Scott Lehrer, Rodgers and Hammerstein's South Pacific__
Dan Moses Schreier, *Gypsy*

Best Sound Design of a Play
Simon Baker, *Boeing-Boeing*
Adam Cork, *Macbeth*
Ian Dickinson, *Rock 'n' Roll*
*__Mic Pool, The 39 Steps__

Special Tony Award
Robert Russell Bennett (1894-1981), in recognition of his historic contribution to American musical theatre in the field of orchestrations, as represented on Broadway this season by *Rodgers and Hammerstein's South Pacific*.

Special Tony Award for Lifetime Achievement in the Theatre
Stephen Sondheim

Regional Theatre Tony Award
Chicago Shakespeare Theater

Tally of Tony Winners:
South Pacific: 7
August: Osage County: 5
In The Heights: 4
Gypsy: 3
Boeing-Boeing: 2
The 39 Steps: 2
Les Liaisons Dangereuses: 1
Passing Strange: 1
The Seafarer: 1

Other Theatre Awards

Covering the 2007-2008 Broadway Season

THE PULITZER PRIZE FOR DRAMA
August: Osage County by Tracy Letts

NY DRAMA CRITICS' CIRCLE AWARDS
Best Play: *August: Osage County*
Best Musical: *Passing Strange*

DRAMA DESK AWARDS
Outstanding Play: *August: Osage County* by Tracy Letts
Outstanding Musical: *Passing Strange* by Stew and Heidi Rodewald
Outstanding Revival of a Play: *Boeing-Boeing* by Marc Camoletti
Outstanding Revival of a Musical: *South Pacific* by Rodgers and Hammerstein
Outstanding Revue: *Forbidden Broadway: Rude Awakening* (OB)
Outstanding Actor in a Play: Mark Rylance, *Boeing-Boeing*
Outstanding Actress in a Play: Deanna Dunagan, *August: Osage County*
Outstanding Actor in a Musical: Paulo Szot, *South Pacific*
Outstanding Actress in a Musical: Patti LuPone, *Gypsy*
Outstanding Featured Actor in a Play: Conleth Hill, *The Seafarer*
Outstanding Featured Actress in a Play: Linda Lavin, *The New Century* (OB)
Outstanding Featured Actor in a Musical: Boyd Gaines, *Gypsy*
Outstanding Featured Actress in a Musical: Laura Benanti, *Gypsy*
Outstanding Director of a Play: Anna D. Shapiro, *August: Osage County*
Outstanding Director of a Musical: Bartlett

The cast of *The 39 Steps*, shortly after winning the 2008 Drama Desk Award for Unique Theatrical Experience at the Drama Desk ceremony at F. H. LaGuardia Concert Hall at Lincoln Center.

Sher, *South Pacific*
Outstanding Choreography: Rob Ashford, *Cry-Baby The Musical*
Outstanding Music: Stew and Heidi Rodewald, *Passing Strange*
Outstanding Lyrics: Stew, *Passing Strange*
Outstanding Book of a Musical: Douglas Carter Beane, *Xanadu*
Outstanding Orchestrations: Jason Carr, *Sunday in the Park With George*
Outstanding Set Design of a Play: Scott Pask, *Les Liaisons Dangereuses*
Outstanding Set Design of a Musical: Michael Yeargan, *South Pacific*
Outstanding Costume Design: Katrina Lindsay, *Les Liaisons Dangereuses*

Outstanding Lighting Design: Kevin Adams, *The 39 Steps*
Outstanding Sound Design: Scott Lehrer, *South Pacific*
Outstanding Projection and Video Design: Timothy Bird & Knifedge Creative Network, *Sunday in the Park With George*
Outstanding Solo Performance: Laurence Fishburne, *Thurgood*
Unique Theatrical Experience: *The 39 Steps*
Outstanding Ensemble Performance: *The Homecoming*
Outstanding Ensemble Performance: *The Dining Room* (OB)
Special Award to Edward Albee on his 80th birthday
Special Award to 59E59 Theaters for imaginative curatorial vision
Special Award to James Earl Jones for being a commanding force on the stage for nearly half a century
Special Award to Playwrights Horizons for ongoing support of theatre artists and new work

OUTER CRITICS CIRCLE AWARDS
Outstanding New Broadway Play: *August: Osage County*
Outstanding New Broadway Musical: *Xanadu* and *Young Frankenstein* (tie)
Outstanding New Off-Broadway Play: *Dividing the Estate* (OB)
Outstanding New Off-Broadway Musical: *Adding Machine* (OB)
Outstanding New Score (Bway or Off): *Adding Machine* (OB) and *Next to Normal* (OB)
Outstanding Revival of a Play: *The Homecoming*
Outstanding Revival of a Musical: *South Pacific*
Outstanding Director of a Play (Lucille Lortel Award): Anna D. Shapiro, *August:*

Stew of *Passing Strange*, with Marian Seldes at the New York Drama Critics' Circle Awards ceremony at the Algonquin Hotel, at which *Passing Strange* was named Best Musical of 2007-2008.

Other Theatre Awards

Covering the 2007-2008 Broadway Season

Osage County
Outstanding Director of a Musical: Bartlett Sher, *South Pacific*
Outstanding Choreographer: Rob Ashford, *Cry-Baby: The Musical*
Outstanding Set Design: David Farley/Timothy Bird, *Sunday in the Park With George*
Outstanding Costume Design: Katrina Lindsay, *Les Liaisons Dangereuses*
Outstanding Lighting Design: Ken Billington, *Sunday in the Park With George*
Outstanding Actor in a Play: Kevin Kline, *Cyrano de Bergerac*
Outstanding Actress in a Play: Deanna Dunagan, *August: Osage County*
Outstanding Actor in a Musical: Paulo Szot, *South Pacific*
Outstanding Actress in a Musical: Patti LuPone, *Gypsy*
Outstanding Featured Actor in a Play: James Earl Jones, *Cat on a Hot Tin Roof*
Outstanding Featured Actress in a Play: Laurie Metcalf, *November*
Outstanding Featured Actor in a Musical: Danny Burstein, *South Pacific*
Outstanding Featured Actress in a Musical: Laura Benanti, *Gypsy*
Outstanding Solo Performance: Laurence Fishburne, *Thurgood*
John Gassner Award (New American Play): Liz Flahive, *From Up Here* (OB)

THE DRAMA LEAGUE AWARDS

Distinguished Production of a Play: *August: Osage County*
Distinguished Production of a Musical: *A Catered Affair*
Distinguished Revival of a Play: *Macbeth*
Distinguished Revival of a Musical: *South Pacific*
Distinguished Performance Award: Patti LuPone, *Gypsy*
Distinguished Achievement in Musical Theatre Award: Paul Gemignani
Julia Hansen Award for Excellence in Directing: Bartlett Sher, *South Pacific*
Unique Contribution to the Theatre: Ellen Stewart, LaMaMa ETC (OB)

THEATRE WORLD AWARDS

For outstanding Broadway or Off-Broadway debuts:
de'Adre Aziza, *Passing Strange*
Cassie Beck, *Drunken City* (OB)
Daniel Breaker, *Passing Strange*
Ben Daniels, *Les Liaisons Dangereuses*
Deanna Dunagan, *August: Osage County*
Hoon Lee, *Yellow Face* (OB)
Alli Mauzey, *Cry-Baby The Musical*
Jenna Russell, *Sunday in the Park With George*
Mark Rylance, *Boeing-Boeing*
Loretta Ables Sayre, *South Pacific*

Mel Brooks reacts when his *Young Frankenstein* is named Outstanding New Broadway Musical of 2007-2008 by the Outer Critics Circle at Sardi's.

Jimmi Simpson, *The Farnsworth Invention*
Paulo Szot, *South Pacific*

THE CLARENCE DERWENT AWARDS

From Actors' Equity for "most promising female and male performers on the New York metropolitan scene."
Zoe Kazan, *Come Back, Little Sheba*
Michael Esper, *Crazy Mary* (OB)

THE RICHARD SEFF AWARDS

From Actors' Equity, to "female and male character actors 50 years of age or older."
Hallie Foote, *Dividing the Estate* (OB)
David Rasche, *The Seagull* (OB)

OTHER ACTORS' EQUITY AWARDS

Joe A. Callaway Award for best performances in a classical play in the New York metropolitan area: Lauren Ambrose *Romeo and Juliet* (OB) and Byron Jennings, *Is He Dead?*
St. Clair Bayfield Award for the best supporting performance by an actor in a Shakespearean play in the New York metropolitan area: Jay O. Sanders, *A Midsummer Night's Dream* (OB)
Extraordinary Excellence in Diversity on Broadway: *110 in the Shade* and *Les Misérables*
Patrick Quinn Award for Distinguished Service to Actors: Alan Eisenberg

THE IRENE SHARAFF AWARDS

From the Theatre Development Fund, for outstanding costume design:

Robert L.B. Tobin Award for Lifetime Achievement: John Conklin
Memorial Tribute Award: Tanya Moiseiwitsch
Artisan Award: Bessie Nelson
Lifetime Achievement Award: Robert Fletcher
Young Master Award: Fabio Toblini

FRED AND ADELE ASTAIRE AWARDS

Best Choreographer on Broadway: Rob Ashford, *Cry-Baby The Musical*
Best Female Dancer on Broadway: Karen Olivo, *In The Heights*
Best Male Dancer on Broadway: Spencer Liff, *Cry-Baby The Musical*
Douglas Watt Lifetime Achievement Award: Tommy Tune

OTHERS

Grammy Award for Best Musical Show Album: *Spring Awakening*
Obie Award for Best New Theatre Piece: Stew, Heidi Rodewald, Annie Dorsen, *Passing Strange*
Obie Award for Ensemble Performance: Cast of *Passing Strange*
Obie Award for Sustained Excellence of Costume Design: Jane Greenwood, *Thurgood* and *Cat on a Hot Tin Roof*
Actors Fund Medal of Honor: Stewart F. Lane, Bonnie Comley
Commercial Theater Institute's Robert Whitehead Award: Nick Scandalios
Lincoln Center's Martin E. Segal Award: Thomas Kail, *In The Heights*
NAACP Theatre Award, Lifetime Achievement: Harold Wheeler, *Hairspray*

Tom Wopat and Faith Prince at the 74th Annual Drama League Awards at the Marriott Marquis where their show, *A Catered Affair*, won Distinguished Production of a Musical.

Faculty

The Shubert Organization

Gerald Schoenfeld
Chairman

Philip J. Smith
President

Robert E. Wankel
Executive Vice President

Photos by Ben Strothmann

Jujamcyn Theatres

Front Row (L-R): Nicole Kastrinos, Joanna Gang, Lauren Schmiedel, Joe Tropia, Cathy Cerge, Thia Calloway, Willa Burke, Stephanie Wallis, Pamela Rajkumar.
Second Row (L-R): Raphael Santos, Allison Buddenhagen, Amy Birnbaum, Bess Eckstein, Jennifer Hershey, Laurice Farrell, Meredith Villatore, Clark Mims Tedesco.
Third Row: (L-R): Rasim Hodzic, Jordan Roth, Jack Viertel, Rocco Landesman, Albert Kim, Holly Sutton, Jeff Hubbard, Justin Karr, Paul Libin.
Back Row (L-R): Daniel Adamian, Matt Fox, Ed Lefferson, William Caramanica, Chris Caramanica, Jeremy Scott Blaustein, Jay Turton.
Not Pictured: Hal Goldberg, Des McAnuff, Christian Sislian and Jerry Zaks.

Faculty

The Nederlander Organization

James M. Nederlander
Chairman

Freida Belviso
Chief Financial Officer

Jim Boese
Vice President

Susan Lee
Chief Marketing Officer

Jack Meyer
Vice President Programming

James L. Nederlander
President

Charlene S. Nederlander
Vice President Corporate Development

Kathleen Raitt
Vice President Corporate Relations

Nick Scandalios
Executive Vice President

Herschel Waxman
Senior Vice President Labor Relations

All photos by Anita & Steve Shevet except where otherwise noted.

Photo courtesy Nederlander Organization

NEDERLANDER STAFF
Front Row (L-R): Rina Beacco, Alyce Cozzi, Phyllis Buono, Lisa Lent, Maleka Musliwala, Maria Manduca, Brian Harasek, Renee Pressley.
Second Row (L-R): Alice Gold, Blair Zwillman, Julia Barr, Carmen Santiago, Susan Knoll, Nancy Santiago, Josh Salez, Rachel Jukofsky, Rebecca Velazquez, Jennifer McKnight, David Perry, Nevolia Corbett-Williams, Marjorie Stewart.
Back Row (L-R): David Vaughn and Ken Happel.

Not pictured: Kim Angad-Jugmohan, Thuy Dang, Jey Moore and Erin Porvaznik.

Faculty

Disney Theatrical Group

Front Row (L-R): Kymberly Tubbs, Shaina Low, Kerry McGrath, Sarah Bills, Thomas Schlenk, Tom Kinsley, Jessica Doina, Wilfredo Hernandez Jr.
Second Row (L-R): Dimitri Pankas, Anne Quart, Todd Lacy, Marshall Purdy, Robbin Kelley, David Scott, Andy Singh, Eric Kratzer, Dana Torres.
Third Row (L-R): Barbara Toben, Nick Judge, Liza Breslin, Dana James, Liz Schwarzwalder, Canara Price, Stephanie Cheek, Michael Cassel, Steven Downing, Fiona Thomas.
Fourth Row (L-R): Jason Zammit, Isander Rojas, June Heindel, Seth Stuhl, Harry Gold, Ron Kollen, Jonathan Olson, Joe Quenqua, Kevin McGuire, Anthony Lyn, Cara Moccia.
Fifth Row (L-R): Kyle Young, Michele Groner, Andrew Flatt, Alan Levey, Rick Elice, Jewel Neal, Dayle Gruet, Janine McGuire, Joy Brown, Amy Caldamone.
Sixth Row (L-R): Laura Eichholz, Dave Ehle, Myriah Perkins, Gregory Hanoian, Tara Engler, Verity Van Tassel, Lauren Daghini, Craig Buckley, Dusty Bennett, Shillae Anderson, Bryan Dockett, David Schrader.
Seventh Row (L-R): John Tiggeloven, John Loiacono, Dana Amendola, Karl Chmielewski, Suyin Chan, Ken Cerniglia, Nick Falzon, Peter Avery, Jen Rudin, William Boudiette.
Eighth Row (L-R): Alyssa Somers, Suzanne Jakel, Shawn Baker, Neil Markman, Michele Steckler, Clifford Schwartz, Lisa Mitchell, Colleen Rosati, Cyntia Leo, Tom Kosis.
Back Row: Ryan Pears, Cristina Fowler, Benjy Shaw, Thomas Schumacher, Randy Meyer, Carl Lembo, Margie Freeswick.

Dodger Theatricals

Back Row (L-R): Michael David, Lauren Mitchell, John Haber, Abigail Kornet, Tim Sulka, Edward Strong.
Middle Row (L-R): Jessica Ludwig, Paula Maldonado, Gordon Kelly, Pamela Lloyd, Sandy Carlson, Dean Carpenter, Jeff Parvin, Andrew Serna.
Front Row (L-R): Flora Johnstone, Laurinda Wilson, Sally Campbell Morse, Ashley Zimmerman, Anne Ezell and Jennifer Vaughan.

Faculty

Manhattan Theatre Club

Front Row (L-R): Barry Grove, Florie Seery, Mandy Greenfield, Daniel Sullivan.
Second Row (L-R): Debra Waxman, Darren Robertson, Lindsey Brooks Sag, Christina Prints, David Shookhoff, Darra Messing.
Third Row (L-R): Charles Graytok, Erin Moeller, Raphael Martin, Kristin Svenningsen, Kelly Gillespie, Ashley Dunn, Jeff Bledsoe, Sarah Ryndak, Amy Harris.
Fourth Row (L-R): Ann Mundorff, Jessica Sadowski Comas, Sage Young, Samantha Mascali, Rebecca Stang, Lisa McNulty, Annie MacRae, Jill Turner Lloyd, Amy Gilkes Loe.
Standing (L-R): Holly Kinney, Tom O'Connor, Laurel Bear, Andrea Paul, Jon Haddorff, Adam Cook, Antonello Di Benedetto, Vijay Mahadeo, Mark Bowers, Mendy Sudranski, Dilshan Keregala, Eric Gerdts, Rosanna Consalva Sarto, Philip Naudé, Kelsey Martinez, Kurt Gardner, and Kevin Emrick.

Lincoln Center Theater

(L-R): André Bishop (Artistic Director) and Bernard Gersten (Executive Producer).

Faculty

The Roundabout Theatre Company

Front Row (L-R): Julia Levy (Executive Director), Todd Haimes (Artistic Director), Harold Wolpert (Managing Director).
Second Row (L-R): David Steffen (Director of Marketing), Scott Ellis (Associate Artistic Director), Jeffory Lawson (Director of Development), Greg Backstrom (Associate Managing Director), Rebecca Habel (General Manager, Steinberg Center), David Miller (Education Director), Nancy Hirschmann (General Counsel), Stephen Deutsch (Human Resources Manager), Charlie Garbowski (Director of Sales Operations), Daniel Weiss (Director of Telesales and Special Promotions).
Third Row (L-R): Victoria Pardo (standing), Tania Camargo, David Solomon, Maggie Cantrick, Dee Beider, Jessica Nash, Elisa Papa, Gavin Brown, Amanda Hinkle, Jay Gerlach, Jennifer DiBella, Kate Bartoldus, Joy Pak.
Fourth Row (L-R): Wendy Hutton (standing), Joshua Poole (standing), Nick Nolte, Allyson Stewart, Jill Rafson, John LaBarbera, Susan Fallon, Nancy Mulliner, Josh Cohen, Yonit Kafka, Nicholas Caccavo, Richard Holst, Robert Dowling.
Fifth Row (L-R): Denise Cooper (standing), Brent McCreary (standing), Jeff Goodman (standing), Steve Schaeffer, Ashley Firestone, Kara Kandel, Ashleigh Awusie, Margaret Casagrande, Nicole Nicholson, Lise Speidel, Sara Curtin, Jaclyn Verbitski, Frank Surdi.

Standing First Row (L-R): Julie D'Andrea, Nick Lyndon, Ted Sod, Glenn Merwede, John Haynes, Ethan Ubell, Maggie Western, Carly Difulvio, Erica Rotstein, Shannon Marcotte, Amber Jo Manuel, Kaitlin Cherichello, Dan Curley.
Standing Back Row (L-R): Daniel Pellew, Robert Montgomery, Darnell Franklin, Ellen Holt, Jeff Monteith, Scott Kelly, Dylan Norden and Micah Kraybill.

The Cooper Company

(L-R): Amanda Taylor, Pamela Cooper, Eric Louie and Adam Reiders.

Faculty

The Broadway League

Nina Lannan
Chair

Charlotte St. Martin
Executive Director

Front Row (L-R): Karen Hauser, Charlotte St. Martin, Zenovia Varelis, Laura Fayans, Ed Sandler, Jean Kroeper, Jan Friedlander-Svendsen.
Second Row (L-R): Patty Casterlin, Eddie Lieber, Joy Axelrad, Colin Gibson, Alan Cohen, Lindsay Florestal, Jennifier Stewart, Ben Pesner, Jessica Storm, Rachel Reiner, Roxanne Rodriguez, Amy Steinhaus.
Back Row (L-R): Andy McGibbon, Braden Chapman, Brian Moran, Chris Brockmeyer, Erica Ryan, Shoshana Parets, Seth Popper, Britt Marden, Josh Cacchione, Robert Davis.
Not pictured: Irving Cheskin, Tom Ferrugia, Robin Fox.

The Frankel Viertel Baruch Routh Group

Front Row (L-R): Michael Naumann, Laura Green, Richard Frankel, Marc Routh, Thomas Viertel, Steven Baruch.
Second Row (L-R): Michael McDonough, Leslie Ledbetter, Katie Adams, John Kivlen, Heidi Libby, Townsend Teague, Amy Clarke, Christina Papagjika, Kendra Swee, Ronni Mandell, Tim Grassel.
Third Row (L-R): Diane Alianiello, Lori Steiger-Perry, John Retsios, Josh Saletnik, Tania Senewiratne, Michael Sinder, Tracy Geltman, Annie Grappone, Melissa Marano, Sue Bartelt, Simma Levine, Shannon O'Neil.
Fourth Row (L-R): Maria Sutton, Joe Watson, Ashley Pitman, Gena Chavez, Margie Kment, Heather Allen, Amanda Johnson, Aliza Wassner, Jennifer Cohen, Josh Sherman, Cait Davis, Allison Engallena and Roddy Pimentel.

Faculty

American Theatre Wing

Photo by Steve Shevett

BOARD OF DIRECTORS AND STAFF
Seated (L-R): Enid Nemy, Douglas Leeds (Board President), Sondra Gilman (Board Chairman), Dasha Epstein, Pia Lindström, Alan Siegel.
Middle Row (L-R): Anita Jaffe, Jo Sullivan Loesser, Barbara Toy, Raisa Ushomirskiy, Randy Lutterman, Myra Wong, Gail Yancosek, Ted Chapin.
Back Row (L-R): Howard Sherman (Executive Director), William Craver, Christopher Rovente, David Brown, Joanna Sheehan, Robb Perry, Lexie Pregosin.
Not Pictured: Lucie Arnaz, Mallory Factor, Jeffrey Eric Jenkins, Ronald S. Konecky, Michael Price, Jane Safer, Peter Schneider and Sir Howard Stringer.

ATW Theatre Intern Group

Photo courtesy The American Theatre Wing

Front Row (L-R): Irina Zheleznyak, Randi Fields, Rebecca O'Connell, Julia Davis, Sophie Aung.
Second Row (L-R): Kaitlin Davis, Dana Enis, Marianne Miller, Elaine Wong, Cory Phillips.
Third Row (L-R): Jeremy Sandler, Courtney Reed, Emily Hammond, Amelia Phelps and Lexie Pregosin (Program Manager).
Back Row (L-R): Travis Ferguson, Kate Cherichello, Taylor Carey, Shari Tischler, Brian McMahon, Brian Weiss and Dan Holzberg.

Faculty

Broadway Cares/Equity Fights AIDS

Front Row (L-R): Christopher F. Davis, Carol Ingram, Wendy Merritt Kaufman, Chris Giarmo.
Second Row (L-R): Rose James, Skip Lawing, Yvonne Ghareeb, Keith Bullock, Bobby McGuire.
Third Row (L-R): Dennis Henriquez, Janice Mayer, Cat Domiano, Janie Smulyan, Ngoc-Ha Bui, Andy Halliday, Denise Roberts Hurlin.
Fourth Row (L-R): Scott Tucker, Scott Stevens, Christopher Economakos, Michael Simmons-DeFord, Madeline Reed, Michael T. Clarkston, Brian Schaaf, Frank Conway.
Back Row (L-R): Larry Cook (Director of Finance and Administration), Roy Palijaro, Nathan Hurlin, Ed Garrison, Chris Kenney, Michael Palm, Michael Graziano (Producing Director), Charles Hamlen, Joe Norton, Andy Smith, Peter Borzotta and Tom Viola (Executive Director).

Producers and Producing Companies

Roger Berlind

Bob Boyett

John Breglio,
Vienna Waits
Productions

Bill Haber/
Ostar Productions

Cameron Mackintosh

Arielle Tepper

Barry and Fran
Weissler

(L-R): Anita Waxman
and Elizabeth Williams,
Waxman/Williams
Entertainment

Faculty

Tony Awards Productions

Don't Say "Break a Leg!"

Kit Ingui, Sue Wagner, Elizabeth I. McCann, John Johnson and Steve Sosnowski.

Yonkers Meet *Jersey*

Joey Parnes with John Lloyd Young.

Ladies and Gentlemen, the TAPettes!

Trini Huschle, Sue Wagner, Kit Ingui and Emily Campbell.

Our Little Shutterbug

Anthony Chisholm and Gaydon Phillips

You Wouldn't Recognize Him Without It.

John Johnson

You Wouldn't Know It To Look at Them But These Gorgeous Girls Spend Their Days Doing Manual Labor

Katrina Dibbini, Maddie Felix and Caryn Morrow.

There's Got to Be a Morning After

Michelle Perna

TonyAwards.com

(L-R): Andrew McGibbon and Ben Pesner.

Faculty

Theatre Development Fund and TKTS

Photographed at the construction site of the new TKTS Booth in Father Duffy Square.

Front Row (L-R): Ann Mathieson, Joy Cooper, Veronica Claypool, Victoria Bailey, Charles Parks, Sarah Aziz, Cheryl Schoonmaker, Branden Huldeen, Patty Allen.

Second Row (L-R): Paula Torres, Catherine Lizima, Eve Rodriguez, Richard Price, Campbell Ringel, Rob Neely, Amy Svoboda, Tymand Staggs, Christophe Mentor, William Castellano, Terrence Erkkila, Michelle St. Hill.

Third Row (L-R): Sal Polizzi, Julie Williams, Ginger Bartkaski, Lisa Carling, George Connolly, Marianna Houston, Howard Marren, Tom Westerman.

Fourth Row (L-R): Tina Kirsimae, Julian Christenberry, Fran Polino, Jessica Wells, Doug Smith, Ray Atherton, Stephen Cabral, Costas Michalopoulos, Gregory Poplyk and Robert Gore.

Not Pictured: David LeShay

TKTS TREASURERS

Front row (L-R): Lawrence Paone, John Sheehan, Charles Stuis, Jr., Laura Turcinovic, Corinne Dorson.

Back row (L-R): Brian Roeder, Robert Kitson, Wesley Heron and William Castellano.

Faculty

Actors' Equity Association

Mark Zimmerman
President

John Connolly
Executive Director

NATIONAL COUNCIL
Front Row (L-R): President Mark Zimmerman, First Vice-President Paige Price, Third Vice-President Ira Mont. Back Row (L-R): Secretary/Treasurer Conard Fowkes, Eastern Regional Vice-President Arne Gundersen. Missing: Second Vice-President Jean-Paul Richard, Central Regional Vice-President Dev Kennedy, Western Regional Vice-President Doug Carfrae.

Photos by Ben Strothmann

Front Row (L-R): David Lotz, Steve DiPaola, Marie Gottschall, Kathy Herrera, Ann Fortuno.
Second Row (L-R): Joe De Michele, Chris Williams, Joyce Vinzani, Karen Nothmann, Spring Streetman, Stephanie Masucci, Flora Stamatiades.
Third Row (L-R): Karen Master, Tom Miller, Megann McManus, Julie Coppola, Doug Beebe, Robert Fuller.
Back Row: Frank Horak.

Front Row (L-R): Joe Erdey, Zalina Hoosein, Benjamin Brooks, Dragica Dabo, Tara Mora, Pearl Brady.

Middle Row (L-R): Kathy Mercado, Val LaVarco, Maria Cameron, Thomas Kaub, Jenifer Hills, Diane Raimondi, Melissa Colgan.

Back Row (L-R): Russell Lehrer, Matthew Summersgill, Dwane Upp, Lawrence Lorczak, Ellen Carter.

Front Row (L-R): Catherine Jayne, Sylvina Persaud, Michelle Lehrman, Eastern Regional Director Carol Waaser, Erin Denton, Ian McGovern, Marvin Nieves.
Second Row (L-R): Jeffrey J. Bateman, David Westphal, Jennifer Herr, Louise Foisy, Quin Chia, Lincoln Hayes, Kevin Pinzon, John Baron, Rick Berg.
Back Row (L-R): Walt Kiskaddon, Barry Rosenberg, Deborah Johnson, Kathy Herrera, Caleb Hammons, William Adriance, Michelle Kelts, Jessica Palermo.

Front Row (L-R): Courtney Godan, Jillian Williams, Allison Plotkin.

Back Row (L-R): Karlene Laemmie, Jonathan Black, Kristine Arwe and David Thorn.

Faculty

United Scenic Artists, IATSE Local 829

(L-R): Joe Saint, Michael McBride, Carl Baldasso, Cecilia Friederichs and Beverly Miller.

IATSE Local 306 Motion Picture Projectionists, Video Technicians and Allied Crafts (Ushers)

Front Row (L-R): Margie Blair, Joe Rivierzo, Roseann Cipriano, Ken Costigan, Rita Russell.
Second Row (L-R): LuLu Caso, Kevin Costigan.
Back Row (L-R): Mike Terr and Dotty Rogan.

Faculty

Association of Theatrical Press Agents and Managers

Seated (L-R): Press Agent Chapter Chair David Gersten, Secretary-Treasurer Gordon G. Forbes, Vice-President David Calhoun, Manager Chapter Chair Robert Nolan.
Middle Row (L-R): Maria Somma, Susan Elrod, Board Member Emeritus Shirley Herz.
Back Row (L-R): Robert Reilly, Mark Schweppe, Board Member Emeritus Merle Debuskey, Kevin McAnarney.
Not Pictured: President Bruce Cohen, Kevin O'Connor, Rick Miramontez, Barbara Carroll, Penny Daulton and Laurel Ann Wilson.

Society of Stage Directors and Choreographers

Seated (L-R): Gretchen M. Michelfeld (staff), Larry Carpenter (Executive Vice President), Karen Azenberg (President), Laura Penn (Executive Director), Sue Lawless (Secretary).
Middle Row (L-R): Michele Holmes (staff), Tracy Mendez (staff), Sheldon Epps (Board), Marcia Milgrom Dodge (Board), Barbara Wolkoff (staff), Renée Lasher (staff), Edie Cowan (Board).
Back Row (L-R): Samuel Bellinger (staff), Kim Rogers (staff), Mauro Melleno (staff), Mary B. Robinson (Board), Ronald H. Shechtman (Counsel), Evan Shoemake (staff) and Lena Abrams (staff).
Not Pictured: Randy Anderson (staff), and Board Members Julie Arenal , Rob Ashford , Walter Bobbie, Mark Brokaw (Vice President), Tisa Chang, Gerald Freedman, Michael John Garcés, Wendy C. Goldberg, Richard Hamburger, Doug Hughes (Treasurer), Paul Lazarus, Kathleen Marshall, Ethan McSweeny, Tom Moore, Amy Morton, Sharon Ott, Lisa Peterson, Lonny Price, Susan H. Schulman, Oz Scott, Daniel Sullivan, David Warren and Chay Yew.

Faculty

Treasurers & Ticket Sellers Union, IATSE Local 751

OFFICE STAFF
Front Row (L-R): Patricia Garrison and Kathy McBrearty.
Back Row (L-R): Gene McElwain, Matthew Fearon, Joseph Scanapicco Jr. and Jim Sita.

Front Row (L-R): Diane Heatherington, Karen Winer, Stanley Shaffer, Lawrence Paone, David Heveran.
Middle Row (L-R): Paul Posillico, A. Greer Bond, Noreen Morgan, Joseph Scanapicco Jr.
Back Row (L-R): Matthew Fearon, Gene McElwain, William Castellano Jr., Michael Loiacono, Peter Attanasio Jr., John Nesbitt, Fred Santore Jr., Robert Begin and Harry Jaffie.

Theatrical Wardrobe Union, IATSE Local 764

Front Row (L-R): Sergeant-at-Arms Terry LaVada, Linda Geley, Dolores Jones, Pamela Pierzina, Luana Michaels, Pattie Barbosa, Board Member Patricia Sullivan.
Second Row (L-R): Jane Rottenbach, Naomi Slavin, James Cavanaugh, Board Member Rochelle Friedman, Mildred Del Rio, Kyle O'Connor, Bobby Condon, Dave Rogers.
Third Row (L-R): Natalie Arango, Laisi Rogovin, Janna Notick, Elizabeth Goodrum, Monica Ruiz Ziegler, Peggy Danz Kazdan, Marilyn Knotts, Board Member Charles Catanese, Board Member Danajean Cicerchi, President Patricia A. White.
Back Row (L-R): Business Representative James Hurley, Charles Crutchfield, David Ruble, Marcel Schmid, James Kabel, Secretary-Treasurer Jenna Krempel and Business Representative Frank Gallagher.

Faculty

Theatrical Teamsters, Local 817

EXECUTIVE BOARD
Front Row (L-R): Francis J. Connolly, Jr. (Business Agent & Union Trustee), Jim Leavey (Recording Secretary), Ed Iacobelli (Vice President).
Back Row (L-R): Mike Hyde (Union Trustee), Thomas R. O'Donnell (President), Thomas J. O'Donnell (Secretary-Treasurer), Kevin Keefe (Union Trustee).

STAFF
Front Row (L-R): Christine Harkerss (Human Resources), Tina Gusmano (Union Secretary).
Back Row (L-R): Terry Casaletta (Casting Director Organizer), Marge Marklin (Fund Secretary).

Not Present: Kathy Kreinbihl (Fund Administrator), Margie Vaeth (Union Secretary).

Service Employees International Union Local 32BJ

EXECUTIVE OFFICERS
(L-R): Kevin Doyle (Executive Vice President), Héctor J. Figueroa (Secretary-Treasurer) and Michael P. Fishman (President).

International Union of Operating Engineers Local 30

BUSINESS MANAGER
Jack Ahern

462

Faculty

Coalition of Broadway Unions and Guilds

Photos by Ben Strothmann

Seated (L-R): Tracy Mendez (Executive Assistant at SSDC), Gene McElwain (President, Local 751), Tony DePaulo (Int'l Vice President, IATSE), Bill Dennison (Local 802), Gordon Forbes (ATPAM), Martin Schulman (Local 798), Frank Connolly Jr. (Local 817).
Standing (L-R): Bruce Cohen (ATPAM), Mike Wekselblatt (Local 1), David Faux (Dramatists Guild), Ralph Sevush (Dramatists Guild), Valerie Gladstone (Local 798), Ira Mont (AEA), Larry Lorczak (AEA), Dwane Upp (AEA), Steve Gelfand (AFM), Mary Landolfi (Local 802), Cecilia Friederichs (USA-829), Deborah Allton (AGMA), John Diaz (Local 1), Frank Gallagher (Local 764) and Joseph Scanapicco Jr. (Local 751).

Binder Casting

Standing (L-R): Mark Brandon, Jay Binder, Jack Bowdan.
Seated (L-R): Karen Young, Nikole Vallins, Sara Schatz, Scout Schatz and Mitzi Michaels.

Faculty

IATSE Local One, Stagehands

Replacement Room Chairperson Daniel Thorn, Administrative Secretary Edmond F. Supple, Sr. and Financial Secretary Anthony Manno.

Seated (L-R): Chairman, Board of Trustees John M. Diaz, Sr., Recording-Corresponding Secretary Robert C. Score, President James J. Claffey, Jr., Vice-President William J. Walters, Treasurer Robert McDonough.

Standing (L-R): Television Business Manager Robert C. Nimmo, Television Business Manager Edward J. McMahon, III, Theatre Business Manager Michael Wekselblatt, Theatre Business Manager Kevin McGarty, Trustee William Ngai and Trustee Daniel D. Dashman.

American Federation of Musicians, Local 802

Mary Landolfi
President

Bill Dennison
Recording Vice President

(L-R): Bud Burridge, Maxine Roach, Jay Blumenthal, Andy Schwartz, Al Hunt, Ethan Fein, Mary Landolfi, Maura Giannini, Jay Schaffner, Ken Rizzo, Bill Dennison and Mark Johansen.

Faculty

The Dramatists Guild

DRAMATISTS GUILD COUNCIL - STEERING COMMITTEE
(L-R): David Auburn, John Weidman (President), Theresa Rebeck and David Ives (Secretary).

Not Pictured: Marsha Norman (Vice President), Jonathan Reynolds (Treasurer), Susan Birkenhead, Sheldon Harnick, David Henry Hwang, Stephen Schwartz and Jeanine Tesori.

STAFF
Front Row (L-R): Abby Marcus (General Manager), Madelena Ryerson (Executive Assistant, Creative Affairs), Tari Stratton (Director of Education, Events & Outreach), John Minore (Executive Assistant, Business Affairs).
Center Row: Joshua Levine (Director of Membership).
Standing (L-R): David Faux (Director of Business Affairs), Patrick Shearer (Membership Assistant), Robert Ross Parker (Director of Publications), Gary Garrison (Executive Director, Creative Affairs) and Ralph Sevush (Executive Director, Business Affairs).
Not Pictured: Sue Drury (Administrator Dramatists Guild Fund).

Faculty

Hudson Scenic Group

Back Row (L-R): Gabriel Tepoxteco, Hector Roman, Matt Bell, Adam Cohan, Pete McGovern, Jim Starr, Josh Braun, Carlos Ramos, Kevin Tedorko, Bill Berry, Chris Labudde, Anthony Robinson.
Second Row (L-R): Kyle Weidner, Michael DiMarco, Ludwig Hnatkowycz, Drew Williamson, Phil Giller, Mike Madravzaki, Ronnie Walsh, Doug Sinclair, Leo Drondin, Tommy Devitt, Boris Shulman, Dean Kozelek, Chris Prava, Rob McGarvie.
Third Row (L-R): Candice Dukehedin, David Kidd, Shawn Larkin, Fernando Colon, Richie Fuggetta, Matt Saide, David Steiner, Joe Hamlin, Jim Geyer, Will Ball, Freddie Sanchez, Elisio Rodriguez, Drew Lanzarotta, Jerry Valenzuela, Hector Pena.
Fourth Row (L-R): Alan Grudzinski, Riccardo Valentin, Bart Coviello, Kasey Walker, Grace Uffner, Erik Nelson, Rick Mone, Rise Abramson, Carla Messina, Grace Brandt, Flo Frintzilas, Walter Murphy, Mary Burt, Dominick Godfrey, Scott Stevens, Dave Rosenfeld, Chuck Adomanis, Roger Bardwell.
Front Row (L-R): Barbara Bloomfield, Melissa McGhee, Jose Ortiz, Russ Stevens, George Sibbald, Jordan Gable, Carrie Silverstein, Dana Gracey, Job Guzman, Mike Stone, Joann Venizano, Rich Chebetar, Delia Washington, Midge Lucas, Lynn Nickels, Kyle Higgins, Beth Leiberman, Carrie Irons, Polly Holland, Tom Sullivan, Kristen Emerv, Tom Ferguson, Ben Grannucci, Pete Weigand, Corky Boyd and Joe Doughney.

The Lawrence Company

(L-R): Ben Bucher, Michael P. Lawrence, Nellie Beavers, Joanna B. Cepler and Richard A. Fromm.

Faculty

The Actors Fund of America

BOARD OF DIRECTORS
Seated (L-R): John Hall, Mark Zimmerman, Brian Stokes Mitchell, Phil Birsh, Merle Debuskey, Scott Weiner, Phil Smith.
Standing (L-R): John Erman, Joe Benincasa, Paul Libin, Kate Edelman Johnson, Anita Jaffe, Jed Bernstein, Fran Gordon, Bebe Neuwirth, George Zuber, Stewart Lane and Charles Hollerith.

STAFF
Front Row (L-R): Suzanne Tobak, Louie Anchondo, Jay Haddad, Connie Yoo, Wally Munro.
Second Row (L-R): Carlos DeJesus, Dave Gusty, Joy Pascua-Kim, Stephanie Linwood-Coleman, Icem Benamu, Amy Picar, Elizabeth Avedon.
Third Row (L-R): Lynne Hoppe, Amanda Clayman, Jose Delgado, Carol Harris-Mannes, Tamar Shapiro, Ina Clark, Barbara Davis, unknown, Liz Tripp.
Fourth Row (L-R): DJ Brumfield, Joe Moretti, Harry Ballard, Judy Fish, Zehava Krinsky, Erica Chung, Alice Vienneau, Gloria Jones, unknown, Rick Martinez, Tony Lopez-Linus.
Back Row (L-R): Victor Mendoza, Megan Quinn, Tim Pinckney, Sam Smith, David Engelman, Charlene Morgan, Jim Brown, Marjorie Roop, Robert Rosenthal and Kent Curtis.

Faculty

Boneau/Bryan-Brown

Chris Boneau

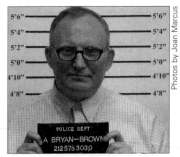

Adrian Bryan-Brown

Ian Bjorklund

Jim Byk

Brandi Cornwell

Adriana Douzos

Jackie Green

Kelly Guiod

Juliana Hannett

Linnae Hodzik

Jessica Johnson

Kevin Jones

Amy Kass

Aaron Meier

Christine Olver

Joe Perrotta

Matt Polk

Matt Ross

Heath Schwartz

Susanne Tighe

Faculty

Barlow•Hartman Public Relations

Photo courtesy Bethany Larsen

(L-R): Richard Prioleau, Tom D'Ambrosio, Michael Hartman, Sam Morris, Bethany Larsen, Ryan Ratelle, The Naked Cowboy (Robert Burck), John Barlow, Matt Shea, Leslie Baden, Dennis Crowley, Michelle Bergmann, Melissa Bixler and Wayne Wolfe.

Richard Kornberg & Associates

Richard Kornberg

Don Summa

Billy Zavelson

Alyssa Hart

Photos by Ben Strothmann

Faculty

Jeffrey Richards Associates

Seated (L-R): Elon Rutberg, Jeffrey Richards (with Lottie the dog) and Irene Gandy.
Standing (L-R): Foster Kamer, Diana Rissetto, Judy Hansen.

The Publicity Office

Standing (L-R): Jeremy Shaffer and Michael Borowski. Seated: Marc Thibodeau (with Berger).

Springer Associates

(L-R): Gary Springer and Joe Trentacosta.

O&M Co.

(L-R): Rick Miramontez, Philip Carrubba, Molly Barnett, Richard Hillman, Elizabeth Wagner and Jon Dimond.

Not Pictured: Jaron Caldwell.

Faculty

G. ANDERSON
ART CLUB

B. AQUART
BASKETBALL

J. AQUINO
TRACK & FIELD

M. BARRY
BADMINTON

A. BIZJAK
JAZZ TEAM

G. COLEMAN
THEATRE TECHIE

J. COOPER
4-H

T. COPPOLA
CHORUS

D. COX
HISTORICAL SOCIETY

G. CRADDOCK
EAGLE SCOUTS

T. CREWS
TECHNOLOGY CLUB

A. CRUZ
GLEE CLUB

A. DAVIS
BLACK HISTORY CLUB

P. DUFFY
BALLET

C. FENTON
THATCHERITE

S. FITZPATRICK
CHEERLEADING

J. FRAENKEL
HILLEL

T. FRANCIS
STUDY CLUB

G. GREEN
PEP SQUAD

K. HALL
WEIGHTLIFTING

L. HUNTER
ICE HOCKEY

L. JOHNSON
DANCE TEAM

L. KAISER
YEARBOOK

H. LEE
DRILL TEAM

SpotCo Class of 2008

D. HODGES
PRINCIPAL

J. EDWARDS
VICE PRINCIPAL

B. BERK
DEAN OF STUDENTS

T. GREENWALD
AV SQUAD

N. LINDEMAN
PING PONG

M. LITTELL
COLOR GUARD

S. MAYA
FORENSICS

T. McCANN
EQUINE CLUB

M. McCRACKEN
DUNGEON MASTER

J. McNICHOLAS
BROADCAST CLUB

P. MILANO
GOLF

W. MITCHELL
DRAMA SOCIETY

D. PRESTON
MATHLETES

L. PRICE
PROM COMMITTEE

K. RATHBUN
QUIZ BOWL CAPTAIN

M. RHEAULT
WRESTLING

J. ROGERS
DRUMLINE

A. ROTHENBERG
HALL MONITOR

V. SAINATO
DEBATE

C. SEES
CLASS CLOWN

J. SOCHACZEWSKI
EXCHANGE STUDENT

S. SOSNOWSKI
FENCING

A. SPIELMAN
NEWSPAPER

D. SUYAMA
SOCCER

E. VICIOSO
BAND

B. WATSON
YOUNG DEMOCRATS

M. WILSTEIN
ASTRONOMY CLUB

Faculty

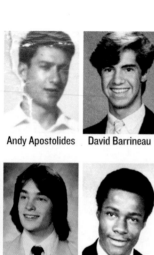

Andy Apostolides   David Barrineau   Sandy Block   Matt Britt   Denise Brown   Tom Callahan   Hilda Chiquito

Cara Christman   Greg Corradetti   Bruce Council   Nancy Coyne   Moira Deakin   Lauren D'Elia   Angelo Desimini   Stephen Elms

Joaquin Esteva   Joe Figliola   Valerie Gorham   Ryan Greer   Beth Griffin   Peter Gunther   Noriko Ishikawa   Scott Johnson

Marci Kaufman   Zack Kinney   Burt Kleeger   Neal Leibowitz   Jean Leonard   Charles MacLachlan   Kathryn Marotta   Joette Martin

Roger Micone   Heather Millen   Jim Miller   David Molina   Marguerite Morea   Diane Niedzialek   Brad Pattinian   Trudy Priatno

Andrea Prince   Catherine Reid   Jim Russek   Beth Schefflan   Aileen Siu   Natalie Serota   Ginger Witt   Scott Yambor

Faculty

From top left: Richard Robertson Terry Newberry Clint White Elizabeth Findlay Suzanne Hereth
Sasha DeFazio Jovan Villalba Pamela Bush Frank 'Fraver' Verlizzo Gita Wisnu
Jon Bierman Lianne Ritchie Steve Knight Davlynn Gundolff Andrew McCarthy
Mary Costa Patrick Flood Simona Tanasescu Sondra Behan Janice Brunell
Adam Neumann DeWayne Snype Bob Levine Lucy Lamela Taryn O'Bra
Barbara Eliran Ann Murphy

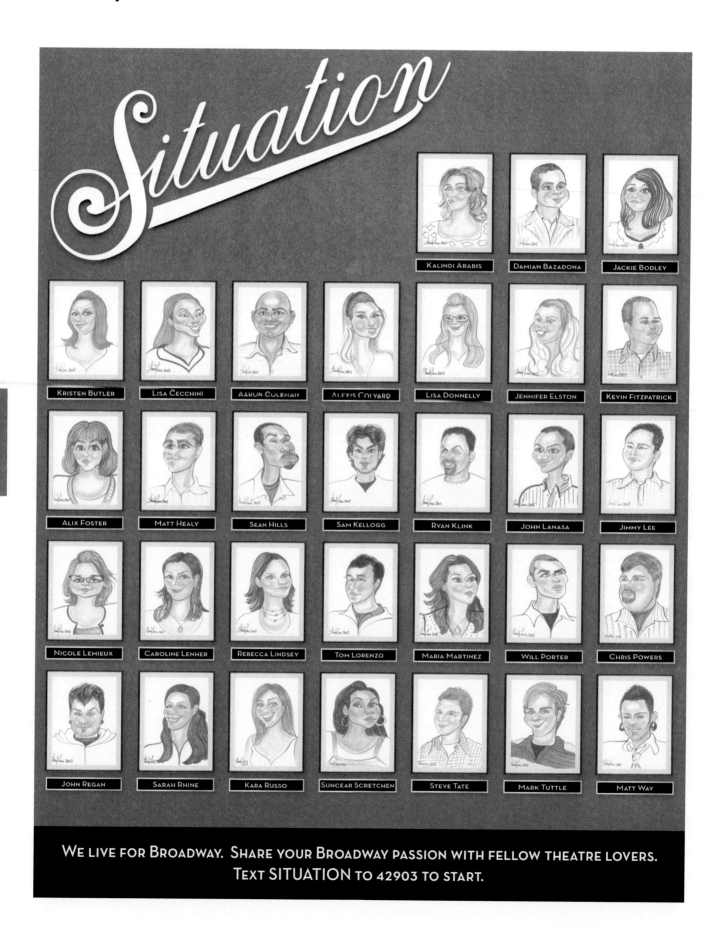

WE LIVE FOR BROADWAY. SHARE YOUR BROADWAY PASSION WITH FELLOW THEATRE LOVERS.
TEXT SITUATION TO 42903 TO START.

Faculty

Playbill / Manhattan Office

Philip S. Birsh
Publisher

Clifford S. Tinder
*Senior Vice President/
Publisher, Classic Arts
Division*

MANHATTAN OFFICE
Front Row (L-R): Jil Simon, Cliff Tinder, Ira Pekelnaya and Diana Leidel.
Second Row (L-R): Louis Botto, Yajaira Marrero, Esvard D'Haiti, Joel Wyman, Wanda Young, Ruthe Schnell, Judy Samelson, Theresa Holder, Jan Meiselman and Harry Haun.
Third Row (L-R): Arturo Gonzalez, Larry Miller, Anderson Peguero, Kristen Luciani, Clara Barragan-Tiburcio, Maude Popkin, Bruce Stapleton, Alex Near, Amy Asch and Irv Winick.
Back Row (L-R): Ari Ackerman, Ben Finane, Elias Seda, Daniel Beaver-Seitz, Robert Viagas, David Gewirtzman and Glenn Asciutto.

EDITORIAL
Front Row (L-R): Harry Haun, Robert Viagas and Ben Finane.
Back Row (L-R): Ira Pekelnaya, Louis Botto, Cliff Tinder, Maude Popkin, Judy Samelson, Alex Near and Diana Leidel.

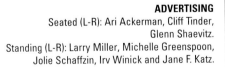

ADVERTISING
Seated (L-R): Ari Ackerman, Cliff Tinder, Glenn Shaevitz.
Standing (L-R): Larry Miller, Michelle Greenspoon, Jolie Schaffzin, Irv Winick and Jane F. Katz.

Faculty

Southern Playbill / Miami Office

Arthur T. Birsh
Chairman

Joan Alleman
Corporate Vice President

Laura Goldman
Publisher/ Southern Division

ACCOUNTING/SALES STAFF
Standing (L-R): Nubia Romo, Tom Green and Raquel Romero.
Sitting (L-R): Sara Smith, Ruth Ingram, Lacy Carter and Donald Roberts.

SOUTHERN PLAYBILL STAFF
Front Row (L-R): Nubia Romo, Silvia Cañadas, Maritza Lopez, Sara Smith, Lacy Carter and Linda Clark.
Second Row (L-R): Carolina Diaz, Eric Schrader, Michelle Campos, Raquel Romero, Laura Goldman, Donald Roberts, Maria Chinda and Ruth Ingram.
Back Row (L-R): Baldemar Albornoz, Carlos Engracio, Milton McPherson, Lance Lenhardt, Christopher Diaz, Tom Green and Ruben Echevarria.
Photos were taken at the Arsht Center for the Performing Arts. Not Pictured: Sally Smith.

ART STAFF
(Front to Back):
Maritza Lopez,
Silvia Cañadas,
Carolina Diaz,
Maria Chinda,
Milton McPherson
and Lance Lenhardt.

PRODUCTION STAFF
(L-R): Baldemar Albornoz, Michelle Campos, Eric Schrader,
Christopher Diaz, Ruben Echevarria, Carlos Engracio and Linda Clark.

Faculty

Playbill / Woodside Office

PRODUCTION CHIEFS
(L-R): Louis Cusanelli, Robert Cusanelli and Patrick Cusanelli.

PRODUCTION
(L-R): Patrick Cusanelli, Benjamin Hyacinthe, David Porrello and Sean Kenny.

PRINTERS
Front Row (L-R): John Matthews, Domingo Pagan, Mary Roaid, David Rodriguez, Gilbert Gonzalez.

Second Row (L-R): Carlos Robinson, Manuel Guzman, Joseph Lucania, Ray Sierra, Nancy Galarraga, Arnold Jacklitsch, Scott Cipriano.

Back Row: Robert Cusanelli, Fabian Cordero, Louis Cusanelli, Fran Divirgilio, Ramdat Ramlall and Lennox Worrell.

PRINTERS
(L-R): Elias Garcia, Thomas McClenin, Sadu Greene, Frank Dunn, Kenneth Gomez, Maheshwari Moti, Thomas Pagliaro, Louis Cusanelli II and Carlos Moyano.

Faculty

Playbill / Woodside Office

PLAYBILL.COM
(L-R): David Gewirtzman, Andrew Ku, Kenneth Jones, Ernio Hernandez, Andrew Gans, Matt Blank and Adam Hetrick.

CLASSIC ARTS DIVISION PROGRAM EDITORS
(L-R): Bill Reese, Kristy Bredin, Claire Mangan, Brian Libfeld and Rori Grable.

ACCOUNTING
(L-R): JoAnn D'Amato, John LoCascio, Beatriz Chitnis, Lewis Cole, Theresa Bernstein and James Eastman.

Michael Buckley
Columnist

Harry Haun
Columnist

Jennifer Lanter
Columnist

Mark Shenton
*London
Correspondent*

Robert Simonson
*Senior
Correspondent*

Steven Suskin
Columnist

Not Pictured: Seth Rudetsky, Zachary Pincus-Roth and Tom Nondorf.

Photos by Ben Strothmann

Faculty

Playbill / Woodside Office

PROGRAM EDITORS
(L-R): Scott Hale (Off-Broadway) and Pam Karr (Broadway).

Photo by Ben Strothmann

Playbill Broadcast / Manhattan Office

Photo by Ben Strothmann

PLAYBILL RADIO
(L-R): Amy Asch, Seth Bisen-Hersh, Robert Viagas and David Gewirtzman.

Photo by David Gewirtzman

VIDEO INTERNS
(L-R): Scott Hamilton, Alex Birsh and Noah Siegel.

CONSULTING PRODUCER
Ray Romano

Faculty

Playbill Yearbook Staff

Photo by Ben Strothmann

EDITORIAL
(L-R): Amy Asch (with 2006 edition), Ben Strothmann, Robert Viagas (with working manuscript of 2008 edition), Kristen Luciani (with 2007 edition) and David Gewirtzman (with 2005 edition).
Not Pictured: Kesler Thibert.

PHOTOGRAPHER
Aubrey Reuben

Photo by David Gewirtzman

INTERNS
(L-R): Averi Barron and Craig Stekeur.

Playbill / Regional Advertising Salespersons

Kenneth R. Back
Sales Manager
Cincinnati

Abigail Bocchetto
Sales
Houston

Elaine Bodker
Sales
St. Louis

Carol Brumm
Sales
St. Louis

Bob Caulfield
Sales
San Francisco

Margo Cooper
Sales Manager
St. Louis

Ron Friedman
Sales Manager
Columbus

Betsy Gugick
Sales Manager
Dallas

Michel Manzo
Sales Manager
Philadelphia

Marilyn A. Miller
Sales Manager
Minneapolis

Judy Pletcher
Sales Manager
Washington, DC

John Rosenow
Sales Manager
Phoenix/Tucson

Kenneth Singer
Sales Manager
Houston

Not Pictured: Jennifer Allington, Dory Binyon, Megan Boles, Dick Coffee, Ed Gurien, Nancy Hardin, Jeff Ross and Donald Roberts.

In Memoriam

May 2007 to May 2008

Michael Abbott
Jennifer Alexander
John Almberg
Douglas Anderson
Kip Andrews
Peggy Atkinson
Bobbi Baird
Robert Bakanic
Jeanne Bates
Jeanne Beauvais
Ingmar Bergman
Joey Bishop
Carol Bruce
John Buckwalter
Donny Burks
Leo Burmester
Bart Burns
Donald Babcock
Jess Cain
Ron Carey
Lonny Chapman
John Christopher
Alvin Colt
Shirl Conway
Caris Corfman
James Costigan
Augusta Dabney
Jules Dassin
Frances Dewey
Ivan Dixon
Charles Durand
Michael Evans
Walter Flanagan
Denny Martin Flinn
Karen E. Fraction
Harry Frazier
George W. George
Alice Ghostley
Madeline Gilford
Robert Goulet
Frank Green

Ed Griffenkranz
Merv Griffin
Victor Griffin
George Grizzard
David Groh
Harriet Hall
Preston Hanson
Jay Harris
Charlton Heston
Bill Hart
Harris Hawkins
Dyanne Hochman
Louisa Horton
Peter Howard
William Hutt
Bella Jarrett
Pattie Darcy Jones
Stanley Kamel
Herbert Kenwith
Deborah Kerr
Michael Kidd
Leslie Klein
Edward Kovens
Ben Kapen
Jerry Kravat
Robert Lamont
Dennis Letts
Stephen Levi
Ira Levin
Leo Leyden
Calvin Lockhart
Spain Logue
Edward Lynch
Edith Maison
Martin Manulis
Mary Marsh
Marcel Marceau
Allan Melvin
Skedge Miller
Anna Minot
Ed Mirvish

Alexandra Montano
Marcia Morris
Barry Morse
Tom Murphy
Lois Nettleton
Natalie Norwick
Gian Pace
Leonard Parker
Gedda Petry
Suzanne Pleshette
Joan Potter
Mala Powers
Jack Rains
Charles Nelson Reilly
Harry L. Rogers
DD Ryan
Steve Ryan
Anne Sargent
Reuben Schafer
Roy Scheider
David Shaw
Paul Shiers
Robert Sidney
Brett Somers
Joanne Spiller
Philip Steele
Allan Stevenson
Oscar Stokes
Robert Symonds
Claude Thompson
Mel Tolkin
John Tyers
Miyoshi Umeki
Henrietta Valor
Terry Violino
Thomas J. Walsh
Anna Minot Warren
Mark Wright
Gretchen Wyler

Index

Index

Index

Index

Index

Caruso, Danny 256
Caruso, Jim 434
Caruso, Joe 303
Carvajal, Celina 375-377
Carver, Steve 100, 175, 176, 381
Casablanca, Adriana 197, 231
Casagrande, Margaret 205, 283, 289, 317, 334, 368, 385, 452
Casal, Melissa 270
Casaletta, Terry 462
Casanova, Marianna 407
Case, Jenny 123, 189
Casella, Carl 272, 273, 410
Casey, Warren 132
Cashman, John 277
Caskey, Marilyn 144, 145, 146, 151, 297, 299, 306
Caso, Lulu 114, 459
Caspare, Cissy 199
Cass, Erin 424
Cassan, Christian 290, 291, 293
Cassano, Tom 102
Cassel, Michael 226, 233, 450
Cassidy, Craig 247, 249
Cassier, Brian 139, 141, 145
Cassin, Olivia 81
Castaldo, Eric 191, 192, 423, 424
Castellana, James 116, 123, 189, 294
Castellana, Lance 10, 116, 123, 143, 164, 189, 242, 278, 294, 362, 414
Castellano, William 457
Castellano, William Jr. 461
Casterlin, Patty 453
Castillo, Raquel 205, 283, 289, 316, 333, 368, 385
Castle, Matt 66, 67
Castner, Fred 198, 199
Castree, Paul 419-421, 425
Castro, Eduardo 379, 380
Castro, Jessica 131
Castro, Lou 369
Caswell, Jeff 228
Cataldo, Christina 150, 159, 424
Catanese, Charles 79, 81, 114, 116, 461
Catron, Andy 256
Cattaneo, Anne 92, 93, 96, 352
Catullo, Patrick 408
Catuy, Gustavo 187
Caudle, David 95, 96, 352
Caulfield, Bob 480

Caulfield, Maxwell 42
Cavanaugh, Ann 413, 414
Cavanaugh, Anne 187
Cavanaugh, James 17, 18, 157, 461
Cavari, Perry 115, 116, 420, 424
Cave, Lisa Dawn 59, 60
Cavenaugh, Matt viii, ix, 28, 29, 33, 138, 140
Cavett, Wendy Bobbitt 244, 247
Caza-Cleypool, Damian 232
Cearcy, Darlesia 54, 55, 56
Cecchini, Lisa 60, 89, 170
Cecere, Anthony 12
Cecil, Derek 201, 202
Celustka, Stephanie 123
Cennamo, Jack 141, 143
Cennamo, Michael 413
Centalonza, Richard 40, 43
Centeno, Francisco 153, 158
Cepler, Joanna B. 466
Ceraso, Chris 64, 238, 262, 393
Cerge, Cathy 448
Cerney, DL 60
Cerniglia, Ken 19, 226, 233, 257, 381, 450
Cerveris, Michael vii, 92, 94, 235, 236, 431
Chabay, Gregory 249
Challis, Marianne 232
Chamberlain, Andrea 113
Chamberlin, Kevin vi, 330, 331, 335, 336
Chambers, Lindsay Nicole 193-195, 200
Chambless, Anne Devon 116
Champion, Charise 303
Chan, Claire 123
Chan, Suyin 225, 450
Chandran, Clarence J. 34
Chandrashaker, Amith 214
Chang, Paul 150, 176, 239
Chang, Tisa 460
Channing, Carol 429
Channon, Steve 414
Chao, Caroline 205, 289, 352
Chapin, Chloe 294
Chapin, Ted 352-454
Chapman, Braden 453
Chapman, Graham 264, 270
Chapman, Kate 210
Chapman, Lonny 481
Chapman, Matthew

170
Chapman, Susannah 29, 31
Chappelle, Dave 295
Chappelle, Keith Eric 97, 98
Charles, Douglas 95
Charlier, Paul 101, 102
Charters, Lanene 244, 245, 248
Chase, David 75, 78, 83, 227
Chase, Myles 244
Chase, Will 326
Chase-Boyd, Meredith 225
Chastain, Sheffield 179
Chavez, Gena 453
Chavez, Mike 422
Chayefsky, Paddy 28
Chazanof, Ilene 408
Chebetar, Rich 466
Checklick, Susan 360, 362
Cheek, Stephanie 19, 226, 233, 257, 381, 450
Chen, Minglie 9
Cheretun, Deborah A. 60
Cherichello, Kaitlin 205, 368, 452, 454
Chernick, Jeremy 108, 313
Cherpakov, Howie 322, 342, 344
Cherques, Luciana 322
Cheskin, Irving 453
Chesney, Suzanne 64
Cheyette, Herb 108
Chia, Quin 458
Chico 193
Chie, Dana 199
Child, Tom 19
Childs, Terri 240, 371
Childs, Timothy 240, 371
Chimples, John 369
Chinda, Maria 476
Ching, Cory 128, 199, 269
Chiquito, Hilda 472
Chiroldes, Tony 171-173
Chisholm, Anthony 319, 320, 456
Chisolm, Alessandra 36
Chisolm, Marissa 34, 35, 38
Chitnis, Beatriz 478
Chittick, Joyce 132, 135
Chloe 193, 200
Chmielewski, Karl 19, 226, 233, 257, 381, 450
Choi, Chuck 226
Chong, Connie 32, 81, 192, 214, 389
Chotto, Ryan
Christopher 156
Christ, Bill 166, 167, 169

Christenberry, Julian 294, 457
Christensen, Emily 50
Christensen, Tom 111
Christensen, Tracy 18, 232
Christenson, Mitch 17
Christian, Eric 57, 58, 75, 76, 82,
Christiano, Jana 19
Christianson, Mike 420
Christie, Ed 10
Christine, Ellen 150
Christine, Mark 131
Christman, Cara 74, 136, 472
Christopher, John 481
Christy, Roberta 328
Chryst, Gary 39
Chudoba, John 47
Chung, Erica 467
Chung, Junah 213
Chung, Wendy 262
Church, Carson 166, 167, 169
Church, Jonathan 242
Church, Joseph 226
Churchill, Caryl viii, 390, 391
Ciaccio, Tom 432
Ciccarone, Rock 219
Cicerchi, Danajean 461
Ciego, Julian 99
Cilento, Wayne 401, 404
Cilibrasi, Joseph 355, 358
Cimino, Michael 380
Cintron, Joseph 17, 231
Cipriano, Rose Ann 180, 211, 459
Cipriano, Scott 477
Cipriatti, Juliette 26, 30
Citron, Jill L. 19, 225, 233, 257, 381
Claffey, James J. Jr. 108, 464
Clancy, Elizabeth Hope 290
Clancy, Hamilton 204, 282, 288, 316, 333, 368, 384
Clancy, John 133, 136
Clapton, Eric Patrick 5
Clar, Steven 70, 150
Clark, Amy 232,408
Clark, Chris 406, 408
Clark, Dwayne 375, 377
Clark, Harriet 297, 299, 303, 305, 306
Clark, Ina 467
Clark, Iryna 312
Clark, James 260
Clark, Jocelyn 143
Clark, John 114
Clark, Joseph 205, 283, 289, 317, 334, 369, 385
Clark, Kristina 350
Clark, Linda 476

Clark, Michael 183
Clark, Phillip 61, 62
Clark, Tom 9, 49, 72, 107, 112, 174, 196, 267
Clarke, Amy 453
Clarke, Gregory 190, 314
Clarke, Natalie 322
Clarke, Tracey 274
Clarkston, Michael T. 455
Claus, Nathan K. 278
Clay, Caroline Stefanie 61, 62
Clay, Paul 323
Clay, Thom 344
Clayman, Amanda 467
Claypool, Veronica 457
Clayton, Lawrence 89
Cleale, Lewis 267
Cleary, Mary 249
Cleary, Michael 247
Cleese, John 264, 266, 270
Cleghorn, Andrew 170, 192
Clem, Steve 135
Clemens, Matt 208, 209, 214
Clement, Sally 399
Clements, Andrew 205, 283, 289, 317, 334, 369, 385
Clements, Bradley 70
Clements, Ron 227
Clemmons, Dave 373
Cleveland, La'Shone 36
Clifford, Maura 423, 424
Clifton, Tina 198
Climer, Jacob A. 60
Cline, Cathy 360, 362
Cline, Elizabeth 136
Cline, James 148, 361
Clinton, Bill 400
Clinton, Chelsea 400
Cloer, Travis 183, 184, 185
Close, Glenn 270
Clow, James 89
Clow, Virginia 233
Clynes, Justin 330, 332
Coates, Sarah 242
Cobb, Clifford 36, 212
Cobb, Lee 249
Cobb, Steve 249
Cobbin, Angela 255, 256
Cobbold, Lorna 128
Cobbs, Jeffrey 4
Coble, Kurt 298, 302
Cocchiara, Christina 406
Cocchiara, Rich 380
Cochran, Beth 116
Cochrane, Anthony 92, 93, 94
Cochrane, Jessica Perlmeter 96, 352
Cochrane, Steve 294
Cockrum, Dennis 125, 126

Coco, Edward 362
Coey, Dan 23, 27, 143, 150, 199
Coffee, Dick 480
Coffey, Timothy 239
Cohan, Adam 466
Cohen, Alan 453
Cohen, Avishai 64, 238, 262
Cohen, Bruce 460, 463
Cohen, David 73, 103, 340, 341
Cohen, David M. 74
Cohen, Elizabeth 226
Cohen, Eric 298, 302
Cohen, Gregory 18
Cohen, Jennifer 70, 453
Cohen, Jonathan 180, 212
Cohen, Joshua 205, 283, 289, 317, 334, 368, 385, 452
Cohen, Randy 70, 76, 81, 131, 136, 143, 150, 176, 408, 414, 420, 424
Cohen, Sherry 248, 249
Cohn, Ben 402, 407
Coid, Marshall 40, 43
Colavin, Charlotte 64, 238, 262, 393
Cole, Gary 5
Cole, Lewis 478
Cole, Michael 408
Cole, Newton 67, 69, 70
Coleman, Cy 440
Coleman, Kris 183, 185
Coleman, LaTrisa A. 54-56, 60
Coleman, Liz 204
Coleman, M. Graham 60
Coleman, Michelle 44
Coleman, Rosalyn 319, 320
Coley, Gwen 192, 293
Colgan, Bill 180
Colgan, Melissa 458
Colgan, Robert 108
Colhns, Ralph 303
Colin, Margaret 280-282
Collado, Maria 158
Colledge, Shaun 304
Collett, Ned 313, 424
Collichio, Gregg 19, 233
Collier, Brian 251-254
Collins, Chrissie 343, 388
Collins, Jennifer 10, 328
Collins, Jessica 201, 202
Collins, Joseph 337, 338
Collins, Kelly 197
Collins, Kenneth 96, 352

Index

Index

Index

Index

Index

Index

Index

Index

Index

Index

Index

Index

Index

Index

Index

Index

Index

Index

Index

Index

Index

Index

Index

Index

Index

Index

Index

Index

Autographs